MW00760047

THE BLUE GUIDES

Albania
Austria
Belgium and Luxembourg
China
Cyprus
Czechoslovakia
Denmark
Egypt

FRANCE
France
Paris and Versailles
Burgundy
Loire Valley
Midi-Pyrénées
Normandy
South West France
Corsica

GERMANY
Berlin and Eastern Germany
Western Germany

GREECE
Greece
Athens and environs
Crete

HOLLAND
Holland
Amsterdam

HUNGARY
Budapest

Ireland

ITALY
Northern Italy
Southern Italy
Florence
Rome and environs
Venice
Tuscany
Umbria

Sicily

Jerusalem
Jordan
Malta and Gozo
Mexico
Morocco
Moscow and Leningrad
Portugal

SPAIN
Spain
Barcelona
Madrid

Sweden
Switzerland
Tunisia

TURKEY
Turkey
Istanbul

UK
England
Scotland
Wales
London
Museums and Galleries of London
Oxford and Cambridge
Country Houses of England
Gardens of England
Literary Britain and Ireland
Victorian Architecture in Britain
Churches and Chapels of Northern
    England
Churches and Chapels of Southern
    England
Channel Islands

USA
New York
Boston and Cambridge
Museums and Galleries of New York

Core (Cored Sculpture), *an austere basalt sculpture (1978) at the*
Isamu Noguchi Garden Museum, Long Island City; Queens.
(Courtesy of the Isamu Noguchi Foundation, Inc. Photo: Shigeo Anzai)

BLUE GUIDE

MUSEUMS AND GALLERIES OF NEW YORK

Carol von Pressentin Wright

A & C Black
London

W. W. Norton & Company
New York

First edition 1997

Published by A & C Black (Publishers) Limited
35 Bedford Row, London WC1R 4JH

A CIP catalogue record of this book
is available from the British Library.

ISBN 0-7136-3938-5

Published in the United States of America by
W. W. Norton & Company, Inc
500 Fifth Avenue, New York, NY 10110

The text of this book is composed in Egyptienne F.
Composition by The Maple-Vail Book Manufacturing Group.
Manufacturing by The Courier Companies, Inc.

The author and the publishers have done their best to ensure the accuracy of all the information in *Museums and Galleries of New York,* however, they can accept no responsibility for any loss, injury, or inconvenience sustained by any traveler as a result of information or advice contained in the guide.

Carol Wright, born on Staten Island, is the author of *Blue Guide New York* and therefore is cognizant of what is outside the city's museums as well as what is in them. She holds a Ph.D. in Comparative Literature, has written travel articles for the *New York Times* and other publications, and is currently working on a book on women's health for Yale University Press.

The publishers and the author welcome comments, suggestions and corrections for the next edition of this Blue Guide. Writers of the most informative letters will be awarded a free Blue Guide of their choice.

Library of Congress Cataloging-in-Publication Data
Wright, Carol (Carol von Pressentin).
Museums and galleries of New York / Carol von Pressentin Wright.—
1st ed.
   p.   cm.—(Blue guide)
Includes index.
1. Museums—New York (N.Y.)—Guidebooks.   2. New York (N.Y.)—
Guidebooks.   I. Title.   II. Series.
AM13.N5V66   1996
069'09747'1—dc20   95-1020

ISBN 0-393-31341-7

1 2 3 4 5 6 7 8 9

CONTENTS

MUSEUMS IN THE BRONX

MUSEUMS IN BROOKLYN

MUSEUMS IN QUEENS

MUSEUMS IN STATEN ISLAND

COMMERCIAL ART GALLERIES

MAPS

FLOOR PLANS

INTRODUCTION

The museums of New York are among the city's superb assets, their holdings constituting an astonishing and surprisingly thorough record of the artistic and technological achievements of humanity. New York's museums range from encyclopedic storehouses that, like Noah's Ark, seem to have collected a small sampling of every object in their domain, to more modest institutions that express the culture of one ethnic group or the achievements of one person. Some, like the Frick Collection or the Cooper-Hewitt, occupy buildings constructed as opulent mansions; others, like the Lower East Side Tenement Museum, reflect the city's humbler past. While most are preoccupied with history of some kind, a few are fiercely contemporary and show only the work of artists at the cutting edge.

New York boasts several internationally famous institutions and others that are hardly known beyond their own neighborhoods. About 4.5 million visitors, from all over the world, flock each year to the Metropolitan Museum of Art. The Nicholas Roerich Museum, tucked away in a quiet neighborhood on the Upper West Side, welcomes perhaps a dozen people a day, but some of these visitors also come from afar.

This book covers more than 150 museums, and though it is unlikely that anyone other than a guidebook writer will visit each of them, the book lays out their riches for all to see. New Yorkers have the opportunity to go back again and again to places that appeal to them, whereas visitors on tight schedules have to make do with hurried sprints through the major collections. This guide is for both groups. If you are a New Yorker, this guide hopes to lure you to explore institutions beyond your usual territory. If you are a visitor to the city, this book will help you use your time more efficiently.

Each entry is organized with practical information first, followed by a brief outline and a list of highlights, if appropriate. If the permanent collection is the focus of the museum, as in the Metropolitan Museum of Art, that is described first. If the changing exhibition program is the museum's first priority, for example, at the National Academy of Design, then that is described first. The same is true for the history section, where included. The number in parentheses is keyed to the number of the museum on the appropriate borough or neighborhood map.

Unfortunately the time lag between writing and publication has made it impossible to write about current exhibitions. But to give a general feeling for the fare a particular museum has to offer, I have included descriptions of interesting or important past exhibitions.

Practical Information

When to Go: Most museums are open six days a week. Many are closed Monday, for example, the Metropolitan Museum of Art, The Cloisters, the Brooklyn Museum, the Frick Collection, and the Whitney Museum of American Art. The Guggenheim Museum is closed on Thursday and the

Museum of Modern Art on Wednesday. The Brooklyn Museum is also closed on Tuesday, as is the Whitney, except to school groups.

Several large museums have evening hours, which can be less crowded than peak daytime periods. The Metropolitan is open Friday and Saturday evenings; there is beverage service and music on the Balcony overlooking the Great Hall. The Museum of Modern Art and the Whitney Museum remain open on Thursday evenings.

On occasion an exhibition, for example, the 1992 Matisse show at the Museum of Modern Art, will be so popular that advance planning is wise. During such exhibitions it may be better to plan a visit near the middle of the run and to arrive either early in the day or toward closing hours.

Admission Fees: Some museums are free, but most have admission charges which range from suggested donations to required entrance fees. Since the 1970s the Metropolitan Museum, for instance, has had a pay-what-you-wish policy, suggesting a donation but requiring only that you pay something. Some museums have specific hours in which admission is free or offered on a pay-what-you-wish basis. Many museums have reduced rates for children, seniors, and students.

Facilities: Most major museums have cafeterias or restaurants, whose food is usually adequate if not as inspiring as the exhibits on the walls. In recent years several museums, such as the Guggenheim, the Whitney, and the Museum of Modern Art, have updated their menus and/or facilities. Nevertheless, museum food tends to be expensive for what you get, since you are to some extent a captive audience.

Most museums also have gift shops, which provide them with another source of revenue. The fine Brooklyn Museum gift shop was a pioneer in expanding this idea. Gift shops generally mirror the focus of the museum, so that you can expect to find Victoriana at the Alice Austen House and items with a medieval cast at The Cloisters. Some of the gift shops offer extensive selections of art books. The American Museum of Natural History also has a major bookstore and a gift shop with items that reflect its holdings in natural history and ethnography.

The majority of museums have restrooms; the entry notes only those that do not.

Museum Programs: Almost all museums offer memberships that allow free admission and entitle members to special privileges. In addition to exhibitions, most museums have programs of films, lectures, concerts, and activities for children, which are worth investigating. Some offer walking tours of the city and sponsor trips that may range from a day's outing somewhere within the perimeter of the five boroughs to a tour of China's Buddhist monasteries.

Many museums also have holiday programs, the most elaborate coming around Christmas. The Metropolitan has a traditional Neapolitan crêche and a beautiful, large tree hung with Baroque 18C angels. The American Museum of Natural History has an equally large tree decorated with origami figures. The city's botanical gardens have special displays at Christmas and Easter.

> **NOTE:** Although brief driving directions are given to museums in the outer boroughs, it is advisable to take along a road map just in case.

EXPLANATIONS

ACCESSION NUMBERS. Accession numbers have been used to help identify or locate certain small objects in collections. Usually the first digits (before the first period) indicate the year the museum acquired the object. Other digits can help identify the donor. For example, in the Metropolitan Museum, the objects donated by J. Pierpont Morgan all bear accession numbers 17.190.xx; paintings in the Havemeyer bequest have accession numbers 29.100.xx.

ABBREVIATIONS. In addition to self-explanatory abbreviations, the following have been used:
act. = active, refers to an artist's period of productivity
attrib. = attributed to
B.C.E. = before the common era
c. = *circa* (approximately)
TT/TTD = Text Telephone/Telecommunications Device for the Deaf

SYMBOLS.

 = Restaurant

 = Restroom and telephone (it will be assumed that each museum has a restroom and telephone; these symbols will be used only if restroom and/or telephone are **not** available.)

 = Gift shop

 = Wheelchair accessibility

 = Prohibitions

 = Subway

 = Bus

 = Directions by foot

 = Car/parking

= Commuter train

= Ferry

ACKNOWLEDGMENTS

I would like to thank all the museum staff members who have provided information, corrected errors, checked facts, and allowed me access to their facilities. In particular, I would like to mention Ann Marie Sekeres of the Brooklyn Museum, and Jonathan Kuhn, parks department archivist, who have graciously shared their expertise. I am indebted to Hilary Buchanan for additional research, and to Amanda Taylor for her work on the commercial art galleries and for undertaking last-minute interborough expeditions to track down minutiae; to Ann Adelman, copyeditor, who has rooted out errors of style and substance; to Nicole Wan, who helped with the illustrations and details of mapmaking; and to Adam Sass, for updating museum hours and other ephemera. Iva Ashner has patiently read this entire manuscript more than once, ultimately advising me that it was time to stop. I am grateful to Mildred Marmur, my agent and friend, for her encouragement and her sustained efforts on my behalf. Finally I wish to thank Fred Wright, my husband, friend, and patron in these endeavors, and my daughter Catherine, whose broad knowledge of New York's museums, galleries, and period houses is remarkable in one so young.

A NOTE ON BLUE GUIDES*

The Blue Guide series began in 1915 when Muirhead Guide-Books Limited published *Blue Guide London and Its Environs*. Findlay and James Muirhead already had extensive experience of guide-book publishing: before World War I they had been the editors of the English editions of the German Baedekers, and by 1915 they had acquired the copyright of most of the famous "Red" Handbooks from John Murray.

An agreement made with the French publishing house Hachette et Cie in 1917 led to the translation of Muirhead's London guide, which became the first *Guide Bleu*—Hachette had previously published the blue-covered *Guides Joannes*. Subsequently, Hachette's *Guide Bleu Paris et Ses Environs* was adapted and published in London by Muirhead. The collaboration between the two publishing houses continued until 1933.

In 1933 Ernest Benn Limited took over the Blue Guides, appointing Russell Muirhead, Findlay Muirhead's son, editor in 1934. The Muirheads' connection with the Blue Guides ended in 1963 when Stuart Rossiter, who had been working on the Guides since 1954, became house editor, revising and compiling several of the books himself.

The Blue Guides are now published by A & C Black, who acquired Ernest Benn in 1984, so continuing the tradition of guide-book publishing which began in 1826 with *Black's Economical Tourist of Scotland.* The Blue Guide series continues to grow: there are now 50 titles in print, with revised editions appearing regularly and many new Blue Guides in preparation.

*Blue Guides is a registered trade mark.

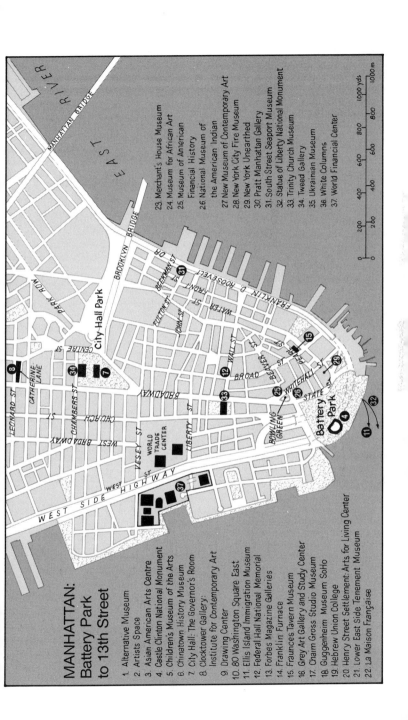

MANHATTAN:
Battery Park
to 13th Street

1. Alternative Museum
2. Artists Space
3. Asian American Arts Centre
4. Castle Clinton National Monument
5. Children's Museum of the Arts
6. Chinatown History Museum
7. City Hall: The Governor's Room
8. Clocktower Gallery:
   Institute for Contemporary Art
9. Drawing Center
10. 80 Washington Square East
11. Ellis Island Immigration Museum
12. Federal Hall National Memorial
13. Forbes Magazine Galleries
14. Franklin Furnace
15. Fraunces Tavern Museum
16. Grey Art Gallery and Study Center
17. Chaim Gross Studio Museum
18. Guggenheim Museum SoHo
19. Hebrew Union College
20. Henry Street Settlement: Arts for Living Center
21. Lower East Side Tenement Museum
22. La Maison Française

23. Merchant's House Museum
24. Museum for African Art
25. Museum of American
    Financial History
26. National Museum of
    the American Indian
27. New Museum of Contemporary Art
28. New York City Fire Museum
29. New York Unearthed
30. Pratt Manhattan Gallery
31. South Street Seaport Museum
32. Statue of Liberty National Monument
33. Trinity Church Museum
34. Tweed Gallery
35. Ukrainian Museum
36. White Columns
37. World Financial Center

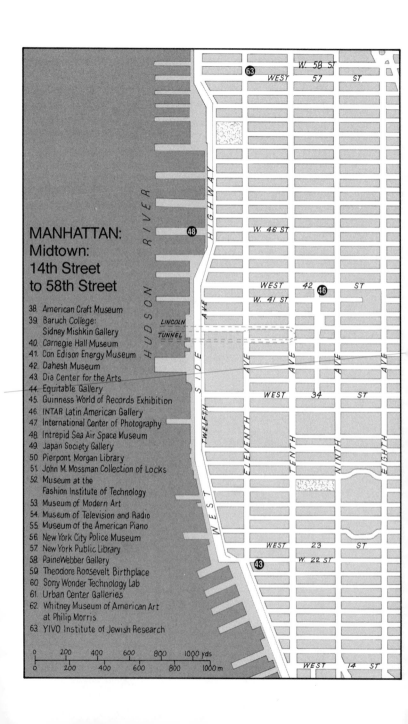

MANHATTAN:
Midtown:
14th Street
to 58th Street

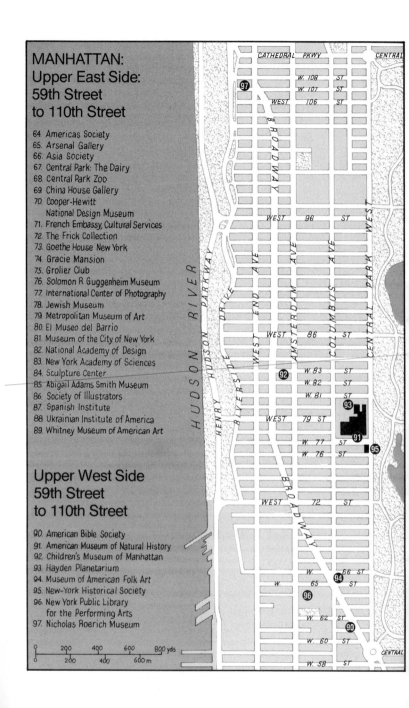

MANHATTAN:
Upper East Side:
59th Street
to 110th Street

64. Americas Society
65. Arsenal Gallery
66. Asia Society
67. Central Park: The Dairy
68. Central Park Zoo
69. China House Gallery
70. Cooper-Hewitt
    National Design Museum
71. French Embassy, Cultural Services
72. The Frick Collection
73. Goethe House New York
74. Gracie Mansion
75. Grolier Club
76. Solomon R. Guggenheim Museum
77. International Center of Photography
78. Jewish Museum
79. Metropolitan Museum of Art
80. El Museo del Barrio
81. Museum of the City of New York
82. National Academy of Design
83. New York Academy of Sciences
84. Sculpture Center
85. Abigail Adams Smith Museum
86. Society of Illustrators
87. Spanish Institute
88. Ukrainian Institute of America
89. Whitney Museum of American Art

Upper West Side
59th Street
to 110th Street

90. American Bible Society
91. American Museum of Natural History
92. Children's Museum of Manhattan
93. Hayden Planetarium
94. Museum of American Folk Art
95. New-York Historical Society
96. New York Public Library
    for the Performing Arts
97. Nicholas Roerich Museum

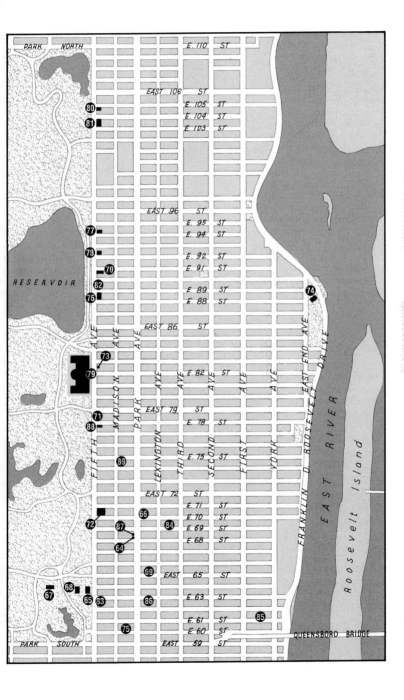

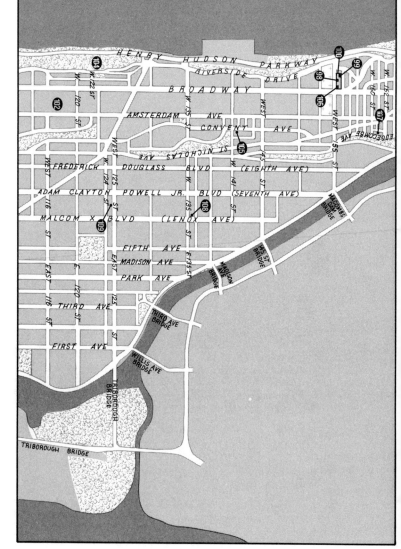

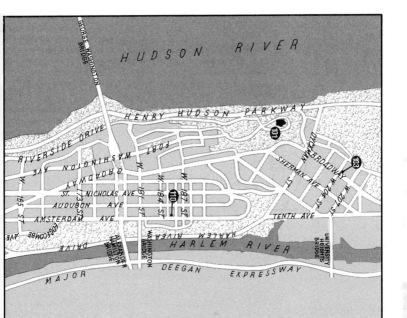

UPPER MANHATTAN:
North of 110th Street

MUSEUMS IN MANHATTAN

The Alternative Museum (1)

594 Broadway (near Houston St), Suite 402, New York 10012. Tel: (212) 966-4444.

ADMISSION: Open Tues–Sat 11–6. Closed Sun, Mon, New Year's Day, mid-Aug to mid-Sept. Suggested donation.

Symposia, panel discussions, lectures, concert series of new music, special events. Publications, catalogues, calendar.

✘ No restaurant.

🛍 Museum shop with catalogues, T-shirts, posters, occasional prints accompanying shows.

♿ Accessible to wheelchairs; elevator to 4th floor.

🚇 IRT Lexington Ave local (train 6) to Spring St or Bleecker St. BMT Broadway local (N or R train) to Prince St.

🚌 Bus M1 downtown on 5th Ave, Park Ave South, and Broadway (make sure you get a bus labeled South Ferry; otherwise walk south from 8th St or transfer to the M6 at 8th St) or uptown on Centre St and Lafayette St to Grand or Canal St. M5 downtown on 5th Ave. M6 downtown on Broadway and uptown on 6th Ave. M21 crosstown on Houston St.

"Ahead of the Times and Behind the Issues" proclaims the motto of the Alternative Museum, an exhibition space in SoHo where art and politics co-exist purposefully if not necessarily harmoniously. Founded (1975) by a group of artists as the Alternative Center for International Arts, its first home was on the Lower East Side, where the counterculture of the early 1970s put down its roots. After a stint in TriBeCa the Museum moved to its present location, where it continues to explore the far reaches of art and contemporary culture, freed by its status as a nonprofit organization from the constraints of the commercial art world.

"Artists of Conscience," the inaugural show in the new Museum space (1991), surveyed 16 years of exhibitions, highlighting some 70 artists who had previously shown at the gallery. Works ranged from figurative painting to installations to video, and included such figures as Leon Golub, Adrian Piper, Martha Rosler, and Nancy Spero, giving viewers a fairly comprehensive notion of the many ways art and politics have interacted over the past two decades. The show touched on such themes as domestic violence, the human devastation of the Persian Gulf War, and social misery in the postindustrial era.

The Museum also emphasizes the work of nonestablished artists, including those who live outside major art centers or whose work has not found acceptance in the city's mainstream galleries. More than 50% of the artists and musicians presented at the Museum have been from "minority" backgrounds and more than 50% have been women.

In addition to its program of changing exhibitions, the Alternative Museum attracts attention for its concerts and performances of jazz and experimental music.

The American Bible Society: Museum Gallery (90)

Bible House, 1865 Broadway (61st St), New York 10023. Tel: (212) 408-1200.

ADMISSION: Open Mon–Fri 9–4:30. Closed weekends and national holidays. Free.

Group tours on request (age 12 and over). Films, lectures.

✘ No restaurant.

🛍 Shop with Bibles in English and other languages, pamphlets, bookmarks.

♿ Accessible to wheelchairs.

🚇 IRT Broadway-7th Ave local (train 1 or 9), IND 8th Ave express or local (A or C train), or IND 6th Ave express (B or D train) to 59th St / Columbus Circle.

🚌 M5 uptown via 6th Ave and Broadway. M7 uptown via 6th Ave and Broadway. M104 via Broadway.

The American Bible Society (founded 1816) exists to make the Scriptures available to every literate person in a language each can understand, at an affordable price. Bible House, the administrative headquarters of the Society, maintains a library that displays the fruits of these efforts. Included in the collection are some 50,000 volumes—books of scripture and books about the Bible—written in over 1,900 languages, as well as complete Bibles in 310 languages. The American Bible Society Archives maintains a trove of photographs, printed sermons on the Bible, and handwritten letters, including 19C correspondence with missionaries and translators in the Near East, Far East, and Latin America.

On the second floor of Bible House is the Museum Gallery (1966), with a permanent display that includes Helen Keller's imposing stack of Braille volumes, an 1849 Nu Testament in Fonetic Shorthand, a Chinese Torah scroll made for a community of Chinese Jews who lived in Honan in the 13–15C, and a full-scale reproduction of the 15C Gutenberg printing press. Changing exhibitions usually focus on Bibles from the collection and have centered on such themes as miniature Bibles, Bible woodcuts, polyglot Bibles, and Bibles in Chinese.

The American Craft Museum (38)

40 West 53rd St (bet. 5th / 6th Aves), New York 10019. Tel: (212) 956-3535.

ADMISSION: Open Tues 10–8; Wed–Sun 10–5. Closed Mon, July 4, Thanksgiving, New Year's Day, and Christmas Day. Admission charge; children 12 and under free. Group visits by appointment.

Demonstrations; lectures; docent tours, films, family workshops, special group activities.

✘ No restaurant.

🛍 Sales desk with exhibition catalogues, museum publications, postcards, handcrafted jewelry, glass, and other items.

♿ Accessible to wheelchairs.

⊘ No photography; visitors must check bags, coats, and umbrellas in checkroom.

🚇 IRT Broadway-7th Ave local (train 1 or 9) to 50th St. IND 6th Ave local or express (B or D train) to 7th Ave. BMT Broadway local or express (N or R train) to 57th St. IND 6th Ave local (F train) or 8th Ave local (E train) to 53rd St and 5th Ave.

🚌 M2 or M3 downtown on 5th Ave, uptown on Madison Ave. M5 downtown on 5th Ave, uptown on 6th Ave. M7 downtown on Broadway-7th Ave, uptown on 6th Ave. M104 downtown on Broadway.

The American Craft Museum is the single most important place in the nation to look at 20C craft. Historically an uneasy relationship has existed between "craft" and "art," and in the past artists who worked in clay, fiber, glass, or metal were often considered less important than artists who worked with paint or marble. Today, however, craft is taking its rightful place among the fine arts, and institutions like the American Craft Museum (founded 1956 as the Museum of Contemporary Crafts) are exploring its full potential.

EXHIBITION PROGRAM

The Museum mounts changing exhibitions of beautifully designed and handcrafted objects in wood, fiber, glass, clay, and metal. The objects range from utilitarian teapots, rocking chairs, and pieced cotton quilts to less conventional renderings of simple objects (jewelry made of canvas, gold paper, or rubber; sculptural glass chairs; bicycles of laminated and carved wood), to objects created primarily for their aesthetic value.

The inaugural show in the present building (1986) surveyed craft in America today, emphasizing its increasing technological sophistication and its artistic rather than utilitarian qualities. Other exhibitions explore in depth the work of a particular artist: e.g., an exhibition on George Ohr, "the mad potter of Biloxi," brought this maverick, long-forgotten genius to the public consciousness.

Some shows are thematic: "Who'd a Thought It: Improvisation in African-American Quiltmaking" offered a group of quilts as remarkable for their intense use of color as for their stitchery.

PERMANENT COLLECTION

In addition to the changing exhibitions, the Museum keeps on view selections from its permanent collection of works in clay, metal, fiber, glass, and wood by American artists; though the earliest objects date back to the turn of the century, the collection emphasizes artists working after World War II.

THE BUILDING

Unlike some smaller midtown museums which depend on the largesse of major corporations for exhibition space, the American Craft Museum owns and controls its own territory as a condominium within the building. This happy situation is the outcome of the astute trade of its former brownstone headquarters plus the air rights of that building for a sizable chunk (15,000 sq ft) of the present one plus funds to offset the costs of finishing the interiors.

The American Museum of Natural History (91)

Central Park West at 79th St, New York 10024. Tel: (212) 769-5000. For recorded information, call (212) 769-5100. For the Naturemax Theater, call (212) 769-5650.

ADMISSION: Open Sun–Thurs 10–5:45; Fri and Sat 10–8:45. Closed Thanksgiving and Christmas Day. Suggested admission fee; some contribution required. Fixed admission fee at the Planetarium serves as entrance fee to Museum also. For Hayden Planetarium hours and information, see p. 128. Large numbers of children visit the Museum in groups (usually between 10–2 on school days); if you wish to enjoy the Museum at its quietest, come later on weekday afternoons.

Special exhibitions, highlights tours, lectures, films, concerts, educational programs, symposia. Naturemax Theater with films on space, flight, natural history, and geography. Courses in astronomy, navigation, aviation, and related subjects. Library open to the public Tues–Fri 11–4.

✘ Diner Saurus cafeteria (no bag lunches) on ground floor, open daily 11–4:45. Garden Cafe: brunch Sat and Sun 11–4; lunch: Mon–Fri 11:30–3:30; dinner: Fri and Sat 5–7:30.

▥ Main Shop near 77th St lobby carries posters, cards, toys, crafts, shell and mineral specimens, outstanding collection of books on natural history. The Junior Shop on the lower level carries educational materials and a wide range of inexpensive toys and novelties (rubber dinosaurs, pins, magic tricks).

♿ Accessible to wheelchairs. Services for the hearing-impaired. Check at Information Desk for services and schedule of sign language tours.

▐ IRT Broadway-7th Ave local (train 1 or 9) to 79th St. IND 6th Ave express (B train, rush hours only). 8th Ave local (C train) to 81st St.

🚌 M7 and M11 uptown on Amsterdam Ave, downtown on Columbus Ave. M10 via Central Park West. M79 crosstown on 79th St. M104 via Broadway.

🚗 Limited car parking (fee) in museum lot on W. 81st St.

The American Museum of Natural History (founded 1869), enjoyed by 3 million people yearly, should delight anyone of any age who is interested in anthropology, astronomy, biology, mineralogy, paleontology, or zoology. The collection contains some 36 million specimens (not all on display) ranging from world-famous dioramas of animal habitat groups and spectacular dinosaur exhibits to models of microscopic protozoa. The Museum is currently pursuing an active program to modernize the presentation of its peerless collection. The Museum is also an educational institution, which sponsors research on subjects ranging from current Asian family rituals to the evolution of long-extinct cephalopods.

HIGHLIGHTS

The Museum offers guided tours of its most popular exhibitions; check with the Information Desk for schedule.

Dinosaurs: The two Halls of Dinosaurs, which reopened after renovation in 1995, are the high point of the Museum for many visitors.

The Hall of Human Biology and Evolution, reinstalled in 1993, with state-of-the-art exhibits, including dioramas of earliest human ancestors.

The Hall of Meteorites, with a 34-ton chunk of the meteorite *Ahnighito* and three *moon rocks.*

The Hall of Minerals and Gems. Among the gems are the *Star of India sapphire,* the *DeLong Star ruby,* and the *Schettler emerald.*

The Animal Habitat Dioramas, especially the African and North American Halls.

PERMANENT COLLECTION

First Floor

The barrel-vaulted lobby in the Roosevelt Memorial wing is known as the ROTUNDA. In the center of the room, a 55-ft skeleton of a *Barosaurus,* one of prehistory's largest creatures, towers toward the ceiling, defending its young from an attacking *Allosaurus.* The 150-million-year-old fossilized skeleton of the *Barosaurus* was found in the southwestern United States; the exhibit, the tallest freestanding dinosaur exhibit in the world, is a resin-and-foam replica, since the original bones are too fragile to be mounted vertically.

In BIOLOGY OF BIRDS, an older exhibit, dioramas, skeletons of giant flightless birds (living and fossil), and hundreds of mounted specimens illustrate the major families of birds (e.g., 40 varieties of hummingbirds). The hall contains only a small fraction of the Museum's million specimens of birds (96% of all known species).

NOTE: For the Hayden Planetarium, see p. 128.

The HALL OF NORTH AMERICAN MAMMALS offers remarkable dioramas of habitat groups of musk oxen, Osborn caribou, mountain goats, bison, Alaska brown bears, grizzly bears, mountain lions, wolves, coyotes, and lynxes. Background paintings were executed by recognized masters of the genre, e.g., Perry Wilson and C. S. Chapman.

The HALL OF BIOLOGY OF INVERTEBRATES. Overhead hangs a model of a *giant squid* (39 ft), the average of several found stranded in Newfoundland in the 1870s. Other imposing invertebrates on view are a *spider crab* (spread of 11 ft), the shell of a *Tridacna gigas clam,* the world's largest bivalve mollusk, and a 34-lb *lobster.* Cases of beautiful glass models of invertebrates demonstrate one way of interpreting the microscopic world before microscopes were readily available. They were made by Herman O. Mueller, descendant of a long line of glassblowers, who worked for the Museum for 40 years, retiring in 1943.

The *Discovery Room* near the entrance of the Hall of Ocean Life and Biology of Fishes is open Sat–Sun 12–4:30, except holidays; it accommodates 25 children (with accompanying adults), who may experiment with a variety of scientific entertainments (admission by ticket, free at the first-floor Information Desk).

The HALL OF OCEAN LIFE AND BIOLOGY OF FISHES. Hanging overhead in this dimly lit hall is a 94-ft model of a *blue whale,* molded from polyurethane, supported by steel, and coated with Fiberglas. The upper-level

AMERICAN MUSEUM OF NATURAL HISTORY
First Floor

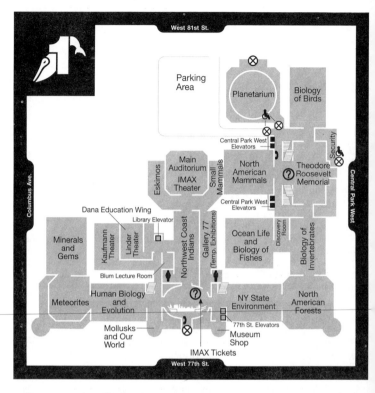

gallery contains displays on biology and the classification of fishes, beginning with fossil fish. The lower level contains dioramas of fish and marine mammals: sharks, walrus, killer whale, and others.

In the entrance corridor to the HALL OF NORTH AMERICAN FORESTS is a display, 24 times larger than life, populated with outsized creatures of the forest floor: gigantic earthworms and other specimens. Further dioramas reproduce the primary North American forest environments: giant cactus forest, mixed deciduous forest, and others.

The trees are made of wire frames with wood supports, covered with real bark. The leaves are crêpe paper dipped in beeswax and individually strung on wires, which are tapered by immersing them in nitric acid and hanging them up to drip.

Between this hall and the HALL OF NEW YORK STATE ENVIRONMENT is a cross section of a *Giant Sequoia* (harvested 1891), cut from a tree that weighed 6,000 tons and had a diameter of 16 ft 6 in.

In the 77TH ST FOYER, originally intended as the main entrance to the Museum, an exhibit shows a Chilkat Indian chief and his followers paddling a 64-ft seagoing war canoe on a ceremonial visit.

The HALL OF NORTHWEST COAST INDIANS has an outstanding collection of artifacts made by Indians whose territories stretched along the Pacific Coast from southeastern Alaska to northern California. Most imposing are two towering rows of carved totem poles which range down the center of the room. Also on display are sculpture, clothing, tools, and ceremonial objects of the Nootka, Kwakiutl, Chilkat, and Tlingit Indians. The Tlingit armor, made of carved wood or hides, was abandoned after the introduction of firearms by white traders. Other cases contain objects made by the Haida, Bella Coola, and Coast Salish tribes.

The HALL OF MOLLUSKS AND OUR WORLD is devoted to the biology of mollusks. In 1874, when shell collecting was a popular enthusiasm, the Museum acquired a collection of some 50,000 shells. Exhibits explore shell forms as well as the life cycles, distribution, and anatomy of mollusks. A full-scale photograph of Shell House (1740s) in Goodwood, Chichester, England, virtually every surface encrusted with shells, shows the excesses to which enthusiasm for shells could lead.

In the HALL OF HUMAN BIOLOGY AND EVOLUTION (opened 1993), dazzling state-of-the-art exhibits celebrate the biology of the human body, human evolution, and the beginnings of human culture. Near the entrance a skeletal female gorilla extends her finger toward the outstretched finger of a skeletal woman, in a scene some observers have found reminiscent of Michelangelo's rendering of the creation of Adam on the Sistine Chapel ceiling.

The biology section begins with a hologram and a 3-ft plastic model of the *double-helical structure of DNA*. Other exhibits illustrate the interactions of muscles and bones and retrace the course of evolution. A short film of a ballet troupe uses computer imaging to show how lungs, kidneys, and other organs work.

The highlight of the hall, however, is a group of four startling dioramas showing the hominid ancestors of human beings in their prehistoric habitats. In the most provocative, a male and female *Australopithecus afarensis* walk side by side through a plain of white volcanic ash in what is now Tanzania. The figures leave footprints which were copied for the diorama from actual footprints, made by these creatures some 3.5 million years ago and still preserved today in rock. A second diorama depicts hominids of the species *Homo ergaster* butchering a carcass while protecting the meat from animal predators. A third shows a Neanderthal family preparing hides at the mouth of the Le Moustier cave in southwest France some 50,000 years ago. A fourth, set 15,000 years ago in what is present-day Ukraine, shows an Ice Age family of Cro-Magnon humans near their hut made of mammoth bones. Displayed along with the dioramas are examples and casts of the most famous hominid skulls ever found.

The exhibit also includes early examples of human culture: reproductions from the *Lascaux* and *Altamira caves.* Among the early artifacts are 28,000-year-old fertility figures with exaggerated breasts and buttocks, a flute made of mammoth bone, and a beautiful small sculpture of a female head.

The centerpiece of the HALL OF METEORITES (opened 1981) is a 34-ton fragment of *Ahnighito* (the Eskimo name means "the Tent"), the Cape York meteorite discovered in 1897. This chunk, jocularly known among scientists as "the largest meteorite in captivity," was shipped back to New York from northern Greenland by explorer Robert Peary, who spent four Arctic summers digging it out of the frozen ground. It is surpassed in size only by a meteorite in southwest Africa which is still in the ground.

In front of a photomontage of the back side of the moon stands a case containing three *moon rocks*, representing the three major lunar types.

In the HALL OF MINERALS and the HALL OF GEMS directly beyond the Hall of Meteorites are some 6,000 of the Museum's 120,000 specimens of minerals. A cylindrical case near the entrance contains large specimens (as found) of fluorite, hematite, and sulphur, among others, chosen to illustrate the nature of minerals. Along the left wall a display of Systematic Mineralogy classifies minerals by composition and by structure. At the far end of the hall are Esthetic Stones, whose form or color makes them natural masterpieces. Elsewhere are spectacular geodes, a giant *topaz crystal* (597 lbs or 1,330,040 carats), glittering azurite and gold crystals, and agates from Brazil and Uruguay.

Near the entrance to the HALL OF GEMS stands a 4,700-lb slab of *nephrite* (more commonly known as jade) from Poland. In the hall itself, a cylindrical case opposite the door contains diamonds and star sapphires, including the world's largest blue sapphire, the *Star of India* (563 carats, mined 300 years ago in Sri Lanka), donated to the Museum (1901) by J. Pierpont Morgan. Not quite so large is the *Midnight Star* (116.75 carats), also a gift from Morgan. Equally dazzling are the rubies, including the *DeLong Star ruby* (100 carats); the emeralds, including the *Schettler engraved emerald* and the uncut *Patricia emerald* (632 carats); and an array of "fancy" (i.e., not blue) sapphires, including the *Padparadschah sapphire* (100 carats), one of the finest on display anywhere.

Second Floor

Dioramas in the WHITNEY HALL OF OCEANIC BIRDS display birds of the Pacific in a latitudinal sequence from Antarctica northward. Harry Payne Whitney, a member of one of New York's monied families, financed expeditions (1920–40) during which Museum researchers visited 1,000 islands; his widow, Gertrude Vanderbilt Whitney, and children donated this hall, as well as the Rothschild Collection of 280,000 bird specimens.

The AKELEY MEMORIAL HALL OF AFRICAN MAMMALS is known for its dramatic dioramas, including habitat groups of gorilla, rhinoceros, lion, buffalo, giraffe, and zebra. Settings are recreated from photographs and sketches made on site, and vegetation is carefully simulated: a blackberry bush in the gorilla diorama with 75,000 artificial leaves and flowers took eight months to make and cost $2,000 (in the 1930s). Special efforts were made to present the animals in characteristic actions: hyenas and vultures devouring a dead zebra, giraffes browsing.

AMERICAN MUSEUM OF NATURAL HISTORY
Second Floor

Carl Akeley (1864–1926), already famous for his innovations in taxidermy, began working for the Museum in 1909, eventually winning recognition also as a great field collector and explorer, an author and sculptor, and the inventor of a panoramic motion-picture camera and a cement gun.

The hall was completed in 1936, ten years after Akeley's death during an expedition in the Belgian Congo (now Zaire), where he was buried near Mt Mikeno, the volcano seen furthest to the right in the gorilla diorama. When, decades later, a Peace Corps worker found his grave ravaged, the Museum responded with funds to restore it.

Earlier taxidermists usually just skinned their specimens and stuffed them, but Akeley pioneered a technique of mounting that began with observing the living animal in its habitat and photographing it in motion. Akeley then copied the skeleton of the specimen and filled out the muscles and tissues with clay; from this he made a plaster cast and from that a papier-mâché mold onto which the skin was glued.

The HALL OF ASIATIC MAMMALS. Considered the best collection of such mammals in the world, the display includes a group of Indian elephants and dioramas showing habitat groups of tigers, wild boar, water buffalo, and lions, as well as a dramatic diorama of a sambar being attacked by a pack of wild dogs.

The HALL OF ASIAN PEOPLES documents traditional Asia, with exhibits of costumes, artifacts, paintings, and photographs. The display focuses on such anthropological themes as the relationship of the individual to family and society, the unifying beliefs of a culture, and the adaptation of a society to its environment.

The exhibit on *Korea* includes examples of Korean celadon, an important ceramic glaze, and movable type, invented c. 200 years before the Gutenberg Bible. Traditional cultures of *Japan* include an 18C wooden Buddha covered with gold leaf and exhibits exploring the concept of style in Japanese life.

China: On the left are cases devoted to ancestor worship and the gods of traditional China. Another case contains a beautiful bridal chair of glass, copper, wire, gilt, and kingfisher feathers. Also shown is a display on traditional Chinese science and medicine, as well as theater masks and costumes, and musical instruments.

The galleries devoted to *India* focus on village life. They include a fine diorama of an Indian village wedding, examples of theater masks and costumes, a display on Hinduism, polychromed wooden horses and musicians from a western Indian temple (19C), and wooden dancing figures (southern India, 17C).

A painting of the Grand Mosque of Mecca dominates the exhibit on the *Islamic World.* Along one wall are women's costumes from Kashmir, Afghanistan, Baluchistan, Yemen, Palestine, and Turkey, illustrating the geographical spread of Islam.

Included in a section on *Siberia* are carvings in wood, bone, and ivory, a diorama on Siberian shamanism, and artifacts of tribes who hunt, fish, and herd reindeer. The cases in the long corridor between the Siberian and Tibetan exhibitions contain rugs, furniture, jewelry, crafts, and clothing of the *tribes of Central Asia.*

The religious aspect of the culture of *Tibet* appears in the collection of *thankas* (religious paintings of deities and saints) and in Tantric ritual implements and religious sculptures.

The HALL OF BIRDS OF THE WORLD offers large dioramas organized by environment: the Canadian tundra, the New Forest in the south of England, the Alps, the Gobi Desert, Japan, the East African plains, and the South Atlantic region near Antarctica.

MAN IN AFRICA begins with two introductory rooms devoted to the origins of man and society in Africa and to river valley civilizations (the Nile, Niger, Zambesi, and Congo). The main part of the exhibition is organized environmentally, treating *Grassland, Forest-Woodland,* and *Desert* cultures.

Exhibits in the HALL OF MEXICO AND CENTRAL AMERICA use archeological finds (primarily pottery and stone carvings) as well as full-sized replicas of large monuments and architectural scale models to document the pre-Columbian cultures of *Mesoamerica.*

The rear of the room is devoted to *Maya* and *Aztec* cultures. Among the more spectacular objects are a cast of a large animal form and two 35-ft stelae, also casts, from the Maya site of Quirigua in eastern Guatemala, as well as casts of stelae and actual architectural elements from Uxmal brought back by John Lloyd Stephens, a principal discoverer of the ancient Maya ruins. Dominating the Aztec section is a full-sized replica of an Aztec stone of the sun, sometimes mistakenly thought to be a calendar.

Other objects include Toltec pottery, clay and stone sculpture from the Vera Cruz area, a tall terracotta figure (Toltec) of a man wearing the skin of a flayed sacrificial victim, and objects from the pre-Classic period (1500 B.C.–A.D. 1).

The HALL OF SOUTH AMERICAN PEOPLES portrays artifacts of aboriginal cultures from Colombia to the southern tip of Chile. Highlights include brilliantly colored textiles, pottery, and carefully crafted gold and silver ornaments.

A section on *Andean archeology* offers textiles and gold ornaments from a 2,200-year-old mummy bundle from the Paracas culture in southern Peru, photographs of the mysterious ground drawings from the Nazca culture (100 B.C. to A.D. 600), and a headdress with a rainbow of feathers from the Peruvian Chancay culture (A.D. 1100–1475). An exhibition on metallurgy and mining includes the mummified body of the "Copper Man" (A.D. 500), a Chilean miner killed when the shaft collapsed on him.

A display on ethnology uses films, artifacts, and manikins to describe *Amazonian cultures.* Particularly impressive is a plaque used during an initiation ceremony of the Wayana Indians of the Guianas: the plaque, filled with hundreds of stinging ants, is strapped to the initiate's chest as a harrowing test of endurance.

Third Floor

Exhibits in the HALL OF REPTILES AND AMPHIBIANS include mounted skins, wax-impregnated specimens, and models and plastic casts of specimens from the collection of the Department of Herpetology. Directly in front of the entrance is a giant *Galapagos tortoise,* which died some decades ago in the Bronx Zoo. Among the specimens are a reticulated python (25 ft), a rock python, a king cobra, egg-laying leatherback turtles, Komodo dragons (the world's largest lizards), an alligator, and a crocodile.

The HALL OF PRIMATES uses taxidermic specimens, skeletons, and diagrams to illustrate the distinctive characteristics and relationships of different groups of primates. Beginning with the lowly tree shrew (near the restrooms), and proceeding through lemurs, lorises, macaques, mangabeys, langurs, and baboons, the display leads up to the cases on the higher primates and, finally, man.

The next hall documents EASTERN WOODLANDS AND PLAINS INDIANS of the United States and Canada from prehistoric times to the early 20C. The Eastern Woodlands Hall is organized thematically and includes displays of clothing, houses, cooking, and fishing. On the left is an extensive display of beautiful costumes from tribes of Canada, New England, and the eastern seaboard. One case contains grotesque wooden masks from the Iroquois False Face Society.

Behind this hall is the room devoted to the Plains Indians, nomadic or seminomadic tribes living west of the Mississippi.

AMERICAN MUSEUM OF NATURAL HISTORY
Third Floor

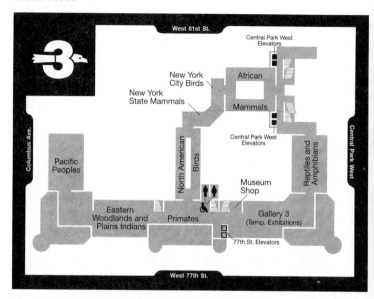

The MARGARET MEAD HALL OF PACIFIC PEOPLES, named after the anthropologist who spent 53 years at the Museum as a curator of ethnology, is the only hall of its kind in the world. It contains artifacts reflecting the Pacific cultures of *Polynesia, Micronesia, Melanesia, Australia, Indonesia,* and *the Philippines,* that is, the cultures of almost 70 separate tribal groups. Artifacts on display date from a carved stone representation of a god from 14C Java to pieces acquired after World War II.

The darker side of Pacific culture is apparent in a set of dried, smoked, and tattooed human heads prepared to honor departed chiefs by the Maori people of *New Zealand.* From *Micronesia* ("small islands") are examples of armor woven from coconut fiber and woodcarving. From *Indonesia,* including the large islands of Java, Bali, and Sumatra, are examples of household goods, theatrical equipment, beaded weapons, and batik textiles. The functional tools of the aborigines of *Australia* include the boomerang and other ingeniously designed implements.

The HALL OF NORTH AMERICAN BIRDS (completed late 1960s) succeeds an earlier hall (1909), the first ever completely devoted to habitat groups. Clockwise from the entrance are groups of game birds, Canada geese, wood stork and limpkins, western marsh birds, golden eagle, whooping crane, warblers, wading birds of the Everglades, boobies, and frigate birds. On the other walls are displays of hawks, the California condor, great horned owl, American egret, bald eagle, wild turkey, and peregrine falcon.

Fourth Floor

> **NOTE:** The Dinosaur Halls, currently in the final stages of renovation, include two HALLS OF MAMMALS AND THEIR EXTINCT RELATIVES (opened 1994) and two HALLS OF DINOSAURS (1995); the final phase, an orientation center and HALL OF PRIMITIVE VERTEBRATES, will open in 1996.

The fossil exhibitins are organized in pathways that trace the evolution of dinosaurs with a main route (marked by a stripe down the center of each galley floor) representing the "trunk" of the family tree, and branches leading to alcoves showing related groups of dinosaurs. When the reinstallation is complete, visitors can walk through some 500 million years of evolution, beginning with primitive vertebrates and ending with such giant mammals as mammoths and mastodons. The Museum has the world's largest and finest collection of fossil bones (only about 5 percent on display), including magnificent fossilized skeletons from the Jurassic period (180–120 million years ago) and the Triassic period (225–180 million years ago). Remarkably, 85 percent of the bones on display are real fossils, not casts.

HALLS OF SAURISCHIAN DISOSAURS. Dinosaurs developed from a common ancestor, whose salient evolutionary characteristic was a hole in its hip socket, a feature that allowed dinosaurs to walk upright (unlike turtles or lizards, whose legs sprawl out to the sides). Saurischian dinosaurs are further marked by a grasping hand or claw.

> **NOTE:** To follow the evolutionary path, enter from the Hall of Vertebrate Origins (open 1996); if you enter from the main corridor, the displays will run backwards chronologically. However, the following description begins at the main corridor, the only entrance open at the time of writing.

HIGHLIGHTS

Tyrannosaurus rex, mounted in a new low-slung posture; *Apatosaurus* (formerly known as *Brontosaurus*) with a longer tail and new head; two cannibalistic *Coelophysis* skeletons with bones of young *Coelophysis* inside; and the first *Velociraptor* skull ever found.

To the right of the doorway are Ornithomimids ("bird mimics"), once thought to be the ancestors of modern birds. On the other side of the hall are Maniraptors, small carnivorous dinosaurs now considered the actual ancestors of birds. It was in the Maniraptors that feathers evolved from modified reptilian scales, thus allowing flight. On view are several casts of *Archaeopteryx,* the earliest known bird. The skeleton of *Deinonychus* is the only real fossil of this non-avian Maniraptor on view anywhere in the world. One of the treasures of the Museum's current expeditions in the Gobi Desert is an egg containing an embryo (cast) of *Oviraptor* ("egg robber"), collected in 1993. From the same nest came a partial baby skull of *Velociraptor,* with bits of eggshell adhering to it. No one knows why the baby *Velociraptor* was in the oviraptorid nest.

On the left of the central walkway is a spectacular *Tyrannosaurus rex,* whose threatening posture—its massive jaws looming overhead, its tail thrust out for balance—reflects modern thinking about how history's greatest predator walked. This specimen has several healed broken ribs

AMERICAN MUSEUM OF NATURAL HISTORY
Fourth Floor

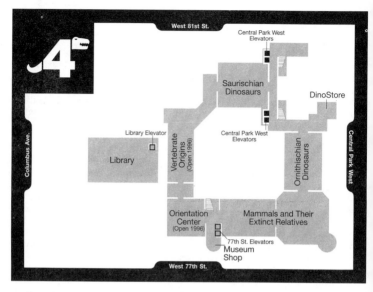

and evidence of a facial abscess, as well as several fused vertebrae in neck and lower back, indications of the traumas of a fighting life.

Across from *Tyrannosaurus rex* is *Apatosaurus*, the correct name for a dinosaur formerly known as *Brontosaurus*. The confusion dates to the 19C, when paleontologist O. C. Marsh gave different names to different fossils of the same species. This mount first appeared at the Museum in 1905; the reinstallation added 20 feet to the tail and substituted a new skull.

Near *Apatosaurus* (climb the steps to the overlook) is the *Glen Rose Trackway*, part of a long series of tracks discovered in the Paluxy River in Texas. Once thought to represent a single plant eater pursued by a single carnivore, it is now known to incorporate at least five trackways, perhaps made at widely different times.

Beyond the Apatosaurus are the most primitive Saurischian dinosaurs, the plant-eating prosauropods (alcove, right wall), including *Plateosaurus*.

Alcoves on the left side of the gallery feature Ceratosaurs (horned dinosaurs with three-toed feet) and giant, meat-eating Carnosaurs. The cast of *Allosaurus* eating *Apatosaurus* was mounted in 1908. *Apatosaurus*'s tail bones bear scratches, perhaps inflicted by an *Allosaurus*'s teeth. On the end wall are two *Coelophysis* skeletons with bones of juvenile *Coelophysis* visible inside, evidence suggesting that these carnivores were cannibals.

HALL OF ORNITHISCHIAN DINOSAURS. The exhibits are described from the entrance from the central corridor.

HIGHLIGHTS

Display includes all-time favorites *Stegosaurus* and *Triceratops*, as well as dinosuar eggs, and several examples of dinosaur "mummies" with evidence of skin and soft tissues.

Ornithischian dinosaurs, developmentally characterized by a backward-pointing extension of the pubis bone, were once thought to have a hip structure similar to that of birds. They include armored dinosaurs, duck-bills, and horned dinosaurs.

Near the entrance are the armored dinosaurs, including *Stegosaurus.* The Museum's specimen came from the Bone Cabin Quarry in Wyoming, a site named after a sheep herder's hut built on a foundation of dinosaur bones. The mistaken notion that *Stegosaurus* had two brains can be traced to the same O. C. Marsh who named one species both *Brontosaurus* and *Apatosaurus.* Describing the *Stegosaurus* in the 1890s, Marsh emphasized its small cavity and the expansion of the spinal column in the pelvis; this gave rise to the notion that *Stegosaurus* needed a second "brain" to drive its hindquarters. Also on view here are *Ankylosaurs,* creatures with clublike tails, some of them so completely plated that even their eyes could be shielded with bony curtains.

Further along are two *Robotic Skulls* (real fossils), whose chewing actions show the difference between animals that crush and grind (duck-bills) and animals that slice and dice (horned dinosaurs). On the left of the central corridor are the horned dinosaurs (Ceratopsians), beginning with a nest of dinosaur eggs originally believed to belong to *Protoceratops,* a primitive member of this group. Dinosaur eggs were first found (1923) in Mongolia by Museum researchers, a stupendous discovery confirming the hypothesis that dinosaurs indeed did lay eggs. Further along are *Triceratops,* with its big, bony neck frill, and *Styracosaurus* ("spiked reptile"), whose neck frill and nose are adorned with long spikes.

On the other side of the walkway are duck-billed dinosaurs (Hadrosaurs) and their relatives. The "mummified" skeleton of *Edmontosaurus* ("reptile from the Edmonton Formation") is displayed lying on its back with its knees drawn up just as it was found; it is remarkable in showing evidence of skin and other soft tissues. Two 30-ft duck-billed dinosaurs of the genus *Anatotitan* ("giant duck") are mounted in standard postures, but now paleontologists believe that they walked on all fours, stretching out their tails to counterbalance their necks. A skeleton of *Corythosaurus* ("Corinthian-helmet reptile") retains fossilized impressions of skin with scales of different sizes and shapes.

The HALLS OF MAMMALS AND THEIR EXTINCT RELATIVES. Begin at the square room facing Central Park, *Primitive Fossil Mammals.* Among the distant relatives of mammals are *Dimetrodon,* a dramatic fossil with a large sail-like structure on its back. *Moschops capensis,* a near relative of mammals, had a skull whose bone is almost 4 in thick. In the center of the room is a display of mammal diversity which shows the important evolutionary characteristics in the development of mammals.

An alcove on the right features Monotremes (egg-laying mammals) and Marsupials (pouched mammals). The next alcove features Edentates (toothless mammals, though actually they had teeth), including prehistoric sloths, armadillos, and anteaters. One spectacular fossil is the skel-

Dimetrodon, *an early ancestor of mammals, in the American Museum of Natural History, Hall of Primitive Mammals. The fossil collections of the Museum, unsurpassed in this country, have recently been reinstalled to reflect modern scientific theories about evolution. (American Museum of Natural History Photo Studio)*

eton of *Panochthus frenzelianus*, an armadillo-like creature, completely covered with a shell of fused bony plates.

In the next hall, *Advanced Fossil Mammals*, are carnivores, including cats, dogs, bears, and seals. A fossil of *Smilodon necator*, a saber-toothed cat, has a broken upper canine, showing how fragile these imposing teeth really were. A skeleton of *Ursus spelaeus*, a cave bear, shows the animal in a threatening posture, as it may have confronted early humans. Across the corridor from the carnivores are Glires (rabbits and rodents), insectivores, bats, and primates.

Further along (left side) are Artiodactyls (animals with an even number of toes), including pigs, deer, and camels. Facing the central corridor is a dramatic exhibit showing a bearlike *Amphicyon* ferociously pursuing its prey, and an ancestral antelope, *Ramoceros*. Nearby is *Megaloceros*, the largest deer in history, with huge, broad antlers and large neck bones to hold them up. The horse display on the central corridor shows the evolution of this animal from a small Eocene *Hyracotherium*, the earliest known horse, to the modern *Equus*.

In the alcove devoted to horses, rhinos, and tapirs is a fossil of a mare, *Protohippus simus*, that may have died giving birth; the head and limbs of the foal are visible behind the mother's rib cage.

On the other side of the corridor are prehistoric Cetaceans (porpoises and whales) and Sirenians (sea cows). Concluding the exhibit are spectacular examples of Proboscideans and Desmostylians (mammoths and mastodons), including the mummified trunk, head, and leg of a baby mammoth that was freeze-dried by the Alaskan tundra some 25,000 years ago.

As part of the restoration of the fossil halls, the Museum has restored the famous murals by Charles R. Knight, one of the first artists to use fossil remains in reconstructing the appearance of prehistoric animals.

CHANGING EXHIBITIONS

In addition to its imposing permanent collection, the Museum mounts changing exhibitions on subjects related to its collections. The most heavily attended in recent years was a cooperative effort between the Museum and the Dinosaur Society, "The Dinosaurs of Jurassic Park," based on the film *Jurassic Park*. The exhibit featured some of the life-size dinosaurs created for the movie, as well as sets and props, and important dinosaur fossils from the Museum's collection.

THE BUILDING

The Museum occupies the equivalent of four city blocks (77th to 81st Sts between Central Park West and Columbus Ave), an area once called Manhattan Sq and intended by the designers of Central Park to complement the park. The first Museum building (1877) is now almost walled in by the wings and additions that have made the present Museum an architectural hodgepodge of some 22 buildings.

The oldest visible part of the facade (1892; J. Cleveland Cady & Co.) facing West 77th St is also the most attractive. This wing, Romanesque in style, faced with pink granite has a central granite stairway that once swept up over a carriage entrance. The central portion of the facade facing Central Park is the Theodore Roosevelt Memorial, its heroic arch framing a 16-ft group showing *Theodore Roosevelt* (1940; James Earle Fraser), the 26th President, as an explorer, flanked by guides who symbolize Africa and America.

HISTORY

The American Museum of Natural History was founded (1869) during a period of intense interest in the natural sciences stimulated by the discoveries of Charles Darwin and other great Victorian scientists. Albert Smith Bickmore, a professor of natural history trained by Louis Agassiz, urged a group of philanthropic New Yorkers to obtain a state charter for a museum and to donate money for the original acquisition, some 3,400 specimens, mostly stuffed birds. This purchase was soon outclassed by the acquisition of the collection of Prince Maximilian of Neuwied, a German explorer of Brazil, who had gathered some 4,000 mounted birds, 600 mounted mammals, and 2,000 mounted and pickled fishes and reptiles.

From these beginnings the Museum has grown to its present stature: among the 36 million artifacts and specimens in the collections are 8 million insect specimens and more birds, spiders, fossil mammals, and whale skeletons than any other institution can boast. The library has a research collection of 420,000 volumes.

The collections were first housed in the Wall St banking firm of Brown Brothers. In 1871 the specimens were moved to the Arsenal in Central Park, where the public could view them. On June 2, 1874, President Ulysses S. Grant laid the cornerstone for the present building with a ceremonial trowel purchased from Tiffany's. Both trowel and cornerstone disappeared, the first during the festivities, the second over the years as builders added a profusion of wings and auxiliary buildings to the original structure. During the centennial year (1969), however, the cornerstone was finally located at the northeast corner of the Hall of Northwest Coast Indians, though the disappearance of the trowel remains unsolved.

The Americas Society Art Gallery (64)

680 Park Ave (68th St), New York 10021. Tel: (212) 249-8950.

ADMISSION: Open Tues–Sun 12–6. Closed Mon, major holidays. Suggested donation.

Lectures, concerts, group visits and guided tours by appointment, films, outreach program including lecture / slide presentations and dance demonstrations.

✖ No restaurant.

▯ Catalogues, posters, magazines, books on Latin-American culture, history.

ظ Entrance up two steps from street level; gallery on ground floor.

◯ Photography by permission. Children must be accompanied by an adult.

▆ Lexington Ave IRT local (train 6) to 68th St.

🚌 M1, M2, M3, or M4 uptown on Madison Ave, downtown on 5th Ave. M101 or M102 uptown on 3rd Ave, downtown on Lexington Ave. M29 crosstown on 66th–67th Sts.

The Americas Society (founded 1965) is a national, not-for-profit institution committed to educating Americans about their western hemisphere neighbors. Some of its programs deal with the economic, social, and political problems facing Latin America, the Caribbean, and Canada; others focus on the cultural heritage of these countries. Since 1967, the Society has mounted exhibitions documenting the artistic achievements of the western hemisphere.

EXHIBITION PROGRAM

The gallery offers three or four shows yearly, which range from pre-Columbian to contemporary art. The inaugural exhibition, "Precursors of Modernism, 1860–1930," was the first survey to place painting from North, Central, and South America in a common historic context. Fernando Botero's first solo show in the United States took place here. The gallery exhibits well-known artists, e.g., Camille Pissarro (born in the Virgin Islands), Rufino Tamayo (Mexico), and Matta (Chile), as well as younger artists virtually unknown outside their native countries.

Some historical shows have emphasized indigenous Indian cultures and their pre-Columbian heritage, with exhibitions of Aztec stone sculpture, Maya hieroglyphic writings, and bark-cloth painting by the Tikuna people of the Amazon. "The Book in the Americas" celebrated the 450th anniversary of printing in the western hemisphere (Mexico, 1539) and the 350th anniversary of printing in British America (Cambridge, Mass., 1639) with a selection of rare books from the Colonial period.

A retrospective of works on paper by Wifredo Lam, an extraordinary artist who developed a style that synthesized Cubism with elements of his native African-Cuban culture, promoted Lam as one of the foremost modernists of the Americas.

THE BUILDING

The Society enjoys the architectural amenities of what was originally an elegant private house, built (1911) for Percy Pyne, a financier. The house was designed by the distinguished firm of McKim, Mead & White. The street-level gallery has been remodeled from the former corner billiard room and the former servants' dining room. The formal rooms upstairs, used by the family, have been largely preserved as they were when the house was private.

The Arsenal Gallery (65)

In the Arsenal, 3rd floor, Central Park opposite 64th St and Fifth Ave, New York 10019. Tel: (212) 360-8163.

ADMISSION: Open Mon–Fri 9–4:30. Closed Sat, Sun, national holidays. Free.

Changing art exhibits, occasional special events.

✗ No restaurant.

🏛 No gift shop.

♿ Gallery on 3rd floor; call ahead for ramp installation at entrance. Elevator. Restrooms accessible to wheelchairs.

🚇 BMT Broadway express or local (N or R train) to 60th St and 5th Ave.

🚌 M1, M2, M3, M4 downtown on 5th Ave, uptown on Madison Ave to 60th St. M5 downtown on 5th Ave and uptown on 6th Ave. Q32 crosstown on 59th and 60th Sts, downtown on 5th, uptown on Madison Ave.

Housed in a former towered and crenelated armory at the edge of Central Park, the Arsenal Gallery (founded 1976) mounts eight to ten exhibitions yearly; many focus on contemporary art or emphasize such themes as urban parks, recreation, the environment, and local history.

EXHIBITION PROGRAM

Past shows have included exhibitions on puppetry by the Park Department's Marionette Theatre, the building of Orchard Beach and outdoor public pools, contemporary painters of the Hudson River, and the art and architecture of the Robert Moses era. An exhibition of photographs by Alice Austen celebrated the 125th anniversary of her birth.

For the annual winter holiday show, "The Wreath: Interpretations," artists, horticulturalists, and landscape architects design conventional and unconventional versions of this familiar symbol, using either ordinary natural materials (berries, leaves, flowers) or unexpected ones (glass, latex, Indian hemp cord, a raccoon skull).

THE BUILDING

The Arsenal (1848; Martin E. Thompson) was built by New York State to stockpile weapons and ammunition; replacing an older armory downtown on Centre and Franklin Sts so decrepit that thieves could easily break in and help themselves to cannonballs and small arms. When the new Arsenal was proposed, the location drew criticism as being too remote to be strategically useful—by the time the militia had gathered and fetched their weapons the disturbance would be out of control.

In 1857, during the construction of Central Park, the Arsenal was purchased by the city to serve as a station for the 11th Police Precinct; it later housed the Municipal Weather Bureau, the American Museum of

Natural History, and even, for a while, the menagerie which became the Central Park Zoo. The rifle balusters and cannon newel posts along the exterior staircase, and the eagle on the facade with its wings spread out over two piles of cannonballs, remain from the Arsenal's military past.

Artists Space (2)

223 West Broadway (bet. White / Franklin Sts), New York 10013. Tel: (212) 226-3970.

ADMISSION: Open Tues–Sat 11–6. Closed Sun, Mon, major holidays, month of Aug, Dec 25–Jan 1. Free admission to exhibitions, but charge for performances and special events.

Exhibitions, music, films and videos, lectures, artists' talks. Exhibitions catalogues and brochures.

✘ No restaurant.

▥ No gift shop, but artists' multiples—T-shirts, lithographs, photograph portfolios—available for purchase to benefit museum.

♿ Limited wheelchair access. Entrance is six steps up from street. Main gallery space on one floor, but video program and additional gallery space are down a flight of stairs.

🚋 IRT Broadway-7th Ave local (train 1 or 9) to Franklin St. IND 8th Ave express or local (A, C, or E train) to Canal St.

🚌 M6 uptown on 6th Ave, downtown on Broadway. M10 downtown on 7th Ave and Varick St, uptown on Hudson St and 8th Ave.

Artists Space was founded (1973) by the Committee for the Visual Arts at a time when the city had few galleries devoted to contemporary art and even fewer alternative art spaces. Its purpose as a nonprofit corporation was to help emerging artists surmount the obstacles confronting them, by offering financial and professional assistance. Artists Space still offers direct financial aid (e.g., to defray exhibition costs) and provides exposure through an active schedule of exhibitions, performances, and screenings. By helping artists financially and by mounting exhibitions which are not influenced by what is currently commercially successful, Artists Space hopes to encourage artists to take risks and remain true to their own vision. In supporting these artists, the gallery has garnered a reputation for integrity and independence.

Some past shows have made their mark on contemporary art history. A series entitled "Persona" launched a generation of performance artists, including Laurie Anderson. Other exhibitions provided initial exposure for such prominent figures as Scott Burton, Judy Pfaff, David Salle, and Cindy Sherman. A show in 1977 entitled "Pictures" broke new ground, displaying the work of young urban artists specifically interested in mass media culture, an interest that would later become a standard theme of contemporary art.

In 1989, the National Endowment for the Arts rescinded a grant to Artists Space because an essay in the catalogue of an exhibition about AIDS made derogatory comments about prominent political and religious leaders. Though the grant was later reinstated for the exhibition (but not for the catalogue), the incident had nationwide repercussions.

EXHIBITION PROGRAM

Exhibitions embrace painting, drawing, photography, sculpture, architecture, performance, video, and site-specific installation. Many have a political or social agenda. A show by the Border Arts Workshop based in southern California offered installations that touched on such political and social issues created by the border with Mexico as immigration and the use of pesticides by the United States in Mexico. Also on view were paintings on velvet, a traditional Mexican art form, whose subjects included both traditional and unexpected residents of the area: women in local costume, bikers. A show of work from Eastern Europe before the demolition of the Berlin Wall spotlighted the work of artists from Poland, Hungary, Czechoslovakia, and Yugoslavia.

One show annually focuses on mature artists, those who have been working for at least 20 years, but most of the artists displayed have not appeared elsewhere and none have commercial gallery affiliations.

The gallery maintains a computerized slide file of New York and New Jersey artists, open by appointment to anyone interested in seeing a body of contemporary work not easily available elsewhere. Now registering more than 3,000 artists according to style, medium, material, and scale, the file is a significant resource for curators, collectors, gallery dealers, and other artists.

The Asia Society (66)

725 Park Ave (70th St), New York 10021. Tel: (212) 288-6400. For information on current events at the Society, call (212) 517-NEWS; for ticket information, call (212) 517-ASIA.

ADMISSION: Open Tues–Sat 11–6, with extended hours Thurs evening until 8; Sun 12–5. Closed Mon, major holidays. Admission charge, except Thurs evenings 6–8.

Changing exhibitions, lectures, gallery tours (Tues–Sat 12:30; Thurs 6:30; Sun 2:30), group tours by appointment (tel: 288-6400), concerts, films, arts programs, performances of music, theater, and dance, special events.

✘ No restaurant.

▥ Bookstore with one of the nation's largest selections of books on subjects relating to Asian art, history, cultures, crafts, and cooking, as well as a good collection of children's books. Also tapes, videos, crafts, jewelry, cards, toys, gift wrap, and postcards related to Asian cultures.

♿ Accessible to wheelchairs.

⊘ No photography.

🚇 IRT Lexington Ave local (train 6) to 68th St.

🚌 M1, M2, M3, M4 uptown on Madison Ave, downtown on 5th Ave. M29 crosstown on 66th and 67th Sts.

In 1951, John D. Rockefeller III made a trip to Japan that awoke his interest in the Far East. One of the fruits of that trip was the Asia Society, which he founded five years later to deepen and enrich American understanding of Asian cultures—the arts, history, and contemporary affairs of a diverse group of peoples. Today, the Asia Society offers a full program of exhibitions and events that focus on a geographical area defined broadly to include some 30 countries—from Japan to New Zealand, from India to Indonesia.

EXHIBITION PROGRAM

The most visible part of the Asia Society's agenda is the exhibition program, which offers about four major exhibitions a year, some of them spectacular. "Court Arts of Indonesia," a sumptuous exhibition focusing on an ancient but still living civilization, brought together objects that spanned more than ten centuries. The galleries were transformed into a *kraton,* an Indonesian palace where rulers would display the treasures of the realm on ceremonial occasions; gold jewelry, metalwork, court regalia, shadow puppets, dance masks, musical instruments, and royal textiles were brought together, many of them never before seen by the public. An Indonesian fashion show, performances of shadow puppets and Balinese dance, and lectures on Indonesian history, mythology, religion, and art accompanied the exhibition.

A Festival of Korea offered 12 months of programs on Korea in cities through the United States as well as exhibitions at the Society. The centerpiece was "Korean Arts of the Eighteenth Century: Splendor & Simplicity," an exhibition which included Korean paintings, ceramics, furniture, textiles, and imperial regalia. Many of the pieces had never been seen outside Korea before. In addition, the Society sponsored exhibits of the Korean martial art tae kwondo; a film series exploring South Korean cinema in 1983–93; and a performance by shamans and musicians from the island of Chindo in southwestern Korea, who performed a ritual ceremony to invoke the presence of spirits.

Other exhibitions, some of them drawn from the Society's own collection, focus on particular genres—Japanese paintings, Chinese ceramics, or Hindu and Buddhist sculpture. At a time when the art community was up in arms over government censorship, the Society offered "Undercurrents in the Floating World: Censorship and Japanese Prints." Texts accompanying the 60 woodblock prints from the mid-18–20C showed the exercise of governmental control of the arts during the Tokugawa Shogunate. A show of 50 paintings by the 20C Chinese artist Chang Dai-chien was the first major American retrospective of this remarkable painter. The show brought together accomplished forgeries of ancient paintings that found their way into the collections of great museums, paintings in the scholar-artist tradition, and works that blended traditional Chinese painting and Western Abstract Expressionism.

PERMANENT COLLECTION

The permanent collection, whose nucleus was gathered by Mr. and Mrs. John D. Rockefeller III, is shown on a rotating basis except when major shows occupy all the gallery space. Though small in scale and personal in its reflection of the Rockefellers' tastes, it is nonetheless of uniformly high quality. It includes ceramics, sculpture, painting, woodcuts, and illustrated manuscripts from China, India, Southeast Asia, Nepal, and Japan.

THE BUILDING

The galleries are housed in the Society's headquarters building (1981; Edward Larrabee Barnes). Finished with red Oklahoma granite, the facade sports the Society's logo, a leogryph or winged lion adapted from an 18C bronze Nepalese figure.

The Asian American Arts Centre (3)

26 Bowery (Canal St), 2nd floor, New York 10013. Tel: (212) 233-2154.

ADMISSION: Open Tues–Fri 12–6; Sat 3–6. Free admission to galleries, admission charge for performance events.

Changing exhibitions, classes in traditional Chinese arts, panel discussions, video programs, lectures, special events.

✘ No restaurant.

▥ Catalogues; folk art items and small gifts sold during Chinese New Year folk art exhibition.

♿ Not accessible to wheelchairs.

⃠ No commercial photography.

🚇 IRT Lexington Ave local (train 6) to Canal St. IND 6th Ave express (B or D train) to Grand St. BMT Broadway local (N or R train) to Canal St.

🚌 M102 downtown on 3rd Ave to Chatham Square. M15 downtown on 2nd Ave to Chatham Square.

Founded 1974, the Asian American Arts Centre is one of the oldest Asian-American arts organizations in the country, sponsoring programs that support both the traditional arts of Asia and the work of contemporary artists.

EXHIBITION PROGRAM

The Centre mounts five to seven exhibitions annually that focus on the work of Asian-American artists and on issues of interest to the Asian-American community. In 1989, to commemorate the abortive uprising in Tiananmen Square, "China: June 4, 1989," a year-long exhibition, featured small works and photo documentation and drew the participation of some 270 artists of different cultural and racial backgrounds. This inspired a similar exhibition in Los Angeles, and eventually became part of a memorial show in Hong Kong.

Other exhibitions have included the annual "From 'Star Star' to Avant Garde: Nine Artists from China" and " 'Folk' Tradition New York, New York," a photographic documentation of nine artists in the Chinese-American community who work in such traditional arts as Chinese origami, embroidery, and dough figures. "And He was Looking for Asia" explored the meanings of Christopher Columbus's discovery from the point of view of nine culturally diverse artists. To celebrate the Chinese New Year and keep alive these authentic customs and folk art forms, the Centre each year presents a festival featuring artists working in traditional media. Solo shows have showcased the work of contemporary Korean-American,

Chinese-American, Japanese-American, and Philippine-American artists.

The Artists Archive of more than 400 Asian-American visual artists is the only one of its kind in the nation, and is a resource for scholars, curators, and researchers.

Audubon Terrace (100)

American Numismatic Society, American Academy and Institute of Arts and Letters, Hispanic Society of America at Audubon Terrace, Broadway at 155th St, New York 10032.

Audubon Terrace, a complex of formal, classical buildings grouped around a central courtyard, was the inspiration of Archer Milton Huntington, founder of the Hispanic Society of America. His goal was to create an intellectual center available not only to scholars and students but to the public as well. In 1904, Huntington bought parts of Audubon Park, which had been the estate and game preserve of artist John James Audubon, and hired his cousin, architect Charles Pratt Huntington, to design a master plan and most of the buildings, including the Hispanic Society.

At the time Audubon Terrace was conceived, the neighborhood was still suburban. Trinity Church had established its cemetery between West 153rd and West 155th Sts in 1876 and in 1914 would build the Church of the Intercession at 155th St. Around the corner on 156th St, Charles Huntington built the Church of Our Lady of Esperanza (1912), whose stained-glass windows and skylights were given by the king of Spain. But the promise of the neighborhood to evolve like Morningside Heights never quite materialized. Audubon Terrace remains stranded in a neighborhood known more for its ethnic diversity than for its intellectual achievement.

The American Academy and Institute of Arts and Letters (99)

Audubon Terrace, Broadway at 155th St, New York 10032. Tel: (212) 368-5900.

ADMISSION: Open during exhibitions, Tues–Sun 1–4. Free.

Changing exhibitions.

✗ The Museum is in a remote neighborhood, with few choices for restaurants.

🏛 No gift shop.

♿ Not accessible to wheelchairs.

🚇 IRT Broadway-7th Ave local (train 1) marked 242nd St to 157th St and Broadway.

🚌 M4 via Madison Ave to 155th St / Broadway. M5 via 6th Ave and Broadway to 155th St / Broadway.

🚗 Henry Hudson Pkwy to 158th St exit. Go east to Broadway and south to 155th St. Some street parking.

The American Academy and Institute of Arts and Letters is the nation's most prestigious society honoring the fine arts, literature, and music. It implements its goal—furthering interest in the arts—by singling out individual artists and recognizing them. In addition to offering annual awards to established artists, it also offers prizes or fellowships to promising younger artists, exhibitions of art and manuscripts, and readings and performances of new work.

PERMANENT COLLECTION

The Academy-Institute (its shortened name) has a permanent collection of original manuscripts of musical and literary works by members, who include such major historical figures as Mark Twain, Sinclair Lewis, John Dos Passos, Elliott Carter, Edward MacDowell, and Eugene O'Neill. The fine arts collection includes paintings, sculpture, drawings, lithographs, etchings, and photographs of works of art by members. The library holds more than 21,000 books by or about members. The art, book, and manuscript collections are open to accredited scholars by appointment.

EXHIBITION PROGRAM

The annual exhibition schedule begins in March with an invitational show of painting and sculpture by candidates for the Academy-Institute's art awards. In May, when new members are formally inducted, an exhibition of manuscripts, books, art and architecture, and musical scores presents the work of newly elected members and award recipients. The autumn exhibition, held in November–mid-December, includes contemporary paintings purchased by the Academy-Institute and donated to museums; sometimes this exhibition includes memorial shows featuring the life work of deceased members or special exhibits of material from the permanent collections.

THE BUILDINGS

The Academy-Institute occupies two buildings facing one another across the courtyard of Audubon Terrace. The Administration Building, on the south side, was designed by McKim, Mead & White (1923). The North Gallery was designed by Cass Gilbert, a member of the Academy, most famous for the Woolworth Building on Broadway near City Hall Park. The imposing bronze doors facing Audubon Terrace are by Herbert Adams, a member of the Academy, and are decorated with classical figures representing inspiration and the various arts. The back doors facing 155th St, the work of Academy member Adolph A. Weinman, are dedicated to the now-obscure novelist Mary E. Wilkins Freeman, one of the first women elected to the Institute, and to "women writers of America."

HISTORY

The American Academy and Institute of Arts and Letters owes its cumbersome name to its history. The National Institute of Arts and Letters was founded in 1898, its members chosen to represent the highest artistic achievement of the era: among them were Henry Adams, the James brothers (William and Henry), and two future presidents—Woodrow Wilson and Theodore Roosevelt—selected for the merit of their literary works. Then, in 1904 the American Academy of Arts and Letters was founded as the inner circle of this already august group. Its membership would be limited to 50 people, of whom the first 7 were chosen by the Institute. These 7 then chose 8 more; then the 15 chose 5 more, and so on until the full 50 were chosen. The original seven were (in order of votes received): William Dean Howells, Augustus Saint-Gaudens, Edmund Clarence Stedman, John LaFarge, Mark Twain, John Hay, and Edward MacDowell.

In 1913, the Institute was incorporated by an Act of Congress; the Academy followed suit three years later. In 1976, the two organizations voted to merge. The Institute is limited to 250 painters, sculptors, architects, composers, and writers, who are nominated and elected by members.

The American Numismatic Society (98)

Broadway at 155th St, New York 10032. Tel: (212) 234-3130.

ADMISSION: Open Tues–Sat 9–4:30; Sun 1–4. Closed Mon and holidays. Library open Tues–Sat 9–4:30. Free. Ring bell for entrance.

Changing exhibitions, lectures, seminars for graduate students.

✘ No restaurant. No easily available choices in the neighborhood.

🏛 No gift shop, but publications of the Society are available for purchase.

♿ Not accessible to wheelchairs.

🚆 IRT Broadway-7th Ave local (train 1) marked 242nd St to 157th St and Broadway.

🚌 M4 via Madison Ave to 155th St / Broadway. M5 via 6th Ave and Broadway to 155th St / Broadway.

🚗 Henry Hudson Pkwy to 158th St exit. Go east to Broadway and south to 155th St. Some street parking.

The American Numismatic Society was founded (1858) to promote knowledge of coins and coinage, particularly as related to history, art, archeology, and economics. Since that time, the Society has gathered a collection of some 750,000 numismatic objects (coins, medals, tokens, paper money, and glass weights) and established a world-famous research library of some 50,000 volumes, to serve Society members, scholars, and collectors.

Strong areas of the collection include Greek and Roman coins, Latin-American coins, Islamic coins, and, not surprisingly, U.S. coins. There are also unusual and unexpected areas of strength: coins from 17–18C Germany, Swedish and Polish coins, and tokens from 17–18C England. During periods when the national currency collapsed—e.g., in England during the Civil War—private individuals who needed change to conduct business (notably pub owners and grocers) issued tokens which temporarily served as coins.

Most of the collection has come through donations; Edward T. Newell, president of the Society from 1916 until his death in 1941, gave one such bequest of some 60,000 Greek, Roman, Islamic, South Asian, and Chinese coins. The Society has augmented the collection through purchases, making a number of wise acquisitions during the Depression.

PERMANENT EXHIBITION

In the WEST GALLERY, "World of Coins" traces the history of coinage from about 500 B.C. to the present. Objects on display range from ancient Greek coins to that ubiquitous contemporary numismatic object, the plastic credit card. Although specific displays within the exhibit are occasionally rotated, certain highlights are usually on view: an early Greek *elektron*, Roman copper coins, a Byzantine gold *scyphates*, Carolingian silver pennies, a Standing Caliph dinar (one of the earliest Arab coins struck), early German *thalers*, and Spanish pieces of eight.

In the EAST GALLERY is a display of American coinage redesigned between 1892 and 1922, including a proof Morgan dollar, a high-relief double eagle designed by Augustus Saint-Gaudens, and the plaster model for the Lincoln cent. Also on view are commemoratives from the 1920s, struck to celebrate such events as the Maine and Missouri centenaries. The hall contains examples of medals and decorations as well, some of them very elaborate.

Like coins, medals reflect contemporary taste, and preserve for future generations the likenesses of famous people. Among the medals usually on view are some devoted to the American Revolution, to Napoleon, and to the French Revolution. Orders and decorations, often elaborate and colorful, comprise British Orders of Knighthood, including the "Most Noble Order of the Garter," as well as American and European decorations.

Also in the East Gallery are changing exhibitions, often related to lectures and conferences sponsored by the Society. One exhibition drew on the Society's holdings of Mexican coins, considered among the best in the world. Another focused on coinages during the bullion shortage in the United States in the 1780s, an exhibition that ironically had to demonstrate a lack of coins.

THE BUILDING

The building (1907) was designed by Charles Pratt Huntington, as part of the Audubon Terrace complex.

The Hispanic Society of America (106)

In Audubon Terrace, Broadway at 155th St, New York 10032. Tel: (212) 926-2234.

ADMISSION: Open Tues–Sat 10–4:30; Sun 1–4. Closed Mon, Easter weekend, major holidays, and part of the Christmas season (call for information). Reading room open Tues–Fri 1–4:30; Sat 10–4:30. Closed Easter weekend, the month of Aug, Thanksgiving weekend, and part of the Christmas season; call for information. Free.

Changing exhibitions. Group tours by appointment.

✗ No restaurant. No neighborhood restaurants easily available.

▥ Sales desk with books, postcards, color prints, catalogues.

♿ Not accessible to wheelchairs.

⊘ Only hand-held still cameras without flash permitted. Visitors not permitted to touch objects.

🚃 IRT Broadway-7th Ave local (train 1) marked 242nd St to 157th St and Broadway.

🚌 M2, M3, M4 via Madison Ave to 155th St / Broadway. M5 via 6th Ave and Broadway to 155th St / Broadway.

Behind the austere classical facade of the Hispanic Society of America (1904) is one of the city's most beautiful exhibition spaces and one of its more remarkable collections. Both the interior courtyard decorated with carved red terracotta and the collection displayed within express the passionate commitment to Spanish culture of Archer Milton Huntington (1870–1955), who founded the Society. Huntington, son of railroad magnate Collis P. Huntington, became fascinated with the Iberian peninsula early in life and visited Spain as a young man, when he began collecting archeological fragments from Italica, the earliest Roman colony in Spain. The collection today, most of it gathered by Huntington, ranges from the prehistoric period, through the epochs of Roman and Moorish domination, to the present; it contains examples of painting, sculpture, and decorative arts as well as archeological objects. The library has thousands of manuscripts and more than 200,000 early and modern books on Spanish and Portuguese history, literature, and art. In the Iconography Collection are prints, maps, and globes, as well as an extensive photographic reference archive.

PERMANENT COLLECTION

The entrance hall opens into the MAIN COURT, two stories high and illuminated in part by skylights. In the central section are three treasures of the collection: two portraits by Francisco de Goya, *The Duchess of Alba* and *Manuel Lapeña, Marquis of Bondad Real,* and a 13C polychromed wood *Mater Dolorosa.* Also displayed are pieces of antique furniture, including several elaborately decorative 17C *vargueños,* which opened to serve as desks and whose many drawers and hidden places could conceal valuables.

In the Main Court but outside the arches are panels from a 14C Catalan retable (Spanish, *retablo,* an altarpiece that stands on the back of an altar or on a pedestal), and a 15C *retablo* from northern Spain whose panels depict the Assumption of the Virgin. Between the Main Court and the Sorolla Room, a small corridor contains a display of tiles and glazed 18–19C earthenware from Valencia and Toledo.

The corridor opens into the SOROLLA ROOM, decorated with a series of murals by Joaquín Sorolla y Bastida Bastida, which depict Spanish regional scenes and festivals. Sorolla, a prolific 19–20C painter and graphic artist who worked mainly in Valencia, produced portraits of celebrated political and literary figures, intimate family scenes, history paintings, and religious works, but is best known for his sun-drenched landscapes.

The main stairway near the entrance to the building, decorated by a display of Hispano-Moresque tiles and mosaics, leads to the UPPER LEVEL of the MAIN GALLERY. Here are displays of ceramics and glass from prehistoric times onward, including the best collection of Spanish ceramics in the United States. Of particular interest are the examples of His-pano-Moresque lusterware, in which metal particles are fired onto the surface of the piece, giving a luminous finish, a technique developed by Islamic ceramists. Luisa Roldán, the only woman to hold the position of royal sculptor, is represented by several polychromed terracotta groups, *The Mystical Marriage of St. Catherine, The Repose in Egypt,* and *The Death of Mary Magdalene.* Paintings by Spanish artists include: Francisco de Goya, *Alberto Foraster* and *Pedro Mocarte;* El Greco, *Pietà, St. Jerome, The Holy Family,* and *St. Luke;* Francisco de Zurbarán, *St. Rufina* and *St. Lucy;* Diego Velázquez, *Portrait of a Little Girl;* and Luís de Morales, *The Holy Family.*

OUTDOOR COURTYARD

Huntington's wife, Anna Vaughn Hyatt Huntington, was a sculptor known for her renderings of animals, and over a period of some 20 years she decorated the courtyard with works inspired by the history and culture of Spain. The equestrian statue of *El Cid Campeador* (1927) dominates the group: the central figure of the 11C knight who led Spain in the reconquest against the Moors is shown rising in his stirrups, waving a pennant. On either side of *El Cid* are limestone reliefs, one representing *Don Quixote* (1942), romantic hero of Cervantes's epic, and the other *Boabdil* (1943), last Moorish king of Granada. Hyatt also sculpted the stone lions (1930) guarding the entrance door to the Hispanic Society.

Baruch College: Sidney Mishkin Gallery (39)

135 East 22nd St (Lexington Ave), New York 11010. Tel: (212) 387-1006.

ADMISSION: Open during the academic year Mon–Fri 12–5; Thurs until 7. Closed weekends, academic holidays, some Jewish holidays, Jan for semester break, June, July, Aug. Free.

Changing exhibitions, lectures, symposia, gallery talks, gallery tours, educational programs.

✕ No restaurant.

⛉ Catalogues; no gift shop.

♿ Accessible to wheelchairs.

⊘ No photography.

🚋 IRT Lexington Ave local (train 6) to 23rd St.

🚌 M1, M2, M3 downtown via 5th Ave and Park Ave South. M23 cross-town on 23rd St.

The Sidney Mishkin Gallery (founded 1983) of Baruch College offers a program of highly regarded exhibitions that stake out original territory in the New York art scene. Located on the ground floor of the Administration Center of Baruch College, a branch of the City University of New York, the Gallery mounts five shows yearly, often accompanied by lectures, symposia, and other events.

EXHIBITION PROGRAM

Exhibitions include both contemporary and historical shows, scholarly shows, multicultural shows, and one-person exhibitions of mature artists. Recently the Gallery mounted a retrospective of prints by the well-known contemporary artist Elizabeth Murray. A historical show that gained widespread critical praise, "The Indian Space Painters: Native American Sources for American Abstract Art," focused on painters of the 1940s and 1950s who were influenced by the art of the Pacific Northwest Coast Indians.

Other exhibitions reflect the multiculturalism of the student body, e.g., a display of photography by jazz bassist Milt Hinton; collages by Romare Bearden; "Venezuela: The Next Generation," a group show of nine young painters; and "Changing Cultures: Immigrant Artists from China," which paired work by the artists before and after immigrating.

Because the college is a research institution, some shows are related to the course of study. A retrospective of the work of Esphyr Slobodkina, painter, sculptor, textile designer, and illustrator, included a lecture by the artist to education students.

Exhibitions on artists shown widely in New York concentrate on a particular aspect of the work. When some murals by the young Franz Kline were discovered in Pennsylvania, the Gallery mounted a show of his early work, and a Marsden Hartley exhibition focused on a period the artist spent in Bavaria painting the Alps.

PERMANENT COLLECTION

In 1992 the college received an important gift from Sidney Mishkin, an accountant and businessman, including ten works by modern European and American artists: Marsden Hartley, Alexander Calder, Barbara Hepworth, Max Ernst, Matta, and Andre Masson. The small permanent collection also includes works on paper, prints, and photographs.

Carnegie Hall Museum (40)

Carnegie Hall (2nd floor), 154 West 57th St (7th Ave), New York 10019. Tel: (212) 903-9629.

ADMISSION: Open to public Thurs–Tues, 11–4:30 Museum also open to concertgoers: ½ hr before event through intermission. Closed Wed, New Year's Day, Memorial Day, July 3–4, Labor Day, Thanksgiving, Dec 24–25. Free.

Changing exhibitions.

✗ Restaurant; cafe connected to Museum and concert hall, open to concertgoers.

⌂ Gift shop with books, records, tapes, items associated with music.

&. Accessible to wheelchairs.

⊘ No photography. No food or drink in Museum.

🚇 IRT Broadway-7th Ave local (train 1 or 9) to 59th St / Columbus Circle. IND 8th Ave express or local (A, B, C, D, or E train) to 59th St Columbus Circle. BMT Broadway express or local (R or N train) to 57th St / 7th Ave.

IND 6th Ave express or local (B, D, E train) to 7th Ave at 53rd St.

🚌 M5, M6, or M7 uptown via 6th Ave. M10 uptown on 8th Ave. M104 uptown via 8th Ave. M30, M57, or M58 crosstown on 57th St.

Founded in 1991, Carnegie Hall's centenary year, the Museum plays host to a permanent collection of Carnegie Hall memorabilia and changing exhibitions relating to music and the history of the Hall.

PERMANENT COLLECTION

In the permanent collection of some 300 items are photographs of famous classical musicians, jazz artists, and lecturers who have appeared at Carnegie Hall. Memorabilia include Benny Goodman's clarinet, Toscanini's baton, and a collection of posters and programs, including one signed by the Beatles at the time of their Carnegie Hall debut.

EXHIBITION PROGRAM

The opening exhibition, entitled "Tchaikovsky at Carnegie Hall: Centennial of an American Journey," commemorated the Russian composer, then 51 years old, who came to New York in 1891 to take part in the festival that celebrated the opening of the Music Hall, as Carnegie Hall was then named. Handsomely displayed were documents recording the composer's arrival (including a picture of the French steamer that brought him) and his diaries, in which he entered practical queries about how to get on in New York ("Can you drink from the faucet?") and observations about the city (the downtown buildings were, even in 1891, "senselessly colossal: How can one live on the 13th floor?"). Other shows have included a display of Beethoven manuscripts, which coincided with a performance cycle of the composer's piano sonatas, and an ambitious exhibition on Leonard Bernstein to celebrate the 50th anniversary of his debut at Carnegie Hall.

THE BUILDING

Carnegie Hall was built in 1891 by Andrew Carnegie as the home for the Oratorio Society, of which the philanthropic industrialist was president for a time. A musical landmark, the building came close to demolition in the 1960s when its owners began yearning for larger profits (Andrew Carnegie never made money on it either). A committee of preservationists headed by violinist Isaac Stern saved it, to the relief of traditionalists throughout the country.

In 1986, the Hall was refurbished. Unfortunately, by common consensus, although the restoration returned the auditorium to its former physical beauty, it diminished the formerly legendary acoustics.

Castle Clinton National Monument (4)

In Battery Park, New York 10004. Tel: (212) 344-7220.
ADMISSION: Open daily 8:30–5. Closed Christmas Day. Free.

Information kiosk on parade ground. Brochures on all National Park Service sites in Manhattan. Ticket booth for Statue of Liberty and Ellis Island ferries. Ticket kiosk open 8:30–3 in winter; extended hours in summer.

✗ No restaurant; coffeeshops and restaurants on lower Broadway.

🛍 Kiosk with books, postcards.

& Accessible to wheelchairs.

🚇 IRT Broadway-7th Ave local (train 1 or 9) to South Ferry; IRT Lexington Ave express (train 4 or 5) to Bowling Green. BMT Broadway local (N or R train) to Whitehall St.

🚌 M1 (marked South Ferry) downtown via 5th Ave, Park Ave South, and Broadway. M6 downtown via 7th Ave and Broadway. M15 downtown via 2nd Ave and Allen St. Rush hours only (southbound mornings, northbound afternoons): express bus X25 from Grand Central to Wall St; X92 from 92nd St / Yorkville Ave to Wall St.

Although most people go to Castle Clinton (1811) only to get tickets for the ferries to the Statue of Liberty and Ellis Island, the low brick structure has had a long and illustrious history serving the city and the nation. A permanent exhibit chronicles its splendid past.

HISTORY

Castle Clinton, built as a fort to protect the harbor during the War of 1812, has been reincarnated over the years as a theater, an immigration station, an aquarium, and a historical museum. It was probably designed by John McComb, Jr., one of the city's earliest native architects, most famous for his work on City Hall.

In 1807, when the British attacked the American frigate *Chesapeake* in New York Harbor, the city realized that it was virtually undefended from the sea and quickly raised five forts, including Castle Clinton (then called the South-west Battery) and Fort Wood on Bedloe's (now Liberty) Island. The placement of paired forts across a strategic waterway was a common 19C notion of coastal defense.

The South-west Battery at the time stood in 35 ft of water, about 100 yds from shore. The walls facing the harbor were fortified by 28 cannon, while those facing the land housed powder magazines and quarters for the officers.

Briefly renamed Castle Clinton after the war to honor De Witt Clinton, mayor of the city and later governor of the state, it was remodeled in 1824 as Castle Garden, a "place of resort" for entertainment. Ladies and gentlemen promenaded atop its thick sandstone walls and took refreshments in its officers' quarters. Famous people, notably the marquis de Lafayette and Andrew Jackson, were publicly received here; on Sept 11, 1850, Jenny Lind, the "Swedish Nightingale," appeared under the sponsorship of the redoubtable P. T. Barnum in a wildly successful concert.

In 1855 the building became an immigrant station. Earlier, Castle Garden had been joined to the mainland by landfill and now it was fenced off from the surrounding park to protect the new arrivals from the omnipresent swindlers who lurked around the station. The old fort remained the gateway to America until 1889, when the federal government took over the immigration service.

In 1896 the building became the popular New York Aquarium, surviving until 1941, when Robert Moses, then Commissioner of Parks, resolved to tear it down. The fish were taken to Coney Island, but a citizens' group managed to delay demolition until Congress declared the fort a national monument in 1946.

PERMANENT EXHIBITION

Directly in front of the main gate, a statue entitled *The Immigrants* (1981; Luis Sanguino) pays homage to the 8 million immigrants who passed through these gates during its 35 years as an immigrant station. On the right side of the passageway a small museum recreates the history of the building with dioramas, photographs, and artifacts.

Central Park: The Dairy (67)

In Central Park, near 65th St transverse, west of the Zoo and north of Wollman Rink. Central Park Visitor Center, Central Park, New York 10019. Tel: (212) 360-3444 for recorded information on park events. To reach a live person, call 1-800-201-PARK.

ADMISSION: Open mid-Feb–mid-Oct: Tues–Thurs, Sat–Sun 11–5, Fri 1–5; mid-Oct–mid-Feb closes at 4. Open Memorial Day and Labor Day. Closed Mon, New Year's Day, Thanksgiving, Christmas Day, and most city holidays; call ahead to check holiday closings. Free.

Video on history of park. Family workshops (free but reservations required), concerts, performances, map for self-guided walking tour of park, information on Central Park, calendars of events.

✕ No restaurant. Cafe at Central Park Zoo.

⊩ Restrooms nearby in park or at Central Park Zoo.

▥ Gift shop with maps, books on Central Park, T-shirts, souvenirs, postcards.

♿ Accessible to wheelchairs.

⊘ No pets.

🚊 BMT Broadway express or local (N or R train) to 60th St and 5th Ave.

🚌 M1, M2, M3, M4 downtown on 5th Ave, uptown on Madison Ave to 60th St. M5 downtown on 5th Ave and uptown on 6th Ave. M30 crosstown on 72nd St, downtown on 5th Ave.

The Dairy, a fanciful little Victorian building (1858) once used to supply milk to urban children, since 1981 has served as an information center for Central Park. Exhibits include a 12-ft, three-dimensional map of the park, and a video, *Oasis in the City,* which explores the past, present, and future of the park. A touch-screen video shows park highlights and offers information about cultural institutions nearby, while a small permanent display of photographs documents the restoration of the building.

HISTORY

When Frederick Law Olmsted and Calvert Vaux designed Central Park (1858), they set aside for children and their parents the southern portion, the part most accessible to the city, which in the mid-19C was sparsely developed this far north. Their plans included the Dairy, the Children's Cottage with rental play equipment, the Carousel, two rustic shelters—the Kinderberg and the Cop Cot—and a ballfield or playground. At a time when fresh milk was not readily available in the city (the two prime sources were the herds of cows kept by breweries to eat the leftover mash and the surplus milk brought in by dairy farmers outside the city), the Dairy was more than just a romantic pastoral feature. Its herd of cows was stabled in the Children's Cottage and grazed in the field between the Dairy and what is now Wollman Rink. After years of decline, the Dairy was restored in 1981, the ornate wooden loggia recreated from the original drawings and painted in Victorian colors.

The Central Park Wildlife Center (formerly Central Park Zoo) (68)

In Central Park at 64th St near Fifth Ave, New York 10019. Tel: (212) 439-6500.

> **NOTE:** The Central Park Children's Zoo, currently closed, is scheduled to reopen in 1997.

ADMISSION: Open every day of the year 10:30–4:30. Tickets sold until a half hour before closing. Admission charge.

Changing exhibitions of art and photography on animal themes. Wildlife Conservation Center gallery devoted to the environment and conservation. Educational programs; catalogue of classes and special lectures available; call Education Department weekdays at (212) 439-6538.

✗ Zoo Cafe serves sandwiches, light meals, other refreshments.

🏛 Gift shop with souvenirs, books, games, T-shirts, stuffed animals, items related to wildlife and wild places.

&. Accessible to wheelchairs.

⊘ Pets and radios not permitted.

🚇 BMT Broadway express or local (N or R train) to 60th St and 5th Ave. IRT Lexington Ave local (train 6) to 68th St.

🚌 M1, M2, M3, M4 downtown on 5th Ave, uptown on Madison Ave to 60th St. M5 downtown on 5th Ave and uptown on 6th Ave. M30 crosstown on 72nd St, downtown on 5th Ave.

Elegantly designed and appropriately scaled, this 5-acre zoo is one of Central Park's treasures, a delight to young and old since 1935. The zoo is divided into three zones, *Temperate, Tropic, and Polar,* with animal exhibits and environments to match: real and artificial vegetation, an elaborate sprinkler system that exhales a humid jungle atmosphere, and a man-made pseudo-Antarctic icepack. Among the animals are red pandas, river otters, and penguins, all chosen for their interest to the visitor and their ability to adapt to zoo conditions.

HISTORY

Although the designers of Central Park, Frederick Law Olmsted and Calvert Vaux, disapproved of caging animals in urban zoos, park commissioners were soon deluged with gifts of animals. To provide shelter for them they established a menagerie in the Arsenal, which remained there until 1934. In 1935 the menagerie was replaced by the Central Park Zoo, which featured both large and small animals, most confined to barred cages. The zoo was redesigned and renovated (1988) by the firm of Kevin Roche, John Dinkeloo & Assocs to make the exhibits more suitable to their urban setting. The new zoo retains the much-loved sea lions and polar bears, but otherwise concentrates on smaller animals.

The Children's Museum of Manhattan (92)

212 West 83rd St (bet. Broadway / Amsterdam Ave), New York 10025. Tel: (212) 721-1234.

ADMISSION: Open Mon, Wed, and Thurs 1:30–5:30; Fri, Sat, and Sun 10–5. Closed Tues, New Year's Day, Thanksgiving, and Christmas Day. Call for hours on school holidays. Summer hours (June 15 through Labor Day) open Wed–Mon 10–5; closed Tues. Admission charge.

Changing exhibitions; art and nature workshops, interactive exhibitions; puppet shows, performances, films, storytelling, holiday celebrations, outreach programs (including parenting classes for teen parents), programs for homeless children and those in temporary housing.

✗ No restaurant.

▥ Gift shop with educational toys, craft supplies, books, cross-cultural toys, toys related to exhibitions.

& Accessible to wheelchairs.

⊘ IRT Broadway-7th Ave local (train 1 or 9) to 86th St. IND 6th Ave express (B train) to 81st St / Central Park West.

▦ M104 via Broadway; M11 uptown on 10th Ave / Amsterdam Ave, downtown on Columbus Ave / 9th Ave. M10 uptown on 8th Ave / Central Park West, downtown on Central Park West / 7th Ave. M7 uptown on 6th Ave / Broadway / Amsterdam Ave, downtown on Columbus Ave / 7th Ave. M79 crosstown on 79th St. M86 crosstown on 86th St.

While the Children's Museum of Manhattan (founded 1979 as the Manhattan Laboratory Museum) may seem to its youthful devotees like a four-story playground, it is in fact a technologically and educationally sophisticated museum for children from early toddlerhood to adolescence.

The Museum offers a whole building full of interactive exhibits and activities. The Main Exhibition Hall on the first floor features long-term, large-scale exhibits accompanied by hands-on activities. There is a gallery devoted to children's art and another to children's book illustration. Elsewhere in the building are activity centers for children of different ages.

EXHIBITION PROGRAM

In addition to its permanent facilities, the Museum has long-term changing exhibitions. "Discovering Dinosaurs" set children digging for dinosaur fossils in a sand-covered table and constructing their own 4-ft dinosaurs from skeleton puzzle parts. A Chroma-key wall let children see themselves on television in prehistoric settings. Overseeing these paleontological activities was a 34-ft robotic *Apatosaurus* that emitted reptilian sounds and a *Protoceratops* family that included real dinosaur bones and egg fragments on loan from the American Museum of Natural History.

A major exhibition on children's collections (Pez containers, baseball cards, Barbie dolls, chopstick rests) explored not only the collections themselves but the motivations and values behind them. Among the exhibit spaces was a mirrored triangular room where visitors were surrounded by a floor-to-ceiling collection of Mickey Mouse souvenirs and models, reflected and re-reflected by the walls to create an infinitude of mouse memorabilia.

The Environmental Center (opened 1992) is a permanent steel frame structure made of recycled materials and installed outside the Museum. Environmental exhibitions in this "Urban Tree House" include "Get to Know Your Trash," where children can fish with magnets as they learn about waste management, and "Underground New York," where visitors can explore the complex underground systems that supply New York with light, power, water, and steam.

The Early Childhood Center and the Family Learning Center offer activities for preschoolers and the grownups who accompany them.

The Media Center has a fully equipped television news studio and control room. Nearby is the media studio, a theater and rehearsal hall, which on weekends features performances by children's theater groups, dancers, puppeteers, and storytellers, as well as productions by children and teenagers.

The Children's Museum of the Arts (5)

72 Spring St (near Broadway bet. Crosby / Lafayette Sts), New York 10012. Tel: (212) 941-9198 for recorded information; to reach a live person, call (212) 274-0986.

ADMISSION: Open Tues–Sun 11–5. Closed Mon, New Year's Day, Thanksgiving, and Christmas Day. Museum remains open many New York City school holidays; call for schedule. Summer hours (June–Aug) Thurs 11–7; Fri–Sun 11–5; closed Mon–Wed. Admission charge. Children under 18 months and adults over 65 free.

Changing exhibitions. Daily activities in the Artist Studio include workshops (giant animal sculpture, Valentine's Day cards, mural making, beadwork, self-portraiture). Also performances, storytelling, interactive theater, musical activities. Birthday parties, play groups.

✘ No restaurant.

🏛 Gift shop with craft kits, arts materials, books, videotapes, educational materials, board games, building blocks, reproductions from the Museum's collection of children's art; handcrafted children's furniture.

♿ Accessible to wheelchairs and strollers.

⊘ Children must be accompanied by an adult. Photography of art works by permission.

🚇 IRT Lexington Ave local (train 6) to Spring St. IND 6th Ave express or local (B, D, F or Q train) to Broadway / Lafayette St. BMT Broadway local or express (N or R train) to Prince St.

🚌 M1 downtown on 5th Ave, Park Ave South, and Broadway (make sure you get a bus labeled South Ferry; otherwise walk south from 8th St or transfer to the M6 at 8th St). Uptown on Centre St and Lafayette St to Grand or Canal St. M5 downtown on 5th Ave. M6 downtown on Broadway and uptown on 6th Ave. M21 crosstown on Houston St.

The Children's Museum of the Arts (founded 1988) is a hands-on, fingersdirty, do-it-yourself place that stands somewhere between a conventional museum where art hangs sedately on the wall and a studio where art comes into being in bursts of creative energy. Founded by Kathleen Schneider, an artist, educator, and museum administrator, the Museum offers programs designed to give children the chance to learn about art while creating it. Museum exhibitions and activities, geared for children from 18 months to 10 years of age, embrace both the visual and the performing arts.

LONG-TERM EXHIBITIONS AND ACTIVITY AREAS

Ongoing exhibitions include the Monet Ball Pond, a carpeted alcove surrounded with a mural of water lilies (whose inspiration stands uptown at the Museum of Modern Art). The "pond" allows children to roll around on large and small balls, while developing motor skills. The Lines and Shapes area includes computer sketch pads and monitors as well as a Magnetic Masterpiece exhibit that allows children to arrange and rearrange magnetic puzzles of artworks by painters as different as Vincent van Gogh and Helen Frankenthaler. The Artist Studio, designed by artist Carol May, is used for ongoing activities.

CHANGING EXHIBITIONS

These shows, held about three times a year, emphasize children's art and multicultural themes. "War Through Children's Eyes," artwork by refugee children from Bosnia and Croatia, brought together some 50 works created by children ages 6–16 living in refugee camps. "Maloca Ticuna and the Amazing Amazon" allowed children to learn about the Ticuna tribe and their life in the rain forests of South America by exploring a replica of their architecture, a Maloca house.

PERMANENT COLLECTION

The Museum has a collection of about 2,000 works of art by children from around the world. Approximately 100 are on view in rotating exhibitions in the International Children's Art Gallery. The Museum also commissions art specifically for children, e.g., Pepon Osorio's chandeliers (near the entrance), which are covered with fanciful found objects: beads, toys, and figurines.

China House Gallery (69)

125 East 65th St (bet. Park / Lexington Aves), New York 10021. Tel: (212) 744-8181.

ADMISSION: Open Mon–Sat 10–5; Sun 1–5. Closed national holidays, Jewish holidays, Lunar New Year. Suggested donation.

Gallery tours, lectures, demonstrations, symposia, programs for schools and community organizations, children's programs, film and video. The China Institute offers courses in Mandarin and Cantonese, calligraphy, Chinese culture, and cooking. Travel programs of the Institute offer opportunities for exploring areas seldom accessible to Western visitors. Lunar New Year festivities.

✗ No restaurant.

▥ No gift shop. Catalogues, postcards, gift items.

♿ Not accessible to wheelchairs.

🚇 IRT Lexington Ave local (train 6) to 68th St.

🚌 M1, M2, M3 or M4 uptown via Madison Ave, downtown via 5th Ave. M101 or M102 uptown via 3rd Ave, downtown via Lexington Ave.

China House Gallery, the exhibition space of the China Institute in America (1926), a nonpolitical, nonprofit cultural organization, offers two major exhibitions yearly. Eminent scholars serve as guest curators for the exhibitions, which draw on museums and private collections from around the world. Though the shows are small in scale and usually low-keyed, they are recognized by authorities on Asian art to be outstanding.

EXHIBITION PROGRAM

Some shows focus on particular artists, e.g., a small exhibition entitled "Mind Landscapes: The Paintings of C. C. Wang," which surveyed the work of a little-known New York City resident who has been praised as the best Chinese artist of his time. Wang began painting in China in 1921 as an adolescent, receiving traditional training; he emigrated to this country in 1949 and eventually developed the techniques that freed him from some of the limitations of traditional Chinese landscape painting. Critics praised the show as an example of the interactions between Chinese art and Abstract Expressionism.

"Treasures of the Last Emperor: Selections from the Palace Museum, Beijing" celebrated the reign of the last emperor of the Qing Dynasty (1644–1922), who formed a bridge between 4,000 years of dynastic rule in China and the birth of the modern nation. The show offered a selection of "Henry" Puyi's personal possessions, ranging from jeweled toys to lacquer scholar's tools and jeweled insignia of office to the menu card of a Western-style meal.

Many shows emphasize classical Chinese arts and archeology; one traced the development of Chinese ceramics from the Neolithic period in about 5000 B.C. to the end of the Sung Dynasty in the 13C; another documented the ancient Chinese art of bronze casting. There are also occasional exhibitions on traditional folk art and the arts of China's ethnic minorities.

Each year the China Institute celebrates the Lunar New Year with a special exhibition. According to the Chinese Zodiac, the Year of the Rooster is especially auspicious, and in 1993 the Institute mounted "Year of Good Fortune," an exhibition drawn from several museums and private collections, which included objects for ensuring an auspicious future, e.g., oracle bones, jade carvings, and ancestral tablets, set in the context of the rooster as a good luck symbol.

The Chinatown History Museum (6)

70 Mulberry St (Bayard St), New York 10013. Tel: (212) 619-4785.

ADMISSION: Open Sun–Fri 12–5; open to school groups Thurs–Fri. Closed Sat, New Year's Day, Chinese New Year, Washington's Birthday, Good Friday, Easter, Memorial Day, Independence Day, Labor Day, Thanksgiving, and Dec 25–26. Admission charge. Children under 12 free.

Changing exhibitions, group tours by arrangement, walking tours of Chinatown area, lectures, performances, literary workshops and readings, programs for children, newsletter.

✕ No restaurant.

▥ Bookshop with excellent selection of books by Asian-American authors and on Asian-American subjects.

♿ Not accessible to wheelchairs. The Museum is on the 2nd floor.

🚊 IRT Lexington Ave express or local (train 4, 5, or 6) to Canal Street.

🚌 M101 or M102 downtown via Lexington Ave, 3rd Ave, and the Bowery.

The Chinatown History Museum, founded (1980) as the Chinatown History Project, seeks to reconstruct the century-old history of New York's Chinatown and its people. Housed in what was once P.S. 122, a public school that served an immigrant population of Italians, Jews, and Chinese, the Museum has become the largest Asian-American resource center on the East Coast, with an archives collection, a program of changing exhibitions, and a library. Note: At press time, the Museum's name was changed to Museum of Chinese in the Americas.

EXHIBITION PROGRAM

At the center of the program is "Remembering New York's Chinatown," a permanent, interactive exhibit that focuses on the lives of three residents of Chinatown, following their stories through photographs and other images, artifacts, and supplementary information. Although the people whose stories are told change from time to time, the themes of the exhibition remain constant.

The Museum also mounts changing artistic and historical exhibitions, some lasting one or two months, others remaining on view for about six months. One important early exhibition, accompanied by a video shown on public television, was "Eight Pound Livelihood," which detailed the history of Chinese laundry workers in the United States from the 1850s, when Chinese first entered the trade in California, to the present-day conditions of New York laundry workers. "In the Shadow of Liberty: Graphics of Chinese Exclusion, 1870s–1890s," mounted at the time of the centennial celebrations for the Statue of Liberty, used rare 19C prints to delineate the discrimination and violence that the Chinese faced in this country during the later 19C.

Although the Museum focuses primarily on the Chinese who live in New York's Chinatown, occasional exhibitions—e.g., a show on Puerto Rican garment workers—detail the experience of other immigrant groups.

PERMANENT COLLECTION

Among the objects in the collection are some 200 oral history tapes of Chinatown residents, more than 16,000 historic and contemporary photographic prints, 200 ft of archival material, and a library of 1,800 books related to Chinatown and the Chinese-American population, as well as costumes, musical instruments, and memorabilia.

City Hall: The Governor's Room (7)

City Hall (City Hall Park), New York 10007. Tel: (212) 788-3071.

ADMISSION: Open Mon–Fri 10–4; closed weekends, major holidays. Free.

Group tours by appointment; tel: (212) 788-3071.

✗ No restaurant.

🛍 No gift shop.

&. Accessible to wheelchairs.

⊘ Special photography by permission only.

🚇 IRT Lexington Ave local or express (train 4, 5, or 6) to Brooklyn Bridge. IRT 7th Ave express (train 2 or 3) to Park Place. BMT Broadway local (R train) to City Hall.

🚌 M1 via 5th Ave and Broadway or M6 via 7th Ave and Broadway to City Hall.

City Hall (1811), one of the city's architectural treasures, houses a noteworthy collection of portraits of New York mayors and 19C celebrities, including 13 paintings by John Trumbull, best known for his depiction of people and scenes associated with the Revolutionary War. The most important works in the collection hang in the Governor's Room on the second floor, though portraits and busts are located throughout the public areas of the building.

THE BUILDING

Novelist Henry James, with his usual keen eye, hailed City Hall for its "perfect taste and finish . . . reduced yet ample scale . . . harmony of parts . . . and modest classic grace." Less articulate observers have called it the best City Hall in America. Constructed (1803–11) during the opening decades of the 19C when the nation was searching for an architectural style that would reflect its youthful republican ideals, the building is an outstanding example of the Federal style. One of the architects, Joseph-François Mangin, was a French immigrant; the other, John McComb, Jr., was a native New Yorker, brought up in the tradition of master builders. The two won a prize of $350 for their design.

The cost of the original marble on the facade distressed the city fathers, who wanted a cheaper brownstone finish; McComb lobbied for marble at least for the front and sides, leaving only the rear facade a dull brown (Alabama limestone replaced both brownstone and the original marble in 1956).

INTERIOR. The lobby and the rotunda, with its beautiful double staircase, are always open to the public during business hours. In the lobby (east end) stands Jean-Antoine Houdon's statue of *George Washington*, one of six bronze copies of an original marble now in Richmond, Va. Benjamin Franklin and Thomas Jefferson, ministers to France, negotiated for Houdon's work; the famous sculptor came to the United States for a year, spending time at Mount Vernon where he made life casts for the statue.

Other rooms well worth seeing (open when in use for public hearings) are the BOARD OF ESTIMATE CHAMBER and the CITY COUNCIL CHAMBER. With its white bench pews, wooden rail, raised dais, and lovely chandelier, the Board of Estimate Chamber suggests a courtroom of the Federal period. The public hearing chamber of the City Council was added when New York became Greater New York, incorporating the present five boroughs, a union commemorated in the decoration of the ceiling, whose central painting (1903; Taber Sears, George W. Breck, and Frederick C. Martin) depicts *New York Receiving the Tributes of the Nation.*

PERMANENT COLLECTION

In 1790, while New York was enjoying its brief fling as capital of the nation, the Common Council, chief legislative body of the city, commissioned John Trumbull to paint portraits of George Washington and George Clinton, the state's first governor. In 1805 the Council expanded the program to include all the governors and mayors who had served since the Revolution. Seven years later, with the country embroiled in the War of 1812, the Council decided to honor several heroes of that struggle by adding their likenesses to the roster. This tradition of officially sponsored portraits of governors and mayors continued through the mayoralty of Fiorello La Guardia (1934–45), with subsequent portraits donated as gifts. The collection also chronicles changing styles of portraiture during the 19C. Especially noteworthy are works by the first generation of post–Revolutionary artists—John Wesley Jarvis, Thomas Sully, Samuel F. B. Morse, John Vanderlyn, Samuel L. Waldo, George Catlin, and Rembrandt Peale.

> **NOTE:** Occasionally the pictures are relocated, but 12 of the 13 Trumbull portraits are traditionally on display in the Governor's Room. The 13th, *DeWitt Clinton* (acquired in the group of 1805), usually hangs in the City Council offices.

The GOVERNOR'S ROOM (completed 1815–16) first served as an office for the governor when he visited the city and as a reception room. Although the room was repeatedly refurbished, refitted, and repaired in the 19C (sometimes with unpopular results), in 1907 it was restored as much as possible to its original appearance by architect Grosvenor Atterbury, who had access to the original drawings by McComb and Mangin.

The Governor's Room contains a pair of high-backed settees and a writing table used by George Washington. In 1844, the writing table which the first President had used at Federal Hall was brought from the Alms House at Bellevue, where it had been relegated for storage, and installed here.

Two portraits by John Trumbull, hung on the end walls of the central section of the room, show the artist at the height of his powers. Trumbull, who served as Washington's aide de camp, depicts *George Washington* as commander in chief of the Continental Army on Evacuation Day (Nov 24, 1783), against a background showing Bowling Green and the Upper Bay. Trumbull's portrait of *George Clinton*, brigadier general in Washington's army, seven-term governor of the state, and opponent of the U.S. Constitution, shows also the Hudson Highlands and American ships burning, a reference to Clinton's unsuccessful defense of Fort Montgomery during the Revolution. Other men of means painted by Trumbull for the collection are: Governor *John Jay*, Secretary of the Treasury *Alexander Hamilton*, Mayor *James Duane*, Mayor *Richard Varick*, Mayor *Edward Livingston*, Governor *Morgan Lewis*, Governor *Daniel D. Tompkins*, Mayor *Marinus Willett*, and Mayor *Jacob Radcliff*. He also added a copy of a portrait of *Peter Stuyvesant*.

The other portraits, some of which may or may not be on display at a given time, are grouped by painter in the list that follows. English-born John Wesley Jarvis received the commission for most of the heroes of the War of 1812: Commodore *William Bainbridge*, General *Jacob Brown*, Commodore *Isaac Hull*, Commodore *Thomas MacDonough*, Commodore *Oliver Hazard Perry*, and General *Joseph G. Swift*. Thomas Sully, who got most of the remaining commissions for the heroes of the War of 1812, was also born in England and influenced by the English painters of the time, particularly Sir Thomas Lawrence. His portrait of Commodore *Stephen Decatur,* accorded a hero's welcome for his naval victories when he visited the city in 1812, cost the city fathers $500. Also in the collection is Sully's portrait of engineer General *Jonathan Williams,* after whom Castle Williams on Governors Island is named.

Samuel L. Waldo picked up the remaining commission for the War of 1812, a portrait of General *Alexander Macomb,* and also painted Mayor *Cadwallader C. Colden,* and *John McComb, Jr.,* architect of City Hall.

John Vanderlyn was advised by Aaron Burr to study in Paris, to absorb the style of the French Neo-Classic and Romantic painters. Vanderlyn's portraits in the collection are President *James Monroe,* General *Andrew Jackson,* Mayor *Philip Hone* (known less for his administrative skills than for his diary, which detailed city events in the 1830s and 1840s), Governor *Joseph C. Yates,* and President *Zachary Taylor.* Vanderlyn spent much of his career in Paris, with occasional trips to Rome; he was highly regarded in France but less successful in this country.

Samuel F. B. Morse, who later became known as the inventor of the telegraph, had ambitions as a history painter, but failing to receive major commissions, painted portraits to make a living. His portrait of the *Marquis de Lafayette* is considered one of the most important works in the collection. In 1824 when the work was painted, Lafayette was on a triumphal tour of the country. He is shown as an old man with busts of Washington and Franklin in the background. Morse was commissioned by the city to paint Mayor *William Paulding* and *Christopher Columbus.*

George Catlin later achieved renown as a painter of the American West, documenting the way of life of the Great Plains Indians with more than 600 canvases. First trained as a lawyer, he became an artist in the early 1820s and was completely self-taught. *DeWitt Clinton* is typical of his early work. Rembrandt Peale was the son of the more famous Charles Willson Peale; the younger Peale, whose reputation rests largely on his portrayals of Washington and Jefferson, contributed a portrait of the jurist *James Kent* to the City Hall collection.

Later portraits include works by Charles Wesley Jarvis, Henry Inman, Charles L. Elliott, William Page, Thomas Hicks, Robert W. Weir, and William H. Powell. Of particular interest are *Grover Cleveland* by Eastman Johnson and Governor *John A. Dix* by Anna Lea Merritt.

The Clocktower Gallery: Institute for Contemporary Art (8)

108 Leonard St (Broadway), 13th floor, New York 10013. Tel: 233-1096.

ADMISSION: Open Wed–Sat 12–6. Closed Sun–Tues, major holidays; closed mid-June–Aug. Requested donation.

Changing exhibitions, studio program.

✗ No restaurant.

🏛 No gift shop. Catalogues.

♿ Not accessible to wheelchairs.

🚇 IRT Lexington Ave local (train 6) to Canal St. BMT Broadway local (N or R train) or Nassau St local or express (J train) to Canal St.

🚌 M1 (marked South Ferry) or M6 downtown via Broadway.

Founded in 1971, the Institute for Contemporary Art (formerly the Institute for Art and Urban Resources) began by devoting itself to salvaging abandoned buildings (or parts thereof) and using them as studio and exhibition space for new and experimental artists. The Clocktower is one such rehabilitated space; P.S. 1 in Long Island City is another. The Clocktower Gallery mounts four or five shows yearly. Exhibitions, which concentrate on one-person shows, focus on painting, sculpture, installations, and other media by American and European artists.

Among memorable exhibitions in the Clocktower's history was "This Is Tomorrow," which opened first at the Whitechapel Gallery in London (1956) and was reinstalled, in part, at the Clocktower three decades later. In 1956, the Whitechapel show heralded popular culture as a force in its own right, not just as a subject for artists. The reinstallation commented on the earlier notions of "Tomorrow." It featured a wooden lean-to surrounded by a patio of sand and a wood fence: house and garden were decorated with junk, discarded wheels, bits of painted tile, and other found objects.

An exhibition entitled "Kapital" showed the work of a collaborative group of five painters from the former Republic of Slovenia, Yugoslavia, who gained notoriety after crashing the 1986 Venice Biennale and gradually achieved international recognition for their responses to the conflicting ideologies of East and West. The exhibition included a series of heavily framed, thickly painted oil paintings hung salon style on floor-to-ceiling photos of prior installations by the group, their imagery drawn from the iconography of contemporary politics.

After closing for several years because of fiscal problems, the Clocktower reopened (1993) with an exhibit by Maura Sheehan called *Do You Know How to Pony?*, an installation that projected the image of a horse moving around the walls, referring to the passing of time and the clock a flight above.

THE BUILDING

The Clocktower occupies a landmarked building, originally the New York Life Insurance Co. Building (1870; Griffith Thomas; remodeled 1895, McKim, Mead & White). In its glory days, the building had two cupolas above the clocktowers and a great iron globe with an eagle on top gracing the Broadway entrance. It still has the largest weight-driven clock in the city.

The Cloisters: The Metropolitan Museum of Art (101)

Fort Tryon Park, New York 10040. Tel: (212) 923-3700.

ADMISSION: Open March–Oct: Tues–Sun 9:30–5:15; Nov–Feb: Tues–Sun 9:30–4:45. Closed Mon, New Year's Day, Thanksgiving, and Christmas Day. The tax-deductible admission fee is mandatory, but visitors may pay more or less than the suggested amount.

Information Desk. Gallery tours (3 P.M. Tues–Fri; Sun noon). Programs of recorded music, concerts, family workshops (usually first Sat of month), Sat gallery talks for adults at 12 and 2, special events, changing exhibitions. Group tours by appointment; call (212) 650-2280.

✘ No restaurant; the Museum is some distance from local streets. Picnicking permitted in the park. Fort Tryon Park Cafe in Fort Tryon Park south of Museum open every day except Mon (except during very snowy weather), about 10–6; tel: (212) 923-2233.

▥ Gift shop with books, cards, reproductions, gifts with a medieval theme; children's items, recordings and tapes, catalogues, jewelry, china, glassware.

♿ Visitors in wheelchairs should notify Museum in advance to arrange access. Restrooms and telephones are accessible to wheelchairs.

⊘ Hand-held cameras only. No flash attachments, no video cameras.

🚊 IND 8th Ave express (A train) to 190th St / Overlook Terrace. Exit by elevator and take bus M4 or walk through park to the Museum.

🚌 M4 marked "Ft. Tryon Park / The Cloisters" goes to door of Museum.

🚗 Henry Hudson Pkwy north to first exit after the George Washington Bridge. Some free parking around Museum, crowded on pleasant weekends.

The Cloisters, the sole branch museum of the Metropolitan Museum of Art, is named after the colonnaded medieval courtyards around which the building is constructed. Indoors, it has outstanding medieval collections—architectural elements, examples of painting, sculpture, stained glass, furniture, metalwork, and tapestry. Outdoors, there are lovely gardens in season and breathtaking views of the Hudson River.

HIGHLIGHTS

The architectural elements from five medieval cloisters, reassembled in a beautiful setting.

The *Unicorn Tapestries.*

The *Altarpiece of the Annunciation* in the Campin (Spanish) Room.

Among the individual precious objects usually on display in the Treasury, the carved walrus ivory *altar cross,* perhaps from the abbey of Bury St. Edmunds. Also the *Book of Hours* of Jeanne d'Evreux and the *Belles Heures de Jean, Duc de Berry,* exquisitely illuminated manuscripts.

HISTORY

George Grey Barnard (1863–1938), an American sculptor of some renown, gathered the nucleus of the collection. A self-taught medievalist and admirer of what he called "the patient Gothic chisel," Barnard lived in France for years, scouring the countryside around abandoned monasteries and churches for examples of medieval art and architecture which he bought up piece by piece. He found treasures stowed away unrecognized in barns, farmhouses, cellars, and, on occasion, pigsties. Among the nearly 700 pieces he brought to New York were large sections of the cloisters of four medieval monasteries—one Romanesque, three Gothic—and such treasures as the tomb effigy of Jean d'Alluye and a Romanesque wooden torso of Christ whose original polychromy was protected by layers of later gilding and gesso during the period when it served as a scarecrow.

In 1914, Barnard put his collection on display in a building he designed and called The Cloisters, located on Fort Washington Avenue. In 1925, with money from John D. Rockefeller, Jr., the Metropolitan Museum purchased Barnard's collection. Five years later Rockefeller gave the city the land for Fort Tryon Park; to ensure a perpetually unspoiled view, he also bought land across the river along the Palisades, which he gave to New Jersey for a park—a prudent piece of foresight.

PERMANENT COLLECTION

Whereas the medieval collections in the Metropolitan Museum span the period from the barbarian invasions to the close of the 14C, the works in The Cloisters focus on the two principal styles of the late Middle Ages, the Romanesque and the Gothic. The Museum is organized more or less chronologically, beginning with the Romanesque Hall and ending with the Late Gothic Hall and the Froville Arcade. (The accession numbers beginning 25.120 on the labels indicate works purchased from the original Barnard Collection.)

The ROMANESQUE HALL incorporates three portals which illustrate the evolution of the sculptured church doorway in the 12–13C: the round-arched Romanesque French *Entrance Doorway* (c. 1150), the late 12C *Reugny Door* from the Loire Valley with a pointed, more deeply recessed arch, and the magnificent 13C *Moutiers Door* from Burgundy, whose decoration shows the full flowering of the Gothic style. The freestanding figures of the two kings in the niches might represent David and Solomon, but in the 16C they were identified as Clovis, first Christian king of France, and his son Clothar, who according to legend exempted the monastery of Moutiers-Saint-Jean from royal and ecclesiastical jurisdictions. Although the monastery was sacked repeatedly, and ultimately almost destroyed during the French Revolution, the sculptures of the kings survived because they had been moved to a private garden.

The wooden *torso of Christ* from the Auvergne is flanked by 13C Italian figures of the Virgin and St. John. Also displayed are *frescoes of a lion and winged dragon* from Spain, similar in style to the illustrations in illuminated manuscripts, which were sometimes used as models for frescoes.

The FUENTIDUEÑA CHAPEL, like other rooms in The Cloisters, contains works of art brought together from different places. The main architectural feature of the room, the apse, comes from the church of San Martín in Fuentidueña, about 100 miles north of Madrid, and dates from the mid-12C. The apse of limestone blocks with a barrel-vaulted roof is decorated with limestone sculpture, including large pier figures of *St. Martin* (left) and an *Annunciation* group (right). St. Martin of Tours was a much-venerated saint who as a young knight took his sword and slashed his cloak in half, to share it with a beggar. The two large capitals supporting the arch have biblical themes: the *Adoration of the Magi* (left) and *Daniel in the Lions' Den* (right). The *fresco* depicting the Virgin and Child with the three Magi and the archangels Michael and Gabriel comes from another Spanish church in the Pyrenees region (c. 1130–50), and is a true fresco, painted onto wet plaster.

THE CLOISTERS
Ground Floor

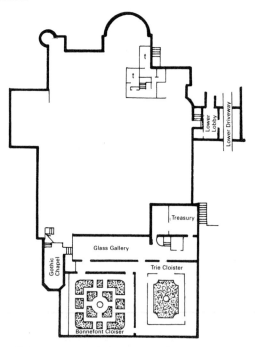

On the wall is a 12C Spanish *crucifix* of carved, painted white oak, whose symmetrical anatomy, flatly executed drapery, and golden crown (instead of the later crown of thorns) mark it as one of the finest surviving examples of the Romanesque type.

The SAINT-GUILHEM CLOISTER is built around a series of capitals, shafts, and columns (before 1206) from the Benedictine abbey of Saint-Guilhem-le-Désert, founded near Montpellier in 804 by Guilhem, count of Toulouse and duke of Aquitaine. Guilhem was one of Charlemagne's paladins, and medieval legends tell how he performed notorious exploits, smuggling his soldiers into a besieged city in wine casks, losing the tip of his nose in a battle to free Rome from the pagans. This is the stuff of legend, but it is historical fact that Guilhem became a monk in the monastery he founded.

The columns are medieval versions of classical Corinthian columns, but unlike their classical predecessors, the medieval columns are decorated with all sorts of designs—one resembling a stylized acanthus tree, another incised with a chevron pattern. The capitals, too, have a variety of designs—traditional acanthus leaves, biblical figures, and the mouth of Hell. The Mouth of Hell capital, with its cloven-hoofed demons forcing sinners into the flaming maw of Hell, represented by an upside-down monster, exemplifies the freer Gothic style.

THE CLOISTERS
Main Floor

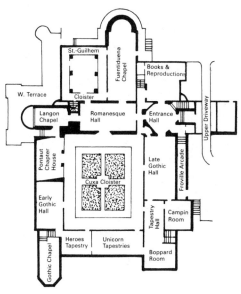

Incorporated in the walls of the LANGON CHAPEL is stonework from the 12C Romanesque church of Notre-Dame-du-Bourg at Langon near Bordeaux. The two large crowned heads on the capital of the column nearest the altar (right side) may represent Henry II of England and his wife Eleanor of Aquitaine, who visited Langon in 1155. In the chapel are two statues of the *Enthroned Virgin and Child,* one from Autun in northeast Burgundy, the other from the Auvergne region. Sculptors of 12C France produced many such statues, symbolizing the abstract notion of Mary as the Throne of the New Solomon and the child as Divine Wisdom. Most of them are rigidly frontal, formal, and symmetrical, impressing with their remote, majestic calm. The *Autun angel,* with fluttering drapery and feathered wings, comes from a side portal of the cathedral of Saint-Lazare at Autun in Burgundy.

The CHAPTER HOUSE FROM PONTAUT is an architectural reconstruction (except for the plaster vaults and the floor), stone by stone and brick by brick, of the chapter house from the former abbey (12C) of Notre-Dame-de-Pontaut in Gascony. It served as a meeting room where the monks gathered to discuss monastery business, and in its original setting had a dormitory above. The windows in the west wall were never glazed but have hinges for shutters and holes for iron bars. Architecturally, the room shows a transition between Romanesque and Gothic styles, the arches round but the ceiling rib-vaulted.

The CUXA CLOISTER, at the heart of the Museum, comes from one of the most important abbeys in southern France, the Benedictine monastery of

The Cloisters: Abacus and capital from the cloister of St.-Guilhem-le-Desert.
(Courtesy of the Metropolitan Museum of Art, The Cloisters Collection)

Saint-Michel-de-Cuxa (founded 878). The stonework here dates from the 12C. Cuxa suffered the fate of other monasteries—sacked in periods of hostility, deserted after the Revolution, left to fall into ruins, when its architecture was dispersed. George Grey Barnard could purchase only part of the original stonework, but a plan dated 1779, notes and drawings by 19C visitors, and the study of fragments and excavations on the site have enabled scholars to determine that the original was approximately twice the size of the present reconstruction.

The simplest and perhaps the earliest of the marble capitals are undecorated; more elaborate ones include pine cones, scrolled leaves, and a variety of lions: in the company of apes, devouring hapless people, or gnawing their own forelegs; there are also eagles, monkeys, and a mermaid.

In the center of the cloister is a garden with fragrant plants.

The entrance from the Cuxa Cloister to the NINE HEROES TAPESTRIES ROOM is a 15C French doorway in the flamboyant Gothic style, with "flamelike" double curves and stylized leaf forms. The room features the major part of a 14C set of French tapestries probably made for Jean, duc de Berry, one of only two known existing sets from that period (the others are the *Apocalypse Tapestries* in Angers). The Nine Heroes—Hector, Alexander, and Julius Caesar (pagan), David, Joshua, and Judas Maccabeus

(Hebrew), and Arthur, Charlemagne, and Godfrey of Bouillon (Christian)—were a popular theme of medieval legend and appear frequently in 14C painting and sculpture. The set, cut up and dispersed over the centuries, was reassembled from 95 fragments over a period of 20 years and now constitutes about two-thirds of the original work.

Around the doorway from the Cuxa Cloister is the largest section, with Joshua and David seated on Gothic thrones and dressed in medieval costumes. Clockwise from here the tapestries depict pagan heroes Hector or Alexander, Julius Caesar, and King Arthur, the only Christian hero recovered.

The EARLY GOTHIC HALL contains statues from the 13–14C as well as paintings and architectural elements (ceiling beams and stained-glass windows). Among the sculptures are an early 14C Flemish *statue of a Young King* and a *pair of Angels* carved of oak. A sandstone *Virgin from Strasbourg Cathedral* (c. 1250) is one of the most important pieces in the collection, expressing in its dignified grace the noble ideal of Gothic sculpture. Originally part of the choir screen, the Virgin stood with the Christ Child seated on a rosebush at her side; two angels held her veil while another hovered above her head. The limestone *Virgin and Child from the Île de France,* with her softly draped garment and curved, relaxed pose, is a masterpiece of the mid-14C; the figure is in an excellent state of preservation, lacking only the points of the crown and the scepter she once held in her right hand.

From this room a short stairway leads down to the GOTHIC CHAPEL, designed as a setting for stained glass and tomb sculpture. All the glass in the chapel is from the 14C. The *Tomb effigy of Jean d'Alluye,* showing a young man fully armed, with his hands joined in prayer and his feet resting against a crouching lion (a frequently used foot rest, symbolizing knightly courage), was one of George Grey Barnard's major acquisitions. Other important pieces in this room are the *tombs of the Spanish counts of Urgel* in Catalonia, whose identities have not been positively confirmed. Included are the effigy of a boy (with the family coat-of-arms on his shoulder strap), a double tomb with the slabs tilted so that we may get a good view of the couple lying on them, and the figure of an armored knight wearing a padded surcoat with rosettes and the family arms.

The gray-white marble columns and capitals of the BONNEFONT CLOISTER, outside the Glass Gallery, come from the former Cistercian abbey of Bonnefont-en-Comminges near Toulouse, founded in 1136, and used for burial of the counts of Comminges until the mid-14C. Although the cloister, still standing in 1807, had virtually disappeared 50 years later, plundered by local inhabitants, Barnard recovered some 50 double capitals and a few shafts from scattered locations, including a stream where they had been used to dam up a drinking pond for cattle. The capitals (first half of the 14C) over slender paired columns are carved to represent natural and imaginary plants.

Next to the Bonnefont Cloister is the TRIE CLOISTER from the Carmelite convent of Trie-en-Bigorre, southwest of Toulouse, destroyed (except for the church) before 1571 by the Huguenots. The capitals, probably carved in 1484–90, show scenes from the Bible, as well as saints' legends, grotesques, and coats-of-arms of local families. In the south arcade is a fine Nativity capital.

The fountain in the garden, whose plants were selected from those shown in the *Unicorn Tapestries,* is surmounted by a cross with Christ between Mary and John on the front and St. Anne with the Child and Virgin among unidentified saints on the back. The octagonal fountainhead has seven apostles and John the Baptist in traceried niches.

The GLASS GALLERY takes its name from the 75 panels and roundels of stained glass (15–early 16C) in the south windows. These panes were usually found in secular buildings but had sacred subjects. Sculpture includes a *female saint holding a book,* perhaps St. Catherine of Alexandria, famed for her learning; *St. Barbara* holding her attribute, a tower; and two *Angels* playing musical instruments. Among the reliquaries is a shoe of boiled leather, probably a case for a metal receptacle holding a foot bone of St. Margaret of Antioch.

Beyond the doorway to the Trie Cloister is the elaborately carved *Abbeville woodwork* from a late-15–early-16C house at Abbeville in Piccardy, which was destroyed during World War II.

In the TREASURY (three rooms) are smaller objects of exceptional quality and value. The 12C walrus ivory *Altar cross* may have come from the abbey of Bury St. Edmunds in Suffolk, England. Its elaborate carving encompasses more than 100 small figures and 60 Greek and Latin inscriptions. The exquisitely detailed miniatures in the 15C *Belles Heures de Jean, Duc de Berry,* were commissioned for a famous bibliophile and collector, who also owned the *Nine Heroes Tapestries* and the *Book of Hours of Jeanne d'Evreux.* This tiny prayer book, made (c. 1325–28) for the queen of France, is remarkable for its masterful drawing. A rare and wonderfully preserved silver and silver gilt beaker, known as the "Monkey Cup," is decorated with freely painted enamel; its surface depicts playful monkeys robbing a sleeping peddler.

The BOPPARD ROOM is on the main floor. It contains six stained-glass panels dating from the second quarter of the 15C, arguably the finest ensemble of late Gothic stained glass in this country. Originally made for the church of the Carmelite convent at Boppard on the Rhine, the windows depict (left to right) a bishop saint trampling a dragon, the Virgin Mary, another bishop saint, St. Catherine of Alexandria, St. Dorothea of Caesarea, and St. Barbara.

Behind the altar is an alabaster retable (altarpiece) from Spain (mid-15C) with scenes from the lives of St. Martin and St. Thecla. The central panel shows the day of Pentecost, with the Holy Spirit descending upon the apostles as tongues of flame.

Dominating the TAPESTRY HALL, adjacent, is a tapestry of the *Glorification of King Charles VIII,* representing the French monarch during his youth in scenes iconographically related to the Old Testament story of Esther and Ahasuerus. The *Armorial Tapestry* bears the arms of John,

Lord of Dynham, who held high office under five English kings during the turbulent Wars of the Roses.

The HALL OF THE UNICORN TAPESTRIES contains a superb series of six late medieval tapestries along with fragments of another which depict *The Hunt of the Unicorn.* They were probably woven in Brussels around 1500, but neither the occasion nor the commissioner is known. The tapestries belonged to the duc de la Rochefoucauld in the 17C. In 1793, during the Revolution, they were removed and for some years used to protect peasants' fruit trees and vegetables from freezing, a period during which they must have sustained considerable damage. During the 1850s they were rediscovered lying in a barn and were once again hung in the château.

According to medieval legend, the unicorn could be caught only by a virgin, whose presence tamed the normally wild, swift, and powerful creature. This story was interpreted both as an allegory of human love and as an allegory of the Incarnation (the unicorn a symbol of Christ). The subjects of the tapestries include: the Start of the Hunt; the Unicorn at the Fountain; the Unicorn Tries to Escape; the Unicorn Defends Himself; the Unicorn Is Captured by the Maiden; the Unicorn Is Killed and Brought to the Lord and Lady of the Castle; and the Unicorn in Captivity—the last said to symbolize both the Resurrection and the consummation of the marriage, which the tapestries were presumably woven to celebrate.

The *Unicorn Tapestries* are remarkable for their naturalistically rendered animals and flowers and human figures, the range of color, and the profusion of detail: over 100 different species of plants appear, of which 85 are recognizable. The plants, rendered with botanical accuracy, would also have conveyed allegorical meanings to medieval viewers: e.g., the roses symbolized attributes of the Virgin Mary; the pomegranates would have recalled human fertility as well as the Church's promise of immortality.

Woven of wool and silk and colored from only three dye plants, the tapestries are works of such excellence that it is remarkable that their origin and the names of their designers should remain unknown. John D. Rockefeller, Jr., donated them to The Cloisters.

The SPANISH ROOM (also known as the CAMPIN ROOM) with its 15C painted Spanish ceiling has been furnished like a domestic interior, the furnishings serving as a backdrop to the masterful *Altarpiece of the Annunciation* by Robert Campin (c. 1425). The work has three panels: two kneeling donors on the left; the Annunciation; and St. Joseph in his workshop on the right. Campin was one of the first painters to place the mysteries of religion, such as the Annunciation, in bourgeois settings.

The LATE GOTHIC HALL, sometimes used for changing exhibitions, contains works from the late 15C, including sculpture and painting. A carved oak relief depicting *The Death of the Virgin* from Cologne shows the apostles gathered at the Virgin's bedside as St. Peter administers the sacrament of extreme unction. A Hispano-Flemish altarpiece depicting *The Lamentation* shows the influence of northern painting in the figures of St. John and the Magdalen wiping her tears, both of whom are derived from Rogier van der Weyden. During the Middle Ages, *the Three Magi* were often believed to have descended from the Sons of Noah, and thus were representative of the three races of mankind; a *group of the magi,* originally part of the high altarpiece of a convent in Baden-Baden (c. 1490) belongs to this tradition.

The FROVILLE ARCADE, just outside the Late Gothic Hall, is constructed around nine pointed arches from the 15C Benedictine priory of Froville. The arches, grouped in threes and separated by buttresses as they were in their original setting, are typical of 14–15C cloisters, which depended for effect on their proportions rather than on great skill in decoration or stonecutting as in the earlier Gothic and Romanesque arcades.

THE BUILDING

Although The Cloisters (1934–38; Charles Collens of Allen, Collens & Willis) was not copied from any single medieval original, it was built around medieval architectural elements with an effort to make modern additions as unobtrusive as possible. The exterior millstone granite was quarried by hand near New London, Conn., according to the dimensions of building blocks in Romanesque churches. The Italian limestone of the interior was hand-sawn to suggest weathering. The gardens within the walls are based on medieval precedents known through manuscript illumination, paintings, and tapestries.

Columbia University: Wallach Art Gallery (102)

Schermerhorn Hall, 8th floor, Broadway and 116th St, New York 10027. Tel: (212) 854-7288.

ADMISSION: Open Wed–Sat 1–5 during the academic year. Closed Sun–Tues, holidays, summer months. Free.

Changing exhibitions. Occasional lectures and symposia; occasional gallery talks by students.

✖ No restaurant.

🏛 No gift shop.

&. Accessible to wheelchairs.

🚃 IRT Broadway-7th Ave local (train 1 or 9) to 116th St.

🚌 M4 uptown via Madison Ave / 110th St / Broadway. M104 uptown on Broadway.

Columbia University's Wallach Gallery (founded 1987) serves as an adjunct to the cultural life of the university. Its exhibitions, usually two each semester, reflect the interests of students and faculty, particularly those in the departments of Art History and Visual Arts. Most shows are curated by faculty members or students, drawing on the resources of the university and borrowing work from private and public collections. A show of Han Dynasty tomb sculpture from the Arthur M. Sackler Collection displayed pieces which students had been examining in a course on Asian art.

On occasion exhibitions are curated elsewhere, e.g., "Money Matters," which originated at the Museum of Fine Arts in Houston, and which offered photos and documents illustrating the history of bank architecture in the United States and Canada.

Con Edison Energy Museum (41)

145 East 14th St (3rd Ave), New York 10003. Tel: (212) 460-6244.

ADMISSION: Open Tues–Sat 9–5. Closed Sun, Mon, holidays. Free.

Changing exhibitions; group tours by appointment.

✘ No restaurant.

🏛 No gift shop. Free pamphlets and educational materials.

♿ Accessible to wheelchairs by prior arrangement.

⊘ No photography.

🚊 IRT Lexington Ave local or express (train 4, 5, or 6) to 14th St. BMT Broadway local or express (N or R train) to Union Sq. 14th St-Canarsie local (L train) to Union Sq.

🚌 M1, M2, or M3 downtown on 5th Ave / Park Ave South. M14 crosstown on 14th St. M101 or M102 downtown on Lexington Ave, uptown on 3rd Ave.

The Con Edison Energy Museum (1979), located on the ground floor of the headquarters building of the Consolidated Edison Company, offers interesting, interactive displays on the past, present, and future of electrical energy in New York City.

There is a model of Charles Edison's historic Pearl St Station (1882), the first generating plant in the city; also a model kitchen of yesteryear with examples of old-time electrical appliances, including such wonders as electric stoves, toasters, and "ice boxes." A primitive recording device known as an Ediphone suggests the impact of the new technology on industry. Historical photos show New York at the turn of the century, when electrical power was just coming into its own as a public utility.

The centerpiece of the exhibition is a model of subterranean New York with a maze of electrical, gas, water, steam, and sewer lines. Lights flash on and off demonstrating the purpose of various pieces of equipment as a simulated subway races by with a deafening roar.

Cooper-Hewitt, National Design Museum: Smithsonian Institution (70)

2 East 91st St (5th Ave), New York 10028. Tel: (212) 860-6868.

ADMISSION: Open Tues–Fri 10–9; Wed–Sat 10–5; Sun 12–5. Closed Mon and major holidays. Admission charge.

Changing exhibitions, lectures, gallery tours, city tours, catalogues, special events. Reference collection for design research (by appointment). Classes and workshops, programs for young people; performing arts and concerts in garden in summer.

✘ No restaurant.

🏛 Shop with excellent selection of books, catalogues, slides. Gift items emphasize good design and include unusual jewelry, stationery and cards, toys, tableware, designer scarves and neckties, and home accessories.

♿ Completely accessible to wheelchairs (call ahead if possible). Enter from parking lot east of main entrance and ring for attendant.

🚫 Strollers must be parked at main entrance.

🚇 IRT Lexington Ave local or express (train 4, 5, or 6) to 86th St.

🚌 M1, M2, M3, or M4 uptown on Madison Ave, downtown on 5th Ave.

Ensconced in the mansion built for steel magnate Andrew Carnegie, Cooper-Hewitt Museum (1897) offers the nation's largest collection devoted to the history of design, almost a quarter of a million objects gathered from all over the world.

PERMANENT COLLECTION

The Museum was planned as a kind of visual reference library where scholars and designers could study historical styles of the past. Thus the broad and eclectic collection includes a little bit of a lot of things. There are American wood engravings, Northern European woodcuts, designs for theater costumes and scenery, 19C American drawings. Ceramics include European and Asian examples, and a collection of 19C figurines. There is a growing collection of glass, as well as furniture, architectural woodwork and hardware, wallpaper, bandboxes, goldsmiths' work, jewelry, and locks and keys. Among the textiles are Near Eastern, Egyptian, and Mediterranean fabrics. Valentines, Christmas tree ornaments, feather pictures, and sand toys add a note of whimsy. Donald Deskey, best known for his Art Deco design work in Radio City, contributed the contents of his studio, including a scheme for an underwater lounge. Isamu Noguchi, whose site-specific sculpture graces the city at several locations, is represented by a plastic *Intercom Transmitter,* shaped like a human head.

EXHIBITION PROGRAM

Although selections from the astonishing collection remain permanently on display, the Museum has an active program of exhibitions, which draws also on the resources of other museums. "L'Art de Vivre: Decorative Art and Design in France 1789–1989" recalled the Hewitt sisters' preference for 18C French design. "The Intimate World of Alexander Calder" included designs for kitchen utensils, toys, jewelry, labor-saving gadgets, and such whimsical if marginally useful Calderiana as a "cachenez," or nose cover of bent wire and fabric made for a friend suffering from a cold. Other shows have focused on the movies, the art of India, food, and even the normally humble dog house, featured in an exhibit of architect-designed abodes for man's best friend. Artifacts in "The Power of Maps" ranged from Mesopotamian clay-tablet maps from 2500 B.C. to computer-generated charts showing the Antarctic ozone hole.

THE BUILDING

Andrew Carnegie (1835–1919), an immigrant from Scotland, amassed a fortune in iron, coal, steel, and steamship and railroad lines. In 1898 he announced his intention to build "the most modest, plainest, and roomi-

Silver tea service (c. 1903), designed by Jan Eisenloeffel (1876–1957).
In the collections of Cooper-Hewitt, National Design Museum.
(Cooper-Hewitt, National Design Museum: Smithsonian Institution)

est house in New York." For his plain and roomy house, he chose a rocky, semirural plot between Yorkville and Harlem, far north of the fashionable areas where his wealthy peers resided. In 1891, Carnegie and his family moved into this 64-room mansion, remarkably comfortable and technically advanced for its time, well suited for his domestic needs and for the philanthropic projects he administered from his first-floor library and office. The subbasement was filled with pumps and boilers, the most advanced and sophisticated available, with a backup for each major piece should the primary one malfunction. Up in the attic great fans pulled air through cheesecloth filters over tanks of cool water in a primitive system of air conditioning. The house was the first private residence in the city with a structural steel frame, an Otis passenger elevator, and central heating.

On 91st St, an ornate copper and glass canopy shelters the door. The marble vestibule leads to the GREAT HALL, paneled in Scottish oak, an indication of Carnegie's affection for his homeland, to which he returned yearly. On the west end of the hall was Carnegie's STUDY, now used as a gallery. Carnegie was 5 ft 2 in tall, and the doorways leading into the library and office are appropriately scaled. Along the south side of the first floor facing the garden were public rooms.

The MUSIC ROOM, on the west, has a large crystal chandelier and musical motifs, including a Scottish bagpipe, in the ceiling moldings. Next to it is the GARDEN VESTIBULE, with leaded-glass windows by Louis Comfort Tiffany. The formal DINING ROOM was east of the vestibule, and adjacent to it a BREAKFAST ROOM faced the garden and conservatory, which had an elevator to the potting shed below. All these rooms are currently used as exhibition space.

THE GARDEN

One of Carnegie's reasons for choosing the upper reaches of Fifth Ave for his mansion was the availability of land for a garden. Although it has been redesigned since Carnegie's day, the garden still remains a pleasant spot to rest.

HISTORY

Sarah, Eleanor, and Amy Hewitt, granddaughters of industrialist Peter Cooper, impressed by the South Kensington Museum (now the Victoria and Albert) in London and the Musée des Arts Décoratifs in Paris, founded (1897) the Cooper Union Museum for the Arts of Decoration. Helped by friends like J. P. Morgan, who donated three European textile collections, they began amassing decorative objects, prints and drawings, and such items as napkins, gloves, and cookie tins, which appealed to them as good design. The Hewitt sisters admired both European culture and the kind of American industrial savvy represented by their grandfather (who along with his other accomplishments had designed the first American locomotive), and their acquisitions reflect these preferences.

The Museum galleries at first were installed on the fourth floor of the Cooper Union for the Advancement of Science and Art, a school established by their grandfather. The collection has continued to grow in size and quality over the years, broadening its focus after the last of the Hewitt sisters died in 1930. By 1963, Cooper Union could no longer maintain the collection financially, and supporters engineered its adoption by the Smithsonian Institution. In 1972, the Carnegie Foundation deeded the mansion to the Museum, which reopened there in 1976.

The Dahesh Museum (42)

601 Fifth Ave, 2nd floor (48th St), New York 10017. Tel: (212) 759-0794.

ADMISSION: Open Tues–Sat 11–6. Closed Sun, Mon, major holidays. Free.

Changing exhibitions. Gallery talks; symposia.

✗ No restaurant.

▥ No gift shop. Posters, postcards of works in the collection.

♿ Accessible to wheelchairs.

🚃 IRT Lexington Ave local (train 6) to 51st St. IND 6th Ave local (F train) to Rockefeller Plaza.

🚌 M1, M2, M4 downtown on 5th Ave, uptown on Madison Ave.

The Dahesh Museum (opened 1995) contains the private collection of its namesake, Salim Moussa Achi (1909–1984), a Lebanese collector and intellectual, who took the name "Dahesh" ("Wonder" in Arabic). Dahesh's taste ran to conservative European academic painting from the 19–20C and for about half a century he acquired some 50 paintings yearly, which now comprise the permanent collection. Among the painters in the collection, most of them obscure today, are Luc-Olivier Merson, Henri-Pierre Picou, and Ernest-Auguste Gendron.

HISTORY

Dr. Dahesh led a universalist religious movement called Daheshism, which drew some of its devotees from the Lebanese political elite and still has followers today. He believed in reincarnation and the spiritual life of plants; he wrote numerous books, including a multivolume *Inferno of Dr. Dahesh* which refined the Dantesque conception of Hell, relegating sinners to 50 strata of punishment, describing and how and why they suffer.

EXHIBITION PROGRAM

The Museum mounts about three exhibitions a year. The opening exhibition, entitled "When Art Was Popular," offered a panoramic view of the subjects explored by academic artists: heroic and mythological themes, genre scenes, landscapes, paintings of animals and flowers. Subsequent exhibitions have explored these themes individually and at greater depth.

The Dia Center for the Arts (43)

548 West 22nd St (11th Ave), New York 10011. Administrative headquarters at 542 West 22nd St, New York 10011. Permanent exhibition spaces in SoHo: "The New York Earth Room," 141 Wooster St. "Broken Kilometer," 393 West Broadway. Tel: (212) 989-5566.

ADMISSION: Main exhibition space open Thurs–Sun 12–6. Closed Mon–Wed, major holidays. "The New York Earth Room" and "Broken Kilometer" open Wed–Sat 12–6. Both exhibits closed late June through Labor Day. Suggested donation.

Changing exhibitions. In its facility at 155 Mercer St, Dia offers symposia, readings in contemporary poetry, and dance rehearsal space and performances.

✗ No restaurant.

🛍 Printed Matter shop, with catalogues, publications, artists' books.

♿ Accessible to wheelchairs.

⊘ Photography by permission.

🚇 IND 8th Ave local (C or E train) to 23rd St. Walk west three long blocks or take bus M23.

🚌 M11 uptown on 10th Ave, downtown on 9th Ave. M23 crosstown on 23rd St.

At the far western edge of Chelsea, the Dia Center for the Arts (founded 1974 as the Dia Art Foundation) maintains a capacious four-story exhibition space and a well-earned reputation for exhibiting the best in international avant-garde art. Both the size (9,000 sq ft on each of four floors) and the "raw" condition of the exhibition space—with natural light, unfinished floors, and industrial amenities—allow the installation of major shows of a scale or character that might not be possible in traditional gallery spaces.

The name comes from the Greek *dia* meaning "through," and suggests the Center's role in realizing extraordinary projects that could not easily find sponsorship elsewhere.

EXHIBITION PROGRAM

Most exhibitions consist of specifically commissioned works created with the space and capabilities of the Center in mind. Exhibitions usually remain on view for about a year to allow for repeated visits.

The inaugural exhibition in the space was a show of large-scale works by Joseph Beuys. Since then, the Center has mounted highly regarded exhibitions of the work of Robert Ryman, Tim Rollins + K.O.S., Brice Marden, Lawrence Weiner, and Francesco Clemente. The generous exhibition space favors such installations as Jenny Holzer's *Laments,* a group of 13 stone sarcophagi with chiseled inscriptions along with a vertical electronic sign programmed with new texts.

Artists are asked to consider the size and character of the exhibition space and to cooperate with Dia in creating appropriate work. For his untitled installation in 1992, for example, Robert Gober hired scene painters to surround the gallery space with a wooded landscape. Along each of two walls four sinks jutted out, water pouring from their faucets. Piercing the painted scenery were barred windows, like those in a jail. Around the room stacks of newspaper with altered pages included texts that referred to sexual discrimination, death, AIDS, abortion, and other socially painful issues.

PERMANENT COLLECTION

Between 1974 and 1984, Dia collected in depth a small group of artists: Joseph Beuys, John Chamberlain, Walter De Maria, Dan Flavin, Donald Judd, Barnett Newman, Cy Twombly, and Andy Warhol. Works from the permanent collection are on view in changing exhibitions in the Center and elsewhere in collaboration with other organizations. Outstanding among these collaborative efforts was a joint project with the Carnegie Institute in Pittsburgh to form a permanent museum for the works of Andy Warhol in that city.

OTHER EXHIBITION SPACES

The Center maintains two other exhibition spaces in SoHo, both installations by Walter de Maria. "The New York Earth Room" (1977) is just that, a room in which 250 cu yds of raked earth fill the gallery to a level of 22 in. "Broken Kilometer" (1979) is an arrangement of 500 solid brass rods, each 2 meters long, which if laid out end to end would measure 1 kilometer.

HISTORY

The Dia Art Foundation was founded (1974) by Philippa de Menil Friedrich, a daughter of Houston art patron Dominique de Menil, and her husband Heiner Friedrich, an art dealer. Their goal was to provide support for a chosen group of artists in a variety of settings outside the usual institutional environment. Among the artists whom the Foundation helped in its early years were Dan Flavin, La Monte Young, Walter De Maria, and Donald Judd.

In the early 1980s the Foundation overreached itself financially, and in 1984 the generous single-patron support of Mrs. Friedrich ended. Since 1986, Dia has been funded by a broad base of contributors, including corporations, individuals, foundations, and the government. In 1987, the Center opened in a newly rehabilitated

19C loft building in Chelsea, a neighborhood that offers several other centers of the visual and performing arts.

The Drawing Center (9)

35 Wooster St (bet. Grand / Broome Sts), New York 10013. Tel: (212) 219-2166.

ADMISSION: Open Tues, Thurs, Fri 10–6; Wed 10–8 and Sat 11–6. Closed Sun, Mon, Aug, major holidays. Suggested donation.

Lectures, symposia, paper conservation workshops, educational programs for school groups. Viewing Program allows emerging artists to bring in work for consideration in exhibitions. Catalogues of major historical shows. Slide archive of works presented in Viewing Program.

✗ No restaurant.

🛍 No gift shop.

♿ Accessible to wheelchairs.

⊘ No photography.

🚇 IRT Lexington Ave local (train 6) to Canal St. BMT Broadway local (N or R train) to Prince St.

🚌 M1 marked South Ferry downtown on 5th Ave / Broadway, uptown on Centre St / Lafayette St to Grand or Canal St. M6 downtown on 7th Ave / Broadway, uptown on Church St / 6th Ave to Grand or Canal St.

The Drawing Center was founded (1977) to foster appreciation of drawing as a major art form. Since 1986 it has been located in a historic (1886) cast-iron building in SoHo whose pristine white walls and Corinthian columns make a handsome background for the exhibitions.

EXHIBITION PROGRAM

Each year the Center offers five or six shows of unique works on paper. At least one show is usually historical, while the others focus on the work of contemporary artists. Past exhibitions, often organized to suggest the diversity of the medium, have focused on theatrical and cinematic drawings, architectural renderings—including a noteworthy show of drawings by Spanish architect Antoni Gaudí—music manuscripts, artists' postcards, sketchbooks, and drawings by creative people in other fields. Exhibitions have drawn from the collections of the Victoria and Albert Museum, the Courtauld Institute, and the National Museum in Stockholm.

One outstanding show, "Picasso's Parade: From Paper to Stage," brought together for the first time 60 of the artist's preliminary studies for the once-scandalous ballet *Parade,* for which Picasso designed the sets, curtain, and costumes, including two in the new Cubist style. The unpublished material in the exhibition allowed viewers to see Picasso's initial impulses, his second thoughts, and his final resolutions, as well as his sources and his discarded notions.

Another important exhibition, "Seeing Through 'Paradise': Artists and the Terezin Concentration Camp," told the moving story of artists imprisoned in the camp in 1941–45 who were forced to churn out Nazi propaganda. While their official efforts advertised Terezin to the outside world as a model ghetto, many of the artists at great risk covertly drew and painted the brutal day-to-day realities of the camp.

An unusual exhibition of collaborative drawings, "The Return of the *Cadavre Exquis,*" revived the old parlor drawing game in which one player draws a head, folds over the paper, and hands it to the next player, who adds a torso, and so on. In the exhibition were examples by Surrealist practitioners of the art (including André Breton and Salvador Dali) and modern drawings by well-known and emerging contemporary artists (Richard Artschwager, Georg Baselitz, Louise Bourgeois, Chuck Close, Elizabeth Murray, Donald Sultan, and others).

To encourage emerging artists, the Center sponsors a Viewing Program which gives artists a chance to present work for inclusion in future exhibitions. The museum maintains an archive of slides, now representing some 3,000 artists, which is consulted by curators, art dealers, collectors, and the interested public. The Selections exhibitions, in general drawn from this archive, show only the work of emerging artists—those who have not had solo shows in New York and who have no New York gallery affiliation.

Dyckman Farmhouse Museum (103)

4881 Broadway (204th St), New York 10034. Tel: (212) 304-9422.

ADMISSION: Open Tues–Sun 11–4. Call to check hours Sun in winter. Closed Mon and legal holidays. Requested donation.

Group tours by appointment.

✗ No restaurant.

▥ No gift shop.

♿ Not accessible to wheelchairs.

🚇 IND 8th Ave express (A train) to 207th St / Broadway. IRT Broadway local (train 1 or 9) to Dyckman St; walk west to Broadway and then south.

🚌 M104 to 125th St, transfer to the M5 to 168th St, transfer to M100 to Dyckman House. The trip takes up to an hour from midtown depending on traffic and bus connections.

Once the center of the 300-acre Dyckman family farm, whose meadows reached the Harlem River, Dyckman House (opened as a museum 1916) is one of the few surviving buildings from the 18C, when upper Manhattan was rolling farmland tended by prosperous farmers, many of Dutch descent. The house, built c. 1785, is the only Dutch Colonial farmhouse on Manhattan, replacing an earlier Dyckman homestead that was destroyed during the Revolutionary War. The present house is believed to incorporate materials from the earlier one, which was probably not on this site.

THE BUILDING

The exterior has the wide overhanging eaves and gambrel roof of the Dutch Colonial style. The walls at ground level are stone, built 2 ft thick; above the foundation, construction is wood frame finished with wide clapboards; the front is surfaced with brick, a sign of wealth.

On the south side of the building a small wing, originally a summer kitchen or bakehouse, predates the rest of the house by perhaps 50 years; it served as a shelter for the Dyckman family while the house was rebuilt during the Revolution.

On the GROUND FLOOR is a WINTER KITCHEN, its staircase built around a slab of Inwood marble, the local bedrock, which was too large to dig out. An assortment of kitchen equipment—kettles, skillets, and long-handled cooking tools, from the 18–19C—suggests the kind of cookery that took place in the large fireplace.

A central hallway, leading from the entrance, divides the FIRST FLOOR in half. The two front PARLORS have fireplaces opening from the two end chimneys. Original woodwork in the right parlor includes the wide board floors, mantelpiece, and corner cupboard.

In the left parlor, furnished as a DINING ROOM, are ladder-back chairs that belonged to the father of Samuel F. B. Morse, a friend of the Dyckman family.

Behind the Dining Room is the RELIC ROOM, originally probably a small bedroom, now used to display objects excavated in the vicinity and Dyckman family memorabilia. Among the archeological fragments are specimens of porcelain and pottery found in the military huts after the war, old bottles, crocks, shoe and belt buckles, melted bullets, buttons, and a bullet mold found in a hut nearby. Behind the Parlor is a small room restored as a FARM OFFICE.

Upstairs, two bedrooms have been furnished. On view are a field bed, a commode that belonged to the Dyckman family, several Windsor chairs, and the Dyckman cradle.

Behind the house are a reconstructed smokehouse and a well. In another corner of the garden is the reconstruction of a small military shed, a crude shelter similar to those used during the Revolutionary War.

HISTORY

The Dyckman family was one of early Manhattan's most prominent, headed by Jan Dyckman, who arrived (1661) from Holland via Westphalia in Germany. A book-keeper and woodcutter, Dyckman went into partnership with Jan Nagel (after whom nearby Nagle Ave is named) and bought land for a farm. As members of the Dyck-man family continued to acquire land, the farm grew, eventually becoming the largest in Manhattan.

During the Revolutionary War, northern Manhattan saw the comings and goings of the Continental and British armies. Washington and his forces were driven from the island following the Battle of Harlem Heights and briefly occupied the original Dyckman farmhouse during the retreat. The British used the house dur-ing the occupation of Manhattan, while Hessian mercenaries and British soldiers lived in primitive shelters on the farmland. The Dyckman family, who had moved to Peekskill, returned to find their home destroyed by the British, who torched it as they withdrew at the end of the war.

William Dyckman, a grandson of Jan Dyckman, rebuilt the house (prob. c. 1785), incorporating materials from the earlier structure. The farm continued to remain active until 1868, and the house remained in the Dyckman family until 1871.

After the turn of the century, when land values in upper Manhattan began ris-ing, it was inevitable that a developer would cast a cold eye on Dyckman House, attractively located on a corner of Broadway. Two Dyckman descendants, Mary Alice Dean (wife of Bashford Dean, curator of arms and armor at the Metropolitan

Museum) and Fannie Fredericka Welch, bought back the house to save it from demolition. They furnished it with family heirlooms, period furniture (from different periods), and other family souvenirs and memorabilia, restored it, and donated it to the city in 1916.

80 Washington Square East Galleries (10)

80 Washington Square East (bet. W. 4th St and Washington Place), New York 10003. Tel: (212) 998-5747.

ADMISSION: Open during academic year (Sept–mid-May) Tues 11–7; Wed and Thurs 11–6; Fri and Sat 11–5. Mid-May–July open Mon–Fri 11–5. Closed Sun and Mon during academic year; part of Aug. Free.

Changing exhibitions.

✖ No restaurant.

▣ No gift shop.

♿ Accessible to wheelchairs by previous arrangement.

⊘ No photography.

🚇 IRT Lexington Ave local (train 6) to Astor Place. IRT Broadway / 7th Ave local (train 1 or 9) to Christopher St. IND 8th and 6th Ave trains, local or express (A, B, D, E, or F train) to W. 4th St. BMT Broadway local (R train) to 8th Street / Broadway.

🚌 M1, M2, M3, M5, downtown via 5th Ave. M6 downtown via 7th Ave and Broadway.

Located in a pleasant town house, the galleries at 80 Washington Square East (1976) showcase the work of graduate students in fine arts at New York University. As part of the degree requirement students must have at least one public show, and the eight galleries are filled with exhibitions that run the gamut of media, from painting, sculpture, glassmaking, photography, and printmaking to video installations. Each year there is a juried show of small works, none larger than 1 ft in any dimension, submitted by artists from all over the world. There are also occasional loan shows from other institutions—e.g., an exhibition of quilts mounted in cooperation with the Museum of American Folk Art.

Ellis Island Immigration Museum (11)

Statue of Liberty National Monument, New York 10004. Tel: (212) 363-3200 for recorded information; to reach a live person, call (212) 363-7620.

ADMISSION: Museum open daily 9–5 (last sailing from Manhattan at 3:30). Closed Christmas Day. Museum is free; charge for ferry transportation.

> **NOTE:** Plan to arrive early, since sailings and the Museum itself are crowded, especially on weekends and in good weather.

Information Desk in Baggage Room. Films, permanent exhibitions. No guided tours, but Park Rangers available throughout the Museum. Research library and Oral History Center open by appointment; write to

Ellis Island in 1905.
(Library of Congress, 1905)

the Museum Services Division at Statue of Liberty National Monument, Liberty Island, New York 10004.

✗ Cafeteria.

🛍 Shop with souvenirs, books, postcards, posters, T-shirts and clothing, dolls, toys, mugs, international gifts.

♿ Complete wheelchair accessibility. Other services for the sight- and hearing-impaired available; write to the Interpretation Division, Statue of Liberty National Monument, Liberty Island, New York 10004.

🚫 No smoking, eating, or drinking in the exhibit areas.

🚇 IRT Broadway-7th Ave local (train 1 or 9) to South Ferry; IRT Lexington Ave local or express (train 4 or 5) to Bowling Green. BMT Broadway local (N or R train) to Whitehall St. Then take ferry from Battery Park.

🚌 M1 (marked South Ferry) downtown via 5th Ave, Park Ave South, and Broadway. M6 downtown via 7th Ave and Broadway. M15 downtown via 2nd Ave and Allen St. Rush hours only: express bus X25 from Grand Central to Wall St; X92 from 92nd St / Yorkville Ave to Wall St. Then take ferry from Battery Park.

⛴ Ferry leaves from Battery Park at the foot of Broadway. Schedule subject to seasonal change; call the Circle Line at (212) 269-5755. The ticket kiosk, located in Castle Clinton, the low red sandstone structure on the west side of the park, is open ½ hr before first sailing. Additional sailings from Liberty State Park in Jersey City, N.J.

> **NOTE:** Some ferries stop also at the Statue of Liberty; check with the Circle Line for details.

Of the places that stir the American imagination, Ellis Island (1892; opened as a museum 1980) is one of the most poignant, its symbolism of hope and rebirth now woven into the national mythology. Built by the federal government to deal with the multitude of immigrants arriving at the nation's doorstep in 1892–1924, it saw about 17 million people pass through its portals, some seeking the realization of lofty ambitions, others looking merely to survive. Today, about 100 million Americans, or 40% of the population, can trace their lineage back to these immigrants who entered the nation through Ellis Island.

THE MAIN BUILDING AND EXHIBITIONS

FIRST FLOOR. "The Peopling of America" exhibit occupies what was once the railroad ticket office. Its displays, based on population statistics, show the effects of 400 years of immigration on the American population. "The Word Tree" explores the effects of immigration on the American language.

SECOND FLOOR. Dominating the floor is the historic **Registry Room,** a large hall (200×100×56 ft) with a majestic vaulted ceiling. Although it has been left largely empty today to heighten its emotional impact, until 1911 it was divided by barriers of iron pipe into smaller areas reminiscent of cattle pens. The tile vaulting was added (1916) after an explosion of ammunition stockpiled in the harbor brought down the earlier ceiling. Engineered by the firm of Rafael Guastavino, an immigrant from Spain, the self-supporting tile proved so resilient that during the recent restoration only 17 of the 28,880 individual tiles had to be replaced.

One of the most effective of the second-floor exhibits, "Through America's Gate," recreates through photographs, oral histories, and objects the process by which immigrants were screened and finally admitted or rejected.

THIRD FLOOR. The **Ellis Island Galleries** offer four exhibits. "Treasures from Home" displays artifacts and photographs brought by immigrants to their new land. "Ellis Island Chronicles" depicts the history of the island.

During 1954–84, when the station was abandoned, it fell prey to vandals and the weather. Thieves tore out its plumbing and wiring; the roof deteriorated and let in the rain; the remaining furniture was scattered and broken. Gradually the place assumed a haunting, melancholy beauty documented by a photographic exhibition, "Silent Voices." "Restoring a Landmark" documents the process of reclaiming the abandoned ruin. Also on the third floor are a restored dormitory with canvas cots, where detained immigrants slept, awaiting their fate.

THE AMERICAN IMMIGRANT WALL OF HONOR

Outside the building, overlooking the harbor, enrolls the names of thousands of immigrants whose descendants donated $100 to have the names included on the wall.

HISTORY

Ellis Island, like most of the other masses of land in the waters surrounding New York, was reserved for people or purposes the city preferred to keep at a distance. In the years before the Revolution it acquired the name Gibbet Island and a reputation as a hanging place for pirates or traitors. Toward the end of the 18C, a man named Samuel Ellis owned its 3 acres of low mudflats, which would gradually be increased by landfill to the present 27.5 acres. The state bought it from Ellis in 1808 and sold it to the national government for $10,000, as a site for harbor fortifications in the War of 1812. In 1890, the federal government took over control of immigration and built an immigration station—several wooden buildings—on it, replacing the old state-run facilities at Castle Garden (now Castle Clinton National Memorial in Battery Park). When the wooden immigrant station burned down in 1897, the government commissioned architects Boring & Tilton to design a new complex, the architectural center of which is the copper-domed brick Main Building that today houses the Museum.

During the heaviest years of immigration, the staff comfortably processed as many as 5,000 people daily; on the peak day of the peak year (April 17, 1907), 12,000 immigrants were herded through its rooms. The figure represented slightly more than 8% of the record 1 million immigrants who arrived that year.

In 1924, the Immigration Act halted mass immigration and Ellis Island evolved into a facility for detaining and deporting illegal aliens. In November 1954, it closed and the last detainee, a Norwegian sailor who had jumped ship, was moved elsewhere. Ellis Island was declared surplus government property and left to deteriorate. Although it became part of the Statue of Liberty National Monument in 1965, only in 1982 was action taken to rescue the complex from its derelict condition. In 1990, after massive restoration, Ellis Island reopened as a national monument and museum of immigration.

The Equitable Gallery (44)

787 Seventh Ave (51st St), New York 10019. Tel: (212) 554-4818.

ADMISSION: Open Mon–Fri 11–6; Sat 12–5. Closed Sun, holidays. Free.

Occasional gallery talks, symposia.

✗ No restaurant.

🛍 No gift shop. In Equitable Building lobby are two gift shops of the Cathedral of St. John the Divine: the Scriptorium, with paper goods, stationery, and books; and the Treasury, with gift items, including jewelry. Catalogues to Equitable Gallery exhibitions on sale in Scriptorium.

♿ Accessible to wheelchairs.

⊘ No photography.

🚇 IND 6th Ave express (D train) to 53rd St / 7th Ave. BMT Broadway local or express (N or R train) to 49th St / 7th Ave. IRT Broadway-7th Ave local (train 1 or 9) to 50th St / 7th Ave.

🚌 M1, M2, M3, M4, M5, or Q32 downtown on 5th Ave, uptown on Madison Ave. M7 downtown on 7th Ave-Broadway, uptown on 6th Ave. M5 downtown on Broadway-5th Ave, uptown on 6th Ave. M104 downtown on Broadway, uptown on 8th Ave.

The Equitable Gallery (1992), located in the lobby of the headquarters of the Equitable Life Assurance Society of the United States, offers visitors a chance to see traveling shows that would not otherwise have exposure in New York or exhibitions from nonprofit New York collections.

PERMANENT EXHIBITION

Dominating the 80-ft atrium is Roy Lichtenstein's *Mural with Blue Brushstroke,* a 68-ft painting whose images span the artist's career and include references to his early Pop period and his later paraphrases of art history. In the center of the atrium is Scott Burton's *Atrium Furnishment,* a

40-ft semicircular settee and circular table (19 ft in diam.) made of marble.

In the north corridor, Thomas Hart Benton's muscular murals *America Today* (1930–31), painted for the New School of Social Research, reflect the life of rural and urban America and the development of technology in what appears to be a halcyon period. They communicate a positive attitude which seems, with historical hindsight, at odds with Depression America; but as the artist pointed out, the Depression hit hard only when he had almost completed the work. The murals have been beautifully restored.

Directly to the east of the building in the Galleria, an open-air space, is Sol LeWitt's *Wall Drawing: Bands of Lines in Four Colors and Four Directions Separated by Gray Bands* (1985). At the north and south ends are Barry Flanagan's bronze *Young Elephant* (1985) and *Hare on Bell* (1983).

EXHIBITION PROGRAM

The inaugural show, entitled "Nineteenth-Century Narrative Paintings," organized by the Pennsylvania Academy of Fine Arts, offered works that "told a story." Included were paintings on historical, biblical, literary, and mythological themes, genre paintings with scenes of everyday life, and a group of fantasies produced during the Gilded Age. Among these was Elihu Vedder's rendering of the Sphinx, whose excavation in the 19C evoked considerable interest. An important exhibition from a local source brought watercolors and drawings from the New-York Historical Society, including a watercolor by John James Audubon never before exhibited.

Federal Hall National Memorial (12)

26 Wall St (Broad St), New York 10005. Tel: (212) 825-6888 or 264-4367.

ADMISSION: Open Mon–Fri, 9–5. Closed all federal holidays except Washington's Birthday and July 4. Free.

Changing exhibitions. Weekly concerts Wed at 12:30 P.M., classical and semiclassical music.

✖ No restaurant.

⌂ Gift shop with books, posters, maps, postcards, historical toys.

♿ All facilities completely accessible to wheelchairs. Ramp entrance at 15 Pine St.

🚇 IRT 7th Ave express (train 2 or 3) to Wall St. IRT Lexington Ave express (train 4 or 5) to Wall St. BMT Broadway express or local (N or R train) to Rector St. BMT Nassau St local (M train) to Broad St.

🚌 M1 or M6 downtown on 5th Ave and Broadway to Wall St. M15 downtown on 2nd Ave and Water St to Wall St.

Federal Hall (opened as a museum 1955), overshadowed by the lofty skyscrapers of Wall St, offers exhibitions on the history of the city and the site. Though the present building is a monumental example of Greek Revival architecture, its more modest predecessor witnessed momentous events.

HISTORY

In the early 18C the second British City Hall (begun 1699) stood on the site. In it, John Peter Zenger, the feisty publisher of the *Weekly Journal,* was tried (1735) for libeling the royal governor; Zenger's acquittal on grounds of freedom of the press would later be reaffirmed in the Bill of Rights.

For a brief period after the Revolution, New York was the nation's capital and the Congress met in City Hall, which was renamed Federal Hall to reflect its new prestige. The nation's first President, George Washington, was inaugurated (1789) on the balcony of the building. The city's political good fortune turned out to be transitory, and the federal government was moved to Philadelphia in 1790. The old Federal Hall was torn down in 1812, when the city government moved to the present City Hall.

THE BUILDING

The present Federal Hall was constructed as the U.S. Custom House and later functioned as one of the six government subtreasuries (hence the massive safe in the rotunda). Begun 1834, and completed 1842, at the height of the Greek Revival period when, as one of its architects noted, even privies were made to resemble Greek temples, it is one of the city's purest examples of that style. The architects—Ithiel Town, Alexander Jackson Davis, William Ross, and John Frazee—were among the city's most eminent.

PERMANENT EXHIBITION

Exhibits on the FIRST FLOOR focus on New York in 1789, on Washington's inauguration (dioramas, prints, and memorabilia, including the rather plain brown suit he is said to have worn for the occasion), and on the history of the site (models of the building in its various incarnations, a piece of the balcony on which Washington stood during the inaugural ceremonies).

Upstairs on the SECOND FLOOR are changing exhibits on historical subjects and a permanent exhibit on the U.S. Constitution. On the GROUND FLOOR are the old coin vaults (1878) dating from the building's stint as a U.S. subtreasury.

The Forbes Magazine Galleries (13)

62 Fifth Ave (W. 12th St), New York 10011. Tel: (212) 206-5548.

ADMISSION: Open Tues–Sat 10–4. Thurs reserved for group tours, by advance reservation only. Closed Sun, Mon, legal holidays. Free.

Group tours by appointment.

✘ No restaurant.

▥ No gift shop. Catalogues available by mail order.

♿ Accessible to wheelchairs.

⊘ Children under 16 must be accompanied by an adult.

🚇 IRT Broadway-7th Ave local or express (train 1, 2, 3, or 9) to 14th St / 7th Ave. IRT Lexington Ave local or express (train 4, 5, or 6) to 14th St / Union Sq. IND 6th Ave local (F train) or IND 6th Ave-14th St-Canarsie local

(L train) to 14th St / 6th Ave. BMT Broadway express or local (N or R train) to 14th St / Union Sq.

M2, M3, or M5 downtown on 5th Ave. M6 downtown via 7th Ave / Broadway, uptown on 6th Ave. M14 crosstown on 14th St.

The late Malcolm Forbes—publisher of *Forbes* magazine, balloon enthusiast, collector, and society celebrity—opened the Forbes Magazine Galleries (1985) as an exhibition space for the corporate collection, which largely reflects his own ebullient personal tastes. Delightfully unorthodox, the collection includes toy boats, lead soldiers, and unusual trophies, as well as important American presidential manuscripts and related historical documents and a famous group of jeweled Fabergé eggs and objets d'art.

PERMANENT COLLECTION

"Ships Ahoy: A Century of Toy Boats" features more than 500 boats manufactured between 1870 and 1955. There are ocean liners, warships, and riverboats, as well as sailboats, speedboats, rowboats, and even the occasional Noah's Ark. All the major German manufacturers and important French and American firms are represented.

Equally impressive is the display of more than 12,000 lead soldiers. The exhibition opens with a history of the toy soldier, told in tableaux displaying figures from the major manufacturers of Germany, France, Britain, and the United States. Tableaux include a Wild West shoot-out and the sack of Troy.

The collection of trophies contains all kinds of oddities, including a commemorative inkwell (or box) made from a horse's hoof and a plaque commemorating the victory of the white Leghorns in the British Northamptonshire egg-laying trials of 1929–30. The trophies, acquired at auctions and in flea markets, are displayed to reflect on the brevity of fame and perhaps the vanity of aspiration.

Historically the most important part of the collection is the "Presidential Papers," which contains more than 3,700 American manuscripts and historical documents. Included here are a request for souvenir Confederate flags for Lincoln's son Tad at the time of Robert E. Lee's surrender at Appomattox, Paul Revere's expense account submitted to John Hancock for his famous ride, a collection of signatures of the signers of the Declaration of Independence, and a message from General Dwight Eisenhower to the U.S. and British Chiefs of Staff announcing the surrender of Germany in 1945.

The most dazzling display is that of jeweled eggs and luxurious objects created by Peter Carl Fabergé, jeweler to Czars Alexander II and Nicholas II. The czars commissioned 54 Imperial Eggs, of which 45 are known to have survived; 12 are on view at the Galleries, including the *First Imperial Egg* (commissioned 1885) and the *Cross of St. George Egg* (1916), which belonged originally to Maria Feodorovna, wife of Alexander III, who was in the Crimea when the Revolution broke out in 1919. It is the only egg to have left Russia in the hands of its original owner. The *Orange Tree Egg* is a little jeweled tree with jade leaves and diamond-centered enamel blossoms, bearing "oranges" of amethyst and citrine. Concealed within its branches is a mechanical bird (with real feathers) that emerges and sings when one of the "oranges" is turned. Along with the eggs are such luxurious objects as jeweled cuff links and picture frames, a silver-gilt glue pot, jade clocks, and vodka glasses with gold and enamel decoration.

Franklin Furnace (14)

112 Franklin St (near West Broadway), New York 10013. Tel: (212) 925-4671.

ADMISSION: Open Tues–Sat 12–6. Closed Sun, Mon, major holidays. Free.

Changing exhibitions, occasional lectures, performances, educational programs.

✘ No restaurant.

⌹ Catalogues and publications; no gift shop.

♿ Exhibition space a few steps up from street. Accessible with advance notice.

⛴ IRT Broadway-7th Ave local (train 1 or 9) to Franklin St. IND 8th Ave express or local (A or E train) to Canal St.

🚌 M6 uptown on 6th Ave, downtown on Broadway. M10 downtown on 7th Ave and Varick St, uptown on Hudson St and 8th Ave.

Founded (1976) by performance artist Martha Wilson, Franklin Furnace is dedicated to artist books, performance art, and "time-based" exhibitions—site-specific, contemporary, and historical exhibitions that emphasize ephemeral objects. Franklin Furnace, whose name suggests both its TriBeCa street address and Ben Franklin's historic stove, began as a nonprofit store for artist books, a genre that uses the book format to combine images, language, and typography into a mass-producible art form.

In the late 1970s, Wilson began amassing the Franklin Furnace Archive, an eccentric collection of multiple-edition artist-designed books, magazines, pamphlets, record jackets, postcards, and other printed matter that might otherwise have been destined for the wastebasket. The announcement card for Gilbert and George's *Walk Through Hyde Park* (1960) contains blades of grass from the famous park. *Passport from Poland,* a real passport altered by the artist, who felt he would never be able to use it and mailed it to the Museum, is one of many works by artists in countries whose governments suppressed their work. Other unusual publications include *Bikini Girl Magazine* and *Paranoids Anonymous Newsletter.*

By 1993 the archive, encompassing about 13,500 objects, presented increasing problems, spilling over into the exhibition space and incurring larger maintenance costs. Franklin Furnace's 19C wood and brick building was far from ideal for purposes of conserving fragile paper objects, so the Museum sold the collection to the Museum of Modern Art, retaining a right to use the objects in exhibitions.

Franklin Furnace embraces political art and has dealt with issues of gender, sexuality, and free speech. At a time of political and artistic conservatism, for example, Franklin Furnace (dependent in part on the National Endowment for the Arts) boldly mounted "The Lesbian Museum: Ten Thousand Years of Penis Envy."

EXHIBITION PROGRAM

Franklin Furnace mounts monthly exhibitions, many related to printed work; some are organized by guest curators; some travel to other institutions; others are site-specific installations. Over its 20-year history Franklin Furnace has offered "A Million Menus: Chinese Takeout Food in America," "The King Is Gone But Not Forgotten" (a trove of Elvis memorabilia), Cubist artist books, Jenny Holzer's 1978 window of "Truisms," Russian Samizdat art, and "Fluxus: A Conceptual Country"—a look at the early years of this group of alternative artists. More recently, a retrospective of Vincent Fitz Gerald's work showed books that integrated handmade paper, hand-cast type, and hand-knotted bindings, their contents ranging from 13C Persian parables and fables to the "Epiphanies" of James Joyce.

PERFORMANCE PROGRAM

When Franklin Furnace was still a bookstore, its artist-writers presented readings in the basement. In 1977 William Wegman, for example, showed up to read excerpts from *War and Peace,* accompanied by his dog Man Ray. As the artists continued to improvise and invent, donning costumes and bringing props, the readings evolved into performance art. Among those who performed at Franklin Furnace and went on to later prominence are Karen Finley, John Cage, and Eric Bogosian. Wilson herself has appeared as Nancy Reagan, Barbara Bush, and Tipper Gore.

The original basement performance space was closed by the fire department in 1990 (following an anonymous tip that Franklin Furnace was an illegal social club); since that time the performance series has been presented at Judson Memorial Church, Cooper Union, P.S. 122, and the Knitting Factory. Performances include video, photography, movement, images, writing, and music.

Fraunces Tavern Museum (15)

54 Pearl St (Broad St), New York 10004. Tel: (212) 425-1778.

ADMISSION: Open Mon–Fri, 10–4:45; Sat 12–4. Closed national holidays except Washington's Birthday and July 4. Admission charge.

Changing exhibitions, lectures, occasional symposia and demonstrations on subjects related to early American life, children's programs (call the Education Department for arrangements). Small reference library available by appointment to researchers.

✗ The Museum is upstairs from the Fraunces Tavern Restaurant.

🏛 Gift shop with posters, books, exhibition catalogues, antique reproductions, toys, items relating to early American history.

♿ No wheelchair access. Museum up a flight of steep stairs.

⊘ No photography of changing exhibitions.

🚇 IRT Lexington Ave express (train 4 or 5) to Bowling Green. IRT Broadway-7th Ave local (train 1 or 9) to South Ferry. BMT Broadway local (R train) to Whitehall St. IND 8th Ave local (E train) to World Trade Center.

🚌 M1 (marked South Ferry) downtown via 5th Ave and Broadway to

South Ferry. M6 downtown via 7th Ave and Broadway to South Ferry. M15 downtown on 2nd Ave and Allen St to South Ferry.

Fraunces Tavern Museum (1907), upstairs in a restored historic building, explores early American history and culture through its permanent collection, changing exhibitions, and period rooms.

HISTORY

Fraunces Tavern earned its niche in American history in 1783, when George Washington, retiring as commander of the American forces in the Revolutionary War, chose it as the site of his farewell dinner for his officers. The present tavern is a conjectural reconstruction of the historic one, which dated back to about 1719.

The building was constructed as a house for Etienne De Lancey, who married Anne Van Cortlandt. In 1762, Samuel Fraunces bought the building and opened it as a tavern the following year. Fraunces, highly regarded as a cook, supervised the kitchen, even preparing the desserts himself, and perhaps his culinary skill influenced Washington's choice of the tavern for his farewell dinner. In 1785, Fraunces leased the building to the Department of Foreign Affairs, the Treasury, and the War Department for office space, and then sold it to a Brooklyn butcher. Thereafter its fortunes declined until 1904, when the Sons of the Revolution in the State of New York bought the building and restored it.

PERIOD ROOMS

On the second floor are two period rooms. The LONG ROOM, where Washington's farewell actually took place, has been reconstructed and furnished as an American tavern of the late 18C. Across the hall is the CLINTON DINING ROOM, furnished in the Federal style and notable for its historic wallpaper (1834). One panel depicts the surrender of the British at Yorktown (apparently thought by the artist to have been located on the Hudson River); the other shows George Washington after the war.

EXHIBITION PROGRAM

The changing exhibition program focuses on American history, emphasizing the Colonial and Federal periods, New York City history, and George Washington. There have been shows on early American taverns, on the practice of medicine in Colonial America, and on the Bill of Rights. One exhibition, "Chroniclers of Corruption: Moral Commentary by America's Political Cartoonists," offered a collection of political cartoons ranging from Elkanah Tisdale's figure of *The Gerrymander* to work by Thomas Nast, Herblock, and Bob Englehart.

"The Changing Image of George Washington" gathered together paintings of the first President illustrating changing attitudes toward the most revered man of his era. Beginning with pictures based on the famous likenesses of John Trumbull and Gilbert Stuart, the exhibition traced a course from idealized portraits that suggested the President's connections to the great heroes of antiquity to more domestic renderings showing him as a private person and family man.

Of more local interest was an exhibition entitled "Wall Street: Changing Fortunes," which traced the evolution from the 17C to the present of a street whose name is synonymous with money and power. Among the earliest objects in the exhibit was a string of wampum, used as currency by the Canarsie, Mohawk, and other Indian tribes. Along with early views of the street, the exhibition included objects unearthed from recent archeological excavation sites on Wall Street—18C Delft tiles, as well as other domestic objects.

PERMANENT COLLECTION

The Museum has a small permanent collection that includes prints, 18–20C genre paintings and portraits, photographs, decorative arts, sculpture, textiles, Revolutionary War relics, and documents relating to the history of the city and country from the late 17C to the early 19C.

The French Embassy: Cultural Services (71)

972 Fifth Ave (79th St), New York 10021. Tel: (212) 439-1400.

ADMISSION: Open Mon–Thurs 10–5. Closed Fri, Sat, Sun, holidays. Free.

Changing exhibitions, cultural programs.

✗ No restaurant.

♯↘ No restroom. No telephone.

🏛 No gift shop.

⚲ Not accessible to wheelchairs.

🚊 IRT Lexington Ave local (train 6) to 77th St.

🚌 M1, M2, M3, or M4 uptown on Madison Ave, downtown on 5th Ave. M79 crosstown on 79th St.

The Cultural Services of the French Embassy (1974) uses the second-floor parlor of the former Payne Whitney House as a gallery for showing painting, sculpture, and photography by French artists. Exhibitions, which change monthly, have included "Through the Lenses of Three French Photographers," a look at contemporary French photography, and an installation of the work of Richard and Hervé di Rosa, which filled the gallery with colorful paintings and sculptures of people, vegetable forms, and animals.

THE BUILDING

The Cultural Services are housed in an elegant town house designed by the stellar architectural firm of its time, McKim, Mead & White. Built in 1904, it was one of the earliest mansions in the Italian Renaissance style north of 72nd St, during the period when the city's richest families were vying to outdo one another in domestic splendor. The exterior is interesting for its facade of gracefully curved and elaborately carved granite. The house belonged first to Payne Whitney, a financier, philanthropist, and aficionado of horse racing who kept stables in Kentucky and on Long Island. Whitney's daughter, Joan Whitney Payson, was the principal owner of the New York Mets baseball team until her death in 1975. His son, John Hay (Jock) Whitney, was publisher of the *New York Herald Tribune* and ambassador to Great Britain.

The Frick Collection (72)

1 East 70th St (bet. 5th / Madison Aves), New York 10021. Tel: (212) 288-0700.

ADMISSION: Open Tues–Sat 10–6; Sun, Feb 12, Election Day, and Nov 11 1–6. Closed Mon, New Year's Day, July 4, Thanksgiving, and Dec 24–25. Admission charge.

Lectures on art history and on the collection. Concert series (write for tickets in advance). Special exhibitions. Group visits by appointment.

✖ No restaurant.

🏛 Gift shop with publications, postcards, art books, gardening books, posters, and prints.

♿ Accessible to wheelchairs.

⊘ Children under 10 not admitted to the Collection; children age 10–16 must be accompanied by adults. No photography.

🚊 IRT Lexington Ave local (train 6) to 59th or 68th St.

🚌 M1, M2, M3, or M4 uptown on Madison Ave or downtown on 5th Ave.

The Frick Collection (1935), housed in one of the few great remaining Fifth Ave mansions, is a monument to the passion for acquiring European art that beset Henry Clay Frick and other wealthy men around the turn of the century. It contains a superb group of European paintings, mainly from the Renaissance to the end of the 19C, as well as fine Renaissance bronzes, French 18C furniture, enamels, prints and drawings, and porcelains. The house remains much as it was when the Fricks lived there, so that a visit to the Frick Collection, considered one of the great small collections in the world, also gives insight into the privileged lives of famous industrialists and financiers around the turn of the century.

HIGHLIGHTS

Clearly one of the highlights of the Frick Collection is the interplay between the superb paintings, the opulent house, and the fine collection of decorative arts, which all work together to provide an experience unlike anything else in New York.

The Living Hall contains some of the finest paintings in the collection, including works by Bellini, Titian, Holbein, and El Greco.

Other outstanding works displayed in several galleries are the three paintings by Vermeer, Ingres's famous portrait, *Comtesse d'Haussonville,* and fine paintings by Rembrandt, Goya, and Velázquez.

Frick was drawn to the aristocratic art of 18C France, and the collection has rooms devoted to Fragonard and Boucher. In these bright, frivolously decorative rooms, ornate furniture, sculpture, and decorative arts complement the painted panels on the walls.

HISTORY

Henry Clay Frick (1849–1919) came from humble beginnings and rose to wealth and power as a pioneering developer of the coke and steel industries. An appraiser of his prospects as a young man remarked that he worked industriously all day and

Jean-Auguste-Dominique Ingres, The Comtesse d'Haussonville, *one of the best-loved paintings in the Frick Collection. (The Frick Collection, New York)*

did the bookkeeping in the evenings, but might be "a little too enthusiastic about pictures."

Frick began collecting art seriously around 1895 and continued until the end of his life, at first indulging a penchant for works by Daubigny, Bouguereau, and the painters of the Barbizon School. As his taste matured, he sold earlier acquisitions and began buying the Flemish, Dutch, Italian, and Spanish paintings which pres-

FRICK COLLECTION

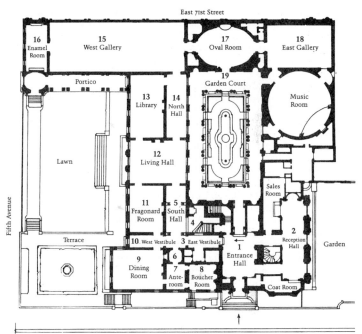

East 71st Street

| 16 Enamel Room | 15 West Gallery | | 17 Oval Room | 18 East Gallery |

Portico

Music Room

13 Library

14 North Hall

19 Garden Court

Lawn

12 Living Hall

Sales Room

11 Fragonard Room

5 South Hall

4

2 Reception Hall

Garden

Terrace

10 West Vestibule

3 East Vestibule

1 Entrance Hall

9 Dining Room

6

7 Ante-room

8 Boucher Room

Coat Room

Fifth Avenue

East 70th Street

ently grace the collection, aided by English dealer Joseph Duveen, whose taste he greatly admired.

When Frick died, he bequeathed the house and the works of art to a board of trustees to be made available to the public and as a center for the study of art. Since his death, the collection has been increased by about a third. The Frick Art Reference Library, with some 750,000 study photographs of works of art and 174,000 books and catalogues, ranks as one of the nation's finest.

PERMANENT COLLECTION

EAST VESTIBULE. Giovanni Battista Tiepolo, *Perseus and Andromeda* (prob. 1730); this oil sketch of Andromeda being rescued by Perseus aboard the winged horse Pegasus was a preliminary study for a ceiling fresco in Milan that was destroyed in World War II.

FOOT OF STAIRS AND LANDING. Sir Anthony Van Dyck, *Ottaviano Canevari* (c. 1625–27). The *Longcase Regulator Clock* (1767) by Balthazar Lieutaud is a masterpiece of its genre.

SOUTH HALL. Johannes Vermeer, *Officer and Laughing Girl* (c. 1655–60). There are fewer than 40 paintings universally accepted as works by Vermeer; the Frick Collection has three, of which this is the earliest. The exaggerated size of the officer in the foreground may have resulted from

Vermeer's use of a *camera oscura,* a sort of pinhole camera that threw the image of a scene or object onto a sheet of paper so that the outlines could be traced. François-Hubert Drouais, *The Comte and Chevalier de Choiseul as Savoyards* (1758). Johannes Vermeer, *Girl Interrupted at Her Music* (c. 1660). François Boucher, *Portrait of Madame Boucher* (1743); a delectable portrait of Boucher's wife, in their charmingly disordered apartment. Pierre-Auguste Renoir, *Mother and Children* (mid-1870s).

ANTEROOM. Hans Memling, *Portrait of a Man* (c. 1470), perhaps Memling's earliest known portrait. Jan van Eyck, *Virgin and Child, with Saints and Donor* (prob. early 1440s); the saints are St. Barbara on the left and St. Elizabeth of Hungary on the right. Barna da Siena, *Christ Bearing the Cross, with a Dominican Friar* (c. 1350–60). El Greco, *Purification of the Temple* (c. 1600), a theme which El Greco treated both earlier and later in his career. Pieter Bruegel the Elder, *The Three Soldiers* (1568), one of the few examples of this artist's work in the United States.

The BOUCHER ROOM. The walls of this small sitting are decorated with panels by François Boucher entitled *The Arts and Sciences* (c. 1750–52). They show plump, rosy-cheeked children playing at adult occupations: *Fowling and Horticulture, Fishing and Hunting, Architecture and Chemistry, Comedy and Tragedy, Astronomy and Hydraulics, Poetry and Music, Singing and Dancing,* and *Painting and Sculpture.* Mme de Pompadour, mistress of Louis XV and patroness of the arts, may have originally commissioned them as designs for chair coverings. They later were painted as decorative panels in the library of her château at Crécy, and still later were installed in Mrs. Frick's second-floor boudoir.

Among the period furniture are pieces by Jean-Henri Riesener—one of the preeminent cabinetmakers during the reign of Louis XV—André-Louis Gilbert, and Martin Carlin. The *Bust of a Young Girl* was made in the 19C after a model of 1750 by François-Jacques-Joseph Saly; the bust also appears in Boucher's figure of *Painting and Sculpture* on the west wall of the room.

If the Boucher Room shows Frick's taste for the 18C in France, the DINING ROOM demonstrates his affection for the same period in England. Adorning the walls is a gallery of aristocratic 18C English portraits. William Hogarth, *Miss Mary Edwards* (1742). Sir Joshua Reynolds, *General John Burgoyne* (prob. 1766); Burgoyne is known best in this country for his efforts in the Revolutionary War and his defeat at the crucial Battle of Saratoga in 1777, but the portrait probably celebrates earlier victories. George Romney, *The Countess of Warwick and Her Children* (1787–89). Thomas Gainsborough, *Richard Paul Jodrell* (c. 1774); Jodrell was an antiquarian, a philologist, a member of Parliament, and a dramatist. *The Mall in St. James's Park* (1783), one of Gainsborough's best paintings, shows London's fashionable set strolling in the Mall, which was near his London residence. His portrait of *Mrs. Elliott* (prob. 1782) depicts the former Grace Dalrymple, mistress of a number of men including the Prince of Wales. John Hoppner, *The Ladies Sarah and Catherine Bligh* (c. 1790).

The four panels by Boucher in the WEST VESTIBULE represent *The Four Seasons* (1755) and were painted for Mme de Pompadour.

The FRAGONARD ROOM, decorated with paintings (1771–73 and 1790–91) by a master of Rococo art, demonstrates Frick's taste toward the end of his collecting career. The four largest panels depict *The Progress of Love* and were commissioned by Mme du Barry, who succeeded Mme de Pompadour in Louis XV's affections. The paintings are entitled *The Pursuit* (south wall left), *The Meeting* (right of fireplace), *Love Letters* (south wall right), and *The Lover Crowned* (left of fireplace). Fragonard, a student of Boucher, had the ill luck to outlive the taste for the style he had perfected. Though these paintings are often considered his masterpieces, Mme du Barry rejected them, perhaps because they were too old-fashioned. Fragonard brought them to his cousin's house in Grasse, where he complemented them with *Love the Avenger* (over mirror), *Love the Sentinel* (over mirror), *Hollyhocks, Love the Jester* (over door), *Reverie, Love Triumphant,* and *Love Pursuing a Dove.* Fragonard also painted three more Hollyhock panels, which now hang in the Music Room.

Sculpture includes Jean-Antoine Houdon, *Comtesse du Cayla* (1777), on the mantel, and two terracotta groups by Clodion, *Satyr with Two Bacchantes* (1766) and *Zephyrus and Flora* (1799).

In the northwest corner of the room is a gilt-bronze *tripod table* with Sèvres porcelain plaques (c. 1783), attributed to Martin Carlin, which is remarkable both for the beauty of the bronze work and the painted plaques; it has been called the finest small porcelain table of the Louis XVI period. Furniture includes a set of armchairs covered in Beauvais tapestry after designs by Boucher and Jean-Baptiste Oudry.

The LIVING HALL. Paintings here include some of the glories of the collection: Hans Holbein the Younger, *Sir Thomas More* (1527); More was an author and statesman, who served as Lord Chancellor to Henry VIII and was eventually accused of treason and executed. El Greco, *St. Jerome* (c. 1590–1600); the Metropolitan Museum of Art has another version of this painting of the ascetic saint, who translated the Bible into Latin. Hans Holbein the Younger, *Thomas Cromwell* (c. 1532–33); Cromwell worked hard to Protestantize the English Church under Henry VIII and was largely responsible for Thomas More's execution. He later alienated the king and was in turn accused of treason and beheaded.

Titian, *Portrait of a Man in a Red Cap* (c. 1516), an early work. Giovanni Bellini, *St. Francis in Ecstasy* (c. 1480), a masterpiece by this genius of Venetian painting. Among Bellini's virtues were a mastery of perspective and color, a knowledge of iconography, and a facility for capturing the details of the real world, all of which are evident in this depiction of the founder of the Franciscan order. Titian was Bellini's greatest student; this second portrait, *Pietro Aretino* (c. 1550), depicts a poet whose pen dripped satirical verses, which earned him the moniker "scourge of princes."

Most of the furniture is in the style of André-Charles Boulle, cabinetmaker to Louis XIV and Louis XV. Boulle garnered a reputation for furniture of ebony or ebonized wood richly decorated with inlays of metals, tortoise shell, and mother-of-pearl.

In this room are examples of the small Renaissance bronzes Frick began to collect toward the end of his life, purchasing many from the estate of J. Pierpont Morgan (died 1914), who himself had swept up large numbers of bronzes from European collections. Here are works by such major artists in this genre as Riccio and Massimiliano Soldani.

The LIBRARY contains further examples of Frick's interest in 18C English portraits, Chinese porcelains, and Renaissance bronzes. Thomas Gainsborough, *Mrs. Charles Hatchett* (c. 1786); *Lady Innes* (c. 1757). George Romney, *Lady Hamilton as 'Nature'* (1782); beautiful Emma Hart, later Lady Hamilton, captivated Romney (who painted her several times), as well as Charles Greville (whose mistress she was when he commissioned this portrait), and Lord Horatio Nelson, with whom she had a notorious affair. Sir Joshua Reynolds, *Lady Skipwith* (1787). John Constable, *Salisbury Cathedral from the Bishop's Garden* (1826). Over a period of ten years Constable painted several versions of the cathedral from the bishop's grounds; a full-scale oil sketch for this sunlit, serene rendering is in the Metropolitan Museum. Sir Joshua Reynolds, *Lady Taylor* (c. 1780). Joseph Mallord William Turner, *Fishing Boats Entering Calais Harbor* (c. 1803), and *Mortlake Terrace: Early Summer Morning* (1826): the picture shows the Thames River west of London from the lawn of an estate named "The Limes." Sir Henry Raeburn, *James Cruickshank* (c. 1805–08). Raeburn was the leading Scottish portrait painter of his time; his sitter was a Scottish businessman who grew wealthy from sugar plantations in the West Indies. Gilbert Stuart, *George Washington* (1795–96), an early copy of Stuart's likeness of Washington as President painted for John Vaughan of Philadelphia. Stuart executed three types of Washington portraits—the Vaughan type, the Lansdowne type (a standing figure), and the Athenaeum type (which appears on the dollar bill)—all of which he copied repeatedly. Sir Thomas Lawrence, *Lady Peel* (1827).

Among the bronzes in the room are those by Bertoldo di Giovanni and Riccio. The portrait bust by Antoine Coysevox of *Louis XV as a Child of Six* (1716) is probably the first of four the sculptor made of the boy who would be king. Coysevox, one of the favored sculptors of Louis XIV, is known for the naturalism and spontaneity of his portrait busts.

NORTH HALL. Antoine Watteau, *The Portal of Valenciennes* (1709–10). Watteau is best known for his rather melancholy depictions of love, but he painted several small military paintings while he was in his 20s. Catherine the Great bought two, which are now in the Hermitage in St. Petersburg; this is the only one in the United States, a major addition (1991) to a collection rich in 18C French painting.

Jean-Siméon Chardin, *Lady with a Bird-Organ* (1753?); *Still Life with Plums* (c. 1730). Théodore Rousseau, *The Village of Becquigny* (c. 1857); Rousseau was the central figure of the Barbizon School, whose work attracted Frick in the early years of his collecting career. Jean-Auguste-Dominique Ingres, *Comtesse d'Haussonville* (1845); Louise, princesse de Broglie, was the granddaughter of Mme de Staël and a woman of self-confessed social ambitions. Claude Monet, *Vétheuil in Winter* (1878–79).

Also in the Hall are a bronze relief of *The Resurrection* (1472) by Vecchietta and Andrea del Verrocchio's *Bust of a Young Woman* (shortly before 1460). Houdon's marble *Bust of Armand-Thomas Hué, the Marquis de Miromesnil* (1777) shows the minister of justice under Louis XVI in his robes and wig.

The WEST GALLERY, planned by Frick as a setting for the major part of his collection, permits the kind of interesting juxtaposition of paintings he preferred.

Jean-Baptiste-Camille Corot, *The Lake* (1861). Sir Anthony Van Dyck,

Frans Snyders (c. 1620), one of his finest portraits; Snyders, a fellow painter, was a friend of Van Dyck. Jacob van Ruisdael, *Landscape with a Footbridge* (1652). Sir Anthony Van Dyck, *Margareta Snyders* (c. 1620). Joseph Mallord William Turner, *The Harbor of Dieppe* (1826?). Frans Hals, *Portrait of an Elderly Man* (c. 1627–30). Meyndert Hobbema, *Village with Watermill Among Trees.* Frans Hals, *Portrait of a Woman* (1635). John Constable, *The White Horse* (1819); Constable admired this painting, bought it back for himself in 1829, and kept it until his death. Agnolo Bronzino, *Lodovico Capponi* (c. 1550–55); Lodovico Capponi was a page at the court of Cosimo I de' Medici, where Bronzino worked as court painter for most of his career.

Paolo Veronese, *Allegory of Virtue and Vice (The Choice of Hercules)* and *Allegory of Wisdom and Strength* (both c. 1580), two rather heavy allegorical paintings.

Gerard David, *The Deposition* (c. 1510–15). Frans Hals, *Portrait of a Painter* (prob. early 1650s). Rembrandt, *The Polish Rider* (c. 1655), an evocative and mysterious painting whose meaning still remains elusive, though some critics see it as an evocation of the journey of life. Frans Hals, *Portrait of a Man* (c. 1660). Hals, now reckoned one of the preeminent Dutch portraitists, was much in demand with the generation of rich American collectors that included Frick. This is one of the more somber paintings of his late period. Attributed to Étienne de La Tour, *The Education of the Virgin* (c. 1650, formerly attrib. to his father, Georges de la Tour).

Joseph Mallord William Turner, *Cologne: The Arrival of a Packet Boat* (1826). Turner made numerous trips abroad after 1817, searching out subjects for compositions. The bright, luminous coloring of this painting drew criticism when it was first exhibited in the Royal Academy. Rembrandt, *Nicolaes Ruts* (1631), an early portrait of a merchant who traded with Russia. Aelbert Cuyp, *Dordrecht: Sunrise* (c. 1650). Rembrandt, *Self-Portrait* (1658). Rembrandt created a magnificent series of more than 60 self-portraits, including this one, admired for its psychological depth and its monumental design, painted when he was 52 years old. Johannes Vermeer, *Mistress and Maid* (c. 1665–70). This is the latest Vermeer in the collection; the background and details of the mistress's hands seem unfinished.

Diego Velázquez, *King Philip IV of Spain* (1644); the subject requested that his portrait be painted wearing an elaborate white and rose-colored campaign outfit to commemorate a victory over the French in Catalonia. El Greco, *Vincenzo Anastagi* (c. 1571–76); Anastagi was a defender of Malta during the Turkish siege of 1565. Francisco de Goya, *The Forge* (c. 1815–20), a somber, forceful painting of blacksmiths laboring in a forge, typical of Goya's later work. Both the proletarian subject and the dark energy make it atypical of Frick's usual choices.

The beautifully paneled ENAMEL ROOM, the smallest of the Museum, contains Frick's collection of painted French enamels dating from the late 15C to the 17C. They were made in the workshops at Limoges and most were acquired from J. Pierpont Morgan's estate after his death. Piero della Francesca (or his workshop), *Augustinian Nun.* Gentile da Fabriano, *Madonna and Child with Sts. Lawrence and Julian* (c. 1423–25). Duccio di Buoninsegna, *The Temptation of Christ on the Mountain* (1308–11); this panel, once part of an altarpiece, shows Christ tempted by Satan with the kingdoms and riches of the world, which are depicted in small scale at the bottom of the painting. Piero della Francesca (or workshop), *Augustinian Monk; Crucifixion.* Piero della Francesca, *St. Simon the Apostle(?);* one of the few works of this master outside Italy. Paolo and Giovanni Veneziano, *Coronation of the Virgin* (1358).

The OVAL ROOM at the other end of the West Gallery was added during the remodeling in 1935 when the house was adapted to its role as a museum. Sir Anthony Van Dyck, *Sir John Suckling* (1632–41). Suckling, who was a minor poet and a member of the court of Charles I, holds an edition of Shakespeare. Van Dyck, *Countess of Clanbrassil* (prob. 1636). Thomas Gainsborough, *Mrs. Peter William Baker* (1781); *The Hon. Frances Duncombe* (c. 1777).

The room also contains a terracotta statue of *Diana the Huntress* (1776–95) by Jean-Antoine Houdon, one of only five life-size terracottas by this master of portrait sculpture.

EAST GALLERY. James Abbott McNeill Whistler, *Robert, Comte de Montesquiou-Fezensac* (1891–92); this dandified figure is said to be a source for the baron de Charlus in Proust's *Remembrance of Things Past.* Francisco de Goya, *Don Pedro, Duque de Osuna* (prob. 1790s). Joseph Mallord William Turner, *Antwerp: Van Goyen Looking Out for a Subject* (1833). Jan van Goyen was a Dutch painter, here seen wearing a turban and standing in a wind-tossed boat, searching for a scene to paint. Goya, *Doña María Martínez de Puga* (1824). Sir Anthony Van Dyck, *James, Seventh Earl of Derby, His Lady and Child* (1632–41). Goya, *An Officer (Conde de Tepa?)* (c. 1804).

Jean-François Millet, *Woman Sewing by Lamplight* (1870–72); although Millet is remembered primarily as a landscape painter, this genre scene recalls the influence on his work of the Dutch 17C painters. James Abbott McNeill Whistler, *Lady Meux* (1881), originally entitled *Harmony in Pink and Grey.* Edgar Degas, *The Rehearsal* (prob. 1878–79). Claude Lorrain, *The Sermon on the Mount* (1656); this poetic landscape shows Christ preaching from the summit of Mt Tabor; Claude was much admired not only by English collectors but by Turner, a painter whom Frick in turn admired. Jean-Baptiste-Camille Corot, *Ville-d'Avray* (c. 1860); the artist's own house can be discerned at the center. Whistler, *Mrs. Frederick R. Leyland* (1872–73): Mrs. Leyland is wearing a dress the artist himself designed; Whistler exhibited it with the title *Symphony in Flesh Colour and Pink.* His musical titles were intended to suggest the notion that painting should not suggest literary or moral ideas, but, like music, which is more abstract, should exist for its own sake.

Jacques-Louis David, *Comtesse Daru* (1810). Aelbert Cuyp, *River Scene.* Sir Anthony Van Dyck, *Paola Adorno, Marchesa di Brignole Sale* (1622 / 27); in 1621 Van Dyck went to Italy, where he painted a series of portraits of Genoese aristocrats. Jacob van Ruisdael, *Quay at Amsterdam* (c. 1670). Jean-Baptiste Greuze, *The Wool Winder* (prob. 1759). Whistler, *Miss Rosa Corder* (1875–78); the artist called this portrait of a young painter *Arrangement in Black and Brown.*

The GARDEN COURT with its fountains and greenery was designed by John Russell Pope on the site of the original carriage court when the house was remodeled as a museum. Around the outside of the room are portrait busts. Jacques Jonghelinck, *Duke of Alba* (1571); the duke, who served as Spanish viceroy in the Netherlands, had a reputation for brutal repression. Antoine Coysevox, *Robert de Cotte* (early 18C); de Cotte served as architect to Louis XIV. Federico Brandani, *Antonio Galli* (c. 1560); Galli was ambassador from the court of Urbino to the papacy and to the Venetian Republic. Danese Cattaneo, *Bust of a Jurist* (prob. mid-16C). Attributed to Antoine Coysevox, *Henri de La Tour d'Auvergne, Maréchal Turenne* (early 18C). In the central part of the court is a lovely bronze *Angel* by Jean Barbet, dated 1475 on the left wing.

EXHIBITION PROGRAM

In addition to the permanent collection, the Frick offers a program of changing exhibitions. "Henry Clay Frick, the Young Collector," made clear that Frick's taste matured as he became more deeply involved with his collection and less concerned with business. Other shows have looked at less well-known artists like François-Marius Granet, a watercolorist whose portrait by Ingres belongs to the Frick Collection, and Nicolas Lancret, a fellow student and imitator of Watteau.

THE BUILDING

The mansion (1914; Carrère & Hastings) was renovated as a museum in 1935 (John Russell Pope).

In 1905, after abandoning plans for a new house and gallery in Pittsburgh because he felt that pollution from the steel mills would be hazardous to his collection, Frick bought the site of the former Lenox Library. At art dealer Joseph Duveen's urging, he commissioned Thomas Hastings to build a home that would suitably display his collection and eventually become a museum. After several false starts, Hastings designed this opulent limestone mansion with a front portico in the style of Louis XVI and a Beaux-Arts axial plan. Frick was not unaware of Carnegie's mansion at Fifth Ave and 90th St, which had been completed in 1901; his own, he opined, would make Carnegie's look like a miner's shack.

Goethe House New York (73)

1014 Fifth Ave (bet. 82nd / 83rd Sts), New York 10028. Tel: (212) 439-8700.

ADMISSION: Gallery and library hours: Open Wed and Sat, 12–5; Tues and Thurs 12–7 P.M. Closed Fri, Sun, Mon, national holidays, Christmas week, and mid-July–early Sept. Free admission to exhibitions at Goethe House; charge for some events and for exhibitions held at other institutions.

Changing exhibitions, lectures, concerts, films, symposia, performances. Catalogues, newsletter. Library.

✗ No restaurant.

🛍 No gift shop.

♿ Limited wheelchair access.

🚇 IRT Lexington Ave local or express (trains 4, 5, 6) to 86th St.

🚌 M1, M2, M3, M4 uptown on Madison Ave, downtown on 5th Ave.

Established (1957) as a private American institution, Goethe House New York became in 1969 one of 150 branches of the Munich-based Goethe Institute, funded by the German government and dedicated to promoting the study of the German language and furthering international cultural cooperation. In addition to offering special programs and information for teachers of German, Goethe House New York mounts exhibitions on German art and culture. It is located in a Beaux-Arts town house built in 1907, which was renovated and reopened in 1991.

EXHIBITION PROGRAM

Goethe House offers exhibitions on a wide range of subjects, some organized in collaboration with other city museums and galleries. In 1991, when the Fifth Ave town house was reopened after extensive remodeling, Goethe House sponsored a program of German art and sculpture which was installed at the Queens Museum. The exhibition, entitled "Interrelations and Migration: Contemporary Sculpture from Germany," included works of four sculptors and suggested the importance of travel, cultural exchange, and even migration among artists who must come to grips with global social and political problems.

Other programs have explored the Jewish experience in Germany after 1945, e.g., an exhibition of photographs entitled "Jewish Portraits" by Herlinde Koelbl, who photographed and interviewed surviving representatives of Central European Jewry.

THE LIBRARY

The collection contains some 16,000 books and periodicals in German and English, as well as cassettes, records, and CDs featuring readings, plays, classical and contemporary music, German rock, and New Wave music. There is a small collection of film on video. The Library offers up-to-date information on political and cultural developments through its airmail subscriptions to some 11 German daily and weekly newspapers and 130 magazines and journals.

Gracie Mansion (74)

East End Ave at 88th St, New York 10128. Tel: (212) 570-4751.

ADMISSION: Tours Wed at 10 and 11 A.M. and 1 and 2 P.M. Reservations required. School tours Thurs mornings. Admission charge. Students with I.D. and children free.

Guided tours by appointment.

✘ No restaurant.

🏛 Gift shop with postcards, stationery, books, gifts, tote bags.

♿ Accessible to wheelchairs.

⊘ No photography inside house.

🚇 Lexington Ave express or local (train 4, 5, or 6) to 86th St.

🚌 M15 uptown on 1st Ave, downtown on 2nd Ave. M86 crosstown on 86th St. M31 uptown and downtown on York Ave between 58th St and 91st St. M101, M102, or M98 uptown on 3rd Ave, downtown on Lexington Ave.

Gracie Mansion, originally a country estate built (c. 1799) by shipping merchant Archibald Gracie, is the home of the mayor of New York and a setting for press conferences, meetings, and ceremonial occasions. The Mansion was restored (1984) during the mayoralty of Edward I. Koch, and its public rooms have been furnished to recreate the Federal period. The Gracie Mansion Conservancy, a not-for-profit group of supporters, which includes designers and architects, works to preserve and restore the Mansion and its furnishings, and offers guided tours of the building.

HISTORY

The first recorded owner of the land where Gracie Mansion now stands was Sybout Claessen, a carpenter who lived in the village of New Amsterdam near the foot of Manhattan Island. In 1770, Jacob Walton, member of a successful merchant family, bought the land and built a house. Walton was a Loyalist; aware of intensifying political strife and the possibility of war, he took precautions for his safety by building a tunnel from the house to the river. In September 1776, the British sailed into the East River and bombarded the house, completely destroying it. Archibald Gracie, an immigrant from Scotland and a successful merchant, bought the land in 1798 and built a 16-room country home, using the foundations of the wrecked house.

Gracie extended his hospitality to Louis Philippe, later king of France, the marquis de Lafayette, Alexander Hamilton, John Quincy Adams, and Washington Irving—early arrivals in a long line of celebrities who would enjoy the Mansion's pleasures. Gracie's shipping business foundered during the War of 1812, and he sold the Mansion in 1819.

The city bought it in 1896, briefly using it as a home for the Museum of the City of New York (1924–30). In 1942 the house became the mayor's residence after Fiorello La Guardia rejected another major contender, the ostentatiously opulent Charles M. Schwab château on Riverside Drive (now demolished). "What," said the 5-ft 2-in fiery proletarian mayor, "me in that?" Although he objected to Gracie Mansion for the same reasons, he was eventually persuaded, in part by Parks Commissioner Robert Moses, who had pushed the city to use the Mansion for its present purpose.

THE BUILDING

The leaded-glass sidelights flanking Gracie Mansion's main doorway (looking out over the East River), the semicircular fanlight above it, and the elegant railings around the roof and above the main floor exemplify Federal domestic architecture at the upper end of the scale.

PERIOD ROOMS

The ENTRANCE HALL is remarkable for the *faux-marbre* painting on the floor and stair risers. Although the Gracies could well afford the best in furnishings and building materials, *trompe l'oeil* effects—the false wood graining on the doors as well as the false marble on the floor—were popular decorative techniques. The unusual five-chairback settee (c. 1800–04) was discovered in the attic of City Hall; the tall case clock dates from c. 1800.

Surprisingly enough, the hand-painted scenic wallpaper in the DINING ROOM is original, manufactured in France (c. 1830). Originally ordered for a private home in upstate New York, it was never used, but preserved in storage until it was hung at Gracie Mansion. Produced by the Dufour brothers in Paris, the paper celebrates that city's classical and modern monuments.

In the PARLOR is a desk-bookcase (1830s), decorated with leaf and floral designs. On one wall is a portrait of *Mrs. Marinus Willett,* wife of a mayor, painted by John Vanderlyn.

The MAYOR'S STUDY. Although the decoration is largely contemporary, the carved mantel is one of the finest in the house. The lithographs of New York street scenes are by Childe Hassam, an American exponent of Impressionism, known for his paintings of New York.

The SITTING ROOM and the FAMILY DINING ROOM both have mantels salvaged from demolished Greenwich Village houses; the mantel in the BALLROOM was recovered from the Bayard family mansion on State St (near Battery Park). In the FAMILY DINING ROOM are portraits of *Archibald Gracie, Jr.,* and *Elizabeth Wolcott Gracie* (c. 1815), the latter painted by John Trumbull.

PERMANENT EXHIBITION

Downstairs in the Wagner Wing, an exhibit of photographs, drawings, and memorabilia describes the history of the house.

General Grant National Memorial (Grant's Tomb) (104)

Riverside Park (Riverside Dr and W. 122nd St), New York 10027. Tel: (212) 666-1640.

ADMISSION: Open daily 9–5. Closed New Year's Day and Christmas Day. Free.

Changing exhibitions. Guided tours if booked in advance. Annual celebration on Grant's birthday, April 27.

✗ No restaurant. Food available at cafeteria in nearby Riverside Church (closed Sat).

† No restrooms.

▥ Small gift shop with postcards, books, slides, information on Grant and the Civil War.

♿ Not accessible to wheelchairs.

▦ IRT Broadway-7th Ave local (train 1 or 9) to 116th St / Broadway. Walk west two blocks to Riverside Park and north three blocks to the Memorial.

▰ M5 via 6th Ave / Central Park South / Broadway / Riverside Dr.

▰ Accessible from Henry Hudson Pkwy; take Riverside Dr exit at 96th St. Drive north on Riverside Dr to 122nd St. Street parking near Memorial.

Grant's Tomb (1897), officially named the General Grant National Memorial, is one of the city's most imposing formal monuments. The massive granite sepulchre contains the remains of Ulysses S. Grant (1822–1885) and his wife, Julia Dent Grant, as well as exhibitions on Grant's accomplishments as a soldier and private citizen.

HISTORY

After an illustrious career as commander in chief of the Union armies in the Civil War and a scandal-ridden presidency (1868–76), Ulysses S. Grant died in 1885. Grant had expressed a preference to be buried in New York City, St. Louis, Mo., or Galena, Ill., and insisted that a space be reserved next to him for his wife, Julia. The mayor of New York, William Grace, offered the family a burial site in the city, assuring a place for Mrs. Grant. After one of the most spectacular funeral processions ever to pass through the city streets, Grant's body was temporarily interred in a brick structure at 123rd St while a committee decided on a design for a permanent structure. Five years later, John H. Duncan won the architectural competition for the tomb, which would cost about half a million dollars (eventually 90,000 subscribers contributed about $600,000). Ground was broken in 1891 and the general's remains were quietly brought to the finished tomb in 1897.

THE BUILDING

Architecturally, Grant's Tomb is unmistakably tomblike, and at first aroused objections that it would give the neighborhood a funereal tone. Duncan's design was based in part on reconstructions of the Mausoleum at Halicarnassus (now in Turkey), the great marble tomb of Mausolus, one of the Seven Wonders of the Ancient World, and an appropriate model for the tomb of a great military hero.

The building consists of a cubelike base topped by a drum supporting a stepped conical dome. A broad flight of steps flanked by two large eagles leads to the Doric portico and entrance. The raised stone blocks above the portico were originally intended to support equestrian statues of Union generals. Above the cornice a tablet contains Grant's words, "Let us have peace," spoken upon accepting the presidential nomination of 1868; figures of two lamenting women recline against the tablet. The stepped cone was to have been crowned by a statue of Grant in a triumphal chariot.

INTERIOR. The austere interior, like that of Napoleon's Tomb at the Hôtel des Invalides in Paris, is cruciform in plan and dominated by the sunken crypt set directly below the dome. Above the windows, mosaics (1966; Allyn Cox) depict Grant's victories at Vicksburg and Chattanooga, and the surrender of Robert E. Lee at Appomattox. A double staircase in the north arm leads down into the crypt containing the imposing polished red granite sarcophaghi of General and Mrs. Grant. Niches in the wall at the crypt level contain bronze busts (1938; William Mues) of Grant's generals William Tecumseh Sherman, Philip Sheridan, George Thomas, Edward Ord, and James McPherson (sculptor, Jens Juszko). Originally the windowpanes were clear glass over which were drawn dark purple curtains symbolizing mourning; but the curtains deteriorated and the windows were redesigned by the Tiffany studios and glazed with purple glass, which in its turn was found to be too somber and dark. The present yellow color is a compromise.

PERMANENT EXHIBITION

Two permanent exhibition rooms on the north wall offer photographic displays devoted to Grant's civil and military career. There is also a permanent photographic display of sites related to his life: Grant's home, his birthplace, the battlefields where he waged war, and the architectural progress of the Memorial.

The Grey Art Gallery and Study Center (16)

33 Washington Place (Washington Square East), New York 10003. Tel: (212) 998-6780.

> **NOTE:** The gallery will be closed until Sept 1996; thereafter call for hours.

Lectures, seminars, symposia, special events. Occasional gallery talks. Research facilities by appointment.

✗ No restaurant.

🏛 Catalogues and posters.

♿ Galleries accessible to wheelchairs; elevator to restrooms.

⊘ Photography by permission.

🚇 IRT Lexington Ave local (train 6) to Astor Place. IRT Broadway / 7th Ave local (train 1) to Christopher St. IND 8th and 6th Ave trains, local or express (A, B, D, E, or F train) to W. 4th St. BMT Broadway local (R train) to 8th Street / Broadway.

🚌 M1, M2, M3, M5, downtown via 5th Ave. M6 downtown via 7th Ave and Broadway.

The Grey Art Gallery and Study Center (founded 1975), which functions as New York University's museum of fine arts and is located in a historic building facing Washington Square, has attracted the attention of the city's art community for the quality and imagination of its exhibitions.

HISTORY

The Department of Fine Arts at NYU harks back to 1835, when Samuel F. B. Morse founded it as the first such academic department in the country. Among the painters with studios in the department were Winslow Homer and George Inness. In the 1830s, Morse conceived the idea of the telegraph and invented the code that bears his name. Disappointed because he could not obtain commissions as a history painter and was reduced to making his living as a portraitist, Morse left painting and turned his attention to his inventions, with well-known and lucrative results. In 1975, Mrs. Abby Weed Grey, a Minneapolis-based collector seeking a home for her collection of contemporary Asian and Middle Eastern art, donated funds to establish the present museum.

PERMANENT COLLECTION

The Gallery's holdings focus on two areas. The New York University Art Collection, devoted primarily to late-19C and 20C art, is especially strong in American paintings from 1940 onward, including works by Jane Freilicher, Arshile Gorky, Adolph Gottlieb, Lee Krasner, Kenneth Noland, and Ad Reinhardt. Another area of strength is European prints, with work by Picasso, Miró, and Matisse. The Ben and Abby Weed Grey Collection of

Contemporary Asian Art contains works from Japan, Turkey, India, and Iran. Both the NYU Art Collection and the Abby Weed Grey Collection are shown in rotating exhibits on a regular basis.

EXHIBITION PROGRAM

The Gallery offers about five exhibitions a year, some of them boldly attractive. Years before Frida Kahlo became popular with collectors, the Gallery mounted "Frida Kahlo/Tina Modotti," an exhibit of painting and photography by the two women artists who had met in Mexico in the 1920s. Equally ambitious was "Krasner / Pollock," an exhibit that explored the careers and working relationship of two important American postwar painters who were married from 1945 until Pollock's death in 1956.

The Gallery garnered praise from the art world with " 'Success is a Job in New York . . .': The Early Art and Business of Andy Warhol," an exhibition that complemented and even upstaged a major Warhol retrospective at the Museum of Modern Art. The show began with paintings and drawings Warhol made while still an art student in Pittsburgh, then followed his career as a successful commercial artist, casting new light on his subsequent life as a Pop artist and art star.

Another exhibition, "18. Oktober 1977," was a provocative installation of Gerhard Richter's black-and-white canvases depicting events surrounding the imprisonment and deaths of the terrorist German Baader-Meinhof group (also known as the Red Faction). The show evoked critical commentary on the place and effects of ideology in art. "Against Nature: Japanese Art in the Eighties" brought together a group of young artists not often seen outside of Japan who view themselves as struggling with the stereotypes of Japanese art. Instead of the cherry blossoms and tributes to nature that are traditionally associated with Japanese culture, the show offered images of a consumerist, information-saturated, urban society.

The Grolier Club (75)

47 East 60th St (bet. Madison / Park Aves), New York 10022. Tel: (212) 838-6690.

ADMISSION: Open Mon–Sat 10–5. Closed Sun, New Year's Day, Washington's Birthday, Memorial Day, Labor Day, Election Day, Thanksgiving, Dec 25–26, and every Sat in June, July, and Aug. Free.

Changing exhibits on books, manuscripts, prints; exhibition catalogues. Lectures. Library for scholars and collectors, by appointment. Groups by appointment.

✖ No restaurant.

🛍 No gift shop. Publications.

♿ Limited wheelchair access; the exhibition hall is on the ground floor, but the entrance to the club is a few steps up from the street.

🚇 IRT Lexington Ave express or local (train 4, 5, or 6) to 59th St.

🚌 M1, M2, M3, or M4 uptown on Madison Ave, downtown on 5th Ave.

The Grolier Club (founded 1884), named for the 16C French bibliophile Jean Grolier, is dedicated to furthering interest in the traditional arts of the book—printing, papermaking, illustration, book design, and binding.

PERMANENT COLLECTION

Included in the permanent collection are incunabula (books printed before c. 1500), among them two Gutenberg leaves on vellum, early printed books, books about books, catalogues of book auctions and private libraries (including those of Mme de Pompadour), and several autograph manuscripts, including a letter from Thomas Jefferson to his French bookseller.

EXHIBITION PROGRAM

In 1884, the club offered its first show, a group of miscellaneous etchings; since that time it has mounted a wide range of exhibitions, most with bibliophilic or literary themes. The scope can be wide-ranging: notable shows have focused on such themes as "The Maya Scribe and His World" (Mayan pottery decorated with text) and "Honored Relics," an exhibit of objects belonging to authors, including such trophies as Samuel Johnson's teapot, Emily Dickinson's hourglass, and Sylvia Plath's typewriter. One of the most original exhibits, "Four Centuries of Dance Notation," detailed various ways of recording choreography before the era of sequential photography or videotape. Thematically more predictable are anniversary and birthday celebrations of literary figures, of which the one commemorating the 400th anniversary of the birth of John Donne was exemplary, including most of his manuscripts, letters, and portraits, as well as a ring that had belonged to him.

"Voices of Scotland," an exhibition of books, manuscripts, prints, and painting from 15–20C Scotland, brought Scottish national treasures never before displayed in this country, including the 16C *Bannatyne Manuscript* (an 800-page anthology of works by writers who worked in the Scots dialect), a rare set of first proof sheets for Boswell's *The Life of Johnson* with corrections in Boswell's own hand, and the manuscript of J. M. Barrie's *Peter Pan*.

Exhibitions of fine contemporary and historical book binding and printing have included such events as a celebration of the 50 years of Leonard Baskin's Gehenna Press, noted for its brilliant images combined with innovative typography.

THE BUILDING

The present club house was designed (1917) by Bertram G. Goodhue, better known for his work on the city's major (and upper-crust) churches: St. Thomas' on Fifth Ave, St. Bartholomew's on Park Ave, and the Church of the Intercession on Broadway at 155th St.

Chaim Gross Studio Museum (17)

526 LaGuardia Place (bet. W. 3rd / Bleecker Sts), New York 10012. Tel: (212) 529-4906.

ADMISSION: Open Fri 11–6. Closed Sun–Thurs, Sat, major holidays. Open by appointment Tues and Thurs to groups and individuals. Free.

Changing exhibitions of work related to sculpture of Chaim Gross. Gallery talks; lectures; tours of collection.

✗ No restaurant.

🗐 No gift shop.

♿ Accessible to wheelchairs, except for studio floor, which is down a short flight of steps. Entire studio visible from ground floor.

🚇 IRT Lexington Ave local (train 6) to Bleecker St. IND 8th Ave express or local (A, C, or E train) or IND 6th Ave express (B or D train) to W. 4th St; walk four blocks east to LaGuardia Place and one block south to W. 3rd St.

🚌 M1 downtown via 5th Ave / Park Ave South / Broadway to Bleecker St; walk west to LaGuardia Place. M5 downtown via Broadway / 5th Ave / Broadway / Houston St to LaGuardia Place; walk north to Bleecker St. M21 crosstown on Houston St to LaGuardia Place.

The Chaim Gross Studio Museum (opened 1994), located in the Greenwich Village home where sculptor Chaim Gross (1904–1991) lived and worked for more than 30 years, celebrates the career of this prolific artist. The small, very personal Museum contains examples of Gross's artistic output from more than 70 years—from his arrival in this country as a 17-year-old immigrant until his death in 1991. In addition to sculptures in wood, stone, and bronze, visitors can see the sculptor's studio as he left it at the time of his death.

HISTORY

Chaim Gross was born in a small village in the Carpathian Mountains in eastern Austria, where his father ran a lumber business. Gross spent his early childhood surrounded by woodsmen, whose avocations often ran to carving and whittling, surely influencing his later choice of materials. During World War I, he and his family fled the Russian invasion, enduring poverty and separation. Gross eventually made his way to Vienna and, in 1921, to America, to New York's Lower East Side. Here he studied at the Art School of the Educational Alliance, meeting Adolph Gottlieb, Ben Shahn, Raphael Soyer, and Barnett Newman, all of whom became lifelong friends. Among his teachers during his first years in New York were Elie Nadelman and Robert Laurent. The earliest work in the collection dates from this period.

By 1932, Gross's career and reputation were becoming firmly established, and he had his first one-person exhibition of sculptures and drawings. That same year he married Renee Nechin, now his widow, who still lives in the building that houses the Museum. His sculpture found a wide and appreciative audience and his career flourished, culminating in Gross's election to the American Academy of Arts in 1964, one of 50 Americans in all the arts so honored at one time. Gross occupied chair #44, formerly held by R. Buckminster Fuller. In 1991, still working hard at his art, Gross died of a heart attack. His work is on view at major museums throughout the country and abroad.

PERMANENT EXHIBITION

Altogether about 80 sculptures are on view, along with clay and plaster maquettes, bronze portrait busts, and other works. Gross's skylit studio, on the lower level of the Museum, contains his workbench, tools, and the last sculpture on which he worked, still clenched in its vise. Among the works displayed here are *Balancing on a Unicycle* (1956), carved of ebony, and *Leap Frog* (1931), of lignum vitae, one of the hardest woods.

On the street level are some two dozen pieces of sculpture in stone and the woods he preferred—lignum vitae, mahogany, walnut, and ebony. Of particular interest are *Roosevelt and Hoover in a Fistfight* (1932) and *The Lindbergh Family* (1932), two works influenced by the Cubism of Pablo Picasso and Jacques Lipchitz, both uncharacteristic of Gross's usual style, which is figurative and chunky. *Novice* (1941), carved of mahogany, shows the robustly rounded forms of two female circus acrobats riding a wheel. The wheel is attached to the self-base, in which can be seen the trunk of the tree from which the entire sculpture emerges.

On the second floor are 26 works in bronze, mostly from later in Gross's career. Included are *Eternal Mother* (1967) and *Happy Children* (1968), works that deal with two of Gross's favorite themes.

CHANGING EXHIBITIONS

In addition to the permanent collection, the Museum mounts one small exhibition each month, featuring some aspect of Gross's work or career. Some shows are thematic, dealing with motifs that have recurred in Gross's work: acrobats, dancers, circus performers. Others have offered clay models and plaster maquettes or tiny bronze castings to give a suggestion of the creative process. One exhibition featured the work of well-known photographers who had taken pictures of Gross, his work, and his family over his lifetime. Occasional shows focus on work in other media, for example, Gross's fantasy watercolors, tapestries, vases for flowers, menorahs, and designs for memorial monuments.

The Solomon R. Guggenheim Museum (76)

1071 Fifth Ave (88th St), New York 10128. Tel: (212) 360-3500 for recorded information. To reach a live person, call (212) 423-3600.

ADMISSION: Open Sun–Wed 10–6; Fri, Sat 10–8. Closed Thurs, New Year's Day, and Christmas Day. Admission charge; lower rates for seniors and students with valid I.D.; children under 12 accompanied by an adult, free. Fri evening, 6–8, pay what you wish.

Changing exhibitions, gallery talks, lectures, panel discussions, symposia, films, concerts, multimedia performances, poetry readings. Group visits by appointment.

✗ Cafe open Fri–Wed 8 A.M.–9 P.M.; Thurs 8 A.M.–3 P.M.

🏛 Two Museum stores, on ground floor and off large rotunda's 6th-floor ramp. Museum stores open daily 10–6, except Thurs, 11–6. Art books, publications relating to Frank Lloyd Wright, posters, notecards, videos, jewelry, and textiles; many gift items designed exclusively for the Guggenheim.

♿ Visitors in wheelchairs are requested to use the 5th Ave entrance. Wheelchairs available in the coatroom. Inquire with the Visitor Services

Department at (212) 423-3555 for services for the hearing- and sight-impaired. For TDD / TT service, call (212) 423-3607.

◎ No strollers in the Museum. Baby carrier packs are allowed; a limited number of packs available in coatroom. Photography with hand-held cameras on rotunda floor only. No flash photography.

🚇 IRT Lexington Ave local or express (train 4, 5, or 6) to 86th St.

🚌 M1, M2, M3, M4, uptown on Madison Ave, downtown on 5th Ave.

The Solomon R. Guggenheim Museum (founded 1939) is justly famous both for its landmark building (1959) by Frank Lloyd Wright and for its permanent collection, rich in early-20C European modernists and outstanding in its holdings of Vasily Kandinsky (205 works). A controversial renovation and expansion that include a satellite museum in SoHo and a tower (1992; Gwathmey Siegel & Assocs) adjacent to Wright's original building have preserved the building, restored it to its original beauty, and made the collection more accessible to the public.

HISTORY

Solomon R. Guggenheim began as an itinerant peddler and made a fortune based on mining and smelting. Like other American millionaires, Guggenheim set out to collect art, concentrating at first on Old Masters, until in 1927 he met Baroness Hilla Rebay von Ehrenwiesen, an artist from whom he commissioned a portrait. Rebay had developed a philosophy of modern art according to which non-objective art, the creation of the artist's imagination alone, held a superior spiritual position. Rebay introduced Guggenheim to her friends, painters like Robert Delaunay, Albert Gleizes, Fernand Léger, Marc Chagall, Vasily Kandinsky, and Rudolf Bauer. Guided by her enthusiasm, Guggenheim began collecting modern paintings.

In 1939, the Solomon R. Guggenheim Collection of Non-Objective Painting was shown in rented quarters at 24 East 54th St, with the baroness in charge.

The idea of building a splendid museum and of hiring Frank Lloyd Wright to design it apparently came from Rebay. Solomon Guggenheim died long before the museum could be built, though he left an endowment for its construction, and the realization of the building was left to Hilla Rebay and Harry Guggenheim, Solomon's nephew.

James Johnson Sweeney succeeded her as Museum director, and under his guidance the Guggenheim Museum became less restrictive in its purchases. Sweeney added some 250 paintings to the collection, including works by Picasso and Cézanne, which Rebay would have outlawed on grounds that they were objective.

The collection of Peggy Guggenheim—niece of Solomon Guggenheim and a highly successful collector in her own right—remains in the Palazzo Venier dei Leoni in Venice where she housed it, though it was legally transferred to the Museum upon her death (1979). Since she stipulated that the paintings should remain in the palazzo unless Venice sank, the Solomon R. Guggenheim Foundation refurbished the palazzo and reinstalled the paintings (1980), including important works by Braque, Picasso, Picabia, Pollock, Brancusi, Ernst, and Arshile Gorky, which are seen in New York at times through exchanges.

PERMANENT COLLECTION

The collection, rich in European modern paintings, was shaped by several tastes and represents the amalgam of several private collections. When Hilla Rebay introduced Solomon Guggenheim to Vasily Kandinsky in 1929, Guggenheim purchased several paintings and works on paper, including *Composition 8* (1923), which would form the beginning of the collection. Guggenheim's purchases, guided by Rebay, continued until

*The skylight of the Solomon R. Guggenheim Museum, designed by
Frank Lloyd Wright, restored 1992.
(© 1992 Solomon R. Guggenheim Foundation. Photo: David Heald)*

the end of his life, and focused on such contemporary European artists as
Chagall, Delaunay, Lyonel Feininger, Gleizes, Kandinsky, Léger, Amedeo
Modigliani, and László Moholy-Nagy. He also purchased many works by
Rudolf Bauer, Rebay's lover and confidant for many years. In 1948, the
Museum acquired the estate of New York art dealer Karl Nierendorf, who
specialized in German painting, including significant numbers of paint-
ings by Kandinsky, Feininger, and Paul Klee.

In addition to purchases made by James Johnson Sweeney to broaden
the scope of the collection, the Museum was fortunate when Justin K.
Thannhauser, a leading dealer and collector, agreed to donate (1963) a
large part of his private collection, which contained important Impressionist, Post-Impressionist, and modern French paintings, filling in visible gaps in the collection. The most recent private collection to enter the
Guggenheim was that of Giuseppe Panza, whose acquisitions concen-
trated on Minimal art, embracing the work of painters Robert Mangold,
Brice Marden, and Robert Ryman, and sculptors Carl Andre, Dan Flavin,
Donald Judd, Robert Morris, Bruce Nauman, and Richard Serra.

Finally, the Guggenheim is enriched by the art acquired by Peggy Guggenheim, Solomon's niece, whose interests ran to Surrealism (she was married for a year to Max Ernst), Cubism, and Abstract Expressionism.

NOTE: Since works on view in the permanent collection are rotated, highlights are listed in alphabetical order by category.

Impressionist and Post-Impressionist Paintings

Pierre Bonnard, *Dining Room on the Garden* (1934–35). Paul Cézanne, *Bend in the Road Through the Forest* (1873–75); *Still Life: Flask, Glass and Jug* (c. 1877); *Still Life: Plate of Peaches* (1879–80); *Mme Cézanne* (1885–87); *Bibémus* (c. 1894–95); *Man with Crossed Arms* (c. 1899), a late portrait. Edgar Degas, *Dancers in Green and Yellow* (c. 1903). Paul Gauguin, *In the Vanilla Grove, Man and Horse,* a painting of the Tahitian landscape where Gauguin had recently arrived, and *Haere Mai* (both 1891). Édouard Manet, *Before the Mirror* (1876); *Woman in Evening Dress* (1877–80). Henri Matisse, *The Italian Woman* (1916). Painted in Matisse's characteristic flat style, the painting was reworked from a more realistic portrait. It came to the Guggenheim from the Museum of Modern Art through an exchange for two paintings by Kandinsky.

Amedeo Modigliani, *Nude* (1917); in 1916–19, Modigliani painted about 26 nudes, whose eroticism caused them to be censured. *Jeanne Hébuterne with Yellow Sweater* (1918–19); Hébuterne was Modigliani's mistress and most familiar model. Claude Monet, *Le Palais Ducal vu de Saint-Georges Majeur.* Pablo Picasso, *Le Moulin de la Galette* (1900), painted when Picasso was 19 years old, influenced by Toulouse-Lautrec; *Woman Ironing* (1904), from the end of Picasso's Blue Period, in somber, neutral tones; *Fernande with a Black Mantilla* (1905 / 06?). Camille Pissarro, *The Hermitage at Pontoise* (c. 1867), painted before his Impressionist works. Pierre-Auguste Renoir, *Woman with Parrot* (1871); a subject also explored by Manet and Courbet. The formal composition, traditional rendering of depth, and rather somber use of color precede his later Impressionist style.

Henri Rousseau, *Artillerymen* (c. 1893–95); *The Football Players* (1908), unusual in its stylized depiction of motion. Georges Seurat, *Peasant with Hoe* (1882); *Farm Women at Work* (1882–83); *Seated Woman* (1883). Henri de Toulouse-Lautrec, *Au Salon* (1893), one of many scenes of brothel life painted in the early 1890s. Vincent van Gogh, *Roadway with Underpass* (1887); *Mountains at Saint-Rémy* (1889); *Landscape with Snow* (1888), a row of tumultuously rendered mountains which were visible from the hospital in Saint-Rémy where van Gogh was confined in 1889. Édouard Vuillard, *Place Vintimille* (1908–10); Vuillard lived in a fourth-floor apartment looking down on the square.

20C Pioneers, European Painters (through World War I)

Georges Braque, *Violin and Palette and Piano and Mandola* (both 1909–10) are composed of the fragmented, monochromatically shaded planes of early Analytical Cubism. Marc Chagall, *Rain,* (1911); *The Soldier Drinks* (1912). Also *Paris Through the Window* (1913), a fantastic rendering of the scene from Chagall's studio, with a Janus-faced man and a human-headed cat, an inverted train, and other gravitational, logic-defying wonders. Robert Delaunay, *Saint-Séverin No. 3* (1909–10); *Eiffel Tower* (1911); *Red Eiffel Tower* (1911–12); and *Simultaneous Windows (2nd Motif, 1st Part)* (1912). The seven paintings and numerous drawings of Saint-Séverin are the first series in Delaunay's work. He spoke of these paintings of the 15C Paris church as having been painted in a period of transition from Cézanne to Cubism, or rather, "from Cézanne to the *Windows*."

Albert Gleizes, *Portrait of an Army Doctor* (1914–15); *Brooklyn Bridge* (1915). Juan Gris, *Houses in Paris* (1911), painted in the early period of Gris's involvement with Cubism; *Still Life with Cherries* (1915). Alexej Jawlensky, *Helene with Colored Turban* (1910).

Vasily Kandinsky, *Blue Mountain* (1908–09), reminiscent of his earliest representational work; the theme of horsemen and a mountain appear in his work until 1913. *Painting with White Border* (1913), a painting the artist described as a translation of impressions received on a visit to Moscow; the central motif is a knight attacking a dragon (lower left) with a white lance. *Black Lines* (1913); a network of black lines links brilliant spots of red, green, blue, yellow, and white. *Dominant Curve* (1936); Kandinsky thought this one of his most important paintings.

Ernst Ludwig Kirchner, *Gerda, Half-Length Portrait* (1914); *Artillerymen* (1915). Oskar Kokoschka, *Knight Errant* (1915), a self-portrait in a turbulent landscape, painted before the artist served in World War I; the reclining woman on the right represents Kokoschka's mistress Alma Mahler. František Kupka, *Planes by Colors, Large Nude* (1909–10). In c. 1906–10, Kupka experimented with the traditional reclining nude and formal arrangements of planes of color, experiments that began his development toward abstraction. Fernand Léger, *The Smokers* (1911–12): the painting shows smoke rising upward against a dark urban landscape with foreground figures seen from multiple points of view; *Contrast of Forms* (1913). Kazimir Malevich, *Morning in the Village After Snowstorm*, (1912), one of a series of Neo-Primitivist paintings showing chunky, geometrically stylized peasants at work. Franz Marc, *The Yellow Cow* (1911); for Marc, the colors here have symbolic values: blue, the severe spiritual and intellectual male principle; yellow, the cheerful and sensual female; red representing heavy and brutal matter. *The Unfortunate Land of Tyrol* (1913); the somber colors reflect the devastation of the Balkan War.

Piet Mondrian, *Composition VII* (1913); *Composition No. 8* (1914); *Composition* (1916). Though based on models in the physical world (a tree, Parisian building facades, and a church), the paintings become progressively more restrained and geometric in construction. Emil Nolde, *Young Horses* (1906), two rather abstract silhouettes of rearing horses in a flat landscape. Francis Picabia, *The Child Carburetor* (1919), in 1915–22, Picabia frequently used mechanical symbols for his larger, human concerns.

Pablo Picasso, *Carafe, Jug and Fruit Bowl* (1909); *Accordionist* (1911), painted while Braque and Picasso were summering together in the Pyrenees; *Bouteille de Porto et verre* (1919). Egon Schiele, *Portrait of Johann Harms* (1916), an Expressionistic portrait of the painter's father-in-law. Gino Severini, *Red Cross Train Passing a Village* (1915).

Painting Between the Wars

Max Beckmann, *Paris Society* (1931). Before he fled the Nazis, Beckmann used to winter in Paris. Some of the figures crowded into this small space are identifiable: the one in the lower right corner covering his face is the German ambassador. Marc Chagall, *Green Violinist* (1923–24); violins and violinists appear frequently in Chagall's work as metaphors for the arts in general. Vasily Kandinsky, *Composition 8* (1923); *Several Circles* (1926); *Dominant Curve* (1936). For Kandinsky, the circle had symbolic, almost mystical meaning, representing something in cosmic evolution similar to the spirit taking the form of matter.

Paul Klee, *Nightfeast* (1921), a landscape under a star-filled night sky; the painted frame gives the work a stagelike quality. *In the Current Six Thresholds* (1929), a geometrical abstraction said to represent the Nile Valley landscape. *The Red Balloon* (1922), a painting of a balloon hanging over a city of imaginary architecture, which anticipates Klee's paintings of squares and rectangles, e.g., *New Harmony* (1936). Fernand Léger, *Woman Holding a Vase* (1927).

Joan Miró, *Landscape (The Hare)* (1927). Piet Mondrian, *Composition I A* (1930). By 1921, Mondrian had restricted his color choice to the three primaries, black, and a grayed white; in the early '30s he eliminated color altogether in many paintings, retaining only the white canvas traversed by black lines. Pablo Picasso, *Mandolin and Guitar* (1924); *Pitcher and Bowl of Fruit* (1931); *Woman with Yellow Hair* (1931).

European Painting Since World War II

Horst Antes, *Large Black Figure* (1968). Karel Appel, *Two Heads* (1953). Francis Bacon, *Three Studies for a Crucifixion* (1962); Bacon interprets this religious subject in a secular manner, as an ultimate example of human brutality. Georg Baselitz, *The Gleaner* (1978). Sandro Chia, *Running Men* (1982). Jean Dubuffet, *Archetypes* (1945); *Will to Power* (1946), a brutal male nude, called by the painter a *personnage incivil* and depicted against a "sky of trivial and violent blue." Also *Propitious Moment* (1962); *Nunc Stans* (1965). Alberto Giacometti, *Diego* (1951).

Anselm Kiefer, *Seraphim* (1983–84). Fernand Léger, *The Great Parade* (definitive state, 1954). Victor Vasarely, *Reytey* (1968); the title means "Secret" in Hungarian, and like other works by Vasarely, this one investigates the optical effects of color.

Latin-American Postwar Painting

Fernando Botero, *Rubens' Wife* (1963). Wifredo Lam, *Rumblings of the Earth* (1950); *Zambezia, Zambezia* (1950). Matta, *Years of Fear* (1941); *Each And* (1947). Rufino Tamayo, *Heavenly Bodies* (1946); *Woman in Grey* (1959), a figure similar to Picasso women of the 1920s–30s but reflective also of Tamayo's Mexican heritage.

American Painting After World War II

Josef Albers, *Impossibles* (1931); *Homage to the Square: Apparition* (1959), part of a series begun in 1949 in which the artist explored color relationships within the confines of a geometrical figure of concentric squares. William Baziotes, *Aquatic* (1961). Willem de Kooning, *Composition* (1955); the painting belongs to a transitional period between his series of women and his return to landscape and abstraction. Richard Diebenkorn, *Ocean Park No. 96* (1977); the name refers to part of Santa Monica where the artist's studio was located. Jim Dine, *Pearls* (1961), one of several paintings of that period using a single object and its written name; *Dream #2* (1963). Helen Frankenthaler, *Canal* (1963). Adolph Gottlieb, *Mist* (1961). Richard Hamilton, *The Solomon R. Guggenheim: Black; Black and White;* and *Spectrum* (1965–66), three Fiberglas and cellulose reliefs made from the same mold, inspired by a color postcard of the Museum. Al Held, *Untitled Y* (1960). Hans Hofmann, *The Gate* (1959–60). Neil Jenney, *Media and Man* (1969).

Franz Kline, *Painting No. 7* (1952), executed with housepainters' brushes and commercial housepaint. Lee Krasner, *Past Continuous* (1976). Roy Lichtenstein, *Preparedness* (1968), explained by the artist as "a muralesque painting about our military-industrial complex." Morris Louis, *Saraband* (1959); *I-68* (1962). Kenneth Noland, *Shift* (1964). Jackson Pollock, *Ocean Greyness* (1953), a painting which postdates his poured and dripped work, returning to imagery of his earlier canvases. Robert Rauschenberg, *Red Painting* (1953); *Untitled* (1963), incorporating a plastic lid, a metal box, photographs of rockets lifting off, and a Coca-Cola advertisement. Ad Reinhardt, *Yellow Painting* (1949). Larry Rivers, *Dutch Masters Presidents Relief* (1964). Mark Rothko, *Violet, Black, Orange, Yellow on White and Red* (1949), one of a number of paintings that suggests the organization of his mature work; *Black, Orange on Maroon (#18)* (1963). Clyfford Still, *1948* (1948). Andy Warhol, *Orange Disaster* (1963); beginning in the early '60s, Warhol produced a number of paintings preoccupied with serial images of death.

SCULPTURE

Alexander Archipenko, *Médrano II* (1913–14?); *Carrousel Pierrot* (1913). Jean Arp, *Growth,* (1938); *Classical Sculpture* (1960–63). Ernst Barlach, *The Reader* (1936). Joseph Beuys, *Incontro con Beuys* (1974–84), vitrine containing felt, copper, fat, and cord; *F. I. U. Difesa della Natura* (1983–85), automobile, shovels, copper, pamphlets, and blackboards, dimensions according to installation. Constantin Brancusi, *Portrait of George* (1911); *The Muse* (1912); *Adam and Eve* (1916–21); *The Seal (Miracle)* (1924–36); *King of Kings* (early 1930s); *Flying Turtle* (1940–45).

Alexander Calder, *Romulus and Remus* (1928); *Spring (Printemps)* (1928); *Mobiles* (1934, 1935, 1936?); *Standing Mobiles* (early '40s); *Blondie* (1972); *Red Lily pads (Nénuphars rouges)* (1956). Anthony Caro, *Quiver* (1981). John Chamberlain, *Dolores James* (1962). Joseph Cornell, *Setting for a Fairy Tale* (1942); *Space Object Box: "Little Bear, etc." motif* (mid-'50s–early '60s). Walter De Maria, *Museum Piece* (1966); *Star* (1972). Edgar Degas, *Dancer Moving Forward* (1882–95); *Spanish Dance (Danse espagnole)* (1896–1911). Jim Dine, *Bedspring* (1960). Jean Dubuffet, *Bidon l'Esbroufe* (1967); *Mute Permute* (1971). Max Ernst, *An Anxious Friend* (1944).

Naum Gabo, *Column* (c. 1923, reconstructed 1937), *Linear Construction in Space No. 2* (c. 1957–58), of Plexiglas and nylon monofilament. Alberto Giacometti, *Spoon Woman* (1926); *Woman with Her Throat Cut* (1932, cast 1940); *Nose* (1947); *Standing Woman ("Leoni")* (1947). Eva Hesse, *Expanded Expansion* (1969). Yves Klein, *Blue Sponge* (1959). Jacques Lipchitz, *Standing Personage* (1916). Aristide Maillol, *Woman with Crab (La Femme au crabe)* (1902?–05). Joan Miró, *Portico* (1956); *Alicia* (1965–67). Both these ceramic works executed with Joseph Lloréns Artigas. Amedeo Modigliani, *Head* (1911–13). László Moholy-Nagy, *Dual Form with Chromium Rods* (1946). Henry Moore, *Upright Figure* (1956–60). Robert Morris, *Untitled* (1967). Louise Nevelson, *Luminous Zag (Night)* (1971); *White Vertical Water* (1972). Isamu Noguchi, *Enigma* (1957); *The Cry* (1959). Claes Oldenburg, *Freighter and Sailboat* (1962); *Soft Pay-Telephone* (1963). Martin Puryear, *Seer* (1984). Lucas Samaras, *Chicken Wire Box #5*

(1972). Richard Serra, *Right Angle* (1969). David Smith, *Cubi XXVII* (1965). Tony Smith, *For W.A.* (1969).

EXHIBITION PROGRAM

The Museum has an ambitious exhibition program, which includes large-scale shows as well as more tightly focused exhibitions. "The Avant-Garde in Russia, 1915–1932," which featured over 800 works documenting the development of abstraction in Soviet Russia, brought together paintings, sculpture, textiles, posters, and other objects borrowed from museums in Europe and Russia, and private collections in Tashkent, Uzbekistan, Baku, Azerbaijan, Kiev, Poland, and Ukraine. "Picasso and the Age of Iron" traced the development of the art of assemblage and the use of forged iron, using works by Alexander Calder, Alberto Giacometti, Julio González, Picasso, and David Smith.

Some exhibitions take particular advantage of the Museum's architecture. Jenny Holzer lit up the interior spiral of the rotunda with a continuous strip of electronic signboard, blazoned with her trademark gnomic statements. Dan Flavin's site-specific installation of fluorescent lights, created for the reopening exhibition (1992), bathed Wright's architectural forms with luminous color. The *Osmosis* series, begun in 1992, seeks to relate the architecture of the Museum to different aesthetic disciplines, bringing together visual artists, architects, composers, choreographers, and filmmakers, who work in pairs to create works designed specifically for the Museum.

THE BUILDING

In form, the Museum is a spiral with a ramp cantilevered out from its interior walls sitting above a horizontal slab. The ramp, 1416 ft long (about ¼ mile), rises 1.75 inches every 10 ft to a domed skylight 92 ft above the ground. The ramp diameter at ground level is 100 ft and, at the top, 128 ft. Wright called the building "organic" architecture, imitating the forms and colors of nature, though his critics called it a militaristic bun, a snail, and an insult to art. Artists, including Willem de Kooning and Robert Motherwell, wrote a formal protest declaring the building unsuitable for the sympathetic display of painting and sculpture.

Between the time of Wright's original design and the completion of the building, 16 years elapsed, many of them spent in arguments with New York City's Department of Buildings, whose ideas on construction differed from Wright's. Wright also quarreled with former Museum director James Johnson Sweeney, who argued that Wright's design would create serious problems in storing and hanging the collection, reservations that proved well founded. In particular, the low ceilings along the ramp limited the size of the canvases that could be hung there and the width of the ramp made it impossible to view the paintings from a distance.

In 1990, after almost a decade of planning and controversy, the Museum closed for a major restoration and expansion. The renovation in the large rotunda included reopening the entire ramp (some of which had been partitioned off for storage and conservation space) and replacing the translucent glass in the skylight with clear glass. It also opened to the public the smaller rotunda, known as the Monitor Building, designed originally for administrative space.

The most controversial part of the expansion plans was the addition of a 10-story annex by the firm of Gwathmey Siegel & Assocs. The original plan, to be cantilevered out over the Wright rotundas, evoked the same kind of hostility Wright's first building engendered, with preservationists likening the new complex to a "giant toilet bowl." Consequently, the annex was scaled down to its present size. In June 1992, the Museum reopened with great fanfare and general critical admiration, which focused more on Wright's original work than on the relationship between the new and old structures.

The Guggenheim Museum SoHo (18)

575 Broadway (Prince St), New York 10012. Tel: (212) 423-3500 for recorded information. To reach a live person, call (212) 423-3600.

ADMISSION: Open Sun and Wed–Fri 11–6; Sat 11–8. Closed Mon, Tues, Thanksgiving, and Christmas Day. Admission charge; children under 12 (must be accompanied by an adult), free.

Changing exhibitions; lectures.

✕ Cafe.

⌂ Museum store open Sun–Fri 11–6; Sat 11–8 (even if museum is closed). Store features books and other publications on art and architecture, gift items, Guggenheim-related merchandise.

♿ Accessible to wheelchairs; wheelchairs available in coatroom. Inquire with Visitors Services Department at (212) 423-3555 about other special services for the hearing- and sight-impaired. For access to TDD/TT Service, call (212) 423-3607.

⦸ No flash photography.

🚇 IRT Lexington Ave local (train 6) to Spring St. BMT Broadway local or express (N or R train) to Prince St.

🚌 M1 marked South Ferry downtown via 5th Ave, Park Ave South, Broadway. M6 downtown via 7th Ave and Broadway.

The downtown satellite (opened 1992) of the Solomon R. Guggenheim Museum came into existence as part of the Museum's expansion and renovation. Housed in a former SoHo loft building whose interiors were redesigned by Arata Isozaki, the Museum offers changing exhibitions from both the permanent collection and other sources.

EXHIBITION PROGRAM

The inaugural exhibition at the Guggenheim Museum SoHo, coinciding with the reopening of the uptown Museum, offered an in-depth selection of works from the permanent collection by six artists: Constantin Brancusi, Vasily Kandinsky, Carl Andre, Robert Ryman, Joseph Beuys, and Louise Bourgeois.

"Marc Chagall and the Jewish Theater" brought to the United States for the first time the artist's murals painted for the Moscow Jewish Theater during a brief period of tolerance by the Soviet government. In the first major exhibition to focus on Robert Rauschenberg's early work, the Museum brought together 100 Abstract Expressionist paintings, collages, and conceptual pieces from his formative years in the 1950s. "Industrial Elegance" examined the beauty in everyday objects from a cast-iron kitchen scale (nominated by Julia Child) to the Concorde jet.

THE BUILDING

Constructed in 1881–82 (architect Thomas Stent) for John Jacob Astor III, whose family fortune rested in part on New York real estate investments, the building is a handsome example of the loft buildings, for commerce and manufacturing, which served the area during the later years of the 19C.

The Guinness World of Records Exhibition (45)

On concourse level of the Empire State Building, 350 Fifth Ave (34th St), New York 10118. Tel: (212) 947-2335.

ADMISSION: Open daily 9 A.M.–8 P.M.; until 11 P.M. during summer months. Closed Christmas Day. Admission charge.

Groups by appointment.

✗ Restaurants on street level of Empire State Building.

♯↴ No restrooms.

▥ Small gift shop with souvenirs.

⅄ Accessible to wheelchairs.

⊘ No video cameras.

▆ IRT Broadway-7th Ave express or local (train 1, 2, 3, or 9) to Penn Station. IRT Lexington Ave local (train 6) to 33rd St/Lexington Ave. IND 6th Ave local or express (B, D or F train) to 34th St; BMT Broadway express or local (N or R train) to 34th St.

▆▆ M1 downtown on 5th and Park Ave South. M2, M3, M4, and M5 downtown on 5th Ave. M6, M7, downtown on Broadway, uptown on 6th Ave. M16 or M34, crosstown on 34th St. Q32, downtown on 5th Ave, uptown on Madison Ave.

The Guinness World of Records Exhibition (1976) recreates with photos, videos, laser disks, and life-sized replicas the unusual feats catalogued in the *Guinness Book of World Records.*

PERMANENT EXHIBITION

There are models of the tallest and heaviest people, the biggest buildings, the smallest vehicles, the longest fingernails, necks, hair, and beards. Other displays recreate amazing, and truly nauseating, feats of rapid food consumption.

Music lovers can listen to history's best-selling pop songs while movie buffs can tap into a databank that documents cinematic record breakers: the movies with the largest number of extras, the longest runs, the highest-paid stars. A computerized sports databank contains statistics on sports, from angling to yachting.

In one hall, videos show the actual establishment of various world records; among the physical feats thus documented is a 28-ft dive into

12⅞ in of water. Another particularly mesmerizing video shows 1.5 million toppling dominoes. Arranged to celebrate the establishing of the European Economic Community, the dominoes depict such attractions as the *Mona Lisa* and the Leaning Tower of Pisa as they fall.

The Museum also documents the natural world—from its highest peaks and windiest spots to its rarest animals and most venomous jellyfish. There are videos of great moments in the conquest of space, from the first human orbits of the earth to the achievements of the space shuttles.

Hamilton Grange National Monument (105)

287 Convent Ave (bet. W. 141st/W. 142nd Sts), New York 10031. Tel: (212) 283-5154.

NOTE: Hamilton Grange is currently closed for restoration.

In 1801, when upper Manhattan was still the hinterlands, Alexander Hamilton built what is today known as Hamilton Grange, the only home he and his family had ever owned. The house is a national historic monument, with exhibits celebrating the life and accomplishments of its builder.

HISTORY

Alexander Hamilton (1755–1804), proponent of a strong federal U.S. government, author of some of the most eloquent *Federalist Papers*, and Secretary of the U.S. Treasury under George Washington, declined in political power with the ascendency of Thomas Jefferson. Disappointed in public life, he turned to private pursuits for fulfillment, building his private law practice and his home in the country. This Federal-style house, begun in 1801 by John McComb, architect of City Hall, was completed a year later, situated atop a knoll about 100 yds from its present location. In the garden Hamilton planted 13 gum trees, a present from Washington, which symbolized the original 13 states.

After Hamilton's death in 1804 following the famous duel with Aaron Burr in Weehawken, N. J., his widow, the former Elizabeth Schuyler, lived in the house for 30 years. In 1834, she sold the property and moved to Washington, D.C., and the Grange passed from owner to owner until 1889, when it was donated to St. Luke's Episcopal Church. The church fathers moved it two blocks southeast to its present location. The American Scenic and Historic Preservation Society acquired the building in 1924 and opened it to the public nine years later. The National Park Service has managed it since 1962. It is hoped that eventually the home can be restored to its original appearance.

The Hayden Planetarium: American Museum of Natural History (93)

In the American Museum of Natural History, Central Park West at 79th St, New York 10024. Enter the Planetarium directly from 81st St off Central

Park West or through the main Museum entrance. Tel: (212) 769-5900 to reach a live person. For recorded information, call (212) 769-5920. For celestial information, call the Sky Reporter Hot Line, 769-5917.

ADMISSION: Open Sun–Thurs 10–5:45; Fri, Sat 10–8:45; slight seasonal variation in closing times. Laser light shows Fri and Sat nights, 7, 8:30, and 10 P.M. Closed Thanksgiving and Christmas Day. Admission charge for Planetarium and for laser shows.

Information Desk. Sky Shows, changed about twice yearly, are shown at intervals throughout the day, more frequently on weekends and in the summer (call for schedule); annual holiday show from Thanksgiving through New Year's. Shows for preschool and older children on the first Sat of each month. Laser light shows with rock music on Fri and Sat evenings. Lectures, special events, concerts, courses in astronomy and related sciences.

✘ Restaurants in American Museum of Natural History. Diner Saurus cafeteria (no bag lunches) on ground floor, open daily 11–4:45. Garden Cafe: brunch Sat and Sun 11–4; lunch: Mon–Fri 11:30–3:30; dinner: Fri and Sat 5–7:30.

▥ Gift shop with books, telescopes, gifts, toys, souvenirs, T-shirts, mobiles, posters.

ᕍ Accessible to wheelchairs. Restrooms in American Museum of Natural History accessible to wheelchairs.

⊘ No photography during Sky Shows.

▙ IRT Broadway-7th Ave local (train 1 or 9) to 79th St. IND 6th Ave express (B train), 8th Ave local (C train or K train), to 81st St/Central Park West.

🚌 M7 and M11, uptown on Amsterdam Ave, downtown on Columbus Ave. M10 via Central Park West. M79, crosstown on 79th St or M104, via Broadway.

The Hayden Planetarium (officially the American Museum-Hayden Planetarium), named after investment banker Charles Hayden who donated the original equipment, is actually the astronomy department of the American Museum of Natural History. Its focal point, the Sky Theater (capacity 650), features a Zeiss Model VI planetarium projector that illuminates the interior of the dome with celestial phenomena of the past, present, and future. Although the Zeiss projector dates back to 1969, the new, computer-automated system which incorporates new sound equipment, laser disks, and more than 100 slide, film, and video projectors creates dazzling visual and auditory effects impossible in the days when the shows were projected manually.

> NOTE: In 1995 the Planetarium announced plans for a major expansion to be completed around the year 2000. Highlights will include renovation of the Sky Theater, whose domed roof will be extended to create an 80-ft sphere; a Hall of Planet Earth; and cutting-edge technology to create for visitors the experience of moving through a "virtual" universe.

PERMANENT EXHIBITIONS

On the first floor is the SPACE THEATER, whose 22 screens offer panoramic slide shows on astronomical subjects; a Copernican orrery shows the planets of our solar system moving on tracklike orbits around a central sun. Among the meteorites on display is the impressive 14-ton *Willamette meteorite,* perforated with irresistibly attractive holes into which generations of children have plunged their fists.

On the second floor, the displays in the HALL OF THE SUN explore the relationships between the sun and the earth (energy, climate, time, eclipses) and the place of the sun among other stars. The "Astronomia" exhibition presents an eclectic display of astronomical fact and fiction. Visitors despondent about their earthbound weight can calculate their poundage on smaller planets.

THE BUILDING

The Planetarium building (1935; Trowbridge & Livingston) is tucked into the northwest corner of the Museum complex. The dome is 45 ft high from floor to apex and 75 ft in diameter, only 1 ft smaller in diameter than the world's two largest planetarium domes (in Tokyo and Richmond, Va.).

Hebrew Union College-Jewish Institute of Religion: Joseph Exhibition Room (19)

Brookdale Center, 1 West 4th St (Mercer St), New York 10012. Tel: (212) 674-5300.

ADMISSION: Open Mon–Thurs 9–5; selected Suns for special programs. Closed Fri–Sun; Jewish holidays. Free.

Changing exhibitions, lectures, symposia, programs and events, artist talks, performance events related to exhibitions.

✗ No restaurant.

⌂ No gift shop.

♿ Accessible to wheelchairs. Gallery on ground floor; elevator to other levels.

🚇 IND 6th or 8th Ave local or express (A, B, C, E, F, or Q train) to W. 4th St; walk east. IRT Lexington Ave local (train 6) to Astor Place (walk south on Broadway and west on W. 4th St). BMT Broadway line (R train) to 8th St.

🚌 M1 (marked South Ferry) downtown via 5th Ave and Park Ave South to W. 4th St. M2 or M3 downtown on 5th Ave to W. 8th St and University Place; walk south to W. 4th St. M5 downtown via 5th Ave and Broadway or M6 downtown via Broadway to W. 4th St. M13, 8th–9th St crosstown. M21 crosstown on Houston St.

Located in the Brookdale Center of Hebrew Union College–Jewish Institute of Religion, the Joseph Gallery offers changing exhibitions on Jewish themes. Shows have ranged from the sculpture of Hana Geber—works in silver, bronze, and gold depicting personalities and events central to the Jewish experience—to displays of contemporary illuminated Hebrew manuscripts, to a collection of rare 18–19C *mizrah* plaques—works in various media (watercolor, copper etching, even embroidery) traditionally hung on the wall of a house to indicate the direction of Jerusalem.

In the main lobby is a permanent photographic exhibition of the history of the college. Also within the building is the Petrie Synagogue, whose windows, Torah ark, and eternal light are by Israeli artist Yaacov Agam.

Henry Street Settlement: Arts for Living Center (20)

466 Grand St (bet. Pitt and Willett Sts), New York 10002. Tel: (212) 598-0400. Free.

Changing exhibitions, children's programs, musical events, performances, readings, dance.

✘ No restaurant.

▥ No gift shop.

♿ Steps to smaller gallery. Larger gallery accessible to wheelchairs.

🚇 IND 6th Ave local (F train) to Delancey St.

🚌 M9 downtown on Avenue B and Essex St. M14 crosstown on 14th St. M22 crosstown on Madison Ave.

The arts programs of the Henry Street Settlement (settlement founded 1893; gallery opened 1974) reflect the goals of this venerable social service organization and the ethnic diversity of the Lower East Side community within which it works. Each year the program mounts about six exhibitions, including one of children's art. Except for those in the Alcove Solo Photography Gallery on the ground floor, most are group shows by emerging artists, frequently women and members of minority groups.

Often shows have a specific social context or touch on the concerns of the Lower East Side Community, e.g., homelessness, a theme that dominated shows in the 1992–93 season. "Bushville and The Hill" offered photographs by Margaret Morton documenting the dwellings of these two makeshift Manhattan communities built by homeless people. "All the Way Home," organized by artist Hope Sandrow, exhibited the fruits of a collaboration between women artists and homeless women in the Park Avenue Armory Women's Shelter.

In June 1993, the Henry Street Settlement celebrated its 100th anniversary with a birthday party featuring children's artwork devoted to the concept of birthdays. Accompanying this exhibition was "Voices of Henry Street," black-and-white photo portraits by Harvey Wang of people who have been touched and changed by involvement with the Henry Street Settlement.

HISTORY

The Louis Abrons Arts for Living Center is the cultural center of the Henry Street Settlement, whose original buildings are around the corner at 263–267 Henry St, between Montgomery and Grand Sts. Lillian Wald (1867–1940), who founded the Settlement to minister to the impoverished and largely uneducated immigrants of the Lower East Side, is still remembered as one of New York's great figures—a compassionate, gentle, yet shrewd and worldly woman, who devoted herself tirelessly to the poor. After a visit to a poor family awakened her sense of vocation, she moved to a fifth-floor walkup at 27 Jefferson St and began her rounds, fighting ignorance, disease, malnutrition, rats, and bigotry. Although she came from a bourgeois German Jewish family, she gradually grew to accept these strange Eastern European immigrants as her own people, and became an important liaison between the "uptown" and "downtown" Jews who often found themselves at odds with one another. The organization continues its work today in the original settlement house tradition.

INTAR Latin American Gallery (46)

420 West 42nd St (bet. 9th/10th Aves), New York 10036. Mailing address: P.O. Box 788, New York, N.Y. 10108. Tel: (212) 695-6135.

ADMISSION: Open Sept–June, Mon–Fri 12–6. Closed weekends, holidays, July and Aug. Free.

Changing exhibitions, symposia, lectures. Student internship program.

✗ No restaurant.

▯ No gift shop; catalogues for sale.

♿ Not accessible to wheelchairs.

🚇 IRT Broadway-7th Ave local or express (train 1, 2, 3, or 9) to 42nd St/Times Sq. IND 8th Ave local or express (A, C, or E train) to 42nd St.

🚌 M11 uptown on 10th Ave, downtown on 11th Ave. M10 uptown on 8th Ave, downtown on Broadway. M16, crosstown on 34th St. M42 crosstown on 42nd St.

The INTAR gallery (founded 1979) is located in the brick-walled lobby of the theater with the same name on Theater Row, the western outpost of the Broadway theater district. The name is an acronym for International Arts Relations (founded 1965), a group dedicated to assisting and exhibiting artists of diverse racial and cultural backgrounds. The gallery, which presents six exhibitions each season, focuses on Latino artists, but also exhibits the work of African-American, Asian-American, and women artists.

On occasion, as its name suggests, INTAR mounts exhibitions curated in cooperation with other institutions in the city, e.g., "Re-Discoveries: The Mythmakers," one of a number of observances of the Columbus quincentennial from non-Eurocentric points of view. This exhibition drew on the resources of INTAR, the American-Indian Community House, and the Jamaica Arts Center. It presented nine artists whose works are rooted in the cultures of the Americas and the Caribbean, where African, European, and native traditions have mutually influenced one another, often challenging the traditional Old World distinctions between "sacred" and "secular" art. Among the artists in the exhibition were West Lathern, known for the monumental yard assemblage he has been constructing since the late 1950s at his home in north-central Alabama; James "Son" Thomas, blues singer and sculptor, whose best-known work is a series of clay skulls; and Sara Bates, who translates Cherokee ritual into contemporary art.

International Center of Photography (ICP) (77)

1130 Fifth Ave (at 94th St), New York 10128. Tel: (212) 860-1778.

ADMISSION: Open Tues 11–8, Wed–Sun 11–6. Closed Mon, New Year's Day, July 4, Thanksgiving, and Christmas Day. Admission charge. Free Tues 6–8 P.M.

Exhibitions, lectures, workshops, seminars, courses in virtually every aspect of photography. Publications, catalogues. Library with comprehensive collection of photographic publications and biographical files.

✘ No restaurant.

🏛 Museum shop with catalogues, books, prints, cards, posters, photographic publications.

♿ Accessible to wheelchairs; call ahead for temporary ramp.

⊘ No photography.

🚇 IRT Lexington Ave local (train 6) to 96th St.

🚌 M1, M2, M3, or M4 uptown on Madison Ave, downtown on 5th Ave. M19 crosstown on 96th St.

The International Center of Photography, known as ICP, was founded in 1974 after a 20-year effort by Cornell Capa, a photographer for *Life* magazine. His brother Robert Capa, whose images of the Spanish Civil War and World War II exemplified photojournalism at its peak, was killed by a land mine in 1954 in Indochina, and Cornell Capa determined to establish a museum which would collect and preserve not only his brother's work but that of other photographers and photojournalists. Today, ICP is the foremost showcase for photography in New York, and a center for photographers, editors, artists, and others interested in the medium.

PERMANENT COLLECTION

Holdings include more than 13,000 prints, as well as video- and audiotapes. The collection focuses on important 20C photographers, and offers researchers access to the work of Berenice Abbott, Robert Capa, Weegee, Andreas Feininger, and others.

EXHIBITION PROGRAM

ICP mounts five or six exhibitions yearly, in its three galleries. Some shows are historical, featuring the work of photographers represented in the permanent collection, traveling from other collections. "Henry Peach Robinson, Master of Photographic Art, 1830–1901" investigated the work of this London "art" photographer who tried to mimic the atmospheric effects of contemporary Victorian painting. There have been retrospectives of Margaret Bourke-White and recapitulations of photography for the *National Geographic.* "An Uncertain Grace: The Photographs of Sebastiao Salgado" depicted the lives of people without power—laborers in the gold mines of Brazil, refugees fleeing the droughts of Ethiopia, schoolgirls in Kenya. "Vanishing Spain," which included about 100 black-and-white pictures by five Spanish photographers, spanned the years 1969–87, documenting the remnants of a culture where medieval values still live.

THE BUILDING

The graceful neo-Georgian town house where the Center mounts its exhibitions was built (1914) by architects Delano & Aldrich for Willard Straight, diplomat, financier, and founder of the *New Republic* magazine.

International Center of Photography: Midtown (47)

1133 Sixth Ave (Ave of the Americas) at 43rd St, New York 10036. Tel: (212) 768-4680.

ADMISSION: Open Tues 11–8; Wed–Sun 11–6. Closed Mon, New Year's Day, July 4, Thanksgiving, and Christmas Day. Admission charge. Free Tues 6–8.

Lectures, gallery talks, videos, films, classes (see preceding entry under International Center of Photography.

✗ No restaurant.

▥ Bookstore with photography books, magazines, cards, posters.

♿ Accessible to wheelchairs.

⊘ No photography.

🚇 IND 6th Ave local or express (B, D, or F train) to 42nd St or 47th St/ Rockefeller Center. BMT Broadway local or express (N or R train) to 49th St.

🚌 M1, M2, M3, or M4 downtown on 5th Ave, uptown on Madison Ave. M5 downtown on 5th Ave, uptown on 6th Ave. M6 or M7 downtown on Broadway, uptown on 6th Ave. M42 crosstown on 42nd St.

ICP/Midtown (1985), the satellite branch of the International Center of Photography, occupies a handsome gallery not far from Times Square. The Center mounts up to a dozen changing exhibitions yearly, focusing on both contemporary and historical photography, showing the work of established and little-known photographers.

EXHIBITION PROGRAM

Major shows stress the historical, the political, and the purely aesthetic aspects of photography. A retrospective of Andre Kertesz traced his career from the earliest years around 1912 in prewar Hungary, through his famous middle period in Paris and New York, to some haunting color still lifes taken near the end of his life with a Polaroid. "In Our Time" offered photographs by past and present photojournalists associated with Magnum Photos. An exhibition of Alexander Liberman, "The Artist in His Studio," highlighted his photographic portraits of artists, including Picasso, Braque, Giacometti, and Rouault. Barbara Kasten's "Architectural Sites" showed her large-scale prints of contemporary architecture transformed by mirrors and brilliantly colored by the use of gels. James Balog's posed photographs of wild animals in unnatural settings allowed viewers to see their aesthetic qualities as a basis for asking crucial questions about the environment, while Brian Weil's large, grainy black-and-white prints documented the impact of AIDS around the world.

Rotating exhibitions of historic photographs appear in the PERMANENT COLLECTION GALLERY. The SCREENING ROOM offers videos, many of which are interactive and experimental.

Intrepid Sea Air Space Museum (48)

Pier 86, One Intrepid Square, West 46th St and 12th Ave, New York 10036. Tel: (212) 245-2533.

ADMISSION: Memorial Day–Labor Day, open every day 10–5. Labor Day–Memorial Day, open Wed–Sun 10–5, last admission at 4; open most major holidays that fall on Mon or Tues; call (212) 245-0072 for recorded message. Closed other Mon and Tues, New Year's Day, Presidents' Day, Thanksgiving, and Christmas Day. Admission charge. Lower rates for groups, children, senior citizens.

> **NOTE:** Be prepared in winter for chilling winds on the Flight Deck. Visitors with claustrophobia are warned not to go aboard the *Growler.*

Group tours by appointment; special events often scheduled around military holidays or on summer weekends.

✗ Cafe with light meals; also vending machines.

🏛 Gift shop with books, posters, ship and plane models, naval souvenirs.

♿ Complete wheelchair access to Hangar Deck; elevator, restrooms, and telephones accessible to handicapped visitors. No wheelchair access to Flight Deck.

🚫 No strollers on submarine or destroyer.

🚇 No subway stop near 12th Ave. Take any subway to 42nd St (Grand Central, 42nd St/6th Ave, Times Sq or 42nd St/8th Ave) and transfer to the M42, crosstown on 42nd St to the Hudson River. Walk three blocks north.

🚌 M50 crosstown on 49th–50th Sts makes a loop south along 12th Ave. M16, crosstown on 34th St, makes a loop to 43rd St and 12th Ave.

The great bulk of the aircraft carrier U.S.S. *Intrepid* dominates the Hudson River waterfront in midtown Manhattan, where trans-Atlantic liners once lay at their berths. Exhibits aboard the ship, fitted out as a museum in 1982, focus on the history of naval aviation from World War II to the present, including displays that chronicle the illustrious career of the carrier itself. Visitors can also climb aboard the U.S.S. *Growler,* one of the first guided-missile submarines, and the U.S.S. *Edson,* a destroyer whose guns once pounded the shores of Vietnam.

HISTORY

The *Intrepid* (launched 1943, decommissioned 1974) enjoyed a long, eventful career. Planes launched from the Flight Deck flew against the Japanese over Tokyo, helped sink two battleships, and accounted for some 650 enemy planes. Hit by a torpedo and rammed by kamikaze planes, the *Intrepid* was known toward the end of the war as "Unlucky I," but survived to join the Sixth Fleet in the Mediterranean, recovering the Mercury 7 and Gemini 3 space capsules later and making three combat tours off Vietnam.

In 1981 the Intrepid Foundation acquired the ship from the U.S. Navy, towed her from Philadelphia to New York, and began the ongoing process of rehabilitation.

PERMANENT EXHIBITIONS

The Hangar Deck, portions of the Gallery Deck, and the Flight Deck with its island of bridges and towers are open to the public, as are the *Growler* and the *Edson.*

HANGAR DECK: In the forward CARRIER OPERATIONS THEATER, a film notable for its thrilling camera angles and thunderous sound track shows landings and takeoffs aboard the nuclear-powered carrier *Nimitz*. NAVY HALL, just aft, contains an exhibit of modern Navy aircraft. The next gallery, INTREPID HALL, contains dioramas, kamikaze artifacts, models, and two World War II aircraft commemorating *Intrepid*'s role in the liberation of the Philippines.

PIONEERS HALL features early wood and canvas planes, including a Voison Biplane. TECHNOLOGIES HALL has full-scale mock-ups of the *Apollo command capsule,* the *Lunar Landing Module* from the Apollo 12, a Gemini capsule, and an actual cockpit of a Boeing 707, as well as videos and films on the conquest of space. There is a good view of both shores of the Hudson River from the ship's fantail.

GALLERY DECK: Just above the Hangar Deck, the Gallery Deck has two areas restored to give an idea of life aboard the carrier.

FLIGHT DECK (sometimes closed due to inclement weather): It is on the 900-ft Flight Deck 57 ft above the waterline that the immensity of the ship becomes apparent. The guidelines for takeoff and landing, the painted warnings to stay clear of props and jet intakes, and the array of aircraft suggest how the carrier may have appeared when on active duty. From the bridges there is a good view of the aircraft on display, which date from World War II to the present. Among them: a *Grumman F-11 Tiger* (long nose) *jet fighter,* a *Grumman S-2E Tracker anti-submarine plane,* a *McDonnell Douglas F-4N Phantom fighter bomber,* several Bell, Hiller, Boeing, and Sikorsky helicopters, a *Lockheed SP-2E Neptune anti-submarine patrol plane,* and an *A-12 Blackbird,* a reconnaissance plane built in the 1960s.

A plaque on deck marks the spot where 22 sailors were killed or wounded in a kamikaze attack in 1944 as the ship cruised near the Philippines.

The U.S.S. *Growler* and the U.S.S. *Edson* have been restored to their wartime appearance. Aboard the *Growler,* visitors can experience, though briefly, the constrictions of shipboard life on a submarine. The cramped showers, the narrow bunks where the crew slept in rotation, and the missile-guidance control center are all on display, along with a film outlining the history of the vessel.

EXHIBITION PROGRAM

Changing exhibitions are organized around military themes, e.g., "The War in the Gulf: The Liberation of Kuwait" and a commemoration of the 50th anniversary of the attack on Pearl Harbor. "Proudly We Served" examined the history of African Americans in the Coast Guard and Navy.

Japan Society Gallery (49)

333 East 47th St (bet. 1st/2nd Aves), New York 10017. Tel: (212) 832-1155. ADMISSION: Open during exhibitions Tues–Sun 11–5. Closed Mon, New

Year's Day, and Christmas Day. Closed between exhibitions. Suggested donation.

Changing exhibitions, gallery talks. Guided tours Wed at noon accompany major exhibitions; group tours by appointment. Japan Society also offers films, lectures, symposia, language classes.

✗ No restaurant.

▥ No gift shop, but postcards, catalogues, some books available at reception desk.

ও Accessible to wheelchairs.

⊘ No photography of individual works.

▣ IRT Lexington Ave local (train 6) to 51st St.

🚌 M15 downtown on 2nd Ave, uptown on 1st Ave. M27 crosstown on 49th/50th Sts.

The Japan Society, founded (1907) as a nonprofit cultural organization, offers exhibitions, film programs, and other resources designed to promote greater understanding between Japan and the United States. The Japan Society Gallery, the visual arts department of the Society, opened in 1971 as the first museum in the United States devoted completely to Japanese art.

PERMANENT COLLECTION

The Gallery maintains a small permanent collection of 20C Japanese art, including woodblock prints and ceramics; it is shown in changing exhibitions.

EXHIBITION PROGRAM

The Gallery usually mounts three exhibitions yearly, drawn from private and institutional collections around the world. Some focus on traditional arts: painted screens, ceramics, textiles, and lacquer work; others display artifacts as diverse as Noh robes and masks, helmets from the mid-16C to the 19C, objects from the Japanese tea ceremony, and early *Ukiyo-e* prints (1680–1750), made before the development of the full-color press and therefore colored by hand. "Paris in Japan," the first American exhibition of late-19C and early-20C Japanese painting in the European tradition, featured some 75 oil paintings by artists who had studied in Japan—mainly with French teachers of the academic tradition—or who went to Paris and encountered the Impressionist and Post-Impressionist painters.

THE BUILDING

Japan House, headquarters of the Society, appropriately draws on both Oriental and Western architectural traditions and materials. It was designed (1971) by Tokyo architect Junzo Yoshimura in consultation with the New York firm, Gruzen & Partners. If its walls and ceiling of poured concrete belong to a recognizable moment in Western urban architecture, the louvered ceiling grids, the sliding panels, and the square pool with its carefully placed stones, trickling water, and surrounding bamboo trees introduce a serenity often associated with Eastern and particularly Japanese culture.

The Jewish Museum (78)

1109 Fifth Ave (92nd St), New York 10128. Tel: (212) 423-3230 for recorded information; to reach a live person, call (212) 423-3200.

ADMISSION: Open Sun 10–5:45; Mon, Wed, and Thurs 11–5:45; Tues 11–8. Closed Fri, Sat, major Jewish holidays, and some legal holidays (call ahead to check).

Admission charge except Tues evenings 5–8 when the Museum is free.

Changing exhibitions, lectures, family programs, panel discussions, films, concerts. Educational programs. Group tours by appointment.

✗ Cafe.

▥ Museum shop with books, catalogues, posters and postcards, notecards, ceremonial objects, reproductions, toys. The shop is open during Museum hours and also Fri 11–3. The Jewish Museum Design Shop, located next door at 1 E. 92nd St, contains beautifully designed and limited-edition ceremonial and decorative objects.

& Accessible to wheelchairs.

⊘ No photography.

🚊 IRT Lexington Ave local (train 6) to 96th St.

🚌 M1, M2, M3, or M4 uptown on Madison Ave, downtown on 5th Ave.

The Jewish Museum (founded 1904), which operates under the auspices of the Jewish Theological Seminary of America, houses a collection of ceremonial objects, works of art, and antiquities considered the most important collection of Judaica in the western hemisphere and one of the three most important in the world. In addition to its central permanent exhibition, the Museum offers changing exhibitions drawn from its own collections and from other public and private sources in the United States, Europe, and Israel. The Museum occupies the former mansion of financier and philanthropist Felix Warburg.

PERMANENT COLLECTION

Among its 27,000 objects are an outstanding group of Jewish coins and medals, archeological artifacts, ceremonial objects, paintings, drawings, prints, sculpture, and decorative arts. The Benjamin and Rose Mintz Collection (purchased by Museum 1947) includes 500 objects of Polish Jewish culture: kiddush cups, Torah crowns and mantles, and Hanukkah lamps. The Mintzes brought these works to New York for exhibition at the 1939 World's Fair, and when the Nazis invaded Poland that year, both the Mintzes and the collection were spared. The Benguiat Collection, purchased by the Museum in 1924 with Warburg's help, contains some 400 works collected by Hadji Ephraim Benguiat, the son and grandson of Turkish dealers in antiquities; it includes fine examples of Ottoman Judaica and a large number of Sephardic works. In 1904, Lesser Gieldzinski, connoisseur and adviser to Kaiser Wilhelm II, donated his collection of Judaica to the Jewish community of Danzig, where it was housed in the Great Synagogue. In 1939 leaders from the Danzig Jewish community shipped the collection to the Jewish Theological Seminary for safekeeping. The objects would be sent back to Poland if the community survived for 15 years; otherwise they would remain in New York. This collection, along with ceremonial objects from Danzig synagogues and some owned

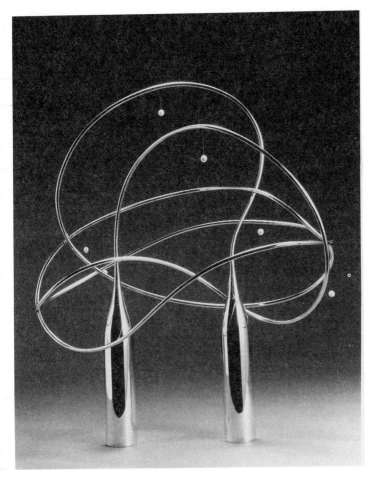

*Silver and pearl torah crown (1959), designed by Moshe Zabari. The
collections of the Jewish Museum span 4,000 years.
(The Jewish Museum, New York. Photo: John Parnell)*

by individual Jews, arrived a month before the German Army occupied
Danzig.

In addition, the Museum collects modern and contemporary art by
Jewish artists or on Jewish subjects. Paintings and sculpture by Leonard
Baskin, Jacques-Émile Blanche, Marc Chagall, Adolph Gottlieb, Max
Liebermann, Jacques Lipchitz, Elie Nadelman, Jules Pascin, Ben Shahn,
Chaim Soutine, Andy Warhol, and Max Weber are rotated through the
galleries in changing exhibitions.

PERMANENT EXHIBITION

The permanent exhibition, "Culture and Continuity: The Jewish Journey," occupies two floors of gallery space. Through ceremonial objects, works of art, and interactive computer exhibits, it traces the history of the Jewish people as they developed their own traditions and interacted with the cultures around them.

The first part, entitled "Forging an Identity," describes the early evolution of the Jews as a people with their own customs and rituals. The initial gallery explores the transformation from Israelite to Jew. On view are terracotta vessels, agricultural implements, and ritual objects, including an Israelite *horned altar* (1000–900 B.C.E.), war implements, and other ornaments. From the period 586 B.C.E.–135 C.E. comes a group of ancient coins, a foundation stone from the fortification wall of Jerusalem (41–70 C.E.), and a group of Hanukkah lamps that begins with ancient terracotta vessels (3–5C B.C.E.) and ends with contemporary renderings of this traditional form.

The second section, "Interpreting a Tradition" (640–1800 C.E.), explores the cultures of three main branches of Judaism—Middle Eastern, Sephardic, and Ashkenazi—and presents a wealth of beautiful objects from the permanent collection. On display are such objects as the *Lord Mayor's Tray,* designed by British silversmith John Ruslen, and presented (filled with candies and sweet things) by Congregation Bevis Marks, the first congregation established after the Jews were readmitted to Britain in 1656. In addition to silver and metalwork there are examples of elaborate needlework, including a *cushion cover* (c. 1900) from the Ottoman Empire, made of velvet and embroidered with gold threads and sequins.

A staircase leads down to a gallery that focuses on ceremonial objects surrounding the Torah. One of the prizes of the collection is an elegant *Torah ark* made for the Jews of Urbino, Italy, in 1533. Like other such Renaissance pieces, it is remarkable for having no external indication of its function, except for a painted inscription; on the inside of the central doors, however, are paintings of the *Tables of the Covenant.*

A portion of a synagogue wall from 19C Persia, made of beautiful faïence tile mosaic, illustrates the artistic influence of Islam. A display of holiday artifacts includes Persian noisemakers, matzoh covers, tiered seder plates, and Haggadahs (books containing the service for celebrating Passover).

The permanent exhibition continues with a space that memorializes the Holocaust, displaying objects that belonged to individuals and communities swept up in this tragedy of Jewish history.

The final section, "Realizing a Future," offers rotating exhibitions of contemporary art that deal with such issues as Jewish identity, life in Israel, and the quest for spirituality. At one corner of the gallery is the plaster model of George Segal's *The Holocaust* (the bronze cast is near the California Palace of the Legion of Honor in San Francisco's Lincoln Park). Constructed using Segal's familiar technique of casting living people in plaster, this powerful work shows a single survivor standing inside a barbed-wire fence, which also encloses a pile of corpses. The composition was based on news photographs taken after the liberation of the death camps, but also contains references to literary and artistic sources.

EXHIBITION PROGRAM

In addition to shows drawn from its own collections, the Museum offers a full range of exhibitions on Jewish art, history, and culture from other sources. Some are based on the work of individual Jewish artists, e.g., Ben Shahn, Marc Chagall, and Jack Levine. Others interpret Jewish art in terms of social history, e.g., "Painting a Place in America: Jewish Artists in New York, 1900–1945; A Tribute to the Educational Alliance Art School," or "Gardens and Ghettos: The Art of Jewish Life in Italy."

An exhibit on Russia and the Jews brought together some 380 rare photographs chosen from the collection of the YIVO Institute for Jewish Research. Entitled "A Century of Ambivalence: The Jews of Russia and the Soviet Union, 1881 to the Present," the show traced the relationships between Russian Jews and the dominant cultures from the period of the czars, through the Holocaust, through the period of Communist domination. "Convivencia: Jews, Muslims and Christians in Medieval Spain" examined the cultural relationships among these three religious groups from the Muslim conquest of Spain in 711 to the defeat of the last Muslim ruler and the expulsion of the Jews in 1492.

A current series, "Cultural Conversations," focuses on contemporary work by Jewish and non-Jewish artists. The first exhibition was "A Postcolonial Kinderhood," an installation by Elaine Reicheck that dealt with issues of assimilation and "Americanization" by Jews.

THE BUILDING

The former Felix Warburg Mansion (1908), a designated New York City Landmark, forms the core of the Museum. Warburg admired the Isaac Fletcher House at Fifth Avenue and 79th St (now the Ukrainian Institute of America) and hired its architect, Charles Pierrepont H. Gilbert (son of the more famous architect Cass Gilbert) to design his house in the French Gothic style reminiscent of the châteaux of the period of Francis I. The mansion remained in the family until 1944, when the financier's widow, Frieda Schiff Warburg, donated it to the Jewish Theological Seminary for a museum.

In 1990–93, the Museum restored and expanded the building, replicating along Fifth Ave its intricately carved limestone facade with stone from the same quarry in Indiana, and doubling the exhibition space.

The Lower East Side Tenement Museum (21)

90 Orchard St (bet. Delancey/Broome Sts), New York 10002. Tel: (212) 431-0233.

ADMISSION: Open Tues–Sun 11–5. Closed Sat and Mon and Jewish holidays. Free admission to exhibitions; charge for walking tours and other events.

Changing exhibitions. Multimedia presentations, walking tours, special events, educational programs. Groups by appointment.

✘ No restaurant.

📖 Books, publications.

&. Not accessible to wheelchairs.

⊘ No photography.

🚌 M15 downtown on 2nd Ave/Allen St, uptown on Water St/Allen St/1st Ave, to Allen and Delancey Sts.

🚇 IND 6th Ave local (F train) to Delancey St; IND 6th Ave express (B or D train) to Grand St; IND 6th Ave local (Q train) to Grand St. BMT Nassau St express or local (J or M train) to Essex St.

The Lower East Side Tenement Museum (founded 1988) seeks to preserve the heritage of the nation's immigrants, honoring the millions who lived on the Lower East Side and in other immigrant ghettos. The Museum, located in an Orchard St tenement at 97 Orchard St, offers walking tours, exhibitions, and other programs that bring alive this segment of the nation's history.

EXHIBITION PROGRAM

Changing exhibitions focus on problems that faced the immigrants of the Lower East Side and the rest of the city. "One Third of a Nation: The W.P.A. Photographs of Arnold Eagle" examined the photojournalism of a photographer whose pictures of tenement life helped in the battle to improve housing. "Meddling with Peddling: The Pushcart Wars" used political cartoons, photos, and documents to examine the disputes between merchants, peddlers, and the city during the 1930s. "Urban Log Cabin: A Tenement Dollhouse" is a scale model of 97 Orchard St, furnished to depict life in the tenement in 1870 (before the passing of housing reform laws), and in 1915 after plumbing and other amenities were required by law.

In addition to the changing exhibitions, the Museum offers a schedule of tours and events to recreate the past of the historic neighborhood. The Peddler's Pack Walking Tour traces the life of a Jewish immigrant family, stopping at such institutions as the former Daily Forward Building, the Educational Alliance, and the Rabbi Jacob Joseph Yeshiva. Other tours visit Little Italy, Chinatown, and the former Free African-American community of 19C New York.

THE BUILDING

The heart of the Museum is the tenement itself, a six-story Italianate brownstone built in 1863 by Lucas Glockner, a tailor who immigrated from Germany. Constructed when there was only casual enforcement of the few housing laws that existed, Glockner had a free hand, but his tenement was better than most. Each floor had four three-room apartments, with daylight reaching one room in every flat. Glockner, who lived there himself, provided clean backyard privies, solidly constructed stairs, and unusually large front and back windows.

As housing laws changed, so did 97 Orchard St. By 1888, the privies were connected to sewers; by 1905, tenement house laws required hallway toilets and ventilating windows between the inner rooms of the building. When stricter laws (1929) required substantial structural changes, the owner decided to rent the building for commercial uses only, and in 1935 the residential apartments were abandoned and sealed.

The Museum's historians have traced with fascinating results the history of many people who lived there. Because landlords conventionally offered a free month's rent at the beginning of a year's lease, tenement dwellers moved frequently, and it is estimated that as many as 10,000 people lived in 97 Orchard St between 1863 and 1935.

About 1870 a family headed by Julius and Nathalia Gumpertz moved in. Gumpertz, who worked cutting heels for shoes in a workshop on Dey St, set out for work one day in 1874 and never returned. His fate was never determined and nine years later his wife, who supported her children as a dressmaker, petitioned to have him declared legally dead.

As with other tenements, increasing age meant decline; by 1900, the residents of 97 Orchard St belonged to humbler trades, mostly in the garment industry. The largest family in the building in 1905 was a Romanian-born peddler, Schlomo Solomowitz, his wife, and their nine children.

Today the Museum, which was added to the National Register of Historic Sites in 1992, is raising money to purchase the building and to continue restoration. Currently tours of the building are restricted to the first floor. The rooms of an apartment rented during the Depression to the family of Adolfo and Rosaria Baldizzi, immigrants from Sicily, are being furnished with the help of memories of a daughter, Josephine, who lived there until she was about seven years old. The Gumpertz apartment is being furnished in the manner of tenement rooms in the 1870s, using trade catalogues, period illustrations, and other documents.

Architectural model of A Living Memorial to the Holocaust—Museum of Jewish Heritage, under construction in Battery Park City opposite the Statue of Liberty and Ellis Island. The Museum (projected opening 1997) will focus on Jewish life in the 20C.
(Kevin Roche John Dinkeloo Assocs.)

La Maison Française (22)

16 Washington Mews (University Place near 8th St), New York 10003. Tel: (212) 998-8750.

ADMISSION: Open during exhibitions Mon–Fri 10–6. Exhibitions are free. Donation requested for film programs.

Occasional changing exhibitions, symposia, lectures (Mon–Thurs evenings at 8:15), French films with subtitles (Fri at 7).

✗ No restaurant.

🏛 No gift shop.

♿ Not accessible to wheelchairs.

🚇 IRT Lexington Ave local (train 6) to Astor Place. IRT Broadway-7th Ave local (train 1) to Christopher St. IND 8th and 6th Ave trains, local or express (A, B, D, E, or F train) to W. 4th St. BMT Broadway local (R train) to 8th St/Broadway.

🚌 M1, M2, M3, M5, downtown via 5th Ave. M6 downtown via 7th Ave and Broadway.

La Maison Française is the French cultural center of New York University, located just off Washington Square in a charming 19C town house. Washington Mews, a private alley, backs up to Washington Square North, the architectural center of New York University. The houses on the north side of the mews were stables, as the configuration of their doors suggests, while those on the south were built in the 1930s on land formerly part of the back gardens of the houses facing Washington Square.

La Maison Française offers a changing program of cultural events. Shows have included an exhibit of paintings by New York artist Pierre Folliet, whose visionary watercolors depicted cityscapes from New York and Paris, as well as the countryside in northern New Jersey and the South of France. A show of photographs by Nancy Crampton offered black-and-white portraits of artists and writers taken over a 20-year period.

The Merchant's House Museum (23)

29 East 4th St (bet. Lafayette St/Bowery), New York 10003. Tel: (212) 777-1089.

ADMISSION: Open Sun–Thurs 1–4, except major holidays. Groups by appointment. Admission charge; lower rates for students and seniors; children under 12 free.

Lectures, special events, changing exhibitions, tours.

✗ No food service. Nearby restaurants on Broadway and E. 4th St.

🏛 Postcards, pamphlets, books, catalogues, souvenirs. Holiday gift shop with 19C items.

♿ Not accessible to wheelchairs.

⊘ No flash photography.

🚇 IRT Lexington Ave local (train 6) to Astor Place. BMT Broadway local (N or R train) to 8th St and Broadway. IND 8th Ave local or express (A, C, or E train) to W. 4th St. IND 6th Ave local (F train) or express (B train) to W. 4th St.

🚌 M1 downtown on 5th Ave. Some M1 buses terminate at 8th St; either walk south to 4th St or transfer to the M6 and continue to E. 4th St. M5 or M6 via Broadway.

The Merchant's House Museum, formerly the Old Merchant's House (opened as a museum 1936), is a treasure among the city's period houses. Through good luck, its architectural details and original furnishings have survived virtually intact from its glory days. The house is an unusual remnant of the period when fashionable architecture was undergoing a transition between the more modest Federal and the more expansive Greek Revival styles.

HISTORY

The house was built (1832) on speculation by Joseph Brewster, a hat merchant. In the early 19C, real estate development was a high road to financial success in New York, and Brewster intended to profit from the general prosperity sweeping the city. After living in the house for three years, Brewster sold it to Seabury Tredwell for $18,000, a handsome sum, but certainly less than the price of houses on nearby Colonnade Row, which went for about $30,000. Tredwell was a prosperous hardware merchant and importer who could afford to fill his home with fine contemporary furniture. About two years after Seabury Tredwell's death (1865), his wife, more in tune with the times than her husband, had some of the rooms redecorated in the fashionable Victorian style and purchased some new furniture to complement the redecoration.

After Mrs. Tredwell's death (1882), the eight Tredwell children inherited the house and furnishings, and in 1900, four unmarried daughters were still living there. The youngest was Gertrude, born in the house in 1840 and the last survivor; she died in the house in 1933. Gertrude was conservative by nature and seems to have thrown nothing away. At the end of her days she lived in genteel poverty, which effectively prevented her from changing the house significantly even had she been so disposed.

After Gertrude's death a kinsman, George Chapman, and Gertrude's niece, Elizabeth Nichols, established a nonprofit organization to preserve the house as a museum. Today it is maintained and is gradually being restored.

EXTERIOR The outside of the house has the red brick facade, steeply slanted dormered roof, and handsomely detailed doorway typical of late Federal period architecture.

GROUND FLOOR On the ground floor are a dining room, used by the family for informal meals and gatherings, and a kitchen. The DINING ROOM retains its original Italian marble coal-burning fireplace. The gaslight fixtures, electrified in 1935, were installed around 1850, but when the Tredwells moved into the house (1835), they used candles and oil lamps for light. The fence and the grilles guarding the downstairs windows are original, security having been a problem in the city even in 1832.

Gertrude Tredwell used the KITCHEN until her death. The Tredwells' original cast-iron stove was removed a century later when the house was first set up as a museum with an open hearth, which replicated the Brewster kitchen in 1832–35. The 1845 cast-iron stove was purchased to replicate the Tredwells' cooking methods. Before the days of modern plumbing, the pump adjacent to the stone sink supplied wash water—rainwater collected in a cistern. Until the Croton System made city water publicly available, drinking water was probably brought to the house

Doorway and ornamental iron railings of the Merchant's House Museum on East 4th St. The original furnishings and architectural details of this home provide detailed insights into the life of a prosperous middle-class New York family in the mid-19C. (Photo: Stan Ries, New York City)

from a nearby well at Broadway and Bleecker St or purchased from vendors.

PARLOR FLOOR This floor contains two beautiful parlors, both used for important occasions—weddings, christenings, and formal parties. The elaborate detailing, including plasterwork, window frames, doors and doorways, suggests Tredwell's affluence. The central recessed ceiling medallions are especially beautiful, with acanthus leaves and anthemion borders. The original 1832 doors are of pine with veneers of Santo Domingo mahogany and silver-plate doorknobs.

The FRONT PARLOR is the most elegant room in the house. Almost all of the furniture here belonged to the Tredwell family—the gondola chairs (1835) covered with black horsehair, the hand-carved Federal sofa with carved eagles, the machine-made pillar and scroll sofa, also covered with black horsehair. The chandelier, now electrified, was originally illuminated by gas and worked on a pulley system.

The REAR PARLOR, separated from the front one by a pair of Ionic columns and two sliding mahogany veneer doors, was first used for family entertaining but later converted for formal dining, when the European custom of dining upstairs became chic in New York.

The *faux marbre* in the VESTIBULE was chosen because it was fashionable, not for reasons of economy. Victorian taste approved of all kinds of *trompe l'oeil* effects, and false marble was considered as desirable as the real thing.

SECOND FLOOR On the next floor are bedrooms, which include exhibition areas with displays of Tredwell family textiles and decorative arts objects. The REAR BEDCHAMBER, decorated with summer matting, has a canopied bed with Victorian gilt flourishes and a mother's chair, whose curved back offered comfort and support to a nursing mother.

The reproduction Greek Revival carpet copies the pattern of the original FRONT BEDROOM floor covering. The American Empire furniture is original from Seabury Tredwell's time, but the bed hangings are Victorian, as are the carved wood leaves which were added to the 1835 bed. The bed curtains were made from an original bolt of fabric, found carefully rolled up and labeled in a trunk. In the HALL BEDROOM is Seabury Tredwell's own Gothic Revival desk.

The Metropolitan Museum of Art (79)

Fifth Ave at 82nd St, New York 10028. For recorded information, call (212) 535-7710. To reach a live person, call (212) 879-5500.

ADMISSION: Open Tues–Thurs and Sun 9:30–5:15; Fri and Sat 9:30 A.M.–8:45 P.M. Closed Mon, New Year's Day, Thanksgiving, and Christmas Day. Suggested admission charge. The tax-deductible admission fee is mandatory, but visitors may pay more or less than the suggested amount. Members and children under 12 free. Reduced rates for students and seniors. Admission booths in the Great Hall and near the Uris Center (ground floor). Some less heavily visited galleries are closed on occasion. Call to determine which, if any, galleries will be closed.

Visitors Center at the **Information Desk** in the Great Hall with information about the Museum and exhibitions at other New York cultural institutions. **Foreign Visitors Desk** in Great Hall with assistance available for visitors who speak Chinese, French, German, Italian, Japanese, or Spanish. Call (212) 879-5500, ext. 2987.

Gallery tours; special group tours in foreign languages. Recorded tours available at the Audioguide desk in the Great Hall and at special exhibitions; call (212) 570-3821. Concerts and lectures. Educational programs for children, adults, families; consult the calendar available at the Information Desk. For information on the Thomas J. Watson Library, the Photograph and Slide Library, and the study rooms, call (212) 879-5500.

Special exhibitions, some of them major events in the city's cultural life, draw large crowds. For the most popular exhibitions, tickets (either free or with a small service charge) are issued to regulate the number of visitors at any one time. For information, call (212) 879-5500.

✗ Cafeteria open Tues–Thurs and Sun 9:30–4:30; Fri and Sat 9:30–8:30. The Museum Bar and Cafe, serving hot food, salads, sandwiches, pastries, afternoon tea, wines by the glass, and a full bar, is open Tues–Sun, 11:30–4:30; Fri and Sat 11:30–8:30. Museum Restaurant with waiter service open Tues–Sun 11:30–4:30; Fri and Sat 5–10 P.M. (last reservation at 8). Call (212) 879-5500, ext. 3964 for reservations. To avoid waiting, eat early or late. The Great Hall Balcony Bar, featuring a string quintet, is open Fri and Sat evenings 4–8. Roof Garden cafe, 5th floor, open May–Nov (weather permitting) Tues–Sun 9:30–4:30; Fri, Sat 9:30–8:30.

🛍 Lavish art, book, and gift shops located off the Great Hall offer a wide selection of Museum publications, books on art and related subjects, postcards, prints, calendars, Christmas items, video and audio cassettes, and reproductions of objects in the collections. The poster shop contains hundreds of posters illustrating objects in the collection or announcing special exhibitions. The children's shop has an impressive selection of books, toys, and games keyed to departments within the Museum. All told, the Metropolitan's gift shops resemble an art-centered department store.

♿ Complete wheelchair accessibility; enter from the garage or from 81st St. Access information available at Information Desk. For information about programs and services for disabled visitors, call (212) 535-7710. For TTD/TT service, call (212) 879-0421.

⊘ No strollers on Sun. No flash photography, video or movie cameras. For permission to sketch, inquire at the Information Desk.

🚇 IRT Lexington Ave local or express (train 4, 5, or 6) to 86th St.

🚌 M1, M2, M3, or M4 downtown on 5th Ave, uptown on Madison Ave. M79 crosstown on 79th St. M86 crosstown on 86th St.

The material on the Metropolitan Museum of Art is organized according to the following plan:

Introductory Material

First Floor
  Arts of Africa, Oceania, and the Americas
  20C Art
  Greek and Roman Art
  Greek and Roman Treasury
  Medieval Art
  Arms and Armor
  Egyptian Art
  European Sculpture and Decorative Arts
  Jack and Belle Linsky Galleries
  Robert Lehman Collection
  American Wing

The Metropolitan Museum of Art is the largest, most comprehensive art museum in the western hemisphere. The building itself occupies 1.5 million sq ft on three exhibition floors, stretching from 80th to 84th St, from Fifth Ave into Central Park. Its collections include more than 2 million objects, whose range includes the whole world and the entire sweep of human civilization.

HIGHLIGHTS

You cannot expect to see the entire Museum in a single or even two or three visits. Yet, amid such a wealth of treasures, it is difficult to select highlights. **First-time visitors** might enjoy the guided tour of Highlights of the Metropolitan Museum of Art, which departs from the Tour Kiosk in the Great Hall three times daily, Tues–Fri; check at the Information Desk for schedule. Otherwise it is probably wisest to confine yourself to one or two departments.

The Metropolitan's holdings in European painting are unrivaled outside Europe. In 1993 the galleries of *19C European paintings and sculpture* were reinstalled. For many visitors these beautiful galleries, with their abundant examples of Impressionist and Post-Impressionist painting, are the high point of a trip to the Museum. The *European Sculpture Court* is a handsome architectural space displaying 18–19C sculpture, much of it French.

The Egyptian collection, probably the best in the western hemisphere, is also a favorite with visitors; the reconstructed *Temple of Dendur* offers a unique opportunity to experience Egyptian architecture.

The galleries of *Arms and Armor,* reinstalled in 1991, are pleasing both for the beauty of individual objects and for the spectacle of the installation.

The *American Wing* has a fine collection of 18–19C American painting and an extensive exhibition of American decorative arts, including fine period rooms.

The *French period rooms* are especially beautiful.

*An early 19C Maori figure from New Zealand in the Michael C. Rocke-
feller Wing of the Metropolitan Museum of Art.
(The Metropolitan Museum of Art. Photo: Charles Uht)*

METROPOLITAN MUSEUM OF ART
First Floor

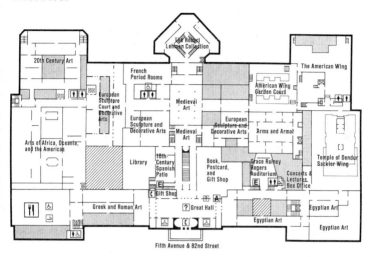

Fifth Avenue & 82nd Street

The Fifth Ave entrance leads directly into Richard Morris Hunt's aptly named **Great Hall,** whose imposing floral exhibits were donated by Lila Acheson Wallace, a founder of the *Reader's Digest* and a significant benefactor of the Museum.

> **NOTE:** Accession numbers have been used to identify small objects in the descriptions that follow.

FIRST FLOOR

Arts of Africa, Oceania, and the Americas
The galleries devoted to the art of Africa, Oceania, and the Americas contain work spanning 3,000 years and three continents, objects of the kind formerly called "primitive" art. The artifacts are not, however, primitive in the sense of being crude or rough, and the societies that fostered them, though nonindustrial, are often complex in their social organization and intellectual achievements. Many of the works on display were made to fill needs that were not purely aesthetic—appeasing the gods, declaring power or status, or adorning the human body.

HISTORY

The wing, given by former New York State Governor Nelson A. Rockefeller, memorializes his son Michael C. Rockefeller, who died in a rafting accident (1961) while on a collecting expedition in Papua, New Guinea. It houses the collection of the former Museum of Primitive Art privately founded by Nelson Rockefeller in 1954, as well as Rockefeller's own personal collection, supplemented by important gifts and other Museum acquisitions.

HIGHLIGHTS

Asmat art from New Guinea, especially the spectacular *mbis* ceremonial poles; African masks and sculpture, especially works from the Court of Benin (Nigeria); and pre-Columbian gold ornaments from South and Central America.

The first of the AFRICAN GALLERIES is devoted to the art of **Western Sudan and the Guinea Coast.** Highlights include wooden sculpture by the Dogon, Bamana, and Senufo peoples of Mali and bronze sculpture from Benin (modern Nigeria). Notable among the many wooden sculptures are a 7-ft male *Dogon figure* (1978.412.322), with upraised arms. Dogon sculpture is among the largest and also the oldest in Africa, preserved by the dry climate. Also on display are Bamana figures, including a *Mother and Child* (1979.206.121), a figure used in fertility rites. Bamana antelope headdresses helped secure the spiritual support of a mythical creature—half man, half antelope—who invented agriculture and taught it to mankind. On the left wall are Senufo helmet masks from the Ivory Coast shaped like monumental bird figures and carried on the heads of dancers.

The second African gallery features the arts of **Central Africa, the Guinea Coast, and Equatorial Africa.** From Central Africa are stools and chairs, including a rare *stool with a caryatid figure* (1979.290) by the Buli Master of the Luba people (Zaire); taken to Europe at the turn of the century, the sculptures of the Buli Master were among the first African sculptures recognized by their stylistic individuality and emotional intensity as the work of one particular artist. In a case on the side wall are a *Kongo fetish of a man or spirit riding on a dog* (1978.412.531) and a *Kongo figure of wood, nails, cloth, beads, and shell* (1979.206.127) believed to embody a spirit with good and evil powers. The little figures hanging from it record prayers to the spirit and the horns are filled with medicinal ingredients. Nearby in a freestanding case is a *Fang reliquary head* (1979.206.229) from Gabon, once owned by sculptor Jacob Epstein. The Fang people believed in the power of ancestors, and each family had a reliquary box with ancestral skulls on which was mounted a carved head, such as this one, to protect the contents against the forbidden gaze of women and uninitiated boys.

One of the remarkable artifacts from the Guinea Coast is an extraordinary early-16C *ivory pendant mask* (rear part of gallery, separate case 1978.412.323), which was made for the Court of Benin in Nigeria; circling the hair is a ring of ornaments representing the heads of bearded Portuguese traders and mudfish. Impressed by the skill of Bini carvers, the Portuguese commissioned ivory spoons, forks, and elaborate saltcellars (e.g., 1972.63a,b), which they took back with them. Also from Benin is a fine collection of bronze and brass objects, e.g. (side wall), a bronze *Horn Player* (1978.412.310) and a group of *dark brass heads* (1979.206.86, 87, 36), which were kept on the royal altars as memorials to ancestors; they wear the royal regalia of coral beads, cap, and choker.

The galleries of THE AMERICAS lie behind the African galleries. Enter the **Mesoamerican Gallery** from the first African gallery. The collection of Aztec stone sculpture includes animals, female figures (perhaps agricultural or fertility goddesses), and a collection of grim-looking rat-tlesnakes. On the entrance wall, the Toltec panel of an *Eagle Devouring a Human Heart* (93.27.2) dates from the 9–12C; in Toltec mythology the eagle represented the sun, which required human blood in order to con-tinue its journey through the sky. Among the ceramics are examples from Huastec, Tlatilco, Colima, Nayarit, and Jalisco cultures. Olmec artifacts include a *jade mask* (1977.187.33), as well as pendants, ornaments, and *"baby" figures* (e.g., 1979.206.1134). These ceramic "baby" figures, big-bel-lied and soft-looking, may represent an early diety. From Veracruz (Remojadas) comes a *smiling figure* (1979.206.1211), the significance of whose expression is not known; it is possible that these figures represent deities, perhaps the god of alcoholic drink. The 6C wooden *seated figure* (1979.206.1063), probably a priest or dignitary, ceremonially posed and elegantly dressed, is one of the few Maya wooden objects that have sur-vived time, moisture, and infestation.

The second gallery of the Americas opens from the first. Against the rear wall in a section devoted to **Central America** are stone sculptures including metates or grinders, and ceramics from Ecuador and northern Peru, including vessels from the Chavin period. This era, roughly the mid-1st millennium B.C., was one of the most artistically fertile periods in ancient South America. Chavin iconography emphasizes feline forms, as well as those of alligators, snakes, and birds of prey. In the TREASURY are ornaments and small objects of gold: *Mohican ear spools* (66.196.40,41) of gold with stone and shell inlay and pendants represent-ing eagles, frogs, sharks, and other creatures. Near the exit is a *gold funerary mask* (1974.271.35) from the Batán Grande burial site in Peru; the cemeteries were used from the mid-2nd millennium B.C. until the late 15C when the Incas rose to power; this mask dates from the 10–14C.

The second Americas gallery leads to the third exhibition area with a small section devoted to **Eskimo and Northwest Coast Indian** cultures of NORTH AMERICA. The *Haida sea-bear mask* (1979.206.830), made of copper with inlaid shell eyes and teeth is exceptional.

The rest of the wing focuses on cultures of OCEANIA. Among the objects in the **Polynesian** section are an 18–19C *temple drum* (1978.412.720) with an elaborate openwork stand from the Austral Islands, a small 19C *ivory figure* (1979.206.1470) from Tonga, and an *anthropomorphic pendant* (1979.206.1587) of a type known formerly only from the writings of the 18C explorer Captain Cook. A *male figure* (1979.206.1466), possibly of the god Rogo, is a rare survival of the enthusiasms of 19C Christian mission-aries, who were notably hard on statues of native gods. A frightening array of clubs from Tonga, Samoa, and Fiji includes specialized clubs styled for assaulting particular parts of the body. One of the more impressive is a *two-handed Fiji club* (1985.317.6) inlaid with whale ivory from Tonga, designed for bashing the opponent's skull, thereby insulting and injuring the most noble part of the body.

The main gallery in this area with its glass wall facing south is devoted to the cultures of **Micronesia,** including New Guinea, New Ireland, and the New Hebrides. On the east wall are cases with large funerary festival carvings from northern New Ireland; these are among the most complex of Oceanic works of art, and were used in feasts to honor the dead and initiate young men into the society which the dead had abandoned. Along with standing slit gongs and figures from the New Hebrides is an impressive collection of artifacts from New Guinea. The Michael C. Rockefeller Collection of Asmat art includes nine *memorial poles* (heights range from 12 to 21 ft) carved with ancestor figures and an openwork phallic projection. According to the Asmat world view all death, even that which seems to occur by natural causes, is brought about by enemies and must be redressed. These *mbis* poles were placed outside the men's ceremonial house when a village had suffered a certain number of deaths. The poles remained in place until a successful headhunt restored the social balance: the heads of the enemy victims were put in the hollows in the lower ends.

20th Century Art

HIGHLIGHTS

The collection, while overshadowed by those of the city's museums devoted solely to modern art, is strong in American painting, notably works by The Eight (a stylistically disparate group of painters, including Robert Henri, John Sloan, and William Glackens, united by their opposition to the National Academy of Design); in American modernist painters whom Alfred Stieglitz nurtured and collected; and in Abstract Expressionist and Color Field painters.

NOTE: This section covers galleries on both the 1st and 2nd floors.

HISTORY

In the early decades of this century the Metropolitan Museum was emphatically disinterested in 20C art, so much so that two outstanding museums, the Whitney Museum of American Art and the Museum of Modern Art, were founded with work rejected by the Metropolitan.

Only after World War II, with the Stieglitz Collection (donated 1949), did the Museum begin to acquire important modern works, and even then the progressive curator of American paintings and sculpture, Robert Beverly Hale, was able to purchase contemporary works only after protracted struggles with the trustees. Eventually (1967) the Department of 20th Century Art was founded; 20 years later the Lila Acheson Wallace Wing (1987; Roche, Dinkeloo & Assocs), named after one of the Museum's greatest benefactors, opened as a permanent home for the department.

To see the galleries in chronological order, begin on the first floor. Because the paintings within galleries are rotated with some frequency, the highlights of the collection are listed below in alphabetical order by artist. Not all of the works mentioned will be on display at any one time.

The general plan of the galleries is as follows: FIRST FLOOR, GALLERIES 1–9, **Chronological Survey of Painting, 1905–40.** GALLERY 10, **Design and Architecture.** GALLERY 11, Changing Exhibitions. MEZZANINE, **Sculpture and Contemporary Painting** and two smaller flanking galleries for **Klee Collection** and changing exhibitions from the **Department of Prints, Drawings, and Photographs.** SECOND FLOOR, GALLERIES 15–22, Continuation of **Chronological Survey of Painting, 1940–Present.** GALLERY 22, the **Lila Acheson Wallace Gallery,** with selected contemporary works, overlooking Central Park.

Magdalena Abakanowicz, *Androgyne III* (1985), the hollow shell of a fragmented human torso on a stretcher of wooden logs. Josef Albers, *Homage to the Square*. As a painter, Albers is best known for a pioneering series of geometrical paintings that explored the interaction of color and form.

Milton Avery, *White Rooster* (1947); *Green Sea* (1954). Avery's interest in color, influenced by Matisse, attracted a later generation of Abstract Expressionists, notably Mark Rothko, and the Color Field painters. Balthus, *The Mountain* (1937). This is one of Balthus's largest works, intended to represent Summer in a cycle of the Four Seasons never executed. Art historians have pointed out the painting's debt to Courbet's *Young Ladies from the Village* (also owned by the Metropolitan) in the forms of the landscape and the studied awkwardness of the figures.

Max Beckmann, *Beginning* (1949); this painting, which focuses on childhood, is the most autobiographical of Beckmann's triptychs. Thomas Hart Benton, *July Hay* (1943). After a five-year stint in Paris where he worked as a Cubist, Benton returned to Missouri and immersed himself in realistic, narrative painting. Pierre Bonnard, *The Terrace at Vernon* (1939). The painting, which depicts the terrace and garden of the painter's home in the Seine Valley, was reworked about 20 years after Bonnard first painted it and is noteworthy for its complex spatial organization and luscious color.

Fernando Botero, *Dancing in Colombia* (1980). Constantin Brancusi, *Sleeping Muse* (1910). Georges Braque, *Le Guéridon* (1921–22). The title refers to the round table in the picture; Braque painted this work at a point in his career when he was beginning to reintroduce naturalistic elements while still maintaining many of the conventions of Cubism.

Alexander Calder, *Red Gongs* (1950). Marc Chagall, *The Market Place, Vitebsk* (1917), an early work, executed before Chagall's tremendous popularity. Robert Colescott, *Knowledge of the Past is the Key to the Future: Some Afterthoughts on Discovery* (1986).

Salvador Dali, *Crucifixion (Corpus Hypercubus)* (1954). Established as a Surrealist in the 1930s, Dali celebrated his return to his religious faith in a series of paintings made in the 1950s; the Vatican declared this one of the most significant Christian works of its time.

Stuart Davis, *Edison Mazda* (1924); *Percolator* (1927); *Semé* (1953). Willem de Kooning, along with Jackson Pollock, was one of the pivotal figures of his time; the Museum is fortunate to own works from different periods in his development. Early figural paintings include *Two Men Standing* (1938) and *The Glazier* (1940). *Seated Woman* (1944), a striking, grotesque image of a woman, breasts bared, hair rolled in curlers, was painted after his early figural work and before a series of women in the 1950s. *Attic* (1949), an early abstract black-and-white painting, may owe its monochromatic coloring to the availability of cheap commercial enamel. The slashing brushwork of *Easter Monday* (1955–56), an abstraction bought by the Museum while the paint was still wet, suggests why the Abstract Expressionists were also called "action" painters.

Charles Demuth, *The Figure 5 in Gold* (1928). The title is taken from a line in his friend William Carlos Williams's poem "The Great Figure." André Derain, *Fishing Boats, Collioure* (1905); *The Table* (1911).

Lyonel Feininger, *Gelmeroda, Number 13* (1936); Feininger made 13 increasingly abstract paintings of the Gothic church at Gelmeroda, a village near Weimar. Lucien Freud, *Naked Man, Back View* (1991–92); a painting of theatrical performer Leigh Bowery, which focuses on the skin and flesh of the subject. Arshile Gorky, *Water of the Flowery Mill* (1944), one of his most beautiful landscapes. Gorky's mature work formed a transition between sophisticated European modernism, especially Cubism, and American Abstract Expressionism, which would emerge after his death. Red Grooms, *Chance Encounter at 3 A.M.* (1984); the painting shows Mark Rothko and Willem de Kooning in Washington Square Park. Philip Guston, *The Street* (1977).

Marsden Hartley, *Portrait of a German Officer* (1914), an abstraction inspired by the death in battle of a German friend, whose initials and age are included in the painting. Childe Hassam, *Avenue of the Allies* (1918). Hassam, considered one of the foremost American exponents of Impressionism, is known for his views of New York; this painting depicts Fifth Ave decorated with flags for a Liberty Bond drive during World War I. David Hockney, *Mount Fuji and Flowers* (1972). Edward Hopper, *From Williamsburg Bridge* (1928); *The Lighthouse at Two Lights* (1929); *Tables for Ladies* (1930). Hopper is known for his evocation of light, and for his depiction of the loneliness and isolation of the human condition.

Wassily Kandinsky, *Improvisation Number 27: The Garden of Love* (1912). Kandinsky often worked in watercolors and in his oil paintings achieved similar effects; discernible in this garden of love are three embracing couples and possibly some animals. Ellsworth Kelly, *Blue Red Green* (1962–63); *Spectrum V* (1969). One of the most important Hard-edge color painters, whose work succeeded that of the Abstract Expressionists. R. B. Kitaj, *Amerika: John Ford on His Deathbed* (1983–84), contains images from the famous director's movies. Paul Klee: the Museum owns some 90 paintings and drawings made by Klee between 1920 and 1940. Among them are *Handbill for Comedians* (1938); *Strange Garden* (1923). Franz Kline, *Black, White and Gray* (1959).

Roy Lichtenstein, *Stepping Out* (1978). After his great success as a Pop artist in the '60s, Lichtenstein began using the benday dots familiar from comic strips to "quote" from art history. This painting refers to Fernand Léger's *Three Musicians* in the Museum of Modern Art and perhaps to Picasso's Surrealism.

John Marin, *Brooklyn Bridge* (c. 1912). Henri Matisse, *Nasturtiums and "The Dance"* (1912). Shown in the famous 1913 Armory Show, this was one of the first paintings by Matisse to be seen by a large American audience. When asked why he painted this second version of a subject he had painted immediately before, the painter replied, "The conception is not the same. Here I was carried away by color."

Amedeo Modigliani is remembered for about 300 pictures—portraits of friends, nudes, and a few landscapes—painted between 1915 and 1919. *Juan Gris,* the Spanish artist, was influenced not only by the Cubists but by Brancusi, with whom Modigliani studied during a period when he was interested in sculpture; *Jeanne Hébuterne* (1918) was his mistress. Robert Motherwell, *Elegy to the Spanish Republic, 70* (1961). Part of a series of some 100 paintings inspired by the Spanish Civil War, this painting, like Jackson Pollock's poured paintings, was executed on the floor.

Louise Nevelson, *Black Crescent* (1971). Kenneth Noland, *Magic Box* (1959). Georgia O'Keeffe, *Cow's Skull: Red, White, and Blue* (1931); *Black Abstraction; Black Iris* (1926). O'Keeffe, a pioneer American modernist, painted a long series of Hard-edge, almost abstract paintings, most of them based on flowers, landscapes, or skeletal parts, some of them sexually suggestive and intended to startle.

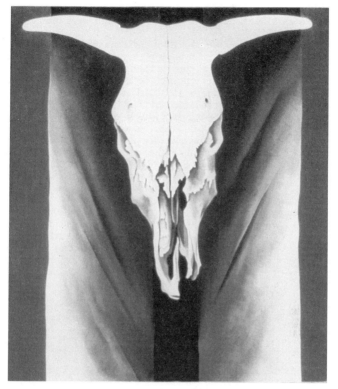

Georgia O'Keeffe, Red, White, and Blue *(1931), Lila Acheson Wallace Wing. O'Keeffe's husband, photographer and art dealer Alfred Stieglitz, left much of his collection of American avant-garde paintings to the Metropolitan.*
(The Metropolitan Museum of Art)

Pablo Picasso, *The Blind Man's Meal* (1903) from the so-called Blue Period; *The Actor* (1904–05). *Gertrude Stein* (1906), his most famous portrait, was executed in Paris when Picasso was 24 and Stein 32. Told that Stein bore little resemblance to the figure in the painting, Picasso is said to have replied, "She will." *A Woman in White* (1923), a calm portrait of Olga Koklova, whom Picasso married in 1918.

Jackson Pollock, an artist of enormous impact, is represented in the collection by two consequential paintings. *Pasiphaë* (1943), hailed as the first important work of Abstract Expressionism, combines references to classical mythology, primitive art, and European modernism with original techniques. Its large size, gestural application of paint, and subdued palette prefigure Pollock's mature style. *Autumn Rhythm* (1950) is one of the monumental poured and dripped paintings—actually they were also splattered, dribbled, slung from sticks or brushes, or spurted from syringes onto an unstretched canvas on the floor—that shocked and fascinated the art world when they appeared. This is a major work from Pollock's most creative period.

Mark Rothko, *Untitled (Number 13)* (1958). Rothko's work from the '40s onward concentrates upon color and simple geometrical shapes; the colors range from bright primary hues to somber purples and browns and, in the years just before his suicide, grays, blacks, and dark browns. James Rosenquist, *House of Fire* (1981). Techniques of Rosenquist's early trade as a billboard painter—large-scale, hard-edged realistic style, and commercial subject matter—influenced his later work.

Charles Sheeler, *Water* (1945). Sheeler, also known as a photographer, depicted industry as the distinctive force in the 20C landscape; this picture shows the powerful geometry of the generators of the Tennessee Valley Authority. John Sloan, *Dust Storm, Fifth Avenue* (1906). David Smith, *Becca* (1965), a welded stainless-steel work named after one of Smith's daughters. Florine Stettheimer, *The Cathedrals of Broadway* (1931); *The Cathedrals of Art* (1942).

Cy Twombly, *Untitled* (1970). Twombly's apparently random scribbles on black or white backgrounds have been described as "drawing into painting," i.e., using the techniques of drawing on a painted canvas surface. Andy Warhol, *Mao* (1973). Grant Wood, *The Ride of Paul Revere* (1931), a very popular painting by a self-consciously primitive painter. Wood's style has been called Precisionist because of its sharp, detailed realism.

Greek and Roman Art

> **NOTE:** The galleries of Greek and Roman art are scheduled for a ten-year reinstallation beginning in 1996. The space currently occupied by the public restaurant, including the skylit central court, will eventually house Roman art. Greek art, including vases now on the Second Floor, will be installed chronologically on the First Floor in the galleries between the Great Hall and the Roman galleries. Cypriot art, now in the barrel-vaulted corridor approaching the restaurant, will be moved to the Second Floor, where the Greek vases are now on view.

The collection of Greek and Roman Art spans several millennia, several civilizations, and several thousand miles—from the Bronze Age civilizations of the Aegean to the remote colonies of the Roman Empire. Chronologically, the earliest pieces come from the Cycladic civilizations of the 2nd–3rd millennia B.C. and the most recent from the Roman Empire at the time of Constantine (emperor A. D. 306–37), whose conversion to Christianity marked a turning point in the acceptance of that religion.

There are currently three gallery areas devoted to Greek and Roman art: the first-floor galleries, with Cypriot, Greek, Etruscan, and Roman art; the second-floor galleries, with an outstanding collection of Greek vases; and the first-floor gallery north of the Grand Stairway, with the Greek and Roman Treasury.

FIRST-FLOOR GALLERIES, WEST SIDE OF CORRIDOR (Begin between the entrance to the restaurants and the entrance to the galleries of African art.)

Cycladic and Greek Bronze Age Cultures. In this room are the earliest pieces in the Cypriot collection, three small *steatite* ("soapstone") *figurines* (e.g., 51.11.5–7) from the 4th or 3rd millennium B.C.

Cycladic culture flourished on several islands in the southern Aegean between 3000 and 1900 B.C. Among the objects surviving from that distant time are numerous small, highly stylized pieces of sculpture, notably large numbers of *female figures* or *idols* (e.g., 68.148) whose features have been reduced to geometrical abstractions; they were buried with the dead, possibly as guardians. *Cycladic* sculptors also created occasional male figures, e.g., the remarkable marble *Seated Harp Player* (47.100.1) from the 3rd millennium B.C., noteworthy for its sculptural form and detail.

The Mycenaean civilization, the greatest of the pre-classical Greek cultures, flourished on mainland Greece and in the Aegean c. 1600–1100 B.C. Mycenaean pottery in the collection includes a *stirrup jar* (53.11.6) from the 12C B.C. decorated with fish and an octopus, whose tentacles surround the swelling body of the jar.

The second gallery contains **Greek and Roman Bronzes,** the earliest dating from the Geometric period. After the destruction of the Mycenaean civilization, probably by unknown invaders and cataclysmic natural events, Greek art entered what is known as the Geometric phase (7–8C B.C.), likened by some historians to the Dark Ages of medieval Europe. Of special interest are a small, stylized *bronze horse* (case in middle of the room, with griffin head, 21.88.24) and a bronze *Centauromachy* (17.190.2072), a bronze group portraying a centaur confronting a standing male figure. The small bronze *Herakles* (1st case against west wall, 28.77), dating from the late 6C B.C., is a muscular hero brandishing a club, one of his traditional attributes. In a separate case is a veiled, *Masked Dancer* (1972.118.95), dating from the 3C B.C., remarkable for its pose and the sensuous swirl of the drapery. Later works include a *Sleeping Eros* (43.11.4) from c. 200 B.C., as well as Roman portrait busts, Greek and Hellenistic figurines, ornaments, helmets, mirrors, wine jugs, and water jars.

The third gallery, next door, contains **Greek Sculpture of the Classic Period, 6–4C** B.C. Except for temple decorations and grave reliefs, most classic Greek sculpture was executed in bronze, very little of which has survived except in later marble copies, many made by admiring Roman sculptors. Among the finer works in the collection are the *Wounded Warrior Falling Backwards* (25.116), a Roman copy of a Greek bronze probably by Kresilas. The marble figure is supporting himself on his spear; the wound under his right arm would have been painted red. The *Wounded Amazon* (32.11.4), formerly thought to be a Roman copy of a Greek original, is now believed to be a Roman original zealously imitating the Greek style. The Roman relief of a *Dancing Maenad* (35.11.3), based on a Greek original by Kallimachos (c. 415 B.C.), shows an ecstatic follower of Dionysius, the folds of her undulating drapery clinging to her body.

Etruscan Art. Next on this side of the corridor is a gallery devoted to the Etruscans, who controlled central Italy from the Po Valley to Naples, and reached the height of their power in the 5C B.C. Etruscan skill in metalwork is apparent in this gallery, whose most spectacular object is a reconstructed *bronze chariot* (late 6C B.C.), found in a tomb near Spoleto. Its repoussé reliefs illustrate episodes from the life of a hero, perhaps Achilles. The Etruscan collection also contains gems, bronze mirrors, tripods, cauldrons and pails, and other utilitarian objects, as well as examples of Etruscan pottery.

Return through the Roman gallery down the CENTRAL CORRIDOR back toward the restaurant. Lining the walls is an array of **Cypriot Sculpture,** a file of archaically smiling votive figures, interspersed with grave reliefs and sarcophagi, most dating from 550–500 B.C. They were gathered by Luigi Palma di Cesnola, an Italian-born adventurer who fought in the American Civil War, became American consul in Cyprus, and later was the first paid director of the Museum (1879–1904). Believing that Cyprus, actually only a cultural crossroads in the Mediterranean, was the cradle of Greek civilization, Cesnola devoted his considerable energies to amassing Cypriot art while other institutions, notably the Boston Museum, were buying up high-quality Greek and Roman works.

EAST SIDE OF CORRIDOR (nearest Fifth Ave)
    The first gallery contains **Greek Sculpture of the Archaic Period (7–6C B.C.).** Outstanding is a fine marble *kouros* (32.11.1), or nude male figure, the earliest (end of 7C B.C.) Greek marble statue in the Museum. The traditional appearance of the *kouros*—frontal pose, left foot slightly forward, blocky form, stylized wiglike hair—shows the influence of Egyptian art. Also in this gallery are funereal monuments: a grave *stele* (11.185) from the Archaic period (c. 540 B.C.) depicts a boy and girl in low relief, guarded by a sphinx atop the monument; the son is shown as an athlete, with an oil bottle strapped to his wrist. Nearby is a 6C B.C. fragment of a marble *kore* (07.306), or statue of a girl; it was found on the island of Paros, known for the high quality of its marble. There is also a grave relief of a *Girl with Doves* (27.45) from c. 450 B.C.; the figure of the girl has been made more mature—actual children or old people do not yet appear in Greek sculpture.

The next gallery contains **Greek Marble Grave Sculpture (4–5C B.C.).** Some of the monuments (e.g., 47.11.2) take the shape of *lekythoi* or oil jars decorated with farewell scenes.

The last gallery along this side of the hall contains **Greek Sculpture from the Hellenistic Period (4–2C B.C.),** a period that began with the death of Alexander the Great (323 B.C.) and ended with the Battle of Actium (31 B.C.), when Augustus consolidated the power of Rome. During this period Greek culture dominated much of the civilized world from Rome to India, and Greek art was created in centers far from Athens. *Old Peasant Woman* (09.39) is perhaps an original from the 2C B.C.; like other Hellenistic sculpture, it portrays a recognizable person in an unidealized situation. The sensuous figure of *Aphrodite* (52.11.5) shows the goddess of love at her bath; the original by Praxiteles stood in her temple at Cnidus on the coast of what is now Turkey.

Adjacent is a large gallery devoted to **Roman Sculpture and Wall Paintings.** The enigmatic *Boscoreale frescoes* are the finest Roman paintings outside Italy; they were removed from a villa in the resort of Boscoreale near Pompeii which was buried by the eruption of Vesuvius in A.D. 79. The room also contains the *Badminton sarcophagus* (55.11.5) dating from

A.D. 220–230, named after Badminton House in England where it remained after the duke of Beaufort bought it (1728), believing it to be the bathtub of the emperor Augustus.

Also in the Roman gallery are fine examples of portrait sculpture, a major contribution of Roman art. Among them is a *portrait of a Man* (26.60.03) from the first quarter of 1C A.D., a portrait transitional between the realism of the republican period and the idealizing tendencies of the later imperial era, exemplified by the portrait of Augustus on the end wall. The larger-than-life nude bronze portrait statue of *Trebonianus Gallus* (05.30), his brow lined with anxiety, his torso grotesquely thickened, dates from A.D. 251–53. A similarly anxious expression, typical of portraits of the 3C A.D., strains the features of the brutish emperor *Caracalla* (40.11.1). Considering the rapid turnover of 3C Roman emperors and the fates of these two, both murdered, their anxiety seems well founded. In the corner of the room, the blocky, colossal *head of Constantine* (c. 325) with its eyes uplifted, possibly to indicate the spiritualism of the emperor who first embraced Christianity, shows a further movement away from naturalism. On the wall near the Great Hall is a lovely marble *portrait bust of a Young Woman* (30.11.11) with skillfully executed drapery (early 3C).

In the long corridor with Cypriot art are the *Boscotrecase frescoes,* excavated from another villa on the slopes of Vesuvius. Nearby is a *portrait statue of a Roman Prince* (14.130.1; late 1C B.C.), possibly Lucius Caesar, a grandson of the emperor Augustus, dressed in a Greek-style robe.

Between the Roman Gallery and the Great Hall (east side) is a *cubiculum* or *Roman bedroom* from Boscoreale. Illusionistic wall paintings depict architectural vistas and an imaginary landscape sweeping away beyond a real window.

Greek and Roman Treasury

The Greek and Roman Treasury, located north of the Great Stairway, contains the Museum's entire collection of Greek and Roman gold and silver plate—some 150 objects, including tableware, offering vessels, and cosmetic accessories. The objects range in date from the 3rd millennium B. C. to the 3C A.D. and represent civilizations that reached as far east as the Black Sea and as far west as the Italian peninsula. On the left of the hallway are objects from the Bronze Age and Archaic periods as well as a group of 50 eastern Greek vases and utensils (6C B.C.), which show the level of taste and craftsmanship in areas of Greece far from the mainland. On the other side of the hallway are objects from the Hellenistic period and examples of Roman plate. One of the rarest objects is a *gold libation bowl* (62.11.1) from the 4C B.C.; decorated with traditional motifs of acorns, beech nuts, and bees, it is incised on the underside with a Carhaginian inscription.

Medieval Art

The collection of the Department of Medieval Art spans 12 centuries, A.D. 300–1500, or from about the time of the fall of Rome to the beginning of the Renaissance—a complex period whose art included styles known as Early Christian, Byzantine, Migration (a term referring to the nomadic tribes that invaded Europe after the collapse of the Roman Empire),

Romanesque, and Gothic. The collection is divided between the Metropolitan Museum proper and The Cloisters, the Metropolitan's only branch museum, in the Inwood section of Manhattan.

The J. Pierpont Morgan bequest (1916–17) formed the original nucleus of the medieval collection. Morgan, a prodigious collector, was chairman of the Museum's board of directors for many years, but did not leave anything directly to the Museum. The bequest, given by his son, comprised about 40% of his collection, which emphasized precious objects, books and manuscripts, and decorative arts. The items in the Morgan bequest bear the accession nos. 17.190.x.

GALLERY 1. EARLY CHRISTIAN ART (south side of Grand Staircase, just west of Great Hall). Near the entrance are tomb reliefs and sarcophagus fragments. Along the staircase wall are examples of early Christian plain and gold glass and gold jewelry. The marble *bust of a Lady of Rank* (66.25), late 5–early 6C, portrays a woman in a heavily draped mantle, her hair covered with a headdress which indicates her high standing. A *sarcophagus lid* (24.240) from the late 3–early 4C illustrates the parable of the sheep and goats, taken by medieval Christians as a symbol of the Last Judgment.

After the Roman Empire fell in the West, the center of power shifted to the Eastern Empire. Byzantine art of the 5–13C includes ivory plaques and caskets, enamels, icons, and jewelry. Byzantine bronze *steelyard weights* (e.g., 1980. 416a,b) were suspended from hooks and moved along a ruled steelyard to establish the weight of some commodity hung from the other side. The *Cyprus Treasure* includes a set of six silver plates with Scenes from the Life of David. Made (628–30) in Constantinople, they were probably a gift for an emperor; art historians believe that they represent a last flourishing of the Hellenistic style of antiquity. Also in the Treasure are a *gold necklace* (17.190.151), a girdle, bracelets, and another *necklace* (17.190.147–153). All these objects from the Morgan bequest reflect the financier's tastes, which in art as in life ran to the luxurious.

Prominent among the objects from the early Christian period is the *Antioch Chalice* (1st half of 6C, 50.4), a liturgical vessel of silver inside an elaborately decorated cup of silver gilt. It is decorated with vines perhaps loaves of bread, and two images of Christ, who is depicted without the beard and flowing hair that became familiar through medieval depictions.

After the fall of the Roman Empire, barbarian tribes overran much of Europe, bringing with them their own artistic traditions. Their art was suited to their nomadic lives: it was small, portable, often of elaborately worked metal and set with precious stones. Beyond the archway are three cases devoted to Barbarian metalwork and jewelry. *Fibulae* (in the last case, e.g., 47.100.19, late 4–5C) were clasps for garments, worn in pairs connected by chains.

GALLERY 2. The ROMANESQUE CHAPEL (on the east wall of Gallery 3). What is today called the Romanesque style began to appear in France and elsewhere in the 8–12C. The chapel contains Romanesque architectural elements: capitals from columns, heads, and columnar statues. On the front wall is a 12C wooden representation of the *Virgin and Child Enthroned* (16.32.194); the stiff, symmetrical, frontal pose was intended to signify Mary as the Throne of the New Solomon and the Child as Divine Wisdom. Nearby is a 13C stained-glass window from the abbey of Saint

Germain-des-Près in Paris; the window shows *St. Vincent in Chains* (24.167). St. Vincent was a 4C Spanish martyr persecuted during the reign of the emperor Diocletian. On a side wall is a 12C limestone *head of King David* (38.180), from the St. Anne portal of the cathedral of Notre Dame in Paris. The other figures on the portal were smashed during the French Revolution; the origin of this one was recognized from drawings made before the Revolution. The compelling eyes were originally inlaid with lead.

GALLERY 3. The MEDIEVAL TAPESTRY HALL. Among the examples of stained glass is a *Tree of Jesse window* (22.25), a kind of divine genealogy which traces the lineage of Christ back to Jesse, father of David.

Tapestries are mounted on the rear wall. Though found in Spain, the rare *Annunciation Tapestry* (45.76) is probably from Arras, the most important center of weaving during the first half of the 15C. The so-called *Rose Tapestries* (09.137.1–2) show courtiers in elegant dress against a background of stripes and stylized rosebushes; metal threads are woven into the clothes and jewelry and also into the flowers and leaves.

In the center of the room is a monumental seated *Virgin and Child* (33.23) from Burgundy (c. 1440–50), remarkable for its naturalism; like many medieval statues, it was originally painted in bright colors and repainted as the need arose. Near the doorway to the Romanesque Chapel is a figure (c. 1150) of an *Old Testament king* (20.157), from the cloister of the abbey of Saint-Denis near Paris, the only complete column figure to have survived from that period.

GALLERY 4. The MEDIEVAL SCULPTURE HALL. At the far end is an impressive 17C *choir screen* (56.234.1) from Valladolid, Spain. The room contains Gothic sculpture in marble, alabaster, limestone, and wood, as well as furniture, majolica, Hispano-Moresque lusterware, paintings, and tapestries. Among the important works usually displayed (case right of door as you face the entrance) is a small polychrome and gilt group representing the *Visitation* (17.190.724), i.e., the visit of the Virgin Mary and Elizabeth, who was at that time also expecting a child (John the Baptist); the crystal ovals probably covered tiny images of the Christ Child and the infant John the Baptist. Nearby is a stylishly dressed *St. Catherine* (50.64, Flemish, c. 1530), carved in walnut. The wheel at her feet is a symbol of her martyrdom, the jester a reminder that she was born to a noble family, the book an emblem of her learning. In a freestanding case is a *reliquary crib* of the Infant Jesus (15C South Netherlandish, 1974.121), which became a popular devotional object during the early 16C. On the other side of the doorway is a marble *bust of Marie de France* (41.100.132), daughter of Charles IV. The *alabaster mourner* (c. 1453, 17.190.389), heavily cloaked in drapery, comes from the Tomb of the duc de Berry in Bourges. Near the entrance to the Treasury is an *eagle lectern* (18.70.20) from Giovanni Pisano's pulpit in the cathedral of Pistoia, dating from c. 1300.

GALLERY 5. The MEDIEVAL TREASURY. This gallery contains objects of gold, silver, ivory, enamel, and leather, as well as textiles. Between the two entrance doors is a glazed terracotta *altarpiece* (82.4) by Andrea della Robbia showing the Assumption of the Virgin. In cases near the door are enamel plaques from the Mosan Valley. On the other side of the door are ivory plaques and caskets, including a *situla,* or holy water bucket (17.190.45), one of four known. Nearby, an *ivory plaque* (c. 1135, 41.100.201) shows the Three Marys at the Tomb of Christ; it is carved from walrus ivory, which was often used instead of elephant ivory in northern Romanesque art. Among the objects from Romanesque Spain is a *plaque* (17.190.47) with the Journey to Emmaus, when the risen Christ appeared to two disciples, and the *Noli Me Tangere* ("Do not touch me"), words uttered by Christ when he appeared to Mary Magdalen at his tomb. Also on display are examples of *châsses,* or boxlike reliquaries in gilt and enamel. The large *reliquary head of St. Yrieix* (17.190.352) from 13C Limoges probably held a piece of the saint's skull, as reliquaries were often crafted to suggest the original relic. Carved ivories include a small *corpus of Christ* (1978.521.3) from the later 13C, a sensitively carved piece intended for an altar cross and remarkable for its rendering of the body: the muscles of the chest, the slight sag of the belly, the twist of the hips. Liturgical vessels and Gothic sumptuary arts include rich vessels of gold, crystal, silver, and horn, elaborately worked. Among the objects from the Hispano-Moresque tradition is a *basin* (41.100.73) glazed in the Islamic lusterware technique, but decorated in the Gothic style, a piece suggestive of the cultural amalgamation taking place in Spain at the time. A small early-15C figure of *St. Catherine of Alexandria* (17.190.905) is crafted in enameled gold and encrusted with jewels.

Gothic utilitarian metalwork includes *aquamanilia* (pitchers) in the form of animals. *Aquamanilia* were used by lay people for washing their hands at meals and by priests for ceremonial hand washing during mass. Among the precious objects for daily use are some grim reminders of life's vanity: a *chaplet* (17.190.306) or shortened rosary, whose middle beads are carved with busts of men and women but whose terminal ones bear skulls and the message "SVE VOT ERIS" ("This is what you will be").

Beyond the Treasury is the gallery of LATE MEDIEVAL SECULAR ART (14–16C), whose objects give a glimpse into daily life. Included are such everyday artifacts as locks and hinges, fireplace equipment, hunting equipment, game boards, and books.

Arms and Armor

Long a favorite with visitors to the Museum, the collection of Arms and Armor contains about 14,000 weapons from Europe, North America, the Middle East, and Asia. Weapons range from simple arrowheads to complicated many-pieced suits of armor. Pieces on display date from the 5C through the 19C.

HIGHLIGHTS

The flamboyant central Equestrian Court, armor from the English royal workshops in Greenwich, Japanese armor, and an outstanding parade helmet by Filippo Negroli.

HISTORY

The collection owes its beginning to Bashford Dean, a zoologist with an interest in armored fishes. Dean founded the Department of Zoology at Columbia University worked with the American Museum of Natural History, and in 1906 became the firs

Japanese armor from the early 14C in the Hall of Arms and Armor. This rare medieval armor, made of lacquered iron, leather, silk, and gilt copper, was generally worn by warriors mounted on horseback. (The Metropolitan Museum of Art)

curator of arms and armor at the Museum. In 1900 his scientific studies took him to Japan. There he became fascinated with Japanese armor and began amassing the finest collection of swords, helmets, and armors outside of Japan.

EQUESTRIAN COURT. In the center of the galleries is the Equestrian Court, overhung with colorful banners bearing the arms of King Arthur and the Knights of the Round Table. In the Court are outstanding examples of **European Tournament and Parade Armor.** On the leading horse a mounted knight wears German armor (1548) attributed to the master armorer Kunz Lochner. The chestplate of the horse armor bears initials for the owner's name and motto, which can be translated as: "In Christ I trust wholly, John Ernest, duke of Saxony."

On the west side of the room is a display of German fluted armor, some from Nuremberg, dated c. 1525. Fluting, which was introduced to imitate fabric folds, rendered armor more dazzling because it reflected sunlight and lighter in weight because it strengthened the steel. Several cases on the same side of the room contain armor made at the royal workshops in Greenwich, established by Henry VIII in 1514. One of the masterpieces in the history of English armor is a *suit of field and tournament armor* (19.131.1,2), whose lavish etched decoration was probably designed by Hans Holbein the Younger; the suit weighs 80 lbs 4 oz. Equally beautiful is the *armor of George Clifford* (32.130.6), made in the royal workshops c. 1585. In 1590, Clifford became Champion of the Queen, a ceremonial position, while continuing to win wealth and fame as a gentleman-pirate, preying on Spanish treasure fleets; on the side he dabbled in mathematics and geography.

Across the room are examples of English, French, and Italian field and tournament armor. In a wall case are pole arms used by the infantry. Among the most efficient of these was the halberd, whose three edges could be used for stabbing (the long end spike), hacking (the ax blade), or grappling a rider off his horse (the apical hook).

The first gallery on the west (toward the American Wing) contains **European Armor: 1400–1525.** Among the finest objects in the collection is a gilded Ostrogothic *spangenhelm* (42.50.1) from the Great Migrations period (early 6C), a style probably brought to the West during the invasion of Europe by the Huns (A.D. 375–453). Constructed as a framework of bronze straps with iron plates fitted between, the helmet is the recreation in metal of the felt caps worn by the steppe nomads. A *Viking sword* with silver-inlaid hilt (55.46.1) has a blade constructed by hammer-welding together strips of steel and iron as the blade core and then adding a separate edge of hard steel.

The standing figure wearing pieces of armor (29.154.3, c. 1400) excavated from the ruins of a Venetian outpost at Chalcis in Greece shows the transition from chain mail to armor plate, needed to defend against the more penetrating bolts of the technically improved crossbow.

In the center of the gallery is a *parade sallet* (23.141) in the shape of a lion's head. The motif alludes to Hercules wearing the skin of the Nemean lion. Also in this gallery are examples of tournament armor, helmets, and shields. A *German tournament helmet* (29.156.67) could be bolted to the breast- and backplates to prevent whiplash; it weighs more than 18 lbs. The one-piece *war hat* or *chapel-de-fer* (4.3.228) is a tour de force, hammered from a single sheet of steel; it weighs 6 lbs 7 oz. Among the *cross-

bows is one dated 1485 that belonged to *Matthias Corvinus* (25.42), king of Hungary and Bohemia.

The next gallery is devoted to **European Parade Armor of the 16C.** The armor used in courtly parades is notable for the beauty of its form and decoration. The *parade helmet* (17.190.1720), signed and dated (1543) by Filippo Negroli, master armorer of Milan, is one of the masterpieces of the collection. Hammered from a single sheet of steel, embossed, and then patinated to look like ancient bronze, it bears on the crest a supine mermaid, her outstretched arms holding a head of Medusa, whose gaze literally petrified those who looked into her eyes.

The Museum owns a suit of *parade armor* (39.121) that belonged to Henry II of France, whose gear was made in his own armor shop; the royal armorers specialized in richly embossed decoration and lavish gilding. A *parade shield* (34.85) that also belonged to Henry II is displayed nearby. It depicts the defeat of the consul Lucius Aemilius Paulus in the Battle of Cannae by the Carthaginian general Hannibal.

Pieces of an early 16C *German costume armor* (24.79 and 26.188.1,2) show the relation between armor and currently fashionable dress. The armor has snugly fitting buttock and hip defenses and dramatically puffed sleeves, which must have challenged the most skillful armorers.

European Firearms include an early double-barreled *wheellock pistol* (49.2) that belonged to the emperor Charles V. The wheellock was the first automatic ignition device, allowing a gun to be loaded and primed ahead of time, ready for instantaneous use. Marin Le Bourgeois is credited with the invention of the flintlock, a more reliable ignition system than the wheellock; a *hunting gun* (1972.223), made c. 1620 in the Bourgeois workshops for King Louis XIII of France, is one of the earliest flintlocks known. A *pair of pistols* (1986.265.1,2) with ivory stocks made (1786) for Catherine the Great illustrates the exquisite workmanship of luxury weapons.

Also in this gallery are examples of German firearms of the 16–17C, and Napoleonic firearms, including a *flintlock rifle* (1970.179.1) made by Nicolas Noël Boutet, court gunsmith to Napoleon.

Until the advent of firearms, the crossbow was the most powerful oneman missile weapon developed; too heavy and thick to be bent by hand, it was armed by means of a winder or *cranequin*, which worked like an automobile jack. One case contains crossbows, including a pellet crossbow, a box for crossbow bolts, and a winder.

European Edged Weapons include daggers, rapiers, and court swords. Rapiers were used in fencing, and the steel gauntlet that formerly protected the hand of the swordsman was considered too ungainly for the elegant fencer. Consequently a complex system of guards for the hilt was developed by the mid-16C. Included in the collection are cup-hilt and swept-hilt rapiers with decoration ranging from cut steel or silver to gilt bronze studded with jewels. Also on display are court swords (known in England as short swords), which served as status symbols and accessories to fashionable attire, though they also could be used for self-defense.

The *parade armor of Luis, prince of Asturias* (b. 1707; 1989.3), manufactured for him when he was about five, is probably the last royal armor made in Western Europe.

The end gallery contains **American Arms,** including firearms and edged weapons. The most famous early American firearm is the *"Kentucky" rifle* (42.22), developed in Pennsylvania by German and Swiss immigrant gunsmiths. The narrow-barreled rifle was suited to wilderness use since the small caliber allowed the hunter to carry more bullets with less weight; the extra barrel length, rifled to give spin to the trajectory of the bullet, ensured a straighter flight. Also in the collection are engraved powderhorns, decorated by soldiers during the French and Indian Wars, the Revolutionary War, and the War of 1812.

The revolver, invented and manufactured by Samuel Colt, was another classic American weapon. On display are presentation sets, e.g., a *police model* of 1862 (1985.264). Marinus Willett's silver-hilted presentation sword, given to him by Congress in 1777, is depicted in Willett's portrait, painted by Ralph Earl. Willett later became mayor of New York.

On the other side of the Equestrian Court are the galleries of **Japanese Armor.** Near the entrance to the gallery are Japanese *face masks* (e.g., 19.115.2) from the Edo period (1615–1868); constructed of lacquered iron and other materials, they were worn for protection in battle like the visored helmets of European armor and designed with savage expressions to intimidate opposing warriors.

In the center of the room is an important example of *early Japanese armor* (14.100.121) from the late Kamakura period (early 14C), which probably belonged to Ashikaga Takauji, the founder of the Ashikaga Shogunate. On the doeskin covering of the cuirass is a stenciled image of a powerful Buddhist deity, Fudō Myō-ō. Another early armor, of a type called *domaru,* dates to the mid-16C. The cuirass closes on the right side; the short skirt with multiple hanging plates facilitated movement on foot. Nearby is a *helmet* (13.112.10) from the Muromachi period (1392–1568); *kuwagata,* antlerlike wings, frame the crest, which served as a kind of personal logo and could be chosen as an emblem of family tradition or for more fanciful reasons. A case of helmets shows an astonishing range of shapes, one designed to resemble an eggplant, another crowned with a crouching rabbit.

On the other side of the room are a beautiful silk jacket and trousers, which would be worn under the samurai's armor. In one corner of the gallery are warriors' accessories. These bows, arrows, lacquer quivers, drinking vessels, and food boxes simultaneously recall the everyday necessities of the warrior and, in their exquisite design and workmanship, the dignity of his role.

At the far end of the gallery is a *helmet* (28.60.2) surviving from the Kofun period; made in the 5C of iron and gilt copper, with individual *lamellae,* or plates, joined together, its construction recalls that of the Ostrogothic *spangenhelm* in the European galleries.

In the next gallery are ceremonial swords and sword furnishings. Samurai swords came in matched pairs. In contrast to European swords, they were constructed of easily assembled parts and could be taken apart and reassembled with decorations appropriate to particular occasions. Among the finest fittings, e.g., a *knife handle, hair-dressing tool,* and *grip ornaments* (45.24.52a–c), were those attributed to Gotō Sōjo (c. 1461–1538) and his school.

The Museum is fortunate to own a fine collection of **Islamic Arms.** Among the more spectacular is a *Mughal dagger* (1984.332), dated c. 1620, from the reign of Jahangir in India. The gold hilt is encrusted with emeralds, rubies, and colored stones. Even more refined is a *ceremonial saber* (23.232.2a,b), whose components came from three important centers of Islam: the blade from 17C Persia, the grip of milky jade inlaid with jeweled flowers from 18C Mughal India, and (according to tradition) the golden scabbard with its inset diamonds and emeralds from 19C Istanbul. Also on display are Islamic firearms, so-called turban helmets with sweeping outlines and silver decoration on dark steel, Iranian mail, and horse armor.

In the center of the room is a glittering *Hispano-Moresque helmet* (1983.413), made of steel overlaid with gold, and inset with plaques of cloisonné enamel, the only known surviving piece of armor from Moorish Spain.

Egyptian Art

The Museum owns the finest collection of Egyptian art in the United States, some 40,000 objects which date from prehistoric times to the Byzantine occupation during the reign of the emperor Justinian (from c. 3000 B.C. to A.D. 641). The galleries are organized chronologically, beginning with the prehistoric material just north of the Great Hall on the east (Fifth Ave) side of the building.

HIGHLIGHTS

A set of wonderful tomb models illustrating aspects of everyday life, collections of royal jewelry, and the Archeological Room with its superb groups of funerary objects (painted coffins, canopic jars, etc.) illustrating burial customs. The *Temple of Dendur* and the *Tomb of Perneb* are notable architectural monuments.

Egyptian art, which conveys such a vigorous picture of life in ancient Egypt, is fundamentally the art of the dead. Although many cultures have assumed survival after death, the ancient Egyptians provided for their future with unrivaled diligence, setting aside the favorite possessions of the deceased and artistically recreating the minutiae of their daily lives to be enjoyed beyond the grave. The dead took with them all the comforts of home: phalanxes of servants either painted on tomb walls or fashioned as statuettes, food, drink, jewelry, clothing, and even games. Most of the objects in the collection, therefore, are funerary objects, and many were uncovered by museum archeologists during a series of excavations that began in 1907 and continued for 35 years.

GALLERY 1. *Predynastic Period (c. 3600–3400 B.C.) and Orientation.* Among the earliest artifacts are examples of Predynastic pottery, some with sophisticated forms, some with painted decoration; one such *jar* (20.2.10; case marked Gerzean Culture, c. 3600–3200 B.C.) depicts scenes with gazelles and ostriches, oared galleys, and female figures in long skirts.

Opposite the entrance stands a reconstruction of the *mastaba* or *Tomb of Perneb* (built c. 2440 B.C.), an official of Dynasty 5 of the Old Kingdom.

The central room of the tomb is decorated with images of Perneb, who is shown at a table receiving food offerings from servants and relatives. At the rear of the chapel is a false door through which Perneb's spirit emerged from a subterranean burial chamber to enjoy the offerings arranged for it on a slab in front of the door.

GALLERY 2. *Dynasties 1–10 (3100–2060 B.C.).* Near the entrance is a small *Lion* (25.2; c. 3100 B.C.) crouched like a Sphinx; hammered out of quartzite with tools of harder stone and polished with abrasives, it may have been a votive offering. Further along on the right, a small diorite statue, *Sahura and a Deity* (18.2.4) depicts the second king of Dynasty 5, who ruled at about the time Perneb was building his tomb. The two *Bound Prisoners* (64.260, same case) kneel in subjugation to the king; they represent hostile enemies of Egypt, crushed by the Pharaoh's power. The statue of *Memi-sabu and His Wife* (48.111, beyond angle in case) shows a couple in an unconventional pose of affection. Originally only pharaohs could expect life beyond the grave, but by the time Memi-sabu, a steward for the king, had this tomb statue carved (c. 2360 B.C.), even middle-level bureaucrats could join the ranks of the immortal.

GALLERY 3. *Dynasty 11 (c. 2009–1998 B.C.).* After the collapse of the Old Kingdom, centered on Memphis in the north, the focus of Egyptian culture shifted south to Thebes, with the establishment of the 11th Dynasty (Middle Kingdom). This gallery and the next two display artifacts from the Museum's excavations at Thebes, including objects from the funerary temple of King Nebhepetra Mentuhotpe (2060–2010 B.C.) and the tombs of his queen and concubines.

GALLERY 4. *Dynasty 11.* On display here is the finest collection of tomb models ever found, discovered in the tomb of Mekutra, a powerful administrator at King Nebhepetra Mentuhotpe's court. The models—figures, boats, scenes from daily life in the stable, granary, brewery, and bakery—assured perpetuation of the activities they depict: Mekutra could be eternally sure of his beer and bread.

GALLERY 5. *Dynasty 11.* In the last of the Theban galleries are tomb reliefs and the papyrus archive of a farmer who lived 4,000 years ago: his letters deal with household affairs, the rationing of food in a time of famine, and the mistreatment of his concubine and younger sons by other members of the family

GALLERY 6. *Amenemhat I (1991–1962 B.C.), Dynasty 12.* Works in this gallery include a relief and altar from Amenemhat's pyramid temple at Lisht and a relief head of the king being greeted by deities.

GALLERY 7. *Senwosret I, also called Sesostris I (1972–1928 B.C.), Dynasty 12.* Senwosret I is represented by a headless *black basalt statue* (25.6) and possibly by a sensitively modeled cedar statue of a *King Wearing the Red Crown of Lower Egypt* (14.3.17).

GALLERY 8. *Dynasty 12–Early Dynasty 18 (c. 1929–1504 B.C.).* In this large gallery are 12th Dynasty royal portrait statues, most notably a black gneiss *figure of Senwosret III as a Sphinx*. Senwosret III (c. 1878–1843 B.C.), a powerful administrator and soldier who reconquered Nubia, is depicted with a solemn, careworn face, both in the Sphinx statue and in an expressive *fragmentary portrait* (26.7.1394) carved in rough brown quartzite. The collection of Middle Kingdom royal jewelry includes a beautiful pectoral with falcons and a belt or girdle of golden cowrie shells, each with a jingling bead inside.

GALLERIES 9–11. *Middle Kingdom, Dynasty 12, Site of Meir.* This is the first of three rooms with material belonging to private individuals from a specific place, each with its own local culture. Among the smaller items displayed here is *"William"* (17.9.1), the blue faïence hippopotamus who serves as a logo for the Metropolitan's Egyptian collections. "William" and his brethren may have been sculpted as protective amulets since the ancient Egyptians, armed with firsthand experience, considered hippos menacing, not cute. GALLERIES 10–11 contain objects from the archeological sites at Lisht and Thebes, including several brilliantly painted coffins. The eyes painted on the coffin allowed the soul of the departed to glimpse the world of the living.

GALLERY 12. *Queen Hatshepsut (c. 1503–1482 B.C.), Dynasty 18.* Hatshepsut, the sister and wife of Tuthmosis II, produced no male heir; her successor, Tuthmosis III, a son of the same king by a lesser wife, was therefore both her nephew and her stepson. When Tuthmosis II died young, Hatshepsut became regent for her stepson-nephew, a position that apparently gave her a taste for power. She declared herself Pharaoh and continued to rule, using the authority of powerful advisers, in particular the chancellor Senemut. It is uncertain whether Tuthmosis III killed Hatshepsut or simply waited for her to die, but upon her death he saw to it that all her memorials were destroyed. Hatshepsut's funerary temple at Deir el Bahri in western Thebes was adorned with some 200 statues of her; 26, all broken, stand in this gallery. The most appealing, known as the *White Hatshepsut* (29.3.2), is a limestone seated figure which shows her in masculine clothing but with a clearly feminine body.

GALLERY 13. *Early Dynasty 18, Private Citizens.* Among the household and funerary objects is a small statue of Hatshepsut's chief official, Senemut, along with portrait sketches in ink, fine furniture, and the gold mask of his mother.

GALLERY 14. *Hatshepsut–Tuthmosis IV (c. 1503–1417 B.C.).* Among the royal objects from the reigns of major 18th Dynasty rulers is the treasure buried with Tuthmosis III's three wives, a magnificent collection of gold jewelry. The articles in the right-hand case—gold finger and toe stalls, collars and amulets of thin sheet gold (c. 1504–1450 B.C.)—were to adorn the dead; the sturdier objects in the case on the other side of the room were for the living.

GALLERY 15. *Amenhotpe III (c. 1417–1379 B.C.).* The objects here, from the middle of Dynasty 18, belong to an age of Egyptian history known for its luxury and elegance. Amenhotpe is represented by three statues, two colossal seated figures in dark stone and a smaller figure in brown quartzite. In a case against the far wall is a blue faïence *statuette*

(1972.125), which portrays him as a Sphinx. The mysterious *yellow jasper fragment* (26.7.1396), with its elegantly incised, sensuous lips, may be one of Amenhotpe's queens, Tiye.

GALLERY 16. *Dynasty 18, The Amarna Reliefs.* Amenhotpe's son, Amenhotpe IV, became a powerful figure in Egyptian history when he redirected the state religion toward Aton, the sun-disk, proclaiming Aton the only true god and himself, now renamed Akhenaton, Aton's only prophet. Running into understandable resistance from the established priesthood of the former state god Amun, Akhenaton built a new capital downriver from Thebes in the vicinity of present Tell el Amarna.

GALLERY 16 contains relief carvings from Akhenaton's temple and palace, which were destroyed by his enemies after his death. The panels are carved in a mannered, expressive style that almost reaches caricature. Akhenaton, pictured in the reliefs as long-jawed and gaunt, was married to Nefertiti, pictured as beautiful. In the center of the room is a fine life-size *statue of Haremhab* portrayed as a scribe. Haremhab was in reality a general, not a scribe, but respect for literacy determined this conventional pose.

GALLERY 17. *The Amarna Room, Late Dynasty 18 (c. 1379–1320 B.C.),* contains artifacts from the reigns of Akhenaton and his successors, Tutankhamun, Ay, and the general Haremhab, probably the power behind their reigns. Noteworthy are a small ivory *gazelle* (26.7.1292, case on the right), and a bevy of Akhenaton's *shawabtys* (servant figurines, who on the recital of a magic spell would leap into action and perform menial tasks, unfortunately as necessary after death as before). Tutankhaton, nephew and successor of Akhenaton, returned the official religion to Amun and switched his name back to Tutankhamun. A statue fragment here shows him being crowned by the god Amun. In the center of the room is a noteworthy alabaster *canopic jar* (30.8.54), which contained those entrails of the deceased that were not embalmed with the mummy; the lid has been carved as a portrait head of a royal lady.

GALLERY 18 contains large-scale pieces and architectural elements from *Dynasties 19–29 (c. 1361–525 B.C.),* including a towering doorpost of red granite, part of a gateway built by Ramesses II.

GALLERY 19. *The Ramesside Room, Dynasties 19–20 (c. 1320–1085 B.C.).* The important sculpture here includes a *kneeling statue of Sety I,* first king of Dynasty 19, and the *stele of Ptahmose,* a scribe and overseer of the royal harem in the early years of Dynasty 19. The sandstone *battle reliefs* (case opposite the entrance) are part of a temple painting showing King Ramesses II vanquishing his bearded Asiatic enemies.

GALLERY 20. *Third Intermediate Period, Dynasties 21–25 (1085–656 B.C.).* Among the few existing objects from this politically and socially chaotic period is a *gold statuette of the god Amun,* considered one of the best examples of ancient Egyptian metalwork to have survived.

GALLERY 21. *The Archeological Room, Dynasties 19–26 (c. 1320–525 B.C.).* Displayed in this properly claustrophobic gallery are superb tomb groups from Dynasty 26, as well as a range of funerary objects from Dynasties

19–26 that illustrate the development of burial customs in Thebes during this period. Included are painted and decorated coffins, canopic chests, *shawabtys,* Osiride figures (with the form and attributes of the dead god Osiris), and mummies.

GALLERY 22. *Late Period Gallery, Dynasties 26–29 (c. 664–380 B.C.).* Dominating this group of works from the last centuries of pharaonic rule is a large section of an uncompleted relief from the tomb of the 26th-Dynasty official Nespakashuty at Thebes. The scarabs, figurines, and precious lapidary objects illustrate a growing taste for the elegant during this period.

GALLERY 23. *Dynasty 30 (c. 380–342 B.C.).* From the Late Period Gallery continue to Gallery 23, where the large stone *sarcophagus of Wennofer* is displayed along with a statue of the falcon god Horus and the *Metternich stele,* named for its former owner, and covered with carved magical incantations.

GALLERY 24, which leads to the Temple of Dendur, contains works from *Dynasties 27–30 (c. 525–342 B.C.).* Within the gallery are two monumental works: the stone sarcophagus of the priest Wereshnefer, and the top of a column from the Temple of Amun at Hibis, in the Kharga Oasis.

GALLERY 25. *The Temple of Dendur (c. 23–10 B.C.).* The Temple was built on the banks of the Nile by the Roman emperor Augustus in part as a public relations gesture to appease a conquered people; some 19 centuries later it came to the United States as a goodwill gesture for contributions to preserve ancient Nubian monuments endangered by the Aswan High Dam. The Temple honors Osiris, a god associated with the Nile and its fertility, as well as two brothers who drowned in the sacred river during military campaigns.

A *Gateway* leads to the Temple; the winged disk on the lintel represents the god Horus, who ascended to the sky in this form. Reliefs on the gateway show the Pharaoh (Augustus) making offerings to local divinities, a theme repeated both inside and outside the structure. Beyond the gateway, the *Temple* itself has three rooms: an entrance room; an undecorated chamber, probably used for storing offerings; and a sanctuary, where the images of the chief temple gods would normally be kept and attended by the priesthood.

In the exterior rear wall a beveled block can be removed to reveal a hidden chamber ($9\frac{1}{2} \times 6 \times 2$ ft) where the drowned brothers might have been entombed.

Throughout its nearly 2,000-year history, the Temple has attracted graffitists, the earliest a man named Pakhom who in 10 B.C. scratched an obscure demotic oath next to a figure of one of the drowned brothers. In time Pakhom was followed by a Coptic priest, a number of venturesome travelers and pioneer Egyptologists, and an American, Luther Bradish, who carved his name in 1821, 29 years before he became president of the New-York Historical Society, and 153 years before his autograph followed him home.

Return to the main part of the Egyptian galleries. Just beyond Gallery 23 (with the sarcophagus of Wennofer) is GALLERY 26, a lounge area, containing *facsimiles of tomb and temple paintings,* many from Thebes, most from the 3rd–11th Dynasties. Copied (1907–39) by Museum staff members, they provide an archive of Egyptian art (many of the temples have since been destroyed) and a source of information on daily life that would be available otherwise only in texts.

From here continue to the remaining galleries, which lead back toward the Great Hall.

GALLERIES 27–28. *Macedonian–Ptolemaic Periods (332–30B.C.).* The objects in these galleries, which date from the time of Alexander's conquest of Egypt (332 B.C.) to the death of Cleopatra (30 B.C.), show the influence of the West upon Egyptian art. When Alexander died (323 B.C.), his generals divided up his empire and Ptolemy, a Macedonian general, got Egypt. In Gallery 27, two long papyrus scrolls bear the inscriptions of the *Book of the Dead,* a collection of magical spells to help the dead surmount the obstacles of the afterlife. In Gallery 28, the painted statue of *jackal-headed Anubis* (38.5, 1st case, left wall), god of the underworld, holds up his hands in a gesture of protection.

Continue past the auditorium lounge (GALLERY 29) with its facsimiles of tomb and temple paintings to Gallery 31. (GALLERY 30 is used for special exhibitions.)

GALLERY 31. *Roman Art from the Time of Augustus (30 B.C.) to the 4C A.D.* The collection of so-called *Fayum Portraits* brings a shock of recognition: the faces depicted could be seen today, though they represent people who lived 18 centuries ago. Found in 2C Greco-Roman cemeteries in the Fayum district (south of modern Cairo), where the customs of the large Greek community merged with the traditional Egyptian ways, the panels, painted in the Greek style, were placed over the faces of mummies wrapped and buried according to Egyptian rites.

GALLERY 32. *Roman and Coptic Periods (30 B.C.–A.D. 641).* Many of the objects here show the influence of Christianity and may seem closer to the Byzantine or the Western tradition of the early Middle Ages than to their Egyptian antecedents.

European Sculpture and Decorative Arts
The galleries of European Sculpture and Decorative Arts offer one of the largest collections in the Museum (some 60,000 objects), including sculpture from the Renaissance to 1900 and a rich variety of decorative arts.

HIGHLIGHTS

The European Sculpture Court (opened 1990) and the Galleries for 19C European Sculpture and Decorative Arts (opened 1991) are recent additions to a long-term reinstallation of the decorative arts' galleries. The French period rooms are exceptional, and unique in this country.

Begin just next to the Tapestry Hall in the Medieval section. The first gallery contains **Sculpture and Decorative Arts from Northern Europe, 16–17C,** including domestic implements, silver relief plaques, steel and brass coffers, earthenware and stoneware vessels, silver-gilt cups and tankards, and a collection of Renaissance bronzes by Flemish, German, and Netherlandish artists. On view in a freestanding case is an automaton in the form of *Diana on a Stag* (17.190.746) made by Joachim Fries in Augsburg (c. 1620). Well-heeled drinkers used these freewheeling devices in drinking games: the body of the stag was filled with the beverage of choice; a mechanism in the base rolled the stag around the table, and when it stopped the reveler sitting in front of it had to drain the contents.

Italian Renaissance Sculpture and Decorative Arts (opened 1991) contains sculpture, furniture, textiles, gems, and glass. Objects in the first part of the gallery reflect the style of the High Renaissance. The central feature of the gallery is a gray sandstone *wall fountain* (1528), designed by the Florentine sculptor Simone Mosca; its proportions and ornamental details recall the style of Michelangelo, with whom Mosca worked. In the center of the second part of the gallery is the famous *Farnese table* (c. 1565–73), elaborately inlaid with colored marble and semiprecious stones, made by Jacopo Barozzi da Vignola. Decorative arts in this part of the gallery show the taste of the Medici dukes and the Venetian nobility in the second half of the 16C.

On the east side of the gallery are three small period rooms. The CHATEAU DE LA BASTIE D'URFÉ features an altarpiece of inlaid and carved woodwork designed by Jacopo Barozzi da Vignola for Claude d'Urfé, French ambassador to the Council of Trent. The piece depicts *The Last Supper,* enframed by an elaborate architectural setting. The SWISS ROOM from the mid-17C has elaborately carved and veneered paneling on ceiling and walls and a stove of faïence tiles painted with scenes from the Old Testament.

Italian Decorative Arts. A corridor gallery with a sedan chair and two gondola prows from Venice serves as an antechamber to the BEDROOM FROM THE PALAZZO SAGREDO, an 18C palace which overlooked the Grand Canal near the Rialto. Such niceties as the ceiling painting and the 32 fluttering stucco cupids were created for eyes other than those of the homeowner, since it was a custom of the time to receive formal visits in bed.

The next gallery contains 18C ITALIAN FURNITURE and a group of allegorical frescoes from the workshop of Giovanni Battista Tiepolo.

English Decorative Arts include 17–18C furniture, needlework, silver, and porcelain.

> NOTE: The galleries of English decorative arts reopened in 1995, too late for inclusion in this book. The following description of the period rooms reflects their appearance before reinstallation.

The DINING ROOM FROM LANSDOWNE HOUSE (1768), Berkeley Square, London, was decorated by Robert Adam in neo-classical style; vases, scrolls, rosettes, and garlands ornament the beautiful plasterwork on walls and ceilings. The silver on the table is by Paul Lamerie and others.

The TAPESTRY ROOM FROM CROOME COURT (1760) shows the contemporary English taste for rooms in the French style, and is remarkable for the *Gobelins tapestries* that cover the walls and the seating. Made to measure in Paris, the wall tapestries incorporate four medallions based on designs of François Boucher.

The STAIRCASE FROM CASSIOBURY PARK comes from a former country house in Hertfordshire. Carved c. 1674, perhaps by Grinling Gibbons, the staircase has deeply carved oak leaf and acorn decoration referring to the "Royal Oak" where Charles II hid during the Civil War.

The DINING ROOM FROM KIRTLINGTON PARK (c. 1748), north of Oxford, is notable for its carved wood doors and Rococo plaster decoration. The room is now furnished as a drawing room with period furniture.

In the long gallery between the English and French period rooms are examples of goldsmiths' work and horology: on display are elaborate watch cases, snuff boxes, and instruments for telling time.

In the anteroom to the Robert Lehman Collection is THE ARTS OF FIRE: DELLA ROBBIA WARES, AND ITALIAN RENAISSANCE MAIOLICA AND GLASS. The Museum has the largest collection of maiolica and glass in the United States, and one of the finest in the world. Works on display include plates, bowls, ewers, and pharmaceutical jars from such important centers of ceramic art and glass as Florence, Faenza, Castel Durante, and Venice.

The French 18C period rooms are highlights of the galleries of **French Decorative Arts.** They recreate within the Museum the luxury and elegance of the reigns of Louis XV and XVI. Turn left and walk to the INTRODUCTORY GALLERY and PARIS SHOPFRONT, the only Parisian shopfront (c. 1775) remaining from the reign of Louis XVI. In the windows are examples of Paris silver, rare survivals from a period when much was melted down on royal orders to finance royal wars. The display of gold boxes includes a *double snuff box* (1967.155.21) with miniature portraits of the French royal family, and a *snuff box* (1976.155.22) with views of the Château de Chanteloup, country seat of the duc de Choiseul.

Two small paneled rooms open from the left side of the corridor. The ROOM FROM THE HÔTEL DE CRILLON is a mirrored boudoir from the residence of the duc d'Aumont in the present Place de la Concorde. Among the furnishings are a daybed and armchair that belonged to Marie-Antoinette. The BORDEAUX ROOM is a circular salon with carved neo-classical paneling; a Beauvais tapestry carpet covers the floor and the table is set with pieces of black Sèvres porcelain.

Beyond the Bordeaux Room is the EARLY LOUIS XV ROOM, whose corner panels are carved with trophies of the Four Seasons. Hyacinthe Rigaud painted the portrait of *Louis XV* (60.6) as a sweet-faced but imperious boy. Jean-Baptiste Lemoyne, Louis's favorite sculptor, made the bust of Louis in 1757. In the SÈVRES ALCOVE are superb examples of porcelain, including part of a famous turquoise blue dessert service ordered by Louis, prince de Rohan (and later cardinal). Also noteworthy is a *rose vase* (58.75.89a,b) in the form of a ship, considered a tour de force of

Sèvres work; the single-masted vessel may allude to a similar craft in the ancient coat-of-arms of Paris.

The SÈVRES ROOM with polychromed paneling from the Hôtel de Lauzun on the Île Saint-Louis, Paris, contains a magnificent collection of furniture set with Sèvres plaques, including several pieces signed by Martin Carlin. The *Negress clock* (58.75.127) on the mantel is one of those complex automata that amused the wealthy before the invention of modern electronics: when the left earring is pulled, the eyes recede and the hour appears in the right eye, the minutes in the left. The right ear originally activated a small pipe organ in the base.

Furniture in the LOUIS XVI GALLERY includes two secretaries and a commode by Adam Weisweiler with panels of Japanese lacquer. The first doorway on the right opens into a ROOM FROM THE HÔTEL DE VARENGEVILLE, the Paris town house of the duchesse de Villars, wife of one of Louis XIV's great generals. Louis XV's own *writing table* (1973.315.1), sometimes described as the most important piece of 18C French furniture ever to have crossed the Atlantic, occupies the center of the room. Designed by Gilles Joubert, the table is japanned in red and ornamented with gilt-bronze mounts; it stands on a Savonnerie carpet, one of 92 woven for the Grande Galerie at the Louvre.

Adjacent is the PAAR ROOM from the Palais Paar in Vienna, built c. 1630 for the baron Johann Christoph von Paar, postmaster of the Holy Roman Empire, and remodeled 1765–71. Among the furnishings are a *writing table* (1976.155.100) with marquetry of tulipwood, rosewood, ebony, and stained horn, and a gilded *dog kennel* (1971.65.45).

The carved and gilded paneling in the CABRIS ROOM was executed in Paris (c. 1775–78) for a home in Grasse, some 12 miles from Cannes. In the center of the room is a *traveling table* (1976.155.99): the upper section was fitted out as a bed table with a book rest and toilet accessories, while the lower section served as an eating table, with drawers for cutlery and a Sèvres breakfast service for two. The next gallery is the DE TESSÉ ROOM, the grand salon of a Paris town house still standing at No. 1 Quai Voltaire. Furniture made by Jean-Henri Riesener for Marie-Antoinette includes a *lacquered secretary* (20.155.11) on the chimneypiece wall and a *mechanical table* (33.12) of adjustable height used to serve the queen her meals in bed after the birth of her first child.

Walk through the De Tessé Room and the Entrance Gallery to the LOUIS XIV STATE BEDCHAMBER. Against the left wall is a wardrobe of tortoise shell, brass, and ebony by André-Charles Boulle, appointed cabinetmaker to Louis XIV in 1672. Behind the balustrade (the construction materials of the room are all modern) is a bed with four needlepoint wall hangings after designs by Charles Le Brun. They were commissioned by the marquise de Montespan, mistress of Louis XIV, and depict the king and three of their children.

Beyond the State Bedchamber are the galleries of **Decorative Arts from Central Europe, 1700–1800.** Here are examples of goldsmiths' work—snuff boxes, candlesticks—and Bohemian, German, and Venetian glass.

Ceramics are richly represented by examples from major factories at Nuremberg, Fulda, and Höchst. Among the Meissen wares are types ranging from an elaborate *Hunting cup* (c. 1741) bearing the arms of Augustus III, elector of Saxony and king of Poland, to figures and decoration influenced by Japanese and Chinese originals, to a large porcelain *Goat and Kid* (central gallery) designed by Johann Joachim Kändler before 1732. There is a table decoration (1727) by Johann Gottlieb Kirchner representing a *Temple of Venus,* with porcelain columns painted to imitate marble.

Furniture includes a set of armchairs, settees, and other pieces of gilded wood covered with a design of trelliswork and flowers. A large pyramid for a *ceramic stove* (1733), decorated with an illustration of St. Francis Xavier Baptizing in a River, shows an important product of German ceramists.

THE EUROPEAN SCULPTURE COURT

This court, which occupies the wing in the Museum between the French period rooms and the Department of 20C Art, represents the last major step in the architectural expansion of the Museum, begun over 20 years ago. Sculptures are arranged in chronological order from east to west (the Central Park side).

Two of the earliest pieces, *Flora and Priapus* (1616) by Pietro Bernini, father of the more famous Gian Lorenzo Bernini, symbolize Spring and Fall and were made for Cardinal Scipione Borghese. *Leda and the Swan* (1640–50) by Jacques Sarrazin is the work of a sculptor influential during the childhood of Louis XIV. East of the central doorway is Pierre-Étienne Monnot's *Andromeda and the Sea Monster* (1700–04), which depicts the Ethiopian princess looking skyward for her rescuer as her would-be devourer climbs from the water. Across the entrance (the original carriage entrance to the Museum from Central Park) is one of the most important pieces in the group, Jean-Louis Lemoyne's *Fear of Cupid's Darts* (1739–40), given by Louis XV to the brother of Mme de Pompadour. The work shows Cupid taking aim at a female figure who delicately flinches before his darts. Closer to the park is *Ugolino and His Sons* (1865–67) by Jean-Baptiste Carpeaux, a dramatic depiction of an incident from Dante's *Inferno,* in which the traitor Ugolino della Gherardesca is imprisoned with his children in a tower and left to starve.

In the arcade along the south side of the Sculpture Court are portrait busts of distinguished 17C and 18C figures.

The gallery facing the park contains examples of **19C French Sculpture,** including Aristide Maillol's *Torso of the "Île de France"* (1910 / 21) and *Night.* The most dramatic piece in the room is Auguste Rodin's *The Burghers of Calais* (1885–95), which shows six citizens of Calais who volunteered for martyrdom at the hands of England's Edward III to spare Calais from destruction. (The burghers were pardoned at the last minute.) The authorities in Calais who commissioned the work in 1884 presumably had a more traditional heroic monument in mind, and it was only after considerable wrangling that Rodin's anatomically distorted and psychologically intense figures were installed.

The JOSEPHINE BAY PAUL GALLERY, leading from the middle of the Sculpture Court, contains French and Italian terracotta, marble, porcelain, and bronze pieces from the 18–19C. Mounted high on the walls are three stucco reliefs by Claude Michel, known as Clodion, depicting *Children and Satyr-Children Sporting with a Goat, Children and Satyr-Children with a Pantheress and Her Cubs,* and *Satyresses and Satyr-Children* (c. 1781–87). Clodion was best known for his lighthearted classical subjects, e.g., the erotic *Nymph and Satyr Carousing.* Also in the room is Jean-Antoine Houdon's *Sabine* (1788), a tender portrait of his one-year-old daughter.

East of the central Sculpture Court are **16C Italian Decorative Arts,** including marble portrait busts and examples of household furnishing from 16–17C Italy. The marble *Faun Teased by Children* is an important early work by Gian Lorenzo Bernini, sculptor, painter, and architect of St. Peter's Cathedral, and preeminent figure of Italian Baroque art. Sculpted in 1616–17, when Bernini was only about 18 years old, the piece has been seen as a key to his later work.

19C European Sculpture and Decorative Arts. These galleries contain works which span the period from the Restoration of the Bourbon dynasty in 1815 to the Art Nouveau period at the beginning of the 20C. In the CENTRAL GALLERY is Antonio Canova's *Reclining Naiad* (1824), and the *Demidoff Table* (1845) by Lorenzo Bartolini, a supposedly allegorical but nonetheless sentimental portrayal of a group of sleeping children.

In the gallery facing Central Park are examples of medals and jewelry. A *four-paneled screen* (c. 1820) in the Biedermeier style shows views of Vienna. The Museum has a rich collection of glass, which includes such objects as a Mughal-inspired *perfume bottle* (1830–40) made of cut, polished, and gilt pink-flashed glass and a turquoise *footed bowl* (c. 1870) made in Venice by a company that at the time was recreating ancient Roman glass techniques.

Also in this gallery are examples of the various styles that rapidly followed one another through the 19C: Neo-Classicism, Gothic Revival, Oriental revivals (including ceramics in Chinese, Islamic, and Japanese modes). Classical revival pieces include 19C Sèvres plates and vases. A *Sèvres coffee set* with pictures of cacao cultivation in South America (bordered with Aztec-inspired designs) is a tour de force commissioned by Louis Philippe in 1837.

Near the entrance to the other flanking gallery (beyond the central Sculpture Gallery) is an elaborate *armoire* (1867), whose silvered bronze ornaments portray the defeat of Attila the Hun by the Merovingians in A.D. 451. In this gallery are examples of Staffordshire and Belleek porcelain. A gilt-bronze and malachite *desk set,* shown at the Crystal Palace Exhibition in 1851, reveals the influence of Moorish, Celtic, and Renaissance sources.

The romantic medievalism of the Pre-Raphaelite and Arts and Crafts movements appears in a *cabinet* (1861) painted by Edward Burne-Jones with a scene of *Backgammon Players.* Christopher Dresser, a prolific designer whose work foreshadowed modern industrial design, is represented by a group of objects ranging from a silver-plated toast rack to a U-shaped vase. The East Gallery closes with examples of international Art Nouveau objects, including medals by Alexandre Charpentier and jewelry with sinuous biomorphic forms by master jeweler René Lalique.

GALLERY 29, between the gallery of Medieval Sculpture and the Sculpture Court, has a collection of **French Decorative Arts, 1760–1820**, including sidechairs by Georges Jacob, a *rolltop desk* (c. 1780; 41.82) with elaborate marquetry by David Roentgen, a German cabinetmaker who had a large French clientele; and a *coin cabinet* (c. 1805, 26.168.77) decorated with Egyptian figures.

Installed in Gallery 57 adjacent to the 16C Spanish Patio are sculptures from the Museum's outstanding collection of **16–17C Bronzes**. Bartolomeo Bellano's *David with the Head of Goliath* (prob. 1440s; 64.304.1) recalls the work of his teacher, Donatello. Pier Jacopo Alari-Bonacolsi, known as Antico because of his reverence for antiquity, produced many scaled-down versions of ancient works, but the figure of *Paris* (c. 1490–1500; 55.93), a youth with gilded hair holding a ring and an apple, seems to have been his own creation. The Paduan Andrea Briosco, known as Il Riccio, created numerous mythological figures, including an imposing *Striding Satyr* (c. 1507; 45.82). Dominating the north wall is Andrea della Robbia's large terracotta *Prudence* (21.116).

The 16C SPANISH PATIO (GALLERY 56) from the castle of Los Vélez in southeastern Spain was donated by George Blumenthal, president of the Museum 1933–41, who had previously installed it in his home on Park Ave at 70th St. It now serves as a sculpture garden containing a group of Renaissance works, notably Tullio Lombardo's *Adam* (c. 1490–95), originally part of the funerary monument of a Venetian doge and the first monumental classical nude carved since ancient times. Antonello Gagini's *Spinario (Boy Removing a Thorn)*, which dates from about 1505, is the work of the leading Sicilian sculptor of the period.

The Jack and Belle Linsky Galleries

The Jack and Belle Linsky Galleries contain a private collection of European paintings, sculpture, and decorative arts, donated to the Museum in 1982. Enter from the Medieval Tapestry Hall, between the staircases.

To the left of the anteroom (Red Room) are **Renaissance Paintings** and small bronzes from the Middle Ages and Renaissance. Outstanding among the Italian paintings are: Vittore Crivelli, *Madonna and Child with Two Angels* (after 1481), painted by the brother of the more famous Carlo. Giovanni di Paolo, *Adoration of the Magi* (after 1423); part of an altarpiece on the infancy of Christ whose companion panels are in Boston. Andrea del Sarto, *Portrait of a Man;* the sitter may be a scholar or cleric, as suggested by his simple clothing and the book in his hand. Fra Bartolomeo, *Portrait of a Man* (after 1497). Bartolomeo, an influential Florentine painter, was inspired by Leonardo and by the Flemish paintings brought to Florence during the later part of the 15C. Also of interest are two paintings by the early Mannerist artist Bacchiacca, *Leda and the Swan* and *Madonna and Child* (c. 1525?). One treasure of the collection is a small panel by Juan de Flandes, *The Marriage Feast at Cana* (c. 1500). The figure outside the columns is thought to be a self-portrait. Gerard David (attrib.), *The Adoration of the Magi*. Lucas Cranach, *Christ Blessing the Children* and *Christ and the Adulteress* (mid-1540s).

Adjacent to this room is a display of Linsky porcelains. Included are German works from Fulda, Nymphenburg, Höchst, and Ludwigsburg, and a collection of Meissen figures, including a series of J. J. Kändler's appealing characters from the *commedia dell'arte.*

Continue to the beige room with its exhibit of **French 18C Decorative Arts and Paintings,** which include three examples by François Boucher, *Angelica and Medoro* (1763), *Jupiter in the Guise of Diana* (1763), and *A View of the Campo Vaccino* (1734). The still life by Luis Egidio Meléndez, *La Merienda* (1773?), is one of his largest and most elaborate. Now recognized the greatest Spanish painter of his specialty, Meléndez was largely neglected in his own time and died in poverty.

Turn right into the blue-gray ROTUNDA, which contains examples of goldsmiths' work and jewels. Also here is Peter Paul Rubens's earliest known dated painting, *Portrait of a Man* (1597); the sitter was possibly an architect or geographer since he holds the tools of those trades.

In the gold room are **17C Dutch Paintings,** notably Jan Steen, *The Dissolute Household* (1660s), and a rare triple portrait by Gerard ter Borch, *The Van Moerkerken Family* (1653–54). Here also are Baroque bronzes, including a small portrait *Bust of Paolo Giordano II Orsini, Duke of Bracciano* (1623–24?), made in Rome by Johann Jakob Kornmann. The single most extravagant decorative object in the collection must be the smoky rock-crystal *ewer,* made in Prague (c. 1680) and then mounted (c. 1810–19) with enameled gold diamond-studded mounts in London by an unknown goldsmith. It was bought by the English collector, writer, and eccentric William Beckford, who thought it the work of Benvenuto Cellini.

Beyond the gold room is a second room of porcelains with examples from Menency and Saint-Cloud; a group of Russian figures showing different ethnic types; Neapolitan figures from the Capodimonte factory; and a group of Danish figures from the Royal Porcelain Manufactory.

The Robert Lehman Collection
Among the great collections donated to the Museum, the Robert Lehman bequest is perhaps the most conspicuous, since a condition of the gift was that it remain permanently intact and that seven period rooms from the Lehman town house be recreated within the Museum. Thus Lehman's superb Italian and Flemish works from the 15–16C, as well as French 19C paintings, decorative arts, and more than 1,600 drawings, now reside in the LEHMAN WING, which is set against the original Victorian Gothic west wall of the Museum.

The GRAND GALLERY, nearest the central courtyard, contains **19–20C French Painting** arranged chronologically. Jean-Baptiste-Camille Corot, *Diana and Actaeon* (1836). Claude Monet, *Landscape Near Zaandam* (1871). Vincent van Gogh, *Mme Roulin and Her Baby* (1888). Paul Gauguin, *Tahitian Women Bathing* (1891 or 1892). Edgar Degas, *Landscape* (c. 1898), an unusual subject for Degas. Suzanne Valadon, *Reclining Nude* (1928); formerly a circus acrobat, a model, and a romantic figure in Montmartre, Valadon eventually became a successful painter. Maurice Utrillo, *40, Rue Ravignan* (c. 1913), a streetscape from the painter's "white period." Utrillo was Suzanne Valadon's son. Balthus, *Figure in Front of a*

Mantel (1955). Also paintings by Alfred Sisley, Camille Pisarro, Pierre-Auguste Renoir, and Pierre Bonnard.

The FIRST ROOM (northwest side of courtyard), arranged as in the Lehman town house, contains the earliest of the **Sienese and Italian Renaissance Paintings.** Giovanni di Paolo, *Bishop Saint* (c. 1460); the elaborate halo indicates sainthood, but the bishop's attributes (open book and whip) are insufficient to identify him. *Sts. John and Mary Magdalen* (c. 1350), probably the work of Roberto d'Odorisio, an artist in the court at Naples. The painting shows the influence of both Florentine and Sienese art: it is Florentine in its half-length, slit-eyed figures with angels diving overhead, Sienese in the gold-tooled halos and borders.

The SECOND ROOM also contains **Italian Renaissance Paintings.** Ugolino da Nerio's *The Last Supper* (c. 1321) shows a primitive attempt at perspective. Lorenzo Monaco belonged to a monastery noted for its miniatures and manuscript illuminations, though Lorenzo worked primarily painting altarpieces; his small *Nativity* (c. 1413) demonstrates a wonderful use of color, the roses and blues of Joseph's and Mary's robes illuminated against a gilded moonlit background. The Flemish tapestry (c. 1510) dominating the DINING ROOM depicts *St. Veronica's Veil Curing the Emperor Vespasian.*

The SPECIAL GALLERY is devoted to **French Painting and Furniture.** Jean-Auguste-Dominique Ingres's *Portrait of the Princesse de Broglie* (1853) dominates the room. The last of Ingres's aristocratic portraits, it shows his mastery of the genre in the depiction of the serenely elegant princess, a respected woman who embodied the best qualities of the Second Empire aristocracy. Also paintings by Georges Braque, Pierre Bonnard, and Henri Matisse.

The RED VELVET ROOM contains wonderful **Paintings by 15C Masters from Siena, Florence, and Venice.** Sassetta, *The Temptation of St. Anthony Abbot* (c. 1444), shows the saint, founder of monasticism, tempted in the desert by a devil with a golden porringer. The devil and the porringer have been scraped off, their location indicated by the grayish spot between the saint and the small rabbit. The style and colors of the bleak landscape and turbulent sky, markedly different from contemporary Italian paintings, give the panel an almost surrealistic quality.

One of the most important paintings in the collection is Giovanni di Paolo's mysterious *Expulsion from Paradise* (c. 1445), originally part of an altarpiece. The angel drives Adam and Eve from a flowering abundant Eden while God points to the cracked arid Earth where they will dwell thereafter. The concentric rings of the universe encircle the Earth, the outermost painted with signs of the Zodiac. Also by Giovanni di Paolo is a large panel, *The Coronation of the Virgin* (1445), which shows the artist still influenced by the Gothic style. Giovanni Bellini's *Madonna and Child* (c. 1460) is an early, serene work by the Venetian master. The iconographic importance of the fruit behind the Madonna's head is not known.

Alessandro Botticelli's *Annunciation* (c. 1490) is a small painting, probably intended for private devotion. The use of a classical architectural setting rendered in perspective was one of the artistic achievements of late 15C Florence. The beautifully drawn figures of the Virgin and angel curving toward one another, the complexity of the composition, and the transparent colors make this one of the most attractive of several *Annunciations* Botticelli painted at this time. Jacometto Veneziano, portrait of *Alvise Contarini,* and a companion portrait, *Nun of San Secondo* (both painted before 1543). Alvise Contarini was a wealthy Venetian merchant, perhaps in the shipping business; the woman's identity is less certain, but her headdress is that of the Benedictine nuns at San Secondo, an order criticized for its worldliness (apparent in the décolletage of her habit). The rare double portraits of *Alessandro di Bernardo Gozzadini* and his wife *Donna Canonici* (c. 1490) are probably by Lorenzo Costa.

Beyond the STAIRCASE LANDING is the SITTING ROOM with **16–18C Spanish and 17C Dutch Painting.** El Greco's *St. Jerome as a Cardinal* (c. 1600–10) is one of the finest of five known versions of this painting; another is in the Frick Collection. The figure of the saint is dramatized by the elongated head, the long beard, and the absence of detail. Rembrandt, *Portrait of Gérard de Lairesse* (1665), a late and sympathetic portrait of an ugly young man, his face virtually destroyed by congenital syphilis. Also by Rembrandt, *Portrait of an Elderly Man* (1638). Francisco Goya, *The Countess of Altamira and Her Daughter* (1787–89), an early portrait, noteworthy for its characterization and use of color.

The final room, the FLEMISH ROOM, contains **15C Northern European Painting and Decorative Arts.** Master of Moulins, *Portrait of a Young Princess* (1490–91), probably Margaret of Austria. She was betrothed at the age of 10 or 11 (though some accounts give her age as 3) to Charles VIII of France and the picture probably shows her at that time—a richly dressed, unhappy child. Hans Memling, *Annunciation* (1482); Mary and the angels are painted in cool, clear colors. The objects in the room—the lilies, the half-filled glass bottle, the candlestick—represent attributes of the Virgin. *Portrait of a Young Man* (1470–75) is one of Memling's finest male portraits. Petrus Christus, *St. Eligius* (1449). St. Eligius, the patron of goldsmiths, is shown in humble garb in the center of his shop; this work, which records the details of the shop, has been cited as an early example of genre painting—the representation of humble scenes and subjects.

Gerard David, two panels, *Christ Bearing the Cross and the Crucifixion* and *The Resurrection with Pilgrims of Emmaus* (the outer sides depict the Archangel Gabriel and the Virgin of the Annunciation). All were painted c. 1500 and deliberately adhere to the older Flemish manner of painting, now superseded by the newer Italian style. Lucas Cranach, *Nymph of the Spring* (c. 1540?). Cranach, a German Protestant court painter, chose mythological subjects as well as religious ones. The inscription means: "I am the nymph of the sacred spring. Don't disturb my sleep; I am resting." Also by Cranach, *Venus and Cupid the Honey Thief* (c. 1530s). The inscription warns that as Cupid, stealing honey, is stung by bees, so we, seeking furtive pleasures, will also garner sadness and pain. Hans Holbein, *Erasmus of Rotterdam* (after 1523), one of Holbein's several portraits of the famous humanist, a man of strong, determined character. Jean Fouquet's illuminated miniature comes from a Book of Hours (c. 1452), with prayers for the canonical hours of the day.

METROPOLITAN MUSEUM OF ART: AMERICAN WING
First Floor, Old & New Wings

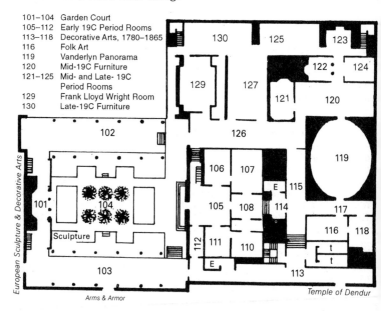

101–104	Garden Court
105–112	Early 19C Period Rooms
113–118	Decorative Arts, 1780–1865
116	Folk Art
119	Vanderlyn Panorama
120	Mid-19C Furniture
121–125	Mid- and Late- 19C Period Rooms
129	Frank Lloyd Wright Room
130	Late-19C Furniture

It shows the *Descent of the Holy Ghost Upon the Faithful,* a biblical event transplanted to Paris. Notre Dame and the Pont Saint-Michel are recognizable in this earliest known topographical view of the city.

The American Wing

NOTE: This section includes all three floors of galleries in the American Wing.

The American Wing holds a superb collection of American painting (late 18C–early 20C), furniture, and decorative arts. When the installation was expanded during the 1980s, the new galleries were wrapped around the previously existing ones; floor plans are provided to unravel the resulting complexities. Period rooms are organized chronologically, with the earliest exhibits on the top floor.

HIGHLIGHTS

American paintings include important work by John Singleton Copley, Thomas Eakins, Winslow Homer, John Singer Sargent, and the Hudson River School of landscape painters. The panorama of Versailles by John Vanderlyn is a remarkable example of a once-popular genre.

First Floor. The centerpiece of the wing is the tranquil GARDEN COURT (GALLERY 104) with fountains, greenery, and views of Central Park. Here are examples of **19C and Early-20C American Sculpture and Architec-**

tural **Elements.** At the north end is architect Martin E. Thompson's dignified marble *facade of the United States Branch Bank* (1824), transported here from Wall St. At the south end (GALLERY 101) is an ornamental *loggia* (c. 1905) with ceramic capitals, glass tiles, and lanterns by Louis Comfort Tiffany, America's foremost master of the Art Nouveau style. The stained-glass window, *View of Oyster Bay* (c. 1905), shows his dazzling technique. Flanking the loggia are two *cast-iron staircases* (1893–94) by Louis H. Sullivan, the outstanding American architect of his period.

The sculpture (exhibition changes from time to time) gives a glimpse of reigning 19C styles. George Grey Barnard, *The Struggle of the Two Natures in Man* (1894), symbolizes the divine element of humanity subduing its baser counterpart; Barnard's collection of medieval architectural elements formed the foundation of The Cloisters, the Metropolitan's branch museum in northern Manhattan. Other sculptors frequently represented here are Gutzon Borglum, Gaston Lachaise, Frederick W. MacMonnies, Paul Manship, William Rimmer, and William Zorach. The gilded figure of *Diana* by Augustus Saint-Gaudens is a reduced replica the statue that once topped off the original Madison Square Garden.

> **NOTE:** Rooms in the wing are not consistently labeled. Some have small placards near an entrance door; others have numbers high on the walls; several are unlabeled.

GALLERIES 105–112. Period Rooms of the Early Federal Period (1790–1820). The era was marked by the influence of English Neo-Classicism, especially the work of Robert and James Adam. The doorway of the United States Branch Bank leads into the FEDERAL GALLERY (105) with distinguished examples of furniture from Boston, New York, Philadelphia, and Baltimore. The BALTIMORE ROOM (106; c. 1812) features a dining table whose light wood inlays exemplify regional characteristics of Baltimore furniture. The BENKARD ROOM (107) has elegant architectural elements salvaged from a derelict house (1811) in Petersburg, Va. Furniture in the NEO-CLASSICAL GALLERY (108) reflects the French Empire style in America. Of particular interest is immigrant craftsman Charles-Honoré Lannuier's marble-topped pier table with gilt-bronze and gilded terracotta ornamentation.

GALLERY 109. The RICHMOND ROOM (110; 1811) contains Federal furniture from the Duncan Phyfe workshop, including a sofa and chairs with "Grecian Cross" legs. The HAVERHILL ROOM (111; c. 1805) from Massachusetts features a distinguished canopied bedstead. The PHILADELPHIA GALLERY (112), accessible through the Federal Gallery, shows representative examples of the distinguished neo-classical tradition of furniture making in that city, e.g., an 8-ft gentleman's secretary with mahogany and satinwood veneers.

GALLERIES 113–117. Furniture and Decorative Arts (c. 1780–1865). This includes other examples of the work of Phyfe and Lannuier, a collection of Windsor chairs (GALLERY 117), and a display of folk art (GALLERY 116). The SHAKER RETIRING ROOM (118) from New Lebanon, N.Y., is furnished in the simple, utilitarian manner associated with that austere religious sect.

In the corridor between the gallery of Early Federal Furniture and the entrance to the Temple of Dendur is an exhibition of **Baseball Cards,** formerly used for advertising. One of the rarities of the collection is an American Tobacco Company card depicting Honus Wagner, who disapproved of having his image used to promote cigarettes and asked that the card be withdrawn from distribution.

GALLERY 119 is given over to John Vanderlyn's *Panorama of the Palace and Gardens of Versailles* (1818–19), the largest painting in the Museum. It was originally exhibited in a rotunda in City Hall Park especially built to suggest the sensation of actually standing on the grounds of Versailles surrounded by its architecture and landscaping. In an age when travel was arduous, panoramas of faraway places were a popular form of entertainment; painted on great canvases, they were rolled up and carried from city to city. Vanderlyn hoped to make his fortune with this work, but the painting failed to attract the public, possibly because of its formality and emptiness.

GALLERY 120. **Mid-19C Furniture.** Groupings reflect 19C Revival Styles —Greek, Gothic, Rococo, Renaissance, and Egyptian—ornate, extravagant, and sometimes amusing to contemporary tastes. The RENAISSANCE REVIVAL PARLOR (121) comes from a house (1868–70) in Meriden, Conn., that belonged to a merchant of carpet bags and hoop skirts. The GREEK REVIVAL ROOM (124) recreates a fashionable New York parlor (c. 1835), with furniture from the workshops of Duncan Phyfe. The ROCOCO REVIVAL ROOM (122) displays the highly ornamented furniture of one of the most original 19C American designers, John Henry Belter. Belter perfected a laminating technique that enabled his furniture to be bent and carved into ornate shapes. The GOTHIC REVIVAL LIBRARY (123), with its handsome ceiling and woodwork, was reconstructed from a house (1859) by architect Frederick Clarke Withers, better known in New York for ornate buildings like the Jefferson Market Courthouse.

The McKIM, MEADE & WHITE STAIRHALL (125) was taken from a shingle-style house (1882), in Buffalo, N.Y. Although meant to be comfortably domestic, the house featured opulent building materials—richly carved oak and Siena marble.

GALLERY 130. **Late-19C Furniture.** On one wall is John La Farge's stained-glass window, *Peonies Blown in the Wind* (c. 1880).

(GALLERIES 127 and 128 are reserved for special exhibitions.)

GALLERY 129. The FRANK LLOYD WRIGHT ROOM recreates a living room (1914) from the Francis W. Little House in Wayzata, Minn. Wright's "prairie houses" were low structures, with open interiors, whose ornamentation avoided embellishment aside from the natural colors and textures of the building materials. The architect also designed and even arranged the furniture.

METROPOLITAN MUSEUM OF ART
Second Floor

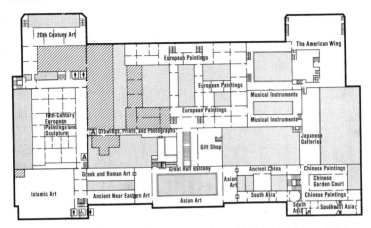

Second Floor

GALLERIES 201–203, on the BALCONY above the Garden Court, contain a survey of **American Decorative Arts, 17–20C.**

GALLERY 202. **Silver.** On view here are coins, silver of the late Colonial and Federal periods (several pieces by Paul Revere), and work by Myer Myers, an important New York silversmith of Dutch descent. The more florid and opulent tastes of the mid- to late 19C are apparent in a group of presentation and exposition pieces (GALLERY 201). Two opulent examples from the Tiffany workshops are the "Adams" vase (04.1) and the "Magnolia" vase (99.2), the latter worked in silver, gold, enamels, and opals.

A reduced copy of Daniel Chester French's grave memorial *Mourning Victory* (1908, this replica 1915) is mounted against the south wall. Also known as the Melvin Memorial, the monument, which commemorates three brothers who died in the Civil War, was commissioned by the surviving brother, who ordered this replica for the Museum.

GALLERY 203. **Glass and Ceramics.** Glassware includes examples from the earliest free-blown tableware to the opalescent "Favrile" glass of Louis Comfort Tiffany. Near the south wall is a beautiful Tiffany lamp (1974; 214.15), with lily pads, bamboo shoots, and lotus flowers.

Ceramics include examples of export ware made for the American market, as well as American domestic pottery, beginning with humble, utilitarian salt-glazed stoneware and the red earthenware of the Pennsylvania Germans. Later examples include early American attempts at true porcelain, Parian ware (a waxy porcelain named for its resemblance to marble quarried on Paros in the Aegean), and porcelain objects from the Union Porcelain Works in Greenpoint, Brooklyn. Also on display is art

METROPOLITAN MUSEUM OF ART: AMERICAN WING
Second Floor, Old & New Wings

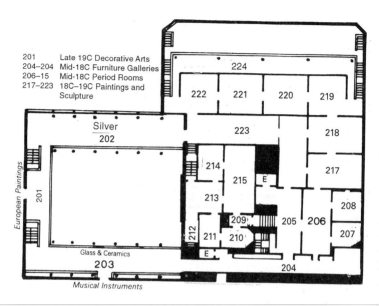

201 — Late 19C Decorative Arts
204–204 — Mid-18C Furniture Galleries
206–15 — Mid-18C Period Rooms
217–223 — 18C–19C Paintings and Sculpture

pottery—i.e., commercial pottery designed by artist-potters who were influenced by the principles of the English Arts and Crafts movement.

GALLERIES 209–15. **Period Rooms of the Late Colonial Period (1730–90)** are in the OLD WING (lower level of SECOND FLOOR). The PENNSYLVA-NIA GERMAN ROOM (210) has furnishings created by German-speaking immigrants who settled in southeastern Pennsylvania, bringing with them their colorful decorative traditions. The carved and molded decoration in the POWEL PARLOR (211) from Philadelphia (c. 1765) is derived from English pattern books; the furniture is in the elegant Philadelphia Chippendale style.

In the NEW ENGLAND FURNITURE GALLERIES (212–213) are exemplary desks, chairs, chests, and secretaries. New England furniture was frequently purchased by residents of the southern colonies, and the ALMODINGTON ROOM (214), a gentleman's bedroom from Somerset County, Md., features a Boston-made fourposter bed. The ALEXANDRIA BALLROOM (215), from a Virginia tavern (c. 1793), has a musicians' gallery and a mahogany spinet in the Queen Anne style.

New Wing of the Second Floor (up the staircase).

GALLERIES 204–205. **Mid-18C Furniture.** Philadelphia Chippendale (204), New England, Queen Anne, and Chippendale furniture (205) is included here. In GALLERY 205 is John Singleton Copley's *Mrs. John*

Winthrop (1773). Copley was the most gifted of the American Colonial painters, noted for his skill at characterization and his rendering of textures.

GALLERIES 206–208. **Mid-18C Period Rooms.** VAN RENSSELAER HALL (206) comes from a manor house (c. 1765), built in Albany, N.Y., by Stephen Van Rensselaer, the last patron of that domain. Its remarkable scenic wallpaper was painted in England. The MARMION ROOM (207) from a Virginia plantation is remarkable for its woodwork—some panels painted to simulate marble, others decorated with urns, leaves, scrolls, and landscapes reminiscent of Dutch paintings. The furnishings of the VERPLANCK ROOM (208) belonged to Samuel and Judith Crommelin Verplank, who lived at 3 Wall St.

The remaining galleries on the SECOND FLOOR AND MEZZANINE contain a chronological display of **American Paintings and Sculpture.** GALLERIES 217–219 contain paintings of 1730–1830. The works in GALLERY 223 (an L-shaped gallery that actually has three rooms) are rotated.

GALLERY 223A. **18C Paintings and Sculpture.** John Singleton Copley, *Augustus Brine, Midshipman* (1782); this picture of 12-year-old Augustus Brine is one of Copley's best European portraits, a painting that reflects his acquaintance with his continental contemporaries and with the Old Masters. John Smibert's *Francis Brinley* (1729) is painted in the prevailing English Baroque style by a wealthy New Englander, who had been trained in Europe before arriving in the colonies in 1710.

GALLERY 217. **18C Painting.** Charles Willson Peale, *George Washington* (c. 1780). Peale's portraits are regarded as the best likenesses of Washington as a general. John Trumbull, *George Washington* (1780). Matthew Pratt, one of James Peale's pupils, painted *The American School* (1765), a depiction of Benjamin West's London studio. West, a self-taught painter and perhaps America's best-known artist before Whistler, emigrated to London to advance his career and became influential as a teacher.

GALLERY 218. **Late-18–Early-19C Painting and Sculpture.** John Trumbull, *The Sortie Made by the Garrison of Gibraltar* (1789); the painting, one of a number of heroic canvases depicting historic scenes, shows a dramatic moment in a three-year siege of the English fortress at Gibraltar by Spanish and French forces; other examples of Trumbull's work adorn the rotunda of the Capitol in Washington, D.C. Among the paintings by Gilbert Stuart are a famous early portrait of *George Washington* (1795), apparently done from life, and one of *General Louis-Marie, Vicomte de Noailles* (1798), Lafayette's brother-in-law.

GALLERY 219. **19C Painting, c. 1812–40.** James Peale, *Still Life: Balsam Apple and Vegetables* (1820s?). George Caleb Bingham, *Fur Traders Descending the Missouri* (c. 1845); this masterpiece of genre painting, remarkable for its luminous mist, was painted by an artist whose professional training was scant, but whose experience of the American West was extensive. Samuel F. B. Morse, *The Muse: Susan Walker Morse* (1835–37), a portrait of Morse's eldest daughter, executed shortly before he turned from painting to telegraphy.

GALLERY 220. **Early Hudson River School.** Thomas Cole, *View from Mount Holyoke, Massachusetts, after a Thunderstorm—The Oxbow* (1836). Cole, virtually self-taught, was widely admired; he is generally considered the father of the Hudson River School, landscapists who celebrated the still unspoiled beauty of the continent. Asher B. Durand, *The Beeches* (1845). Durand started his career as an engraver, reproducing views by Cole and others; his painting shows the meticulous observation of detail typical of his engravings.

GALLERY 221. **Late Hudson River School.** Martin Johnson Heade, *The Coming Storm* (1859); Heade, John Frederick Kensett, Fitz Hugh Lane, and others deeply interested in effects of light and atmosphere, were known as the Luminists. Albert Bierstadt, *The Rocky Mountains, Lander's Peak* (1864). Bierstadt's favorite subject, the wild landscape of the American West, suggested to him the destiny of the nation; he was the first American landscapist to go west. Frederic Edwin Church, *The Heart of the Andes* (1859); like his teacher Bierstadt and his friend Cole, Church sought dramatic landscapes. After making sketches in South America, Church painted this work in his studio; he then surrounded the painting with tropical plants, illuminated it with hidden lights, and exhibited it in a dark gallery to enthusiastic viewers.

GALLERY 222. **Winslow Homer.** Today rated as one of the finest painters of his period, Homer was trained as a lithographer, taught himself to draw and paint, and became a magazine illustrator. *Prisoners from the Front* (1866), a Civil War scene, was one of his first important oil paintings. *Rainy Day in Camp* (1871), an evocation of bleak boredom, was reconstructed from drawings he made during the war. Among Homer's early works are depictions of rural life, e.g., *Snap the Whip* (1872) and *Eagle Head, Manchester, Massachusetts* (1870).

GALLERY 223. **Selected Paintings, 1790–1880.** Paintings are shown on a rotating basis with the exception of Emanuel Leutze's *Washington Crossing the Delaware* (1851), a romantic reconstruction of history, inaccurate in many details but nonetheless deeply imprinted on the American consciousness. Leutze painted this picture while living in Germany, where he spent most of his career. Hiram Powers, *Andrew Jackson* (1837); Jackson himself dictated the realistic rendering of this marble bust, saying he had no desire to look young as long as he felt old.

GALLERY 225 (on the BALCONY). **Trompe L'Oeil Painting, Western Art, and Visionary Painting.** Here are paintings and bronzes by Frederic Remington, chronicler of cowboys, Indians, and army troopers. Frequently on display is *Coming Through the Rye* (1904), once informally known as "Cowboys Shooting up a Western Town." Other late-19C–early-20C sculptures by Solon Borglum, Hermon A. MacNeil, and John Quincy Adams Ward.

Visionary painter Albert Pinkham Ryder's *Moonlight Marine* (c. 1879–90), is an emotional evocation of the sea, the surface cracked from layers of paint and varnish. Also work by Ralph Albert Blakelock. William Michael Harnett, *Music and Good Luck* (1888); Harnett, a masterful *trompe l'oeil* painter, selected commonplace objects and rendered their

METROPOLITAN MUSEUM OF ART: AMERICAN WING
Mezzanine, New Wing

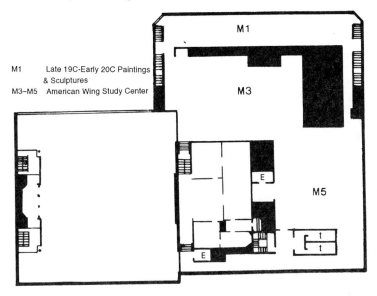

M1   Late 19C-Early 20C Paintings
          & Sculptures
M3–M5 American Wing Study Center

colors and textures so precisely that his paintings almost literally "fool the eye."

A stairway leads down to the MEZZANINE in the New Wing.

GALLERY M1. **Late-19C–Early-20C Realists.** The Museum has an impressive group of paintings by Thomas Eakins, who with Winslow Homer was one of the outstanding painters of the period. *Portrait of a Lady with a Setter Dog* (c. 1885) depicts Eakins's wife, also a painter. *Max Schmitt in a Single Scull* (1871), with Eakins himself rowing in the middle distance, is as much a study of perspective and light as it is of the champion rower working out on the Skuylkill River. *The Thinker* (1900) from his late period is a dark, brooding portrait, noteworthy for its rendering of character.

Mary Cassatt, *Lydia Crocheting in the Garden at Marly* (1880); *Lady at the Tea Table* (1885). Cassatt worked with the French Impressionists Degas and Manet; though she never married, mothers and children were among her favorite subjects. Part of Cassatt's importance lies in her influence on her wealthy compatriots, particularly Mrs. H. O. Havemeyer, to whom she introduced the paintings of the French Impressionists. The Havemeyer bequest, rich in paintings by Degas, Monet, Manet, and Cézanne, is one of the treasures of the Museum.

James Abbott McNeill Whistler, *Arrangement in Flesh Colour and Black: Portrait of Theodore Duret* (1883). Whistler studied in Paris. where Duret was an art critic and collector. As the title here suggests, Whistler was interested more in form and color than in accurate portraiture.

METROPOLITAN MUSEUM OF ART: AMERICAN WING
Third Floor

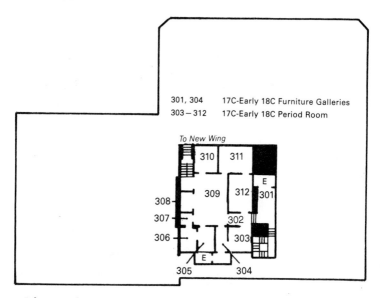

301, 304   17C-Early 18C Furniture Galleries
303 – 312   17C-Early 18C Period Room

John Twachtman's *Arques-La-Bataille* (1885) was painted in subdued tones of gray and green from a sketch made in Normandy near Dieppe; the dark green reeds in the foreground suggest his attraction to Japanese prints. Childe Hassam, *Avenue of the Allies* (1918); Hassam learned the technique of the French Impressionists during a stay in France.

William Merritt Chase, *At the Seaside* (c. 1892); *For the Little One* (c. 1895). Chase, also indebted to the French Impressionists, was a successful printmaker, painter, and teacher, numbering among his pupils Charles Sheeler, Charles Demuth, and Georgia O'Keeffe.

Among Winslow Homer's most memorable paintings are his late seascapes. *Northeaster* (1895) is a masterful example of his late austere style. *The Gulf Stream* (1899) is based on sketches he made in the Bahamas, where he spent winter in the later years of his life; with drama and power Homer renders the vastness of the sea and the loneliness of the solitary figure in the dismasted boat. Also, *Maine Coast: Prout's Neck* (1896); and *Breaking on the Bar: Cannon Rock* (1895).

John Singer Sargent, *Madame X* (1884); a scandalous portrait in its day, both for the real-life behavior of its subject and for her depiction in a dress with a plunging neckline and a wandering shoulder strap (later painted over). Sargent thought it his best work.

Third Floor, Old Wing

GALLERIES 301–309. **Period Rooms of the Early Colonial Period, 1630–1730.** The central MEETINGHOUSE GALLERY (309) features chests—some with Tudor and Jacobean motifs—cupboards, and several pieces in

METROPOLITAN MUSEUM OF ART
Second Floor, European Paintings

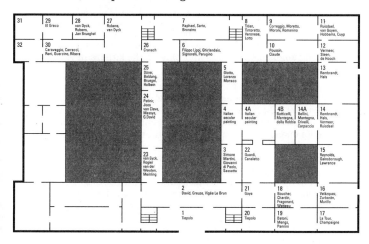

the William and Mary style. Around it are furniture galleries and period rooms. GALLERY 301 contains 17C and 18C chairs. The HART ROOM (303), the earliest (before 1674) in the collection, comes from Ipswich, Mass., and is furnished with 17C oak and pine furniture.

GALLERY 304 shows a variety of chests from Massachusetts and Connecticut. The NEWINGTON ROOM (305), from a mid-18C Connecticut home, is furnished with oak and pine furniture. The HAMPTON ROOM (306), from a New Hampshire farmhouse, and the NEW YORK ALCOVE (308), with paneling from a stone house in Ulster County, show regional variations on Colonial furniture. The Wentworth stair (307), a rare survival (c. 1700), has unusual spiral-turned balusters. The HEWLETT ROOM (310), from a house (c. 1740) on Long Island, has Dutch tiles surrounding the fireplace opening and a painted *kas* (chest) showing Dutch influence. The BOWLER ROOM (311), from a house (c. 1763) near Portsmouth, R.I., recalls the formal elegance of Georgian England. In the WENTWORTH ROOM (312; c. 1700) from Portsmouth, N.H., are such imported luxuries as a Turkey "carpitt" and tin-glazed pottery from Holland and England.

SECOND FLOOR

Greek and Roman Art: Greek Vases
Five rooms are devoted to the Museum's fine collection of Greek vases, which are arranged chronologically (beginning in the elevator lobby adjacent to the Department of Ancient Near Eastern Art).

> **NOTE:** The galleries of Greek and Roman art are scheduled for a major reinstallation beginning in 1996. Greek vases will be moved to the First Floor with the rest of Greek art.

HIGHLIGHTS

The most famous piece in the collection is the *Euphronios vase* (Room 4), but the collection contains many beautifully painted vases: among them are the *prize amphora* (14.130.12) in Room 2 showing a foot race; the *red-figured amphora* (63.11.6) showing Herakles and Apollo struggling over the Delphic tripod in Room 3; and the *amphora* (56.171.38) depicting a musician singing and playing the kithara in Room 4.

In the lobby are three large sepulchral vases from the Geometric period which served as tomb monuments; the term "Geometric" applies to the decoration of 8–7C B.C., describing its schematic, abstract quality. Notable is an Attic *sepulchral vase* (14.130.14, 2nd half of 7C B.C.) almost 4 ft tall, with an open bottom for pouring libations onto the grave below.

Enter ROOM 1 (room number above entrance door) with wares from the **Protogeometric Period** (11–10C B.C.) **to the Attic Black-Figured Ware** of the 6C B.C. In Case 11 is a large black-and-white *neck amphora* (11.210.1, 2nd quarter of 7C B.C.), whose decoration shows the struggle between Herakles and the centaur Nessos. The decoration is curvilinear and, as in much art of the early Archaic period, the background has been filled with ornaments. From Corinth, where the black-figure technique was developed, comes an *oinochoe* (wine jug) decorated with animals and monsters (Case 3, 1972.118.138). The black silhouettes are articulated with incised lines and enhanced with added color. In Case 5 is a fine *neck amphora* (Case 5, 63.11.3) from Chalcidia, with palmettes, sirens, and cocks. One of the kneeling figures has turned his face forward, a gesture rare in Archaic art, used to inspire either fear or humor. Among the black-figured vases are several *kraters,* large bowls for mixing wine with water; the *column krater* is so named because the handles function like columns supporting the lip of the vase. One such *krater* (Case 8, 24.97.95) depicts the struggle between Zeus and the Titans.

ROOM 2 contains **Attic Black-Figured Vases,** including a group (Cases 1–6) of *prize amphorae* of the type used at the Pan-Athenaic Festival held in Athens. The vases, filled with about 40 liters of olive oil from the sacred grove and presented to the winners, depict an armed Athena on one side and on the other a scene of the athletic event for which they were awarded. Especially famous is one depicting a foot race (Case 2, 14.130.12). In Case 7 is a fine *hydria* or water jar (56.171.29) showing Ajax and Achilles playing at draughts, and in Case 9 a *lekythos* or oil jug (56.11.1) depicting a bridal procession, with the bride and groom arriving home at the bridegroom's house, whose doorway has been newly painted. In Case 13 is a small *stand* with a grimacing Gorgon's head. Many of the Gorgon's features are traditional: bared teeth, protruding tongue, beard, frontal pose. This particular Gorgon has six serrated incisors and her canines have been extended to become tusklike.

ROOM 3 is also primarily devoted to **Attic Black-Figured Ware.** On the right side of the doorway a *red-figured amphora* (63.11.6) shows the struggle between Herakles and Apollo over the Delphic tripod. Painted by the Andokides Painter, it is one of the earliest red-figured vases in existence. The red-figured technique—a style in which unpainted figures taking on the color of the fired clay stand out against a black glazed background—was developed c. 530 B.C. On this vase the illustration is separated from the background by an ornamental border. Andokides was the potter; the artist who decorated the vase is named after him.

ROOM 4, devoted to **Red-Figured Ware,** contains (Case 19) the celebrated *Euphronios vase* (1972.11.10). In 1972, the Museum purchased this vase in Switzerland for $1 million; it was said to be from an old collection in Beirut, but some observers, including officials of the Italian government, believed that it had been dug up by grave robbers not long before the sale and smuggled out of Italy in pieces. Dating from about 515 B.C., this *calyx krater* depicts an episode from the Trojan War, the death of Sarpedon, whose body is lifted by Sleep and Death as Hermes looks on. The other side of the vase shows a scene of soldiers donning battle gear. Admired for the design of the individual compositions, for the virtuosity of the brushwork, and the skillful rendering of anatomical detail, the vase is considered a masterpiece of Greek art.

An *amphora* (Case 3, 56.171.38) from c. 490 B.C. by the Berlin Painter, decorated with a picture of a young musician singing and playing the kithara, is a moving depiction of ancient music. The figure, unframed, stands alone as if spotlighted against the black background. Other noteworthy pieces include an *oinochoe* or wine jug (Case 10, 23.160.55) from c. 480–70 B.C., showing Ganymede with a hoop and rooster fleeing Zeus, who is not depicted. The figure is taken from a traditional scene that included more people, but by its typing would have been recognizable to the ancients as Ganymede, in the same manner that saints with their attributes were recognizable to medieval Christians. Another piece which uses the white-ground technique, with an attempt at polychromy, is a *pyxis* or cosmetic box (07.286.36), depicting the Judgment of Paris, whose choice of Aphrodite as the most beautiful of the goddesses eventually led to the Trojan War. On this jar, made about the time mural painting was beginning in Athens, the figures are painted with a brush rather than simply drawn. In Case 17 is a large *volute krater* (07.286.84) showing the battle between the Amazons and the Athenians.

ROOM 5 contains **Attic and Southern Italian Red-Figured Ware of the Late 5–4C B.C.,** by which time vase painting had declined as a major art. Of interest is a rare *calyx krater* (Case 16, 51.11.2) from the third quarter of the 4C B.C. depicting a grotesque comic actor playing the role of a reveler. Also on display in this room is a small but choice collection of **ancient glass,** ranging from early Mycenaean to late Roman times.

Ancient Near Eastern Art

The galleries of Ancient Near Eastern Art contain pre-Islamic works that date from the 6th millennium B.C. up to the Arab conquest of the Near East in the mid-7C A.D. Geographically, the area represented in the galleries extends from Mesopotamia, Syria, Iran, Anatolia, and other regions bounded by the Caucasus in the north, the Gulf of Aden in the south, the western borders of modern Turkey in the west, and the valley of the Indus River, now in central Pakistan, on the east.

The history of the Ancient Near East—unlike that of Egypt, unified by the physical presence of the Nile—is fragmented into different political and cultural areas. While the fertile plains of Mesopotamia between the

Tigris and Euphrates rivers bear evidence of the first traces of civilization, its rivers led to distant regions where over the centuries multiple civilizations rose, flourished, and fell into ruin. In southern Mesopotamia alone were the capital cities of the Sumerians, Akkadians, Babylonians, Seleucids, Parthians, and Sasanians. Yet despite their chronological and cultural remoteness, the objects have an immediacy that often speaks across time and distance.

The galleries begin with a room of monumental Assyrian Art and then proceed chronologically and geographically, focusing on Mesopotamia, Anatolia, Iran, and Arabia.

In the first gallery for **Assyrian Art** stand large stone reliefs and imposing carvings taken from the palace of King Assurnasirpal II (reigned 883–859 B.C.) in Nimrud (now northern Iraq) on the upper Tigris. Two enormous winged creatures, a bull and a lion, both with human heads, defend the door (and originally supported an arch above). Their mere bulk and weight convey power, but their horned caps would have symbolized their might and divinity to ancient observers. Both creatures have five legs. From the side they seem to be striding forward; seen from the front, they stand watchfully.

In the adjacent galleries are objects from the excavations at Nimrud—bowls, clay figurines, and delicately carved ivories in Assyrian, Phoenician, and Syrian styles. Many may have been brought to Nimrud as tribute or loot from lands west of Assyria, where elephants were indigenous and ivory carving had long been an established craft. One small masterpiece is a *Nubian tribute bearer* (60.145.11, 8C B.C.), influenced by Egyptian artistic traditions.

The first gallery of Ancient Near Eastern Art (south of the Nimrud excavations gallery) is devoted to **Mesopotamian Art (5th–1st millennium B.C.)** and focuses on works from the earliest urban societies through the Sumerian, Akkadian, and Babylonian periods. Along the north wall are cylinder seals with geometric symbols, human and animal shapes, and cuneiform inscriptions. Used to seal jars, doors, legal agreements, and personal property, they appear as early as the 4th millennium B.C.

One of the most famous objects in the collection is a gypsum *statue of a bearded Sumerian worshiper* (40.156; c. 2750–2600 B.C.) wearing a long sheepskin skirt with a tufted border. Mesopotamian gods were believed to actually dwell within their images, which were placed in cult buildings and ritually fed and tended every day. Often they were surrounded by statues of other gods and important worshipers, who could pray even while human priests slept.

A *headdress ornament* (33.35.3, c. 2600–2500 B.C.) with gold pendants shaped like poplar leaves comes from the royal tombs of the Early Dynastic period at Ur; neither gold nor silver is native to Mesopotamia, so the use of these metals indicates the development of a system of trade.

Across the room is a neo-Sumerian *statue of Gudea* (59.2; c. 2150 B.C.), governor of the city-state of Lagash. Nearby is a *statue of Ur-Ningirsu* (47.100.86; c. 2100 B.C.), Gudea's son, whose head is joined to a body belonging to the Louvre; the complete statue alternates between the two museums every three years.

The next section of the gallery is devoted to **Anatolian and Syrian Art.** In the case containing golden objects from Mesopotamia is a *bronze foundation figure of a snarling lion* (48.100), buried to commemorate the construction of a building; its form was intended to frighten off evildoers. The yoked *long-horned bulls* (55.137.5; c. 2300–2000 B.C.) served as a finial, maybe for a ceremonial standard or chariot pole; the exaggerated length of their horns is characteristic of ancient Near Eastern art.

In the central part of the gallery are **Pre-Islamic Antiquities from Iran.** Known from biblical stories for his wickedness, Nebuchadnezzar II (reigned 604–562 B.C.) was also a great builder, constructing royal palaces, gateways, and roads in the city of Babylon. The glazed and molded *brick panels* (31.13.2) on the east wall depict lions, symbol of Ishtar, the Mesopotamian goddess of love and war; they once covered a wall along a processional road. Civilizations of the 5th and early 4th millennia B.C. are represented by pottery with geometric and animal designs, e.g., a large ceramic *storage jar* (case in center of the room, 59.52) decorated with silhouettes of mountain goats. The modeled stone *mountain goat* or mouflon (1978.58; Indus Valley, 2nd half of 3rd millennium B.C.) may have been a religious object, ceremonially buried to ensure a plentiful supply of game. A bronze *head of a man* (47.100.80; late 3rd millennium B.C.), whose inherent dignity and power led scholars to believe the figure represented a ruler, is considered a masterpiece of ancient art.

In the case opposite the lions is a silver *kneeling bull* (66.173), from the early 3rd millennium B.C., dressed in a printed skirt, holding between its hooves a vessel; the suppliant posture suggests that it is engaged in some ritual activity. A lovely *gold cup* (62.84; c. 1000 B.C.) shows four gazelles executed in delicate detail.

The final part of the gallery houses **Achaemenid, Parthian, and Sasanian Art.** The Achaemenid dynasty was founded by Cyrus the Great (c. 559–530 B.C.), who led a revolt of the Persians against their Median rulers and then went on to conquer neighboring lands, establishing ceremonial centers in Iran and Mesopotamia. The Achaemenids were noteworthy for their skill in metalwork, and in this art influenced the Greeks who eventually conquered them. A gold *horn-shaped cup* (54.3.3.) ending in the head of a lion dates from the 6–5C B.C. and is made of seven pieces joined almost invisibly. The *silver cup* (47.100.87; 5C B.C.) *in the shape of a horse's head* is decorated with a gold-foil bridle and birds; the mixing of gold and silver in this manner continued into the later Sasanian and Parthian periods.

The Sasanians ruled northwest Iran from the 3rd to mid-7C A.D. and extended their empire east to present Afghanistan and west to Syria, Yemen, and parts of Egypt. The wealth of their empire is reflected in their silver work, and among Sasanian artifacts are many silver and silver-gilt objects, some decorated with banquet or hunting scenes, e.g., a *plate with a king hunting rams* (34.33; late 5–early 6C A.D.). The gold-covered iron *sword* (65.28; A.D. 6–7C) was adapted by the Sasanians from the swords of Hunnish nomads, who were roaming Asia and Europe at the time; the flanges are mountings for straps to hold the weapon to a belt. Equally elaborate is the *head of a Sasanian king* (65.126; late 4C A.D.), with fierce staring eyes and a tall crown.

The period that stretched from the last few centuries before Christ until the Islamic conquests in the 7C witnessed almost continuous warfare between the great empires of Byzantium and Sasanian Iran. The two empires consumed their resources trying to dominate the trade routes and the wealth of Syria and Anatolia, so that by the mid-7C Sasanian Iran as well as half the Byzantine Empire had succumbed to Arab armies from the west, followers of Islam. The art of Islam continues in the galleries across the corridor.

Islamic Art

The galleries of Islamic art offer what is probably the most comprehensive permanent exhibition of this art on view anywhere. Objects date from the 7C to the 19C and have been gathered from a geographical area that reaches west to Spain and east to India and Southeast Asia.

In 622, the year in which the Islamic calendar begins, Muhammad fled Mecca for Medina. Ten years later the prophet and his followers controlled the Arabian peninsula, and in the years to come spread the religion east and west as far as China and Spain. The single dominant force affecting Islamic art across its geographical and chronological boundaries is the religion itself, whose tenets found expression in a restricted, highly stylized art, and whose main energies were focused not on painting and sculpture as in the West but on the decorative arts: pottery, metalwork, glass, ivory carving, and textiles. Objects in the Islamic galleries were created as early as the 8C and as late as the 19C, when European forms and techniques influenced the style of native arts and crafts.

HIGHLIGHTS

Miniatures from the royal courts of Persia and Mughal India, beautiful 16–17C carpets, and glass and metalwork from Egypt, Mesopotamia, and Syria.

GALLERY 1. **Introductory Gallery.** On display here are exquisite objects from the collection as a whole, suggesting the full sweep of Islamic art. Often on display here is a *white slip-painted bowl* (65.106.2; 10C) with an elegant Arabic inscription. In Kufic script, it reads: "Planning before work protects you from regret; prosperity and peace." Because the Koran embodies the divine message received by the prophet Muhammad, the use of Koranic sentences and, eventually, other religious and secular sayings, became a chief element in Islamic decoration. In the center of the gallery is a large bronze *incense burner* (51.56; 1181–82) in the shape of a lion.

GALLERY 2 (to the right of the Introductory Gallery) is devoted to the **Nishapur Excavations.** In 1935–39 and 1947 the Museum sponsored excavations at Nishapur, today a small town in Iran. From the late 9C to the early 13C when Mongol invaders destroyed it, however, Nishapur was a great Islamic city, a center of religious and secular learning. Of particular interest are the central cases displaying a sampling of the great variety of ceramic types produced at Nishapur between the 9C and 12C.

GALLERY 3. **Early Centuries of Islam (7–12C).** This gallery contains artifacts from the Umayyad dynasty (A.D. 661–750), whose capital was at

Damascus; its offshoot, the Spanish Umayyad dynasty (756–1031); the Egyptian Fatimid dynasty (969–1171), with its cultural progeny in Islamic Sicily and southern Italy; and the Abbasid dynasty (750–1258), whose prime cities were Baghdad and Samarra.

Cases along the west wall contain glassware, textiles, and ceramics. The technique of luster painting on pottery, previously used only on glass, was one of the great developments of Islamic potters.

Cases along the east wall contain glassware and delicately carved *ivory plaques* (e.g., 13.141); such plaques were an outstanding achievement of the Spanish Umayyad dynasty; most were made for the royal family and its entourage. Also on the east side of the gallery is a pair of bevel-style *carved doors* (31.119.1,2) from 9C Iraq, and a collection of chessmen and gaming pieces.

Islamic art from the Egyptian Fatimid period is known for its use of human and animal motifs (because of religious restrictions against these motifs, earlier decoration focused on plant forms and calligraphy) and for its high level of craftsmanship, especially in gold work. Fatimid ceramists used the technique of luster painting developed earlier in Iraq to achieve powerful effects, e.g., the eagle-adorned *lusterware bowl* (west wall, opposite the chessmen, 63.178.1).

GALLERY 4A (directly beyond Gallery 3) covers the **Seljuk (11–13C) and Mongol (13–14C) Periods** and focuses on ceramics of the Seljuk period. One unusual exhibit is the *ceramic tabouret* (69.225), a small piece of furniture in the shape of a pleasure pavilion, probably used as a table for food and beverages. Also in this room is the earliest-known virtually complete *chess set* (1971.193, a–ff), which dates from the 12C. Although historians are uncertain, chess seems to have been invented in India in the 7C or perhaps earlier, and then spread to Persia and elsewhere following the Muslim conquests.

GALLERY 4B, also devoted to the **Seljuk and Mongol Periods,** contains metalwork, painting, and sculpture as well as ceramics. On the left end wall near the entrance is an unusual example of figural art, a *stucco head* (42.25.17) from 12–13C Iran, whose facial features (the eye fold, the broad flat face) and pointed cap, suggest ethnic types of the Mongolian steppes. On the left end wall are ceramics of the *mina'i* (i.e., overglaze-enameled) type. The technique, which involved firing the piece twice at higher and then lower temperatures, allowed artists to increase their range of colors. On the right wall are stone and tile niches, and on the far right wall a *ceramic ewer* (32.52.1; 1215–16) with a carved and pierced outer shell. The design has winged harpies and sphinxes, as well as deer, rabbits, and dogs. Cases in the center of the room contain leaves from 14C manuscripts of the *Shah Nameh* of Ferdowsi, the Iranian national epic, as well as other 13–14C manuscript leaves.

GALLERY 4C contains **Objects from Mosque Settings,** including Koran stands, enameled-glass mosque lamps, wood panels, and a historical progression of calligraphic styles as represented in Koran leaves. The centerpiece of the room is a *Mihrab* or prayer niche (39.20; c. 1354) that indicates the direction of Mecca, executed in small pieces of ceramic arranged to form floral and geometric patterns and Arabic inscriptions.

GALLERY 5, which opens off Gallery 4B, contains mainly works from the **Ayyubid (1171–1250) and Mamluk (1250–1517) Periods in Egypt and Syria,** and the **Masrid Period (1230–1492) in Spain.** In the center is a *Mamluk geometric carpet* (1970.105) from the last quarter of the 15C, one of the most famous of its type.

GALLERY 6, **Timurid Period (1395–1501) and Savafid Period (1501–1736) in Iran,** contains changing exhibitions of miniatures from such manuscripts as the *Mantiq at-Tayr* ("Language of the Birds"), dated 1483, the *Haft Paikar* ("Seven Portraits"), from c. 1426, and the Houghton *Shah Nameh,* which was executed over a period of years and consequently affords a picture of the development of Savafid painting over the second quarter of the 16C. The room also contains carpets, and (wall cases) examples of jewelry and metalwork from the Timurid period.

GALLERY 7, **Other Arts of the Savafid Period,** includes ceramics, carpets, metalwork, and book bindings. Of particular interest are (left wall, 5th case clockwise) a *ceramic plate* (65.109.2) following Chinese blue-and-white porcelain ware in its color scheme and design of intertwined dragons; and a Timurid *jug* (91.1.607, northwest case) decorated with arabesques—tendrils ending with bilateral leaves from which spring more tendrils—the most distinctively Islamic design element.

GALLERY 8. **Arts of the Ottoman Empire (1281–1924).** This gallery contains ceramics, including painted and glazed ceramics from Iznik (16–17C), carpets, and textile fragments. The 16C Ottoman court *prayer rug* (22.100.51) is an outstanding example of its type, from the tulips and carnations between the column bases, to the columned central panel with its hanging mosque lamp, to the stylized flora of the light blue border.

GALLERY 9. **Mughal Period in India (1526–1858).** Although Islam reached northern India as early as the 8C, the Mughal period begins with the reign of the emperor Babar, a Muslim invader from Afghanistan. The greatest Mughal emperor was Akbar (1556–1605), who encouraged such cross-cultural ventures as the translation into Persian of Hindu classics. Mughal arts included carpets, miniature painting, jewelry, and jade carving. Mughal painting originally sprang from the Persian tradition but gradually developed in its own direction, showing a more naturalistic representation of nature and also absorbing European influences. Miniatures on display may include pages from the *Dastan-i Amir Hamzeh* (c. 1561–76), the first major work in the Mughal tradition. Opposite the entrance on a marble platform is a dramatic *wool carpet* (17.190.857 alternating with 17.190.858) from the reign (1628–58) of Shah Jahan, builder of the Taj Mahal.

GALLERY 10 (adjacent to the Introductory Gallery) is the luxurious paneled **Nur ad-Din Room** (1707) from Damascus, a traditional reception room of a well-to-do gentleman of the Ottoman period.

19C European Paintings and Sculpture
The Metropolitan Museum has the most outstanding collection of 19C European painting and sculpture in North America. The collection is one

of the high points of the Museum and one of the great cultural attractions of New York. In 1993, the 21 galleries that hold these works were reconstructed in the Beaux-Arts style using early 20C designs by the architectural firms of McKim, Mead & White and Richard Morris Hunt. The goal was to create galleries where the art of the 19C would be displayed in rooms similar to those for which the artists painted their pictures.

HIGHLIGHTS

The collection is rich in works by Courbet, the French Impressionists, Degas, van Gogh, Cézanne, and Rodin. The large central gallery contains a group of celebrated paintings by Manet.

The corridor gallery near the entry to the galleries of paintings contains several bronze sculptures by Antoine-Louis Barye, an artist noted for his Romantic renderings of animals, often in tense or violent poses, e.g., *Panther Seizing a Stag* (c. 1835–40) and *Theseus and the Centaur Bianor* (1849).

Near the entrance to the Neo-Classical Gallery is Gustave Moreau, *Oedipus and the Sphinx* (1864). Also in the corridor are sculptures by Auguste Rodin and Salon Paintings; see p. 207.

The galleries of painting are arranged more or less chronologically from north to south and from east to west (the corridor is on the north side of the galleries).

Neoclassicism. Pierre-Paul Prud'hon, *Andromache and Astyanax* (begun c. 1814). Jacques-Louis David, *General Étienne Maurice Gérard, Marshal of France* (1816). Jean-Auguste-Dominique Ingres, portrait of *Joseph-Antoine Moltedo* (1807–14), a successful industrialist who served as director of the Roman post office (hence the Colosseum and Appian Way in the background). Degas, who admired Ingres, owned the portrait of Moltedo, as well as the portraits of *Jacques-Louis Le Blanc* and *Mme Le Blanc* (both 1823) also on display, and considered them highlights of his collection. Also by Ingres, *Edmond Cavé* and *Mme Edmond Cavé* (both 1844); and *Odalisque in Grisaille* (1824–34), an unfinished replica of the *Grand Odalisque* in the Louvre.

Anonymous French painter, *Portrait of a Young Woman, Called Mlle Charlotte du Val d'Ognes* (c. 1800). François-Marius Granet, *The Interior of the Capuchin Church in Rome* (1815).

Romanticism. Sometimes on view in this gallery is John Constable, *Salisbury Cathedral from the Bishop's Garden.* Constable, a friend of the bishop of Salisbury who appears in the lower left, painted this scene several times; this version is probably a study for the picture (1826) now in the Frick Collection.

Joseph Mallord William Turner, *The Ferry Beach and Inn at Saltash, Cornwall* (1812); *The Grand Canal, Venice* (1835); *The Whale Ship* (1845). Although Turner's use of light and luminosity made him controversial during his own lifetime, much of his work now seems prophetically modern. Émile-Jean-Horace Vernet, *The Start of the Race of the Riderless Horse* (before 1820). Edwin Landseer, *Copy after Rubens's "Wolf and Fox Hunt"* (1824–26).

Théodore Géricault, *Alfred Dedreux as a Child* (1818); *Evening: Land-*

scape with an Aqueduct (1817–19). Henry Fuseli, *The Night-Hag Visiting Lapland Witches* (1799).

Eugène Delacroix offended the establishment by his turbulent use of color and frequently violent subject matter: *Basket of Flowers* (1848); *The Abduction of Rebecca* (1846), a Romantic subject taken from Scott's *Ivanhoe*. Also *The Natchez* (c. 1835) and *George Sand's Garden at Nohant* (c. 1843).

Corot. The Museum has many works by the prolific Jean-Baptiste-Camille Corot, whose painting shares qualities with the Neo-Classicists and the Romantics in the preceding galleries. Among them are: *Hagar in the Wilderness* (1835); *Woman Reading* (1869); *The Letter* (c. 1865); *Ville d'Avray* (c. 1870); *The Destruction of Sodom* (1843); *Bacchante by the Sea* (1865); *A Lane Through the Trees* (1870–73); *Bacchante in a Landscape* (1865); *River with a Distant Tower* (1866); *A Wheelwright's Yard on the Seine* (1865–70); and *A Woman Gathering Faggots at Ville d'Avray* (1870).

The Barbizon School painters took their name from a village near the Forest of Fontainebleau, where several of them went to live during the late 1840s. The group rejected classical conventions and ideals, and shared a Romantic reverence for nature and an interest in landscape painting for its own sake. Théodore Rousseau, *The Forest in Winter at Sunset,* was begun in the winter of 1845–46 and reworked for the following 20 years. Rousseau, a prolific painter, considered it his masterpiece, refusing to sell it during his lifetime. Also *Meadow Bordered by Trees* (c. 1845); *A River Landscape* (c. 1845); *A Path Among Rocks* (1867).

Jean-François Millet, best known for his idealization of peasant life: *Autumn Landscape with a Flock of Turkeys* (1873); *Woman with a Rake* (c. 1856–57); *Calling the Cows Home* (1872); *Haystacks: Autumn* (1874).

Honoré Daumier began as a newspaper caricaturist: *The Third-Class Carriage* (1863–65) is a treatment of a subject—people using public transportation—that interested him for two decades.

Gustave Courbet (gallery near Barbizon painters).

> **NOTE:** The Courbet paintings are divided between two galleries at opposite ends of the Manet gallery.

The Museum has one of the world's largest holdings of the work of Courbet, considered the leader of 19C French Realism. Shown in the Salon of 1866, *Woman with a Parrot* (1865–66) was attacked for its sensuality, critics remarking on the disheveled hair and "ungainly" pose of the nude and on Courbet's general lack of taste. Among the other paintings in the collection are *Portrait of Jo (La Belle Irlandaise)* (1865); *The Source of the Loue* (1864); and *The Woman in the Waves* (1868). Also *The Young Bather* (1866); *Marine: The Waterspout* (1870); *The Calm Sea* (1869); *The Deer* (c. 1861).

Manet. This central gallery is also the centerpiece of the Museum's collection of Impressionist and Post-Impressionist painters. Édouard Manet, *Woman with a Parrot* (1866); this painting was perhaps intended as a comment on the Courbet nude with the same name that shocked the Salon of 1866. *The Dead Christ with Angels* (1864) is an atypical religious subject for Manet. *Mlle. V . . . in the Costume of an Espada* (1862): the same model, Victorine Meurent, posed for *Woman with a Parrot* and two of Manet's most famous paintings, *Olympia* and *Le Déjeuner sur l'herbe* (both in Paris's Musée d'Orsay). *The Spanish Singer* (1861) is one of the two pictures with which Manet made his name in the Salon of 1861, two years before *Le Déjeuner sur l'herbe* was rejected. *Boating* (1874), an outdoor painting, was executed when the painter was working at Argenteuil with Renoir and Monet. Also on view: *Boy with a Sword* (1861); *A Matador* (after 1865); *The Monet Family in Their Garden* (1874); *Jean-Baptiste Faure* (1822–23); *Fishing* (1861–63); *Young Man in the Costume of a Maja* (1863).

Courbet (gallery near Salon Painting). In this gallery are paintings from the 1850s. *Young Women from the Village* (1851–52). Courbet, who was generally at odds with the critics, was attacked for the "ugliness" of the painting and the "common" features of the girls. Also, *Woman in a Riding Habit* (1857); *Mme de Brayer* (1858); *Mme Auguste Cuoq* (completed 1867); *Louis Gueymard as Robert le Diable* (1857); *After the Hunt* (1857); *Alphonse Promayet* (before 1855).

Two galleries which may be reached from the Manet gallery are named for *Louisine and H. O. Havemeyer*. Through her friendship with expatriate painter Mary Cassatt, Mrs. Havemeyer first came to know the Impressionist painters, including Degas, whose work especially captivated her. She eventually changed the focus of her husband's collection from Asian to European art, particularly Impressionist and Post-Impressionist paintings. The Havemeyer bequest contains many of the greatest and most beloved pictures in the Metropolitan's collection of 19C painting.

Degas Sculpture. Degas exhibited only one piece of sculpture during his lifetime, the *Little Fourteen-Year-Old Dancer* exhibited in the next gallery. Toward the end of his life, when his eyesight was failing, however, he made many models in clay and wax, which were cast in bronze after his death. The first series was made for Louisine Havemeyer. Among the outstanding pieces on view are: *Picking Apples* (1881–82, cast 1922); *Dressed Dancer at Rest* (c. 1895, cast 1922); and *Seated Bather Drying Her Left Hip* (c. 1922, cast 1922).

Degas Paintings. *The Ballet from "Robert le Diable"* (1872); *The Dancing Class* (1871); *A Woman Seated Beside a Vase of Flowers* (1858). *Jacques-Joseph Tissot* (1866–68) is a portrait of a painter who fled to England for political reasons; the paintings shown on the wall are both Old Masters and contemporary works. *The Collector of Prints* (1866): in the background are Japanese prints, which attracted Degas as well as other Impressionist painters. Also on view: *Woman Ironing* (1874); *Portrait of a Woman in Gray* (1865); *Dancers: Pink and Green* (c. 1890); *Mme Théodore Gobillard* (1869); *Sulking* (c. 1875). *Little Fourteen-Year-Old Dancer* (modeled 1880–81, cast 1922); the sculpture was originally exhibited with a tutu and real slippers.

Pastels Galleries. Because of their fragility, pastels are rotated in these two galleries with some frequency. Among them: Degas, *The Singer in Green* (c. 1884); *Dancers Practicing at the Bar* (c. 1876–77); *Nude Woman Having Her Hair Combed* (c. 1886–88); *Woman with a Towel* (1904 or 1898); *Three Jockeys* (c. 1900); *At the Milliner's* (1882). Henri de Toulouse-Lautrec, *The Englishman at the Moulin Rouge* (1892); *The Sofa* (c. 1892–96).

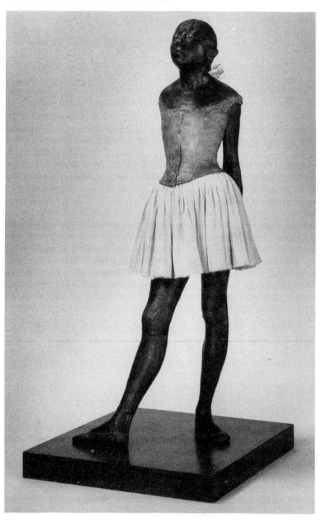

Edgar Degas, Little Fourteen-Year-Old Dancer, *19C European Paintings and Sculpture galleries. This bronze, probably cast in 1922, was given to the Museum by Louisine Havemeyer, one of its greatest benefactors.*
(The Metropolitan Museum of Art)

Next to the later Courbet gallery is a gallery devoted primarily to **Renoir.** Pierre-Auguste Renoir's *Mme Charpentier and Her Children* (1878) is a society portrait of the wife of the wealthy publisher whose clients included Maupassant and Zola. Mme Charpentier, important in intellectual circles, sits in an expensively furnished room. This commission and others that followed rescued Renoir from poverty. Other paintings by Renoir include *A Waitress at Duval's Restaurant* (1875); a touching portrait of *Marguerite (Margot) Bérard* (1879); and a portrait of actress *Tilla Durieux* (1914), painted at the end of Renoir's life. Also by Renoir: *Mme Darras* (1871); *View of the Seacoast Near Wargemont* (1880); *The Bay of Naples* (1881); *A Road in Louveciennes* (c. 1870); *A Young Girl with Daisies* (1889); *By the Seashore* (1883); *In the Meadow* (1888–94).

Berthe Morisot, *Young Woman Seated on a Sofa* (1879); Morisot, granddaughter of Fragonard, student of Corot, and sister-in-law of Manet, was one of the few women painters of her generation recognized by her peers.

Daubigny, Sisley, Boudin. Charles-François Daubigny, *Landscape with a Sunlit Stream; Apple Blossoms* (1883); *Boats on the Seacoast at Étaples* (1871). Alfred Sisley, *Sahurs Meadows in Morning Sun* (1894); *The Seine at Bougival* (1876); *The Bridge at Villeneuve-la-Garenne* (1872).

Eugène Boudin, *Beaulieu: The Bay of Fournis* (1892); *On the Beach at Trouville* (1863); *Beach at Trouville* (1864). Boudin, who painted mainly beach scenes and seascapes, is regarded as a link between Corot and his contemporaries and the Impressionists.

Monet. FIRST GALLERY. The Museum has a fine collection of paintings by Claude Monet from early to late in his career. *The Green Wave* (1865); *Regatta at Sainte-Adresse* (1867). Monet's *Garden at Sainte-Adresse* (1867) was painted while Monet was in his 20s; it combines traditional smooth brushwork with the short strokes and dots of color that would characterize Monet's later technique. Other works include *La Grenouillère (The Frog Pond)* (1869), *The Park Monceau* (1878), *Vétheuil in Summer* (1880); *Path in the Île Saint-Martin, Vétheuil* (1880); *Spring (Fruit Trees in Bloom)* (1873); *The Bodmer Oak: Fontainebleau Forest* (1865); and *Cabin of the Customs Watch* (two versions from 1882; one from 1896–97).

SECOND GALLERY. This gallery contains several paintings from the 1890s and later, a time when Monet had begun to concentrate on series of paintings exploring the effect of changing light on the same subject. *The Houses of Parliament (Effect of Fog)* (1903); *Rouen Cathedral: The Portal (in Sun)* (1894); *Bridge Over a Pool of Water Lilies* (1899); *Morning on the Seine Near Giverny* (1897); *Haystacks (Effect of Snow and Sun)* (1891); *Poplars* (1891); *Ice Floes* (1893); *The Palm Trees at Bordighera* (1884); *Île aux Orties near Vernon* (1897); *Rapids on the Petite Creuse at Fresselines* (1889); *The Manneporte (Étretat)* (1883); *The Manneporte Near Étretat* (1886).

French Still Lifes. Claude Monet, *Chrysanthemums* (1882); *Apples and Grapes* (1879); *Bouquet of Sunflowers* (1881). Pierre Auguste Renoir, *Still Life with Peaches and Grapes* (1881); *Still Life with Peaches* (1881). Camille Pisarro, *Still Life with Apples and Pitcher* (1872).

Henri Fantin-Latour, *Still Life with Flowers and Fruit* (1865–66); *Still Life with Pansies* (1874).

Pisarro. Camille Pisarro, *Barges at Pontoise* (1876); *Poplars, Eragy* (1895); *Morning, An Overcast Day* (1896); *Rue de l'Épicerie, Rouen* (1898); *The Garden of the Tuileries on a Winter Afternoon* (1899). Especially fine are *The Garden of the Tuileries on a Spring Morning* (1899) and *The Boulevard Montmartre on a Winter Morning* (1897).

Cézanne. This gallery has a stunning array of paintings by Paul Cézanne: *Fantasy Scene (The Fisherman)* (c. 1875); *Bathers* (1874–75); *View of the Domaine Saint-Joseph* (1887); *The Pool at the Jas de Bouffan* (1880s). *The Gulf of Marseilles Seen from L'Estaque* (1884–86); Cézanne made multiple paintings of this landscape, studying the changing forms of the houses and mountains from slightly different viewpoints, just as Monet also recorded single scenes in different kinds of light. *Mont Sainte-Victoire and the Viaduct of the Arc River Valley* (1882–85); *Rocks in the Forest* (mid-1880s?); *Mont Sainte-Victoire* (1885–87).

Dominique Aubert (1865–66); *Mme Cézanne in a Red Dress* (c.1890); *Gustave Boyer in a Straw Hat* (1870–71). *The Card Players* (1892) is a genre painting, unusual for Cézanne, who generally preferred still lifes, landscapes, or portraits. In his still lifes he continued to grappled with the problems of space, volume, and the underlying structure of reality. *Still Life with a Ginger Jar and Eggplants* (1890–94) is a fine example of his work in this genre. Also: *Still Life with Apples and Pears* (1885–87); *Still Life with Apples and a Pot of Primroses* (early 1890s); *Still Life with a Jar, Cup, and Apples* (c. 1877).

Seurat, Signac, Redon. Georges Seurat, *Circus Sideshow* (1887–88), is painted methodically with small dots or points of color, which capture the hazy, flickering quality of gaslight. *Study for a Sunday Afternoon on the Island of La Grande Jatte* (1884) is the final sketch for the famous painting in the Art Institute of Chicago. Also: *The Gardener* (1882–83); *View of the Seine* (1882–83); *Forest at Pontaubert* (1881).

Paul Signac, *View of the Port of Marseilles* (1895); *The Jetty at Cassis* (1899); *View of Collioure* (1887). Odilon Redon, *Bouquet in a Chinese Vase* (1912–14); *Flowers in a Chinese Vase* (1906); *Pandora* (1910).

Gauguin, Rousseau, and van Gogh. Paul Gauguin, *Ia Orana Maria* (1892); the title repeats in Tahitian native dialect the opening words of the Angel Gabriel to Mary at the Annunciation. *A Farm in Brittany* (1894); *Two Tahitian Women* (1899). Henri Rousseau, *The Repast of the Lion* (1907).

The Museum has the largest collection of van Gogh's works in America. Vincent van Gogh, *Wheat Fields with Cypresses* (1889), was the artist's first rendering of this important theme. Van Gogh said of the cypress tree: "as beautiful of line and proportion as an Egyptian obelisk. . . . It is a splash of *black* in a sunny landscape." *Cypresses* (1889) is a vertical treatment of the same theme.

Other famous works include the *Sunflowers* (1887) and *Mme Ginoux (L'Arlésienne)* (1888). *Irises* (1890) was painted at the end of his life at Saint-Rémy during a period of calm. Also *Peasant Woman Cooking by a Fireplace* (1885); *The Flowering Orchard* (1888); *Shoes* (1888). A two-sided panel (1886–88) has *The Potato Peeler* on one side and *Self-Portrait with a Straw Hat* on the reverse.

CORRIDOR GALLERY. The long Corridor Gallery contains sculptures by **Rodin** and **Salon Painting**. The sculptures by Auguste Rodin include: *Fallen Caryatid Carrying an Urn* (1893); *Fallen Caryatid Carrying a Stone* (1881); *Final Study for the Monument to Balzac* (1897); *Cupid and Psyche* (c. 1893); *Beside the Sea* (1907); *Orpheus and Eurydice* (before 1887); *Genius of Eternal Rest, Without Head and Arms* (1899); *Eve* (1881); *Adam* (1899); *The Martyr* (1885); *The Thinker* (1880).

"Salon Painting" is a name given to conservative, often commercially successful, 19C French painting that used traditional techniques to render subjects that were often exotic and romantic. Some of the early Impressionists studied with these painters before rebelling to find their own techniques and subject matter. Rosa Bonheur, *The Horse Fair* (1852–53); dressed as a man in order to escape attention, Bonheur went to the horse market in Paris twice a week for a year and a half to make sketches for this large painting. Jean-Louis-Ernest Messonier, *Friedland, 1807* (1875).

Jules Bastien-Lepage, *Joan of Arc* (1879), here shown listening to the voices of the three saints floating in the background. When Germany gained control of the province of Lorraine after the Franco-Prussian War, Joan reemerged as a symbol of rebellion.

Also in the corridor are several allegorical paintings by Pierre Puvis de Chavannes, a painter known for his flat, stylized, symbolic figures; Puvis's work influenced younger artists, including Gauguin, who studied with him. Chavannes, *Sleep* (before 1867); *The Shepherd's Song* (1891).

Arnold Böcklin, *Island of the Dead* (1880). The Swiss Symbolist painter made five versions of this subject; the first was commissioned by a newly widowed Florentine patroness to commemorate her bereavement.

European Paintings

The Museum has one of the world's great collections of European paintings, which dates back to trustee William T. Blodgett's purchase of 174 paintings in about 1870, the time when Old Masters were just becoming popular with new millionaires. With the exception of major gifts from Benjamin Altman, Robert Lehman, and Jack and Belle Linsky, gifts conditional upon specific arrangement within the Museum, the paintings are arranged chronologically and by school. The collection of European paintings spans roughly the late 13C to 18C.

> **NOTE:** 19C paintings and sculpture are exhibited in galleries to the south of the European Painting galleries). The Lehman and Linsky Collections are installed elsewhere in the Museum in their own galleries. The Altman paintings are grouped together within the Galleries of European Paintings.

GALLERY 1. 18C VENETIAN PAINTING: TIEPOLO

> **NOTE:** This gallery was closed for renovation in 1995. The paintings by Tiepolo will be reinstalled.

Giovanni Battista Tiepolo, *The Triumph of Marius* (1729), depicts the victorious Roman general Gaius Marius preceded by his captive, the African king Jugurtha. Tiepolo painted himself at the left in front of the torchbearer. Also, *Allegory of the Planets and Continents* (1752).

GALLERY 2. 18C EUROPEAN PAINTING

> **NOTE:** This gallery was closed for renovation in 1995. It will contain
> works by Jacques-Louis David, Pompeo Batoni, and Anton Raffael
> Mengs.

Italian Renaissance Painting. The right-hand row of galleries is devoted
primarily to the Italian Renaissance. Galleries 3–9 contain paintings from
the 14C to the 16C.

GALLERY 3. 13C–15C ITALIAN PAINTING: MARTINI, SASSETTA, GIO-
VANNI DI PAOLO. Berlinghiero, *Madonna and Child* (early 13C), one of
three known paintings by Berlinghiero, the most important Tuscan
painter of the early 13C. Simone Martini, *St. Andrew;* part of the same
altarpiece to which *St. Ansanus* in the Lehman Collection belongs. Sassetta, *Madonna and Child with Angels* (c. 1440). *Journey of the Magi* (c.
1435), the upper half of a panel showing the kings bringing their gifts to
the Christ child, whose manger (in the lower panel, now in Sienna) lies
below the golden star on the hill. Paolo di Giovanni Fei, *Madonna and
Child,* in its original frame with cabochon gems and glass medallions.
Giovanni di Paolo, *Madonna and Child with Saints* (1445?); *Paradise,*
part of an altarpiece to which the *Expulsion from Paradise* in the Lehman
Collection may have also belonged.

GALLERY 4. ITALIAN SECULAR PAINTING OF THE 15C. Filippo Lippi,
Portrait of a Man and a Woman at a Casement (c. 1440); Tuscan women
of the 15C were usually portrayed in profile, apparently considered their
most flattering aspect. Domenico Ghirlandaio, *Francesco Sassetti and His
Son Teodoro* (1487); *Portrait of a Lady.*

GALLERY 4A. ITALIAN SECULAR PAINTING. Ceiling panels from the
PALAZZO DEL MAGNIFICO in Siena by Bernardo Pintoricchio. Examples
of furniture painted with allegorical and mythological scenes.

GALLERY 4B (also accessible from Gallery 14). ITALIAN RENAISSANCE
PAINTING FROM THE ALTMAN COLLECTION: MANTEGNA, BOTTI-
CELLI, DELLA ROBBIA.

Benjamin Altman, founder of the department store which occupied a Renaissance-
style palazzo on Fifth Ave in New York in 1906–89, was a bachelor who devoted
himself totally to his work and his art collection. On his death in 1913, he left a $15
million collection of paintings and porcelains to the Museum on condition that the
collection be maintained intact in two suitable adjoining rooms—one for the paintings, statuary, Limoges enamels, and rock crystals, a second for the Chinese porcelains.

Andrea Mantegna, *The Holy Family with St. Mary Magdalene* (1490–
1506); painted on canvas instead of the more commonly used wood, it
was probably intended for private devotions. Alessandro Botticelli, *The
Last Communion of St. Jerome* (early 1490s), an unusual portrayal of a
saint characteristically shown as a scholar surrounded by ancient texts.
Also, *Three Miracles of St. Zenobius.* Fra Angelico, *The Crucifixion* (1440–
45?); although the painting is damaged, the saints are still recognizable:
Monica, Augustine, Dominic, Mary, Mary Magdalen, John the Evangelist,

Thomas Aquinas, Francis, and Elizabeth of Hungary. Andrea della Robbia, *Madonna and Child with Scroll* (c. 1455).

(GALLERY 14A, adjacent to Gallery 4B, contains paintings by 15C Venetian painters, including Bellini. See p. 211.)

GALLERY 5. 14–15C NORTHERN ITALIAN PAINTING: GIOTTO, LORENZO MONACO. Giotto, *The Epiphany* (c. 1320); Italian Renaissance painting is traditionally said to begin with Giotto, a younger contemporary of Dante. In this painting one of the Magi lifts up the Christ child, a motif said to derive from religious drama. Lorenzo Monaco, *Noah, David, Moses,* and *Abraham* (all 1408–10), panels from an altarpiece.

GALLERY 6. 15C ITALIAN PAINTING: FILIPPO LIPPI, GHIRLANDAIO, SIGNORELLI, PERUGINO. Fra Filippo Lippi, *Madonna and Child Enthroned with Two Angels* (1437). Domenico Ghirlandaio, *St. Christopher with the Infant Christ* (c. 1475). Luca Signorelli, *Madonna and Child* (1505), shown with grotesque figures, golden putti, and Roman coins instead of the usual background landscape. Also, *The Resurrection* (1st decade, 16C). Piero di Cosimo, *Young St. John the Baptist* (early 1480s); St. John the Baptist was the patron saint of Florence. *A Hunting Scene* is part of a cycle illustrating the life of primitive man, a theme to which the eccentric Piero was drawn. Pietro Perugino, *Sts. John the Baptist and Lucy* (c. 1505); the two saints were painted as mirror images to flank the central panel of an altarpiece.

GALLERY 7. 16C ITALIAN PAINTING: RAPHAEL, SARTO, BRONZINO. Raphael, *Madonna and Child Enthroned with Saints* (1504), part of an altarpiece for a convent in Perugia, painted when Raphael was about 20 years old. The *Agony in the Garden* was painted as part of the predella (small painting or series of paintings below the main panel) of the same altarpiece. Andrea del Sarto, *Holy Family with Infant St. John* (c. 1530), a late work, painted in soft, rich colors; John the Baptist offers Christ a globe, possibly symbolizing Christian dominion. Agnolo Bronzino, *Portrait of a Young Man* (c. 1540); one of Bronzino's finest portraits, the elegant, self-consciously posed nobleman reflects the sophistication of the Florentine court under Cosimo I.

Continue to the right past the stairway.

GALLERY 8. 16C VENETIAN PAINTING: TITIAN, TINTORETTO, VERONESE. Titian, *Venus and the Lute Player* (1560s); the head of Venus and the curtain behind her were probably completed by an assistant. Also, *Venus and Adonis* (1560s), a scene from Ovid's *Metamorphoses,* showing Venus embracing her lover as he departs on the fatal boar hunt. Tintoretto, *The Miracle of the Loaves and Fishes* (1545–50). Paolo Veronese, *Mars and Venus United by Love* (1570s), a work of Veronese's maturity, with uncertain allegorical meanings. Also, *Alessandro Vittoria* (c. 1570?), a portrait of a famous Venetian sculptor with a model of one of his most famous works, a statue of St. Sebastian.

GALLERY 9. 16C ITALIAN PAINTING: CORREGGIO, MORETTO, MORONI, ROMANINO. Correggio, *Sts. Peter, Martha, Mary Magdalen, and Leonard* (c. 1517), identifiable by their attributes. St. Peter with the keys and Magdalen with a jar of ointment are familiar figures. St. Leonard holds the irons of prisoners freed by his intercession, while St. Martha leads a docile dragon that she tamed with holy water. Moretto da Brescia, *The Entombment* (1554), painted the year of Moretto's death; *Portrait of a Man* (1520–25?). Giovanni Battista Moroni, *Bartolommeo Bonghi* (1554): Bonghi, a lawyer, holds a copy of Justinian's *Pandects;* Bergamo can be seen out the window. Moroni's *Abbess Lucrezia Agliardi Vertova* (1556) is a strong portrait of an old woman, the founder of the Carmelite convent of Sant'Anna near Bergamo. Gerolamo Romanino, *The Flagellation* (c. 1540).

GALLERY 10. 17C FRENCH PAINTING: POUSSIN, CLAUDE. Nicolas Poussin, *The Blind Orion Searching for the Rising Sun* (1658), a haunting, mysterious picture painted late in Poussin's career. Orion, a mighty hunter blinded by the king of Chios for trying to rape his daughter, was told by an oracle that the rays of the rising sun would restore his sight. Another painting on a mythological subject, *The Rape of the Sabine Women* (c. 1637?), shows Romulus, ruler of Rome, signaling his men to seize the Sabine women, needed to populate the newly founded city. *The Companions of Rinaldo* (1630s) depicts a scene from Tasso's *Jerusalem Delivered.*

Claude Lorrain, *View of La Crescenza* (c. 1649). The artist came to Rome as an adolescent, apprenticed to a pastry cook. He is known for his idealization of the beauty of the Italian landscape, often portrayed in paintings with subjects drawn from classical literature. *The Trojan Women Setting Fire to Their Fleet* (1643) refers to an episode from the *Aeneid* in which the Trojan women, tired of wandering, try to destroy their ships; Jupiter, however, petitioned by Aeneas, extinguishes the fires with a rainstorm.

Dutch Painting. In Galleries 11–14 are 17C Dutch portraits and landscapes.

GALLERY 11. 17C DUTCH LANDSCAPE PAINTING: RUISDAEL, VAN GOYEN, HOBBEMA, AND CUYP. Several landscapes by Jacob van Ruisdael. Jan van Goyen, *Country House Near the Water* (1646); *The Pelkus Gate, Utrecht* (1646). Van Goyen traveled around the country making drawings on which he based his paintings. Meindert Hobbema, *A Woodland Road* (after 1660), a dramatic landscape by a disciple of Jacob van Ruisdael. Aelbert Cuyp, *Starting for the Hunt* (1653); *Piping Shepherds* (1643–44).

GALLERY 12. 17C DUTCH PAINTING: VERMEER, STEEN. Fewer than 40 universally accepted paintings by Johannes Vermeer have been known to survive; the Metropolitan has five. Johannes Vermeer, *Young Woman with a Water Jug* (c. 1662), a wonderful rendering of light and color. Vermeer painted few portraits; the subtle coloring and enigmatic expression of *Portrait of a Young Woman* (late 1660s) reminded Théophile Thoré, Vermeer's rediscoverer, of the *Mona Lisa.* Also, *Woman with a Lute. Allegory of the Faith* (early 1670s); Faith's pose is histrionic, but the rendering of the glass sphere, the tapestry, and the reflections in the globe demonstrate the painter's technical virtuosity.

Jan Steen, *Merry Company on a Terrace* (after 1669). Steen is the fat fellow on the left with a jug. Nicholas Maes, *The Lacemaker* (1655–60).

GALLERY 13. 17C DUTCH PORTRAITS: REMBRANDT, HALS. The Museum owns 18–20 paintings by Rembrandt as well as about 20 more from the school of Rembrandt. *Aristotle with a Bust of Homer* (1653); a brooding Aristotle rests his right hand on Homer's head; his left hand fingers a gold chain with a medallion of Alexander the Great, Aristotle's student. The Museum bought this exceptionally fine Rembrandt in 1961 for the then astronomical price of $2.3 million. *Portrait of a Man* (1632); *Portrait of a Lady* (1632); *Herman Doomer* (1640); *Henrickje Stoffels* (1660); *The Standard Bearer* (1654).

Frans Hals, *Portrait of a Man* (1630–35). *Portrait of a Man* (early 1650s), painted with slashing brushwork that impressed later painters; van Gogh said Hals had no less than 27 varieties of black, useful for painting somber Dutch garb.

GALLERY 14. 17C DUTCH PAINTING FROM THE BENJAMIN ALTMAN COLLECTION: REMBRANDT, HALS, VERMEER, RUISDAEL. Rembrandt, *Self-Portrait* (1660), one of almost 100 self-portraits, some of them among his finest works. *Woman with a Pink* (1662–65); a child's head has been painted out of this late portrait, possibly to indicate death. *Portrait of a Man Holding Gloves* (early 1640s).

Frans Hals, *Young Man and Woman in an Inn* (1623); *Merrymakers at Shrovetide* (c. 1615). Johannes Vermeer, *A Girl Asleep* (c. 1657); the painting, with its untidy interior scene and drowsing subject, may be an allegory for sloth. Jacob van Ruisdael, *Wheatfields* (1670s). Ruisdael was the preeminent 17C Dutch landscape painter, known for his emotional range as well as his technical virtuosity. Aelbert Cuyp, *Young Herdsman with Cows* (1650s).

GALLERY 14A. 15C VENETIAN AND NORTHERN ITALIAN PAINTERS: BELLINI, MANTEGNA, CRIVELLI, CARPACCIO. Giovanni Bellini, *Madonna and Child* (1480s), a late painting with a fine background landscape; *Madonna Adoring the Sleeping Child* (early 1460s). Andrea Mantegna, *The Adoration of the Shepherds;* an early painting (before 1460?). Mantegna's style was marked by clarity of detail, mastery of perspective, and an interest in archeology. Carlo Crivelli, *Madonna and Child* (1480s?), a small, delicately colored and stylistically archaic painting filled with symbolic flora and fauna. Also, *Pietà* (1476).

Vittore Carpaccio, *Meditation on the Passion* (c. 1510), a devotional painting suggesting Old Testament events that prefigure the coming of Christ. Job (lower right) and St. Jerome sit in front of symbolic savage and fertile landscapes; St. Jerome wrote a commentary on the Book of Job. Antonello da Messina, *Christ Crowned with Thorns* (1470s). Antonello came to Venice from Messina (Sicily) in 1475, bringing with him from Naples a knowledge of the Flemish painters and the technique of using oils. Cosimo Tura, *Flight into Egypt* (c. 1474); the highly individualistic Tura was the most important 15C Ferrarese painter.

GALLERY 15. 18C ENGLISH PORTRAITS: REYNOLDS, GAINSBOROUGH, LAWRENCE. Sir Joshua Reynolds, *Lady Smith and Her Children* (1787); *Colonel George Coussmaker* (1782), a painting by the most successful portraitist of the time, showing the aristocratic grenadier guard and his horse artfully posed in a bucolic setting. Also, *Hon. Henry Fane with His Guardians Inigo Jones and Charles Blair* (1766); the Inigo Jones pictured here is a descendant of the famous architect and stage designer. Thomas Gainsborough, *Mrs. Grace Dalrymple Elliott* (c. 1778), one of Gainsborough's many graceful society portraits. Mrs. Elliott married young and later enjoyed an adventurous romantic career, pleasing, among others, George IV and the marquess of Cholmondeley, who commissioned this portrait. Sir Thomas Lawrence, *Elizabeth Farren* (1790), the work of a young virtuoso.

GALLERY 16. 17C SPANISH PAINTING: VELÁZQUEZ, ZURBARÁN, MURILLO. Diego Velázquez, *Juan de Pareja* (c. 1650); a masterful and celebrated portrait of the painter's assistant, a Spaniard of Moorish descent. Commissioned to paint Pope Innocent X, Velázquez practiced on his assistant before attempting the pope. *The Supper at Emmaus* (1622–23). Francisco de Zurbarán, *The Young Virgin* (1632–33). Bartolomé Esteban Murillo, *Virgin and Child* (1670s), a subject Murillo returned to repeatedly. During his lifetime, Murillo was influential and highly esteemed; his reputation suffered later because of the sentimentality of his work, but is now rising again.

GALLERY 17. 17C FRENCH PAINTING: LA TOUR, CHAMPAIGNE. Georges de la Tour, *The Fortune Teller* (c. 1625). *The Penitent Magdalen* (c. 1638–43?). La Tour is known for his handling of light, particularly candlelight; this is one of four pictures he painted of the repentent Magdalen. Philippe de Champaigne, *Jean-Baptiste Colbert* (1655); Colbert rose to become minister of finance under Louis XIV.

GALLERY 18. 18C FRENCH PAINTING: GREUZE, CHARDIN, VIGÉE LE BRUN. Jean-Baptiste Greuze, *Broken Eggs* (c. 1757). *Aegina Visited by Jupiter* (c. 1767); a subject taken from Ovid's *Metamorphoses:* Aegina, daughter of a river god, is visited by Jupiter disguised as a column of fire. Jean-Baptiste Chardin, *Boy Blowing Bubbles* (early 1730s?), a common metaphor for the transience of life. Louise-Élisabeth Vigée LeBrun, *Madame de la Châtre* (1789). Vigée LeBrun, a charming and witty woman, became a friend of Marie-Antoinette; for the ten years preceding the French Revolution she made her career painting the queen and members of the court, including Mme de la Châtre.

Jacques-Louis David, *Antoine-Laurent Lavoisier and His Wife* (1788); Lavoisier, shown surrounded by elegant scientific glassware, was a celebrated chemist. Adélaïde Labille-Guiard, *Self-Portrait with Two Pupils* (1785); like Vigée LeBrun, Labille-Guiard was a court painter and a member of the French Royal Academy.

GALLERY 19. 18C FRENCH PAINTING: FRAGONARD AND BOUCHER. Jean-Honoré Fragonard, *The Love Letter* (1770s); the fashionable aristocratic lady in her boudoir is possibly the daughter of Fragonard's teacher François Boucher. François Boucher, *Washerwomen* (1768); *Shepherds' Idyll* (1768).

GALLERY 20. GOYA. Francisco de Goya, the outstanding European painter of his time, is handsomely represented in the collection. *José*

Costa y Bonells, called Pepito (c. 1810). *Don Manuel Osorio Manrique de Zuñiga* (c. 1786); the magpie, which the child holds on a string, was a traditional Christian symbol for the soul. *Don Sebastián Martínez y Pérez* (1792); this painting of an aristocratic collector and intellectual shows the influence of 18C French portraiture. *Majas on a Balcony* (c. 1815) is one of the great paintings collected by the Havemeyers (see p. 203); two cloaked sinister men hover behind the two *majas,* women of questionable social status. *The Bullfight* (early 19C), formerly attributed to Goya, now considered to be by a painter working in Goya's style.

GALLERY 21. 18C FRENCH PAINTING: WATTEAU, BOUCHER, FRAGO-NARD. Antoine Watteau, *Mezzetin* (1718–20). Mezzetin was a stock character in the *commedia dell'arte,* a sympathetic figure troubled by unrequited love, here wistfully depicted serenading an unseen lover; even the marble statue turns her back. Also, *The French Comedians* (1720–21). François Boucher, *The Toilet of Venus* (1751). Louis XV's most famous mistress, Mme de Pompadour, patronized Boucher and may have commissioned this for her château at Bellevue, near Paris. Also by Boucher: *The Dispatch of the Messenger* (1765); *The Interrupted Sleep* (1750).

Jean-Honoré Fragonard, a pupil of Chardin and later Boucher, known as the most perfect embodiment of the Rococo spirit. *The Italian Family* (c. 1760); *The Cascade* (1773); *A Shady Avenue* (1773).

GALLERY 22. 18C VENETIAN PAINTING: GUARDI, TIEPOLO, CANA-LETTO. Francesco Guardi, *Venice: Piazza San Marco; Venice: Santa Maria della Salute;* and *Fantastic Landscape* (three canvases from the 1760s). Guardi is most famous for his views of Venice; he was esteemed by the Impressionists for the spontaneity of his rapidly painted works. Giovanni Domenico Tiepolo, the son and assistant of Giovanni Battista Tiepolo, excelled in paintings of contemporary life, of which *A Dance in the Country* (c. 1756) is one of the most attractive. Canaletto, *The Piazza San Marco* (late 1720s).

Renaissance Painting from Northern Europe, Spanish Painting, and 18C Italian Painting (Galleries 23–30) are in the other wing, opening to left of Gallery 2.

GALLERY 23. 15C FLEMISH PAINTING: VAN EYCK, ROGIER VAN DER WEYDEN, MEMLING. Jan van Eyck, *The Crucifixion* and *The Last Judgment* (1425–30). The acutely observed detail shows van Eyck, formerly called the "inventor" of oil painting, as a precursor of Northern European realism. Petrus Christus, *Lamentation Over the Dead Christ* (1450s); *Portrait of a Carthusian* (1446). Rogier van der Weyden, *Christ Appearing to His Mother* (prob. 1440–45); a legend proposes this visit as the first act of Christ after the Resurrection. *Francesco d'Este* (c. 1460), the illegitimate son of the duke of Ferrara, cool and aristocratic like many of Rogier's portraits, against an unusual white background. Hans Memling, *Tommaso Portinari* and his wife, *Maria Baroncelli* (c. 1472); Portinari, a Florentine, represented the Medici banking house in Bruges.

GALLERY 24. 16C FLEMISH PAINTING: GERARD DAVID, JOOS VAN GHENT, PATINIR, JOOS VAN CLEVE, MASSYS. Gerard David, *Rest on the Flight into Egypt* (c. 1500), a beautiful and original treatment of the subject. Joos van Ghent, *The Adoration of the Magi* (c. 1467). Joachim Patinir, *The Penitence of St. Jerome* (after 1515), a triptych showing St. Jerome in the center, the baptism of Christ and the temptation of St. Anthony on the interior wings. Patinir was known for his landscapes; here the panorama is continuous across the panels of the triptych. Joos van Cleve, *The Holy Family* (c. 1513?); *The Annunciation* (c. 1525). Hieronymus Bosch, *The Adoration of the Magi;* possibly an early work whose exotic figures anticipate Bosch's later work. Quentin Massys, *The Adoration of the Magi* (1526).

GALLERY 25. 16C GERMAN AND FLEMISH PAINTING: DÜRER, BALDUNG, HOLBEIN. Albrecht Dürer, *Virgin and Child with St. Anne* (1519). St. Anne, the mother of the Virgin Mary, is depicted with her daughter adoring the sleeping Christ Child; this picture was painted the year after Dürer's conversion to Lutheranism. Hans Baldung Grien, *St. John on Patmos* (prob. by 1510–11), a relatively recent acquisition (1983). Hans Holbein the Younger, *A Member of the Wedigh Family* (1532), possibly a London merchant. The portrait is distinguished by its precise drawing and fine characterization. Jean Clouet, *Guillaume Budé* (c. 1536), his only documented work. The dour-looking Budé was France's greatest Greek scholar, admired by Erasmus for his erudition.

GALLERY 26. 16C FLEMISH PAINTING: BRUEGEL, CRANACH. Pieter Bruegel the Elder, *The Harvesters* (1565), part of a cycle representing the months; Bruegel, who typically painted energetic outdoor scenes, was himself an Antwerp intellectual and included a cardinal among his patrons. Lucas Cranach, *The Judgment of Paris* (c. 1528); Paris, in Cupid's range, awards Venus the golden apple (here made of glass). The plumed hat on the central nude typifies Cranach's coy humor.

GALLERY 27. 17C FLEMISH PAINTING: VAN DYCK, RUBENS. Anthony Van Dyck, *James Stuart, Duke of Richmond and Lennox,* a flattering portrait of the cousin of Charles I. Peter Paul Rubens, *Venus and Adonis* (mid-1630s?), a painting influenced by Titian's treatment of the same subject; the color and technique are indicative of Rubens's maturity. *Rubens, His Wife Helena Fourment, and Their Son, Peter Paul* (c. 1639), a full-size portrait of Rubens and his second wife, whom he married (1630) when he was 53 and she was 16.

GALLERY 28. 17C FLEMISH PAINTING: VAN DYCK, RUBENS, JAN BRUEGHEL. Anthony Van Dyck, *Virgin and Child* (c. 1620); *Study Head of a Young Woman* (1621–27); *Study Head of a Young Man* (1617–20). Peter Paul Rubens, *The Holy Family with the Young Baptist and St. Elizabeth* (c. 1608); *Christ Triumphant over Sin and Death* (c. 1630). Jan Brueghel the Elder, *Woodland Road with Travellers* (1607). Jan Brueghel the Younger, *Still Life: A Basket of Flowers.* Jan Brueghel the Elder was the second son of Pieter Bruegel; Jan Brueghel the Younger was his son.

GALLERY 29. EL GRECO. El Greco, *Portrait of a Cardinal, probably Don Fernando Niño de Guevara* (c. 1600), an unforgettable portrait of the cardinal as a man of power; the cardinal was also Grand Inquisitor and archbishop of Seville. *View of Toledo* (1597): El Greco's only landscape subject (there is a similar view in Toledo), illuminated by an eerie light. *The Miracle of Christ Healing the Blind* (c. 1577). El Greco, born in Crete, studied in Venice, where he was influenced by Titian and Tintoretto.

GALLERY 30. 17C ITALIAN PAINTING: CARAVAGGIO, CARRACI, RENI, RIBERA. Michelangelo Merisi da Caravaggio, *The Musicians* (c. 1595); *The Lute Player* (c. 1597). Mattia Preti, *Pilate Washing His Hands* (1663), an intensely psychological portrait. Annibale Carraci, *The Coronation of the Virgin* (c. 1595), painted shortly after his arrival in Rome; his later work is more monumental. Guido Reni, *Charity* (c. 1630), typical of Reni's influential late style, with its soft colors and depictions of gentle emotions. Jusepe Ribera, *The Holy Family with Sts. Anne and Catherine of Alexandria* (1648); Ribera, a Spaniard, worked all his adult life in Italy.

(GALLERIES 30 and 31 are used for special exhibitions.)

Far Eastern Art
The collection of Far Eastern Art reaches from the 2nd millennium B.C. to the 19C A.D., with objects from China, Japan, Korea, India, and Southeast Asia. It occupies several adjacent areas on the second floor, beginning at the south end of the Great Hall Balcony, encircling the Great Staircase, and then running north and west. This scattered arrangement seems to reflect the history of the collection, undertaken at first in a desultory manner by collectors like J. Pierpont Morgan, who unsystematically picked up Oriental rugs and other objects that pleased him, and Benjamin Altman, who prized classical Chinese ceramics as well as European paintings.

In the past decade the Museum has undertaken a major reorganization of its galleries of Far Eastern Art. The fruits of these efforts can be seen in the Japanese galleries (1987) and the galleries of Ancient Chinese Art (1988), as well as in the earlier Chinese Garden Court and galleries of Chinese painting. In 1994, the Museum completed the project with new galleries for the arts of South and Southeast Asia.

HIGHLIGHTS

A group of monumental Chinese Buddhist sculptures, perhaps the finest collection outside China; the Chinese Garden Court with its gallery of Ming Dynasty furniture; and the new South and Southeast Asian galleries.

The collection of **Chinese Ceramics** is arranged around the GREAT HALL BALCONY. The collection (organized chronologically, with earliest objects in the northeast corner) dates back to the Neolithic period and the legendary Shang Dynasty (15–11C B.C.), the earliest historic Chinese civilization. Included are early pieces of T'ang stoneware, bowls and other objects finished with the greenish glaze known in the West as celadon, e.g., the *bowl* (18.56.36), with swirling dragon decoration, which is one of the high points of the collection, and pieces of porcelain from the Ming Dynasty with superb surface painting. A fine *Bodhidharma* (63.176) is made of a type of porcelain known in the West as *blanc de chine,* outstanding for its finely grained vitreous white body.

In the cases surrounding the Great Staircase are 17–18C *Porcelains from the Benjamin Altman Collection,* grouped together because of a stipulation in the bequest. Altman's porcelains reflect the skill in glazing and decoration of Ch'ing Dynasty potters, particularly those from the Kang-Hsi (1662–1722), Yung-cheng (1722–35), and Chi'en Lung (1736–65) periods. These porcelains include a wide range of types, from extravagantly decorated objects, many for export, to jewel-toned monochromatic glazes, whose simplicity emphasizes the elegant shapes of the objects.

In the center of the balcony stands Antonio Canova's marble *Perseus with the Head of Medusa,* based on the Vatican's Apollo Belvedere captured for France by Napoleon's army. Canova's first version of Perseus was bought by Pope Pius VII to replace the Apollo; this one (completed c. 1808) was commissioned by a Polish countess.

The other galleries along the balcony contain exhibits of Korean porcelaneous stoneware and porcelain from the Koryo (918–1392) and Choson (1392–1910) dynasties.

Chinese Art.

North of the Great Hall balcony is the gallery of **Early Chinese Sculpture from the 5–6C.** During the Northern Wei Dynasty (A.D. 386–534), Buddhism and Buddhist art flourished in northern China. On display are monumental examples of Buddhist sculpture from the Northern Wei, including a Buddhist stele with the *Maitreya Buddha* (65.29.3) dating from about 489–95 and a *Standing Buddha* dating from about 420–23. Another outstanding and complex piece, a stele with scenes from a popular text, the *Vimalakirti Sutra,* dates from the mid-6C.

Beyond the arch on the left are galleries of the **Arts of Ancient China,** which contain works from the Neolithic period (4000–1500 B.C.) through the T'ang Dynasty (A.D. 618–906).

THE NEOLITHIC GALLERY has painted grain jars and pottery vessels from the Yellow River region of northwestern China. Also on view are examples of carved jade (nephrite) from eastern China, especially the lower Yangtze Valley.

THE BRONZE AGE GALLERY contains artifacts from about 1500–2000 B.C., among them a famous *Tuan Fang altar set* (24.721.1–14), with ritual vessels. From the Shang Dynasty (11C B.C.) comes a bronze lobed *tripod cauldron* (1985.214.3) decorated with an animal mask. There are also decorated weapons, hooks for closing garments, jade ornaments, and small sculptures.

IN THE HAN DYNASTY GALLERY (206 B.C.–A.D. 220) are a group of ceramic tomb figurines, appealing to modern sensibilities for their depiction of human activities. A pair of men play a game, one clearly happier than the other with the outcome. A dancing woman with a long robe and hanging sleeves is captured in an expressive pose. Architectural models of houses and farm buildings (complete with livestock) suggest the domestic side of Han life.

THE GALLERY OF THE SIX DYNASTIES PERIOD (A.D. 220–618) focuses on a collection of early Buddhist sculpture from northern China. Prominently displayed is a *Maitreya altarpiece* (38.158.1a–n) dated 524 from the Northern Wei Dynasty; it shows figures from the Buddhist pantheon, including Maitreya, the Buddha of the Future. A 3C *funerary urn* (65.74.2a,b), with its upper portion decorated as a celestial city, was believed to contain the soul of the deceased.

THE T'ANG DYNASTY GALLERY (A.D. 618–906) contains objects from an era when China enjoyed political and cultural influence and its capital (modern Sian) at the end of the Silk Road was among the most technologically advanced cities on earth. Gold and silver vessels and ornaments, and jade belt plaques illustrate the wealth and cosmopolitan spirit of the age. Also of interest are a gilt-bronze statuette of the *Shakyamuni Buddha* (43.24.3) and *ceramic T'ang tomb figures* representing soldiers, servants, guardians, camels, and horses, which buried in tombs to serve the dead.

Return to the large LATER CHINESE BUDDHIST SCULPTURE GALLERY (A.D. 500–1500), opening off the center of the chronological galleries. The large *standing Maitreya* or Buddha of the Future (5C) stands on a lotus pedestal, wearing a monastic robe. The protuberance on his head, the webbed hands, and the elongated arms are divine attributes. The dry-lacquer *seated Buddha* (7C) was made by molding layers of lacquer-soaked cloth over a wooden base to build up the desired form.

In galleries of **Chinese Paintings** some 80 works of Chinese painting from the Sung, Yüan, Ming, and Ch'ing dynasties are shown on a rotating basis along with sculpture, other objects from the same dynasties, and special exhibitions. In the right or east gallery is a permanent display of jades.

The **Chinese Garden Court** between the two galleries is modeled on a 12C original. The courtyard was constructed in China and assembled here according to traditional methods by Chinese engineers and craftsmen. Like other Chinese gardens, this one is carefully designed so that contrasting principles—light and dark, hard and soft, high and low, crooked and straight, dynamic and static—balance and complement one another. The garden becomes a microcosm for the universe as construed by Chinese philosophers, ruled by the complementary principles of Yin and Yang.

In China, many rooms would have been built around the courtyard and, in prosperous families, many courtyards and sets of rooms would extend and enlarge the house as needed. Here the architecture consists of three typical garden structures: the viewing pavilion or *ting;* the winding walkway; and the small main hall (called the Ming Room), with formally arranged furniture.

Japanese Art.

Nine galleries contain Japanese painting, sculpture, ceramics, lacquer, textiles, metalwork, and woodblock prints spanning more than 4,000 years, from the 3rd millennium B.C. up to the present. Prints, textiles, and other fragile works are shown in rotation. The installation is roughly chronological, and the galleries conform to the Japanese sense of appropriateness, displaying objects in settings similar to the temples, houses, and palaces for which they were created.

PRE-BUDDHIST AND SHINTŌ ART. On the left side of this small gallery are objects from the nomadic Jōmon (cord marking) culture (5,000–c. 250 B.C.) and the subsequent Yayoi period (c. 250 B.C.–A.D. 300), including rare Jōmon tools and pottery, as well as *haniwa* figures (cylindrical clay sculptures) from the Kofun culture. In the years c. 300 B.C.–c. A.D. 300, enormous tomb mounds were built for the military aristocracy, and these *haniwa* figures were placed around the mounds, possibly to serve as guardians. On the other side of the gallery is a fierce bronze image of *Zaō Gongen* (11C), a tutelary deity who became the object of a cult incorporating both Buddhist and Shintō beliefs.

BUDDHIST ART. Different schools of Japanese Buddhism, first imported from China in the 6C, are reflected in the images of this room. A 12C *Dainichi Buddha* is seated upon a lotus pedestal in a contemplative posture; the dais supporting him represents Mt. Sumeru, the mystic center of the Buddhist universe. In a nearby corner is a ferocious standing 12C *Fudōo* (the name means "immovable"), a protective deity. An early 14C *Jizōo Bosatsu,* a deity from a sect known as Pure Land Buddhism, is seated on a lotus and dressed as a young monk in a patched robe.

KAMAKURA NARRATIVE PAINTING (paintings on exhibition rotated because of light-sensitivity). During the Heian (794–1185) and Kamakura periods (1185–1333), in which Japan assimilated the borrowings from Chinese of previous periods, a style of uniquely Japanese narrative painting developed. The Museum owns a 13C *Kannon Sutra,* a scroll with illustrations of a sacred text *(sutra)* describing the miracles performed by Kannon, a *bodhisattva* whose acts of mercy included saving believers from demons, fire, and flood. Another important group of illustrations from the Kamakura period is the *Kitano Tenjin Engi,* a set of scrolls remarkable for its depictions of Hell.

ART OF THE MUROMACHI PERIOD. The Muromachi period (1392–1568) saw the reintroduction of Chinese art, particularly monochromatic landscape paintings and screens, of the type shown in this gallery.

MOMOYAMA PAINTINGS AND OBJECTS. In the center of the galleries is Isamu Noguchi's sculptural *Water Stone* (1986), whose design evokes in contemporary terms Japan's tradition of symbolic, spiritual gardens.

THE SHOIN ROOM. Adjacent to the sculpture is a replica of a Momoyama period (1568–1615) *shoin,* modeled on a guest room at a temple outside Kyoto. The *shoin* originated in 14C Zen temples as a place of study for monks and later was adopted by the Ashikaga shoguns as an area for the display of treasured art objects. Here, as in its original setting, the *tokonoma* (recessed alcove) allows for the display and contemplation of art. The mid-17C *Ancient Plum,* attributed to Kanō Sansetsu, is displayed on the sliding doors.

EDO PAINTINGS AND OBJECTS. The arrangement of the objects and the architecture of the ceiling in this room are derived from mansions and palaces of the Edo period (1615–1868). Two early-18C works by Ogata Kōrin, *Eight Plank Bridge* (also called *The Irises*) and *Rough Waves*, are among the most famous in the collection. Also on display here are ceramics, lacquered objects, and later Edo paintings. Influenced by Chinese painting of the Ming and Ch'ing dynasties, these evoke the sophisticated urban ambiance of 18C Kyoto.

CERAMICS. This skylit gallery offers changing selections of Japanese ceramics, including wares from the Arita area of northern Kyushu.

DECORATIVE ARTS OF THE EDO PERIOD. Works from the late Edo period (19C) include textiles with painstaking embroidery, elegant lacquer ware, woodblock prints, and paintings (rotated through the galleries because of light-sensitivity). Among the artists represented in the collection is Hishikawa Moronobu, who popularized the *Ukiyo-e* ("floating world") tradition of printmaking—popular prints made by and for the lower classes of feudal society. Other prominent figures represented here are Kitagawa Utamaro, known for his portraits of women, and Katsushika Hokusai, known for his sensitivity to landscape, whose *Thirty-Six Views of Mt. Fuji* introduced a colorful, dramatic era of Japanese printmaking.

Arts of South and Southeast Asia.

The 18 galleries contain objects from India, Tibet, and Nepal, and from Thailand, Vietnam, Indonesia, Cambodia, Vietnam, and Burma. Objects date from the 3rd millennium B.C. to the 18C. Enter the galleries of **South Asian Art** from northeast corner of Early Chinese Sculpture (off Great Hall Balcony).

GALLERY 1. EARLY INDIA (c. 3000 B.C.–1C B.C.) Among the statues from this early period are those of nature gods and goddesses, dwarfish male figures called *yakshas* (e.g., 1988.354), and female figures called *yakshis* that represent fertility. A terracotta *plaque* (1990.281) depicts the goddess Durga, originally a fertility goddess, later enrolled in the Hindu pantheon. Also on view is a beautiful pair of *gold earrings* (1981.398.3,4) dating from 1C B.C., the most elaborate pieces of early Indian jewelry known to exist.

GALLERY 2. KUSHAN AND IKSHVAKU PERIODS (1C A.D.–4C A.D.). The Kushans were nomadic warriors who conquered much of northwest India, including Gandhara, in present-day Pakistan. They controlled the trade routes from Mediterranean cultures to China and their art reflects contact with Western cultures. *Standing Bodhisattva Maitreya* (1991.75); in Buddhism, bodhisattvas were beings who could have achieved nirvana, but remained instead on earth to help others achieve salvation. In its idealized features and the execution of the robe, this figure of the Buddha of the Future shows the influence of Greek art. *Head of a Bodhisattva* (1986.2; c. 2–3C). *The Gift of Anathpindada* (1987.142.1 ;2–3C), a plaque portraying an episode from the life of Buddha. *Model of a stupa* or building containing sacred relics (1985.387; c. 4C).

GALLERY 3. GUPTA PERIOD (4–7C). The arts flourished under the generous patronage of the politically powerful Gupta rulers of northern India. A sandstone *Standing Buddha* (1979.6; 5C) is one of the most important pieces in the collection; the flowing lines of the robe and the posture of repose suggest the spirituality achieved by the god. The *Serpent King and Queen* (1987, 415, 1,2; 5C) were nature deities; they are surrounded by many-headed cobras. *Krishna Battling the Horse Demon, Keshi* (1991. 300; 5C). The *Standing Buddha* (69.222) and *Seated Buddha* (1987.218.2), both made in the late 6–7C, show the influence of Gupta culture.

GALLERY 4. KASHMIR AND CONTIGUOUS REGIONS (5–11C). The artistic traditions of northwest India were influenced by the art of Central Asia, Iran, and the Greco-Buddhist art of Gandhara. *Vishnu as Vaikuntha Chaturmurti* (1991.301; 8C). *Crowned and Jeweled Buddha* (1970.297; 9C). *Standing Four-Armed Durga* (1984.488; 9C); the extra arms represent attributes of the goddess. *Linga with One Face* (1980.415; 9C). The *linga* (phallus) symbolized the creative power of the Hindu god Shiva; the face is that of the god as he makes himself manifest. *Bodhisattva Maitreya* (1978.536; c. 7C). *Padmapani Lokeshvara Seated in Meditation* (1974.273; 7C). Lokeshvara was a Buddhist deity, a form of the Bodhisattva of Infinite Compassion; the lotus *(padma)* is a symbol of transcendence.

GALLERY 5. KINGDOMS OF NORTHEAST INDIA (7–12C). *Standing Buddha* (1990.115; 8C). *Seated and Crowned Jeweled Buddha* (1993.311a, b; late 10C). *Shiva Seated with Uma* (1978.253; 9–10C). The statue shows the god and his consort; at the base are their two sons, Skanda, a warrior, and Ganesha, god of good fortune, represented with an elephant head. *Durga as the Slayer of the Demon Buffalo* (1993.7; 12C).

GALLERY 6. SOUTH INDIA (8–9C). PANDYA PERIOD. The Pandyas, Cholas, and Pallavas were the most important ruling families in South India. *Garuda Seated in Royal Ease* (1983.518; 2nd half 8C–early 9C). Garuda was Vishnu's mount; part of his wings can be seen behind his arms. *Seated Four-Armed Vishnu* (1984.296; 2nd half 8C–early 9C).

GALLERY 7. SOUTH INDIA. PALLAVA, CHOLA, AND VIJAYANAGAR PERIODS (8–14C). Chola artists were known for producing large-scale cast-metal sculpture of Hindu gods. *Standing Parvati* (57.51.3; 10C). *Shiva as Lord of the Dance* (1987.80.1; late 11C); this famous image shows Shiva in his three roles as creator, preserver, and destroyer of the universe. *Seated Saint, Karaikkal Ammaiyar* (1982.220.11; 14C). *Yashoda and Krishna* (1982.220.8; early 14C). Krishna, an incarnation of Vishnu, is shown as an infant nursed by his foster mother.

GALLERY 8. MEDIEVAL SCULPTURE GALLERY (8–13C). In northern India during the 8–13C many kingdoms flourished, whose arts derived from the styles of the Gupta period. *Chamunda, the Horrific Destroyer of Evil* (1989.121; 10–11C). Indian gods often have both peaceful and destructive aspects; Chamunda, the incarnation of female energy, is shown here as a bloodthirsty figure with a scorpion on her stomach. *Loving Couple* (1970.44; 13C); sexual pleasure was used as a metaphor for spiritual release.

GALLERY 9. KERALA AND SRI LANKA (5–14C). Small bronze figures.

GALLERY 10. INTERIOR CEILING OF A JAIN MEETING HALL (2nd half 16C). A fine example of Gujarati woodcarving.

GALLERY 11. LATER INDIA (15–19C). Shown in this gallery are changing exhibitions of Indian painting of the 17–18C. Muslim invaders began to establish themselves in India as early as the 8C, consolidating their capital at Delhi in the 12C. Their art is displayed in the Department of Islamic Art, but their artistic styles influenced contemporaneous Indian painting, including the miniatures shown here.

GALLERY 12. NEPAL (7–17C). Buddhism and Hinduism were early exported to Nepal, and Nepali sculpture shows the influence of northern Indian styles. *Standing Maitreya* (1982.220.12; 9–10C). The thrice-bent posture *(tribhanga)* is adapted from Indian sculpture; the sacred thread on the chest is a characteristic of Brahma. *Standing Padmapani* (1982.220.2; 11–12C). *Standing Tara* (66.179; 14C) and *Durga as the Slayer of the Demon Buffalo* (1986.498; 14–15C); the ornaments embellishing these figures are typical of Nepali sculpture.

GALLERY 13. TIBET (11–18C). *The Buddha Amoghasiddhi Attended by Bodhisattvas* (1991.74; 1st half 13C). This painted cloth *(thanka),* probably used in religious rites, shows one of the five Cosmic Buddhas, who were associated with different colors, different directions of the compass, and different steeds or mounts. Amoghasiddhi, Buddha of the North, is painted green; beneath his throne stands a group of *kinnaris* (bird-woman musicians).

A staircase leads down to the galleries of **Southeast Asian Art.**

GALLERY 14. SOUTHEAST ASIA, THAILAND, VIETNAM, AND INDONE-SIA (Bronze Age, c. 3rd millennium B.C.–4C A.D.). Terracotta vessels, including a ceremonial vessel in the form of an ax (2C B.C.). Sculptural works from the pre-Angkor period (6–9C) of Cambodia and Vietnam. Unlike Indian statues of the same era, these are carved in the round.

GALLERY 15. INDONESIA (5–15C). Indian culture was transported to the Indonesian archipelago by maritime traders who stopped at the islands en route to China. *Standing Buddha* (1993.64; 7–8C) from Kalimantan (Borneo). Figure of *Krishna on Garuda* (1992.135; 9C). The small bronze sculptures include lamps, water spouts, and images of Hindu and Buddhist deities. There are also Indonesian gold ornaments and a set of temple statues from the *Ngandjuk hoard* (discovered 1913). The statues hold ritual objects and were arranged to form mandalas.

GALLERY 16. THAILAND, CAMBODIA, AND VIETNAM. PRE-ANGKOR PERIOD (6–9C). The culture of mainland Southeast Asia was early influenced by contacts with Indian traders, who exported their religious systems and artistic styles. While reflecting Indian traditions, Cambodian and Vietnamese sculpture, e.g., *Standing Shiva* (1987.17; late 7C–early 8C), is remarkable for its sense of physicality and undecorated simplicity. The facial features of the *Mon Buddha* (1982.220.6; 7–8C) from Thailand reflect local ethnic types. The bronze *Four-Armed Avalokiteshvara* (67.234; 8C) has eyes inlaid with silver and black glass.

GALLERY 17. KHMER COURTYARD. ANGKOR PERIOD (9–13C) of Cambodia, Thailand, and Vietnam. The Khmer kings controlled Cambodia, Vietnam, and parts of Thailand for five centuries, during which artistic traditions remained relatively constant. *Avalokiteshvara, the Bodhisattva of Infinite Compassion, Seated in Royal Ease* (1992.336; late 10C–early 11C), one of the finest early Angkor bronzes to survive. *Kneeling Female* (1972.147; 11C). *Standing Four-Armed Male Deity* (1987.414; mid-11C). *Standing Female Deity* (1983.14; mid-11C). *Bust of Hevajra* (39.96.4; late 12C–early 13C). This many-headed deity was part of a guardian figure on a temple mound built by a king as a ceremonial center.

GALLERY 18. LATER THAILAND AND BURMA (12–16C). Burmese *Seated Amitayus* (23.8; 11–12C). From Thailand, a *Standing Buddha* (1991.423.5) and a *Seated Ganesha* (1983.512; both 15C). Also Thai earthenware from the Sawankhalok kilns.

Musical Instruments

HIGHLIGHTS

A group of rare Baroque violins, the oldest extant piano, and courtly instruments from the Middle Ages and the Renaissance.

The galleries are arranged in a rectangle, with instruments from Europe and the United States on the west (left) side, proceeding through the Americas and the Pacific on the north, the Near East, Africa, and Asia on the east. The instruments have been chosen for their technical and social importance as well as for their physical and tonal beauty.

HISTORY

In the 1870s, Mrs. Mary Crosby Brown, wife of a New York banker, began a collection of musical instruments, enlisting the help of missionaries, foreign officers of her husband's bank, scholars, and diplomats in her global search. By 1914 she had gathered some 3,000 instruments, the nucleus of the present collection.

EUROPEAN GALLERIES. The instruments are arranged by family or by material. There are ivory instruments, including a Baroque oboe, a *cornetto* (52.96.1), and a recorder. Horns include post horns originally used for signaling mail riders and hunting horns, as well as serpent and bass horns. In a central case is a beautiful glazed earthenware *hunting horn* (89.4.1150), possibly made to commemorate a special event; it is decorative rather than functional. Among the reed instruments are saxophones and Sarrusophones (resembling double-reeded saxophones), shawms, oboes, and bassoons. One case has a display of instruments that doubled as walking sticks, including a violin, bow and all, built into a slender cane whose handle converts into the chin rest. Further along are single-reed instruments, including basset horns (a kind of tenor clarinet), bass clarinets, and folk clarinets.

The elaborate marquetry of the Erard & Co. *grand piano* (59.76; c. 1840) shows its function as a status symbol for the wealthy; Liszt favored Erard pianos for their power and, by 19C standards, rapid action. The

Museum is fortunate to own a *piano* (89.4.1219) by Bartolommeo Cristofori, who invented the instrument (c. 1700) at the Medici court in Florence. This is the oldest piano still in existence (1720), one of three surviving from the Cristofori workshop, and it is still in playable condition. Also important is a Venetian *spinettino* (53.6) made in 1540 for the duchess of Urbino. The Italian inscription above the keyboard warns off the morally and musically unworthy: "I am rich in gold and rich in tone; if you lack goodness, leave me alone."

Among the stringed instruments are lutes, mandolins, citterns, guitars, and American folk instruments, as well as a freestanding case with *Baroque violins by Stradivari and Amati.* Antonio Stradivari was the pre-eminent Baroque violinmaker, whose instruments after three centuries maintain a glorious warmth of tone. Although most of the master's other instruments have been modified to produce a larger, more brilliant sound, the finest Stradivari violin (55.86) in the collection is unique in having been restored to its original appearance and tone.

GALLERIES OF THE AMERICAS, ASIA, AND AFRICA. Instruments from the Americas include pottery whistles, whistling jars, and rattles in human and animal forms. *Shaman rattles* (e.g., 89.4.615), carved by the Northwest Coast Indians of British Columbia, were made to depict animals conveying magical powers to the shaman through their tongues. The next cases contain instruments of the South Pacific, North Africa, the Near East, Iran, and Turkey. African instruments include whistles, drums, horns, Benin bells worn around the neck as a badge of rank, rattles, *mbiras* or thumb pianos whose tunable metal tongues produce different tones when plucked, and an imposing *marimba* (89.4.492) with gourd resonators.

Japanese instruments include fiddles, kotos, drums, bells, and gongs. Chinese and Korean instruments include a beautiful *sonorous stone* (89.4.64), carved of nephrite and veined to suggest patterns of energy inherent in the stone. Among the Tibetan instruments are trumpets made from the thigh bones of priests and executed criminals; not unexpectedly, they were assumed to call up fearsome magical powers. A *sesando* from Indonesia (89.4.1489), dating from the late 19C, is made of palm leaf, bamboo, and wire. Indian instruments include sitars in many forms, among them a *mayuri* (89.4.3516) with a tail of peacock feathers, as well as drums, trumpets, and other bowed and plucked stringed instruments.

GROUND FLOOR

The Costume Institute

The Costume Institute contains a collection of more than 60,000 articles of clothing and accessories from the 15C to the present. Garments range from high-style urban garb to regional costumes from Asia, Africa, Europe, and the Americas, from Dior gowns to bullfighters' capes, from tribal headgear to the dress (complete with knife hole) in which the empress Elizabeth of Austria was stabbed.

The Institute not only documents the taste of the past but serves as a resource for designers, fashion illustrators, and craftsmen. It has storerooms, private study rooms, a library, and a conservation room. The library (open to students and researchers by appointment only) contains reference works on costume design and history, fashion journals, pattern books, photographs, and fashion plates from the 19–20C.

The collection is shown in a rotating permanent exhibition in the ground-floor galleries, which were redesigned and reopened in 1992.

HISTORY

The Costume Institute began (1937) as the Museum of Costume Art, founded by a group interested in costume and theater. The original nucleus of the collection came from the private holdings of Irene Lewisohn and her sister Alice Lewisohn Crowley, and from costumes donated by theater designers Aline Bernstein and Lee Simonson. In 1946, the Museum moved to the Metropolitan where it was reincarnated as the Costume Institute. It enjoyed what many recall as a Golden Age during the 1970s when Diana Vreeland, then editor of *Vogue* magazine, served as special consultant and oversaw lavish exhibitions that became star-spangled social events as well as artistic milestones in the city's cultural life.

EXHIBITION PROGRAM

Past exhibitions have consisted of lavish displays, such as "Costumes of Royal India," which placed on view court costumes and textiles from former ruling families of several princely states, including a well-dressed elephant with princely trappings. "Diana Vreeland: Immoderate Style" celebrated a woman who was both a driving force behind the Costume Institute and one of the great tastemakers of 20C America.

ROOF GARDEN

Outdoor Sculpture Garden

The Roof Garden, accessible from the galleries for 20th Century Art, is open May to November, weather permitting. Designed to accommodate large-scale pieces of modern sculpture, it offers, in addition to yearly changing exhibits from the permanent collection, a stunning aerial view of Central Park and the skyline surrounding it.

Impressive among recent exhibitions was an installation of eight bronze sculptures by Auguste Rodin, highlighted by *The Burghers of Calais,* perhaps the sculptor's greatest monument.

HISTORY

The Metropolitan Museum of Art was founded (1870) at a time when the city's financial barons, profiting from the city's rise to eminence after the Civil War, turned their attention to culture. While these civic leaders could see how a local art museum was indirectly good for business, they also believed in the moral power of art to educate and improve the masses. The Metropolitan's first president, John Taylor Johnston, who owed his wealth to railroads, oversaw the negotiations with the state (which authorized the construction of a museum in Central Park) and with the city (which awarded the Museum a handsome tax abatement). Eventually the city took title to the building, while ceding its contents to the trustees, the arrangement that persists today.

The first acquisitions came from the collection of William T. Blodgett, a founder of *The Nation* magazine, who had bought paintings by Anthony Van Dyck, Salomon van Ruysdael, Nicolas Poussin, and Francesco Guardi.

Johnston was followed in office by the controversial Italian-born Luigi Palma di Cesnola, who had fought in the American Civil War and later became consul in Cyprus. Convinced that Cyprus was the cradle of Greek civilization, Cesnola sent back to the Museum tons of Cyprian antiquities, some of which are now marshaled along the corridor leading to the restaurants.

It was during the closing decades of the 19C that the Museum truly began to capitalize on the national wealth. In 1888, H. B. Marquand, another railroad financier, donated 37 paintings, which he had bought for that express purpose; among them were Van Dyck's *James Stewart* and Vermeer's *Young Woman with a Water Jug.* About a decade later, Jacob S. Rogers, a locomotive manufacturer known as Paterson, N.J.'s, meanest man (an adjective that described both his lack of generosity and his behavior toward his relatives), left his estate of some $5 million to the Metropolitan, disappointing family members but delighting the Museum, which now took its place among the ranks of wealthy institutions.

Cesnola, who resisted all efforts to unseat him from his directorship, died in 1904 and was succeeded by Sir Caspar Purdon Clarke, who was pried away from London's Victoria and Albert Museum by the relentless J. Pierpont Morgan. Under Clarke's guidance and later as director himself, Edward Robinson, a classicist by training, oversaw important acquisitions in ancient art, notably the *Old Market Woman,* a Hellenistic statue found during construction in Rome.

Even after Clarke's appointment, Morgan continued to exercise his influence on the Museum. He brought the mighty collectors of his day—e.g., Henry Clay Frick and Stephen Harkness—to serve on the Museum's board and engineered the appointment of art historian Roger Fry as curator of paintings. Fry made significant purchases and recommended paintings by the French Impressionists, who in 1907 had not yet achieved the popularity that would later drive up their prices. When Morgan died (1913), he left a dazzling collection which focused on precious objects (jewels, gold, rare books, illuminated medieval manuscripts), most of which did not come to the Metropolitan because the Museum had not acted to house Morgan's treasures as the great financier saw fit. Fortunately, Morgan's son later gave the Museum some 40% of the holdings that remained after various sales and bequests, a gift that now comprises a significant part of the medieval collection.

In recent decades the Metropolitan has undertaken an intense program of expansion in its efforts to become a truly encyclopedic art museum, rather than one that reflects the spectacular holdings of a few great collectors. Proving its founders' financial instincts correct, the Metropolitan is today the city's single largest tourist attraction, and a great financial and artistic power in the cultural life of New York.

THE BUILDING

As the collections have grown, so has the Museum building—from modest Ruskinian Gothic beginnings to its present mix of the major architectural styles of the past century.

The rear facade (1874–80; Calvert Vaux and Jacob Wrey Mould), in orange brick and white limestone, was originally the front entrance, facing Central Park. Most of the original building has disappeared beneath new additions, but parts of the facade can be seen from the Lehman Wing and the European Sculpture Court.

Later wings were added on the north and south (1894, Arthur L. T. Tuckerman; 1888, Theodore Weston), which have either been demolished or covered by later expansion. The architectural segment that most people identify with the Museum, the central Fifth Ave pavilion—the present front entrance to the Museum—was designed by Richard Morris Hunt (1902) and executed by his son Richard Howland Hunt. To this facade in turn were added north and south wings facing the avenue (1911 and 1913) by the reigning architects of the day, McKim, Mead & White. Recent expansion undertaken by Roche, Dinkeloo & Assocs has resulted in the redesign of the Fifth Ave stairs and the addition of glass-walled wings on the other facades: the Lehman Wing (1975) to the rear; the Sackler Wing (1979) to the north; and the Rockefeller Wing (1982) to the south. The Kravis Wing, which houses European decorative arts, opened in 1990.

The Pierpont Morgan Library (50)

29 East 36th St (Madison Ave), New York 10016. Tel: (212) 685-0008.

ADMISSION: Open Tues–Fri 10:30–5; Sat 10:30–6; Sun noon–6. Closed Mon, national holidays. Suggested donation.

Lectures, publications including books, catalogues, and facsimiles. Gallery talks, guided tours of period rooms, concerts, seminars.

✗ Café serves lunch and afternoon tea in the Garden Court.

▥ Book Shop (in Morgan House) with unusual offerings of books and children's books, toys, catalogues, prints, postcards, and gift items.

♿ Limited wheelchair accessibility; ramp at entrance, but there is a seven-step flight up to the rooms of the original library.

🚫 No photography. No strollers.

🚇 IRT Lexington Ave local (train 6) to 33rd St. IND 6th Ave local or express (B, D, or F train) to 34th St. BMT Broadway express or local (N or R train) to 34th St.

🚌 M1 downtown on 5th Ave and Park Ave South, uptown on Park Ave South and Madison Ave. M2, M3, or M4 downtown on 5th Ave, uptown on Madison Ave. M5 downtown on 5th Ave, uptown on 6th Ave. M6 downtown on 7th Ave / Broadway, uptown on 6th Ave. M16 or M34 crosstown on 34th St. Q32 downtown on 5th Ave, uptown on Madison Ave between 32nd St and 60th St.

The Pierpont Morgan Library, whose collections were largely gathered by the legendary financier J. Pierpont Morgan (1837–1913), was given (1924) by his son, J. P. Morgan, Jr., to the American public as a museum and reference library. It is one of the great repositories of culture in the western hemisphere, known for its Renaissance manuscripts, Old Master drawings (artists before 1800), early and later printed books, early children's books, and ancient written records, notably Assyrian and Babylonian seals, cuneiform tablets, and Egyptian papyri.

HIGHLIGHTS

The West Room (Mr. Morgan's study) reflects Morgan's own personal tastes.

The East Room with its floor-to-ceiling bookcases gives a stunning hint of the riches of the collection. It is difficult to mention only a few highlights, but among the medieval and Renaissance manuscripts the *Stavelot Triptych,* the *Lindau Gospels,* the *Hours of Catherine of Cleves,* and the *Farnese Hours* are undisputed treasures and frequently on view.

Among the printed books, the *Gutenberg Bibles*—of which the Library possesses three, more than any other institution in the world—continue to fascinate both specialists and ordinary viewers.

HISTORY

At a time when other millionaires found themselves attracted to French landscapes or Old Master paintings, J. Pierpont Morgan used his fortune to amass (in the true sense of that word) not only paintings and sculpture but rare books and manuscripts, porcelains, majolica, faïence, fine gold work, and enamel. Morgan's passion

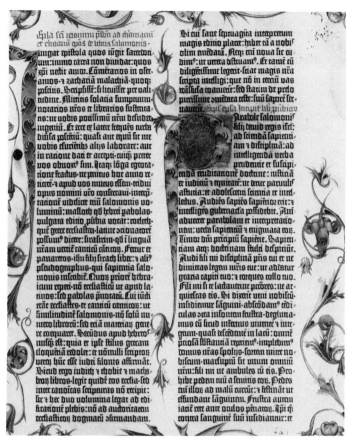

A page from one of the three Gutenberg Bibles acquired by J. Pierpont Morgan. The holdings of the Pierpont Morgan Library are so remarkable that its first director remarked that it contains "everything but the original tablets of the Ten Commandments."
(The Pierpont Morgan Library. Photo: David A. Loggie)

for collecting began when, at age 14, he asked Millard Fillmore for his autograph and received it in an envelope personally franked by the President. As a student in Switzerland and Germany, Morgan began collecting bits of stained glass from old churches and cathedrals; some of these shards are now embedded in the windows of the West Room.

However, it was not until his father died in a carriage accident on the Riviera in 1890 that Morgan's collecting activities began in earnest. During the next decade he purchased a Gutenberg Bible on vellum, the 1459 Mainz Psalter, the famous 9C Lindau Gospels with their spectacular jeweled binding, four Shakespeare Folios, and original autograph manuscripts by Keats and Dickens, among others.

Eventually, when his own good-sized brownstone on the corner of East 36th St and Madison Ave would no longer contain these and other rapidly accumulating treasures, Morgan hired Charles Follen McKim of McKim, Mead & White to design a "little museum building to house his books and collections."

THE BUILDING

Though the original Library was, as Morgan requested of his architect, "a little museum building" whose modest proportions were consistent with the residential scale of the neighborhood, it is often considered the pinnacle of McKim's career. He and his partner Stanford White were leading exponents of the American Renaissance style, an architectural movement that sought models in the monuments of the past and embodied the notion that America had inherited the spirit of the Renaissance and its intellectual and material energies. Pierpont Morgan, not surprisingly, subscribed to these notions.

When the Library became a public museum and research library after Morgan's death, more space was necessary. Morgan's brownstone was torn down (1926) and Benjamin Wistar Morris designed the Annex (1928).

In 1988, the Library purchased the former home of Morgan's son, J. P. Morgan, Jr., on the southeast corner of Madison Ave and 37th St. Built in 1852 for copper king Anson Phelps Stokes, the 45-room brownstone (with its 2,000-bottle-capacity wine cellar) had been acquired in 1904 by Pierpont Morgan for his son, along with the brownstone between the two houses, which Morgan tore down to make a garden. Today, Morgan House (renovated 1991; Voorsanger & Assocs) serves as the Library's education center (with a lecture hall in the former ballroom) and also contains the Book Shop. Between Morgan House and the Library is a glass-enclosed indoor Garden Court (also 1991; Voorsanger & Assocs), which replaces the outdoor garden.

EXTERIOR. The Library is neo-classical in style. The facade was inspired by the Villa Giulia and the Villa Medici in Rome. Sculptured panels designed by Adolph A. Weinman below the frieze represent (east wing, right to left), Truth with Literature, Philosophy, History, Oratory, and Astronomy, and (west wing) Music, accompanied by Fame, Inspiring the Arts of Architecture, Sculpture, Painting, Ceramics, and Textiles. The sphinx in the right panel has been said to wear McKim's profile and serve as his signature because Morgan forbade any signed work; in fact, McKim had a prominent walrus mustache and Weinman signed one of the panels on the facade.

The lionesses guarding the doorway are by Edward Clark Potter, who later placed another more famous pair before the New York Public Library a half dozen blocks uptown.

INTERIOR. The visitors' entrance is part of the 1928 expansion. A corridor leads to the original Library, which was physically quite small, consisting of the domed entrance foyer (the Rotunda), flanked by the East Room (the original library), the West Room (Morgan's study), and the North Room (the librarian's office).

The WEST ROOM was once called "the most beautiful room in America"; surely it is, even now, one of the most opulent. At one end is Morgan's custom-made desk, on whose surface weighty transactions in finance and art were consummated. The marble mantelpiece is ascribed to the studio of Florentine sculptor Desiderio da Settignano. Morgan purchased the antique carved ceiling in Florence and had it reassembled and installed here.

Displayed in the room are some of Morgan's favorite paintings and objets d'art of bronze, faïence, and metalwork, many of them notable for their intricate workmanship.

Paintings. Clockwise from doorway, EAST WALL: Hans Memling, *Portrait of a Man with a Pink* (c. 1475), the most famous painting in the collection. A pair of unidentified donor portraits by Memling flank Cima da Conegliano, *The Virgin and Child with St. Catherine and St. John the Baptist;* a workshop variant of Botticelli's *Madonna of the Magnificat;* a *Portrait of a Knight of Malta,* dated 1499, by Macrino d'Alba.

SOUTH WALL (fireplace wall): Francesco Francia, *The Virgin and Child with Sts. Dominic and Barbara* (c. 1500). Pietro Perugino, *Madonna and Saints Adoring the Child.*

WEST WALL (opposite doorway): The double portrait on the bookcase of *Martin Luther and his wife, Katharina von Bora,* was painted in 1525, the year of their marriage; various replicas were painted after the original in the workshop of Lucas Cranach.

NORTH WALL: Workshop of Giovanni Bellini, *The Virgin and Child with Four Saints and a Kneeling Donor* (c. 1505); *Portrait of a Moor* (c. 1570) from the workshop of Tintoretto.

Sculpture and Objets d'Art. The selection of objects displayed suggests the full range of Morgan's collecting interests. The bronze *Running Eros,* a Hellenistic Greek original, dates from 1C or 2C B.C., and was one of Morgan's favorite pieces. It was found in the ruins of a villa buried by the eruption of Mt Vesuvius in A.D. 79. The wooden sculpture of *St. Elizabeth* dates from the early 16C and was carved in Ulm, southern Germany. On the bookcase is a deep red 17C Chinese porcelain vase, sometimes called the "Morgan Ruby." The Etruscan *cista* (c. 200 B.C.), a bronze container meant to hold jewelry or cosmetics, has a cover whose handle is shaped like a woman acrobat. Morgan's archeological interests are represented by a Babylonian (2300 B.C.) copper sculpture of a *male basket-carrier,* identified as King Ur-Nammu. A faïence *pilgrim bottle,* by Antoine Sigalon (c. 1524–90), a Huguenot craftsman, is decorated with Catholics shown with the heads of monkeys and asses. The marble bas-relief of the *Madonna and Child with Cherubim* was executed by the Florentine sculptor Antonio Rossellino. The bronze *candelabrum* on Morgan's desk is by French sculptor Antoine-Louis Barye.

The decoration of the ROTUNDA is based on but not copied from classical models, with ceiling paintings executed by H. Siddons Mowbray, who traveled to Rome to study Italian Renaissance works. The blue-and-white stucco relief carvings on the apse at the north end of the room were modeled after Raphael's work in the Villa Madama in Rome. The lunettes over the main entrance and the doors to the East and West Rooms, inspired by Pintoricchio's decorations for the Borgia apartments in the Vatican, represent the great ages of poetry.

The work in the central part of the ceiling, inspired by the decoration of Raphael's Stanza della Segnatura, one of the papal rooms in the Vatican, depicts Art, Science, Knowledge, and Religion. The marbles on the floor were brought from ancient quarries in Africa and Italy. Morgan especially liked the deep purple of imperial porphyry and had the large disc in the center of the room carefully delivered by Wells Fargo. The columns include two of lapis lazuli and, at the east and west ends of the room, beautifully veined gray-green columns of an Italian marble known as cipollino, whose striations may indeed suggest the rings on an onion. The bronze portrait bust of *Alfonso d'Avalos, Marquis del Vasto,* by Leone Leoni, wears the Order of the Golden Fleece. The terracotta relief of *The Madonna and Child* over the marble Florentine door is from the workshop of Luca della Robbia; the ones in the hallway by the WEST ROOM are from the workshop of members of the della Robbia family and their followers. The Renaissance furniture—chairs and *cassoni* (marriage chests)—was purchased from the Strozzi family for Morgan and dates from the 15C to the early 16C.

In the EAST ROOM, where Morgan originally kept most of his books, are tiers of rare books and changing exhibitions of autograph manuscripts, music manuscripts, printed books, and medieval and Renaissance manuscripts. The bookcases contain portions of the printed books collection. One of the Gutenberg Bibles is always on display. Above the marble mantelpiece is a 16C Brussels tapestry depicting *The Triumph of Avarice,* with a Latin inscription that warns us that as Tantalus is ever thirsty in the midst of water, so the miser is always desirous of riches. It belongs to a series of *The Seven Deadly Sins,* designed by Pieter van Aelst, father-in-law of Pieter Bruegel the Elder.

The Zodiacal signs in the ceiling decoration of the East Room, also by H. Siddons Mowbray, refer to important dates in Morgan's life. Flanking the door are Morgan's birth sign, Aries, and that of the date of his second marriage in May 1865, Gemini, with Mercury signifying Wednesday as the day of the week. Directly across is Aquarius with the Muse of Tragedy, an emblem that marks the death of Morgan's young first wife in February 1862.

PERMANENT COLLECTION

Belle da Costa Green, the first director of the Library, remarked that it "apparently contains everything but the original tablets of the Ten Commandments." Although this statement is exaggerated, the range and scope of the Library's holdings are astonishing. The main areas of collecting include Medieval and Renaissance Manuscripts, Prints and Drawings, Autograph Manuscripts and Letters, Printed Books, Music Manuscripts, and Ancient Cylinder Seals.

Among the illuminated manuscripts are the *Farnese Hours* (1546) by Giulio Clovio (1498–1578), probably the last of the great Italian illuminated manuscripts. The *Hours of Catherine of Cleves* (c. 1440), a masterpiece of Dutch illumination, is remarkable for showing humble scenes from daily life, e.g., "The Holy Family at Supper," with Joseph sitting by the fire eating porridge. The purchase of the *Lindau Gospels* (back cover late 8C, front cover c. 880), Morgan Manuscript 1, marked the beginning of Morgan's career as the country's greatest collector of medieval manuscripts. The metal covers encrusted with jewels and the 9C illuminated manuscript are outstanding examples of Carolingian book arts. The *Stavelot Triptych* (c. 1150s), intended as a reliquary for fragments of the True Cross, was commissioned by Wibald, abbot of the Belgian abbey of Stavelot. Opulent with enamels, gems, and metalwork, the wings of the triptych are decorated with roundels that tell the legend of the True Cross.

Among the early printed books, in addition to the Gutenberg Bibles, are works by Gutenberg's associates, Fust and Schoeffer; England's first printer, William Caxton; and the great Italian Renaissance printer, Aldus Manutius. Later works include the First Folio edition (1623) of Shakespeare's collected plays; the first printing, first state, of the Declaration of Independence; and William Morris's *The Works of Geoffrey Chaucer* (1896), printed by the Kelmscott Press.

Master drawings include work by artists from Leonardo and Michelangelo to Degas and Matisse. The Library owns eight drawings by Albrecht Dürer, including *Adam and Eve* (1504), a celebrated work made in preparation for the engraving *Fall of Man.* William Blake is represented by a series of watercolor illustrations for the *Book of Job,* as well as illustrations for Milton's *L'Allegro* and *Il Penseroso.* The Library owns an outstanding collection of etchings and drawings by Rembrandt, including two drawings of his wife Saskia asleep.

Among the music manuscripts are autographs of Brahms's First Symphony and Mahler's Fifth Symphony, Beethoven's Violin Sonata in G major, Opus 96, four Schubert Impromptus and the *Winterreise,* Offenbach's operetta *Robinson Crusoe,* and Stravinsky's *Perséphone.*

Highlights among the autograph manuscripts and letters include Charles Perrault's manuscript for *The Tales of Mother Goose* (1695) and Charles Dickens's *A Christmas Carol* (1843). John Milton's autograph manuscript of *Paradise Lost,* Book I, in the hand of various amanuenses, is the sole remnant of the manuscript from which the first edition was printed and one of the most important British literary manuscripts in America. The collection of American manuscripts includes Twain's *Pudd'nhead Wilson,* Thoreau's *Journal,* and Steinbeck's *Travels with Charley.* There are letters autographed by Elizabeth I, Napoleon, George Washington, Thomas Jefferson, and such artists as Piranesi, Manet, Seurat, and Picasso.

In 1992 the Library received the *Gilder Lehrman Collection,* one of the finest private collections of American historical manuscripts in the world, whose treasures include a letter by George Washington, signed copies of the Emancipation Proclamation and the Thirteenth Amendment, and a signed copy of Gerald Ford's pardon of Richard Nixon.

EXHIBITION PROGRAM

The PERMANENT COLLECTIONS GALLERIES (created in the 1991 expansion) contain rotating exhibits from the Library's collections. On a given day, visitors might view a Gutenberg Bible, autograph letters penned by Mozart, illuminated medieval manuscripts, jeweled bindings from the time of Charlemagne, historic English children's books, or Mark Twain's response to Pierpont Morgan's request for the original manuscript of *Pudd'nhead Wilson* (Twain said he was gratified to "have something of mine placed elbow to elbow with that august company which you have gathered together").

The Library also mounts changing thematic exhibitions drawn from its own collections. A major exhibition of British landscape drawings offered exquisite watercolors by Turner, Gainsborough, and Constable. A major show on Johann Gutenberg's development of printing with movable types offered a full-scale model of Gutenberg's press (on loan from Mainz, Germany) as well as all three of the Library's Gutenberg Bibles.

The exhibition program also offers shows that draw on material from other institutions. In the future as in the past visitors will have the opportunity to examine such treasures as Mozartiana from the British Library, major drawings from Florence's Uffizi Galleries, and spectacular architectural renderings from the École des Beaux-Arts in Paris.

The Morris-Jumel Mansion (107)

65 Jumel Terrace (bet. 160th / 162nd Sts near Edgecombe Ave), New York 10032. Tel: (212) 923-8008.

ADMISSION: Open Wed–Sun 10–4. Closed Mon, Tues, major holidays. Admission charge. Children under 10 free, if accompanied by an adult.

Group tours by appointment, workshops, lectures, craft demonstrations; space rental for small private parties.

✘ No restaurant; picnicking permitted on grounds.

🛍 Sales desk with postcards, T-shirts, gift items.

♿ Not accessible to wheelchairs.

⊘ No flash photography.

🚇 IND 6th Ave express (B train) weekdays or 8th Ave local (C train) weekends to 163rd St / St. Nicholas Ave.

🚌 M3 or M18 uptown on Madison Ave, downtown on 5th Ave. M101 uptown on 3rd Ave, downtown on Lexington Ave.

Built before the Revolutionary War (1765) as a country home, the Morris-Jumel Mansion (opened as a museum 1904) briefly served as George Washington's headquarters during his unsuccessful defense of New York City in 1776. Later it was the home of Eliza Jumel—eccentric wife of a wealthy shipper and merchant, favorite of Napoleon's court, and, briefly, wife of Aaron Burr. Situated in a small, high park with a fine view, the house has been restored and furnished with period furniture from the 18–19C, some of it formerly belonging to the Jumels.

HISTORY

One of the city's few remaining pre-Revolutionary structures (1765), the Mansion has a history which is both glamorous and rich in anecdote.

Lt.-Col. Roger Morris, the Mansion's builder, belonged to one of early New York's patrician families; he served in the French and Indian War as an aide de camp to General Edward Braddock and enjoyed the friendship of George Washington. Morris married Mary Philipse, member of a well-landed family of Dutch origins; before her marriage she had been romantically linked, by rumor at least, to Washington.

In 1765 the couple built their 130-acre estate, called Mount Morris, on one of the highest pieces of ground in Manhattan, from which they could see the Hudson River on the west and the Harlem River on the east without looking past their own lands. Like many other wealthy landowners in the city, Roger Morris was a Loyalist, sympathetic to England and anxious to preserve the status quo. When the Revolution threatened, he left for England, while his wife and their children departed for Westchester County.

In 1776, after disastrous losses in battle, Washington withdrew to the northern part of Manhattan and established his headquarters in the Morris home between Sept 14 and Oct 18, as he planned his unsuccessful defense of the city.

When New York fell, the British took this fine and comfortable house for their own use. At the war's end, the American government confiscated the estate, the fate of much Loyalist property, and the house began a downward course. By 1790 it was Calumet Hall, a tavern on the Post Road to Albany.

In 1810, Stephen Jumel, a successful wine merchant from France, bought the property for $100,000 and had it restored. Jumel's wife, née Eliza (Betsy) Bowen of Providence, R.I., was said to be brilliant and beautiful, but had a reputation for an imperious tongue, a scandalous love life, and boundless social ambition. She was Jumel's mistress before she was his wife, and wagging tongues hinted that she had feigned a deathbed crisis to lure him into wedlock. The marriage made her one of America's richest women.

The Jumels spent considerable time in France, where they supported Napoleon and enjoyed the favors of his court. Here Eliza's talents were more cheerfully received than they were in conservative upper-crust New York. During her various stays in France, Eliza Jumel acquired Empire furniture, an extensive wardrobe, and Francophilic tastes.

In 1832, Jumel was injured in a carriage accident and died, leaving his wife a rich widow—a fact not lost on Aaron Burr, who had known her since before her marriage to Jumel. In 1833, the two were married; he was 77 and she was about 60. The marriage was stormy and short. Burr only lived in the house for about a month; Mme Jumel filed for divorce, a process that became final, ironically, the day of Burr's death in 1836. She continued to live in the house, becoming more eccentric and reclusive, until she died in 1865 at the age of about 93.

Today the Mansion belongs to New York City, which cares for the exterior and the grounds, while a private association, Morris Jumel Mansion Inc., maintains the interiors and the furnishings. In 1916 the association purchased at auction much of the Jumel family furniture; later pieces were donated by benefactors.

THE BUILDING

Morris's father, also named Roger, was an English architect and builder, who may have been responsible for its two exceptional features, the Palladian portico and the Octagon Room, both unusual in this country when the house was built.

EXTERIOR. The wide wooden clapboards and wooden corner quoins cover a brick shell. The shutters and the present front door with its Federal-style sidelights were installed by the Jumels when they remodeled their house in 1810. But the Palladian portico, once thought to be an addition, is now known to be original.

FIRST FLOOR. A recessed staircase and handsome arches with keystones adorn the ENTRANCE HALL. The signed Duncan Phyfe sofa has elaborately carved legs; the marble-topped pier table belonged to Mme Jumel.

The FRONT PARLOR, one of the most formal rooms in the house, witnessed the marriage of Mme Jumel and Aaron Burr. The American Empire parlor suite with its black-and-gold chairs was commissioned by Mme Jumel in 1826, while the drop-lid mahogany and satinwood desk (c. 1820) belonged to Burr.

The DINING ROOM, used for formal occasions, has a set of 12 Duncan Phyfe chairs and settee with reeded legs and carved back rails. The 19C Chinese export porcelain belonged to Mme Jumel. The portrait of *Colonel John Chester* was painted (1790) by Joseph Steward. Chester was an aide de camp to George Washington who had earlier distinguished himself at the Battle of Bunker Hill. His wife Elizabeth is portrayed in a companion painting.

The BACK PARLOR, a family sitting room, contains furniture including Mme Jumel's shield-back New York chair, from the late 18C. The OCTA-GON ROOM has been restored to its appearance when the house was built. The Morris family would have used it for entertaining—for games, perhaps, or dancing. The chair rail is original; the pattern of the hand-painted wallpaper has no repeats.

SECOND FLOOR. The upstairs HALL features a portrait of Mme Jumel in her 80s with her two grandchildren, William and Eliza Jumel Chase. (The Jumels, childless, adopted Eliza's stepniece Mary, who married a man named Nelson Chase.) Near the front of the hall is a large pair of carved, gilded wooden wings believed to have decorated Mme Jumel's carriage. Though she claimed Napoleon had given them to her, their workmanship suggests that they were made in this country.

MME JUMEL'S BEDROOM contains furniture brought back from Paris in 1826, when she restyled the interiors to reflect her Napoleonic lean-ings. Napoleon himself is said to have slept in the mahogany sleigh bed when he was First Consul. The "dolphin" chair near the doorway, with its carved dolphins on the arms, also belonged to Napoleon. The slipper chairs near the fireplace first belonged to Queen Hortense of the Nether-lands, daughter of Josephine Bonaparte and mother of Napoleon III. Nearby is her DRESSING ROOM (under restoration).

AARON BURR'S BEDROOM is decorated in the style of the 1830s, the period of his brief marriage to Eliza Jumel. George Washington may have used the OFFICE at the end of the hall during his stay in the house, enjoying its strategic view of the rivers. It is furnished with 18C English and American furniture.

John M. Mossman Collection of Locks (51)

20 West 44th St (bet. 5th / 6th Aves), New York 10036. Tel: (212) 840-1840.

ADMISSION: Open Mon–Fri 9–5. Closed weekends, the month of July, and major holidays. Free.

Permanent exhibition.

✘ No restaurant.

🏛 No gift shop.

♿ Limited wheelchair access; steps up from street. Elevator to 2nd floor.

🚇 IRT Lexington Ave express or local (train 4, 5, or 6) to Grand Central Station. IRT Flushing line (train 7) to 5th Ave.

🚍 M1, M2, M3, M4, Q32 downtown on 5th Ave, uptown on Madison Ave. M5 downtown on 5th Ave, uptown on 6th Ave. M7, uptown on 6th Ave, downtown on Broadway / 7th Ave. M104 downtown on Broadway, cross-town on 42nd St. M42 crosstown on 42nd St.

The J. M. Mossman Collection of Locks is the fruit of the collecting passion of a member of the General Society of Mechanics and Tradesmen, in whose building the locks are displayed.

HISTORY

One of the oldest institutions in the city is the General Society of Mechanics and Tradesmen of the City of New York, founded in 1785 as a professional society. Before the days of free public education, the Society offered free instruction to apprentices in the trades, and in 1820 it formed a library which circulated books free to members. By the end of the 19C, when the Society moved to its present location, it also offered courses in stenography, typewriting, and freehand drawing to both men and women.

PERMANENT COLLECTION

Mossman (1850–1912), a member of the Society, gathered the approximately 400 locks that make up the collection, which is installed in weighty old-fashioned cases on a gallery above the Library. The locks, mostly intended for safes and strongboxes rather than for doors, range from ancient and Renaissance locks to spring-tension locks, electric locks, time locks, calendar time locks, and even a liquid time lock. The Very Complicated Lock more than justifies its name. Visitors may explore the intricacies of lock design with a little book, *The Lure of the Lock*, supplied as a guide to the collection.

THE BUILDING

The Society is housed in the first important private school building (1891; Lamb & Rich) in the city. It belonged originally to the Berkeley School, a prep school for boys, which emphasized physical education and military drill along with academic courses. Today the Library of the Mechanics and Tradesmen Society occupies the former gymnasium and drill hall on the ground floor.

El Museo del Barrio (80)

1230 Fifth Ave (bet. 104th / 105th Sts), New York 10029. Tel: (212) 831-7272.

ADMISSION: Open Wed–Sun, 11–5. Closed Mon, Tues, and holidays. Voluntary contribution. Children under 12 free.

Gallery talks by appointment, lectures and symposia on Hispanic art and culture, concerts, film and theater festivals, school programs.

✗ No restaurant.

🗋 Posters and catalogues. No gift shop.

&. Accessible to wheelchairs; ramp at 5th Ave entrance.

⊘ No photography.

🚇 IRT Lexington Ave local (train 6) to 103rd St.

🚌 M1, M2, M3, or M4 uptown on Madison Ave, downtown on 5th Ave. M19 crosstown on 96th St.

Founded (1969) as a neighborhood museum in an East Harlem school-room, El Museo del Barrio is today the only museum in the United States devoted to preserving and documenting the art of Puerto Rico and Latin America, both traditional folk arts and the contemporary urban art of the *barrio,* the city's Spanish-speaking enclave.

PERMANENT COLLECTION

The permanent collection, shown in changing exhibitions, contains pre-Columbian objects, paintings and works on paper, films, sculpture, photography, and folk arts. Permanently on view are selections from the extensive collection of *Santos de Palo,* carved and painted wooden figures of saints usually used for home devotions. The collection contains *Santos* from Mexico, Guatemala, Colombia, Spain, and the Philippines, most dating from the 19C and early 20C.

EXHIBITION PROGRAM

Each year, El Museo mounts about four exhibitions of painting, sculpture, photography, and graphic arts. One emphasis of the program is on disseminating the work of contemporary Puerto Rican and Latin-American artists, especially those living and working in New York. Noteworthy was a 20-year retrospective of *El Taller Boricua* (The Puerto Rican Workshop), an artists' collaborative formed (1969) during a period of cultural and political activism to address the artistic and cultural problems facing Puerto Rican artists in New York.

Other exhibitions concentrate on folk art, craft, or the artistic heritage of the Puerto Rican community. "Folklore!" displayed traditional arts that originated in Cuba, the Dominican Republic, and Puerto Rico, but were made in New York by artists who for the most part had learned from their parents. Included were handcrafted musical instruments, little black rag dolls *(conguitas),* piñatas, masks and costumes, and paper sculpture.

Finally, the exhibitions at El Museo emphasize history and community, the background and life of the people of El Barrio whom it serves. One show documented photographically the city's Puerto Rican community from the '30s to the present; others have looked at the *bodegas* as key social centers for the Latino community in New York. "Emblems of His City: José Campeche and San Juan," presented in conjunction with the Metropolitan's Campeche exhibit, examined the secular and religious painting of this 18C Puerto Rican painter. The "International Art Show for the End of World Hunger," which traveled through the United States stopping at El Museo before continuing on to Europe, placed Latin-American artists in an international context, focusing on a theme of great importance to the Latin-American community.

Coinciding with the 5th centenary of Columbus's voyages to the New World, El Museo showed a portion of its pre-Columbian Taino collection, highlighting the ancient history and cultures Columbus found there. At the same time, an exhibition entitled "Rethinking History through Contemporary Latino Art" presented artists whose work examined the distortion or neglect of Latin-American history.

The Museum at the Fashion Institute of Technology (52)

Shirley Goodman Resource Center, S.W. corner 27th St and Seventh Ave, New York 10001. Tel: (212) 760-7760.

ADMISSION: Open during exhibitions Tues–Fri 12–8; Sat 10–5. Closed Sun, Mon, legal holidays. Free.

Group tours by appointment. Occasional lectures and seminars with major exhibitions. Costume, accessory, textile collections available to members of Design Laboratory. Library.

✗ No restaurant.

⬚ No gift shop.

♿ Accessible to wheelchairs.

⊘ No photography.

🚇 IRT Broadway-7th Ave local (train 1 or 9) to 28th St. BMT Broadway local (N or R train) to 28th St.

🚌 M4 downtown on 5th Ave, uptown on Madison Ave. M5 downtown on 5th Ave, uptown on 6th Ave. M6 or M7 downtown on 7th Ave-Broadway, uptown on 6th Ave. M10 downtown on 7th Ave, uptown on 8th Ave. M11 downtown on 9th Ave, uptown on 10th Ave. M16 or M34 crosstown on 34th St.

The Museum at F.I.T. (1975) provides a showcase for exhibitions relevant to the fashion industry and for work by students and faculty of the Fashion Institute of Technology (F. I. T.). Part of the New York State university system, the Institute is one of the city's major professional schools of art, design, business, and technology, for students who want to enter some aspect of the fashion industry.

PERMANENT COLLECTION

The Institute maintains a research facility begun in concert with the Brooklyn Museum during World War I, when American designers were isolated from developments in Europe. Two block-long storerooms hold indexed collections of clothing and more than 4 million textile swatches. Among the articles of dress are both men's and women's clothes, furs, foundation garments, lingerie, and an outstanding selection of work by 20C American designers and major European couturiers. The collection also contains selected costumes from the stage and screen and period costumes ranging back to the mid-1700s.

EXHIBITION PROGRAM

Each year, along with a half dozen smaller shows, two major exhibitions are mounted with the panache, drama, and occasional humor expected of the fashion industry. Some are thematic or historical; others focus retrospectively on the work of important designers. Smaller shows may examine the use of particular fabrics, featuring lace, embroidery, velvet, or brocaded silk.

One exhibition entitled "Fashion and Surrealism" included such wondrous garments as a dress designed by Karl Lagerfeld for Chanel, which had black and white patternings resembling the keys of a piano; costumes whose form or decoration emphasized lips or eyes, birds' nests,

furniture, and undersea creatures (a red crêpe dress pleated like the artic-
ulations of a lobster shell and another beaded and sequined in grays and
browns like fish scales). In addition to costumes by Giorgio di Chirico and
other Surrealists not usually associated with the fashion industry, there
were photos, drawings, and objects by Dali, Tchelichew, and Magritte; a
suite of furniture based on shoe motifs; and a tableful of hats made to
look like food—wedding cakes, salads, tureens of onion soup, giant cup-
cakes.

Other exhibitions have included "Splash! A History of Swimwear";
"Paper Clothes, 1966–1991"; "Giorgio Armani: Images of Man," which documented the designer's changing concept of masculine style; and "Frock
'n' Roll," which looked at the history of rock music and its influence on
clothing. "The Golden Cut" examined 50 years of style by Pauline Trigère.

The Museum for African Art (24)

593 Broadway (bet. Houston / Prince Sts), New York 10012. Tel: (212) 966-
1313.

ADMISSION: Open Tues–Fri 10:30–5:30; Sat, Sun 12–6. Open Tues to school
groups by appointment. Closed Mon and major holidays. Admission
charge. During periods when only the Focus gallery is open, no admission
is charged.

Educational programs. Fri evening programs of film and video, music,
dance, and performance art. Hands-on workshops for children and adults.

✗ No restaurant.

🏛 Gift shop with traditional textiles, pottery, jewelry, clothing, and other
crafts from Africa. Also museum catalogues and books for children and
adults about African art and culture.

⚲ No flash photography.

◯ Accessible to wheelchairs.

🚇 IRT Lexington Ave local or express (train 4, 5, or 6) to Spring St and
Lafayette. IND 6th Ave local (Q train) to Prince St. IND 8th Ave express or
local (A, C, or E train) to Spring St. BMT Broadway line express or local (N
or R train) to Prince St.

🚌 M6 downtown via 7th Ave / Broadway to Houston St. M5 downtown
via Riverside Dr / 5th Ave to corner of Houston and Broadway.

Since opening in 1984, the Museum for African Art has carved out its
own territory in the city's cultural domain, working to increase public
awareness of the richness and the variety of art produced by different
African cultures.

The Museum's exhibitions have shown an eye for quality, a taste for
originality, and a willingness to embrace controversy. Every year two or
three such exhibitions are mounted, which draw on many sources—private collections and museums in Africa, Europe, and the United States.
Some shows focus on the arts of particular ethnic groups, e.g., exhibitions of Yoruba (Nigeria), Guro (Ivory Coast), or Luba (Zaire). Others deal
with particular themes that are treated cross-culturally, such as
"Secrecy: African Art That Conceals and Reveals," the inaugural show in
the new building. This exhibition presented about 100 works from sub-

The Museum for African Art. Seated figure, Bembe, Republic of the Congo. Known and admired for its exhibitions of a kind of art not intended for museum walls, the Museum for African Art draws on collections from Africa and Europe as well as the United States. (University Museum, Zurich)

Saharan Africa, including masks, initiation and reliquary objects, and even a secret association's dance enclosure.

Finally, the Museum is well known for shows that reflect on the nature of the art on view—art that was not created with exhibition as its prime purpose. Of these shows, "ART / artifact" was perhaps the best known, addressing the question of whether African art is "art" or "artifact." African art was presented in various settings: in dioramas, as in a museum of natural history; in exhibition cases, as in an art museum; and in Victorian curio cabinets, as it was exhibited by early collectors who brought home these objects as novelties.

The Museum's Focus series, with two shows yearly, looks at the work of contemporary African artists. Shows in the Focus gallery and the main exhibition space overlap, so that the Museum will never be closed.

The Museum of American Financial History (25)

24 Broadway (Bowling Green), New York 10004. Tel: (212) 908-4110.

ADMISSION: Open Mon–Fri 11:30–2:30, and by appointment. Closed weekends, New Year's Day, Good Friday, Memorial Day, July 4, Labor Day, Thanksgiving, and Christmas Day. Free.

Changing exhibitions. Publications. Group tours by appointment.

✕ No restaurant.

⁑ No restrooms. No public telephone.

▦ No gift shop but memorabilia of financial history available by mail.

♿ Not accessible to wheelchairs.

🚇 IRT Lexington Ave express (train 4 or 5) to Bowling Green. IRT Broadway-7th Ave local (train 1 or 9) to Rector St or Wall St. BMT Broadway local or express (N or R train) to Whitehall St / South Ferry. BMT Nassau St local (M train) to Broad St.

🚌 M1 marked South Ferry downtown via 5th Ave, Park Ave South, and Broadway. M6 downtown via 7th Ave and Broadway.

The Museum of American Financial History, founded (1988) by John E. Herzog, a collector and chairman of a firm that makes markets in over-the-counter securities, is the only museum in the country to document the ups and downs of America's capital markets. Ensconced in a small lobby of the building where John D. Rockefeller once made his New York headquarters, the Museum offers examples of antique stock market equipment, memorabilia, and documents.

Not unexpected among the antique equipment on view is a stock ticker (1880) invented by Thomas Edison, the kind of machine that churned out the miles of ticker tape showered over lower Broadway on celebratory occasions. A metal annunciator number from the New York Stock Exchange floor and a machine (c. 1960) from the Dow Jones service that printed breaking news on "broad tape" recall the pre-electronic days of Wall St. More surprising for its outmoded appearance is an early electronic Quotron machine from the '60s, with which a broker could see the price of a stock at the push of a button.

Stock market memorabilia include a cigar box (c. 1900) depicting Wall St and a commemorative poster (1903) sporting a view of the newly completed New York Stock Exchange. Bordering the central picture of the building are images of 112 members of the exchange, including such notables as J. Pierpont Morgan (front-center), Marshall Field, John D. Rockefeller, Marcus A. Hanna, Jay Cooke, Henry Clay Frick, and Jacob H. Schiff.

EXHIBITION PROGRAM

Exhibitions change about twice yearly. The inaugural one in the Museum's present home highlighted the evolution in design of engraved stocks and bonds. Antique security certificates displayed advances in techniques of engraving (and of avoiding counterfeiting) as well as vignettes of the nation's burgeoning industry in the 19C, when the securities were issued to raise capital. Certificates commemorated such familiar entities as the Pennsylvania Railroad and the Waldorf-Astoria Hotel; others recalled from obscurity such long-departed enterprises as the Mayflower Bullfrog Consolidated Mining Co. or the Moon Motor Car Co. An exhibition commemorating the bicentennial of Alexander Hamilton's appointment as first Secretary of the U.S. Treasury offered photographs, documents, and memorabilia tracing Hamilton's achievements in American finance and his presence in New York City. "The Financial Roots of the Civil War" assessed the relative financial strengths of North and South, suggesting the economic reasons for the victory of the Union.

PERMANENT COLLECTION

The permanent collection of some 10,000 items includes stock and bond certificates, historic photographs and engravings, newspaper clippings of events important in American financial history, books on finance and financial history, and stock market memorabilia.

The Museum of American Folk Art (94)

Two Lincoln Square (Columbus Ave bet. 65th / 66th Sts), New York 10023. Tel: (212) 977-7298.

ADMISSION: Open daily Tues–Sun 11:30–7:30. Closed Mon. Free.

Information Desk. Free brochures describing exhibits. Publications, lectures, gallery talks, educational programs, workshops, seminars, photographic archives. For group tours, tel: (212) 595-9533. Folk Art Institute offers accredited courses in folk art, folk life, conservation, the commercial folk art market. Crafts Heritage Division offers hands-on workshops in quilting, basketmaking, and other folk arts. Library open by appointment. Special events include the Great American Quilt Festival, held every other spring.

✗ No restaurant.

▥ Gift shop at Two Lincoln Sq: Open Mon 11–6; Tues–Fri 11–7:30; Sat 11–7; Sun 12–6. Tel: (212) 496-2966. Gift shop at 62 W. 50th St (bet. 5th / 6th Aves): Open Mon–Sat 10:30–5:30. Tel: (212) 247-5611. Both shops contain handcrafted items, catalogues, cards, traditional toys, jewelry, wide selection of books on folk art and craft.

♿ Complete wheelchair accessibility. Museum also sponsors programs for the visually impaired, including special tactile exhibits, Braille, and large-print labeling.

⊘ No food in gallery areas.

🚇 IRT Broadway-7th Ave local (train 1 or 9) to 66th St / Lincoln Center. IRT 7th Ave express (train 2 or 3) to 72nd St / Broadway. IND 8th Ave express or local (A or C train) to 59th St / Columbus Circle. IND 6th Ave express (B or D train) to 59th St / Columbus Circle.

🚌 M5 or M7 uptown on 6th Ave and Broadway. M10 uptown on Central Park West. M66 crosstown on 65th and 66th Sts. M104 uptown and downtown on Broadway.

Founded (1961) by a group of collectors, the Museum of American Folk Art is the only urban institution in the country devoted solely to American folk art. While a larger permanent home awaits construction, the Museum's current gallery space offers an attractive setting for viewing selections from its outstanding collection and other exhibitions.

PERMANENT COLLECTION

The more than 2,500 objects include painting, sculpture, textiles, and decorative arts from the 18–20C. Paintings include 18–19C portraits by some of the thousands of painters who traveled from town to town selling "likenesses" of those who could pay for them. Among the masterpieces in this field is Ammi Phillips's *Girl in Red Dress with Cat and Dog* (1834–36). Other paintings include mourning pictures, miniatures, landscapes and seascapes, examples of cut paper (paper dolls, Valentines), and folk paintings by contemporary artists. Equally impressive is the collection of sculpture and three-dimensional objects, whose most familiar icons are perhaps *Flag Gate*, a painted wooden gate with a blue field of white stars and rippling red slats, and the imposing *St. Tammany Weather Vane*, a large molded copper figure of an Indian, standing on an arrow. Other forms of folk sculpture include architectural ornaments, weathervanes and whirligigs, trade signs, and a famous collection of decoys.

"Animal Carnival," a group of contemporary New Mexican carvings by a group of artists formerly led by patriarch Felipe Benito Archuleta, includes a catfish, a seated tiger, and other creatures carved in wood and painted with housepaint. Equally imaginative is the work of America's best-known living folk artist, the inspired and prolific Rev. Howard Finster, who uses "other people's junk" to create artistic and devotional objects.

Among the furniture are examples of boxes and mirrors, case clocks, work tables, and dower chests. Shaker stands, rocking chairs, and rugs illustrate the utilitarian design of this austere religious sect.

Textiles are another artistically superb area of the collection. There are counterpanes, samplers, coverlets, hooked and braided rugs, and quilts, which illustrate the skillful and imaginative needlework of American women from 18C to the 20C.

EXHIBITION PROGRAM

The Museum mounts about a half dozen exhibitions yearly. They range from shows of individual artists (Grandma Moses, Harry Lieberman) to shows of a particular craft ("Stitched from the Soul: Slave Quilting in the Ante-Bellum South" and "American Primitive: Discoveries in Folk Sculpture"), to thematic shows and exhibitions of the folk art of different cultures. Among the thematic shows, "America Eats: Folk Art and Food," the first full-scale show to treat cookery as a folk craft, offered biscuit cutters, wafer irons, candy molds, and food-oriented painting and sculpture, as well as recipes for those viewers who wished to go home and try their

Flag Gate, *artist unknown, Jefferson County, New York, c. 1876. A signature piece of the American Museum of Folk Art, whose collections include quilts, furniture, paintings, and artful renderings of useful objects.*
(The Museum of American Folk Art. Photo: Helga Photo Studio)

own hand. A celebration of the quincentenary of Columbus's voyage to the New World included displays of *Santos de Palo,* the carved wooden household saints of Puerto Rico, and a comprehensive exploration of contemporary Latin-American folk art.

THE BUILDING

In 1989 the Museum moved into its present space, a formerly barren and unused public plaza at Two Lincoln Square facing Columbus Ave. When Two Lincoln Square was constructed (1975), the developers negotiated for a profitable 63,000 sq ft of extra space by providing an open-air mall within the office tower, but made the space so unattractive that the public never used it. Because the consequent trade-off between the city and the owners required that the space remain public and free to all, the Museum remains open 12 hours daily. After its permanent home on West 53rd St is completed, this space will become a satellite museum.

The Museum of Modern Art (53)

11 West 53rd St (bet. 5th / 6th Aves), New York 10019. Tel: (212) 708-9500. For information on current exhibitions, call 708-9480; for information on daily film screenings, call 708-9480.

ADMISSION: Open Thurs, Fri noon–8:30; Sat–Tues 11–5:45. Closed Wed, New Year's Day, Thanksgiving, and Christmas Day. Admission charge. Pay what you wish Thurs and Fri 5:30–8:30 P.M.

Information Desk in lobby. Current exhibitions, film screenings, gallery talks, and lectures listed in the monthly calendar available in the lobby. Gallery talks weekdays 12:30 and 3; Thurs evenings 5:30 and 7, but check at the Museum, as schedule may vary. Daily film screenings; tickets (included in the price of admission) available at the Information Desk. Lectures, video and educational programs. Library and study centers open by appointment.

✘ Informal Garden Cafe open Fri–Tues 11–5; Thurs 11–8. Closed Wed. Cafe, open during museum hours, closes 1/2 hour before Museum. Sette MoMa, the formal restaurant open to the public as well as to Museum visitors, serves lunch 12–3 and dinner 5–11:30; no dinner Sun. Entrances from the Museum and at 12 W. 54th St. Closed Wed. Reservations recommended: call (212) 708-9864.

▥ The MoMA Book Store, east of the lobby, carries a wide selection of art books, posters, postcards, slides, calendars, and gift items. Tel: (212) 708-9700. The MoMA Design Store, across the street at 44 W. 53rd St, carries glassware, furniture, lamps, jewelry, and other items selected for their superior design. Tel: (212) 767-1050.

♿ Complete wheelchair accessibility. wheelchairs available in the checkroom. For TT / TDD service, call 247-1230. Sign language-interpreted gallery talks every third Thurs of the month at 7 P.M. Personal amplification headsets available in Education Center for all gallery and slide talks. For blind and severely visually impaired visitors, a sculpture touch-tour of the Collection is offered by advance appointment. To schedule, call (212) 708-9369 or TT / TDD at (212) 247-1230.

⊘ Photography with hand-held camera and electronic flash permitted in Permanent Collection galleries only.

🚇 IND 6th Ave local (F train) or IND 8th Ave local (E train) to 53rd St / 5th Ave.

🚌 M1, M2, M3, M4, or Q32 downtown via 5th Ave or uptown via Madison Ave. M5, M6 or M7 uptown via 6th Ave. M27 crosstown on 49th / 50th Sts.

The Museum of Modern Art (1929) owns one of the world's outstanding collections of European and American art from the end of the 19C to the present. In addition to its marvelous collections of painting and sculpture, MoMA also has outstanding examples of modern photography, film, and industrial design, and in fact pioneered the inclusion of these arts' contemporary museum collections. In addition to its stunning permanent collection, the Museum offers a full schedule of changing exhibitions, some of which are major events in the city's cultural life.

HIGHLIGHTS

The permanent collection is notable as a synopsis of modern art from the late 19C through about 1960. It is strong in European modernist movements, beginning with Cubism.

MoMA has an outstanding collection of works by Picasso and Matisse, as well as masterworks by van Gogh, Braque, and Mondrian.

The collection of postwar avant-garde American Abstract Expressionists is superb.

The design collection is unique in this country, as are the holdings in film and photography, which are shown in changing exhibitions.

PERMANENT COLLECTION

Ground Floor Sculpture Garden. In addition to housing the Education Center and galleries for temporary exhibitions, the ground floor opens into the Sculpture Garden, a favorite midtown oasis. David Smith, *Cubi X* (1963); the *Cubi* series, created toward the end of Smith's life, includes works constructed only of cubes, cylinders, or multiples of these forms. Alexander Calder, *Black Widow* (1959). Henri Matisse, *The Back, I–IV.* Made over the years 1909–31, the four images grow more abstract with the passage of time.

Aristide Maillol, *The River,* c. 1939–43. Jacques Lipchitz, *Figure* (c. 1939–43). Gaston Lachaise, *Standing Woman* (1932). Auguste Rodin, *Monument to Balzac* (1897–98; bronze cast 1954). Though generally considered one of Rodin's masterpieces nowadays, the Balzac monument was rejected by the committee that had commissioned the work. The towering figure, larger than life, depicts the writer wrapped in a voluminous, swelling cloak, his massive head thrusting forcefully upward.

Henry Moore, *Large Torso: Arch* (1962–63). This monumental piece reflects Moore's abiding interest in the handling of positive and negative volumes, i.e., the relationship of voids or concavities to solid masses. Pablo Picasso, *She Goat* (1950). Tony Smith, *Free Ride* (1962, refabricated 1982).

Second Floor

The **Painting and Sculpture Collection** is installed chronologically on the second and third floors. The installation traces the movements and events of modernism from the Post-Impressionists through Pop Art and the mid-1960s.

> **NOTE:** Paintings and sculptures are reinstalled from time to time, or may occasionally be on loan to other museums as part of traveling exhibitions.

GALLERIES 1–3. Post-Impressionism.

GALLERY 1. Near the door stands Rodin's *St. John the Baptist Preaching* (1878–80). Paul Cézanne, *The Bather* (c. 1885). Museum director Alfred Barr wrote of this important painting that the figure "rises like a colossus who has just bestrode mountains and rivers—for Cézanne, adapting a landscape from another painting, has again fumbled his naturalistic scale while achieving artistic grandeur." Both *Pines and Rocks (Fontainebleau?)* (1896–99) and *Still Life with Apples* (1895–98) show Cézanne's interest in the underlying geometry of natural shapes. Also *Melting Snow, Fontainebleau* (c. 1879–80).

Henri de Toulouse-Lautrec, *La Goulue at the Moulin Rouge* (1891–92). *"La Goulue"* ("The Glutton") was the nickname of dancer Louise Weber, whose hearty appetite eventually led her to become grossly fat. Edgar Degas, *At the Milliner's* (c. 1882). Mary Cassatt served as the model for the woman trying on the hat.

MUSEUM OF MODERN ART
Ground Floor

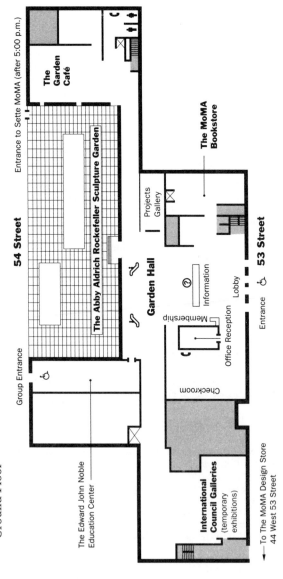

International Council Galleries

Projects Gallery

MUSEUM OF MODERN ART
Second Floor

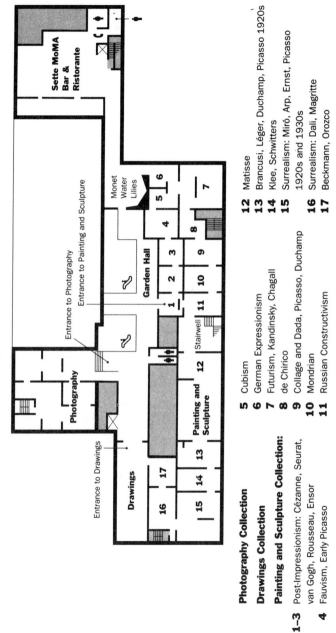

Photography Collection

Drawings Collection

Painting and Sculpture Collection:

1–3 Post-Impressionism: Cézanne, Seurat, van Gogh, Rousseau, Ensor

4 Fauvism, Early Picasso

5 Cubism

6 German Expressionism

7 Futurism, Kandinsky, Chagall

8 de Chirico

9 Collage and Dada, Picasso, Duchamp

10 Mondrian

11 Russian Constructivism

12 Matisse

13 Brancusi, Léger, Duchamp, Picasso 1920s

14 Klee, Schwitters

15 Surrealism: Miró, Arp, Ernst, Picasso 1920s and 1930s

16 Surrealism: Dali, Magritte

17 Beckmann, Orozco

GALLERY 2. Georges Seurat, *The Channel at Gravelines, Evening* (1890); *Port-en-Besssin, Entrance to the Harbor* (1888); *Evening, Honfleur* (1886).

Paul Gauguin, *The Moon and the Earth* (1893). The square-bodied, native woman who here represents the moon is a physical type the painter developed to represent monumental, mythological figures. *Still Life with Three Puppies* (1888); Gauguin admired the work of Cézanne, as the foreground of this painting suggests.

Vincent van Gogh, *The Starry Night* (1889). This visionary painting with its tumultuously radiant night sky is one of the most popular pictures in the Museum. *Portrait of Joseph Roulin* (1889): van Gogh painted five portraits of Roulin, the postman at Arles.

GALLERY 3. James Ensor, *Tribulations of St. Anthony* (1887); *Masks Confronting Death* (1888). Typically Ensor's nightmarish paintings contain skeletons and grotesque carnival masks—images of death and human brutality—in vivid, bright colors. Edvard Munch, *The Storm* (1893).

Henri Rousseau, *The Sleeping Gypsy* (1897); *The Dream* (1910). Although Rousseau claimed to have done military service in Mexico, the exotic foliage of *The Dream,* his last painting, was drawn from his imagination and perhaps from his visits to the Botanical Garden in Paris. Édouard Vuillard, *The Mother and Sister of the Artist* (c. 1893).

GALLERY 4. **Fauvism, Early Picasso.** André Derain, *London Bridge* (1906). Derain, one of the Fauve painters, was commissioned by his dealer to paint the Thames as Monet had done earlier; the brilliant unnaturalistic color shocked critics, who found the painting "the barbaric and naïve sport of a child." Also, *Fishing Boats, Collioure* (1905); *L'Estaque* (1906); *Bathers* (1907). Georges Braque, *Landscape at La Clotat* (1907). Henri Matisse, *Woman Beside the Water (La Japonaise, Mme Matisse)* (1905); *Male Model* (1900). Near the male nude is a bronze statue by Matisse, *The Serf* (c. 1900–06).

At one end of the gallery is Pablo Picasso's *Les Demoiselles d'Avignon* (1907), one of the most important paintings in the collection. Studies show that Picasso first conceived *Les Demoiselles* as a brothel scene (on Avignon St in Barcelona) with a sailor, a medical student, and five prostitutes. Eventually the picture evolved into the present expressionistic rendering of the five women only. The gallery also includes two studies for *Les Demoiselles d'Avignon,* an untitled study and *Bathers in a Forest* (1908). Also on view are two other works from about the same period, *Two Acrobats with a Dog* (1905) and *Repose* (1908).

GALLERY 5. **Cubism.** This gallery contains early examples of what is commonly called "Analytical" Cubism, a radical style developed largely by Picasso and Braque, in which forms were analyzed into geometrical components and rendered, usually in subdued colors. Pablo Picasso, *"Ma Jolie"* (1911–12); *Landscape* (1908); *Fruit Dish* (1908–09); *Girl with a Mandolin (Fanny Tellier)* (1910); *Violin and Grapes* (1912); *Still Life with Liqueur Bottle* (1909); *Woman's Head (Fernande)* (1909).

Georges Braque, *Man with a Guitar* (1911); *Soda* (1912). Juan Gris, *Guitar and Flowers* (1912); *Still Life* (1911). On the partition leading into the next gallery is Henri Matisse's *Bather* (1909).

GALLERY 6. **German Expressionism.** Gustav Klimt, *Hope II* (1907–08). Klimt's ornamental, Oriental stylization and the frequently erotic nature of his images, even allegorical ones like this, have made him the embodiment of fin-de-siècle Vienna. Egon Schiele, *Portrait of Gertrude Schiele* (1909).

Wilhelm Lehmbruck, *Standing Youth* (1913). Some critics find in Lehmbruck's elongated figures a precursor of Giacometti; the downward gaze and vaguely defensive postures of both these figures suggests the theme of alienation common to the German Expressionists.

Oskar Kokoschka, *Hans Tietze and Erica Tietze-Conrat* (1909); *Self-Portrait* (1913); *Dr. Emma Veronika Sanders* (1909). Lyonel Feininger, *Uprising* (1910). Otto Dix, *Nuns* (1914).

Ernst Ludwig Kirchner, *Street, Berlin* (1913); *Street, Dresden* (1908). With several other students from Dresden, Kirchner was a founder of the early German Expressionist group, *Die Brücke* ("The Bridge"), a circle of painters concerned with bridging the gap between old traditions and avant-garde styles. Kirchner's intense and nightmarish depiction of German society branded him as a degenerate during the Nazi period, when some 600 of his works were confiscated.

Franz Marc, *The Cow* (1913). Karl Schmidt-Rottluff, *Houses at Night* (1912).

GALLERY 7. **Futurism, Kandinsky, Chagall.** Roger de la Fresnaye, *The Conquest of the Air* (1913). This large painting, influenced by the spatial concepts of Cubism, was painted during the early heroic years of aviation.

František Kupka, *The First Step* (1910–13); *Red and Blue Disks* (1911–12). Kupka's color theories led to experimental paintings with astronomical overtones. Robert Delaunay, *Simultaneous Contrasts: Sun and Moon* (1913). The title came from a book on color theory whose principles appealed to Delaunay as a rationale for his artistic play with color. Sonia Delaunay-Terk, *Portuguese Market* (1915).

Wassily Kandinsky, *Painting #198; Painting #199; Painting #200; Painting #201* (all 1914). Kandinsky painted his first purely abstract work in 1910. These four numbered paintings were commissioned for the New York apartment of a collector.

Gino Severini, Giacomo Balla, and Umberto Boccioni were the outstanding figures in the movement known as Futurism, which used Cubist techniques of spatial dislocation to render motion. Umberto Boccioni's powerful *Dynamism of a Soccer Player* (1913) evokes both the form and the energy of the striding athlete. His bronze *Unique Forms of Continuity in Space* (1913; cast 1931) suggests the same forceful energy of a moving figure.

Marc Chagall, *Over Vitebsk* (1915–20); *Birthday* (1915); *I and the Village* (1915). Vitebsk, Chagall's native village, appears in many of his paintings, including several replicas of *I and the Village*.

Also by Boccioni, *States of Mind: Those Who Go, The Farewells, Those Who Stay* (1911); *The Laugh* (1911); *Development of a Bottle in Space* (1912). Gino Severini's *Dynamic Hieroglyphic of the Bal Tabarin* (1912) is an abstraction of an evening scene in a Paris café. Giacomo Balla, *Swifts: Paths of Movement + Dynamic Sequences* (1913).

Fernand Léger, *Exit the Ballets Russes* (1914). Léger had met Picasso and Braque in 1910, but developed his own approach to Cubism in which he used certain restricted colors, often with black outlines and white contrasts, to create strong, geometrical forms. Kasimir Malevich, *Woman with Water Pails: Dynamic Arrangement* (1912–13); *Contrast of Forms* (1913).

GALLERY 8. **Giorgio de Chirico.** *The Nostalgia of the Infinite* (1913–14?); *Gare Montparnasse (The Melancholy of Departure)* (1914); *Song of Love* (1914); *The Duo (Les mannequins de la Tour Rose)* (1915); *The Great Metaphysician (1917); The Enigma of a Day* (1914). Chirico was interested in presenting objects to awaken "sensations of revelation" in the viewer. His scenes, which often recall the architecture of Italian cities, have a sense of silence and mystery that appealed to the Surrealists.

GALLERY 9. **Collage and Dada, Picasso, Duchamp.** Man Ray, *The Rope Dancer Accompanies Herself with Her Shadows* (1916). The artist drew a ballet dancer in several positions on large sheets of colored paper, cut out the figure, and retained scraps with their negative images.

Marcel Duchamp, *The Passage from Virgin to Bride* (1912). Duchamp saw this picture as a personal transition from the formal analysis of Cubism to his own intellectual concept of painting, which he thought of as "reduction" rather than abstraction. This painting has its own esoteric symbolism, which has given rise to considerable explication; it also suggests its subject in its warm, organic coloring. Also by Duchamp, *To Be Looked At (From the Other Side of the Glass), with One Eye, Close To, for Almost an Hour* (1918); *Bicycle Wheel* (1951; 3rd version, after lost original of 1913); *Network of Stoppages* (1914).

The gallery also contains works from the years around 1914 of the great Cubists, Picasso, Braque, and Juan Gris. Juan Gris, *Breakfast* (1914). Along with Braque and Picasso, Gris is usually considered the third giant of Cubism, though his style, which included the notion of traditional perspective, remained his own.

Another of Picasso's radical innovations was the kind of sculpture represented by a small piece, *Glass of Absinthe* (1914). It combines Cubist notions of dismantled objects viewed simultaneously from different perspectives with the Cubist practice of including found objects in a sculptural composition. Also by Picasso, *Green Still Life* (1914); *Student with a Pipe* (1914); *Harlequin* (1915); *Card Player* (1913–14); *Man with a Hat* (1912). Georges Braque, *Still Life with Tenora* (1915).

GALLERY 10. **Mondrian.** The Museum has a fine collection of the works of Piet Mondrian, which outlines the development of his painting over most of his career. *Dunes and Sea* (1909–10); *Pier and Ocean* (1914); *Composition, V* (1914); *Composition with Color Planes* (1917); *Composition in White, Black, and Red* (1936); *Trafalgar Square* (1939–43). *Broadway Boogie Woogie* (1942–43), the last painting completed by Mondrian, attempts to abstract the frantic energy of the urban scene (Mondrian came to New York during World War II). The artist also theorized that American jazz, with its deemphasis of traditional melody and stress on rhythm, was the musical equivalent of what he was trying to achieve visually.

Theo van Doesburg, *Rhythm of a Russian Dance* (1918): the conclusion of a series of eight studies which begins with a realistic drawing of a dancer and ends with an abstraction of her form.

GALLERY 11. **Russian Constructivism.** Kasimir Malevich, *Private of the First Division* (1914). Malevich was the chief developer and practitioner of a Russian movement in abstract art that he named Suprematism. In 1915 he painted a series of 35 *Suprematist Compositions,* all of them geometrical abstractions using such basic forms as squares, circles, triangles, and rectangles, painted in a narrow range of colors. Among them are *Suprematist Composition: Red Square and Black Square* (1915) and *Suprematist Composition: Airplane Flying* (1915). His ideas reached their conclusion in a series of paintings of white squares on a white background, e.g., *Suprematist Composition: White on White* (1918).

Among his followers was El Lissitzky, who was also a student of architecture and engineering. The name "Proun" refers to the "interchange station between painting and architecture": *Proun 19D* (1922?).

Aleksandr Rodchenko, *Hanging Construction Number 12* (c. 1920); *Non-Objective Painting: Black on Black* (1918). László Moholy-Nagy, *Nickel Construction* (1921); the artist came under the influence of Malevich and Lissitzky after World War I in Vienna. Gustav Klucis, *Maquette for Radio Announcer* (1922); the work is a small-scale version of a propaganda kiosk designed for the fifth anniversary of the Russian Revolution, to be placed at main intersections for the radio transmission of a speech by Lenin.

STAIRWELL. Oskar Schlemmer, *Bauhaus Stairway* (1932). Schlemmer was a teacher of ballet and theater at the Bauhaus, the German school of the arts and architecture in Dessau, as well as a painter and designer; the painting depicts an actual stairway in the Bauhaus. Pierre Bonnard, *The Breakfast Room* (c. 1930–31); *Basket of Fruit Reflected in a Mirror* (c. 1944–46). Amedeo Modigliani, *Anna Zborowska* (1917). Also Modigliani's last figure painting, *Reclining Nude* (1919); this nude is perhaps his greatest.

GALLERY 12. **Matisse.** This large room is one of the glories of the Museum, with its collection of painting and sculpture by Henri Matisse. *The Red Studio* (1911): the studio is Matisse's and the paintings and objects are those on which he was working during this period (1898–1911) in his career. *The Moroccans* (1915–16); *The Dance* (1909; 1st version): this painting is a study for a commission by the great Russian collector, Sergei Shchukin, who had seen Matisse's *Joy of Life* in Paris. The circle of dancers in that painting was based on some Catalan fishermen whom Matisse had seen performing the traditional *sardana.*

Goldfish and Sculpture (1912); *Moroccan Garden* (1912); *View of Notre Dame* (1914); *Piano Lesson* (1916): the child playing on the Pleyel piano is Matisse's son; the green triangle is the garden visible through the window. The painting behind the boy is *Woman on a High Stool* (1914), hung nearby. *The Blue Window* (1913); *The Rose Marble Table* (1917); *Artist and Goldfish* (1914). *Variation on a Still Life by de Heem* (1915). Jan Davidsz de Heem was a Dutch painter of the 17C. Early in his career Matisse had copied paintings of the Old Masters in the Louvre to study formal structure and to earn money through the sale of copies. This picture was painted some 20 years after Matisse's student days.

GALLERY 13. **Brancusi, Léger, Duchamp, Picasso 1920s.** *Three Women at the Spring* (1921); *Three Musicians* (1921). The second picture is said to epitomize Picasso's "Synthetic" or decorative Cubism; the flat, rectilinear quality of the figures has reminded some observers of a jigsaw puzzle or of the Cubist technique of collage. The year before the *Musicians* was painted, Picasso designed costumes for Stravinsky's *Pulcinella,* a ballet based on the *commedia dell'arte* from whose tradition the figures of Harlequin and Pierrot (playing the clarinet) are drawn.

Fernand Léger, *Three Women (Le Grand déjeuner) (1921).* Léger once remarked that the human figure should be considered not for its sentimental value but for its plastic value; hence since 1905 he had purposely rendered the human figure in inexpressive poses.

Marcel Duchamp, *Rotary Demisphere* (1925); *Fresh Widow* (1920).

Constantin Brancusi, *Bird in Space* (1913), *Mlle Pogany* (1913); *Endless Column, Version I* (1918); *The Newborn* (1920); *Magic Bird* (1910–12); *Young Bird* (1928); *Fish* (1930); *The Cock* (1924); *Blond Negress II* (1933). Le Corbusier, *Still Life* (1920). Brancusi, one of the most admired 20C artists, shaped the course of modern sculpture. His simplification of natural forms to the point of abstraction drew admirers as different as Alexander Archipenko and Henry Moore.

GALLERY 14. **Klee, Schwitters.** Lyonel Feininger, *The Viaduct* (1920). Feininger, though born in America, lived his adult life in Germany and was acquainted with the work of the French Cubists; he was an instructor at the Bauhaus, and the luminous planes of his painting are often suggestive of architecture even when the subject is not itself overtly architectural. George Grosz, *The Engineer Heartfield* (1920).

Paul Klee, *Pastoral* (1927); *Cat and Bird* (1928): the bird is in the mind of the cat. *Around the Fish* (1926), a painting filled with Klee's personal symbolism. The symbols around the fish may suggest religion, the sun and moon, nature, even the atomic constituents of matter. *Mask of Fear* (1932); *Actor's Mask* (1924). Klee was fascinated by the theater and in his early years was influenced by Ensor, himself fascinated by carnival masks. *Heroic Strokes of the Bow* (1938); *Vocal Fabric of the Singer Rosa Silber* (1922); *Twittering Machine* (1922).

Kurt Schwitters, *Picture with Light Center* (1919); *Merz Picture 32A. Cherry Picture* (1921); *Merz Drawing* (1924). The Cubists had used scraps of newspaper and other patterned papers in collages, but Schwitters extended this range, incorporating bits of waste paper, string, wire, cork, buttons, old tickets, driftwood, and other found objects into his paintings, some of which he called *Merzbild* ("trash pictures").

GALLERY 15 (FIRST ROOM). **Surrealism: Picasso, 1920s–1930s.** This gallery contains works from the late 1920s through the mid-1930s. *Painter and Model* (1928); *Seated Bather* (1930). With its undertones of aggression and violence, *Seated Bather* is sometimes compared to the work of the Surrealists. *Girl Before a Mirror* (1932): a modern equivalent of the traditional "vanity" picture in which a woman, gazing at her reflection in a mirror, sees instead a skull. The girl on the right is Marie-Thérèse Walter, Picasso's lover at the time, a frequent subject for paintings of this period. Also in this gallery: *Studio with Plaster Head* (1925); *Head of a Woman [Marie-Thérèse Walter]* (1932); *Interior with a Girl Drawing* (1935). Julio Gonzalez, *Woman Combing Her Hair* (1936); Gonzalez was a pioneer in iron sculpture and had a significant influence on Picasso, David Smith, and others.

(SECOND ROOM). **Surrealism: Miró, Arp, Ernst.** Joan Miró, *The Hunter (Catalan Landscape)* (1923–24). Miró explicated the picture, explaining that the yellow area is both the sea and the sky; the beetle-shaped object in the sky is the sun; the letters "SARD" in the foreground stand for "sardine," the object to the left. *Person Throwing a Stone at a Bird* (1926); *Dutch Interior, I* (1928); *The Birth of the World* (1925); *Hirondelle / Amour* (1933–34).

Jean Arp, *Bell and Navels* (1931); *Enak's Tears (Terrestrial Forms)* (1917). Max Ernst, *Rendezvous of Friends—The Friends Become Flowers* (1928).

GALLERY 16. **Surrealism: Dali, Magritte.** Alberto Giacometti, *Woman with Her Throat Cut* (1932); *The Palace at 4 A.M.* (1932–33). Frida Kahlo, *Self-Portrait with Cropped Hair* (1940). Kahlo was the second wife of the painter Diego Rivera; many of her paintings are self-portraits with psychological overtones.

Meret Oppenheim, *Object* (1936). This fur-covered teacup and spoon became an icon of Surrealism. Salvador Dali, *The Persistence of Memory* (1931). The soft, oozing watches, painted with photographic meticulousness, are among the most famous images of Surrealist art. René Magritte, *The Menaced Assassin* (1926); *The Empire of Light, II* (1950). *The False Mirror* (1928) contains one of Magritte's most famous visual puns, in which external reality and inner vision are interchanged.

Balthus, *The Street* (1933); *The Living Room* (1942); *André Derain* (1936). Balthus, the son of aristocratic, artistic Polish parents, was encouraged in his youth by Bonnard and Derain. Hans Bellmer, *Doll* (1936).

GALLERY 17. **Orozco, Beckmann.** David Alfaro Siqueiros, *Collective Suicide* (1936); *Echo of a Scream* (1937). Siqueiros, who belonged to the second generation of Mexican muralists, studied in Europe and fought in the Spanish Civil War, which inspired this painting, a general outcry against the brutality of war. Jackson Pollock would later become the dominant figure of Abstract Expressionism, probably the most important movement in American painting in this century, and the Museum is fortunate to own 18 of his works, including *Flame* (1934–38), an early work painted well before his dripped and poured abstractions of the late '40s. José Clemente Orozco, *Zapatistas* (1931).

Max Beckmann, *Departure* (1932–33). Beckmann was driven from his academic post in Frankfurt by the Nazis in 1933, at the time when he was working on this allegorical triptych, the first of a series of nine. The paintings, which occupied him until his death, expressed in powerful symbolism his horror at human cruelty. They have been received as a powerful comment on German culture and politics during his lifetime.

Department of Drawings. The last three galleries on this floor are occupied by this department, whose collection is shown in changing exhibitions. The Museum planned a Department of Drawings at its opening in 1929, when it acquired its first drawing, George Grosz's *Portrait of Anna Peters.* Until the new building opened in 1984, the drawings were not regularly exhibited, though the Museum continued to acquire them. Today the collection numbers more than 6,000 unique works on paper and is acknowledged to be the most comprehensive in existence.

Department of Photography. The photography collection of the Museum, which reaches back to the beginnings of photography in c. 1840 and continues to the present, has been said to be the best of any art museum in the world. It is especially notable for its list of photographers working since World War I. The collection is shown in changing exhibitions.

CORRIDOR. Francis Picabia, *Comic Wedlock* (1914); *This Has to Do With Me* (1914). Diego Rivera, *Agrarian Leader Zapata* (1931); the painting is a copy from a mural commissioned by the Mexican government for the Palace of Cortés in Cuernavaca. The panel depicts the reformer Zapata anachronistically holding Cortés's white stallion. Umberto Boccioni, *The City Rises* (1910). Joan Miró, *Mural Painting* (1950–51). Fernand Léger, *The Divers, II* (1941–42); toward the end of his life, Léger made a conscious effort to make his art, always entranced with machinelike forms, more accessible and public. David Smith, *Australia* (1951). Critics have likened Smith's linear sculpture to the painting of the Abstract Expressionists; here its proximity to the Picasso suggests an affinity with another kind of linearity. Pablo Picasso, *The Kitchen* (1948); the painting shows a view through Picasso's studio door into the kitchen, which has a collection of plates hanging on the wall.

Monet Water Lilies. Facing the Sculpture Garden, between the corridor and the restaurant, is a gallery containing Claude Monet's *Water Lilies* (c. 1920). Between the early 1890s and the end of his life in 1926, Monet, an ardent gardener, was preoccupied with several series of paintings of the pond in the beautiful garden he created at Giverny outside Paris. His intention was to render the surface of the water, the water-lily blossoms and pads, and the reflections of the trees and sky as faithfully as possible under different conditions of light, weather, and season. The Museum's triptych and additional panel are the largest holding of the *Water Lilies* outside France. Also in the same gallery is Monet's *The Japanese Footbridge* (c. 1920–22).

Third Floor

GARDEN HALL (CORRIDOR). Elizabeth Murray, *Dis Pair* (1989–90). Anselm Kiefer, *The Red Sea* (1984–85). Chuck Close, *Robert / 104,072* (1976).

The chronological installation of the collection of **Painting and Sculpture** continues on the third floor, beginning in Gallery 18, west of the escalators.

GALLERIES 18–19. **Europe and the United States, 1940s.**

GALLERY 18. Alberto Giacometti, *Man Pointing* (1947); *City Square* (1948); *Dog* (1951); *Chariot* (1950). Giacometti's characteristic elongated style appeared in the late '40s and his isolated figures have been said to

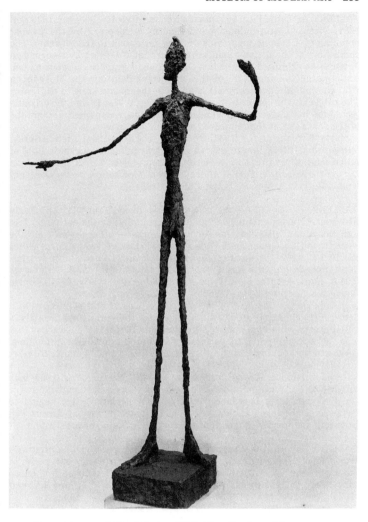

Alberto Giacometti, Man Pointing *(1947). The collections of the*
Museum of Modern Art are renowned for painting and sculpture,
architecture, design, photography, and film.
(Photograph © 1947 The Museum of Modern Art)

carry the burden of Existentialist tragedy; he was a friend of philosopher
Jean-Paul Sartre, who wrote about his work.

Jean Dubuffet, *Childbirth* (1944); *Grand Jazz Band (New Orleans)*
(1944); *Wall with Inscriptions* (1945); *Joë Bosquet in Bed* (1947); *Portrait*
of Henri Michaux (1947). Francis Bacon, *Painting* (1946).

GALLERY 19. Pablo Picasso, *Charnel House* (1944–45). Between 1939 and 1981, Picasso's stupendous mural *Guernica*, inspired by the Fascist bombing of a Basque town, was on long-term loan to the Museum. The conditions of the artist's loan stipulated that *Guernica* be returned to Spain to be exhibited there when the regime of Francisco Franco ended. Anticipating the departure of this important painting, the Museum in 1971 purchased *Charnel House*, similar in theme and style to *Guernica*. The subject is the concentration camps of World War II, and the grisaille technique has suggested to some observers the newspaper photographs of the death camps that appeared at the end of the war.

Matta, *Listen to Living* (1941); *The Vertigo of Eros* (1944). Arshile Gorky, *Summation* (1947). Gorky was an important influence on the school of American painting that flowered in the years after World War II. Joan Miró, *Escape Ladder* (1940). André Masson, *Meditation on an Oak Leaf* (1942). Herbert Ferber, *He Is Not a Man* (1950).

GALLERY 21 (GALLERY 20 is accessible from GALLERY 21). **Early Abstract Expressionism.** This gallery, dominated by the early Abstract Expressionists, also contains American works in other styles from the same period. Joseph Cornell, *Taglioni's Jewel Casket* (1940); *Object (Roses des Vents)* (1942–43); *Untitled (Hôtel Beau-Séjour)* (1954). Alexander Calder, *Constellation with Red Object* (1943). David Hare, *Magician's Game* (1944). Mark Rothko, *Slow Swirl by the Edge of the Sea* (1944). Louise Bourgeois, *Sleeping Figure* (1950).

Arshile Gorky, *The Leaf of the Artichoke Is an Owl* (1944); *Diary of a Seducer* (1945); *Agony* (1947). *Agony*, executed the year before the artist's suicide, exemplifies his mature style and also suggests the darkness that was gathering around Gorky's personal and professional life at this time.

Willem de Kooning, *Painting* (1948). Bradley Walker Tomlin, *Number 20* (1949).

Jackson Pollock, *Stenographic Figure* (1942). *The She-Wolf* (1943) was the first of Pollock's paintings to be purchased by a museum and one of the first paintings in which Pollock's own personal style begins to coalesce. The subject is the mythological foster mother of Remus and Romulus, founders of Rome. Herbert Ferber, *Jackson Pollock* (1940).

GALLERY 20. **United States, 1920–1945.** Andrew Wyeth, *Christina's World* (1948). This painting, with its technical virtuosity and sense of emptiness, brought Wyeth into the public eye and launched him on an immensely successful career. Edward Hopper, *House by the Railroad* (1925); *New York Movie* (1939); *Gas* (1940).

Stuart Davis, *Lucky Strike* (1921); *Visa* (1951). Georgia O'Keeffe, *Lake George Window* (1929). Florine Stettheimer, *Family Portrait, II* (1933). Arthur G. Dove, *Grandmother* (1925).

GALLERY 22. **Jackson Pollock.** *Gothic* (1944). By 1947, Jackson Pollock had begun placing his canvas on the floor and dripping or pouring paint directly from the can, then manipulating it with sticks or trowels. This room contains examples of Pollock's mature "drip and splash" style: *Full Fathom Five* (1947); *Number #1* (1948); *Echo (Number 25)* (1951); *White Light* (1954). *One (Number 31, 1950)* (1950), a monumental painting, exemplifies Pollock's "classic" style. The effect derives in part from the flickering, mysterious effects of light suggested by the built-up surface of the painting and in part from the monumental scale of the work.

Lee Krasner, *Untitled* (1949); Krasner was the wife of Jackson Pollock, a fact which both overshadowed and enhanced her career.

GALLERY 23. **1950s: Newman, Reinhardt, Still.** Barnett Newman, *Onement, I* (1948); *Onement, III* (1949); *The Voice* (1950). Also *Vir Heroicus Sublimis* (1950–51); like *Onement, III,* the painting consists of a single color field crossed by thin vertical stripes. The title of this huge red canvas refers to the heroic and sublime nature of man.

Ad Reinhardt, *Abstract Painting: Red* (1952); *Number 107* (1950). Clyfford Still, *Painting 1944-N* (1944). Alberto Giacometti, *Tall Figure* (1949).

GALLERY 24. **1950s: Motherwell, Rothko, Kelly, Kline, de Kooning, Bacon.** Clyfford Still, *Painting* (1951). Robert Motherwell, *Elegy to the Spanish Republic 108* (1965–67). Motherwell painted more than 100 of these *Elegies,* all with heavy black egglike shapes and vertical rectangles against a white background. Though the painter denied that they had any overt symbolism, he also said that the pictures represent "contrasts between life and death, and their interrelation." Adolph Gottlieb, *Blast, I.*

Mark Rothko, *Magenta, Black, Green on Orange* (1949); *Number 10* (1950); *Red, Brown, and Black* (1958). From the late 1940s, Rothko was concerned with the effects of color and simple geometrical forms, usually large, soft-edged rectangles, which created for him a feeling of the sublime. As time passed, his colors became darker and more somber.

Antoní Tàpies, *Gray Relief on Black* (1959). Francis Bacon, *Dog* (1952); *Study of a Baboon* (1953). Willem de Kooning, *Woman, I* (1950–52). De Kooning returned several times in his career to paintings of women. This aggressive, predatory, but nonetheless humorous image marked the painter's transition to a less figural style. The figure reminded him of a landscape, "with arms like lanes, and a body of hills and fields . . . a panorama all squeezed together."

Franz Kline, *Chief* (1950). David Smith, *History of LeRoy Burton* (1956). Ellsworth Kelly, *Colors for a Large Wall* (1951). Color Field painting was a logical outgrowth of Abstract Expressionism. Kelly's use of color fields is notable for the flatness of the color and for the hard-edge technique separating one field from another. Leon Polk Smith, *Anitou* (1958).

GALLERY 25. **Abstract Painting c. 1960: Johns, Rauschenberg, Twombly.** Jasper Johns, *Flags* (1954–55); *Target with Four Faces* (1955). Robert Rauschenberg, *Bed* (1955); *Green Target* (1955); *First Landing Jump* (1961). Cy Twombly, *The Italians* (1961).

GALLERY 26. **Abstract Painting, c. 1960: Fontana, Stella, Martin. Pop Art: Warhol, Oldenburg, Lichtenstein.** Agnes Martin, *The Tree* (1964). Ad Reinhardt, *Abstract Painting* (1963). Frank Stella, *The Marriage of Reason and Squalor, II* (1959). Yves Klein, *Blue Monochrome* (1961). Lucio Fontana, *Spatial Concept* (1957).

Andy Warhol, *Orange Car Crash Fourteen Times* (1963); *Gold Marilyn Monroe* (1962). Jasper Johns, *Map* (1961). Donald Judd, *Untitled* (1968). Claes Oldenburg, *Hamburger* (1962); *Two Cheeseburgers with Everything (Dual Hamburgers)* (1962); *Giant Soft Fan* (1966–67). James Rosenquist, *Marilyn Monroe, I* (1962). Roy Lichtenstein, *Girl with Ball* (1961) and *Drowning Girl* (1963).

STAIRWELL. Henri Matisse, *Memory of Oceania* (1952–53). This large abstraction was created at the end of Matisse's life, when age and illness prevented him from working standing at an easel. The title recalls a visit to Tahiti made some 20 years earlier.

The galleries beyond the stairwell contain changing exhibitions or selections from the Museum's collection of **Contemporary Art.** There is also a gallery for video, accessible from the Garden Hall.

Although the Museum's collection of **Prints and Illustrated Books** is not the largest in the country, it is one of the finest, since much of the collecting was accomplished before copies of works became difficult to find. It also is unusually diverse, containing prints by artists of some 64 countries.

A selection of prints from the permanent collection is usually on view, offering an overview of the medium from the time of Gauguin and Cézanne to the present. The prints are displayed in reduced light, necessary for their preservation. The largest gallery contains a changing selection of contemporary prints, suggesting recent choices made by the curators.

Fourth Floor

Design Collection. When the Museum was founded in 1929, the idea of amassing a collection focusing on architecture and design was a radical notion, and even today MoMA is still the only institution in the country with a curatorial department devoted to these aspects of art. The design collection focuses on mass-produced utilitarian objects created to serve a specific need, while the architectural archives include models and photographs of buildings as well as architectural drawings. Many of these drawings have their own intrinsic value as works of art in addition to their significance as records of architectural history. The Mies van der Rohe Archive contains more than 20,000 of his drawings.

Included in the more than 3,000 objects in the collection are household and office furniture, textiles, tools, tableware, and examples of industrial design. There are objects as diverse as pillboxes, nylon tents, vacuum cleaners, Tiffany lamps, self-aligning ball bearings, and an entrance arch to the Paris Métro. There are such classic objects as the Gerrit Rietveld *"Red and Blue" chair* and the Le Corbusier *tubular steel armchair,* as well as such ephemera as modern packaging materials. One of the most memorable objects is an automobile, the *Cisitalia "202" GT,* designed in 1946, the first auto to have entered a museum collection and a remarkable example of aerodynamic design. Equally imposing is a *Bell & Howell helicopter* which hangs in the stairwell.

The graphics collection—posters, typography, and other printed combinations of word and image—includes more than 4,000 items, notably a stellar collection of European and American posters.

Certain key works are kept permanently on display. Others are rotated several times a year. The architecture gallery is devoted to changing exhibitions of the work of major architects or seminal ideas of 20C architecture.

CHANGING EXHIBITIONS

In addition to its permanent collection, the Museum has through the years mounted outstanding changing exhibitions. The inaugural show, held in November 1929, was entitled "Cézanne, Gauguin, Seurat, van Gogh," and examined these precursors of modernism. A 1934 exhibition, "Machine Art," mounted by architect Philip Johnson, filled the building with examples of modern design and industrial engineering and formed the core of the design collection, since 100 objects—many by anonymous designers—were acquired from the show.

Later exhibitions have illustrated the continuing and changing concerns of the Museum. During World War II, the Museum began collecting American artists and established a commitment to avant-garde Americans which has resulted in rich holdings in Abstract Impressionism, for example. In the 1950s, the Museum mounted retrospectives of such important mid-career artists as David Smith and Jackson Pollock (who died a few months before his show opened). Major exhibitions in the '50s and '60s, such as "The Package" and "The Architecture of Japan," accompanied the growth of the architecture and design collections. Perhaps the most impressive exhibitions in a rich and varied program were the restrospectives of the work of Pablo Picasso (1980) and Henri Matisse (1993), the latter seen by 950,000 people.

HISTORY

When the Museum of Modern Art first opened its doors in 1929, the whole notion of "modern art" was still suspect with the public and also with the traditional museum establishment. In Buffalo, for example, the trustees of the Albright Art Gallery forced its president to resign because he had purchased a Picasso painting of the late Rose Period.

That the Museum came into being was the work of three influential women: Lillie P. Bliss, daughter of a textile manufacturer and a close friend of the painter Arthur B. Davies; Mary Quinn Sullivan, a former art teacher and later the wife of a successful attorney and collector; and Abby Aldrich Rockefeller, daughter of Senator Nelson W. Aldrich and wife of John D. Rockefeller, Jr. Mrs. Rockefeller had become interested in art as a young woman, traveling to Europe with her father and later developing a taste for modern art. In 1929 the three women asked A. Conger Goodyear, the former head of the Albright Art Gallery, to head a committee to form the proposed museum.

The first board of directors hired Alfred H. Barr, Jr., to direct the Museum. Through his studies and European travels Barr had developed the concept of a museum of modern art that would embrace all the arts of contemporary life, not just painting and sculpture. As a result of his vision the Museum of Modern Art through the years became a truly international, interdepartmental institution. Its first gift, eight prints and a drawing, has now grown to a collection of more than 100,000 objects.

Today, ironically, MoMA finds itself a conservative institution. Its strengths are those of a traditional museum, conserving the best of the past, offering a historical view of the sweep of "modern" art from the period of the Post-Impressionists to relatively recent times.

THE BUILDING

The Museum first opened in temporary quarters in the Heckscher Building at 630 Fifth Ave. In 1933 it moved to a house leased from John D. Rockefeller, Jr., at 11 W. 53rd St, now part of the Museum site. In 1939 the Museum moved to its new six-story building (now its central wing), designed by Philip L. Goodwin and Edward D. Stone, a building hailed as an exemplar of the International Style. The first Sculpture Garden, designed by John McAndrew, was installed behind the Museum on land also donated by John D. Rockefeller, Jr., and quickly became the urban oasis it remains today.

By the '60s the Museum facilities had become seriously inadequate and new wings designed by Philip Johnson (1964) were opened east and west of the 1939 building; at the same time Johnson redesigned the Sculpture Garden, which was renamed to honor Abby Aldrich Rockefeller.

A decade later, as the collections and the number of visitors continued to grow, the Museum again found its facilities inadequate. In 1976 it announced a program to expand its physical plant and to develop new sources of revenue. The air rights over its prime midtown location were sold to a developer, who raised a condominium apartment tower above a new museum wing west of the 1939 structure. Through a trust arrangement with the city, the Museum receives the benefits of most of the municipal real estate taxes generated by the apartment tower. Designed by Cesar Pelli & Assocs, the new building (1984) has allowed the Museum once again to show much of its magnificent collection.

The Museum of Television and Radio (54)

25 West 52nd St (bet. 5th / 6th Aves), New York 10019. Tel: (212) 621-6800 for recorded information on scheduled daily activities; to reach a live person, call 621-6600

ADMISSION: Open Tues–Sun 12–6; Thurs 12–8. Theaters and screening rooms remain open until 9 P.M. Fri for evening shows. Closed Mon, New Year's Day, July 4, Thanksgiving, and Christmas Day. Suggested donation.

Changing exhibitions, tours, special screenings. Lectures and seminars, often with TV and radio critics, performers, producers. Special events, educational programs, screenings of special interest to children (Sat and Sun).

✗ No restaurant.

🛍 Shop with T-shirts, posters, catalogues, museum publications, cassettes, gift items.

♿ Completely accessible to wheelchairs.

🚇 IND 8th Ave local (E train) to 5th Ave / 53rd St. IND 6th Ave local or express (B, D or F train) to 47–50th St / Rockefeller Center or (D or F train only) to 5th Ave / 53rd St. BMT Broadway line (N or R train) to 49th St / Broadway. IRT Lexington Ave local (train 6) to Lexington Ave / 51st St. IRT Broadway-7th Ave local (train 1 or 9) to 50th St.

🚌 M1, M2, M3, M4, downtown on 5th Ave, uptown on Madison Ave. M6 or M7 uptown on 6th Ave, downtown on Broadway.

The Museum of Television and Radio (formerly the Museum of Broadcasting) was founded (1975) by William S. Paley at a time when only a few private collectors and media buffs were recording and saving radio and TV programs. Today, because of the importance of radio and TV as documentary media, the collections of the Museum have grown to form not only an archive of radio and TV productions but a window onto the events and cultural trends of the last seven decades.

Visitors can explore the collection by viewing a program privately in the console rooms or by attending a television screening or radio presentation as part of an exhibition. There are also three gallery spaces with photographs and other artifacts relating to radio and TV.

PERMANENT COLLECTION

The collection (some 25,000 television programs, 15,000 radio shows, and 10,000 commercials) dates back to the dawn of broadcasting, when radio KDKA sent out its first signals over the airwaves in Pittsburgh in 1920. Documentary programs include decisive moments in 20C history, the earliest a 1920 broadcast by Franklin D. Roosevelt, then running for Vice President. The list includes an eyewitness account of the crash of the *Hindenburg* (1937), Adolf Hitler's address to the Reichstag in 1939, the Hiroshima news bulletin of 1945, and the signing of the 1968 Civil Rights Bill. There are also international events, including the abdication of Edward VIII (1936), the pageantry of Queen Elizabeth II's coronation (1952), and the diplomacy of Anwar Sadat in Israel (1977). More recent events include the Iran-Contra hearings (1987), the fall of the Berlin Wall (1989), and the Rodney King videotape of police brutality in Los Angeles (1991).

Radio nostalgia buffs can hear again the shows of yesteryear: Humphrey Bogart and Lauren Bacall in the Lux Radio Theatre's production of *To Have and Have Not* or Tallulah Bankhead in Theatre Guild on the Air's rendition of *All About Eve.*

The TV collection begins with such early pieces as an excerpt from a 1936 drama entitled *Poverty Is Not a Crime* and the 1944 historic broadcast by the NBC Symphony of Verdi's "Hymn of the Nations," with Arturo Toscanini conducting. TV drama includes episodes from Philco Television Playhouse, Producers' Showcase, and Robert Montgomery Presents (with Helen Hayes as Victoria Regina). Childhood TV favorites from *Kukla, Fran and Ollie* and *Howdy Doody* to the Muppets and Charlie Brown will entertain present and former children. Other performers in the collection include Sid Caesar, Lucille Ball, the Beatles, Elvis Presley, Ernie Kovacs, and Jackie Gleason.

EXHIBITION PROGRAM

Changing exhibitions drawn from the permanent collection have included a seven-month retrospective of the work of Jack Benny that showed how the Benny character was created and developed over a period of 40 years. A tribute to radio comedians Bob and Ray brought to life once again such zany characters as Bert and Harry Piel and Mary Backstayge, Noble Wife. A gallery exhibit and screening series highlighted the achievements of *Star Trek: The Next Generation* in using allegory to examine social and moral issues.

The Museum has a strong children's program that includes workshops where young people reenact classic radio programs, reading the script and working the sound effects. Other events include favorite stories narrated by famous actors and repeat performances of such beloved children's programs as the Muppets, *Sesame Street,* and the Flintstones.

Exhibits in the three gallery spaces have included the line drawings of Al Hirschfeld, who portrayed famous personalities of radio and television, and poster art of *Masterpiece Theatre* and *Mystery!*

THE BUILDING

In 1991 the Museum opened its new 17-story, high-tech facility (John Burgee Architects with Philip Johnson, design consultant). The six-story space features two theaters, two screening / listening rooms, and a radio listening room, as well as 96 television and radio consoles for individual viewing. The heart of the sophisticated retrieval system is a set of video library machines developed by Sony, each of which holds 800 videotapes and services 32 individual viewing consoles.

The Museum of the American Piano (55)

211 West 58th St (bet. 7th / 8th Aves), New York 10019. Tel: (212) 246-4646.

ADMISSION: Open Mon–Fri by reservation only. Closed weekends, holidays. Suggested donation. Call 10–4 weekdays. Group tours by arrangement. Ring doorbell for admission.

Lectures, recitals on historic instruments, newsletter, calendar of events. The Museum also offers specialized services to the musical community, including courses in piano tuning and technology, assessments and consultation in acquisition or maintenance of antique pianos, research on the history of older pianos, and piano restoration.

✖ No restaurant.

🛍 No gift shop.

&. Limited wheelchair accessibility. Museum on ground floor; wheelchairs may enter through sales room.

◎ Visitors may play the pianos in the exhibition but are asked to do so briefly.

🚇 IRT Broadway-7th Ave local (train 1 or 9) to 59th St / Columbus Circle; IND 6th or 8th Ave express (D or A train) to 59th St / Columbus Circle; IND 6th Ave local (B train) to 57th St / 6th Ave; BMT Broadway express or local (N or R train) to 57th St / 7th Ave.

🚌 M1, M2, M3, or M4 uptown on Madison Ave, downtown on 5th Ave. M5 uptown on 6th Ave, downtown on 5th Ave. M6 or M7 uptown on 6th Ave, downtown on 7th Ave and Broadway. M10 uptown on 8th Ave, downtown on Central Park West, Broadway, and 7th Ave. M27 / M50 crosstown on 49th and 50th Sts. M30 crosstown on 72nd and 57th Sts. Q32 crosstown on 59th and 60th Sts. M104 uptown on 8th Ave and Broadway, downtown on Broadway.

During the 19C, the piano played a significant role in American life, both socially and economically. The Museum of the American Piano (chartered 1981, opened 1984) was founded by Kalman Detrich to preserve and document the history of this important instrument. On view is a small, highly specialized exhibition of interest to anyone with a curiosity about pianos or the history of music in America.

PERMANENT COLLECTION

The collection contains examples of instruments by major American piano manufacturers, including Chickering, Steinway, and Weber. The earliest instrument in the collection is a clavichord, ancestor of the 19C square piano. Among the most historically important pieces are a *square piano by John Geib* (c. 1812), an American piano maker of German descent who had learned his craft in England before immigrating to the United States, and another *square piano* (c. 1825) by a nephew, *William Geib,* more heavily built and with a more robust tone. A *Nunns & Clark square piano* (c. 1850) illustrates techniques of stringing before the invention of the full plate, a cast-iron hitch-plate which would better support the strings. An *Emerson square piano* (1887) shows the advance of technology toward the end of the 19C; it is essentially a modern instrument with the exception of the rectangular shape of the case.

Several of the pianos in the collection are interesting as instrumental oddities. A *Kroeger "Giraffe" piano* (c. 1880) looks like a small upright with the strings extending above it on a gilded harp-shaped support. The purpose of the unusual configuration was social, not musical—to show off the performers (i.e., Victorian ladies) at their best physical advantage. An 1850 *Timothy Gilbert square piano* with a reed organ attachment is typical of a class of 19C pianos with add-ons that imitated other instruments, drums and bells, for example.

The Museum of the City of New York (81)

Fifth Ave at 103rd St, New York 10029. Tel: (212) 534-1672.

ADMISSION: Open Wed–Sat 10–5; Sun 1–5. Open to pre-registered school and group tours Tues 10–2. Closed to the public Mon, Tues, and legal holidays. Special rate for families. Suggested contribution.

Lectures, special events, concerts, walking tours of the city, free gallery talks associated with exhibits, films, guided tours for groups by reservation. Programs for children, including puppet shows, family workshops.

✘ No restaurant.

🏛 Interesting gift shop with a good collection of books about New York, miniatures, reproduction antique toys, ornaments, postcards, posters, exhibition-related merchandise.

♿ Accessible to wheelchairs. Ramp entrance on 104th St.

🚇 IRT Lexington Ave local (train 6) to 103rd St.

🚌 M1, M2, M3, M4, uptown on Madison Ave, downtown on 5th Ave.

The Museum of the City of New York (founded 1923) keeps alive the city's history by preserving its artifacts and documenting its past in a program of permanent and changing exhibitions. The collections, which number more than 3 million objects, include everything from fire engines to stripper Gypsy Rose Lee's hand-embroidered garter belt. Changing exhibitions may focus on a particular part of town, an urban problem, an artist, or some other aspect of the city's 300 years of artistic and political life.

HIGHLIGHTS

The dolls' houses, especially the *Stettheimer dollhouse.*
"Broadway!", an ongoing exhibition.
The silver collection.
The Rockefeller period rooms (closed occasionally).

PERMANENT COLLECTIONS

Among the historical objects in the collections are several lengths of wooden pipe from the city's first water-delivery system. The Prints and Photographs Collection has an outstanding group of Currier & Ives prints, as well as an extensive photo archive that includes the Jacob Riis Collection and the Byron Collection. The Theatre Collection is the most complete history of the New York stage ever assembled, and the Costume Collection, with clothing and accessories either worn by or designed by New Yorkers, is also outstanding. The collections of silver and furniture include work by well-known silversmiths and cabinetmakers, pieces owned in many cases by members of prominent New York families. Children and adults alike are drawn to the toys and dolls' houses and to the period rooms, all of which portray domestic life during various eras of the city's history.

Ground Floor

The FIRE GALLERY contains antique fire engines, prints and paintings of famous New York fires, fire engine models, and memorabilia. The display includes a section of wooden water pipes laid down by the Manhattan Company starting in 1799, not primarily for drinking water, but to fight fire. The Museum is fortunate to own one of the fire engines, "Big Six," formerly known as "Americus Six," that belonged to the company where William M. ("Boss") Tweed got his start. The engine (built 1851) is indeed large for the period and seems to have been unwieldy, for in 1855 it ran over two members of the company who were trying to fight a fire at Lord & Taylor's.

The Big Apple, a 22-min film on view in the ground-floor AUDITORIUM, summarizes more than 450 years of city history.

The COMMUNITY GALLERY houses changing exhibits which focus on the city's cultural and ethnic diversity.

Second Floor

At the north end of the corridor, six period alcoves recreate New York interiors from the late 17C to the early 20C, some of them from the homes of well-to-do New Yorkers.

The earliest of the period rooms is the 17C DUTCH ALCOVE. Some of the household items, silver, and Delft dishes are typical of wares imported by the Dutch Colonial settlers, but the room also contains American products, including a slat-back armchair (1680–1700) that once belonged to the Riker family of Newtown (now Elmhurst, Queens), and a linen press that belonged to the Bowne family of Flushing, Queens (see p. 395).

The ENGLISH COLONIAL PARLOR (1760–80) and the BERTHA KING BENKARD MEMORIAL BEDROOM (c. 1740–60) represent the late Colonial period. The STEPHEN WHITNEY DRAWING ROOM (c. 1830), from a house at 7 Bowling Green near Battery Park, and a VICTORIAN DRAWING ROOM (1856–57) from Brooklyn Heights represent changing tastes in the 19C. The most recent interior is the HARRY HARKNESS FLAGLER DRAWING ROOM from the Flagler town house at 32 Park Ave, built by Richard Morris Hunt, society architect of the Gilded Age. The room illustrates the lifestyle (and possibly the yearnings) of wealthy Americans at the turn of the century who attempted to live in the grand European manner.

In the CORRIDOR outside the period rooms is the ALEXANDER HAMILTON COLLECTION, including family furniture and portraits. The posthumously painted portrait of Hamilton (1806) is by John Trumbull; Ralph Earl painted his wife, *Elizabeth Schuyler Hamilton* (1787). Hamilton used the cylinder desk (c. 1800) of mahogany and satinwood late in his public career. Other portraits in the corridor are by John Durand, an artist probably of French origin, who painted portraits in New York beginning c. 1766.

J. CLARENCE DAVIES AND SILVER GALLERIES. In the J. Clarence Davies Gallery are changing selections of paintings, prints, maps, and documents reflecting the history of the city. Davies began his remarkable collection in 1892; at his death in 1934, it numbered 15,000 items. Among its treasures are the *Hartgers view* (1651), which is the earliest known view of the Dutch settlement on Manhattan, and the *Commissioners Map* (published 1811), engraved by Peter Maverick. It depicts the laying out of the future city into the systematic lots, streets, and avenues that exist today.

The Museum owns one of the finest collections of silver in the country. Selections are shown in the Davies Gallery as well as in the adjoining Silver Gallery. Among the most beautiful objects are 18C pieces made by New York silversmiths of Dutch, English, and French background. The craftsmen represented in the collection include Cornelius Kierstede, a native New Yorker and one of the most accomplished artists in the history of the craft; Jurian Blanck, Jr.; Benjamin Wynkoop; Charles Le Roux; his grandson Bartholomew Le Roux; and Nicholas Roosevelt. Myer Myers, a freeman of the city active in Jewish affairs, was president of the New York Silver Smith's Society after the Revolution.

Among the florid 19C silver are pieces by the city's premier firm of the period, Tiffany & Co.

On the walls are portraits of illustrious 18–19C New Yorkers, which are rotated from time to time. The Museum owns a notable portrait of *Robert R. Livingston* by Gilbert Stuart. Livingston was one of the drafters of the Declaration of Independence and later supported Robert Fulton in his experiments with steam navigation; as a statesman his supreme achievement was negotiating the Louisiana Purchase. Also in the collection is one of the finest of Stuart's portraits of *George Washington* (1795). John Singleton Copley painted Loyalist *Henry White* in London between 1782 and 1786, where he had moved after his American property was confiscated in 1779.

Nearby is the MARINE GALLERY, with ship models, figureheads, paintings, photographs, and maps to trace the history of New York as a port from 1524 to the present. Near the entrance is a 2-ton zinc statue of Robert Fulton, promoter of steamboat travel, whose efforts enhanced the city's commercial success. Among the resources on which the exhibitions may draw is the Andrew Fletcher Collection of paintings of steamers.

Third Floor

At the north end is the TOY GALLERY, which has a collection of New York toys from the late 18C onward. The most famous exhibit in the gallery is the permanent DOLLS' HOUSE GALLERY of period dolls' houses and furniture from 1769 to the present, including the *Goelet House* (1845), modeled on the former family brownstone at 890 Broadway (19th St), and the *Stettheimer House* (1925), which was decorated by Carrie Stettheimer, one of three sisters active in the city's artistic community during the 1920s. The interiors, meticulously executed, include wonderful miniature reproductions of works of art by Marcel Duchamp, Gaston Lachaise, and William Zorach, as well as dolls representing such celebrities as writer Gertrude Stein, composer Virgil Thomson, and photographer Edward Steichen. The other two Stettheimer sisters were Florine, a painter whose work is in the Metropolitan Museum of Art and the Museum of Modern Art, and Ettie, who wrote novels under the *nom de plume* "Henri Waste."

Portraits on this floor depict men and women who shaped the economic and social growth of the city during the period 1820–1920, when it rose to dominance. Included here are: *William Henry Vanderbilt* (1881), by Eastman Johnson; *August Belmont* (cast 1891), sculpted in bronze by John Quincy Adams Ward; *Nicholas Fish* (1823), by Henry Inman; and *Caroline Slidell Perry Belmont* (1859), by George Peter Alexander Healy. Healy was the leading society painter of his day; Mrs. Belmont was the niece of naval hero Oliver Hazard Perry and the wife of August Belmont, representative of the Rothschild banking interests.

"Broadway!", a long-term exhibition, looks at the development of this famous street from its early days as a humble footpath to its glittering present as "The Great White Way." Tintypes and contemporary photographs, early maps and views of the city, 19C newspapers, and modern oil paintings illuminate the history of this famous thoroughfare.

Fifth Floor

The ROCKEFELLER ROOMS, a master bedroom and dressing room from the home of John D. Rockefeller, Sr, date from the early 1880s. When the Rockefeller residence at 4 East 54th St was demolished (1937) to make way for the Museum of Modern Art, John D. Rockefeller, Jr, offered two rooms in the "Japanese" and American Renaissance styles to the Museum. The MASTER BEDROOM, decorated in a style made popular by Charles Eastlake, English writer of works on art and decoration, has a stenciled ceiling and dark ebonized woodwork with light wood inlays of "Japanese" flora. Beyond the archway with its stained-glass screen is a cozy "Turkish corner," whose presence along with the "Japanese" woodwork may seem excessively eclectic to modern tastes. However, during the 1880s through the turn of the century such Turkish—or Persian, Indian, or Moorish—nooks were said to provide their owners with a particular sense of rest. The weary industrialist, exhausted by commercial strife, could sink into his retreat and, soothed by soft carpets, embroideries, and gleams of art metalwork and porcelain, refresh himself for the next day's struggle.

The DRESSING ROOM has light maple woodwork with rosewood and mother-of-pearl inlay, a marble sink with a hand-painted porcelain basin, and an imposing clothes press and dresser decorated with carved cherub heads and footed urns.

EXHIBITION PROGRAM

Special exhibitions have included shows on subjects as diverse as the New York of Walt Whitman, the urban poor as seen through the lens of Jacob Riis, and the elegant artistic milieu of Louis Comfort Tiffany. An ongoing exhibition entitled "Broadway!" offers a survey of musicals from *The Black Crook,* which opened in 1866 abd provoked attention with scantily clad women and stunning special effects, through the great years of the Gershwins and Rodgers and Hammerstein, to a revival of *Showboat* in 1994. "Ladies' Mile: Emporia and Entertainment" offered a glimpse of New York in the Gilded Age. A lavish exhibition that included concerts, walking tours, and theatrical events commemorated the genius of Duke Ellington.

HISTORY

Originally located in Gracie Mansion, now the mayor's official residence, the Museum moved to its present red brick neo-Georgian Colonial home (architect Joseph Freedlander) in 1931. The Museum focuses on material directly connected to the city—either objects made in the city or directly related to its history.

The National Academy of Design (82)

1083 Fifth Ave (bet. 89th / 90th Sts), New York 10128. Tel: (212) 369-4880.

ADMISSION: Open Wed, Thurs, Sat, and Sun 12–5; Fri 12–8. Closed Mon, Tues, major holidays. Admission charge except Fri 5–8, when admission is free.

Changing exhibitions, lectures, symposia. Guided tours for groups by appointment. Research facilities by appointment.

✘ No restaurant.

▥ Bookshop with art books, catalogues, postcards, posters.

&. Accessible to wheelchairs; elevator to upstairs galleries.

🚇 IRT Lexington Ave express or local (train 4, 5, or 6) to 86th St.

🚌 M1, M2, M3, or M4 uptown on Madison Ave, downtown on 5th Ave. M86 crosstown on 86th St. M19 crosstown on 96th St.

The National Academy of Design (1825), headquartered in an elegant Fifth Ave town house, draws its members from the ranks of the nation's established painters, sculptors, graphic artists, and architects. Its exhibition program includes not only the work of the members but loan exhibitions from here and abroad.

THE BUILDING

The house (1914; Ogden Codman, Jr.) was donated to the Academy in 1940 by Archer Milton Huntington, whose wife, sculptor Anna Hyatt Huntington, belonged to the Academy. Cool, elegant, and formal, with an abundance of marble, classical detail, and a sweeping spiral staircase, the house suggests at once the lifestyle of the rich and famous and the conservatism often associated with the academic tradition.

HISTORY

Founded in 1825 as a school and exhibition center by painters Samuel F. B. Morse and Rembrandt Peale, architect Ithiel Town, sculptor John Frazee, and engraver Peter Maverick, the Academy still maintains a school (around the corner at 5 East 89th St). Among its members during the last century were Thomas Eakins, Winslow Homer, Augustus Saint-Gaudens, and John Singer Sargent; those elected more recently include painters Isabel Bishop, Raphael Soyer, Robert Rauschenberg, Willem de Kooning, and Jim Dine; sculptors Marisol, Bruno Lucchesi, and Isamu Noguchi; and architects I. M. Pei, Hugh G. Hardy, and Philip Johnson.

The collection of more than 2,000 paintings, 200 works of sculpture, and 1,000 drawings also contains architectural renderings, prints, and photographs; in part it is the product of a ruling that members supply a representative sample of their work, which in the case of painters has often been a self-portrait. Since the collection has been gathered over a 150-year span, it also suggests important currents in American art over that period, and is particularly strong in landscapes of the Hudson River School and Realism of the 1930s and 1940s. Selections from the permanent collection are shown on a rotating basis.

EXHIBITION PROGRAM

Some of the 10 to 12 yearly exhibitions are drawn from the collection, e.g., an exhibition of Hudson River School paintings or a show entitled "Artists by Themselves," which focused on portraits and included works by Asher B. Durand, Eastman Johnson, Robert Henri, William Glackens, and Reginald Marsh.

The Academy also mounts loan exhibitions from here and abroad and an annual juried show every spring. To celebrate the New York Botanical Garden's centennial year, the Academy offered "Illustrating Nature: The Art of Botany," which included drawings, watercolors, and dried specimens from their collection. Among the loan exhibitions have been "The Art of Babar: Drawings by Jean and Laurent de Brunhoff," and "The Drawings of Henry Fuseli," a small show of extraordinary work, outstanding in its thematic and chronological breadth.

The National Museum of the American Indian, Smithsonian Institution: George Gustav Heye Center (26)

In the Alexander Hamilton U.S. Custom House, One Bowling Green (Broadway at Battery Park), New York 10004. Tel: (212) 668-6624 for recorded information. To reach a live person, call (212) 825-6700.

ADMISSION: Open 10–5 every day except Christmas Day. Free.

Resource Center; changing exhibitions; demonstrations and performances; films; publications; school programs. Group tours and gallery talks by appointment.

✗ No restaurant.

🏛 Gallery Shop with jewelry, baskets, rugs, textiles, carvings, pottery, and prints by Native American artists; publications, books. Museum Shop with souvenirs, craft items, gifts, books, and toys.

♿ Completely accessible to wheelchairs.

🚫 No flash photography.

🚇 IRT Broadway-7th Ave local (train 1 or 9) to South Ferry. IRT Lexington Ave express (trains 4 or 5) to Bowling Green. BMT Broadway express or local (train N or R) to Whitehall St.

🚌 M1 (marked South Ferry) downtown via 5th Ave, Park Ave South, and Broadway. M6 downtown via 7th Ave and Broadway. M15 downtown via 2nd Ave and Allen St.

The National Museum of the American Indian, Smithsonian Institution (chartered by Congress 1989; George Gustav Heye Center opened 1994), is the world's largest and finest museum of Native American artifacts. It merges the collections of the Smithsonian Institution with those of the former Museum of the American Indian / Heye Foundation (1916). The George Gustav Heye Center, opposite Battery Park, is the New York branch of the institution and offers exhibitions drawn from the collection as well as ongoing public programs devoted to Native American culture.

HISTORY

The Museum of the American Indian was born from the obsession of George Gustav Heye (1874–1957), who gathered most of its astonishing collection. The son of a wealthy German oil baron who sold out handsomely to John D. Rockefeller, George Heye (pronounced "High") took a job after college in Arizona as an electrical engineer. One day he saw the wife of a Navajo foreman biting on what seemed to be a piece of skin; in fact, she was chewing the seams of her husband's deerskin shirt to kill the lice. Heye bought the shirt, the first object in his collection, only to find that he also wanted moccasins and a rattle to go with it. After that, he wrote later, the "collecting bug" seized him and he was lost.

At first Heye, who eventually became an investment banker, acquired individual objects a few at a time. Later he collected wholesale, over the years repeatedly criss-crossing the West and even financing expeditions to Central and South America, which combined archeological inquiry with acquisition. Heye initially stored his collection in his apartment; outgrowing that, he moved it to a loft building on East 33rd St and later (1922) to Audubon Terrace (Broadway at 155th St).

Although the Museum flourished in the early years after it opened on Audubon Terrace, the death of two generous trustees and the collapse of the stock market weakened it financially. Its location, far from the cultural center of the city in a neighborhood increasingly afflicted with crime and poverty, exacerbated these problems.

After several years of failed negotiations with institutions in New York City, the Museum merged (1989) with the Smithsonian Institution. The Custom House, federal property vacant since 1973, was chosen as the site for the Heye Center. The Smithsonian will also construct a building for the National Museum of the American Indian on the Mall in Washington, D.C. Scheduled to open in 2001, this building will house both the bulk of the Heye Foundation collection and the Smithsonian's own holdings. A conservation and research facility, the Museum Support Center (opening 1997), in Suitland, Md., will contain the library and archives.

The present Museum's goals reflect attitudes toward Indian cultures and art that have evolved in the decades since Heye died. First, the Museum aspires to show

American Indian art as art, not as natural history, anthropology, or handcraft. Second, in its commitment to Indian culture and its recognition that much Indian art has ceremonial and spiritual as well as aesthetic importance, the Museum relies on the advice of Indian people in preparing exhibitions that will be accurate and sensitively presented. Heye's own insatiable methods of collecting are no longer condoned and the Museum is by law required to return to the tribes sacred objects and human remains.

THE COLLECTION

Known both for its depth and breadth, the collection includes artifacts of aboriginal peoples from North, Central, and South America, from the Eskimos of the Arctic region to the inhabitants of Tierra del Fuego. The objects span more than 10,000 years, ranging from prehistoric stone clovis points to contemporary silkscreen prints. Strengths within the collection are *horn, wood,* and *stone carvings* by the *Northwest Coast Indians; Kachina dance masks and dolls;* rare Caribbean archeological objects; textiles from Peru and Mexico; Southwest American basketry; goldwork from Colombia, Mexico, and Peru; and jade from the Olmec and Maya people. Among the articles of personal memorabilia are *Sitting Bull's drum* and *Geronimo's hat.* Altogether the collection has more than 1 million objects and a photo archive of some 86,000 prints and negatives.

EXHIBITION PROGRAM

The inaugural exhibition consisted of three displays. "All Roads Are Good: Native Voices on Life and Culture" presented works chosen from the permanent collection by 23 Native Americans—artists, storytellers, scholars, and tribal leaders. On view were intricately beaded Ojibwe bandolier bags, a Sioux parasol, a Haida hat closely woven of spruce roots, and a large collection of simple and decorated moccasins from Arapaho, Assiniboin, Athabaskan, Comanche, Osage, Tuscarora, Yurok, and Zuni tribes. The Native Americans who picked these objects recorded, often in moving words, the reasons for their choices.

"Creation's Journey," closing in 1997, offers a selection of 165 masterworks. On view are objects, all of them wonderfully crafted and many of them stunningly beautiful, used for everyday and ceremonial purposes. Among them are Tuscarora and Mohawk beaded caps; a Chilkat Tlingit hat with a bear crest; Chochiti Pueblo pottery figures; a Seminole man doll dressed in patchwork clothing; carved duck decoys (A.D. 200) from Humboldt County, Nev.; a Northern Cheyenne quillwork mask for a horse; Haida house posts with carved animal faces; feather ornaments from Brazil and Peru; and fabrics from Chile.

The inaugural exhibit also included a collaborative installation by 15 contemporary Native American artists. Containing items as disparate as TV sets and a burial platform, it focused on themes of creation, sacred places, and conflicts between Indian and Euro-American beliefs.

THE BUILDING

The Alexander Hamilton U.S. Custom House (1907) is a superb example of Beaux-Arts architecture. It sits at the foot of Broadway, originally an Algonquian trade route, on a spot once occupied by the fort protecting the original Dutch settlement. While the Custom House is one of the city's

Shield with Snapping Turtle, Northern Plains people. The National
Museum of the American Indian (opened 1994) merges the collections
of the Smithsonian Institution and George Gustav Heye (1874–1957),
an impassioned private collector.
(National Museum of the American Indian, Smithsonian Institution:
George Gustav Heye Center)

important architectural monuments, the organization of its interior spaces makes it less than a perfect site for exhibiting art.

EXTERIOR. The Custom House, designed by Cass Gilbert, was constructed as a monument to commerce. The four pedestals at the entrance support seated female figures symbolizing the four continents; they were designed by Daniel Chester French, creator of the statue of Abraham Lincoln at the Lincoln Memorial in Washington, D.C. Not surprisingly, the groups reflect early-20C cultural attitudes. Asia and Africa, meditative and somnolent, sit at the periphery. America (left of stairs) looks dynamically forward. On her right, Labor turns the wheel of progress; on her left, an Indian kneels, eyes downcast, subjected to her power.

INTERIOR. The LOBBY is a grand monument of high arches and columns, walls covered with marbles of different colors and textures. It leads to the central ROTUNDA, with an immense arched ceiling. Constructed of tile and plaster according to engineering principles of immigrant Rafael Guastavino, the arch with its 140-ton elliptical skylight contains no metalwork and has no visible means of support. Beneath it, murals by New York painter Reginald Marsh show early explorers of America and the progress of a ship entering New York Harbor. One of the most celebrated panels depicts Greta Garbo, on deck, surrounded by reporters and photographers.

The New Museum of Contemporary Art (27)

583 Broadway (bet. Prince / Houston Sts), New York 10012. Tel: (212) 219-1355 for recorded information; to reach a live person, call (212) 219-1222.

ADMISSION: Open Wed, Thurs, Fri, and Sun 12–6; Sat 12–8. Closed Mon and Tues, New Year's Day, July 4, and Christmas Day. Admission charge; children under 12 free. Free hours, Sat 6–8.

Lectures, panels, visitor programs, seminars, films, publications, catalogues, performances of art and music. Educational programs for high school students, high school art learning guide.

✘ No restaurant.

🛍 Catalogues, books, and limited-edition prints.

♿ No ramp, but all galleries are on ground-floor level.

⊘ No photography.

🚇 IRT Lexington Ave local (train 6) to Spring St or Bleecker St. IND 8th Ave line (A, C, or E train) to Spring St. BMT Broadway local (N or R train) to Prince St. IND 6th Ave line (B, D, or F train) to Broadway / Lafayette St.

🚌 Bus M1 downtown on 5th Ave, Park Ave South, and Broadway (make sure you get a bus labeled South Ferry; otherwise walk south from 8th St or transfer to the M6 at 8th St). Uptown on Centre St and Lafayette St to Grand or Canal St. M5 downtown on 5th Ave. M6 downtown on Broadway and uptown on 6th Ave. M21 crosstown on Houston St.

The New Museum of Contemporary Art (founded 1977) is the only museum in the city devoted exclusively to contemporary art; it is concerned with the work of living artists and is committed to looking at their work in relation to contemporary ideas and the issues of society.

EXHIBITION PROGRAM

Three major exhibitions are mounted annually in the primary gallery space. Not unexpectedly, the Museum searches out emerging talent and was the first institution in the city to exhibit such now prominent artists as Jenny Holzer and David Hammons; it also gave major solo shows to John Baldessari, Leon Golub, Hans Haacke, Ana Mendieta, and Martin Puryear, long before their places in the art world were established. Other shows have included exhibitions of established artists in mid-career and mature artists whose work has not engaged serious scrutiny, as well as retrospectives of older artists outside the mainstream.

Exhibitions explore a variety of themes ranging from chaos theory, to television and its impact, to such social problems as AIDS. The New Museum has mounted installations by AIDS activist groups Act Up! and Gran Fury; in one exhibition, artists from the collaborative group General Idea reworked Robert Indiana's four-letter graphic LOVE image, which captured the popular imagination in the 1960s, re-spelling it as AIDS.

Other shows explore the relationship between the artist, the work of art, and the viewer. In a 1988 exhibit, "The Living Paintings," three spray-painted artists actually hung from their own paintings six hours a day and discussed art with gallery goers.

In keeping with its interests in exploring experimental art and introducing lesser-known artists, the New Museum mounted "Bad Girls," a two-part multimedia show of works by and about women marked by conspicuous humor and dubious taste. Included were Stephanie Ellis's *Pink Satin Panties,* foundation garments blown up to billboard size, Portia Munson's cloying collection of pink objects, Elizabeth Berdann's copper miniatures *Topless Hall of Fame,* and Chuck Nanney's photographic self-portraits of himself done up in women's clothes. An audiotape piped through the women's and men's bathrooms during the exhibition featured two hours of nonstop "Bad Blues, Ballads, and Boogie," with such hits as the Derivative Duo's "PMS Aria" and Ethel Waters's "No Man's Mama."

The On View program occupies the Workspace and the New Work Gallery, at the rear of the first floor behind the primary gallery space, and the Window on Broadway. The program mounts smaller exhibits planned with a quick turnaround time.

The Museum also offers performance art—an experimental genre that mixes literature, theater, music, video, and dance. One landmark program was a seven-year performance project by Linda Montano, a sculptor and ex-nun best known for having been tied by a rope to another artist for a year without the two touching one another. Montano appeared in the Mercer Street Window on specified dates from 1984 to 1991 to discuss life and art with Museum visitors.

SEMIPERMANENT COLLECTION

The New Museum has a semipermanent collection of works that are constantly being acquired and sold off, thus maintaining a constant focus on recent works of art. In addition to donated works, the collection (currently numbering some 120 objects) includes pieces chosen from the changing exhibits to serve as a matter of record for the Museum. Works in the collection, which must have been created within the last decade, are retained for a period of at least 10 but not more than 20 years, and then are deaccessioned in order to acquire more recent art.

HISTORY

The New Museum of Contemporary Art was founded by its present director, Marcia Tucker, a former curator of painting and sculpture at the Whitney Museum of American Art. Tucker's ideas about showing living artists outside the mainstream and her misgivings about established museum management led her to start a museum that would focus on truly contemporary art, displaying only works created in the past decade. The premise of the New Museum was that art and its political and social contexts are inseparable. Thus the Museum would be current, responsive to artists, and democratic in its management style, unlike most museums, whose power structure is hierarchical and authoritarian.

In 1983 the Museum moved from temporary quarters in the New School of Social Research to its present SoHo home, a Beaux-Arts landmark building constructed by John Jacob Astor, whose fortune owed a great deal to speculation in New York real estate.

The New York Academy of Sciences (83)

2 East 63rd St (5th Ave), New York 10021. Tel: (212) 838-0230.

ADMISSION: Open Mon–Fri 10–4. Closed weekends, legal holidays, July and Aug. Free.

Changing exhibitions.

✗ No restaurant.

⌂ No gift shop.

♿ Call ahead for portable wheelchair ramp.

🚆 IRT Lexington Ave local (train 6) to 68th St.

🚌 M1, M2, M3, or M4 uptown on Madison Ave or downtown on 5th Ave.

The New York Academy of Sciences (founded 1817) seeks to advance scientific research and to enhance public understanding of science and its implications for society. In the lobby of its handsome building, the Academy offers a program of changing exhibitions showing the interaction between the arts and sciences. There are some six shows yearly, which have ranged from Mexican artist Remedios Varo's "Science and Surrealism" to photographs by Berenice Abbott demonstrating "The Beauty of Physics." Abbott's pictures documented visually the working of physical laws e.g., in a series of multiple exposures, recording the path of a thrown wrench as it spun through the air or the trajectory of a steel ball shot vertically upward. "Chemistry Imagined," by Vivian Torrence, working with Roald Hoffmann, Nobel Laureate in Chemistry, offered a series of watercolors based on objects associated with chemistry. Other shows have touched on pinhole photography, Darwinian evolutionary theory, geology, and the classic figures of Euclidean plane geometry.

Each spring during National Science and Technology Week, the Academy offers a high school student art show, with paintings, drawings, and photographs on scientific subjects or inspired by scientific concepts.

THE BUILDING

The Academy is housed in a former Fifth Ave mansion built (1920) by William Ziegler, Jr., president of the Royal Baking Powder Company. Members of the Woolworth family lived there and later gave it to the Academy.

The New York City Fire Museum (28)

278 Spring St (bet. Hudson / Varick Sts), New York 10013. Tel: (212) 691-1303.

ADMISSION: Open Tues–Sun 10–4. Closed Mon, holidays. Admission charge.

Changing exhibitions. Group tours by appointment.

✘ No restaurant.

🛍 Gift shop with fire memorabilia, toys, T-shirts, books, souvenirs.

♿ Ground floor accessible to wheelchairs; 2nd floor currently inaccessible.

⊘ Special photography by appointment only.

🚇 IRT Broadway-7th Ave local (train 1) to Houston St (walk south) or Canal St (walk north). IND 8th Ave local (C or E train) to Spring St (walk west).

🚌 M10 downtown via Central Park West, 7th Ave, and Varick St to Spring St. Any north-south bus line (M1, M5, M6, M15, M102) that intersects the M21 Houston St crosstown; then M21 to Varick and Spring Sts.

Housed in a restored former fire station, the New York City Fire Museum (founded 1987) holds one of the richest collections of firefighting memorabilia in the nation, combining the acquisitions of the New York City Fire Department and the Home Insurance Company, a firm with vested interest in fire prevention. Exhibits trace the history of firefighting in the city, from the first fires in New Amsterdam fought by amateur fire brigades, through the heady days of the Volunteer Fire Department when firefighting was something of a competitive high-risk sport, the creation of the Metropolitan Fire Department (1865), the first municipal fire department, to the present FDNY, which extends its services throughout the boroughs.

PERMANENT COLLECTION

GROUND FLOOR. The exhibits here focus on the technical side of firefighting—equipment and firefighting techniques. The main gallery houses a group of horse-drawn vehicles, including both steamers and pumpers: a 1901 *American La France engine* that could deliver some 700 gallons per minute; a horse-drawn *hook and ladder* (1882) made by Gleason & Bailey; and two *early 19C hand pumpers* made by the prominent New York firm of James Smith. From a later period is a *"Metropolitan" steamer* (1912), originally fitted with a front-wheel-drive tractor.

Other displays on this floor include the *Tool Wall,* with axes, hooks, saws, and other antique tools, as well as a modern roof saw and hand tools with wrench attachments for shutting off gas lines. An exhibit of

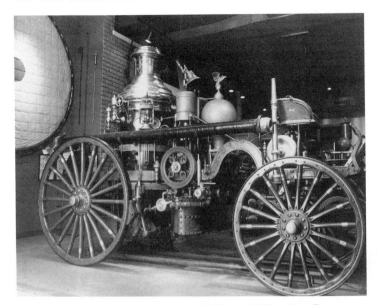

This La France engine steam pumper (1901) could deliver 700 gallons per minute. Exhibits at the New York City Fire Museum, which combine collections of the FDNY and the Home Insurance Co., trace the history of firefighting in the city.
(Collection of the New York City Fire Museum)

fire-alarm boxes traces the development of the fire call box from the old keyed type through boxes whose messages were sent by voice communication, to the present electronic type. Photos and models bring to life the age of horse-drawn fire engines and document such innovations as the quick release harness, which greatly decreased the time it took a company to hitch up and get under way.

SECOND FLOOR. Upstairs, the exhibits concentrate on the pomp and pageantry of firefighting, with a large collection of parade hats, trumpets, badges, portraits, and the world's largest collection of fire insurance marks, fastened on buildings to inform fire brigades that the property was insured.

Among the silver ceremonial objects is an extravagant *Punch Set* (1872), its cups and bowl supported by silver firemen, hydrants, and hoses, its ladle shaped like a helmet. Here also are engines, including two especially fine ones, the elaborately painted *"Hope"* and the *"Bolton Quick Step,"* dating back to 1765 and fitted with unusual pivoting brakes. William M. ("Boss") Tweed got his start in city politics as a volunteer firefighter with Americus Engine Company Number 6; the Museum has his helmet frontpiece and trumpet.

Other displays on this floor include photographs and paintings documenting the most devastating fires in the nation's history, including the historic conflagrations of Chicago and San Francisco, and New York's Triangle Shirtwaist fire.

CHANGING EXHIBITIONS

A separate small gallery on the ground floor is set aside for special exhibits, which have included exhibitions on New York City firehouses, women firefighters, and the city waterworks.

THE BUILDING

Constructed in 1904–05 (architect Edward Pierce Casey), the Renaissance Revival style firehouse was formerly the home of Engine Company 30.

The New York City Police Museum (56)

235 East 20th St (bet. 2nd / 3rd Aves), New York 10003. Tel: (212) 477-9753.

ADMISSION: Open Mon–Fri 9–2. Closed weekends, major holidays. During school year, groups admitted by appointment only. Museum closed to groups July–Aug. Visitors are advised to call ahead since the Museum is occasionally closed during training sessions. Free.

Changing exhibitions.

✖ No restaurant.

⛫ No gift shop.

♿ Not accessible to wheelchairs.

🚇 IRT Lexington Ave local (train 6) to 23rd St.

🚌 M15 downtown on 2nd Ave, uptown on 1st Ave. M101 or M102 uptown on 3rd Ave, downtown on Lexington Ave.

Since 1929 the New York City Police Department Museum, located on the second floor of the Police Academy, has been a repository of memorabilia of New York's Finest, housing one of the largest collections of police memorabilia in the world.

PERMANENT COLLECTION

The collection contains some 50,000 objects, including guns, knives, nightsticks, badges and uniform articles, and a large collection of photographs. Among the guns are examples of pepperbox pistols, tommy guns, and early rapid-fire guns, including the first submachine gun used to kill anyone in New York. There are "Saturday night specials" (.38-caliber pistols), Uzi submachine guns, and even a machine gun in a violin case, confirming the actual existence of this piece of equipment which achieved legendary status during Prohibition years.

The Museum owns a run of every type of New York City Police badge issued from 1845 to the present, as well as a collection of uniform articles dating back to 1870, including police caps. There are albums of photographs showing policemen of the past wearing these articles and police blotters detailing sensational and run-of-the-mill crimes.

A growing international section offers uniform articles, hats, batons, and other accoutrements from police forces throughout the world, with artifacts from Germany, Holland, England, Israel, and elsewhere. The display shows the continuity of symbolism from one force to another— the use of traditional and symbolic colors (white, green, or blue) and insignia.

CHANGING EXHIBITIONS

Changing exhibits focus on such topics as Police Fraternal Organizations, medals of honor, and the career of Al Capone.

HISTORY

Much of the collection was gathered by Alfred J. Young, who served the Police Department as a detective and for ten years was curator of the Museum. Some objects have been donated by police officers and their families, while others—weapons, for example—were confiscated by the police and donated to the Museum by the police property clerk.

The New-York Historical Society (95)

170 Central Park West (W. 76th / 77th Sts), New York 10024. Tel: (212) 873-3400.

ADMISSION: Open Wed–Sun 12–5. Closed Mon, Tues, and national holidays. Library open Wed–Fri 12–5. Suggested donation.

Changing exhibitions, lectures, gallery tours, events for children and families.

✘ No restaurant.

▥ No gift shop.

♿ Accessible to wheelchairs, but visitors are requested to inquire about facilities at the Admissions Desk or by telephoning ahead.

⃠ No photography without permission.

🚇 IND 8th Ave local (C train) to 81st St / Central Park West. IND 6th Ave express (B train marked 168th St / Broadway, weekdays only) to 81st St / Central Park West. IRT Broadway-7th Ave local (train 1 or 9) or IRT 7th Ave express (train 2 or 3) to 79th St / Broadway.

🚌 M10 uptown on 8th Ave / Central Park West. M79 crosstown on 79th / 81st Sts.

The New-York Historical Society (1804) is one of the city's most venerable museums, as the old-fashioned spelling of the name, New-York, suggests. Its impressive collections make it an important resource in studying the early years of the American experience as well as the history of New York City. Housed in a granite landmark building, the Society maintains a museum with fine holdings of art and Americana and a library with a major research collection.

HISTORY

The Museum was founded in 1804 by lawyer John Pintard, who had earlier represented George Washington in New York. The Society began as a repository of historical documents related to the city's role during the founding of the nation. Over the years its holdings expanded to include Americana, European paintings, and, for a while during the 19C, botanical, zoological, and mineralogical specimens, as well as fossils, coins, and medals. Today, the focus of the Museum is the history of the city and state of New York.

During recent years, the Society has fallen upon fiscal hard times. It was forced to shut its doors to the public from 1993 to 1995, and in 1995 it auctioned off paintings and other objects to raise money. The Society reopened as a museum in May 1995, with an exhibition that showcased the remarkable holdings of the permanent collection.

PERMANENT COLLECTION

Among the highlights of the collection are John James Audubon's watercolors for *The Birds of America.* Published (1827–38) by London engraver Robert Havell, this became one of the most valued books ever printed, and the Society is fortunate to own all but two of the 435 original watercolors.

The Society owns other fine American paintings, including genre paintings and landscapes as well as works with allegorical and heroic subjects: Thomas Cole, *The Vale and Temple of Segestae, Sicily* (1844); Albert Bierstadt, *Autumn Woods* (1886); John Vanderlyn, *Ariadne Asleep on the Island of Naxos* (before 1831); Benjamin West, *Aeneas Parting with His Family* (1771); Daniel Huntington, *Sowing the Word* (1868).

Among the landscapes by members of the Hudson River School are: Asher B. Durand, *White Mountain Scenery: Franconia Notch, New Hampshire* (1857); Albert Bierstadt, *Black Mountain from the Harbor Islands, Lake George, New York* (1875); and Frederic Edwin Church, *Cayambe* (1858). Other important paintings include a grandiose allegory by Thomas Cole, *The Course of Empire.* Although Cole is best known as a landscape painter and founder of the Hudson River School, during a visit to Europe in 1829–32 he came under the influence of both Turner and John Martin, a popular English painter famous for his depiction of catastrophic events. Thereafter, Cole painted a number of grand allegorical and historical paintings, of which this series is one of the most admired. Its five paintings—*The Savage State* (1834–36), *The Arcadian or Pastoral State* (1834–36), *The Consummation of Empire* (1835–36), *Destruction* (1836), and *Desolation* (1836)—present a romantic rendering of the evolution of civilization from its animalistic beginnings to its ruin-strewn endings.

Portraits of wealthy and prominent New Yorkers—Livingstons, De Peysters, and Beekmans—illustrate the development of American portraiture in the 18–19C. Included are Rembrandt Peale's likeness of *Stephen Decatur* (c. 1815–20) and Alexis Joseph Perignon's undoubtedly flattering rendering of *James Gordon Bennett* (1867), heir to the *New York Herald* fortune. Most arresting, however, is an anonymous early 18C portrait of Edward Hyde, Viscount Cornbury, who served as governor of New York and New Jersey (1702–08). He is depicted dressed as a woman, something he occasionally did because, he said, he acted in the person of his cousin, Queen Anne.

Other portraits include Benjamin West's *Charles Willson Peale* (1767–69), and three works by Charles Willson Peale: *The Peale Family* (c. 1770–73); *Self-Portrait* (1824); and *George Washington* (1795). Peale—naturalist, soldier in the militia during the Revolutionary War, craftsman, and painter—was the paterfamilias of an illustrious family of artists, some of whose children were named for artists and became artists. Also, Charles Willson Peale and Rembrandt Peale, *Gilbert Stuart* (1805). Rembrandt Peale, *George Washington* and *Mrs. George Washington* (both 1853).

The LIBRARY has some 600,000 books and over a million manuscripts. Among the documents and letters are slave diaries, the correspondence between Alexander Hamilton and Aaron Burr which led to their historic duel, and manuscripts relating to the Constitution. Other important documents include a first edition of Champlain's *Voyages,* one of the 23 surviving copies of the original broadside of the Declaration of Independence, a rare first printing of Lincoln's Second Inaugural Address (one of fewer than ten known copies), and one of three manuscript copies of Ulysses S. Grant's terms of surrender written to Robert E. Lee at Appomattox Court House.

The Society has important collections of silver, including objects from the Colonial through Victorian periods, with examples of the characteristic New York style, which resulted from the convergence within the city of Dutch, English, and Huguenot craftsmen. The Society owns flatware that once belonged to Roosevelts, Schuylers, De Peysters, and Verplanks, and work by such outstanding figures as Cornelius Kierstede and Myer Myers. Among the fine American 18–19C furniture is a Federal desk (c. 1780) attributed to Pierre L'Enfant and used by members of the Continental Congress. The Neustadt Collection of Tiffany Lamps, with 132 stained glass and Favrile lamps, embraces practically every type created by Louis Comfort Tiffany. Children will enjoy the antique toys and dolls, including metal coin banks, one depicting the infamous politician "Boss" Tweed, which slips into its pocket any coin placed in its hand.

Other important areas of the collection include prints and photographs of New York scenes, the Pach Collection of Photographs of Distinguished New Yorkers (1867–1937), thousands of engraved portraits, and a group of political caricatures from the first half of the 19C. The Bella C. Landauer Collection of Business and Advertising Art (over 1 million items) contains posters, tradecards, handbills, broadsides, and other advertising material (18–20C), hawking everything from chewing tobacco to cocaine (said to cure dandruff and prevent falling hair). The architectural collections, among the Society's most significant, include drawings of the city's most famous buildings by the city's most famous architects.

EXHIBITION PROGRAM

Over the years the exhibition program has featured works both from the Society's own collections and from other museums. "McKim, Mead & White's New York" celebrated the buildings and monuments of these famous architects; "Building City Hall" featured the remarkable architectural designs of John McComb, Jr., and Joseph-François Mangin for City Hall. "The Judicial Court System," marked the 300th anniversary of the New York State court system.

The Society reopened in 1995 with "Treasury of the Past," chronicling 200 years of city history. Each year from 1750 to 1950 was represented by an object in the collection. On view were a cot used by George Washington at Valley Forge (1778) and the tag end of the ticker tape printed on Black Friday (1929), as well as more traditional fare, for example, the authorization for the Louisiana Purchase signed by Napoleon. An installation of the personal belongings of an anonymous New Yorker, organized by Conceptual artist Christian Boltanski, and "On the Avenue, Fifth Avenue," a history of that famed thoroughfare, accompanied the primary exhibition.

The New York Public Library: Central Research Library (57)

Fifth Ave and 42nd St, New York 10018. Tel: (212) 869-8089 for recorded announcement of exhibitions and events at Central and Branch libraries. For library hours, call (212) 661-7220.

ADMISSION: Exhibition hours: Mon–Wed 11–7:30; Thurs–Sat 10–6. Closed Sun, national holidays. Free.

Lectures, changing exhibitions, tours of library building and of major exhibitions, concerts. Exhibition tours offered Mon–Sat at 12:30 and 2:30; building tours Mon–Sat at 11 and 2; for information about group tours, call (212) 930-0501. Calendars of events.

✗ No restaurant. Outdoor cafe, weather permitting, during warm months, usually April–Sept.

☐ Gift shop with books, jewelry, publications, gifts for children, fine printing and letterpress items (notecards, wrapping paper, address books) based on the collections of the Library and museums.

♿ Accessible to wheelchairs. Elevators. Restrooms equipped for handicapped visitors.

⊘ No smoking, food, or drink.

🚌 M1, M2, M3, M4, Q32 downtown on 5th Ave, uptown on Madison Ave to 42nd St. M5 downtown on 5th Ave, uptown on 6th Ave. M6 and M7, downtown on 7th Ave and Broadway, uptown on 6th Ave. M104 downtown on Broadway. M106 crosstown on 42nd St.

🚇 IRT Broadway-7th Ave local or express (train 1, 2, 3, or 9) to 42nd St / Times Sq. IRT Lexington Ave local or express (train 4, 5, or 6) to 42nd St / Grand Central. IND 6th Ave local or express (B, D, F train) to 42nd St. BMT Broadway express or local (N or R train) to Times Sq. IRT Flushing Line (train 7) to 5th Ave.

The Central Research Library of the New York Public Library (1895) is one of the world's great libraries, holding in its collections some 6.2 million books and a total of about 36 million items altogether. In addition the New York Public Library has an extensive program of exhibitions, both in the Central Research Building and in some of the specialized branch libraries.

PERMANENT COLLECTION

The Library is known for its SPECIAL COLLECTIONS, which are housed in different areas of the building. The *Berg Collection* (Room 320) contains some 127,000 items, mostly in the fields of American and English literature: manuscripts of the 15–20C, authors' corrected proofs, family correspondence, and rare books. The *Prints Division* (Room 308) has some 180,000 prints, including the Phelps Stokes Collection of American Historical Prints, one of whose treasures is an engraving by Paul Revere of

A 1907 view of the uncompleted New York Public Library on 42nd St. Itself an architectural treasure, the Library owns such masterworks as Jefferson's handwritten copy of the Declaration of Independence. (The New York Public Library)

the British landing in Boston in 1768. The *Spencer Collection* (Room 308) has illuminated manuscripts of the 9–16C, and finely illustrated and bound books, including a 14C Tickhill psalter. The *Arents Collection* (Room 324) consists of two sections, a collection of books published in serial form, acquired unbound as originally issued; and a collection of manuscripts, printed works, and other documents (1507–present) concerned directly or tangentially with tobacco, a resource for researchers interested in the early history of America or such matters as taxation.

The *Rare Book Division* (Room 303) contains more than 122,000 volumes and 21,500 broadsides, including such treasures as a Gutenberg Bible, the only known copy of the original folio edition (in Spanish) of Christopher Columbus's letter describing his discoveries (dated 1493), the first full folio of Shakespeare (1623), and a Bay Psalm Book (1640) from Cambridge, Mass., the first book printed in America in the English language. Selections from the permanent collection are on view in these rooms.

EXHIBITION PROGRAM

The largest exhibition space in the Central Research Building is GOTTESMAN HALL (restored 1984), directly beyond the marble entrance hall. About four major exhibitions are mounted yearly, drawing on the collections of the Library as well as other institutions here and abroad. Noteworthy shows have focused on the bicentennial of the Federal Constitution, the centennial of the Statue of Liberty, and the history of Spanish books, which included items as diverse as illuminated manuscripts and a Bible illustrated by Salvador Dali. "Kingdoms of Land, Sea, and Sky: 400 Years of Animal Illustration" offered 200 zoological illustrations from 1500 to 1900 by such scientists and artists as Charles Darwin, John James Audubon, and Albrecht Dürer. Along with the expected furred and feathered creatures were such unusual offerings as the mythical jackalope (a kind of antlered hare), an offbeat herbivorous mollusk, and Robert Hooke's (1665) huge rendering of that ubiquitous parasitical pest, the flea.

Smaller shows appear in the THIRD-FLOOR GALLERY, usually prints from the *Prints and Photographs Division* that are often chosen to complement the main exhibition in Gottesman Hall. Featured here have been the prints of Reginald Marsh; American historical prints documenting the evolution of New York from the 17C to the 19C; and Otto Dix's celebrated etchings entitled *The War,* made by an artist who served in the trenches in World War I.

ROOM 381 is used to mount exhibitions from the Berg Collection, a great archive of American and English literature, among whose treasures are manuscripts, authors' proofs, first editions, and correspondence of Dickens, Yeats, T. S. Eliot, Dylan Thomas, W. H. Auden, and Virginia Woolf. Shows have included recent acquisitions—e.g., Washington Irving's *Sketchbook* and the manuscript of Joseph Conrad's *The Secret Sharer*—or treasures of the collection—Dickens's own copy of *A Christmas Carol*—displayed along with letters, manuscripts, and illustrations to give a portrait of the novelist at work.

The EDNA BARNES SALOMON ROOM (third floor, east of the Rotunda) serves as the Library's main picture gallery, originally designed by Library architects Carrère & Hastings for that purpose and restored (1984) preserving where possible their intentions. The portraits, which came originally from the Lenox and Astor collections, reflect the history of the Library: they are primarily pictures of founders and donors and of notable figures in the arts and in American history.

WEST WALL: Paintings from the Lenox Library. At the center are five portraits of *George Washington* by James Peale, Rembrandt Peale, and Gilbert Stuart. Surrounding them are Lenox family portraits by John Wesley Jarvis, Gilbert Stuart, and John Trumbull. The Lenox portraits are of interest because James Lenox's donation of books and manuscripts forms the core of the Library's Rare Book and Manuscripts Division.

NORTH WALL: This wall is devoted to donors, principally the Astor family: Léon J. F. Bonnat, *John Jacob Astor IV* (1896); Eastman Johnson, *William Backhouse Astor* (1883).

EAST WALL: This wall contains a group of topographical views, primarily from the collection of Isaac Newton Phelps Stokes. Stokes, member of an illustrious family, was the architect of St. Paul's Chapel at Columbia University and the author of the imposing six-volume *Iconography of Manhattan Island.* The most famous painting on the wall is Asher B. Durand's *Kindred Spirits* (1849), which shows a romanticized Catskill landscape with author William Cullen Bryant and artist Thomas Cole communing with nature. Cole was the acknowledged founder of the Hudson River School of painting. Also on display are busts of *Voltaire* (c. 1778–1800) by Jean-Antoine Houdon and *George William Curtis* (1899) by John Quincy Adams Ward. Samuel F. B. Morse's portrait *Fitz-Greene Halleck* (1827) commemorates a poet more highly esteemed in his time than in ours. Halleck also worked as a private secretary to John Jacob Astor.

SOUTH WALL: One of James Lenox's favorite poets was John Milton, an interest reflected in Mihály von Munkácsy's *Blind Milton Dictating "Paradise Lost" to His Daughters* (1877), the most famous work of that painter. George Romney's *Sir Timothy Shelley* (1795) and *Lady Elizabeth Shelley* (1795) depict the parents of poet Percy Bysshe Shelley.

On the remaining part of the West Wall are English and American portraits. The Gilbert Stuart portrait, *George Washington* (1797), was commissioned for Alexander Hamilton and given to the Astor Library by Hamilton's grandson. Other portraits are: John Singleton Copley, *Hannah White Cowell Hooper* (c. 1767) and *Frances Deering Atkinson* (1765); Sir Henry Raeburn, *Peter Van Brugh Livingston* (1819) and *Penelope Macdonald Hamilton, Lady Belhaven and Stenton* (c. 1800); Sir Joshua Reynolds, *Kitty Fisher* (c. 1764–65); Gilbert Stuart, *John Campbell* (c. 1794–1810), *Ann Woodward Haven* (1824), *John Haven* (1824), and *Mary White Morris* (c. 1795); and Samuel F. B. Morse's well-known *Marquis de Lafayette* (1825).

The cases in the center of the room contain objects from the collections and special exhibitions. Often on display are a *Gutenberg Bible,* one of 48 known to exist, and the *Hunt-Lenox globe* (c. 1510), the earliest existing globe from the period following the discovery of the New World.

The SECOND-FLOOR GALLERY contains an ongoing exhibition entitled "Building the New York Public Library," whose documents and photographs trace the history of the Central Research Building.

THE BUILDING

Regarded as one of the city's finest, the Library sits on a wide terrace running the length of the Fifth Ave facade. In the center a broad flight of steps leads to three deep entrance arches framed by Corinthian columns. Flanking the steps, which have long attracted tourists, pigeons, footsore shoppers, and the usual urban eccentrics, are two famous couchant marble lions by Edward Clark Potter (1911), originally criticized as mealymouthed, complacent creatures but now securely ensconced in public affection. In niches behind the fountains against the facade are statues (1913; Frederick W. MacMonnies) of Truth, a man leaning against a sphinx, and Beauty, a woman seated on the winged horse Pegasus. Above the entrance on the frieze are six allegorical figures by Paul Wayland Bartlett representing (left to right) History, Romance, Religion, Poetry, Drama, and Philosophy. The pediment figures at the ends of the facade are Art (south) and History (north) by George Grey Barnard.

INTERIOR. The entrance hall is finished in white Vermont marble, with an elaborate vaulted ceiling, heroic marble candelabra, and wide staircases.

Take the elevator (end of the right corridor) to the third floor, or walk up the marble stairs that crisscross back and forth under marble barrel vaults. Visible from the stairway are the large interior courts that provide natural light for the Catalogue and Reading rooms.

The stairway rises to the McGRAW ROTUNDA (third floor), decorated with murals (1940) by Edward Laning depicting the *Story of the Recorded Word.* The Public Catalogue in Room 315 formerly held more than 10 million cards; these have either been photographed and bound into books (pre-1972) or recorded electronically in the library's computerized catalogue system, CATNYP.

Beyond is the monumental MAIN READING ROOM, with a shelf collection of about 40,000 reference books. The beautifully decorated ceiling, the tall, arched windows, and the furniture designed by Carrère & Hastings make this one of the city's great interiors. Beneath the Reading Room are the original stacks, to whose 88 miles of shelves have been added another 81 miles of stacks beneath Bryant Park behind the Library.

HISTORY

The research collections of the New York Public Library developed from the consolidation of two great privately endowed libraries, the Astor and Lenox libraries, with the Tilden Trust, a bequest of $2 million and 15,000 books from Samuel J. Tilden, lawyer, governor, and unsuccessful presidential candidate. Immigrant John Jacob Astor, hardly a bookish man, was persuaded by his friend Joseph Green Cogswell, a scholar, to establish a public library as a fitting testimonial to his adopted country. The books, largely chosen by Cogswell, provided a general reference service in the fields of greatest public interest, including works on the "mechanic arts and practical industry" and on languages. James Lenox, on the other hand, was a scholar whose particular interests are reflected in the strengths of his collection: American literature and history, the Bible, Milton, Shakespeare, Bunyan, and Renaissance literature of travel and discovery. Lenox built his own library (1875) on the site of the present Frick Collection (Fifth Ave between 70th and 71st Sts), but at his death in 1880 left his 85,000 peerless books and an endowment of $505,000 to the New York Public Library. The gift of bachelor Samuel J. Tilden, a bequest reduced from $4 million to $2 million by his relatives who contested the will, was sorely needed as by 1886 the Astor and Lenox libraries already lacked funds for new books and maintenance. In 1895 the three gifts were united as the New York Public Library, Astor, Lenox, and Tilden Foundations to become the Central Research Library as it exists today. In 1901, Andrew Carnegie, aware that New York lacked the public circulating systems of Boston and other American cities, gave $52 million for the building of branch libraries.

The New York Public Library for the Performing Arts (96)

40 Lincoln Center Plaza (W. 65th St), New York 10023. Tel: (212) 870-1600 for recorded announcement of library hours; to reach a live person, call (212) 870-1630.

ADMISSION: Open Mon and Thurs 12–8; Tues, Wed, Fri, and Sat 12–6. Closed Sun, holidays. Free.

Information Desk near entrance from Lincoln Center Plaza. Changing exhibitions, tours every Wednesday at 2 (meet on 1st floor at Lincoln Center Plaza entrance). Concerts, lectures, films, panel discussions, readings, children's programs.

✘ No restaurant.

🏛 Gift shop for Lincoln Center in Metropolitan Opera building, concourse level. Wide selection of recordings, tapes, posters, and books relating to performing arts. Also stationery, cards, toys, T-shirts, mugs, and gift items.

♿ Accessible to wheelchairs.

🚇 IRT Broadway-7th Ave local (train 1 or 9) to 66th St. Underground concourse to all buildings at Lincoln Center.

🚌 M7 via Broadway and Columbus Ave. M5 uptown via 6th Ave / Broadway; downtown via Riverside Dr / Broadway / 5th Ave. M30 crosstown on 72nd St. M29 crosstown on 65th St. M104 via Broadway.

The New York Public Library for the Performing Arts, founded in 1965 and located at Lincoln Center, is a priceless and celebrated repository of information on dance, the theater, and music. Used by both professionals and amateurs, it is known especially for its outstanding collections of nonbook materials—historic recordings, autograph manuscripts, sheet music, stage designs, press clippings, posters, programs, and photographs. Choreographers use videotapes or printed materials to create new dances or recreate older ones; stage designers may study historic theater productions; musicians may study published or unpublished scores. Ordinary aficionados of the arts may take advantage of rich collections of circulating materials, including books, periodicals, records, cassettes, compact discs, and VHS tapes. Professionals in the field of performing arts administration have more than 1,500 books and periodicals aiding them in their work.

EXHIBITION PROGRAM

Within the Library are four gallery spaces, whose exhibitions highlight the riches of the collections: the Amsterdam Gallery (on the Amsterdam Ave level); the Plaza Gallery (near the Lincoln Center Plaza entrance); the Main Gallery (on the second floor); and the Vincent Astor Gallery (off the Main Gallery).

In 1991, to celebrate its 25th anniversary documenting and preserving the arts, the Library mounted an ambitious program to show how documentation inspires the creation of new works. The exhibition occupied all the galleries and explored such themes as "Inventions of Notation" (choreographic diagrams for *Annie Get Your Gun*, Luther Adler's script of *Fiddler on the Roof* with notes made to himself in Yiddish) and "The Impact of Media and Technology" (control board, plots, and other materials from the Rolling Stones' 1975 tour).

Another outstanding show, "Arturo Toscanini, 1915–1946: Art in the Shadow of Politics," documented the great conductor's anti-Fascist feelings and activities. The exhibition brought together original materials assembled for the first time in this country, including a transcript from a wiretap made by the Fascist secret police in Milan, a flattering but unavailing letter from Hitler (Toscanini refused to conduct in Germany, Austria, or Italy until after the war), and a letter from President Franklin D. Roosevelt.

PERMANENT COLLECTION

The research collections are housed on the third floor and intended for advanced researchers. The *Dance Collection,* which embraces ethnic, modern, social, and folk dancing, as well as ballet, contains more than 30,600 books, which nonetheless account for only 3% of its holdings; there are also manuscripts, costume and set designs, taped interviews with famous dance personalities, and the Jerome Robbins Archive of Recorded Moving Image, a collection of dance performances on film and videotape.

The Music Division is even more remarkable, with autograph scores and an *American Collection* that has jazz, popular music, and 18C imprints. The Rodgers & Hammerstein Archives of Recorded Sound contain more than 460,000 recordings and music-related videotapes. Among them are early operatic performances preserved on wax cylinders and historic broadcasts of celebrated personalities and world leaders.

The *Billy Rose Theatre Collection* is the world's most widely used documentary archive of the theater, including also drama, film, radio and television, the circus, vaudeville, and magic. Its vast clipping files, organized under 25,000 headings, include hundreds of thousands of photos, prints, posters, and programs. The *Theatre on Film and Tape Archive* (TOFT), housed in the Lucille Lortel Room, contains more than 1,600 films and tapes of live theatrical performances, including excerpts of early Rodgers and Hart musicals.

New York Unearthed (29)

17 State St at Battery Park (in courtyard facing Pearl St bet. Whitehall / State Sts), New York 10004. Tel: (212) 748-8628.

ADMISSION: Open Easter to Christmas: Mon–Sat 12–6; Christmas to Easter: Mon–Fri 12–6. Closed Sun, major holidays. Free.

Educational programs, tours, and workshops for schoolchildren, special needs groups, and adults. Groups by appointment; call Group Tours at the South Street Seaport, (212) 748-8590.

✖ No restaurant.

🏛 Small gift shop, with educational items, books on New York City archeology.

♿ Accessible to wheelchairs.

🚇 IRT Broadway-7th Ave local (train 1 or 9) to South Ferry. IRT Lexington Ave express (train 4 or 5) to Bowling Green. BMT Broadway express (N or R train) to Whitehall St.

🚌 M1 (marked South Ferry), M6, M15.

This small archeological museum (founded 1990), a satellite of the South Street Seaport Museum, offers a unique view of historical New York from the Dutch period up to the 20C, through exhibitions of artifacts dug up from beneath the city streets. When the Dutch settled New Amsterdam in 1625 at a spot near Battery Park, lower Manhattan was much smaller than it is today. Through landfill, the shoreline of the southern tip of the island has been built up and extended. Consequently excavations for the foundations of today's skyscrapers sometimes reveal artifacts buried many feet beneath the earth's surface. Small household articles—bottles, clay pipes for smoking, jugs and other ceramic objects—foundations of old buildings, and even ships' timbers have been unearthed.

The Museum provides a look not only at the artifacts themselves but at the history they represent. There is a three-dimensional cross section of an archeological site that demonstrates how the layers containing artifacts were deposited. An exhibition of Native American artifacts provides a glimpse of pre-Colonial New York. A permanent exhibit with dioramas relates archeological finds to different facets of the city's history, e.g., the social interactions of the city's 17–18C taverns and tenement life in the late 19C. A simulated trip down beneath the city streets in an "elevator" (actually an interactive video) provides a look at the workings of a dig, and a simulated "emergency" provides thrills for the younger set (recommended for ages 8 and older) as the elevator descends beneath Wall St.

In addition to its function as a museum, New York Unearthed offers a state-of-the-art glass-enclosed laboratory where workers can be seen restoring and stabilizing the archeological collections donated to the South Street Seaport Museum. Conservators are often willing to answer questions about their work.

The PaineWebber Gallery (58)

1285 Ave of the Americas (51st St), New York 10019. Tel: (212) 713-2885 for recorded information.

ADMISSION: Open Mon–Fri 8–6. Closed Sat and Sun, and holidays when the stock market is closed: New Year's Day, Washington's Birthday, Good Friday, Memorial Day, Independence Day, Labor Day, Thanksgiving, and Christmas Day. Free.

Changing exhibitions.

✕ Cafeteria on 2nd floor closes at 2:30 P.M.

♦↰ Restrooms on 2nd floor.

⌂ No gift shop.

♿ Accessible to wheelchairs. Parking available.

🚇 IND 6th Ave local or express (B, D, or F train) to 47th / 50th Sts. BMT Broadway local (R train) to 49th St.

🚌 M5, M6, M7 or M104 uptown on 6th Ave. M5 downtown on 5th Ave. M6, M7, or M104 downtown on Broadway.

The PaineWebber Gallery (1985), located on the ground floor of the corporate headquarters of the PaineWebber Group Inc, mounts four exhibitions a year, most from nonprofit arts and cultural groups in the New York area that seek midtown exhibition space. Exhibitions have included carousel animals from the Museum of American Folk Art, contemporary works on paper from the Drawing Center, antique dolls and banks from the Museum of the City of New York, and circus and theater posters from the New-York Historical Society. An exhibition of the garden designs of Gertrude Jekyll was presented by the Brooklyn Botanic Garden in conjunction with a book about the work of this important English landscape artist and gardener. As part of a citywide celebration of Mexican art, the

Gallery offered "The Universe of the Amate," a show that explored a style of regional painting executed by the Nahuas in the state of Guerrero on *amate* paper, produced by the Otomies of Puebla from the bark of regional trees.

Every other spring the Studio in a School Association offers a show of artwork by New York's public school children. The children, encouraged and assisted by professional painters, illustrators, and sculptors, create an exuberant display of animals, portrait masks, quilts, puppets, and cityscapes.

Pratt Manhattan Gallery (30)

295 Lafayette St (E. Houston St), 2nd floor of Puck Building, New York 10012. Tel: (212) 925-8481.

ADMISSION: Open Mon–Sat 10–5. Closed Sun, holidays. Free.

Changing exhibitions of painting, sculpture, graphic arts, architecture.

✗ No restaurant.

▥ No gift shop.

♿ Accessible to wheelchairs; ask on ground-floor level to have elevator to gallery opened.

🚇 IRT Lexington Ave local (train 6) to Spring St or Bleecker St. IND 8th Ave line (A, C, or E train) to Spring St. BMT Broadway local (N or R train) to Prince St. IND 6th Ave line (B, D, or F train) to Broadway / Lafayette St.

🚌 Bus M1 downtown on 5th Ave, Park Ave South, and Broadway (make sure you get a bus labeled South Ferry; otherwise walk south from 8th St or transfer to the M6 at 8th St). Uptown on Centre St and Lafayette St to Grand or Canal St. M5 downtown on 5th Ave. M6 downtown on Broadway and uptown on 6th Ave. M21 crosstown on Houston St.

The Pratt Manhattan Gallery (founded 1975) is the Manhattan showcase of Pratt Institute in Brooklyn, whose degree programs include majors in fine art, design, and architecture. The gallery, which mounts about nine shows yearly, features the work of students, faculty, and alumni of the Institute. There are curated shows in architecture and design, as well as drawing, painting, and sculpture. Exhibitions have included "The Nature of Science," works in mixed media by artists who use the processes and imagery of the natural sciences; "Imaging Sappho," a series of paintings based on surviving fragments of verse by the ancient Greek poet; and "Pratt Profile," a panorama of graphic design work by some of the school's successful recent alumni (with examples of illustration, packaging, and corporate-identity campaigns). "Goddess in the Details" presented products designed by women; the objects ranged from refrigerators and washer-dryers to medical equipment and auto batteries.

THE BUILDING

The gallery is installed in the imposing brick Romanesque Revival Puck Building, built 1885–86 (later addition 1892–93) by architects Albert Wagner and Herman Wagner. Now a designated landmark, the building long served the printing industry, first as the home of the humor magazine *Puck;* later it housed a commercial publishing firm whose 30 large lithographic presses turned out steamboat and railway posters, stationery, and certificates. At the corner of Houston St and above the main entrance on Lafayette St are figures of Puck, top-hatted and cherubic, by Caspar Buberl (died 1889), an immigrant from Bohemia.

The Nicholas Roerich Museum (97)

319 West 107th St (Riverside Dr), New York 10025. Tel: (212) 864-7752.

ADMISSION: Open Tues–Sun 2–5. Closed Mon and holidays. Ring bell for admission. Requested donation.

Poetry readings, changing exhibitions, musical programs, occasional lectures.

✗ No restaurant.

🏛 Postcards, reproductions, books by and about Roerich.

⅄ Not accessible to wheelchairs; two long flights of stairs.

🚇 IRT Broadway-7th Ave local (train 1 or 9) to 110th St.

🚌 M4 via Madison Ave and 110th St to Broadway; walk west to Riverside Dr and downtown to 107th St. M5 via 6th Ave, Broadway, and Riverside Dr. M104 via Broadway.

This small, quiet museum (1923) commemorates the life and work of Nicholas Roerich, the Russian-born painter, mystic, archeologist, writer, and humanitarian, who was nominated for the Nobel Peace Prize but is virtually unknown today. The exhibit contains about 200 of his paintings, a display of his writings, and a small collection of Indian and Asian artifacts.

HISTORY

Born in St. Petersburg (1874), Roerich was early attracted to the legendary Russian past and to the natural beauty of his country. As a young man he studied painting and developed an interest in archeology, visiting the ancient Russian cities and writing about legends and remote history. His later work included stage settings for Russian ballets and operas, and he established an international reputation working with Sergei Diaghilev. Roerich first came to the United States for an exhibition tour in 1920, remaining for three years and painting such subjects as Santa Fe and the Grand Canyon. He also lectured on art, designed for the stage, and publicized his ideals and humanitarian philosophy.

In 1923–28, Roerich lived in India, leading an artistic-scientific expedition that followed the ancient caravan route across the Karakoram Pass through Tibet and Mongolia. He was deeply moved by the spirituality of Buddhist culture and the austere beauty of the Tibetan Highlands, which dominated his paintings thereafter.

Roerich's philosophy, which emphasized the primacy of artistic and cultural values and the unity of mankind, led him to propose a treaty stipulating that educational, artistic, scientific, and religious institutions and all sites of cultural and historic importance should remain inviolate in times of war. Roerich designed a banner that would fly over the buildings and sites to be so protected. His efforts led to the signing of a treaty in 1935 by the United States and 21 Latin-American countries, and its later ratification in Paris in 1955 by 39 nations participating in the Hague Conference. Roerich spent the last years of his life in the Himalayas, where he died in 1947.

PERMANENT COLLECTION

Most of the paintings are rendered in startlingly bright, clear colors and illuminated by a strange, almost mystical light. Many celebrate the beauty of the Himalayas and the spiritual quality of its people. There are also paintings of gods and goddesses, of history's great religious leaders, and of the grandeur of nature elsewhere in the world. The portraits of the artist are by his son, Svetoslav Roerich.

EXHIBITION PROGRAM

On the third floor are changing exhibitions of the work of emerging artists.

The Theodore Roosevelt Birthplace (59)

28 East 20th St (5th Ave), New York 10003. Tel: (212) 260-1616.

ADMISSION: Open Wed–Sun 9–4; tours on the hour. Closed major holidays. When a federal holiday falls on Mon, the Museum is closed the following Wed. Admission charge; children under 16 free.

Guided tours. Films upon request. Occasional lectures.

✘ No restaurant.

🏛 Gift shop with brochures, books on Roosevelt, cards, Teddy bears.

♿ Entrance several steps down from street. Elevator to period rooms on 2nd floor. Restrooms not equipped for handicapped visitors.

🚇 IRT Lexington Ave local (train 6) to 23rd St. BMT Broadway express (N train) to 14th St or local (R train) 23rd St.

🚌 M2, M3, M5 downtown on 5th Ave, uptown on Madison Ave. M6, M7 downtown on Broadway. M26 crosstown on 23rd St.

The Theodore Roosevelt Birthplace (opened to the public 1923), a brownstone reconstruction of the original Roosevelt House dating from the mid-19C, has been restored as a museum, whose period rooms and exhibits of documents and memorabilia commemorate the life and achievements of the 26th President of the United States.

PERMANENT EXHIBITION

There are two exhibition spaces and five period rooms, furnished in the Victorian style of Roosevelt's youth. About 40% of the furnishings come from the original house; another 20% were donated by members of the Roosevelt family; the rest are period pieces.

GROUND FLOOR. The contents of a small but excellent MUSEUM recapitulate important events in Roosevelt's life. The exhibit includes personal belongings, e.g., his parents' wedding garments and T.R.'s own christening gown; the uniform he wore as a "Rough Rider" in the Spanish-American War; and a toy tea set complete with little lace-edged napkins, which Roosevelt's mother gave to one of his childhood friends, who would later become his second wife. First editions of his books and publications and drafts of his speeches suggest the wide range of T. R.'s interests. Also on

display are his Nobel Peace Prize certificate and a series of political cartoons documenting his public life.

PARLOR FLOOR. In many New York brownstones the parlor floor is
raised above a high basement and the front door reached by a flight of
stairs. Both the name of the stairs ("stoop" from the Dutch *stoep*) and the
elevation of the most formal rooms above flood level recalls the city's
Dutch origins.

The Rococo Revival-style PARLOR, with its pale blue damask uphol-
stery, large mirrors, high ceilings, and crystal chandelier, was the most
formal room in the house.

The LIBRARY, the middle room on the parlor floor, contains souvenirs
of trips abroad, including two obelisks that recall a family trip to Egypt.
The small red velvet chair belonged to T.R.

The tall windows of the DINING ROOM once overlooked the backyard
of the Goelet family mansion with its collection of tropical birds. Some
Roosevelt family china is still preserved on the sideboard. The family
crest, the basis for the pattern on the china, shows three red roses springing from a field of green, a symbolic rendering of the family name "Roosevelt."

A second exhibition space known as the LION ROOM contains memorabilia of Roosevelt's lust for the outdoor life—hunting trophies including
the eponymous stuffed lion, birds mounted for a childhood museum of
natural history, chaps and spurs from his adventures in the West—and a
desk he used when he was Assistant Secretary of the Navy, early in his
career. Apparently the "Teddy bear" had its origins on a hunting trip
when T.R. spared the life of a bear, though urged by his guides to shoot
it to win a hunting trophy. When a Brooklyn toy salesman saw a cartoon
recalling the incident, he asked Roosevelt's permission to sell toy bears
called "Teddy's Bear."

THIRD FLOOR. The NURSERY contains a sleigh bed and examples of
period toys and children's Lilliputian-sized furniture. Beyond is an open-
air porch which was used as a "gymnasium." Because "Teedie"—as T.R.
was known to his family—had severe asthma and other illnesses as a
child, his father installed the gymnasium on the rear porch, where Teedie
could exercise to improve his health.

In the MASTER BEDROOM, with the Roosevelts' own rosewood and
satinwood veneered furniture, hangs a portrait of Martha Bulloch Roosevelt, T.R.'s mother, a gracious and beautiful southern woman. All the furniture in this room is original.

HISTORY

When Theodore Roosevelt's parents were given a typical three-story brownstone in
1854, East 20th St was a quiet, tree-lined byway in a socially desirable neighborhood. In 1865, as the family fortunes waxed, the Roosevelts hired one of the city's
leading interior decorators, Leon Marcotte, to refurbish the rooms as befitted their
status and to add an extra story. In 1872, when Theodore Jr. was 14, the family
moved to a more fashionable home on West 57th St, and the E. 20th St house began
a period of decline, eventually becoming commercial space. In 1916 it was demolished, but its mirror image built for T.R.'s uncle Robert remained next door. Only
three years later, after T.R.'s death (1919), a group of admirers, urged on by Roosevelt's sisters, decided to reconstruct his boyhood home as a memorial. Using archi-

tectural details from the adjacent house and relying on color schemes, furniture layouts, and other details provided by T.R.'s sisters and his wife, the house was restored as closely as possible to its appearance during the President's childhood.

In 1963 the Theodore Roosevelt Association gave the house to the National Park Service, which now administers it as a National Historic Site.

The Schomburg Center for Research in Black Culture: New York Public Library (108)

515 Malcolm X Blvd (Lenox Ave at 135th St), New York 10037. Tel: (212) 491-2200.

ADMISSION: Open Mon–Wed 12–8; Thurs–Sat 10–6. Closed Sun, holidays. Free admission to exhibitions; charge for events in the Langston Hughes Auditorium.

Changing exhibitions, seminars, film screenings, performing arts presentations, educational programs, scholarly programs. Group tours by appointment.

✖ No restaurant.

🛍 Gift shop with books, posters, jewelry, prints, memorabilia.

♿ Accessible to wheelchairs.

⊘ Photography by permission.

🚈 IRT 7th Ave express (train 2 or 3) to 135th St.

🚌 M1 or M2 uptown on Madison Ave, downtown on 5th Ave. M7 uptown on 6th Ave / Amsterdam Ave / Lenox Ave, downtown on Lenox Ave / Columbus Ave / Broadway. M102 uptown on 2nd Ave, downtown on 3rd Ave. BX33 crosstown on 135th St.

Located on Malcolm X Blvd (formerly Lenox Ave) in Harlem, the Schomburg Center for Research in Black Culture (founded 1925) is a major research center of the New York Public Library and one of the finest facilities in the world for the study of the meaning of the black experience and heritage. The Library is named for Arthur A. Schomburg (1874–1938), a black scholar and bibliophile, who gathered the nucleus of the collection.

EXHIBITION PROGRAM

In 1991 the Center opened a handsome new gallery space in the former 135th St Branch of the New York Public Library, later the first building of the Schomburg Center. The inaugural exhibition, "African Presence in the Americas," explored the different cultures and peoples of African descent living in the Americas for the past 500 years. Other shows have included "Black Photographers Bear Witness: 100 Years of Social Protest"; "Drum," photographs from the magazine *Drum,* which chronicled black urban life and the beginnings of political activism in South Africa in the 1950s; and "African Americans in Space Sciences," which documented the achievements of black physicists, astronauts, and mathematicians.

PERMANENT COLLECTION

The collection has grown to more than 5 million items, which range from literary works by black authors to the United States Federal Population Census (1790 through 1900). In addition to more than 125,000 printed books (most in English but some in languages of parts of the world with sizable black populations—Africa, the Caribbean, and South America), there are more than 400 black newspapers and 1,000 black periodicals from around the world. The Ernest D. Kaiser Index to Black Resources, now being converted to a computerized database, is a file of a quarter million citations to articles in thousands of issues of black magazines and newspapers, some of which ceased publication decades ago.

Among the rare books are important finds by Arthur Schomburg himself, including *Ad Catholicum,* a book of Latin verse published in Spain (1573) by Juan Latino, the black African who held the chair of poetry at the University of Granada during the reign of Philip V. More recent works include early editions of poetry by the American slave Phillis Wheatley, the original manuscript of Richard Wright's *Native Son,* and the records of the New York Urban League and the Civil Rights Congress.

The visual arts play an important part in the collection, including the work of black American artists, African art, Caribbean art, stereographic views of slave life through the Civil War, and buttons and posters. A photographic collection documents major historical events, depicts black life throughout the world, and contains portraits of prominent 19C and 20C black figures.

HISTORY

In 1925, the New York Public Library opened its division of Negro Literature, History, and Prints at the 135th St Branch in Harlem. The next year Arthur Schomburg donated his own private collection—some 5,000 volumes, 3,000 manuscripts, 2,000 etchings and portraits, and several thousand pamphlets—to the division. Schomburg served as curator of the division between 1932 and his death in 1938, and in 1940 the Center was renamed to honor him.

The Sculpture Center (84)

167 East 69th St (bet. Lexington / 3rd Aves), New York 10021. Tel: (212) 879-3500.

ADMISSION: Open Tues–Sat 11–5. Closed Sun, Mon, holidays, and July–Aug. Free.

Changing exhibitions; poetry readings, panel discussions.

✘ No restaurant.

🛍 No formal gift shop, but some merchandise for sale, including artist-designed T-shirts.

♿ Accessible to wheelchairs.

🚇 IRT Lexington Ave local (train 6) to 68th St.

🚌 M101 and M102, uptown on 3rd Ave, downtown on 2nd Ave. M15 downtown on 2nd Ave, uptown on 1st Ave. M66, crosstown on 67th / 68th Sts.

Founded (1928) on West 8th St in Greenwich Village by sculptor Dorothea Denslow, the Sculpture Center Gallery offers prime exhibition space both to emerging sculptors and those in mid-career whose work remains outside the mainstream. The gallery occupies a former carriage house, whose 14-ft ceiling allows the showing of large-scale work. In addition, the Center is an important source of information for the art community, maintaining a slide file that serves collectors, artists, and consultants.

Each year the Center mounts about eight group, solo, and thematic exhibitions. In the summer an artist-in-residence develops a site-specific work, which serves as the opening exhibit of the season each September, and in recent years some of these installations have attracted great interest. Since 1986 the Center has held an annual exhibition that has become known as an event for previewing the work of emerging artists before they become fixtures on the scene.

Several generations of distinguished artists have shown at the Center. In the '40s and '50s, Isamu Noguchi, David Smith, Ibram Lassaw, Gaston Lachaise, and Louise Nevelson showed here. More recently George Sugarman, Mia Westerlund Roosen, Alison Saar, Petah Coyne, and Mel Edwards have been exhibited, some in their first major New York appearances.

The Abigail Adams Smith Museum (85)

421 East 61st St (bet. 1st / York Aves), New York 10021. Tel: (212) 838-6878.

ADMISSION: Open Mon–Fri 12–4; Sun 1–5 Sept–May; Thurs in June, July open until 6:30. Weekdays 10 A.M. until noon the Museum is open only for group tours; 12–4 it is open to the general public. Closed Sat, the month of Aug, and major holidays. Admission fee. Members and children under 12 accompanied by parents, free. Ring bell for admission.

Tours, lectures, workshops, special events, musical programs, walking tours. Workshops and programs scheduled one Sun of each month. Thurs evening programs during June and July.

✘ No restaurant.

⌂ Small gift shop.

♿ Not accessible to wheelchairs.

⊘ No flash photography. No baby carriages.

🚇 IRT Lexington Ave local or express (train 4, 5, or 6) to 59th St. BMT Broadway express or local (N or R train) to Lexington Ave (and 59th St).

🚌 M15, downtown on 2nd Ave, uptown on 1st Ave. M31, via York Ave. M103, crosstown on 59th St.

The Abigail Adams Smith House (built 1799; opened as a museum 1924) through good fortune has survived from the early years of the American republic, when the area attracted wealthy families seeking country estates close to the city. Although Abigail Adams Smith, daughter of President John Adams, and her husband, William Stephens Smith, never actually lived in the house, her connection with the property contributed to its survival and to its interest as a museum. Today, the house (originally a carriage house) has been painstakingly restored, furnished with period furniture and carefully researched period reproductions.

PERMANENT EXHIBITION

GROUND FLOOR. Over the windows in the entrance hallway are brick arches, indicating the building's intended function as a stable and carriage house.

The KITCHEN with its traditionally unvarnished floor is furnished with a tavern table, chairs, cupboards and chests, and an assortment of cooking utensils that date back to the early 19C.

Across the hall is the MUSIC ROOM, furnished to suggest French Empire and Greek Revival influences. Among the furnishings are a Hepplewhite spinet (Thomas Tomkison, London, 1790) and a gilded English harp. In the corner is a standing barrel organ.

In the DINING ROOM, the American Sheraton table is surrounded by painted "fancy" chairs with woven rush seats, a type that predates the better-known Hitchcock chairs. The arrangement of "country-style" chairs around a formal table may seem strange today, but the grouping of furniture as well as the selection of individual pieces is historically accurate.

A wide staircase with a handsome bannister leads upstairs. The carpet is a reproduction, based on a "point paper" from an English rug manufacturer, and even the brass rods holding the carpet firmly against the risers are accurate as to period.

SECOND FLOOR. This floor, at ground level on the west end of the building, was once the storage area for carriages, which were rolled through the large doorways into what is presently the Library. At the top of the stairs is the UPPER HALL. On the south wall a painting by an unknown artist shows the neighborhood c. 1850.

During the 1930s the LIBRARY was completely reconstructed. It contains cases with Adams family and other memorabilia, including a record of Abigail's mother's marriage to John Adams, a piece of canvas from George Washington's field tent, and a mourning pin with a snippet of Washington's hair.

In the BEDROOM, the only room in the house without a fireplace, is an American Sheraton-style mahogany bedstead and a linen press with an embroidered muslin dress made by Abigail Adams Smith at the White House when her father was President.

Across the hall is a DRAWING ROOM or PARLOR with a fine Chinese black-and-gold lacquer desk (c. 1810) and an Aubusson rug. On one of the small tables is a candlestand, or screen, for protection from the heat of the candle. Ladies did not necessarily have more tender skin in the early 19C, but their complexions were often pockmarked and the blemishes filled with wax to conceal them.

On the card table in the GAME ROOM a hand of unnumbered, hand-painted cards is laid out along with poker chips that belonged to John Adams. On the wall is a precise, finely executed sampler, the work of a ten-year-old girl.

THIRD FLOOR. This floor, not open to the public, was originally the hay-loft. Behind the house is a modest but pleasant garden with herbs and other plantings reminiscent of those popular in c. 1800.

HISTORY

In 1795, Col. William Stephens Smith bought 23 acres of land along the East River from the Van Zandt family and set about planning a mansion suitable for a man of his social position. He called his estate "Mount Vernon" to honor his former commander, George Washington, but before the mansion was completed, Smith fell on hard times and had to sell the property. The site became known locally as "Smith's Folly," but William T. Robinson bought it in 1798 and completed the house, as well as the stable and carriage house.

After Robinson's tenure the mansion began a long decline, becoming first the Mount Vernon Hotel (noted for its turtle soup) and later a female academy. In 1826, fire destroyed the main building. The stables, however, were in turn converted into a small hotel also called the Mount Vernon Hotel. A family named Towle owned it in 1833–1905, eventually selling the house and land to the Standard Gas Light Co.

In 1919 an antiques dealer, Jane Teller, rented and restored the house, using it to display a collection of early American furniture. The Colonial Dames of America bought it five years later, furnished it, and opened it to the public.

The Society of Illustrators: Museum of American Illustration (86)

128 East 63rd St (Park Ave), New York 10021. Tel: (212) 838-2560.

ADMISSION: Open Tues–Fri 10–5; Sat 12–4. Tues evenings until 8. Closed Sun, Mon, month of Aug, legal holidays. Free.

Changing exhibitions. Tours and gallery talks for groups by appointment. Lecture series twice yearly.

✗ No restaurant.

▥ Museum shop with catalogues, books relating to the art of illustration, posters, prints, calendars, T-shirts, greeting cards.

& Ground-floor exhibition space accessible to wheelchairs; a few steps at the back of the main gallery.

🚊 IRT Lexington Ave local or express (train 4, 5, or 6) to 59th St.

🚌 M1, M2, M3, or M4 uptown via Madison Ave, downtown via 5th Ave. M66 crosstown on 66th–67th Sts. M30 crosstown on 72nd St.

The Museum (1981) is the exhibition space of the Society of Illustrators, formed in 1901 to stimulate interest in the art of illustration "past, present and future." That goal is perhaps especially pressing today when television is preeminent among the media and illustration is often shouldered aside by photography.

EXHIBITION PROGRAM

The Society mounts about a dozen exhibitions yearly, which put before the public the best of contemporary and historical American illustration, in solo, group, and thematically organized shows. The "Bicentennial Show" explored 200 years of American illustration; "American Beauty" suggested how illustrators delineate the American ideal of feminine beauty. There have been shows on "New Wave" illustration and "America's Great Women Illustrators (1850–1950)." Other topics have included science fiction and the art created by the *National Geographic* magazine on the occasion of its 100th birthday. Each spring a college-level student scholarship competition and a juried show, which dates back to 1959, bring together the best work of the year.

PERMANENT COLLECTION

"Illustration," as defined by the Society, includes any artwork commissioned for commercial reproduction: book illustrations, advertisements, posters, record jackets, magazine covers, even annual reports. The permanent collection comprises some 1,400 original works from 1838 to the present. Among the outstanding illustrations are an original frontispiece by N. C. Wyeth for Robert Louis Stevenson's *The Black Arrow,* a volume in Scribner's Books for Young Readers, and J. C. Leyendecker's original 1934 Easter cover for the *Saturday Evening Post.*

THE BUILDING

The Society's headquarters, a remodeled carriage house (c. 1875), once belonged to J. Pierpont Morgan's private secretary, William Read.

HISTORY

Among the Society's early members were such stellar figures as Charles Dana Gibson, remembered nowadays for the Gibson Girl; William Glackens, member of the group of painters called "Ash Can School"; and Frederic Remington, best known for his renderings of horses, cowboys, Indians, and other western subjects. Norman Rockwell, famous for his *Saturday Evening Post* covers, which depicted sentimental and traditional moments in American life, and N. C. Wyeth, paterfamilias of a famous American family of painters, also appeared on the Society's roster.

During two world wars, the Society and its members turned out illustrations for the war effort, the most famous of which was James Montgomery Flagg's World War I poster of Uncle Sam pointing at the viewer and intoning "I Want You!", a remark which by now has entered the annals of American folklore.

Sony Wonder Technology Lab (60)

550 Madison Ave (56th St), New York 10022. Tel: (212) 833-8100.

ADMISSION: Open Tues–Sat 10–6; Sun 12–6. Weekends and school vacations: admission by numbered ticket (with specific time slot); tickets must be picked up in person; try to arrive early, since all tickets are usually distributed by 2:30 P.M. Closed Mon, New Year's Day, Memorial Day, July 4, Labor Day, Thanksgiving, Christmas Day. Free.

Group tours; call for reservations.

✘ No restaurant.

🏛 Gift shop with Sony products, science-related books, toys, and gifts.

♿ Accessible to wheelchairs.

🚇 IRT Lexington Ave local or express (train 4, 5, or 6) to 51st St. IND 6th Ave express (B or D train) to 47th / 50th St. IND 6th Ave local (F train) to 5th Ave; IND 8th Ave local (E train) to 51st St.

🚌 M1, M2, M4 downtown on 5th Ave, uptown on Madison Ave.

Sony Wonder Technology Lab (1994), a glittering, computerized, hands-on introduction to information-age technology, offers technophiles a chance to experiment with robotics, medical imaging, and music and video technology. Visitors pick up a plastic identification card in the lobby and log in at a station on the fourth floor by recording their name, an image of their face, and a sample of their voice. The next part of the exhibition, the *Communication Bridge,* offers a short history of communications from the invention of photography to the present.

In the *Technology Workshop* you can experiment with cameras, computers, and video monitors. In the *Audio Lab* you can edit sound waves and make your own musical composition. The *High-Definition Interactive Theater* offers a video adventure movie, whose outcomes the audience can influence by pushing buttons on the arm rests of their comfortably padded seats.

The *Professional Studios* afford the opportunity to make digital recordings, operate robots, and deal with simulated environmental crises (take your pick between an oilspill and a hurricane threatening New York). The *Medical Imaging Lab* displays the capabilities of ultrasound equipment and an endoscopic camera. The final exhibitions, which also inform visitors about Sony products, display high-definition television and industrial design processes.

The South Street Seaport Museum (31)

Visitors Center, 12 Fulton St (bet. John / South Sts), New York 10004. Tel: (212) 748-8600 for recorded information; for sailing reservations, call (212) 748-8786.

ADMISSION: Open mid-May–mid-Sept: daily 10–6; mid-Sept–mid-May: 10–5. Closed New Year's Day, Thanksgiving, and Christmas Day. Admission fee. Admission tickets sold until 1 hr before closing at Visitors Center or at the ticket booth on Pier 16.

Changing exhibitions, tours (of Seaport and ships; also seasonal early morning tours of Fulton Fish Market), films, gallery talks, children's programs. Exhibitions of maritime crafts, traditional boat-building techniques, printing. Special events. Sailing cruises aboard the sloop *Pioneer:* tel: (212) 748-8786. Melville Library, 213–215 Water St, open to researchers by appointment.

✕ Numerous restaurants in Pavilion Building on Pier 17 and in the Fulton Market Building.

❙❮ Restrooms in Fulton Market Building and the Pavilion Building on Pier 17.

▥ Museum Shop adjacent to the Visitors Center has ship models, toys, and souvenirs. The Container Store on Pier 16 near the ticket booth offers children's gifts and souvenirs. There is extensive shopping in the Pier 17 Pavilion and in the Fulton Market Building. The Chandlery, 207–209 Water St, offers fine jewelry, books, and nautical gifts; the Beken Gallery, in the same building, has photographs, engravings, and posters.

♿ Wheelchair access limited. No ramps, no elevators. Most shops and galleries are up or down a few steps. Restrooms in Fulton Market Building are on 2nd floor, accessible by escalator. Restrooms on Pier 15 at ground level and in Pier 17 shopping facility.

⊘ No pets in buildings or on ships; commercial photography by permission only.

🚇 IRT 7th Ave express (train 2 or 3) to Fulton St. IRT Lexington Ave express (train 4 or 5) to Fulton St. BMT Nassau Street local (J or M train) to Fulton St. IND 8th Ave express or local (A or C train) to Broadway / Nassau. The Broadway / Nassau subway station is huge, labyrinthine, and confusing. Unless you are adept at the subway system, it is easier to walk above ground to Broadway and board the IRT Lexington Ave line there.

🚌 M15 downtown on 2nd Ave and Allen St to Pearl and Fulton Sts.

The South Street Seaport Museum (1967) is a collection of restored ships, historic buildings—countinghouses, saloons, hotels, warehouses—and exhibition galleries clustered around Fulton St on the East River, once the center of the city's maritime industries. The district, which decayed when its importance to the city's economic life diminished, has been reconstructed both as a historic restoration and as a commercial development featuring shops, restaurants, and office space.

HIGHLIGHTS

The centerpiece of the Museum is its fleet of historic ships, several of which have been restored and opened to the public. The *Peking,* one of the last commercial sailing ships; the *Ambrose Lightship;* and the *Wavertree,* a three-masted iron-hulled square-rigger, are among the treasures of the collection.

THE SHIPS

The Pilothouse on Pier 16 was once part of the steam tugboat *New York Central No. 31,* built for the railroad in 1923 to ferry passenger and freight cars across the rivers. Moored on the north side of Pier 16 is the former *Ambrose Lightship.* Built in 1908, the lightship marked the entrance to New York Harbor, through the deepwater Ambrose Channel, whose construction opened the harbor to large-scale ships. The *Ambrose Lightship* was replaced at its station in 1932 by a tower and beacon. Moored in the slip is the tugboat *W. O. Decker* (1930), which once hauled barges and scows in Newtown Creek across the river and now is a working vessel for the Seaport.

In the next slip is the pride of the Seaport, the *Peking,* a four-masted bark (1911) from Hamburg, Germany, one of the last sailing ships built for commercial purposes and one of the last such vessels left in the world. Carrying more than an acre of sail, this swift ship transported general cargo from Europe to South America and brought back nitrates for fertilizer, until the development of synthetic fertilizers made the South American trade economically unfeasible. On board is an exhibition on life at sea.

The *Lettie G. Howard* (1893), a Gloucester fishing schooner, is typical of many that formerly brought their catches to the Fulton Fish Market.

The *Wavertree* (1885), moored on the north side of Pier 15, is a square-rigged, iron-hulled ship built in England to carry jute from India to Europe; she was dismasted rounding Cape Horn in 1910 and towed to a remote backwater, where a slick of lanoline from a nearby slaughterhouse preserved her hull. Her decks have been rebuilt, and her masts restored and rerigged, but considerable restoration work remains. The public can visit during special Wavertree Restoration tours.

In the Maritime Crafts Center near Pier 15 you can see craftspeople at work on figureheads, carved signs, scrimshaw, and ship models.

THE BUILDINGS

In the triangle formed by the intersection of Water and Fulton Sts is the **Titanic Memorial,** moved here from the former Seamen's Church Institute building on South St near what is now Vietnam Veterans Park. It was erected to commemorate those who went down with the *Titanic.*

Schermerhorn Row (1812, 1880, 1983), the architectural centerpiece of the seaport, stretches along Fulton St from Front to South St. The Schermerhorns, one of the city's earliest families, owed their wealth in part to shrewd real estate investment and in part to their recognition of the importance of the coastal trade to the city's economic life. In 1793, Peter Schermerhorn, a shipowner and merchant, consolidated the family water-lot holdings (land between the extremes of high and low tides, hence underwater half the time), filled them, and constructed a block of 12 red brick commercial buildings with warehouse space downstairs and accounting offices above. When the Fulton Market opened in 1822, Schermerhorn found himself the owner of a piece of prime commercial property.

Sweet's, formerly at 4 Fulton St, a venerable seafood restaurant founded by Abraham M. Sweet in 1847, closed in 1993. The building at **2–4 Fulton St** became a steamboat hotel during the 19C, first called McKinley's, later the Fulton Ferry Hotel. The former Fulton Ferry, developed and owned by Robert Fulton, entrepreneur of the steamboat, crossed from Fulton St in Manhattan to Fulton St in Brooklyn beginning in 1814 (though the streets were named later).

Around the corner at the intersection of John and South Sts is the **Boat Building Shop,** where skilled craftsmen build and restore small wooden vessels using traditional techniques.

Nearby at 167–171 John St the former **A. A. Low Building** (1850), now home of the **Norway Galleries,** houses one of the Seaport's permanent exhibition spaces. It was built by Abiel Abbott Low, a pioneer of the China Trade, who made his fortune on tea, silk, porcelains, and other exotica. Low founded his firm (1840) after spending three years in Canton learning the business; ten years later he built this elegant brownstone-faced countinghouse, demolishing Peter Schermerhorn's older brick buildings on the site. The Lows were princes of the China Trade, and shortly after Commodore Perry opened Japan to trade in 1854, A. A. Low had ships riding at anchor in Shimoda, Nagasaki, and Hakodate.

Next door at 165 John St, in a building first occupied by flour merchants, is the **Children's Center,** whose activities include exhibits, films, workshops, and maritime programs.

The Museum also has exhibits along Water St. **207–211 Water St** (1835–36), with its granite steps, lintels, piers, and cornices, is a group of typical Greek Revival storefronts. **The Beken Gallery** at 207 Water St offers changing exhibits of photographs that document the seaport and the maritime heritage of the city. The **Chandlery** next door carries a good collection of books on local history, ships, the lore of the sea, and historic preservation. 211 Water St has been restored to recreate the 19C printing shop of **Bowne & Co., Stationers,** complete with working 19C presses.

Next door at 213 Water St (1868, remodeled 1975) is the **Museum Gallery** (gallery talks, changing exhibitions) and the **Melville Library.** The building was constructed as a warehouse for a tin company and has a ground-floor facade of cast iron and upper stories of limestone.

On the waterfront between South St and the Pier 17 Pavilion is a building formerly known as the "Tin Building" (1907), sheathed in corrugated metal. It is the fourth home of the famous **Fulton Fish Market,** which dates back to 1822 when vendors were allowed to set up their stalls in a wooden building on the site of the present Fulton Market Building. Many of the tenants were butchers but there were also produce dealers, fishmongers, sausagemakers, and cheese sellers. By 1834, however, the butchers were complaining that the run-off from the upstairs fish-gutting operations was seeping down to their stands, and so the fish dealers were exiled to their own wooden shed on the water, behind which floated fish cars with live fish. This arrangement persisted until the turn of the century, when the polluted water of the river poisoned the fish. Hanging from the rafters are examples of sailboats, dinghies, canoes, and other small craft.

The large **Pavilion Building** further out on the pier has shops, restaurants, fast-food counters, and a large seating area facing the river with great views of the Brooklyn waterfront and the Brooklyn Bridge.

PERMANENT COLLECTION

The Seaport has a fine arts collection of maritime paintings, prints, watercolors and drawings, ship models, scrimshaw objects, and marine fixtures. Part of the collection, more than 2,000 objects, was gathered by the Seamen's Bank for Savings (founded 1829, closed 1990). The ship models, many painstakingly fashioned by seamen with plenty of time on their hands, include riverboats, Chinese junks, and sidewheelers, as well as clipper ships and British ships of the line. Among the models are rare "Dartmoor" models made by French sailors held in the British prison during the Napoleonic Wars; the ships are crafted with hulls of beef bone and rigging of human hair.

HISTORY

From the first days of settlement until the years after the Civil War, the city's maritime activity focused on the East River, actually an arm of the sea lying on the lee side of Manhattan and less affected than the Hudson by ice, flooding, and the prevailing westerlies. When the Erie Canal opened in 1825, flooding New York with midwestern products, 500 new shipping firms came into existence. The China Trade, spearheaded by the firm of A. A. Low on Burling Slip (now John St), and the California trade both burgeoned. After the Civil War, however, the area slipped into decline as steamships superseded the clippers and trade moved to the deep-water docks on the Hudson.

In the mid-'60s, after a century of neglect, preservationists began working to save the old port, chartering the Museum (1967), and acquiring historic buildings and ships. In 1979 the city approved a plan to merge museum interests with major commercial development, and in 1983 a large part of the present restoration opened, including a rehabilitated Schermerhorn Row and a new Fulton Market. In 1985 the large red steel and glass pavilion housing stores and restaurants was constructed on Pier 17.

The Spanish Institute (87)

The Center for American-Spanish Affairs, 684 Park Ave (68th St), New York 10021. Tel: (212) 628-0420.

ADMISSION: Open during exhibitions Mon–Sat 11–5. Closed Sun, holidays.

Changing exhibitions, lectures and symposia on Spanish politics, economy, culture; language instruction, courses in art history; concerts; publications.

✘ No restaurant.

▥ No gift shop. Exhibition catalogues available.

໓ Not easily accessible to wheelchairs; entrance up three stairs from street. Main gallery on 1st floor; galleries on 2nd floor used for occasional large exhibitions.

▮▬ Lexington Ave IRT local (train 6) to 68th St.

▭ M1, M2, M3, or M4 uptown on Madison Ave, downtown on 5th Ave. M101 or M102 uptown on 3rd Ave, downtown on Lexington Ave. M29 crosstown on 66th–67th Sts.

The Spanish Institute (founded 1954), a nonprofit center devoted to promoting cultural understanding and strengthening ties between Spain and the United States, offers a wide range of programs to achieve those goals—lectures on Spanish politics, economics, history, and literature, language courses in Spanish, Catalan, and English, recitals, concerts, performances, and art exhibitions.

EXHIBITION PROGRAM

Exhibits include some of the finest contemporary Spanish art, as well as historical shows. There are usually four shows yearly, one in the autumn and three in the spring. Notable have been lithographs and pastels illustrating *Don Quixote* by the Surrealist Matta, and drawings by the poet and playwright Federico García Lorca. To mark its 30th anniversary, the Institute mounted an exhibition of prints by Goya, drawing on the five major print cycles made by the artist during his long career and including a group of etchings from the series *Disasters of War,* inspired by the atrocities that followed Napoleon's invasion of Spain.

"Spain Collects," curated by Guggenheim curator of 20C art Carmen Giménez, offered selected works of modern art assembled by Jacques Hachuel of Madrid, and included works by Braque, Picasso, Miró, Julio González, Léger, Giacometti, Antoni Tàpies, Alexander Calder, and Eduardo Chillida. "The Spanish Vision" gave an overview of Spanish contemporary art photography.

Other exhibitions and programs, mounted in coordination with New York institutions elsewhere, allow cultural insights that cross the limits of particular collections. A show on Spanish landscape photography from the turn of the century was mounted contemporaneously with an exhibition of other present-day Spanish photography at the International Center of Photography.

THE BUILDING

Like its Park Ave neighbors, the Americas Society and the Istituto Italiano di Cultura, the Spanish Institute occupies a handsome neo-Georgian block of houses built between 1909 and 1926 by the firm of McKim, Mead & White.

The Statue of Liberty National Monument and Statue of Liberty Museum (32)

Liberty Island, New York 10004. Tel: (212) 363-3200 for recorded information; for a live person, call (212) 363-7620. For boat information, call the Circle Line at (212) 269-5755.

ADMISSION: Statue open every day, 9:30–4, with extended hours sometimes in summer. Admission to Statue and Museum is free; charge for ferry.

> NOTE: Crowds are often very heavy and the time required to ascend the statue lengthens proportionately. To make the ascent with the shortest waiting time, take the first boat (telephone Circle Line for exact time of first sailing), stay downstairs near the gangway, and hurry immediately from the dock to the statue. The round trip by boat takes about 45 min. Visitors arriving at the statue in mid-afternoon may not have time to make the ascent.

Information kiosk in Castle Clinton, near ticket booth, has information on Statue of Liberty, Ellis Island, and other National Park Service sites.

✕ Cafeteria.

▥ Gift shop, with souvenirs, books, postcards.

♿ Complete access for handicapped visitors to Museum, restrooms, and restaurant; no wheelchair access above Museum level.

> NOTE: The crown is a 22-story climb from ground level. An elevator reaches the top of the pedestal but from this level ascent is by spiral stairway only, the equivalent of 12 stories. Although the interior is air-cooled (not air-conditioned), temperatures rise in summer. Visitors with physical disabilities, vertigo, or claustrophobia are urged not to make the climb. There are excellent views from the promenade level, above the original Fort Wood, and at the top of the pedestal, as well as from the crown.

⊘ There are no facilities for checking parcels or strollers, so visitors must carry any paraphernalia they bring to the island or else leave it unguarded.

🚇 IRT Broadway-7th Ave local (train 1 or 9) to South Ferry. IRT Lexington Ave express (train 4 or 5) to Bowling Green. BMT Broadway express or local (N or R train) to Whitehall St / South Ferry. Ferry from Battery Park to Statue.

🚌 M1 or M6 downtown via 5th Ave and Broadway to South Ferry. M15 downtown via 2nd Ave and Water St to Whitehall St. Ferry from Battery Park to Statue.

⛴ Ferry leaves from Battery Park at the foot of Broadway. Schedule subject to seasonal change; call the Circle Line at (212) 269-5755. The ticket kiosk, located in Castle Clinton, the low red sandstone structure on the west side of the park, is open ½ hr before first sailing. Additional sailings from Liberty State Park in Jersey City, N.J. Some ferries continue on to Ellis Island; check with Circle Line for details.

The Statue of Liberty (dedicated 1886; Frédéric-Auguste Bartholdi), surely the most famous piece of sculpture in America, rises in towering majesty on Liberty Island in direct view of ships entering the Upper Bay. *Liberty*'s head is surrounded by a radiant crown; broken shackles lie at her feet. Her uplifted right hand holds a torch and her left grasps a tablet representing the Declaration of Independence.

Located in the base of the statue one level above the ground floor, the Statue of Liberty Museum offers exhibits on the history and construction of the statue. There is also an outdoor display of sculpture by Philip Ratner with bronze figures of people involved in the creation of the statue; included are Eiffel, Bartholdi, and Emma Lazarus.

HISTORY

The inspiration for the Statue of Liberty, originally called "Liberty Enlightening the World," came primarily from two men: Édouard-René Lefebvre de Laboulaye (1811–83), a noted authority on U.S. Constitutional history, and Frédéric-Auguste Bartholdi (1834–1904), a sculptor of monumental ambitions. Laboulaye, wanting to identify the destiny of France with that of the United States, the preeminent modern republic, proposed a joint Franco-American monument in 1865 and introduced Bartholdi to the project. The statue's iron skeleton was devised by Alexandre-Gustave Eiffel (1832–1923), whose reputation at the time rested with his iron trusswork railway bridges.

The French people raised about $400,000 for the statue, which was constructed in Paris by the firm of Gaget, Gauthier, et Cie. In 1884 the statue was shipped in pieces to New York, and the cornerstone laid, but construction was halted for lack of funds. In 1885, newspaper publisher Joseph Pulitzer launched a funding campaign which in a few months raised over $100,000, mostly in modest donations, while quadrupling the circulation of his financially troubled newspaper. On Oct 28, 1886, President Grover Cleveland dedicated the statue during spectacular ceremonies climaxed by fireworks and the unveiling of the face. The statue soon became a tourist attraction, a promise of hope offered to immigrants by the New World, and eventually a powerful symbol for the United States itself.

As such it has been the target of extremist groups: in 1965 four terrorists attempted to blow off the head and arm holding the torch; in 1971 a group of Vietnam veterans occupied it for several days as a war protest.

The centennial year (1986) saw the triumphant unveiling of a restored statue, which had been shrouded for two years in scaffolding. The only visible exterior change is the replacement of the former torch (1916) of glass in a copper grid by a new one gilded with gold leaf as Bartholdi had envisioned. The interior, however, is considerably changed. The corroded iron straps which held the copper skin to the interior framework have been replaced by stainless-steel ones, and the connection between the central pylon and the upraised right arm, swaying since 1916, has been strengthened. The wire mesh that long enclosed the spiral staircase has been cleared away, revealing the interior of the statue itself, the great volumes of the body and the billowing folds and creases of the robe.

The unveiling of the restored statue was climaxed by a July 4 celebration truly American in its exuberant excess. Naval warships fired 21-gun salvos and military planes performed aerobatics over the harbor; a fleet of 150 tall ships—some of them recreations of 18C and 19C traders, fishing schooners, and square-riggers—sailed from the Narrows up the Hudson River; a 40,000-shell fireworks display illuminated the harbor at night. Some 25,000 vessels clogged the harbor. Helicopters, jet fighters, and six stately blimps buzzed, soared, and hovered overhead. An estimated 1.5–2 million people jammed the streets and parks, climbed to the roofs of tall buildings, or crowded into any apartment or office space with a view of the statue.

LIBERTY ISLAND

Renamed in 1956, the island on which the statue stands, was formerly known as Bedloe's Island after Isaac Bedloe, who acquired it in 1667 from the English Colonial governor. Before the Revolution it was used as a quarantine station, particularly for smallpox, and in 1746–57 it was owned by Archibald Kennedy, a wealthy merchant, who summered there. The U.S. government acquired it in 1800 to build Fort Wood (1808–11), designed by Col. Jonathan Williams, who also planned Castle Williams on Governors Island and Fort Gibson on Ellis Island. Named after a now obscure hero of the War of 1812, Fort Wood later served as a Civil War recruitment camp and an ordnance depot; in 1877 the government donated it to the Liberty project.

VITAL STATISTICS

Height of statue alone, 151 ft; pedestal, 89 ft; height of torch above sea, 305 ft; weight, 225 tons; waist measurement, 35 ft; width of mouth, 3 ft; length of index finger, 8 ft. The hammered copper "skin" of the figure is only 3/32 in thick; it is bound together in sections by steel straps, and joined to the trusswork in such a way that it "floats" at the ends of hundreds of flexible attachments and can accommodate both thermal changes and wind.

PERMANENT EXHIBITION

The Statue of Liberty Museum is devoted to the history and construction of the statue and to its symbolism. Exhibits of photographs, models, and documents detail the evolution of Bartholdi's design. Tools, models, photographs, and plans should satisfy the technophile curious about the engineering of the figure, the construction of the interior iron framework (now replaced by steel), the copper repoussé technique of the outer "skin," and the recent restoration.

The next section of the exhibit offers photos, films, and recorded voices to suggest the impact of the statue on arriving immigrants and its evolution from a symbol of New York City to a symbol for the nation itself. A collection of statuettes, photographs (including an astonishing picture of the statue recreated in corn, oats, and wheat for an 1895 Nebraska fundraiser), and posters shows the exploitation of the statue as a commercial image and as a vehicle for political propaganda.

The Studio Museum in Harlem (109)

144 West 125th St (bet. Adam Clayton Powell Blvd [7th Ave] and Lenox Ave [6th Ave]), New York 10027. Tel: (212) 864-4500.

ADMISSION: Open Wed–Fri 10–5; Sat and Sun 1–6. Closed Mon–Tues, holidays. Admission charge.

Changing exhibitions, lectures, workshops, gallery talks, films, artist-in-residence program, school programs, musical events, panel discussions, dance events.

✗ No restaurant.

🛍 Gift shop with books, cards, posters, crafts, and jewelry by African-American, Caribbean, and African artists, gifts, toys, reproductions. To order by phone with a credit card during Museum hours, call (212) 864-4500, ext. 237.

& Complete wheelchair accessibility.

🚇 IRT 7th Ave express (train 2 or 3) to 125th St. IND 8th Ave local or express (C or A train) to 125th St. IND 6th Ave express (D train) to 125th St.

🚌 M2 uptown via Madison Ave / Powell Blvd. M7 uptown via Amsterdam Ave / 116th St / Lenox Ave. M101 uptown via 3rd Ave, crosstown on 125th–126th Sts.

The Studio Museum in Harlem (founded 1968) is the premier museum in the nation devoted solely to the preservation of African-American art and culture. It offers changing exhibitions as well as shows based on a growing permanent collection.

EXHIBITION PROGRAM

The exhibition program focuses on the work of black artists and on African-American culture in a more general sense. "The Black Musician in American Art" used the work of both black and white artists to explore attitudes toward blacks from the time of Revolutionary War through the civil rights movement. "Harlem Renaissance: The Art of Black America" celebrated the work of four Harlem artists of the 1920s, on the one hand emphasizing the rich cultural and social life of the period, on the other taking a hard look at social problems—poverty, crime, inadequate housing—that still plague the area.

In recent years the Museum has expanded its program, working with other museums in the city. "The Decade Show," organized in collaboration with the New Museum of Contemporary Art and the former Museum of Contemporary Hispanic Art, both located in SoHo, presented the work of black, white, and Latino artists. The show looked at major concerns of the 1980s—homelessness, racism, sexism, AIDS, the environment, and war.

"Memory and Metaphor: The Art of Romare Bearden, 1940–1987" was the first major retrospective of Bearden's evolution from social realism through a trail of styles that finally coalesced in the collages for which he is best known. The Museum has presented retrospectives of such other important artists as Archibald J. Motley, Jr., and William H. Johnson.

In addition to providing exposure for black artists, the Museum has organized shows on classic and contemporary African art; its contribution of work by contemporary artists from sub-Saharan Africa to the 1990 Venice Biennale was its first exhibition abroad. "Wifredo Lam and His Contemporaries, 1938–1952" was one of the largest and most important exhibitions in the Museum's history. Works gathered from collections worldwide offered an interpretation of the career of the African-Cuban artist, who was trained in the European tradition but was also influenced by Cuban and American contemporaries.

PERMANENT COLLECTION

Though collecting was not a first priority in its early days, the Museum is gradually acquiring a permanent collection, which will strengthen its role as a major repository of African and African-American art. Among its holdings are works by African-American artists Sam Gilliam, Norman Lewis, Romare Bearden, Jacob Lawrence, Faith Ringgold, and Betye Saar, as well as works by Caribbean and Latino artists. African art includes masks, funerary sculptures, Ashanti gold weights, and Yoruba twin figures. Caribbean and specifically Haitian art includes traditional pieces, as well as the work of contemporary sculptors like Edgar and Murat Brierre who fashion works from metal oil drums. The photography collection embraces the work of such important black photographers as James VanDerZee, Gordon Parks, and P. H. Polk.

HISTORY

Founded as the offspring of the Junior Council of the Museum of Modern Art, the Museum's original purpose was simply to provide studio and exhibition space for working artists, but its location—in a rented loft over a liquor store in Harlem—and the timing of its arrival—in the late '60s when civil rights activism was an intense concern—shaped its course. The Studio Museum quickly shed its general avant-garde image and responded to the needs of the community around it, its mission becoming the interpretation and preservation of the black presence in the western hemisphere. In 1979 the Museum received its present building as a gift from the New York Bank for Savings, where it reopened after renovation in 1982.

Trinity Church Museum (33)

Broadway at Wall St, New York 10006. Tel: (212) 602-0872.

ADMISSION: Open Mon–Fri 9–11:45, 1–3:45; Sat 10–3:45; Sun 1–3:45. Closed major holidays. Free.

Occasional special events, tours of churchyard, lectures; tel: (212) 602-0872. Educational programs by appointment.

✗ No restaurant.

💇 Restrooms located at the west end of the church beyond the chapel, accessible from north aisle.

🏛 No gift shop. Postcards for sale near entrance to nave. Bookstore at 74 Trinity Place.

♿ Limited wheelchair accessibility: church is a few steps up from street level; museum on same level as church. Ramp at rear of church. Restrooms not equipped for wheelchair access.

⊘ No photography during services.

🚇 IRT 7th Ave express (train 2 or 3) to Wall St. IRT Broadway-7th Ave local (train 1 or 9) to Rector St. IRT Lexington Ave express (train 4 or 5) to Wall St. BMT Broadway local (R train) to Rector St.

🚌 M1 (marked South Ferry) downtown via 5th Ave and Broadway to Wall St. M6 downtown via 7th Ave and Broadway to Wall St.

Trinity Church Museum (parish chartered 1697; church built 1846) chronicles the history of this important architectural and historic presence in lower Manhattan.

EXHIBITION PROGRAM

A permanent exhibit, "The Parish of Trinity Church in the City of New York: The Evolution of an Urban Institution," portrays the relationship between the parish and the city as both have evolved over the past 300 years. On display are documents, maps, newspapers, burial records, sermons, and other artifacts which show the life of Trinity as an institution and emphasize its social outreach programs.

The Museum also mounts long-term exhibitions (two or three years' duration) on historical subjects. "An Ocean of Difficulties: The New Nation 1798–1849" offered photographs, diary excerpts, drawings, and the minutes of church meetings to document change and growth in the parish, during a period that began with the passage of the Bill of Rights and ended with the California gold rush.

THE CHURCHYARD

The Trinity Church graveyard contains the earthly remains of illustrious early New Yorkers. Most famous of all is Alexander Hamilton, mortally wounded (1804) by Aaron Burr in a duel. Of only slightly less prominence are Robert Fulton, inventor of the steamboat, and James Lawrence, commander of the frigate *Chesapeake*, whose immortal words, "Don't Give Up the Ship," are inscribed as the last line of his epitaph. The elaborate 39-ft monument in the middle of the north plot commemorates Caroline Webster Schermerhorn Astor (1830–1908), matriarch of New York society in the late 19C.

HISTORY

Trinity Church, the first Episcopalian church in New York, was chartered by William III of England in 1697, though land was not granted to the parish until 1705 by Queen Anne. Queen Anne was indeed generous to Trinity Parish, ceding to it a plot known as the Queen's Farm, which ran north from Fulton St and from Broadway west to the Hudson River. With the later acquisition of some other plots, Trinity's holdings in the 18C reached as far north as Christopher St. Through the years the church has given away two-thirds of the original land grant to other institutions; today only about 6% of the original grant still belongs to the parish.

The church has also placed its stamp on lower Manhattan place names: Barclay, Vesey, Rector, and Vestry Sts, as well as Trinity Place and Church St—are all names connected with the church and its early rectors.

Tweed Gallery (34)

52 Chambers St (City Hall Park), New York 10007. The Art Commission administers the gallery; tel: (212) 788-3071.

ADMISSION: Open Mon–Fri 9–5. Closed major holidays Free.

Changing exhibitions.

✖ No restaurant.

🏛 No gift shop. Publications of the Art Commission available at CityBooks, 61 Chambers St.

&. Complete wheelchair access; ramps, elevator.

🚇 IRT Lexington Ave local or express (train 4, 5, or 6) to Brooklyn Bridge. IRT 7th Ave express (train 2 or 3) to Park Place. BMT Broadway local (R train) to City Hall.

🚌 M1 via 5th Ave and Broadway or M6 via 7th Ave and Broadway to Chambers St. M22 crosstown on Madison and Chambers Sts, Vesey St and Park Row.

NOTE: The gallery will be closed for renovation in 1996.

Established (1984) by the Mayor's Office, the Tweed Gallery presents exhibitions sponsored by city agencies and community groups. It is located in the restored rotunda of the former New York City Courthouse, popularly known as the "Tweed Courthouse."

EXHIBITION PROGRAM

Perhaps to exorcise the unsavory reputation which long clung to the Tweed Courthouse, exhibitions in the gallery often highlight the accomplishments and special programs of the city government. Others reflect the cultural heritage of the city's ethnic groups. To celebrate Black History Month, "Movements of Ten Dance Masters" used archival photographs to highlight the achievements of black dancers and choreographers—Alvin Ailey, Arthur Mitchell, Marie Brooks, and others. The Department of Parks and Recreation organized "Designing Women: Works by Landscape Architects and Sculptors in New York City Parks" to celebrate Women's History Month. In commemoration of Asian American Heritage Month, the Asian American Arts Center worked together with the Mayor's Office for Asian Affairs in mounting "We Count! The State of Asian Pacific America," an exhibition of contemporary works by artists of diverse Asian backgrounds.

THE BUILDING

The "Tweed Courthouse" (1872; John Kellum. Addition to the rear, 1880; Leopold Eidlitz) is famous primarily for how much it cost, a figure estimated between $12 and $13 million, but successfully obscured during the scandal that erupted after its completion. Along with his cronies, William M. ("Boss") Tweed, political kingmaker and Democratic Party potentate, fleeced the city by having contractors pad their accounts and kick back the difference between what the work actually cost and what the city paid for it. Thus a plasterer named Andrew J. Garvey appeared in the records as receiving $45,966.89 for one day's work, thereby earning headlines as the "Prince of Plasterers."

The courthouse, as a symbol of municipal graft, never endeared itself to those in power; it narrowly escaped demolition in the mid-1970s, saved by the combined resistance of preservationists and the high cost of demolition. Despite the graft, however, the Tweed Courthouse is a handsome Victorian building.

The Ukrainian Institute of America (88)

1 East 72nd St (5th Ave), New York 10021. Tel: (212) 288-8660.

ADMISSION: Generally open Tues–Sun 1–6, but sometimes hours vary according to show. Closed Mon, weekends, holidays. Voluntary donation.

Occasional exhibitions, lectures, concerts, artist-in-residence, classes in Slavic and Ukrainian, other cultural events.

✗ No restaurant.

🏛 No gift shop.

♿ Not accessible to wheelchairs.

🚍 IRT Lexington Ave local (train 6) to 77th St.

🚌 M1, M2, M3, M4 uptown on Madison Ave, downtown on 5th Ave.

The Ukrainian Institute of America (founded 1948) is a center for Ukrainian and Slavic cultural activities, including art exhibitions, concerts, and lectures. It is housed in a Gothic-style mansion that formerly belonged to Augustus Van Horne Stuyvesant, last direct male descendant of the Dutch governor Peter Stuyvesant.

EXHIBITION PROGRAM

The Institute presents two or three exhibitions each year, which range from the work of contemporary artists of Ukrainian birth or heritage currently working and living in America, to photography, to traditional costumes and folk arts. Other shows commemorate particular occasions, such as the celebration of the millennial anniversary of Christianity in Ukraine, which offered manuscripts, paintings, and liturgical vestments, among other things.

PERMANENT COLLECTION

The small permanent collection includes work by modern Ukrainian artists. There are examples of sculpture by Alexander Archipenko and painting by Alexis Gritchenko. Also in the collection are church garments, religious books, and manuscripts dating back to the 17C, and examples of folk art, including embroidered textiles and costumes of various Slavic ethnic groups, decorative ceramics, and *pysanky* (traditionally dyed Easter eggs).

HISTORY

William Kzus, an immigrant from Ukraine, founded the Institute and donated the building it presently occupies. Kzus had made his fortune inventing a simple fastener that held together the sheets of aluminum that replaced the fabric and wood formerly used to cover airplane fuselages and wings. The principle of the fastener is still used today, though in orthopedics rather than aeronautics.

The Ukrainian Museum (35)

203 Second Ave (bet. 12th / 13th Sts,), New York 10003. Tel: (212) 228-0110.

ADMISSION: Open Wed–Sun 1–5. Closed Mon and Tues, New Year's Day,

Easter, Thanksgiving, and Christmas Day. Admission charge; children under 12 free.

Educational and cultural programs, courses in embroidery and woodcarving, workshops, lectures, films, concerts, publications. Traveling exhibitions.

✘ No restaurant.

📺 Gift shop with Ukrainian crafts, gift items adapted from the Museum's collection, prints, publications, posters, and greeting cards. Items may be ordered by mail.

♿ Not accessible to wheelchairs.

⃠ No photography.

🚇 14th St-Canarsie local (L train) crosstown on 14th St to 1st or 3rd Ave. IRT Lexington Ave local or express (train 4, 5, or 6) to 14th St.

🚌 M15 downtown on 2nd Ave, uptown on 1st Ave. M14 crosstown on 14th St. M101 or M102 via Lexington and 3rd Aves.

Located in a flourishing Ukrainian enclave in the East Village, the Ukrainian Museum (founded 1976) offers changing exhibitions on Ukrainian art, many drawn from a folk art collection that contains more than 4,000 objects.

PERMANENT COLLECTION

Most objects in the collection date from the late 19–early 20C; they have been chosen to illustrate the regional diversity of Ukrainian folk art and the Eastern and Western influences that characterize it.

Ceramics include stove tiles, jugs, and traditional *kolachi* (ring-shaped vessels) decorated in geometric, floral, and figural motifs.

The collection of folk costumes is perhaps the most important one outside Ukraine. Other textiles include woven and embroidered *rushnyky* or ritual cloths, which Ukrainian girls traditionally embroidered for their trousseaux using some of the 100 different stitches found in Ukrainian embroidery. Metalwork includes a large collection of jewelry made of brass or German silver, peasant substitutes for gold and silver. The influence of Turkish motifs can be seen in the Museum's collection of *kilims,* woven belts, and furniture covers.

The collection also includes some 900 brilliantly decorated Easter eggs *(pysanky),* a tradition that surely dates back to pre-Christian spring fertility rituals. Most decorations are geometric, but sometimes the entire universe—with sun, moon, and stars—is symbolized. Patterns are applied in wax; then the egg is dipped in dyes progressing from light to dark colors. When the wax is melted off in the final stage, the design emerges.

Since 1981 the Museum has been gathering an archive of photographs and written documents, detailing the history of Ukrainian immigration to the United States. Photographs illustrate Ukrainian folk costumes and vernacular architecture. The fine arts collection includes drawings and watercolors of the primitive artist Nikifor, etchings by Nicholas Bervinchak, and works by Mychajlo Andreenko and other Ukrainian artists. A numismatic collection contains coins and printed currency ranging from the 11C *hryvnia* (a bar-shaped Kievan monetary unit) to examples of Ukrainian money produced by the Ukrainian Republic in 1918–22.

EXHIBITION PROGRAM

The collection is shown in special exhibitions, some of which have high-lighted Easter eggs and ritual breads, folk ceramics from the Carpathian Mountains, folk music instruments, houses of worship in Ukraine, and contemporary Ukrainian posters. In 1992, while Ukraine was celebrating its renewed existence as an independent nation, the Museum mounted a show of posters and political cartoons from *Ratusha,* a newspaper published in Lviv. The work, by members of a student political group, celebrated Ukrainian nationalism.

HISTORY

The Ukrainian Museum traces its beginnings to the 1930s, when the Ukrainian National Women's League of America gathered the core of its folk art collection in Ukraine and exhibited it in various cities throughout the country. In 1976 the Museum was formally organized to preserve and document the fine art and the folk art of Ukrainian Americans.

The Urban Center Galleries (61)

457 Madison Ave (bet. 50th / 51st Sts), New York 10022. Tel: (212) 935-3960.

ADMISSION: Open Mon–Wed, Fri 11–5; Sat 12–5. Closed Thurs, Sun, and national holidays. Free.

Changing exhibitions, lectures, discussions, special events, calendar of events, publications.

✖ No restaurant.

📖 Urban Center Book Store, one of finest specialized collections in the city; books on architecture, urban planning, and historic preservation. Excellent selection of guidebooks and other books on New York.

♿ Accessible to wheelchairs from side service entrance on 51st St (bet. Park and Madison Aves).

🚌 M1, M2, M3, M4, M5, or Q32 uptown on Madison Ave, downtown on 5th Ave. M27 / M50 crosstown on 49th / 50th Sts.

🚇 IRT Lexington Ave local (train 6) to 51st St.

The Urban Center (1980), located in the north wing of the restored **Villard Houses,** is the headquarters for four urban planning and architectural organizations: the New York Chapter of the American Institute of Architects, the Architectural League of New York, the Municipal Art Society of New York, and the Parks Council. The Galleries, two of them in former reception rooms of the Villard Houses, offer changing exhibitions on topics related to architecture, urban planning, historic preservation, and urban life.

EXHIBITION PROGRAM

Exhibits range from Andrew Bordwin's stunning photos of the little-known (and now defunct) Cloud Club, a jewel of Art Deco splendor located high in the Chrysler Building, to entries for the "Bioshelter Competition, Cathedral of St. John the Divine," plans for completing the south transept of the cathedral in ways that reflect the contemporary needs of New York. Other shows may examine the uses of specific architectural materials, e.g., the decorative use of terracotta, or showcase the work of particular architects. Every year the Architectural League mounts a "Young Architects" exhibition.

To celebrate its centennial year, the Municipal Art Society (founded 1892), which functions as a watchdog over the urban environment, offered a major exhibit chronicling the history of the City Beautiful movement and another celebrating the work of Stanford White, architect of the Villard Houses.

THE BUILDING

The Villard Houses, a U-shaped group of six neo-Renaissance dwellings, were built (1886) for railroad baron Henry Villard by McKim, Mead & White, the architectural firm favored by those wealthy families contending to build New York's most sumptuous homes. Villard's own home occupied the entire south side of the courtyard; the other five houses were built speculatively for resale. Decades later, after the income tax and changing social mores had taken their toll on Villard and his social peers, business firms and the Archdiocese of New York took over the buildings as offices, fortunately leaving them more or less intact. Exhaustive negotiations led to their preservation and present use.

The Urban Center occupies rooms in the onetime homes of banker and railroad investor Harris C. Fahnestock and his son William. Considering the long struggle to protect the houses from destruction, the presence of the Urban Center here is a happy use of the space. Across the courtyard, Villard's own home serves as a base for a high-rise hotel. The most important ground- and first-floor interiors, now public rooms of the hotel, have been handsomely restored and are worth a visit.

White Columns (36)

154 Christopher St, 2nd floor (between Greenwich / Washington Sts), New York 10014. Tel: (212) 924-4212.

ADMISSION: Open Sept–June: Wed–Sun, 12–6. Closed Mon, Tues, holidays, July and Aug. Free.

Changing exhibitions. Seminar program: "Theoretical Studies in Art" on topics of interest to professionals. Artists' slide file available to curators, art writers, and dealers by appointment.

✗ No restaurant.

▥ No gift shop. Catalogues published occasionally.

♿ Accessible to wheelchairs.

🚈 IRT Broadway-7th Ave local (train 1 or 9) to Sheridan Sq / Christopher St. Walk west.

🚌 M10 uptown on Hudson St, downtown on Varick St. M13 westbound on 9th St / Christopher St, eastbound on Christopher St / 8th St.

Founded (1969) by artists Gordon Matta-Clark and Jeffrey Lew, White Columns is the city's oldest alternative art space. Its chief function is to build new audiences for the experimental work of emerging artists. In the past White Columns has supported such now well-established figures as Richard Serra, Dennis Oppenheim, Carl Andre, and Meyer Vaisman. More recently artists like Glenn Ligon, Marilyn Minter, Cady Noland, and Lorna Simpson, have also exhibited here.

EXHIBITION PROGRAM

Each year, White Columns presents 8–10 group and solo shows of contemporary work in a variety of media. The Main Gallery usually contains group shows, including commissioned installations. There are no thematic restrictions, and White Columns has offered subway graffiti and salt sculpture, as well as works in more traditional media.

The White Room program, which occupies the smaller galleries, mounts simultaneous exhibitions of three artists who have not yet had major exposure, allowing them the opportunity to be seen in a New York show. In choosing exhibitors, the gallery reviews the work of more than 1,000 artists each year, viewing their slides, interviewing them personally, and following up with studio visits.

In the spring White Columns holds a preview exhibition of works that will be sold in the annual benefit auction. Artists who have been supported by White Columns during the initial stages of their careers, as well as those who simply support its goals, donate works to be auctioned. Though the exhibition is by nature eclectic, it also provides an overview of the concerns and activities of the gallery.

The Whitney Museum of American Art (89)

945 Madison Ave (75th St), New York 10021. Tel: (212) 570-3676 for general information. For film and video information, tel: (212) 570-3676. To reach a live person, tel: (212) 570-3600.

ADMISSION: Open Wed 11–6, Thurs 1–8, Fri–Sun 11–6. Closed Mon, Tues, and national holidays. ArtReach Tues for scheduled educational programs only. Admission charge; free evening hours Thurs 6–8.

Changing exhibitions, lectures, gallery talks, symposia, film and video performances. Schedule of tours available at Information Desk in lobby.

✗ Sarabeth's at the Whitney open Tues 12–5, Wed 11–5, Thurs 12:30–8, Fri 11–5, Sat and Sun 10–5. Closed Mon.

▥ Bookshop with catalogues, cards, posters, art books, reproductions. Bookshop open same hours as Museum, and also Tues 10–5, when the Museum is closed. The Store Next Door (just south of the Museum at 943 Madison Ave) is open Tues, Wed, Fri–Sat 10–6; Thurs 10–8; Sun 11–6. The store has books, gifts, reproductions, jewelry, household items, American crafts.

♿ Accessible to wheelchairs. On the first Thurs evening of each month at 6:30 there are gallery talks, accompanied by a certified sign language interpreter. Call the Museum for further information.

🚇 IRT Lexington Ave local (train 6) to 77th St.

🚌 M1, M2, M3, M4 uptown on Madison Ave, downtown on 5th Ave. M30, crosstown on 72nd St. M79 crosstown on 79th St.

The Whitney Museum of American Art, founded (1930) by Gertrude Vanderbilt Whitney, houses a superb collection of 20C American art, the most comprehensive in the world. An active and sometimes controversial exhibition program supplements the permanent exhibition.

HISTORY

In 1907, Gertrude Vanderbilt Whitney, an aspiring sculptor connected by both birth and marriage to two of the city's preeminent families, opened a studio in Greenwich Village, far from the family domains uptown, perhaps to escape the oppression of too much money and too much social position. Her own work fell comfortably within the academic tradition, but her commitments were more daring. In 1914 she bought the house adjoining her studio, remodeled it as a small gallery, and began showing the work of young American artists. In 1918 she organized the Studio Club as an exhibition center and meeting ground. She sponsored the first solo shows of John Sloan, Reginald Marsh, Guy Pène du Bois, and Edward Hopper. Mrs. Whitney purchased many of the paintings she exhibited, and further helped her artists by paying their medical bills and footing their rents.

By 1929, Mrs. Whitney owned some 500 works by American artists and, feeling that they should be available to the public, offered her collection to the Metropolitan Museum of Art. The Museum rejected the offer so quickly that she could not even announce her intention to build and endow a wing to house it. Consequently she decided to start her own museum, and in 1931 the Whitney Museum of American Art opened in three remodeled brownstones on West 8th St. In 1954 the Museum moved uptown to 54th St near the Museum of Modern Art—a move that boosted its attendance from 70,000 to 270,000 annually, quickly necessitating a new building.

That goal was realized in 1966 with the present handsome building designed by Marcel Breuer. Breuer spoke of wanting the building to have the vitality of the streets, the latitude of a bridge, and the weight of a skyscraper. The building that resulted, three tiers of reinforced concrete clad in gray granite and cantilevered out like the steps of an inverted pyramid, has again proven to be too small for the number of viewers and the increasing size of the collection.

The Museum has entertained various plans to expand the present facilities. After years of heated controversy, these are presently on hold. But the Museum has expanded in other ways, opening branch museums in the city and in suburban Connecticut. Currently the Museum maintains branches at the Philip Morris Building and in Stamford.

PERMANENT COLLECTION

Both as a sculptor and as a collector, Gertrude Vanderbilt Whitney was conventional in her tastes. She preferred realism to abstraction, and as a collector preferred painting to sculpture. Today the Whitney continues its founder's interest in supporting contemporary American art but it no longer expresses her personal preferences, although naturally some of the strengths of its permanent collection have their source in her gifts. The 500 works she bought for herself before 1930 and the additional 100 she acquired to broaden her holdings for the Museum when it opened to the public in 1931 still form the nucleus of the collection, which now includes more than 10,000 objects. Paintings by Charles Demuth, Charles Sheeler, Joseph Stella, Charles Burchfield, George Bellows, and The Eight were donated by Mrs. Whitney or purchased with funds she provided. Her support for Edward Hopper and Reginald Marsh led to sizable bequests by their widows to the permanent collection. Mrs. Whitney was not particularly interested in collecting sculpture, and with the exception of some works by Gaston Lachaise, it was only long after her death that the Museum gave equal importance to sculpture in its program of acquisitions. American 20C pioneers—painters like Arthur G. Dove, Marsden Hartley, Oscar Bluemner, and Georgia O'Keeffe—were collected in depth only after Mrs. Whitney's death. The Museum also has strong holdings in the works of Donald Judd, Willem de Kooning, Ad Reinhardt, Mark Rothko, and David Smith.

Installations from the permanent collection are rotated through the gallery spaces at three- or four-month intervals. The following list, in alphabetical order, suggests some of the works which may be on display.

Josef Albers, *Homage to the Square: Gained* (1959). Richard Artschwager, *Construction with Indentation* (1966). Milton Avery, *Dunes and Sea II* (1960). William Baziotes, *The Beach* (1955). George Bellows, *Dempsey and Firpo* (1924). Oscar Bluemner, *A Situation in Yellow* (1933). Louise Bourgeois, *Quarantania* (1941). Patrick Henry Bruce, *Painting* (1930). Scott Burton, *Pair of Two-Part Chairs, Obtuse Angle* (1984). Alexander Calder, *Double Cat* (1930); *Bifurcated Tower* (1950); *Indian Feathers* (1969); *The Brass Family* (1927); *Little Ball with Counterweight* (c. 1930); *Roxbury Flurry* (c. 1948); *The Arches* (1959); *Big Red* (1959). John Chamberlain, *Velvet White* (1962); *Jackpot* (1962). Chuck Close, *Phil* (1969). Ralston Crawford, *Lobster Pots #3* (1960–63). Stuart Davis, *The Paris Bit* (1959); *House and Street* (1931); *Owh! in San Paõ* (1951). Willem de Kooning, *Door to the River* (1960); *Woman and Bicycle* (1952–53). Charles Demuth, *My Egypt* (1927). Richard Diebenkorn, *Ocean Park, #125* (1980). Mark di Suvero, *Hankchampion* (1960). Burgoyne Diller, *Third Theme* (1946–48). Arthur G. Dove, *Ferry Boat Wreck* (1931). Guy Pène du Bois, *Opera Box* (1926). Richard Estes, *Ansonia* (1977).

Helen Frankenthaler, *Flood* (1967). Fritz Glarner, *Relational Painting* (1949–51). Arshile Gorky, *The Artist and His Mother* (c. 1926–36); *The Betrothal, II* (1947). Philip Guston, *Dial* (1956). Marsden Hartley, *The Blast of Winter* (1908); *Forms Abstracted* (1913); *Granite by the Sea* (1937); *Painting, Number 5* (1914–15). Al Held, *The Dowager Empress* (1965). Robert Henri, *Gertrude Vanderbilt Whitney* (1916). Eva Hesse, *Sans II* (1968). Edward Hopper, *Early Sunday Morning* (1930); *Railroad Sunset* (1929); *Second Story Sunlight* (1960). Jasper Johns, *Three Flags* (1958); *Racing Thoughts* (1983); *White Target* (1957). Donald Judd, *Untitled* (1965). Alex Katz, *The Red Smile* (1963). Ellsworth Kelly, *Atlantic* (1956). Edward Kienholz, *The Wait* (1964–65). Franz Kline, *Mahoning* (1956). Lee Krasner, *The Seasons* (1957).

Gaston Lachaise, *Standing Woman* (1912–27); *Dolphin Fountain* (1924); *Torso with Arms Raised* (1935). Roy Lichtenstein, *Little Big Painting* (1965); *Still Life with Crystal Bowl* (1973). Morris Louis, *Tet* (1958). Stanton MacDonald-Wright, *Oriental: Synchromy in Blue-Green* (1918). Reginald Marsh, *Twenty Cent Movie* (1936). Agnes Martin, *Milk River* (1963). Elie Nadelman, *Sur La Plage* (1916); *Tango* (1916–19). Bruce Nauman, *Untitled* (1965–66). Louise Nevelson, *Black Majesty* (1955); *Young Shadows* (1959–60); *Rain Forest Column VI* (1967); *Dawn's Wedding Chapel II* (1959); *Night-Focus-Dawn* (1969). Barnett Newman, *Day One* (1951–52). Isamu Noguchi, *Humpty Dumpty* (1946); *The Queen* (1931). Georgia O'Keeffe, *Abstraction* (1926); *Black and White* (1930); *Summer Days* (1936); *The White Calico Flower* (1951). Claes Oldenburg, *Soft Toilet* (1966). Jackson Pollock, *Number 27* (1950). Maurice Prendergast, *The Promenade* (1913).

Ad Reinhardt, *Abstract Painting: Number 33* (1963). Mark Rothko, *Four*

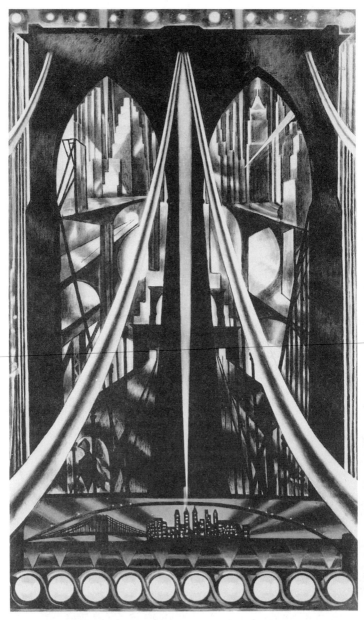

The Whitney Museum of American Art. Joseph Stella, The Brooklyn Bridge: Variation on an Old Theme *(1939). This work epitomizes Gertrude Vanderbilt Whitney's preference for representational American painting. The Museum continues her commitment to living artists. (The Whitney Museum of American Art. Photo: Geoffrey Clements)*

Darks in Red (1958). George Segal, *Walk, Don't Walk* (1976). Richard Serra, *Prop* (1968). Ben Shahn, *The Passion of Sacco and Vanzetti* (1931–32). Charles Sheeler, *River Rouge Plant* (1932). John Sloan, *Backyards, Greenwich Village* (1914); *The Picnic Grounds* (1906–07); *The Blue Sea—Classic* (1918); *Dolly with a Black Bow* (1909). David Smith, *Hudson River Landscape* (1951); *Running Daughter* (1956); *Lectern Sentinel* (1961); *Cubi XXI.* Robert Smithson, *Non-Site (Palisades—Edgewater, N.J.)* (1968). Frank Stella, *Die Fahne Hoch* (1959). Joseph Stella, *The Brooklyn Bridge: Variation on an Old Theme* (1939).

Clyfford Still, *Untitled* (1957). John Storrs, *Forms in Space #1* (c. 1924). Yves Tanguy, *Fear* (1949). Cy Twombly, *Untitled* (1969). Andy Warhol, *Green Coca-Cola Bottles* (1962); *Ethel Scull, 36 Times* (1963). Max Weber, *Chinese Restaurant* (1915). Jackie Winsor, *Bound Logs* (1972–73). Andrew Wyeth, *Winter Fields* (1942).

EXHIBITION PROGRAM

The Whitney runs a full range of exhibitions, including thematic shows and important retrospectives of individual artists. Shows have focused on Scott Burton, who achieved recognition for innovative designs that combined architecture, sculpture, and furniture; Joan Mitchell, one of the few women artists associated with the New York School; and William Wegman, whose world-famous photos of dogs in the guises, postures, and accoutrements of people comment on both the human and the animal condition. The 1992 retrospective of Jean-Michel Basquiat was the first museum survey of the work of this Hispanic-African-American artist who soared to fame in the 1980s.

The Whitney Biennial, which dates back to 1932 and seeks to display what is most important in contemporary art, is the centerpiece of the exhibition program. The Biennials evoke considerable comment that sometimes borders on outright hostility, a suggestion of their importance in the art world.

The Whitney Museum of American Art at Philip Morris (62)

120 Park Ave (42nd St), New York 10017. Tel: (212) 878-2550.

ADMISSION: Gallery open Mon–Fri 11–6; Thurs until 7:30. Sculpture Court open Mon–Sat 7:30 A.M.–9:30 P.M.; Sun 11–7. Free.

Gallery talks Wed and Fri at 1:00. Tours by appointment. Free brochures on exhibitions, informal midday performances, other educational activities.

✘ Espresso bar in Sculpture Court.

🕪 No restrooms.

🏛 No gift shop.

♿ Complete wheelchair access from 42nd St. Steps down to Sculpture Garden from Park Ave.

⃠ Because the location of the Philip Morris Building, near Grand Central Terminal, has attracted the homeless, security is strict. No littering, no panhandling, no carts or bikes, no alcoholic beverages, no sleeping.

🚇 IRT Lexington Ave local or express (train 4, 5, or 6) to 42nd St / Grand Central Station.

🚌 M1, M2, M3, M4, or Q32 uptown on Madison Ave, downtown on 5th Ave to 42nd St. M5 downtown on 5th Ave. M101 or M102 downtown on Lexington Ave, uptown on 3rd Ave. M104 crosstown on 42nd St, uptown and downtown on Broadway north of 42nd St. M106 crosstown on 42nd St.

The Whitney Museum of American Art at Philip Morris (1983), one of the Museum's several ventures into corporate space, adds an enclave of art in midtown, long noticeably short in that commodity. The Museum space is two-fold: a high courtyard used for sculpture, usually large pieces, and a gallery for changing smaller-scale shows.

The SCULPTURE COURT, visible from 42nd St and Park Ave, offers a scale (42-ft high and 5,200 sq ft) that allows installation of works too large to be shown conveniently in the main facility of the Museum on Madison Ave. Major American sculptors who have been represented here include Louise Bourgeois, Alexander Calder, John Chamberlain, Roy Lichtenstein, Elie Nadelman, Louise Nevelson, Claes Oldenburg, Judy Pfaff, and David Smith. Frank Stella's flamboyant *Dove of Tanna* (1977), a 3,500-lb, painted aluminum relief, hangs on the west wall.

EXHIBITION PROGRAM

Exhibitions in the smaller gallery near 42nd St change about five times yearly. Though the emphasis is on 20C painting and sculpture, the program has included exhibits of folk art, photography, design, and architecture. Most are drawn from the collections of the Museum but some have been organized elsewhere.

The World Financial Center: Arts and Events Program (37)

World Financial Center, Battery Park City, New York 10281. Tel: (212) 945-0505.

ADMISSION: Courtyard Gallery open weekdays 12–7; weekends 12–6. Free.

Lectures, performing arts events, changing exhibition program.

✗ Restaurants in World Financial Center.

🏛 No gift shop.

♿ Complete wheelchair accessibility.

🚫 No photography of visual arts exhibitions.

🚇 IRT Broadway-7th Ave local (train 1 or 9) to Cortlandt St / World Trade Center. BMT Broadway local (N or R train) to Cortlandt St / World Trade Center; IND 8th Ave express or local (A, C, or E train) to Chambers St / World Trade Center.

🚌 M9 downtown on Avenue B and East Broadway to Battery Park City. M10 downtown on Broadway and 7th Ave to Battery Park City. M22 crosstown on Madison and Chambers St to Battery Park City.

The Arts and Events Program (begun 1987) offers an ongoing series of performances and visual exhibitions in the handsome public spaces of the World Financial Center, usually in the Winter Garden or the Courtyard Gallery. Some exhibitions showcase works from cultural institutions throughout the city; others are on loan from further afield.

EXHIBITION PROGRAM

The inaugural exhibition, "The New Urban Landscape," offered 28 artists and architects from the United States and abroad the opportunity to create site-specific installations focusing on problems of urban life. Tadashi Kawamata's *Favela in Battery Park City; Inside / Outside,* inspired by the urban slums of South America, constructed a temporary wooden shack that lay half inside, half outside the exhibition space. Video artist Nam June Paik contributed *Ruin,* an apparently random arrangement of 24 state-of-the-art television monitors rising up from 40 consoles dating from the '50s.

In "Celebrate Harlem," three uptown museums—the Studio Museum in Harlem, the Schomburg Center for Research in Black Culture, and El Museo del Barrio—contributed works from their collections. "The Masters of Cartoon Art," a loan exhibition from the Museum of Cartoon Art in Westchester County, N.Y., traced the development of this American art form using original drawings and newspaper pages detailing the exploits of Popeye, Buster Brown, Prince Valiant, Dick Tracy, and Doonesbury. "Cross Section" offered 75 works of three-dimensional art, displayed indoors and outdoors, from the permanent collections of the city's museums.

Other events have included an environmental festival with a film series and several ambitious exhibitions: an installation of ten large aquariums alive with fish, corals, and invertebrates; a sound installation broadcast through 102 hidden speakers that incorporated bird, animal, and other natural sounds from the Amazon rain forest into the music of composer Brian Eno.

Yeshiva University Museum (110)

2520 Amsterdam Ave (185th St), New York 10033. Tel: (212) 960-5390.

ADMISSION: Open Tues–Thurs 10:30–5; Sun 12–6. Closed Sat, Mon, Jewish holidays, Thanksgiving, Memorial Day, Labor Day. Admission charge.

Changing exhibitions, guided tours, lectures, family events (craft projects, Israeli folksongs and dances for young children), educational programs.

✘ Cafeteria in university building across the street. Fast-food restaurants on Amsterdam Ave.

🏛 Gift shop with books, catalogues, children's books, Judaica, jewelry.

♿ Main galleries on 4th floor are accessible to wheelchairs.

🚇 IRT Broadway-7th Ave local (train 1 or 9, marked 242nd St / Broadway) to 181st St. IND 8th Ave express (A train) to 181st St. Walk east to Amsterdam Ave.

🚌 M101 via 3rd Ave to 185th St.

Yeshiva University Museum (founded 1973) seeks to widen public knowledge and appreciation of Jewish culture through exhibitions of Jewish art, architecture, history, and anthropology.

EXHIBITION PROGRAM

The opening exhibition focused on the architectural history of the synagogue through ten beautifully crafted models of historic synagogues, including the Tempio Israelitico in Florence (c. 1875), the Zabludow Synagogue in Poland, destroyed during World War II, and the Touro Synagogue (1763) of Newport, R.I., the oldest extant Jewish house of worship in this country. The models remain in the permanent collection but are not always on display.

Other exhibitions have been drawn from the collections of the Museum and the university, as well as outside sources. "The Jewish Wedding" featured bridal costumes, rings, wedding presents, marriage contracts, and music, from Ashkenazic and Sephardic collections. "Terezin 942–1945: Through the Eyes of Norbert Troller" documented life in the Theresienstadt concentration camp with drawings and paintings secretly made by Troller, an imprisoned Czech architect. "Lights / Orot" featured a dramatic environment produced by electronic technology—lasers, computers, holography, and video disks—and prepared by artists of the Center for Advanced Visual Studies at Massachusetts Institute of Technology. The artworks illustrated Jewish themes: a Star of David that continually emitted light encircling the whole exhibition, the Ten Commandments written by laser beam in a hologram.

"The Sephardic Journey: 1492–1992" traced the Diaspora of the Sephardic Jews after they were expelled from Spain by Ferdinand and Isabella. On exhibit were rare books and documents, costumes from the Ottoman Empire and Morocco, religious and ceremonial objects, including the ark cloth rescued from the Synagogue of Vienna, which was destroyed in 1938, and costumes and furnishings of a Sephardic family that settled in Colonial America in the 17C.

PERMANENT COLLECTION

The permanent collection was started with ceremonial objects and textiles recovered from the Nazis after World War II. After successful exhibitions began attracting donors to the Museum, the collection amassed important Sephardic costumes, paintings and graphics by Israeli artists, cultural artifacts, including the Torah scroll of the Baal Shem Tov, founder of Hasidism, and a 50-year run of a German Jewish weekly newspaper published up until the outbreak of World War II.

YIVO Institute for Jewish Research (63)

555 West 57th St, Suite 1100 (bet. 10th / 11th Aves), New York 10019. Tel: (212) 246-6080.

> NOTE: In 1994, YIVO vacated its former home on Fifth Ave at 86th St, and expects to open at 15 West 16th St, probably in 1997. Library and Reading Room currently open Mon–Thurs 9–5:30. Call for information about off-site exhibitions, Free.

Founded in 1925 in Vilna, Poland, then an intellectual center of East European Jewry, the YIVO Institute, an acronym for *Yiddisher Visnshaft-*

lekher Institut (Institute for Jewish Research), is the repository of a collection equaled only by that of the Hebrew University of Jerusalem. Its more than 300,000 books, 100,000 photographs, 4,000 artifacts and ceremonial objects, and 22 million archival items document the history of Eastern European Jews and their descendants. The Institute specializes in the training of graduate students, and sponsors research in Yiddish, East European, and American Jewish studies. It also mounts informal exhibitions based on its collections.

PERMANENT COLLECTION

Among the treasures of the collection is an underground archive of the Warsaw Ghetto, gathered by Polish Jewish historian and YIVO associate Emmanuel Ringelbaum. The archive was buried for concealment and recovered from the rubble in 1946–50.

The Abraham Cahan Collection reflects Cahan's position as editor of the *Jewish Daily Forward* and includes his correspondence with Socialist leaders of the time and such writers as Theodore Dreiser, Upton Sinclair, and Yiddish playwright I. J. Singer. The Yiddish theater collection begins in the 1920s and continues to 1958. Sheet music, records of Jewish fraternal organizations, family papers including records of the Grossingers whose famous hotel in Liberty, N.Y., was an institution among Catskill resorts, sound recordings of Yiddish speakers, diaries of Holocaust survivors, and periodicals from Czarist Russia further enrich the holdings of the Institute.

The archive is used primarily by scholars: Hannah Arendt researched much of *Eichmann in Jerusalem* in the reading room.

HISTORY

Well before World War II, the YIVO Institute in Vilna, which offered courses in language and culture to graduate students, began collecting diaries, photographs, folkloric material, and other artifacts, not with any premonition that Yiddish culture was doomed but simply as a scholarly activity to document contemporary Jewish life. When the Nazis invaded Poland, Alfred Rosenberg, a Nazi ideologist gathering material on "the Jewish question," ordered the Institute's documents shipped to Germany. But YIVO workers, risking their lives, smuggled items from the building into the Jewish ghetto where they were hidden in attics and buried in milk cans and tin boxes for the duration. After the war many of these documents were recovered, along with others confiscated by the Germans and preserved in a storehouse in Germany. Since 1940 the headquarters of the organization has been in New York.

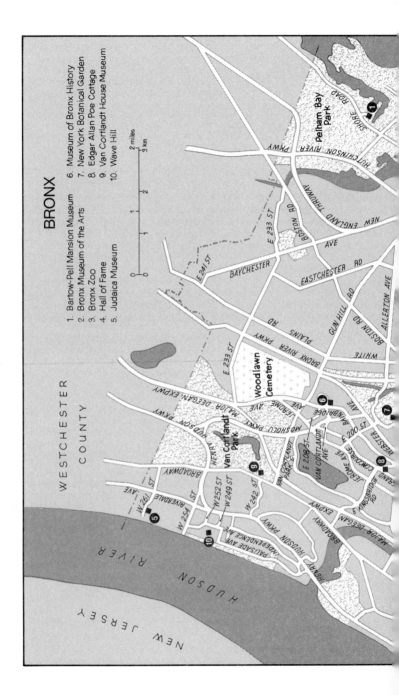

BRONX

1. Bartow-Pell Mansion Museum
2. Bronx Museum of the Arts
3. Bronx Zoo
4. Hall of Fame
5. Judaica Museum
6. Museum of Bronx History
7. New York Botanical Garden
8. Edgar Allan Poe Cottage
9. Van Cortlandt House Museum
10. Wave Hill

MUSEUMS IN THE BRONX

The Bartow-Pell Mansion Museum (1)

Shore Rd, Pelham Bay Park, Bronx, N.Y. 10464. Tel: (718) 885-1461.

ADMISSION: Open Wed, Sat, and Sun, 12–4 and by appointment. Closed Mon, Tues, Thurs, and Fri; New Year's Day, Easter, the last three weeks in Aug, Thanksgiving weekend, and Christmas Day. Admission charge; children under 12 free.

Self-guided tour. Group tours and luncheon tours by arrangement. Children's educational programs. Occasional concerts and special events.

✗ No restaurant. Picnicking permitted.

🛍 No gift shop, but sales table with books, postcards, stationery.

♿ Not accessible to wheelchairs.

🚊 🚌 The Mansion is not easy to reach by public transportation. IRT Lexington Ave local (train 6) to Pelham Bay. Then transfer to Westchester Bee-Line, bus 45, which goes past the gate. The bus does not run on Sun.

🚗 **From Manhattan:** The mansion is about 15 miles from midtown. Take I-95 (from Bruckner Expwy or Cross Bronx Expwy) toward Connecticut. Exit 8B (City Island and Orchard Beach). Take Shore Road north for 1.2 miles to circle for Orchard Beach. Follow signs to Split Rock Golf Course. Bartow-Pell gates on right just past golf house on left. Parking available.

🚆 Metro-North (New Haven line) from Grand Central Terminal to the Pelham Station; then take a taxi to the Mansion.

The Bartow-Pell Mansion (1842; opened as a museum 1914) is a restored country house whose lawns and gardens overlook Long Island Sound. The site, though part of Pelham Bay Park, has a feeling of remoteness that suggests the slower pace of life when the Pells and Bartows lived here.

PERIOD ROOMS

On display are ten rooms furnished with American Empire furniture, paintings, and decorative arts. Though none of the furniture from the family of Robert Bartow, the original owner, remains in the house, a pair of portraits and a needlework mourning picture are associated with Bartow cousins. Some furnishings have been borrowed from the Metropolitan Museum, the Brooklyn Museum, and the Museum of the City of New York, but most belong to the Bartow-Pell Landmark Fund, which operates the museum.

The elegant elliptical staircase may be the work of architect Minard Lafever, a friend of the Bartow family. The most spectacular piece of furniture is a canopied sleigh bed, the work of Charles-Honoré Lannuier, one of the best known New York cabinetmakers of the Greek Revival period.

CARRIAGE HOUSE

This attractive stone building (c. 1840, restored 1993), on the north side of the house, is a rare survival. Inside are sleighs, a traveling carriage (c. 1850) designed by James Goold of Albany, and other objects related to horse-drawn transportation.

GARDENS

Between Shore Rd and the parking lot is the "Treaty Tree," a huge oak where Thomas Pell signed his bargain with the Indians in 1654. Between the house and Long Island Sound are formal gardens planted with azaleas, rhododendrons, and flowering fruit trees. The HERB GARDEN contains a formal array of culinary, aromatic, medicinal, and ornamental herbs. On the south side of the house a path leads past a row of mature horse chestnut trees (spectacular when they bloom in May) to the small Pell family graveyard, located close to an inlet from the Sound.

HISTORY

In 1654, Thomas Pell, an English physician who had previously settled in Connecticut, struck a bargain with the Siwanoy Indians, acquiring by treaty 9,000 acres of land bordering Long Island Sound. The Dutch in New Amsterdam ceded their rights to the English in 1664, and two years later Pell received a royal charter to create the manor of Pelham. It is presumed that Thomas Pell built a house, but no information about it survived. His nephew and heir, Sir John Pell, however, did build a manor house (1675), which served four generations of his descendants until it was destroyed around the time of the Revolutionary War.

Ann Pell, daughter of the fourth lord of the mansion, married her cousin, John Bartow, who acquired the property after the Revolution. For a while it was owned outside the Bartow-Pell family, but John's grandson Robert bought it back in 1836, by then reduced to 200 acres. In 1842, Robert Bartow built the present granite-faced Classical Revival house.

The City of New York bought it in 1888, along with the Carriage House and the 200 acres, as part of the purchase of land for Pelham Bay Park. In 1914, a group of prominent New Yorkers decided to save the mansion and restore it. It opened a year later, presided over by the president of the International Garden Club Inc., which continues to maintain the interior of the building and the gardens while the city cares for the exterior. In 1936, Mayor Fiorello La Guardia used it as a summer office.

The Bronx Museum of the Arts (2)

1040 Grand Concourse (165th St), Bronx, N.Y. 10456. Tel: (718) 681-6000.

ADMISSION: Open Wed 3–9; Thurs–Fri 10–5; Sat–Sun 1–6. Closed Mon, Tues, Thanksgiving, and Christmas Day.

> **NOTE:** The Museum schedule reflects the constraints of recent city budget cuts; check for changes. Suggested donation.

Changing exhibitions, educational programs for children and adults, art classes for children, special events, workshops, films.

✘ No restaurant.

🏛 Gift shop with exhibition catalogues and posters, craft items by New York, Caribbean, and Latin-American artists, notecards, jewelry.

♿ Accessible to wheelchairs.

🚋 IRT Lexington Ave local (train 4) to 161st St / Grand Concourse. IND 8th Ave local (C train) to 161st St / Grand Concourse. IND 6th Ave express (D train) to 167th St / Grand Concourse, except afternoon rush hours.

From Manhattan: BMX Liberty Express bus 4 to 165th St / Grand Concourse.

From Manhattan, East Side: Take the FDR Drive to the Major Deegan Expwy; exit at the Grand Concourse; continue north to 165th St. **From Manhattan, West Side:** Take Riverside Dr to 155th St / Macombs Dam Bridge; cross to Jerome Ave and continue to 165th St / Grand Concourse. Street parking only.

The Bronx Museum of the Arts (1971), the only arts museum in the borough, is a refurbished and expanded former synagogue, located in a handsome glass, aluminum, and granite building on the Grand Concourse. It offers contemporary and historical exhibitions on art, on urban life, and on the past and present of the borough of the Bronx.

EXHIBITION PROGRAM

The Museum's ambitious exhibition program reflects its position as an institution in an ethnically diverse and economically troubled community. Exhibitions frequently focus on African, Latin, or Asian artists and their American counterparts. In recent years there has been a major retrospective of Latin-American art in the United States, an exhibition of sculpture by African Americans, and a show of politicized Mexican revolutionary graphics directed at the plight of the poor. "The Nearest Edge of the World: Art and Cuba Now" (1991) was the first major exhibition of Cuban art to open in the United States since the Cuban revolution.

"Las Casitas: An Urban Cultural Alternative" allowed visitors to experience a *casita,* a one-story urban cottage like those Puerto Ricans build in empty lots as social clubs. Placards on the walls of the Museum's 12-by-12 ft *casita* explained how communities collaborate in building these clubs, what they do there, and how they outmaneuver city officials seeking to eradicate *casitas* which frequently fail to meet building codes.

The "Artist in the Marketplace" program focuses on young New York artists from diverse cultural and economic backgrounds, who have been selected to participate in a series of seminars designed to provide them with the skills to operate successfully in the professional art world. The seminars, led by curators, dealers, tax accountants, and other art professionals, culminate in an exhibition at the Museum, accompanied by a catalogue.

In other shows the Museum examines issues that affect the borough and its struggles to revive. A landmark exhibition, "Devastation / Resurrection: The South Bronx" (1980), used historical and contemporary photographs and videotaped oral histories to chronicle the descent of the South Bronx into poverty, as well as the efforts of individuals and groups to solve the borough's almost intractable problems.

Finally, the Museum offers exhibitions that explore aspects of art in general—Japanese painting and calligraphy, Italian photography, the prints and paintings of American artist Isabel Bishop. The "Emerging Expression Biennial" (inaugurated 1985) focuses on the partnership between art and science; it includes exhibitions of sculpture, installation art, and video by artists using computer technology.

PERMANENT COLLECTION

The Museum maintains a small but growing collection of works on paper by artists from Southeast Asia, Africa, and Latin America, and the American descendants of these groups. In the future an artists' registry, a slide registry, and a video archive focusing on Latino and Latin-American art are planned.

HISTORY

Founded by local community groups and given a helping hand by the Metropolitan Museum of Art, the Museum spent its early years in the lobby of the Bronx Borough Courthouse a few blocks down the Concourse from its present location. The inaugural exhibition combined Impressionist and Post-Impressionist paintings, some borrowed from the Met. In 1983 the Museum moved to its present building, an abandoned and vandalized synagogue, and undertook major renovations (completed 1988).

Bronx Zoo / Wildlife Conservation Park (3)

Fordham Rd and Bronx River Pkwy, Bronx, N.Y. 10460. For recorded announcement of hours, fees, special events, tel: (718) 367-1010; for other information, tel: (718) 220-5100.

ADMISSION: The zoo opens every day of the year at 10 A.M. Closing times: Feb–Oct: Mon–Sat at 5; Sun and holidays at 5:30; Nov–Jan, every day at 4:30. Admission charge except Wed, when admission is free. Children under two always free. Reduced rates for seniors and children 2–12. Reduced admission rates during winter months. Children's Zoo: open Mon–Fri 10–5 (tickets sold until 4); weekends and holidays 10–5:30 (tickets sold until 4:30). Rides and some exhibits closed in winter. Additional fees for Zoo Shuttle, Bengali Express monorail, Safari train, Skyfari aerial tramway, and World of Darkness. Baby strollers for rent (deposit required) at entrances.

✗ Cafeteria near Wildfowl Pond; Flamingo Pub with simple fare in more relaxed surroundings near Flamingo Pond or at African Market. Zoobar outdoors near Children's Zoo with children's food favorites. Some facilities closed in winter. Picnic tables at Wildfowl Terrace and Zoobar. Food stands.

▥ Souvenir shops. Zoo map included with entrance fee.

& Accessible to wheelchairs, which may be reserved in advance; tel: (718) 220-5188.

⊘ No bicycles, radios, skateboards, or pets. Children under 16 must be accompanied by an older chaperone.

▙ IRT 7th Ave express (train 2) to Pelham Pkwy. IRT Lexington Ave express (train 5) to E. 180th St, transfer to IRT 7th Ave express (train 2) to Pelham Pkwy. Walk west to Bronxdale entrance to the zoo.

▤ **City bus:** Bx9 and Bx19 stop at the Southern Boulevard entrance to the zoo. Bx12 stops at the corner of Fordham Rd and Southern Blvd; walk east on Fordham Rd to the Rainey Gate. Q44 from Queens stops three blocks south of the zoo; walk north to the Asia entrance. **Express bus:** Liberty Lines provides air-conditioned express bus service BxM11 between mid-Manhattan and the Bronxdale entrance to the zoo. Bus stops in Manhattan on Madison Ave at various cross streets (return stops on 5th Ave

are slightly different). Exact fare required. For schedule and fare information, call (718) 652-8400.

🚌 **From Manhattan, East Side:** Triborough Bridge and Bruckner Expwy
east to Bronx River Pkwy north. Follow exit signs to Bronx Zoo parking.
From Manhattan, West Side: West Side Highway to Cross Bronx Expwy.
Drive east to Bronx River Parkway north. Follow exit signs to Bronx Zoo
parking. Large lots along Bronx River Pkwy (Bronxdale) near exit 6 and on
Southern Blvd at 182nd St (Crotona). Smaller lot at main gate (Fountain
Circle) often full. Parking fee.

🚆 Metro-North Commuter Railroad to Fordham station from Grand Central Terminal; from station take Bx9 bus to Southern Blvd entrance to the
zoo. For train schedule and fare information, call (212) 532-4900.

The Wildlife Conservation Park (1899), known popularly as the Bronx Zoo,
is the largest urban zoo in the United States, covering 265 acres and
including some 4,000 animals of 561 species. It is well managed, attractively designed, and one of the city's major tourist attractions. In addition
to its exhibition program, the Wildlife Conservation Society (formerly
the N.Y. Zoological Society), the governing body of the zoo, acts to save
wildlife by propagating endangered species, preserving declining animal
habitats throughout the world, and educating people to the need for
conservation.

EXHIBITIONS

The animals live in spacious naturalistic surroundings organized by habitat. **World of Birds** is a handsome indoor display (c. 100 species) exploring the complexities of bird life. An artificial waterfall plummets 40 ft
from a 50-ft Fiberglas cliff. In **World of Darkness,** another indoor exhibit
(40 species), low levels of white, blue, green, and red light turn day into
night so that visitors may see nocturnal animals at their liveliest.
Included is the world's largest captive breeding collection of bats. **Jungle
World** is a fine indoor exhibit recreating tropical Asian habitats and featuring gibbons, hornbills, tapirs, as well as rare and beautiful plants.

Among the many large-scale outdoor exhibits are the **Himalayan Highlands** with snow leopards, red pandas, and cranes. The Bengali Express,
a monorail (25-min guided tour), circles the 40 acres of **Wild Asia** (May–
Oct)—the only way to see this exhibit. The animals on view include elephants, gaur (largest of the world's cattle), antelope, Siberian tigers, and
rhinoceros. The **Baboon Reserve** is home to gelada baboons, Nubian ibex,
and African waterfowl, who share a simulated mountaintop.

CHILDREN'S ZOO

Offers domesticated animals for petting and feeding, as well as opportunities to experience life as animals do. Children can climb around in a
spider web, crawl into a turtle shell, or tunnel through a prairie dog
house.

ZOO BUILDINGS AND ARCHITECTURE

The main entrance to the zoo at *Fountain Circle* is marked by the 36-
ft bronze Rainey Memorial Gate (1934; Paul Manship, sculptor), whose
stylized Tree of Life motif has 22 full-size animals. The stone jaguars
near the stairs are the work of Anna Vaughn Hyatt Huntington (1937) and

BRONX ZOO AND NEW YORK BOTANICAL GARDEN

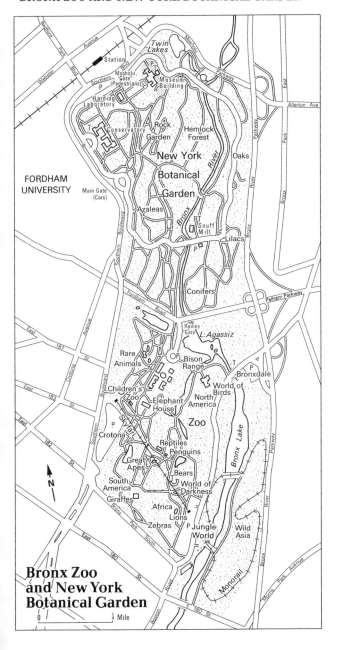

were modeled after Señor Lopez, the first big cat in the Carnivore House (opened 1903). The original Elephant House with its green-tinted dome and sculpted pachyderms is now the **Zoo Reception Center. Astor Court,** once the main exhibit area of the zoo, consisted of the Lion House, the Primate House (1901; later renamed the Monkey House), the Administration Building (1910), the Main Bird House (1905), and the Heads and Horns Building (1922), in addition to the Elephant House.

The Hall of Fame for Great Americans (4)

On the campus of Bronx Community College of the City University of New York, University Ave and West 181st St, Bronx, N.Y. 10453. Tel: (718) 220-6003.

ADMISSION: The Hall is open every day 9–5. The rotunda in Gould Memorial Library is open during the school year every day 9:30–2:30. Free.

Permanent exhibition of sculpture; guided tours on weekdays; call (718) 220-6003 to arrange a tour.

✘ No restaurant.

†↑↘ Restrooms in Gould Memorial Library.

🛍 No gift shop.

♿ The colonnade is accessible to wheelchairs; the rotunda is not.

🚇 IRT Lexington Ave express (train 4) to Burnside Ave / Jerome Ave.

🚌 BX3 from George Washington Bridge Bus Station in Manhattan via University Ave.

The Hall of Fame for Great Americans (1901), a dramatic 630-ft outdoor arcade with heroic portrait busts honoring 97 outstanding Americans, overlooks the Harlem River from the rocky spine of University Heights. The colonnaded arcade was designed by architect Stanford White as part of the University Heights campus of New York University. In 1973 the City University of New York took over the campus, which now serves Bronx Community College, part of the city university system.

The Great Americans are chosen by a college of electors appointed by the trustees of the Hall of Fame. Those honored include such obvious candidates as George Washington, Benjamin Franklin, and Abraham Lincoln, as well as such dark horses as John Lothrop Motley (a 19C historian whose definitive works were *The Rise of the Dutch Republic* and *The History of the United Netherlands*) and Rufus Choate (a notable 19C trial lawyer who completed Daniel Webster's unexpired term in the Senate). Sculptors, too, range from the well known, including Jean-Antoine Houdon (*George Washington* and *Robert Fulton,* both replicas) and Frederick W. MacMonnies (*Simon Newcomb* and *James Abbott McNeill Whistler),* to less renowned figures, e.g., Rudulph Evans (*Grover Cleveland* and *Henry Wadsworth Longfellow).* The most recent honorees were Clara Barton, founder of the American Red Cross; Luther Burbank, the horticulturist; and Andrew Carnegie, industrialist and philanthropist. In 1992 the newest bust, *Franklin Delano Roosevelt,* was installed.

THE BUILDING

Gould Memorial Library is considered one of Stanford White's masterpieces. A long, low stairway leads from the portico facing the campus to
a three-story rotunda, with a shallow dome of Guastavino tile. The dome
is supported by 16 columns of green Connemara marble, probably the
most extensive display of this type of marble in the country. Both the
building as a whole and its interior have been awarded landmark designation by the city.

The Judaica Museum (5)

The Hebrew Home for the Aged at Riverdale, 5961 Palisade Ave (261st St),
Bronx, N.Y. 10471. Tel: (718) 548-1006.

ADMISSION: Open Mon–Thurs 1–4:30; Sun 1–5. Closed Fri and Sat, Jewish
holidays, legal holidays. Free for individuals; admission charge for groups.

Changing exhibitions.

✗ Coffee shop in Home. Groups may make arrangements for luncheon in
the dining room.

▥ No gift shop.

♿ Accessible to wheelchairs.

🚇 IRT Broadway-7th Ave local (train 1 or 9) to 231st St.

🚌 Bx7 from 168th St and Broadway in Manhattan.

The Judaica Museum (1982), housed in two galleries at The Hebrew Home
for the Aged at Riverdale in the Bronx, owes its beginnings to the donation by Ralph and Leuba Baum of over 1,000 pieces of Judaica of Sephardic and Ashkenazic origin. Mr. Baum, an immigrant from Germany who
founded a successful photographic firm, began collecting in response to
the Holocaust, acquiring objects in Europe, Israel, and the United States.
In addition to displays from the permanent collection, the Museum orga-
nizes two or three annual changing exhibitions on subjects related to
Judaism.

EXHIBITION PROGRAM

Some changing exhibitions are drawn from the permanent collection, but
on occasion the Museum collaborates with other institutions for more
ambitious shows. "Family Memories: Transition and Continuity," organized in cooperation with A Living Memorial to the Holocaust: Museum
of Jewish Heritage, explored the way in which Jewish families and individuals maintained their heritage and sense of continuity in the midst of
change. The objects chosen ranged from simple household items to beautiful textiles, photographs, a kosher restaurant sign that once hung on
the Lower East Side, an attorney's robe worn in Berlin by Adolf Hamburger, who fled the Nazis in 1933, and an immigrant inspection card
(dated 1911) that belonged to a teenage Jewish immigrant from Greece.
Complementing the exhibition were lectures, gallery talks, and workshops.

A traveling exhibition mounted by the Bavarian Historical Society,

"Integral and Integrated? Four Hundred Years of Jewish Life in Ichen-hausen, Bavaria," explored Jewish life in a rural German town. On view were objects that showed the integration of Ichenhausen's Jews into the community and photographs showing Jewish firefighters and Jewish sol-diers in World War I.

PERMANENT COLLECTION

Included in the permanent collection are objects that reflect the customs and ceremonies of European and Oriental Jewry over the past three cen-turies. Among the objects, many of them intrinsically beautiful as well as historically important, are an ornamented silver Torah shield (1842) from Nuremberg, an 18C silver spice container from Poland, illuminated wed-ding contracts, Sabbath candlesticks, including a silver pair made in Russia in 1872, prayer books, pewter Passover plates and pitchers, and a Yemenite Hanukkah lamp carved from stone.

Museum of Bronx History, Valentine-Varian House (6)

3266 Bainbridge Ave (Van Cortlandt Ave / 208th St), Bronx, N.Y. 10467. Tel: (718) 881-8900.

ADMISSION: Open Sat 10–4; Sun 1–5. Weekdays open only to groups by appointment. Closed holidays. Admission charge.

Changing exhibitions, educational programs; the Bronx County Historical Society maintains a research library, 3309 Bainbridge Ave.

✘ No restaurant.

▥ Books and publications about the Bronx; notecards, souvenirs, posters, postcards.

♿ Not accessible to wheelchairs.

🚇 IND D train to 205th St and Bainbridge Ave. Lexington Ave IRT express (train 4) to Mosholu Pkwy.

🚗 Major Deegan Expwy (Rte 87) to Van Cortlandt Park exit. Go east on Van Cortlandt Park South, which becomes Gun Hill Rd. Follow Gun Hill Rd east to Bainbridge Ave; turn right and follow Bainbridge Ave to Museum. Street parking.

The Museum of Bronx History (founded 1965) offers a permanent collec-tion and exhibition, as well as changing displays of photographs, prints, paintings, and other artifacts that recall the history of what is now the borough of the Bronx.

EXHIBITION PROGRAM

In the COLONIAL ROOM, a permanent exhibition of photos and historic objects (muskets, cannonballs, dishes, pipes, and a sewing kit used by Colonial soldiers during the Revolutionary War) offers an overview of the development of the Bronx from the Native American period through the beginning of the 19C.

The other two galleries put on special exhibitions, usually two each year, which deal with some aspect of the borough's history. An exhibition on borough politics from 1898 through the present contained such memorabilia as a Tiffany loving cup presented to Jordan Mott when he served on the Board of Aldermen and an ivory ceremonial gavel presented to Louis Haffen, first borough president of the Bronx. Also on view were badges from state and national conventions, programs from Democratic national conventions of 1924 and 1992 held in New York, a turn-of-the-century voting booth, and voter registration cards from the same period.

To celebrate the 70th anniversary of Yankee Stadium, the Museum in conjunction with the New York Public Library, the New York Yankees, and the Baseball Hall of Fame at Cooperstown, N.Y., mounted "The Bronx Bombers and Yankee Stadium." In addition to exploring the history of the stadium itself (the original cement came from a subsidiary company held by Thomas Edison) and the history of the team, the exhibition examined several Hollywood films based on the Yankees.

PERMANENT COLLECTION

The Historical Society collections contain books, photos, slides, clippings, maps, local art, and historic postcards, as well as some 8,000 historic objects dating from the 17C to the 20C. The collections are especially strong in the political and economic history of the Bronx from late 19C to early 20C, when the county emerged from its rural and suburban beginnings to become part of the City of New York. Photos from c. 1850 to the present number about 20,000 images, including some 4,000 glass negatives donated in part by the Bureau of Highways. A file of ephemera contains some 250,000 documents, newspaper clippings, and other items. Books on microfilm include atlases from the 1860s to the 1920s and a full range of directories from 1850 through the 1930s, including city directories from pre-telephone days. Both the clipping and photo collections are ongoing, as researchers and a part-time photographer continue to document the borough.

THE BUILDING

The Museum has as its home the historic Valentine-Varian House, built c. 1758 by a blacksmith named Isaac Valentine. During the Revolution, the house stood between the American and British lines in a no-man's-land continually pillaged by raiders from both sides. Understandably the Valentine family fled the area, leaving the house to Hessian, British, and American troops who successively used it.

Isaac Varian bought the property in 1791 (another Isaac Varian, who belonged to the Manhattan branch of the family, became mayor of New York 1839–41). The house remained in the Varian family until 1905, when William F. Beller bought it. In 1965 his son, William C. Beller, donated the building to the Bronx County Historical Society (founded 1955), which moved it across the street to its present location.

The New York Botanical Garden (7)

200th Street and Southern Blvd, Bronx, N.Y. 10458. Tel: (718) 817-8777 for recorded event information; to reach a live person, call (718) 817-8700.

ADMISSION: Grounds are open year-round Tues–Sun and Mon holidays: April–Oct, 10–6; Nov–March, 10–4. Closed Mon, except New York City holidays. Admission charge except Wed (all day) and Sat (10–12).

Visitor Information booth. 20-min narrated tram tours (fee) circle the grounds and stop at convenient locations. Guided walking tours, ecology tours, gardening demonstrations, changing exhibitions, special events; thematic events planned around the growing season (Tulip Weekend, Chrysanthemum Festival Weekend, Rock Garden Weekend); performances. Education programs: children's gardening programs, family activities (every weekend April–Oct), 250 continuing education courses for adults, School of Professional Horticulture. Research library open to the public, Tues–Thurs 12–6; Fri 12–5. For library information, call (718) 817-8604.

✘ Snuff Mill Restaurant, a restored 19C mill overlooking the Bronx River, open 11–5; Rotunda Cafe, in Main Building, open Nov–March, 11–5. The outdoor Tulip Tree Cafe, near Main Garden Gate (opposite Metro-North train station), open April–Oct 11–5, weather permitting. Cafes serve light refreshments. There are also picnic areas located near Twin Lakes and the Snuff Mill.

▥ The Shop in the Garden in the Main Building offers plants, books, gardening tools and supplies, and gifts with a horticultural theme.

♿ Accessible to wheelchairs. Tram circles grounds (see above). Visitors who require assistance can contact Security at (718) 817-8664.

⊘ Do not touch plants or climb trees. Vehicles allowed only on designated roadways or in parking areas. Picnics allowed only in specified picnic areas near Twin Lakes and south of the Snuff Mill. No barbecue fires, alcoholic beverages, sports activities, or radios. No swimming, wading, fishing, boating, or skating. No pets. Children under 16 must be accompanied by an adult.

🚇 IRT Lexington Ave express (train 4) to Bedford Park Blvd. IND 6th Ave express (D train) to Bedford Park Blvd. Walk eight blocks east to the Garden or take the Bx26 bus.

🚌 Mar–Nov on weekends and Mon holidays, the New York Botanical Garden operates a shuttle bus from the Metropolitan Museum of Art in Manhattan, with a stop at the American Museum of Natural History. For reservations and information, call (718) 817-8700.

🚗 The Main Gate is located at Southern Blvd, with easy access from Pelham, Bronx River, and Henry Hudson Pkwys. Take Bronx River Pkwy north to exit 7W; follow Pelham Pkwy to Southern Blvd; follow signs to Garden. Or take Henry Hudson Pkwy north to exit 24; follow Mosholu Pkwy to Southern Blvd and Main Gate. Large parking lot (fee).

🚆 Metro-North Commuter Railroad from Grand Central Terminal to Botanical Garden station is the easiest transport from Manhattan (20 min). For train information, call Metro-North Railroad at (212) 532-4900.

The New York Botanical Garden (founded 1891) is one of the city's great open spaces. Its 250 acres encompass 27 gardens and plant collections that vary from meticulous formal plots to a 40-acre wilderness forest; plantings range from azaleas to zinnias. The centerpiece of the Garden is the glorious turn-of-the-century Conservatory, whose indoor climates support horticultural exhibits of desert and tropical plants. The Garden is also a leader in botanical research, its efforts centering on collecting and identifying plants and studying their economic uses.

NOTE: The Conservatory is closed for restoration until late 1996.

PERMANENT EXHIBITION

The CONSERVATORY (1901; William R. Cobb for Lord & Burnham, green-house manufacturers) is perhaps the most spectacular area of the Garden. Housed within the restored landmark will be important collections of palms (more than 100 varieties), tropical and desert flora, and spectacular seasonal exhibits (chrysanthemums, poinsettias, spring bulbs). Horticulturalists, scientists, and exhibition planners are designing new displays, which focus on "Plants of the World" and will include an aquatic house, rain forest environments, and desert habitats.

Outside the Conservatory are a series of five DEMONSTRATION GARDENS, which show home gardeners what they may do with their own plots: a fragrance garden, a vegetable garden, a cutting garden, a wildlife garden to attract birds, bees, and butterflies, and a country garden with native and naturalized perennials. Nearby are the PERENNIAL GARDEN, with herbaceous perennial plants like clematis, hydrangeas, and daylilies, planted according to color, and the HERB GARDEN, in a traditional knot design, containing plants grown for flavor, fragrance, and medicinal properties.

From the Conservatory it is a short walk along an avenue of tulip trees to the Main Building (built 1890s), once a museum but now a facility housing the Shop in the Garden, the Library, and the Herbarium.

The *Herbarium* is a systematic collection of some 5.7 million dried plant specimens from around the world. Besides its immense size, the Herbarium is remarkable for its depth (some 125,000 type specimens, i.e., specimens that define their respective species) and its historical interest: some specimens came to the Garden (indirectly) from the Lewis and Clark Expedition and others were gathered by naturalists who went with Captain Cook on his first voyage to the South Pacific. As a cornerstone of botanical research, the Herbarium serves scientists throughout the world.

The ROCK GARDEN and the NATIVE PLANT GARDEN. The Rock Garden, one of the most beautifully designed public rock gardens in the United States, is named for its designer, T. H. Everett, a former director of horticulture and education at the Garden. The rocks, gathered from the grounds, were positioned by man- and horsepower beginning in 1932. Plantings include 2,000 kinds of rock and alpine plants from all over the world. The Native Plant Garden presents plants from Maine to the Carolinas in 11 habitats, including a woodland, meadow, and pine barrens. Highlights include 200 kinds of ferns, a meadow with spectacular peak bloom in mid-Aug, and more than 20 species of endangered plants.

Between these gardens and the Bronx River is the New York Botanical Garden FOREST, 40 acres of uncut woodland, the largest remnant of the forest that once covered New York City. Along with a dense grove of hemlock are examples of American beech, red oak, cherry birch, and white ash. From the Hester Bridge there is a good view of the Bronx River gorge. Throughout the gorge the effects of the Wisconsin glacier can be seen in the striation of the rocks, the scattered boulders, and rocky outcrops.

The SNUFF MILL, about a 20-min walk from the Visitor Information Center or tram, was built by the Lorillard brothers Peter and George (1840; restored 1954) on the site of an earlier mill. The Lorillard family, tobacco growers and merchants, continued to operate this mill until the firm

The Enid A. Haupt Conservatory at the New York Botanical Garden. This beautiful turn-of-the-century building, restored to its original condition, houses a collection of more than 100 different kinds of palms.
(The New York Botanical Garden. Photo: Allen Rokach)

moved (1870) to a more modern factory in Jersey City, N.J. One of the original grindstones was uncovered during restoration and incorporated in the sidewalk between the mill and the parking lot.

Across the road from the Snuff Mill is the LILAC COLLECTION, which surrounds the site of Peter Lorillard's "Acre of Roses," whose petals perfumed the snuff manufactured in the nearby mill. Nearby is the ROSE GARDEN, reconstructed after the designs of Beatrix Farrand. Farrand, a disciple of the famous English garden designer Gertrude Jekyll, began the garden in 1916 and it remained on this site until the '70s. The present reconstruction offers not only roses of every hue and fragrance, but a historic design from the early 20C period of American landscape architecture. Among the 2,700 plants are 230 different kinds of roses.

The nearby FAMILY GARDEN has small plots where children may learn to plant, cultivate, and harvest their own flowers and vegetables. In the DAYLILY GARDEN, which peaks in July, are historic daylilies as well as recently developed hybrids.

Trees in the outlying areas of the Garden are grouped by families. Adjacent to the Snuff Mill Rd are maples and the *Montgomery Conifer Collection* transplanted from Connecticut; the collection contains a grove of the rare dawn redwood, a deciduous conifer known only from fossils until 1945, when three living trees were discovered in China.

EXHIBITION PROGRAM

In addition to the permanent gardens and collections, the Garden presents seasonal horticultural displays. Offerings also include outdoor sculpture and the Holiday Garden Railway Exhibition.

HISTORY

In 1884 the city bought 661 acres of land from the Lorillard family, whose fortunes rested on the broad leaves of the tobacco plants they cultivated, primarily for snuff. Pierre Lorillard (d. 1843) had devised a process for grinding tobacco with millstones instead of rubbing it over graters, an innovation that put the family business a jump ahead of its competitors, causing 19C New York diarist Philip Hone to remark that Lorillard "led people by the nose for the best part of a century and made his enormous fortune giving them to chew that which they could not swallow."

Nathaniel Lord Britton, a Columbia University botanist, and his wife Elizabeth, also a botanist, convinced leading citizens of New York City, including Andrew Carnegie, J. Pierpont Morgan, and Cornelius Vanderbilt II, to lead the fund-raising effort and form the board of a botanical garden. The site selected was the former Lorillard estate. Between 1915 and 1937, the city transferred land and buildings from the estate to the Garden, including the mansion, the Snuff Mill, the carriage house and stables (now a maintenance center), and a stone cottage. The Lorillard mansion burned down in 1923. In 1978, the Conservatory, built to resemble the Palm House and the Royal Botanic Gardens in Kew, England, was restored and reopened.

Edgar Allan Poe Cottage (8)

East Kingsbridge Rd and Grand Concourse, Bronx, N.Y. 10458. Tel: (718) 881-8900 (Bronx County Historical Society).

ADMISSION: Open Sat 10–4; Sun 1–5. Closed Mon and Tues, New Year's Day, Thanksgiving, and Christmas Day. Open for group tours by appointment during the week. Call ahead to confirm hours during Dec and Jan.

Edgar Allan Poe Week observed first week in April to commemorate Poe's arrival in New York on April 6, 1844. Activities of this celebration vary from year to year, but include walking tours of the neighborhood and downtown Manhattan where Poe also lived, slide shows, lectures, and school programs.

✖ No restaurant.

†↑ Restroom in park.

▥ Small gift shop with books by and about Poe, notecards, posters, miscellaneous items.

♿ Not accessible to wheelchairs.

⊘ Commercial photography, film and video photography by permission.

🚆 IND 6th Ave express (D train) or IRT Lexington Ave express to Kingsbridge Rd.

🚌 Liberty Line bus 4A and 4B stops at corner of Kingsbridge Rd / Grand Concourse. Bus leaves Manhattan from stops along Madison Ave between 26th St and 96th St at marked locations. For schedule, call Liberty Lines at (718) 652-8400.

🚗 Take Major Deegan Expwy (I-87) to Fordham Road; go east to Kingsbridge Rd and left to Poe Park. Street parking only.

The poet Edgar Allan Poe (1809–1849) lived in this small country house (opened as a museum 1917) between the spring of 1846 and October 1849. During his stay he wrote "Ulalume," "The Bells," and "Annabel Lee." The cottage has been restored and furnished with period furniture and memorabilia.

PERMANENT EXHIBITION

On the ground floor, the kitchen, parlor, and a bedroom have been restored to the period of the Poes' residence. The iron stove in the KITCHEN along with the fireplace in the parlor served to heat the house. The PARLOR contains a traveling desk similar to the one where Poe composed his poetry. The mirror and rocking chair were donated when the Museum first opened and are believed to have belonged to the Poes. The bed in the BEDROOM was donated along with the rocking chair and mirror, and is believed to be the one in which Virginia Poe died.

Upstairs is Poe's STUDY, now an exhibition gallery, and a second BEDROOM, which now contains an audiovisual presentation on Poe's life in the house.

HISTORY

Always in need of money, Poe along with his wife and his mother-in-law moved to New York in 1844, where he worked as an editor first for a paper called the *Sunday Times* and later for the *Evening Mirror*. He became editor and part-owner of a weekly paper, the *Broadway Journal,* in which he published versions of many of his stories, but the paper failed in January 1846.

Early in their New York stay the Poes lived at several addresses downtown, but by 1846 the poet's young wife was severely ill with tuberculosis and Poe himself was in poor health; the family moved to Fordham, hoping that the country air would help Virginia's condition.

When the Poes moved, the cottage was on Kingsbridge Rd, a few hundred ft south of its present location. Built c. 1812, it was a simple farmhouse, surrounded by trees and fields. "I am living out of town about 13 miles, at a village called Fordham, on the railroad leading north," Poe wrote in a letter. "We are in a snug little cottage, keeping house, and would be very comfortable, but that I have been for a long time dreadfully ill."

The country air of Fordham was not enough to save Virginia Poe, who died there in January 1847. Poe remained in the cottage, ill and poverty-stricken, until 1849, when he went South on a trip; he died on his way back to Fordham.

Around the turn of the century the pressures of development began to threaten the cottage. The New York Shakespeare Society determined to save the building and in 1902 the city created Poe Park. In 1913 the city bought the cottage and moved it to its present location adjacent to the park. Four years later it opened as a museum; it is currently administered by the Bronx County Historical Society.

Van Cortlandt House Museum (9)

North of 242nd St and Broadway in Van Cortlandt Park, Bronx, N.Y. 10471. Tel: (718) 543-3344.

ADMISSION: Open Tues–Fri 9–3; Sat, Sun 11–4. Closed Mon, city holidays. Admission charge. Children under 14 free.

Guided tours; group tours by appointment; special events and seasonal programs.

✗ No restaurant.

▥ Gift shop with cards, gifts, toys, 18–19C reproductions.

&. 1st floor is five steps above ground level; 2nd and 3rd floors accessible by flight of stairs.

⊘ No photography.

▆ IRT Broadway-7th Ave local (train 1 or 9) to 242nd St / Van Cortlandt Park.

� Liberty Line bus BxM3 stops at 244th St and Broadway; there are stops along Madison Ave between 26th St and 96th St at marked locations; the bus runs weekdays at ½-hr intervals between 10:20 A.M. and 4:10 P.M.; on Sun it runs at ½-hr intervals between 11:30 A.M. and 1:30 P.M. For further information, call (718) 652-8400.

Built in 1748 (opened as a museum 1897) by one of New York's reigning Dutch families, this vernacular Georgian-style manor house briefly served as George Washington's headquarters during the Revolution. It has been restored and furnished with fine examples of English and American furnishings, many from the Van Cortlandt family.

THE BUILDING

The mansion, almost square in shape, is constructed of locally quarried rough fieldstone with brick trim around the windows. The grotesque faces of the carved keystones, unique in this country and startling in such an austere dwelling, may have been brought from Holland. The high stoop and half-doors reflect Dutch Colonial influences, while the hipped roof, multipaned windows, window frames, and the general symmetry and proportions of the house suggest the English Georgian tradition. Though the interiors of many 18C houses were stripped and "modernized" in the 19C, Van Cortlandt Mansion has retained many of its original architectural details: the wide floorboards, gracefully manteled fireplaces, carved moldings, paneled and plaster walls, and the U-shaped staircase in the front hall.

PERIOD ROOMS

GROUND FLOOR. The KITCHEN has a large cooking fireplace, surrounded by pots, cauldrons, and other utensils. Important pieces include the green glass milk-setting bowls (where milk was set to let the cream rise) and the Canton hotplate and beefsteak platter.

FIRST FLOOR. The EAST PARLOR was perhaps the most formal in the house. Its fine carved Georgian mantel postdates the house. The portrait (c. 1810) of the first *Augustus Van Cortlandt* (1728–1823) is by John Wesley Jarvis. Furnishings include a blockfront secretary of Massachusetts origin, a Chippendale mirror (1760), and a mahogany pie-crust table that once belonged to General Nathaniel Greene.

George Washington is believed to have briefly used the WEST PARLOR as his headquarters while conducting the defense of New York during the Revolution. The Dutch Colonial painted cupboard (1700–20), or *kast,* from the Hudson Valley is painted with grisaille decorations of fruit and vegetables, which simulate the rich woods and ornate carvings of the Dutch prototypes of these vernacular pieces.

The DINING ROOM contains a portrait (c. 1794) of another illustrious Van Cortlandt in-law, *John Jacob Astor,* by Gilbert Stuart. On the mahogany dining table are Chinese export place settings, silver mounted wine bottles, and mahogany knife boxes, all of which belonged to the Van Cortlandts.

SECOND FLOOR. Bedrooms include the EAST CHAMBER and the WEST ROOM, where George Washington did sleep, as did a Hessian commandant during the British occupation. In the West Room is an early Connecticut Valley chest from Belchertown, Mass., and a Philadelphia Chippendale dressing table. The DUTCH ROOM has been fitted out as a 17C bedroom, with the built-in Dutch bed providing warmth. The *kast* in this room, with its relief foliate work on the doors and its ornately carved cornice, is from Holland, its decoration a model for the humbler painted version downstairs.

THIRD FLOOR. Of all the rooms in the house, the NURSERY is believed to have undergone the least interior renovation. It contains a fine early American dollhouse, dated 1744.

On the grounds behind the house is the SUGAR HOUSE WINDOW. It belonged originally to a warehouse on Duane St, built (1763) for storing sugar brought from the West Indies. When the British occupied the city during the Revolutionary War, the warehouse became a makeshift prison for American soldiers. The stones and iron bars from the window were numbered as they were removed from the building and the window was reconstructed as a memorial to the prisoners.

About a half mile north of the Mansion is VAULT HILL, site of the family burial ground; although the gate is still visible, the vault itself has been sealed. Here Augustus Van Cortlandt, city clerk during the Revolution, hid the municipal records in a strongbox.

HISTORY

In 1646, the Dutch West India Company granted Adriaen Van der Donck, the first lawyer in the colony of New Netherlands, a generous tract of land that included the present site of Van Cortlandt Park (and all the land to the Croton River in what is now Westchester County). After his death some of the land passed to Frederick Philipse (himself a landowner with impressive holdings), whose adopted daughter Eva married Jacobus Van Cortlandt. Jacobus bought 50 acres of what is now the park from his father-in-law and later added more, making his farm one of the largest and most prosperous in the area.

Jacobus Van Cortlandt's father, Oloff Stevense Van Cortlandt, was the first American-born Van Cortlandt; he had come as a soldier for the Dutch West Indies Company (1638) and then decided to stay. Oloff Van Cortlandt went into business brewing, trading, lending money, shipping, and manufacturing wampum, and by 1689 was judged one of the four wealthiest men in New York. His descendants—successful merchants and shipbuilders, and frequent holders of city office—were equally successful in making profitable marriages, allying themselves with the colonies' ranking families: Jays, Livingstons, Van Rensselaers, Schuylers, and Philipses.

Frederick Van Cortlandt, the only son of Jacobus and Eva Van Cortlandt, built the present house (1748) in a fashion that reflects both his family's Dutch heritage and the English Georgian style, which dominated upper-class American tastes of the period. The manor house was surrounded by farmland, where the Van Cortlandts raised stock, food crops, and flax, as well as wheat, their most profitable crop, which was milled on the premises.

Before the Battle of White Plains, George Washington maintained his headquarters at Van Cortlandt Manor. Again at the end of the war, Washington returned to the house on his way back to New York City, and spent one or more nights there between Nov 17 and Nov 20, 1783.

The Van Cortlandts lived in the house until 1889, when the house and land were purchased by the city. In 1896 the house was placed in the custody of the National Society of Colonial Dames in the State of New York, which now operates the museum, while the city maintains the grounds and the exterior of the mansion.

Wave Hill (10)

West 249th St and Independence Ave, Bronx, N.Y. 10471. Tel: (718) 549-3200.

ADMISSION: Open summer (May 15–Oct 15): *Wave Hill House and Grounds:* Tues, Thurs–Sun 9–5:30; Wed 9–dusk. Winter (Oct 15–May 15): Tues–Sun 9–4:30. *Greenhouses:* Open Tues–Sun 10–12 and 2–4. Free admission on weekdays; admission charge on weekends. Children under 6 free.

Garden and greenhouse walks Sun at 2:15. Changing art exhibitions at Glyndor Gallery. Gallery talks; lectures, special events, performances and musical events, activities for seniors, educational programs for families; volunteer work days.

✘ The cafe serves lunch and light refreshments Tues–Sun; open 11–4:30. Call to check about hours on Fri. Picnic area adjacent to Glyndor House.

🛍 Gift shop with merchandise on gardens and gardening, nature and environmental concerns; books, cards, toys, gifts. Open 11:30–4:30.

⚐ Grounds accessible to wheelchairs. Wave Hill House and cafe accessible to wheelchairs; restroom in Wave Hill House not accessible. Glyndor House entrance up a few steps from ground level; restroom accessible to wheelchairs.

⊘ No radios, pets, picnicking on grounds (except in designated picnic area), or Frisbee playing.

🚊 IRT Broadway-7th Ave line (train 1) to 231st St station. **Bus connection:** Take Bx10 or Bx7 at northwest corner of 231st St and Broadway. Leave bus at 252nd St. Walk across parkway bridge and turn left. Walk to 249th St. Turn right onto 249th St and walk to Wave Hill Gate. IND 8th Ave line (A train) to last stop, 207th St. **Bus connection:** Take Bx20 at 211th-Isham St, Broadway corner. Leave bus at 246th St. Walk across parkway bridge and turn right. Walk to 249th St, turn left, and walk to Wave Hill Gate.

🚌 Bronx bus Bx1 or Bx9: Take bus to 231st St and Broadway. Follow bus connections (above) for IRT line. **Express Bus:** Liberty Lines Manhattan–Riverdale service from East and West Side. Leave bus at 252nd St. Follow bus connection directions for IRT-7th Ave subway. For further information, call (718) 652-8400. **Van Service:** Reasonably priced van service from Mosholu Limousine Service available from points in Manhattan and Riverdale. Van stops at Wave Hill Gate. For further information, call (718) 543-6900.

🚗 **From Manhattan, east side:** Take Major Deegan Expwy northbound. Exit at Henry Hudson Pkwy. Take first right to Henry Hudson Pkwy southbound. Exit at 254th St. Turn left at stop sign. Turn left at light. Turn right at 249th St to Wave Hill Gate. **From Manhattan, west side:** Take Henry Hudson Pkwy to 246th–250th St exit. Continue north to 252nd St. Turn left at overpass; turn left again beyond overpass. Turn right at 249th St to Wave Hill Gate. Parking available.

🚂 Metro-North Commuter Railroad from Grand Central Station to Riverdale / W. 254th St. Tel: (212) 532-4900 for schedule and information.

Wave Hill (opened 1965) is a cultural and environmental center with 28 acres of landscaped lawns, beautifully planted gardens, greenhouses, and natural forest. Set on high ground overlooking the Hudson River and the New Jersey Palisades, it is a horticulturalist's paradise. Formerly the home of such celebrated people as Mark Twain (1901–03) and Arturo Toscanini (1942–45), Wave Hill offers concerts, art exhibitions, and a variety of programs in its two historic houses, Wave Hill House and Glyndor. It is, however, the gardens themselves that are the real reason for coming to Wave Hill.

THE GARDENS

The FLOWER GARDEN offers seasonal plantings and annual beds. In the GREENHOUSE are exhibitions of succulents and cacti as well as palms and a variety of seasonal displays. The formal HERB GARDEN offers some 150 varieties of medicinal and culinary herbs, planted in walled and terraced beds, whose foundations remain from horticultural ventures during the residency of George W. Perkins. Gravel paths wander through a profusion of flowers and carefully sculpted shrubs in the beautiful WILD GARDEN.

WAVE HILL

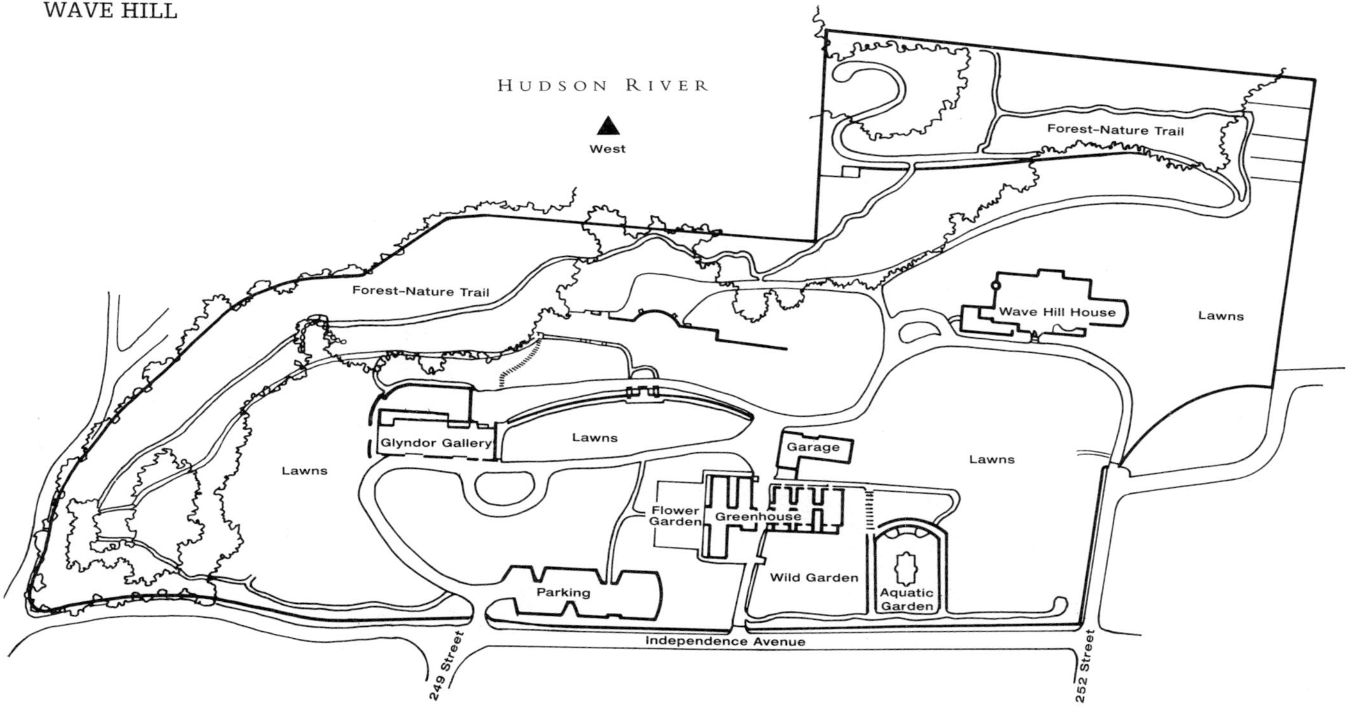

HUDSON RIVER

West

Forest-Nature Trail

Forest-Nature Trail

Lawns

Lawns

Lawns

Lawns

Glyndor Gallery

Parking

Flower Garden

Greenhouse

Garage

Wild Garden

Aquatic Garden

Wave Hill House

Independence Avenue

249 Street

252 Street

Past monocot beds and a large trellis covered with a draped conifer, Weeping Blue Atlas Cedar, paths lead to an AQUATIC GARDEN, with a pool filled with water lilies, cattails, and papyrus plants. On the sloping lawns are mature specimens of native North American trees, some dating back to before the Civil War.

HISTORY

On the grounds are two houses, *Wave Hill House* (central wing, 1843 with later additions; Armor Hall) and *Glyndor* (early 20C). (Neither is restored in period style.) Wave Hill House is a fieldstone mansion built by William Lewis Morris, a successful jurist. Publisher William Henry Appleton bought the property from the Morris family in 1866 as a summer home. In 1903 it passed into the hands of George W. Perkins, a J. Pierpont Morgan partner, who added greenhouses, gardens, stables, an underground recreation building with a bowling alley, and the neo-Georgian mansion called Glyndor, which now serves as an art gallery. Perkins also worked personally with Albert Millard, previously a royal landscape gardener in Vienna, to lay out gardens emphasizing the beauties of the site.

In 1928, Bashford Dean, a curator of arms and armor at the Metropolitan Museum (and also of reptiles and fishes at the Museum of Natural History), who had a lifetime tenancy, hired eminent Riverdale architect Dwight James Baum to add an *Armor Hall* to Wave Hill House for his collection. The Hall is now used for lectures and chamber music and some of the armor can be seen at the Metropolitan Museum of Art.

The estate passed to Perkins's daughter, Mrs. Edward U. Freeman, and in 1960 Wave Hill was deeded to the City of New York by the Perkins and Freeman families. The city now owns the land, but the gardens are maintained through both public and private resources. Since 1967, Marco Polo Stufano has been the director of horticulture. When he arrived, only traces of the formerly beautiful gardens remained visible beneath acres of tangled vegetation. Today, the gardens have taken their place among the most beautiful in the country.

EXHIBITION PROGRAM

In the galleries at Glyndor are rotating exhibitions, dealing with the relationship between human beings and their natural environment. Programs have included "Garden Dreams," a display of paintings by Ferris Cook based on turn-of-the-century cover designs for garden books, and "Images of Cotswold Gardens," paintings and drawings by Simon Dorrell, one of England's premier garden painters. "Alchemical Reconnaissance," an exhibition of the photography of John Huddleston, examined the relationship between landscape photography and high-energy physics, exploring these two disciplines as they focused on the natural world.

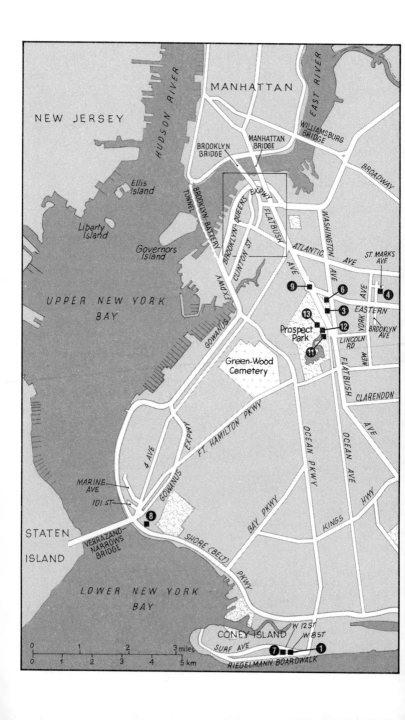

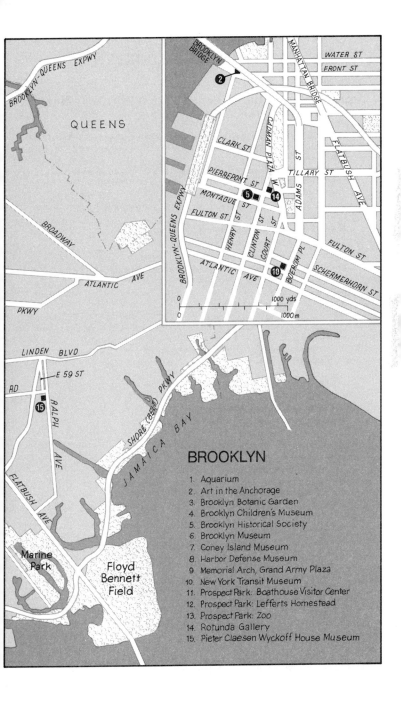

BROOKLYN

1. Aquarium
2. Art in the Anchorage
3. Brooklyn Botanic Garden
4. Brooklyn Children's Museum
5. Brooklyn Historical Society
6. Brooklyn Museum
7. Coney Island Museum
8. Harbor Defense Museum
9. Memorial Arch, Grand Army Plaza
10. New York Transit Museum
11. Prospect Park: Boathouse Visitor Center
12. Prospect Park: Lefferts Homestead
13. Prospect Park: Zoo
14. Rotunda Gallery
15. Pieter Claesen Wyckoff House Museum

MUSEUMS IN BROOKLYN

Aquarium for Wildlife Conservation (formerly New York Aquarium) (1)

West 8th St and Surf Ave, Coney Island, Brooklyn, N.Y. 11224. Tel: (718) 265-FISH for recorded information; to reach a live person, call (718) 265-3400.

ADMISSION: Open every day of the year 10–5; until 6:45 on weekends and holidays from Memorial Day through Labor Day. Admission charge; children under two admitted free.

Exhibitions, marine mammal shows, family programs, lectures, tours, family workshops, school programs.

✗ Snack bar and cafeteria; outdoor picnic area.

🛍 Gift and souvenir shops.

♿ Accessible to wheelchairs.

🚫 No pets, radios, bicycles, or skateboards. No smoking indoors.

🚇 IND 6th Ave express or local (D or F train) to W. 8th St in Brooklyn; a pedestrian bridge from the subway station crosses Surf Ave and leads directly to the Aquarium entrance.

🚗 Belt Pkwy to exit 6 (Cropsey Ave) or exit 7S (Ocean Pkwy South). Follow the blue Beluga Whale signs to the Aquarium. Parking available; fee varies with season.

HIGHLIGHTS

Beluga whales, sharks, and seals.
Sea Cliffs habitat area.
Discovery Cove exhibition.
Shark feeding, 1:30 daily.

One of New York's oldest (1896) and most beloved attractions, the New York Aquarium harbors more than 10,000 specimens of aquatic life, from imposing beluga whales to such humble local species as fluke and sea robins.

EXHIBITIONS

The aquatic animals in the collections—more than 300 species of vertebrates and invertebrates—are housed in some 100 marine environments.

The OCEANIC TANK (180,000 gallons) offers above- and below-water viewing of harbor and gray seals. In the MAIN GALLERY are habitat aquariums representing such environments as the Pacific Reef, an African Rift Lake, and the Red Sea, an intricate vertical reef with colorful fishes unique to this area. In the COLD WATER GALLERY are cuttlefish, toadfish, wolf eels, large Japanese spider crabs, and a giant Pacific octopus.

DISCOVERY COVE is a changing exhibit space with entertaining and educational exhibits. A man-made wave dumps 400 gallons of water every 45 seconds into a man-made tidal pool; a walk-in diorama of a salt-marsh gives visitors firsthand experience of an ecosystem that includes horseshoe crabs, minnows, killifish, and specialized marsh grasses. A mock New England seaside village shows the benefits, including food and pharmaceuticals, that people have traditionally reaped from the sea.

HUDSON RIVER EXHIBIT: A 30-ft illustrated map shows the history and course of the Hudson River, as well as its freshwater and marine habitats from the headwaters of the river to its mouth in New York Bay. The BATHYSPHERE was used in a historic deep-sea dive (1934) by William Beebe and Otis Barton. The NATIVE SEA LIFE exhibit offers a sampling of aquatic life found in local waters.

In the SHARK TANK are nurse, white-tip, and sand tiger sharks, as well as sting rays and horseshoe crabs.

The newest addition (opened summer 1993) is the SEA CLIFFS EXHIBIT, a 300-ft-long coastline habitat for penguins, sea otters, and walruses. Nuka, the city's only Pacific walrus, is a longtime favorite with crowds. Sea otters, formerly an endangered species, harbor seals, and the Aquarium's breeding colony of black-footed penguins all enjoy this spacious area.

HISTORY

The New York Aquarium, a division of the Wildlife Conservation Society, is the oldest continuously operating aquarium in the nation. Its first home was Castle Garden (now Castle Clinton) in Manhattan's Battery Park. The structure, originally a fort, was remodeled (1896) by the prestigious firm of McKim, Mead & White to house the Aquarium. In the '40s, despite the immense popularity of the Aquarium, which attracted some 2.5 million visitors annually, Commissioner of Parks Robert Moses threatened to raze the building. The Aquarium moved to its present location in 1957.

In 1981 the first beluga bred in captivity was born at the Aquarium. In addition to its displays and educational programs, the Aquarium operates the Osborn Laboratories of Marine Sciences, located next door.

Art in the Anchorage (2)

Brooklyn Bridge Anchorage, Cadman Plaza West and Old Front St, Brooklyn, N.Y. Mailing address: % Creative Time, Inc., 131 W. 24th St, New York 10011. Tel: (212) 206-6674.

ADMISSION: Open during exhibitions (spring and summer) Thurs–Sun 1–6. Free.

One exhibition each season; music and dance events, readings, and performances related to themes of exhibitions.

✗ No restaurant.

🏛 No gift shop.

♿ Accessible to wheelchairs.

🚇 IRT 7th Ave express (train 2 or 3) to Clark Street. Walk north on Henry St to Cadman Plaza West; continue toward the river and Anchorage at Old Front St / Cadman Plaza West. IND 8th Ave express or local (A or C train) to High St. Follow Cadman Plaza West toward the river to Old Front St.

Art in the Anchorage (1983) occupies the city's most dramatic exhibition space, the cavernous vaults beneath the eastern tower of the Brooklyn Bridge. The vaults, darkly reminiscent of the Paris sewers or the fantasies of Piranesi, serve as a venue for Creative Time, an organization devoted to sponsoring provocative and innovative art for the city's public spaces. Each year, Creative Time selects a group of emerging or mid-career artists to develop work that will make compelling use of the site and address timely social, artistic, or aesthetic issues.

EXHIBITION PROGRAM

Exhibitions are organized around general artistic or social themes. One year artists explored the sound and light properties of the Anchorage itself. Terry Fox and Yoshi Wada created a sound and performance installation, filling a tunnel with an array of industrial-looking materials; pieces of buckled aluminum sheeting, garbage cans, pipes, and other detritus were used as sound sources along with more traditional gongs, synthesizers, sirens, bagpipes, and some 100 ft of tightly stretched piano wire. The "instruments" were played to dramatic and eerie effect.

Another exhibition presented 28 artists whose work focused on such issues as juvenile runaways, drug and alcohol addiction, racism, aging, the environment, religion, and the First Amendment. Projects included Jim Goldberg's *Memories of Swinging on Swings,* an installation that included documentary photographs of runaway teenagers in San Francisco and Los Angeles; David Nechak's *The Elderly Speak,* a sound installation; Izhar Patkin's *Palagonia,* a large wax sculpture inspired by Bernini's *The Ecstasy of Santa Teresa* and the 17C Baroque grotesques in the Villa Palagonia in Sicily. Outside the Anchorage banners by Paul H-O and Roger Boyce proclaimed: "Demolish the Wall of Censorship."

THE BROOKLYN BRIDGE ANCHORAGE

The completion of the Brooklyn Bridge in 1883 was a remarkable event in the history of the city, making possible closer links between Brooklyn, then a separate city, and New York. The bridge was an architectural and technological wonder, the world's first steel suspension bridge, and the second highest structure in the city, surpassed only by Trinity Church. It is still thought by many to be the world's most beautiful suspension bridge.

Both bridge anchorages—enormous masonry structures in which the cables are embedded—have imposing vaulted spaces within them. For many years the vaults on the Manhattan side, cool, dark, and partly underground, were used as storage by a commercial wine merchant, though they were sealed during Prohibition; an alternative use is presently being sought.

In 1983, the centenary of the Brooklyn Bridge, the president of the borough of Brooklyn asked Creative Time to participate in the anniversary celebrations. The Brooklyn Anchorage, then used for storage of surplus city tires, was refurbished as an exhibition and performance space, with a brick floor, theatrical lighting, and modern plumbing. One hundred fifty visual and performing artists were selected to tour the Anchorage and submit proposals for new works, of which 10 visual works and 18 performances were chosen.

HISTORY

Creative Time is an experimental organization (founded 1973) that has won wide recognition for supporting artists in producing art in public spaces throughout the city. The programs began in the early '70s when a recessionary economy left vacant many office spaces in the financial district. One of the most visible spaces was 88 Pine St, also known as Wall Street Plaza, whose most famous installation was Red Grooms's *Ruckus Manhattan,* a witty three-dimensional reconstruction of part of Manhattan. Creative Time has sponsored art in subway stations, on billboards, on buses, at a refuse transfer station where garbage was formerly loaded onto barges, and on the landfill where Battery Park City now stands.

Creative Time also pioneered Art on the Beach at the sands of the Battery Park Landfill, a series of exhibitions in 1978–85 that dealt with such themes as the urban environment, issues in geology and technology, and stories of mystery and myth. Among the hundreds of artists who have participated in projects sponsored by Creative Time are Laurie Anderson, Judy Pfaff, Michelangelo Pistoletto, Gran Fury, Karen Finley, David Wojnarowicz, and Petah Coyne.

The Brooklyn Botanic Garden (3)

1000 Washington Ave (Eastern Pkwy), Brooklyn, N.Y. 11225. Tel: (718) 622-4433.

ADMISSION: Open April–Sept: Tues–Fri 8–6; weekends and holidays 10–6. Oct–March: Tues–Fri 8–4:30, weekends and holidays 10–4:30. Closed Mon except holiday Mondays, New Year's Day, Thanksgiving, and Christmas Day. Free. *Japanese Garden and Conservatory:* Open April–Oct: Tues–Sun 10–5:30. Nov–March: Tues–Sun 10–3:30. Free.

Public tours Sat and Sun at 1 P.M. meet in front of Garden Shop in the Administration Building. Films, lectures, occasional exhibits of painting and photography, festivals with entertainment. Extensive educational programs for children and adults.

✗ Terrace cafe (sandwiches, hamburgers, snacks) open March–mid-Nov. Cafe moved to Conservatory in winter.

▥ Gift shop with plants, garden tools, horticultural gifts, books, cards.

& Most gardens, Conservatory, and Conservatory restrooms accessible to wheelchairs. Fragrance Garden for the Blind.

⊘ No radios. No pets. No picnicking.

▙ IRT Broadway-7th Ave express (train 2 or 3) to Eastern Pkwy-Brooklyn Museum. IND 6th Ave (D train) to Prospect Park. BMT Nassau St line (Q train) to Prospect Park.

🚗 **From Manhattan:** Take the Triborough Bridge to the Brooklyn-Queens Expwy (Route 278). Exit 27 to Atlantic Ave, turn right onto Washington Ave. Enclosed pay parking lot on Washington Ave between the Garden and the Brooklyn Museum.

The Brooklyn Botanic Garden (1910), 52 carefully tended and intensively planted acres hedged around by asphalt and apartment houses, is an unexpected Eden, clearly enjoyed by neighborhood visitors as well as horticulturists and plant lovers from further away.

PERMANENT EXHIBITION

Outside the main entrance of the ADMINISTRATION AND CLASSROOM BUILDING (completed 1918; McKim, Mead & White) is *Magnolia Plaza,* where magnolia trees of 11 species bloom beginning in early April along with daffodils planted on Boulder Hill (to the right). The figures on the

BROOKLYN BOTANIC GARDEN

N

MAIN ENTRANCES
SUBWAYS
WATER FEATURES
REST ROOMS

IND
D Q B

EMPIRE BLVD.

FLATBUSH AVENUE

CHILDREN'S GARDEN
rhododendrons
dogwood
butterfly bushes
beauty berries
forsythia
ash trees
viburnums
IRIS GARDEN
weigelas
spring bulbs
ROCK GARDEN
honeysuckles
lilacs
hollies
horsechestnuts
roses-of-sharon
witch hazels
rose family
snowberries
quince
cotoneasters
barberries
snowdrops
WISterias
CONSERVATORY
PALM HOUSE
GIFT SHOP
food
food
Japanese
water lilies
annuals
MAGNOLIA PLAZA
ADMINISTRATION
EDUCATION DEPARTMENT
FRAGRANCE GARDEN
SHAKESPEARE GDN.
DAFFODIL HILL
JAPANESE GARDEN
CHERRY WALK
HERB GARDEN
peonies
crab apples
OVERLOOK
barberries
birches
oaks
beeches
conifers
walnuts
hedge wheel
CHERRY ESPLANADE
wisteria
lilacs
crape-myrtles
dogwoods
CRANFORD ROSE GARDEN
azaleas
andromeda
NATIVE FLORA SECTION
mt. laurel
rhododendrons
ALMONT MEMORIAL
WISteria
OSBORNE GARDEN
crab apples
EGGERS TERRACE
IRT 2 & 3
BROOKLYN MUSEUM
PARKING LOT
WASHINGTON AVENUE
EASTERN PKWY.

armillary sphere representing signs of the Zodiac are by Rhys Caparn, daughter of Harold Caparn, landscape architect for much of the Garden.

Continue past the brook to *Cherry Walk* and the *Cherry Esplanade* (on the right), famous for its deep pink Kwanzan cherry trees, spectacular in early May against a backdrop of red foliage provided by Schwedler maples planted on Armistice Day, 1918.

Diagonally across from the *Rose Arc* (on the left) is the Cranford *Rose Garden* (1927) with over 1,200 varieties of roses (more than 5,000 plants).

On the left, toward the hillside, is the *Lilac Collection* arranged, like much of the Botanic Garden, as an arboretum with permanent plantings showing botanic relationships between species. Behind the fence on the left is the *Local Flora Section,* featuring wildflowers, shrubs, and trees normally found within a 100-mile radius of the Botanic Garden. At the top of the stairs the *Overlook,* bordered by fastigiate gingkos, leads east past the Rose Garden to the *Herb Garden* (1938), whose formally planted Elizabethan knots were intended to be seen from above, presumably from one's manor window. The garden contains over 300 different herbaceous plants with culinary and medicinal uses.

A path leads to the *Japanese Garden,* designed and constructed (1914–15) in the traditional Hall-and-Pond style by Takeo Shiota and considered by its maker to be his masterpiece. The Viewing Pavilion with its circular window symbolizes the home of the host, owner of the garden, and the shelter across the lake symbolizes a Waiting House where in an actual Japanese tea garden guests would wait to be received by the host. On the hillside, five small cascades with echo caverns beneath them splash downward in a landscape of dwarfed trees and shrubs.

A path from the Japanese Garden leads to the *Shakespeare Garden,* containing some 80 varieties of plants mentioned in the Bard's works. In the nearby *Fragrance Garden for the Blind* (1955) grow plants chosen for touch, taste, and smell, labeled in Braille and planted in raised beds.

Beyond the Administration Building is the CONSERVATORY (1988). On the UPPER LEVEL to the left of the entrance is the *Bonsai Museum* with the Garden's world-renowned collection of over 750 species of temperate and tropical bonsai, displayed in indoor and outdoor environments. The central exhibit is a *Trail of Evolution,* which traces the development of plant life from the Precambrian era 4 billion years ago to the present, from simple single-celled organisms to "modern" flowering plants. Also on this level is the *Aquatic House* with tropical water lilies and other aquatic plants of economic or cultural significance (papyrus, rice, water chestnuts). Submerged plants can be viewed from windows on the lower level. Other displays include insectivorous plants and orchids.

On the LOWER LEVEL are three environmental pavilions—*Tropical, Desert,* and *Warm Temperate*—with appropriate plantings.

Return to the pathway and continue past the *Children's Garden,* a cherished local institution where hundreds of local children annually learn to grow vegetables and flowers, absorbing in the process the human virtues associated with gardening. The pathway next leads past dogwoods, azaleas, forsythia, and the iris garden (late May–early June) to the *Rock Garden,* with plants normally found on mountain slopes, whose low growth protects them from wind. The *Monocot Bed,* on the other side of the path, is a display border of plants with parallel-veined leaves and includes irises, daylilies, and narcissi, as well as more exotic grasses, cannas, and yuccas. The *Hedge Wheel* has 18 rows of evergreen and deciduous shrubs planted like spokes to show their use in hedges.

CALENDAR OF HIGHLIGHTS

The Cranford Rose Garden peaks in June with a second blooming in Sept. The Herb Garden is at its best in June–early Aug, with the lavender hedge blooming in July. The Water Lily Pools with tropical lilies blossoms in Aug and Sept; lotuses bloom mid-July through Aug. The Fragrance Garden, with Braille labels, is outstanding June through mid-Sept.

HISTORY

The Botanic Garden was founded (1910) as a department of the Brooklyn Institute of Arts and Sciences for the education and enjoyment of the public, a remarkable goal at a time when botanic gardens were still primarily attached to universities. Initially funded with a donation from Brooklyn philanthropist Alfred Tredway White and a matching sum from the City of New York, the Garden, wasteland at first, was enriched in its early years with the by-products of nearby breweries and stables. Its collections have since been expanded to include more than 12,000 species of plants from all over the globe.

The Brooklyn Children's Museum (4)

145 Brooklyn Ave (St. Marks Ave), Brooklyn, N.Y. 11213. Tel: (718) 735-4400.

ADMISSION: Open during school year Wed–Fri 2–5; weekends and school holidays 12–5. During summer vacation, open Wed–Mon 12–5. Closed Mon and Tues, New Year's Day, Thanksgiving, and Christmas Day. Suggested contribution.

Changing exhibitions, children's resource library, workshops, films, special events, family programs.

✗ No restaurant.

🏛 No gift shop.

♿ Accessible to wheelchairs.

🚇 IRT 7th Ave express (train 3) to Kingston Ave; walk one block west on Eastern Pkwy, turn right onto Brooklyn Ave; walk six blocks to St. Marks Ave. IND 8th Ave (A train) to Kingston-Throop Ave station; walk west on Fulton St one block to Brooklyn Ave, turn left (south) and walk six blocks to the corner of Brooklyn Ave and St. Marks Ave.

🚗 **From Manhattan:** Take Brooklyn Bridge onto Adams St; turn left on Atlantic Ave; Atlantic Ave to Brooklyn Ave; turn south onto Brooklyn Ave and continue four blocks to St. Marks Ave. Or follow Flatbush Ave to Eastern Pkwy. Continue east on Eastern Pkwy; turn north onto New York Ave and continue six blocks to St. Marks Ave. Turn right one block to Brooklyn Ave. Street parking only.

The Brooklyn Children's Museum (1899) was the first museum founded solely for the education and delight of children, or as its Victorian founders phrased it, to "stimulate their powers of observation and reflection." Today, occupying subterranean quarters beneath Brower Park, the Museum is a resource for parents and children of Brooklyn and the whole tristate area, offering changing exhibitions, school programs, and workshops for children age two through high school.

EXHIBITION PROGRAM

Visitors enter the Museum through a 1907 trolley kiosk and proceed downstairs along a sewer culvert through which pours a stream whose waterpower children can harness with sluices, gates, and waterwheels. Inside, the brightly painted exhibit areas are divided into several levels connected by a maze of passageways. Most exhibits are interactive, with buttons to push, handles to pull, and objects to pick up. Changing exhibitions last a year or so and are supplemented by workshops and special activities.

One long-term and very popular exhibition is "The Music Studio" with a walk-on floor piano where children can tap out their favorite tunes (in the sense that Fred Astaire tapped things out). "Animals Eat: Different Feasts for Different Beasts" explores the way animals adapt to their environments, showing how they obtain food for themselves and avoid becoming food for others.

Another long-term exhibition, "Night Journeys," features sleep environments where children can try out life-size "beds" from other cultures or pillow their heads on wooden African and Japanese headrests. "Bone Yard Detectives" suggests the purposes and importance of bones, offering human and animal skeletons as well as living animals.

PERMANENT COLLECTION

The permanent collection of more than 27,000 objects includes articles from the natural sciences (a mammoth's tooth, a pickled human brain), anthropology (African masks, jewelry, pottery), and objects related simply to children (a collection of dolls from all over the world). "Collection Connections" in the Children's Resource Library (open Wed–Sun 2–4:30) allows young researchers to make their own inquiries, using objects organized in special study boxes (coins, butterflies, artifacts of the Plains Indians). Recent additions to these collections explore African and Jewish traditions, reflecting the cultural heritage of ethnic groups in the neighboring community of Crown Heights.

HISTORY

The Museum, founded by the Brooklyn Institute of Arts and Sciences (1899), proudly bills itself as "The World's First Museum for Children" and the originator of the kind of participatory exhibitions that make children's museums today so delightful. Its first home, the Adams home in Bedford Park (renamed Brower Park 1923), was a Victorian mansion belonging to historian James Truslow Adams; its many parlors and hallways were converted to galleries and filled with natural history specimens (stuffed birds, minerals, and zoological models) from the permanent collections. The driving force behind the Museum was Anna Billings Gallup, who became curator in 1903 and whose philosophy of education shaped both the collections and the programs.

In 1929 the Museum expanded to a second Brower Park home, the Smith mansion, which had belonged to L. C. Smith, typewriter manufacturer and partner in the Smith Corona Company.

The deteriorating Smith and Adams mansions were declared hazardous in 1967 and closed; in their place rose the present building (1977; Hardy Holzman Pfeiffer

Assocs). Its architectural playfulness—subway kiosk entrance, the "stream," the "people tube" connecting different levels, and the auditorium installed in a huge oil drum—have attracted favorable attention from museumgoers and the architectural community.

The Brooklyn Historical Society (5)

128 Pierrepont St (Clinton St), Brooklyn, N.Y. 11201. Tel: (718) 624-0890.

ADMISSION: Gallery open Tues–Sat 12–5; library open Tues–Sat, 12–4:45. Closed Sun, Mon, national holidays. When national holidays fall on Mon, the Society is usually closed the preceding Sat. Admission charge except Wed. Charge for nonmembers to use library. Children under 6 free.

Information Desk. Lectures, changing exhibitions, walking tours, educational programs for children, concerts. Library with fine research collection, photographs, ephemera, genealogical materials.

✘ No restaurant in Museum; nearby restaurants on Montague St.

▥ Publications, catalogues.

♿ Gallery accessible to wheelchairs. Limited access to library; call ahead for information.

⊘ No photography.

🚇 IRT 7th Ave express (train 2 or 3) to Borough Hall. IRT Lexington Ave express (train 4 or 5) to Borough Hall. BMT Broadway Nassau St local (M train) or BMT Broadway local (R train) to Court St. IND 8th Ave express (A train) or 6th Ave local (F train) to Jay St / Borough Hall.

🚗 **From Manhattan:** Take Brooklyn Bridge to Cadman Plaza West exit. Turn left and continue to Montague St. Turn right on Montague and continue one block to Clinton St. Turn right again. The Society is one block ahead. Garage parking nearby.

Through a program of changing exhibitions, lectures, and borough walking tours, and a remarkable permanent collection, the Brooklyn Historical Society (1863) keeps alive in the hearts and minds of its admirers the borough's real and mythic past. Founded as the Long Island Historical Society (name changed 1985), it occupies a landmark building at the edge of historic Brooklyn Heights.

PERMANENT EXHIBITION

The first-floor gallery was once an auditorium whose seats were removed during World War I so that the Red Cross could convert it to a hospital. Today it houses a permanent exhibit, which chronicles 350 years of local history, focusing on five major themes: the Brooklyn Bridge, the Brooklyn Navy Yard, the Dodgers, Coney Island, and Brooklynites, including the "Guy from Brooklyn," a stereotypical streetwise, fast-talking blue-collar worker popularized by the movies and television. Visitors can see souvenirs from the opening day of the Brooklyn Bridge in 1883, artistic renditions of the bridge ranging from serious paintings to packing for Italian-made bubble gum, and posters from the Navy Yard reminding workers that "Loose Lips Sink Ships." Fans of the long-departed Brooklyn Dodgers can see authentic "crying towels," derisively tossed to opponents on the short end of the score, and photos of the Brooklyn Sym-Phony, known for its rendition of "Three Blind Mice," when the umpires ruled in favor of the opposition. Ralph Kramden, the most famous "Guy from Brooklyn," appears on a mock-up of the set of *The Honeymooners,* the popular TV show featuring Jackie Gleason.

CHANGING EXHIBITIONS

Exhibitions usually focus on historic and mythic Brooklyn and on the multiethnic present of the borough. Historical exhibitions have included "Focus on Weeksville: A Nineteenth Century Black Settlement" established in what is now Bedford-Stuyvesant. Other historical shows have focused on Henry Ward Beecher (whose activities ranged from opposing slavery to endorsing soap), Indian life in 17C Brooklyn, Brooklyn baseball and the Dodgers, including an afternoon with former Dodger stars. One program celebrated the 150th anniversary of Green-Wood Cemetery, offering photographs, paintings, and prints, as well as lectures and walking tours.

Exhibitions frequently spotlight the present multicultural population of the borough. One featured the Italian community of Williamsburg and its traditional Giglio Feast, where the faithful of Our Lady of Mt Carmel carry through the streets an 85-ft tower with a statue of St. Paulinus. "¿Por Qué Brooklyn?" explored the culture of the Latino population, which has been a Brooklyn presence since Puerto Ricans began emigrating to Red Hook and the area around Borough Hall after World War I. On display were such treasured possessions from the homeland as a carved wooden *Santa* representing *La Virgen Santísima,* made by a traditional Puerto Rican carver in 1890 and brought to Brooklyn after World War II.

PERMANENT COLLECTION

The library on the second floor contains an important research collection: some 125,000 volumes and 100,000 photographs of Brooklyn people and places, with special collections of houses and street scenes arranged by geographic location. There are several hundred paintings of Brooklyn personalities, landscapes, and events. The Society owns 500 manuscript collections that range from the 1679 diary and drawings of the Labadist missionaries, to the papers of prominent 18C Brooklyn families, to the record of the Flatbush Taxpayers Assoc in 1890–1914. The periodicals collection includes newspapers predating the Civil War, e.g., *The Long Island Star* (1809–63) and the *Williamsburgh Gazette* (1835–53). In addition there are maps, diaries, legal documents, drawings, church histories, paintings, watercolors, prints, and other historical materials. The genealogical collection is outstanding.

THE BUILDING

In 1868 the members of the Society bought property on the corner of Pierrepont and Clinton Sts and over the next ten years raised money for the present building. George B. Post, soon to become famous for designing the New York Stock Exchange and the New York Times Building in Manhattan, won the architectural competition for the building.

The asymmetrical red brick building (opened 1881) with its slate-roofed tower and terracotta ornament has become one of the city's architectural landmarks. On the facade is a wealth of ornamental detail; busts of worthies including Columbus and Franklin (Pierrepont St side), Shakespeare, Gutenberg, Beethoven, and Michelangelo (Clinton St side), peer out from between the window arches, and a Viking and an Indian (presumably symbolizing Long Island's earliest visitors and inhabitants) overlook the main door.

The interior of the library upstairs remains virtually unchanged. With its tall, round-headed windows designed to admit maximum light, and its black ash bookcases, tables, columns, and railings, it is considered a masterpiece of 19C interior design.

HISTORY

Founded during the Civil War by a group of prominent citizens concerned with preserving and celebrating their own history, the Society was originally a repository where these local aristocrats could deposit their own books, pamphlets, church histories, manuscripts, genealogies and family records, legal documents, and materials recording Long Island's houses, families, and citizens.

The Society began publishing works on the history of Brooklyn and Long Island during the late 1860s; among its first efforts were a translation of the Dutch journal of two missionary visitors to America in 1679 and a book on the Battle of Long Island.

Through the years the Society has continued its work of collecting and preserving documents and artifacts on Brooklyn history. A bequest from real estate investor Ruth Ann Shellens (1989) endowed the Society's first permanent exhibition on Brooklyn history.

The Brooklyn Museum (6)

200 Eastern Pkwy (Washington Ave), Brooklyn, N.Y. 11238. Tel: (718) 638-5000.

ADMISSION: Open Wed–Sun 10–5. Closed Mon and Tues, New Year's Day, Thanksgiving, and Christmas Day. Suggested contribution. Free to members and children under 12 accompanied by an adult.

Lectures, gallery talks, films, artist demonstrations, educational programs for children and adults; children's gallery talks; weekend programs. Group tours by appointment; call ext. 221. Museum library and archives open Wed–Fri by appointment.

✗ Museum cafe open 10–4.

🛍 Shops are open 10:30–5:30 when the Museum is open. Excellent book and gift shop with art books, exhibition catalogues, calendars, notecards, postcards, reproductions from the collection, jewelry, gifts, handcrafted items. Children's gift shop with educational books and toys. There is a branch shop in Manhattan at the Equitable Center, 787 7th Ave (50th / 51st Sts), open Mon–Fri 11–6 and Sat 12–5.

♿ Accessible to wheelchairs. Handicapped parking available in the parking lot. Ramp access to lower-level entrance lobby. Handicapped restroom facilities on 1st and 3rd floors. Sign language-interpreted gallery talks first and third Sats of each month at 2:00; for more information, call (718) 638-5000, ext. 226; for TT / TDD service, call (718) 783-6501.

⊘ Photography permitted only in permanent collection galleries. Lights and / or tripods require special permission.

🚇 IRT 7th Ave express (train 2 or 3) to Eastern Pkwy / Brooklyn Museum.

🚗 **From Manhattan:** Take Brooklyn Bridge left onto Tillary St, right onto Flatbush Ave to Grand Army Plaza. Go left on Eastern Pkwy to the Museum. Parking in large lot (fee) accessible from Washington Ave.

Standing near Prospect Park and Grand Army Plaza—two of the borough's great landmarks—the Brooklyn Museum harks back to the days when Brooklyn was a separate city, fired with ambitious plans to rival New York across the river. Today one of the leading cultural resources of the borough and the city, the Museum has recently completed a major architectural expansion, reinstalling its Egyptian collections and reopening the West Wing to the public. Its wide-ranging collections, embracing 1.5 million objects housed in a grand 19C building, make it one of the nation's largest and most prestigious institutions. The Museum is known not only for its collections of Egyptian art and American painting but, in recent years, for its enterprising program of exhibitions.

HIGHLIGHTS

The Egyptian collection.
18–19C American paintings.
The Rodin Sculpture Gallery.
The period rooms, especially the rooms from historic Brooklyn.

PERMANENT COLLECTION

East Wing

Between the Museum building and the parking lot is the **Sculpture Garden,** a collection of architectural ornaments and sculptures salvaged from demolished New York buildings, from the late lamented Pennsylvania Station to obscure tenements. The large bronze head of a *Longhorn Steer* (1905) by Solon Borglum once graced the entrance to Charles A. Schieren's leather belt factory in Manhattan. (Schieren served for a time as mayor of Brooklyn.) Adolph A. Weinman's figure of *Night* (c. 1910) was commissioned for the former Pennsylvania Station, designed by McKim, Mead & White. Weinman also sculpted a companion figure representing *Day* and other statuary for the station. When the station was destroyed (1963), the statues were broken up and buried in the Jersey Meadowlands; only three have been retrieved.

First Floor

In the Glass Corridor facing the Sculpture Garden are the abstract **Williamsburg Murals** rediscovered in the Williamsburg Housing Project in Brooklyn. Executed by four pioneer American abstract artists, Ilya Bolotowsky, Balcomb Greene, Paul Kelpe, and Albert Swinden, the murals were commissioned (1936) by the New York Mural Division of the Works Progress Administration (WPA). Burgoyne Diller, a painter deeply influenced by Mondrian, headed the Mural Division and selected the artists, a bold choice at a time when murals generally depicted American regional life or Social Realist subjects.

Originally the murals were installed in the public areas of the housing project. In time these public rooms became offices or storage space, and

BROOKLYN MUSEUM
First Floor

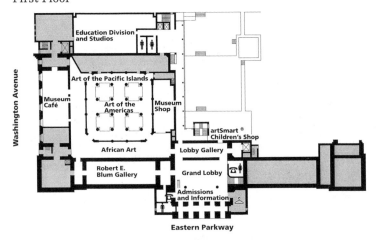

the murals were neglected; some were even covered over with layers of paint. Long believed either lost or destroyed, they were recovered during the 1980s by a combination of a scholarly investigation of the records documenting their creation and a physical search of the building complex. Today, after restoration, they are on long-term loan from the Housing Authority.

The Arts of Africa, the Pacific, and the Americas are located in the GREAT HALL (between the Museum Shop and the Cafe).

In 1995 the Museum reinstalled its collection of **African Art,** putting on view recent acquisitions and pieces long in storage. Works are arranged by cultural and geographic groupings. Highlights include a *Karanse mask* of the Mossi people of Burkina Faso; these masks with projections that tower 6 ft above the head are used in dances that honor ancestors. Other objects include a finely carved *wooden spoon* whose handle incorporates the figure of a water buffalo, an *iron altar* from the Fon people of the Republic of Benin (Nigeria), and a large *equestrian figure* from an altar shrine of the Yoruba people of Nigeria. From Zaire comes a *Kuba mask* of painted parchment, its face decorated with tiny shells and fringed with monkey fur. Also from Zaire is a collection of ivory ornaments.

Because most objects of African art are created from fragile materials, most of the works on view were made in the 19–20C, but there are also a few earlier pieces. Outstanding is a *terracotta head,* which may date back as far as the 11C. The representation of a sacred king from the Ife Kingdom of Nigeria is one of the oldest surviving sculptures from West Africa. A *carved ivory gong* (16–17C) from the Edo people of Benin is equally remarkable for its survival. The wooden figure (early 18C) of King Mishe MiShyaang maMbul of the Kuba people of Zaire is the earliest-known surviving example of a *Ndop,* a figure representing a king's spirit double.

In cases near those displaying African art are **Arts of the Pacific,** an exhibit that focuses on Melanesia (the group of islands northeast of Australia, including New Guinea, the Solomon Islands, and others). Many of the works here functioned as religious and ritual objects. The large basketry *ceremonial shield* (59.63) with shell inlay is one of about 20 known to exist today. The *Bioma figure,* from Papua New Guinea, was cut from a curved slab of wood and placed in the men's ceremonial house, where it was honored with offerings. There is also a remarkable *headdress* decorated with bright feathers, from the highland Huli people of Papua New Guinea.

Large cases in the middle of the room contain **Arts of Central and South America.** From the Huastec culture of Mexico (northern Veracruz) is an almost life-size *Life-Death Figure* (37.2897) carved of stone. The front of the figure shows a young man wearing a conical hat and large ear ornaments; on the back is a skeleton with a grinning skull. Also on display are stone carvings from Mexico and Costa Rica and examples of Panamanian and Colombian goldwork.

"Arts of the Andes" offers textiles, ceramics, and gold objects created between 300 B.C. and A.D. 800, representing the Paracas, Nasca, Topará, and Wari cultures. Among the textiles, one of the most important forms of Andean art, are two vividly colored embroidered mantles recovered from the Necropolis cemetery, where between 200 B.C. and A.D. 400 more than 400 mummy bundles were buried in the desert sand. Ceramics include a group of pots decorated in the early Nasca style, showing life forms native to the south coast of Peru. Also on view are five hammered-gold Nasca ornaments, including a ceremonial winged object that may have ornamented a headdress.

Displayed in a special case is perhaps the most famous piece in the South American collection, the *Paracas Textile.* This rectangular mantle, which has been designated the most exquisitely executed fabric ever produced in the western hemisphere, was excavated (1910–20) either at Nazca or at Paracas in southwest Peru, and is believed to date from c. 300 B.C.

The collection of **Native American Art** is strong in works by the *Northwest Coast, Southwest,* and *Plains Indians.* The Northwest Coast section includes the enormous totem poles and houseposts that have long been on view, as well as wooden potlatch figures, ivory shaman's charms, and a detailed scale model of a Haida chieftain's house built for the Chicago World's Columbian Exposition (1893). In the Plains section are objects from the Nathan Sturges Jarvis Collection, gathered in the 1830s and acquired by the Museum in 1950. Jarvis served as an army surgeon at Fort Snelling, Minn., in 1833–36 and, unlike many of his contemporaries, had the foresight to document what he found, giving his collection special importance. Included along with pipes and war clubs are carefully wrought garments, some decorated with beads, quillwork, and painted designs. Southwest Indian cultures are represented by ceramics and textiles, including a Hopi wedding blanket and several Navajo blankets. The Museum owns a fine collection of historic Pueblo pottery, including beautifully painted Zuni water jars. The collection also includes works by the great artists of modern Pueblo pottery, among them Maria Martinez and Margaret Tafoya.

Second Floor

The Museum's collections of **Islamic and Asian Art,** as well as the exhibition space for the **Department of Prints, Drawings, and Photography,** are on this floor.

Islamic Art. In the collection are ceramics, metalwork (e.g., a Pakistani astrolabe dating from A.D. 1650), glass—including enameled and gilded mosque lamps—and illuminated manuscripts, carpets, and textiles, among them beautiful rugs from the McMullan Collection. Among the manuscripts and books are Islamic prayer books, which illustrate the beauty and importance of Arabic calligraphy, and illuminated manuscripts, including beautifully illustrated poems from such Persian classics as the *Khamseh* or *Quintet* of the 12C poet Nizami. An exquisite watercolor rendering of a *Blue Iris* (86.23) is the only known depiction of a single flower by 17C Iranian artist Muhammad Zaman.

Indian Art includes Buddhist sculpture in stone and bronze. Particularly beautiful is a headless pale green limestone figure of a *Seated Buddha* (86.227.24) from the late 3C. The iconography of the throne upon which it sits suggests that the figure represents the historical Buddha, Sakyamuni, who gave his first sermon in the deer park at Sarnath. A large 9C granite *Buddha Meditating Under the Bodhi Tree* (84.132) shows the Buddha Sakyamuni attaining enlightenment as he meditates under the Bodhi tree; he is represented in a cross-legged meditative pose, his hands in the stylized gesture of contemplation. The Museum owns a collection of Mughal paintings, including pages from the *Hamza-nama,* a cycle of stories about Amir Hamza illustrated during the reign of the emperor Akbar.

A small selection of **Tibetan and Southeast Asian Art** includes a sandstone *head of Shiva* (83.182.5) from 10C Cambodia and a gilt-copper *Seated Maitreya* (67.80) from Tibet.

Japanese Art has been installed in galleries whose appointments suggest the austere serenity of a traditional Japanese room. Among the earlier pieces is a bell-shaped bronze ritual object or *dōtaku* (67.198) from the Yayoi period (2–3C) which corresponds to Japan's Bronze-Iron Age. These objects were buried on hills overlooking the rice paddies to propitiate the spirits of nature. A painted screen (39.87; c. 1624–44) from the Edo period depicts a *Cherry Blossom Viewing Picnic,* enjoyed by a young woman surrounded with her attendants and a young samurai accompanied by his retainers. Also in the Japanese exhibition are selections from the Museum's collection of woodblock prints and drawings.

Korean Art. Ceramics include a *celadon ewer* (56.138.1) with a lid in the shape of a lotus blossom and the knob resembling a lotus bud. A 17C *Dragon jar* (86.139) is decorated with the figure of a sinuous reptile, painted on with iron oxide.

Chinese Art. The collection contains bronze vessels, ceramics, sculpture, and paintings. Among the earliest pieces is a *bronze ritual vessel* (72.163;

BROOKLYN MUSEUM
Second Floor

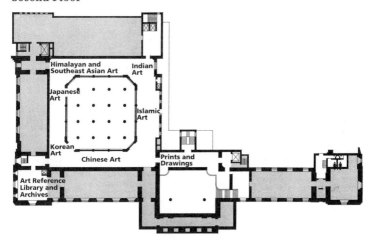

12C B.C.) from the Shang Dynasty in the form of an animal; its surface is covered with designs suggesting dragons and other animal forms. An earthenware *war horse* (37.128; 7–8C) from the T'ang Dynasty, glazed in brown, cream, green, and amber, was buried as a tomb figure, its appointed duty to serve its master in death as a real horse served him in life. One of the most beautifully shaped and decorated porcelain pieces is a blue-and-white *Jar with a design of fishes and water plants* (52.87.1) from the Yuan Dynasty of the 14C. Among the landscape paintings, considered one of the highest art forms along with calligraphy, is a fine *Landscape* showing an idealized view of trees and rocks by Lan Ying, a major painter of the late Ming and early Ch'ing dynasties.

Third Floor

Classical Art, including Greek and Roman antiquities, is arranged around the central courtyard. On one side of the court are Greek red- and black-figured vases, examples of gold jewelry, and Cycladic figures. A *Minoan jug* (37.13E) from Crete (c. 1575–1500 B.C.) is decorated with tentacled nautili and water plants, a form of decoration eminently suitable to the shape of the vase. On the other side of the courtyard are examples of Greek and Roman sculpture and Coptic art.

Ancient Middle Eastern Art. The gallery contains 12 Assyrian reliefs of gypseous alabaster from the palace of Ashurnasirpal II (9C B.C.) in Nimrud. The reliefs depict the king accomplishing his royal duties (performing religious rituals, hunting lions). Cuneiform inscriptions recount major events in the reign of a king who styled himself "King of the World." Also in the gallery are examples of vessels, small animal sculptures, and bronze work.

BROOKLYN MUSEUM
Third Floor

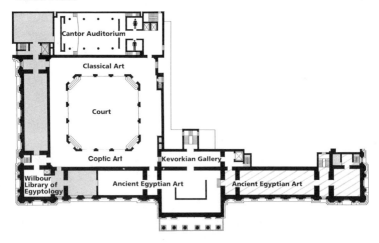

Egyptian Collection. The Brooklyn Museum owns one of the most famous Egyptian collections in the country. Although the Museum had begun collecting antiquities c. 1902, it was with the endowment of Charles Edwin Wilbour (1833–1896) that the collection gained impetus. Wilbour, a successful New York journalist, moved to Europe in the 1870s to study Egyptology in Paris and Heidelberg. After 1880 he spent his winters as an amateur Egyptologist in the Nile Valley, conducting excavations, recording ancient monuments, and building his own collection. When he died, his widow gave his collection and his Egyptological books to the Museum, and in 1932 his children gave an endowment that made possible the establishment of the Department of Egyptology.

The collection covers 4 millennia, from the Predynastic period (4000–3000 B.C.) to the Muslim conquest in the 7C A.D. Some 100 objects from the Predynastic to the Amarna periods and from the Roman and Coptic periods are on view in the EAST WING galleries near the galleries of Assyrian Art; these galleries are slated for reinstallation. Material from Dynasties 18 through 31 is displayed in the new galleries in the WEST WING (described at pp. 373–75).

Fourth Floor

The Museum's collection of decorative arts contains objects from the 14C to the present and 28 period rooms from the New York area and eastern United States. The decorative arts are displayed both in permanent galleries and in changing exhibitions.

PERIOD ROOMS

The most interesting *rooms* come from New York City. The oldest is the two-room Dutch vernacular *Jan Martense Schenck House* (c. 1675), built

*Cartonnage of Nespanetjerenpere, Egypt (prob. 945–271 B.C.) The
Brooklyn Museum's Egyptian collection is one of the finest in the
world, generously endowed by Charles Wilbour, who had made a fortune in the printing business, and became an amateur Egyptologist.
(The Brooklyn Museum. The Charles Edwin Wilbour Fund)*

on Mill Island in the former town of Flatlands (now part of Brooklyn). It
is furnished with period pieces that reflect the comfortable standard of
living Schenck achieved as a mill owner.

The *Nicholas Schenck House* (c. 1771) was built by Jan Martense
Schenck's grandson about a century later in what is now the Canarsie
section of Brooklyn. The furnishings, a mixture of 18C and 19C styles,

BROOKLYN MUSEUM
Fourth Floor

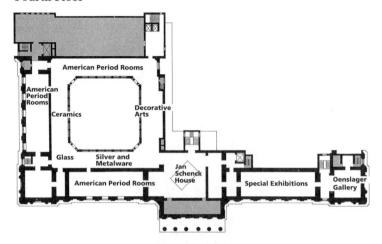

have been chosen to show the house as it might have looked after a remodeling in the early 19C, and to suggest the assimilation of Brooklyn's Dutch-American families.

The *John D. Rockefeller House* at 4 West 54th St was purchased by the oil tycoon in 1864–65 from Arabella Worsham, who later married railroad magnate Collis P. Huntington. The opulent Near Eastern appearance of the Moorish Smoking Room reflects the taste of Worsham, who had the house redecorated by interior designer George Schastey.

The most recent of the period rooms is the *Worgelt Study,* a room from a Park Ave apartment designed by the Parisian firm of Alavoine in 1928–30. The Art Deco appointments include olive and palisander wood paneling, a modernist metal window, and an abstract geometric panel behind the sofa.

Other period rooms include settings from Providence, R.I. (1772); Springfield, Mass. (1755); Saratoga Springs, N.Y. (1853); Edenton, N.C. (c. 1725); and Sumnerville, S.C. (1806).

Around the central courtyard are exhibitions of **Decorative Arts** arranged by type and period. In the 19C section is a piano dating from about 1870, decorated in the Egyptian Revival style, with sphinx heads peering forth at the performer. There is a selection of animal sculpture by Antoine-Louis Barye and an elaborately decorated bed by John Henry Belter, a German-born craftsman known for the pierced carving and elaborately curved shapes of his furniture.

The silver collection contains examples of 17–19C American silver, including pieces by New York's early Dutch and Huguenot silversmiths Cornelius van der Burgh, Nicholas Roosevelt, and Simeon Soumaine. More elaborate 19C pieces include a Gothic Revival-style pitcher and goblet by Zalmon Bostwick, who worked in Manhattan, and an elaborate tray (c. 1890) with a view of the Brooklyn Bridge, manufactured by Gor-

The Brooklyn Museum. Century Vase (1876), designed by Karl Mueller. Made at the Union Porcelain Works in Greenpoint, Brooklyn, this piece won a gold medal at the Philadelphia Centennial Exposition. In its florid, exuberant decoration, it expresses the optimism of the thriving post–Civil War economy.
(The Brooklyn Museum. Gift of Carll and Franklin Chace, in memory of their mother, Pastora Forest Smith Chace)

ham & Co. to commemorate the 25th wedding anniversary of Washington and Emily Roebling. There are selections of Jewish ritual silver and other metalwork, including pewter and toleware.

The glassware collection includes English and American pieces. The ceramics collection offers indigenous American types from salt-glazed stoneware and redware to American porcelain, with several pieces from

Brooklyn's Union Porcelain Works, located in the Greenpoint section of Brooklyn from the 1860s to the 1920s. The most elaborate of these, perhaps, is the *Century Vase* (43.25) exhibited at the Centennial Exhibition (Philadelphia, 1876), every inch covered with American symbolism, from a bas-relief of the Boston Tea Party to a telegraph pole indicating progress.

Fifth Floor

The collections of American painting and sculpture, European painting and sculpture, and contemporary art are shown on the fifth floor, accompanied at times by changing exhibitions of painting and sculpture. (For contemporary art, see West Wing, p. 375.)

American Painting and Sculpture. Galleries surrounding the central courtyard contain selections from the permanent collection arranged more or less chronologically. The exhibition changes from time to time.

> NOTE: Galleries are unlabeled; they form a large square around a central open court. The galleries are described here proceeding counterclockwise from the elevator lobby at the rear of the building, beginning with the first long gallery.

FIRST LONG GALLERY (turn right from elevator lobby). Here are 18C and 19C American paintings, including portraits, religious paintings, and genre scenes. Samuel F. B. Morse, *Jonas Platt* (c. 1827–28); *Mrs. William Eppes* (1769). John Singleton Copley, *Mrs. Benjamin Davis* (c. 1764). John Smibert, *Captain James Gooch* (c. 1740). Benjamin West, *The Angel of the Lord Announcing the Resurrection to the Three Marys at the Sepulchre* (1805). There are two portraits of *George Washington,* one (1776) by Charles Willson Peale; the other (1796), a rendering of the standing figure known as the Lansdowne portrait, by Gilbert Stuart. Francis Guy, *Winter Scene in Brooklyn* (1817–20). Guy, a British-born painter, brought with him the tradition of townscape painting; this view painted from Guy's window on Front St is one of the earliest American genre scenes. Raphaelle Peale, *Still Life with Peaches* (1821). Ammi Phillips, *Portrait of Betsey Beckwith* (1815–20).

Hiram Powers's nude marble statue, *The Greek Slave* (1869), of which the sculptor made six full-scale versions, was one of the most popular and frequently reproduced statues of the 19C. The figure refers to the Greek War of Independence during which Christian Greeks were sold into slavery by the Turks.

In the FIRST CORNER GALLERY are two portraits by Henry Inman, *Young Woman in a Blue Dress* (1815–20) and *Mrs. Robert Lowden* (1837). George Caleb Bingham, *Shooting for the Beef* (1850); Bingham moved as a child from Virginia to frontier Missouri and his art frequently reflects the spirit of pioneer life. William Sidney Mount, *Boys Caught Napping in a Field* (1844). Asher B. Durand, *First Harvest in the Wilderness* (1855).

SECOND LONG GALLERY. Thomas Cole, *View of Two Lakes and Mountain House, Catskill Mountains, Morning* (1844); a founder of the Hudson River School, Cole is often considered this country's first great landscapist. *The Pic-Nic* (1846); his travels in Europe made Cole well aware of the

BROOKLYN MUSEUM
Fifth Floor

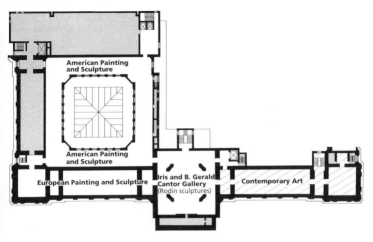

allegorical potential of landscape painting. The guitarist here has been interpreted as a symbol of the ephemeral nature of human endeavor.

Also often on view here in this gallery: George Inness, *Sunset Over the Sea* (1887); *June* (1882). John Frederick Kensett, *Lake George* (1870). Frederic Edwin Church, *Tropical Scenery* (1873); a student of Thomas Cole, Church went to South America and was inspired to paint the grandeur of scenery in climes more exotic than those sought by his mentor.

Emanuel Leutze, *Columbus Before the Queen* (1843). Leutze is best known for his rendering of *Washington Crossing the Delaware* (in the Metropolitan Museum of Art), but this painting touches on similar heroic themes; Leutze also painted portraits and landscapes. Daniel Huntington, *The Sketcher: Portrait of Mlle Rosina: A Jewess* (1858) and *The Republican Court* (1861). The second painting shows Martha Washington and her husband George presiding over a grand party in an imaginary palace, attended by the great men of the early republic, including Alexander Hamilton and Thomas Jefferson. Eastman Johnson, *The Ride for Liberty: The Fugitive Slaves* (c. 1862). After studying in Europe, Johnson returned to the United States (1855) and painted a series of genre scenes of the Old South, including a number of Civil War subjects.

SECOND CORNER GALLERY. Contains one of the best-known paintings in the collection, Albert Bierstadt's *A Storm in the Rocky Mountains—Mt. Rosalie* (1866). Bierstadt traveled the American West in 1859 and again in 1863 searching its momentous scenery for subjects; he made on-the-spot sketches which he later developed into grandiose paintings in his New York studio. Winslow Homer, *In the Mountains* (1877). Homer is best known for his seascapes and watercolors (of which the Museum owns a fine collection), but he also painted other subjects, including children at play, hunters in the Adirondack Mountains, and New England farm scenes. Eastman Johnson, *Not at Home* (c. 1872–80); while studying in

Europe, Johnson went to The Hague to study the Dutch masters of the 17C, whose interiors influenced this painting.

THIRD LONG GALLERY. Thomas Eakins, *Letitia Wilson Jordan* (1888). Alternately ignored and maligned by the public during much of his career, Eakins is now recognized as one of the preeminent American painters of the 19C; his portraits, influenced by Velázquez and Ribera, are remarkable for their revelation of character. *William Rush Carving His Allegorical Figure of the Schuylkill River* (1908): Eakins admired Philadelphia sculptor Rush (1756–1833), who progressed from crafting wooden ships' figureheads to carving freestanding sculpture; *Nymph of the Schuylkill* was one of his most famous works.

John H. Twachtman, *Meadow Flowers* (1890–1900); Twachtman, along with William Merritt Chase and Childe Hassam, belonged to The Ten, a group of painters from New York and Boston interested in Impressionism. Childe Hassam, *Poppies on the Isles of Shoals* (1890). Hassam, the best known of the American Impressionists, studied in Paris in 1886–89; this scene shows the gardens at a hotel on an island off the coast of New Hampshire. Paintings by John Singer Sargent are often on display here. John Singer Sargent, *Paul Helleu Sketching with His Wife.* Albert Pinkham Ryder, *The Hunter* (1870).

THIRD CORNER GALLERY (near entrance to Rodin Sculpture Gallery). William Glackens, *The Country Fair* (c. 1896). Robert Henri, *Laughing Girl* (1910). John Sloan, *Haymarket* (1907). Like other painters of the Ash Can School, Sloan depicted the lower rungs of society with determined realism. The Haymarket was a dance hall of doubtful reputation on Sixth Ave near 14th St.

FOURTH LONG GALLERY. Edward Hopper, *Macomb's Dam Bridge* (1935). Georgia O'Keeffe, *Yellow Leaves* (1926–28); *Pansy* (1926). Stuart Davis, *The Mellow Pad* (1945–46); this painting, with a palette of aquamarines, light blues, and fushia tones, has the density and rhythm typical of Davis's later work. Lyonel Feininger, *Zirchow V* (1916). Marsden Hartley, *Three Pears, Grapes and White Flowers* (1936); *The Last Look of John Donne* (1940).

FOURTH CORNER GALLERY (near elevator lobby). Milton Avery, *The Artist's Daughter by the Sea* (1943). Georgia O'Keeffe, *Ram's Head, White Hollyhock Hills* (1935). Arthur Dove, *Flat Surfaces* (1946). Stuart Davis, two *Landscapes* (1932, 1935). Charles Sheeler, *Incantation* (1946).

Rodin Sculpture Gallery. The central gallery contains the sculpture of Auguste Rodin. In the 1980s Iris and B. Gerald Cantor gave 58 Rodin sculptures to the Museum, a gift that included not only groups from the sculptor's best-known commissions *(The Gates of Hell, The Burghers of Calais,* and the *Monument to Balzac),* but portraits, parts of figures, erotic groups, and mythological subjects, which suggest the entire scope of a long, prolific, and influential career. The Museum owns 12 figures and studies from *The Burghers of Calais,* including *Eustache de St.-Pierre,* (1886–87), *Andrieu d'Andres* (1886–87), and two figures of *Pierre de Wiessant* (1886–87 and 1886–88). The group was commissioned by the town of Calais in 1884 as a memorial to Eustache de St.-Pierre, one of six citizens who in 1347 volunteered to surrender to the English to save the people of besieged Calais from starvation. The Museum also owns a large reduction of *The Age of Bronze* (1876); *The Helmet Maker's Wife* (1880s) from *The Gates of Hell;* and a *Monumental Head* and the *"F" Athlete* from the studies for the *Monument to Balzac.*

European Art. The collection, which has something of the character of a private collection of Old Masters, is installed in a single long gallery east of the Rodin Sculpture Gallery. It includes paintings from the 14–19C and is especially fortunate in its holdings of Italian paintings of the 14–15C and 19C French paintings.

> **NOTE:** The galleries containing the permanent collection of European paintings and sculpture are closed for renovation until early 1996. During the closing, important works are on view in the Rodin Sculpture Gallery. Sculptures include François Rude's terracotta model for *La Marseillaise* (1834–35), the final version of which decorates the Arc de Triomphe in Paris; and Jean-Baptiste Carpeaux, *Une Negresse* (1868).
>
> Among the paintings on view are Jean-Baptiste Corot, *Young Women of Sparta* (1868–70); Francisco de Goya, *Taddeo Bravo de Rivero* (1806); Edgar Degas, *Woman Drying Herself* (c. 1886–92); and Claude Monet, *The Doge's Palace in Venice* (1908).

West Wing

Handsomely redesigned by architects Arata Isozaki and James Stewart Polshek, the West Wing reopened in 1993. Long the home of the Brooklyn Museum Art School (now part of Pratt Institute), the West Wing now contains part of the Egyptian collection, space for temporary exhibitions, and the galleries for contemporary painting and sculpture. The only feature remaining from the original McKim, Mead & White structure is an openwork cast-iron staircase joining the three exhibition floors of the wing.

West Wing, Third Floor

Egyptian Collection. (For the introduction to the collection, see p. 366.) The galleries in the West Wing contain two exhibitions: a chronological exhibit of materials from the Amarna through the Ptolemaic periods, and a thematic exhibition, "Temples, Tombs, and the Egyptian Universe." Displayed within the six galleries are some 500 objects drawn from the Museum's famous collection of more than 8,000 artifacts and works of art.

Chronological Exhibit

GALLERY 1. *Late Dynasty 18 and Amarna Period (1347–1334 B.C.).* When Amunhotep IV became Pharoah in 1352 B.C., he briefly wrenched Egyptian religion from its former course, ordering the construction of shrines dedicated to a new god, a previously obscure solar diety known as the Aten. Amunhotep changed his name to Akhenaten and moved his court from Thebes to a site now known as Amarna. The style that developed during this artistically exhilarating period is one of heightened naturalism. The *Wilbour plaque* (16.48), found by Charles Edwin Wilbour, godfather of the Museum's Egyptian collections, probably was intended as a model for sculptors to follow; it depicts King Akhenaten and Nefertiti, his wife, in the naturalistic style of the period. *Relief of Nefertiti kissing one of her daughters* (60.197.8); the hand holding the ankh sign, or sign of life, is a ray of sunlight, which comes from the solar disk, symbol for the Aten. *Relief of Nefertiti* (78.39); limestone reliefs of scenes from everyday life; sandstone *reliefs of building scene* (61.195.1). *Relief with antelopes* (60.197.5); the naturalism of the Amarna style is evident in the opened mouths and flared nostrils of the antelopes. Faïence monkeys; limestone *torso of Akhenaten* (58.2).

GALLERY 2. *Late 18th Dynasty to Start of Roman Period (c. 1336 B.C. to c. 30 B.C.)*. The Late 18th Dynasty began with the reign of King Tutankhamun (c. 1336–1327 B.C.), who succeeded Akhenaten and strove to bring Egypt back to its former religious *orthodoxy*. Limestone block *statue of Ay* (66.174.1), c. 1336–1327 B.C. *Relief from Tomb of Horemheb* (32.103), c. 1352–1295 B.C., showing a group of soldiers honoring their lord; the two figures at the right are notable for their naturalism, one soldier with a flabby belly and both with unusually high foreheads and distinctive, ethnic features. Face from a *sarcophagus* (86.166) from Dynasty 18 or 19, c. 1336–1250 B.C. The *Model of a Temple Gateway* (49.183) from Dynasty 19, reign of Seti I (1294–1279 B.C.), was purchased at an auction in New York by Lt.-Cmdr. Henry H. Gorringe, who also engineered the transportation from Alexandria of the Obelisk that now stands in Central Park, known (inaccurately) as Cleopatra's Needle.

Dynasties 19 and 20 (c. 1295–1070 B.C.) are referred to as the **Ramesside Period,** since 11 of its 18 pharoahs were named Ramesses. The Ramesside *mummy board* (37.1520E), c. 1295–1185 B.C., shows the deceased in daily dress, not clothed as a mummy. A relief of *Ramesses II* (11.670), c. 1279–1213 B.C., shows the Pharoah with his arms raised offering worship. One of the highlights of the collection is the beautifully decorated *mummy cartonnage of Nespanetjerenpere* (35.1265), a priest of the god Amun. The cartonnage, made of linen or papyrus mixed with plaster, is painted with images that link Nespanetjerenpere with deities and their resurrection. *Statue of Sa-Iset the Younger* (47.120.2), c. 1279–1213 B.C.; the carved wooden figure with its elaborately pleated garment and an intricately curled wig represents an official who was a royal scribe and overseer of the granaries of Upper and Lower Egypt. *Cat and mouse* (37.51E), sketched on limestone, c. 1295–1070 B.C.

From the **Third Intermediate Period** (c. 1070–945 B.C.), a period of political and ethnic disunity, come small faïence objects, jewelry spacers, a papyrus fragment from the *Book of the Dead* (37.1782E), funerary figurines, and reliefs of the *Theban Divine Family* (87.184.1–2).

Late Period, Macedonian Period, and Ptolemaic Periods. The Macedonian period (332–305 B.C.) includes the reign of Alexander the Great, who freed Egypt from Persian domination. Alexander was succeeded by his general, Ptolemy I. From the Late period: *head of Wesirwer, Priest of Montu* (55.175), 384–342 B.C.; *statue of a priest of Amun* (52.89), 380–362 B.C.; *bust of a King* (37.37); alabaster *bust of Alexander the Great* (54.162); *head of Egyptian official* (58.30); steatite busts from Ptolemaic period. Among the objects of faïence and glass is a glass *figure of a King* (49.61.1–4), perhaps used as an inlay in a piece of furniture. Because of its curly hair, the diorite *head of a Priest*, also known as the *Brooklyn Black Head* (58.30), was formerly thought to have been influenced by Hellenistic

Greek sculpture. It is now believed to be typically Egyptian in style, since the representation of the hair has antecedents in earlier Egyptian art. *Egyptian Erotic Composition* (58.13): this erotic group of six male figures and a central nude woman wearing a curled wig has a religious component as well as the obvious erotic content; the male figures are identifiable by their sidelocks as priests associated with the god Osiris. The bound oryx usually symbolized the powers of evil. *Coffin for an ibis* (49.48); this extraordinary object was used to contain a mummified ibis, a bird believed to be a manifestation of the god Thoth. Mummified birds were used as votive offerings.

Temples and Tombs

In an unusual departure from the traditional chronological display of Egyptian art, this exhibit is organized thematically, to suggest the Egyptian concept of the universe and the influence of religion on art.

GALLERY 1. CORRIDOR. Sandstone stela, or funeral monument, of *Ramesses II* (1279–1213 B.C.); cult statuette of *Pepy I and the Horus falcon* (39.10; Dynasty 6, 2292–2252 B.C.). *Nun vessel* (40.298; 1539–1500 B.C.); in the center is a representation of the primordial waters *(nun)*, source of all existence.

GALLERIES 2 AND 3 introduce objects made either for temples or for tombs. On the right side of Gallery 2 are examples of temple art and photographs of archeological work at Karnak, where the Museum is excavating the temple of the goddess Mut. Near the entrance is the temple reconstruction, based on the model of the gateway in Gallery 2 of the Chronological Exhibit. Toward the rear of the gallery are exhibits on goddesses and on personal religion. A fragment of a *stela* (64.174; c. 1295–1070 B.C.) bears images of crocodiles; the crocodile at the top, crowned with a sun disk and plumes, is a divine figure, possibly a representation of the god Sobek.

On the left side of the gallery are pieces associated with tombs and tomb architecture, including objects for containing offerings, figurines associated with Osiris, god of the underworld, a *shrine-shaped coffin* (37.15E) of a man named Kemy, cartonnages, coffins, coffin lids, mummy boards, and other funeral equipment.

GALLERY 3 contains the 2,600-year-old *coffin and wrapped mummy of Thothirdes* (37.152), c. 664–525 B.C. A highlight of the exhibit is a group of 30 limestone blocks (8C B.C.) of carved reliefs (22 ft long) from the *tomb of the vizier Nespeqashuty* (52.131.1–32; 664–610 B.C.). For reasons unknown, the decoration was never completed and the reliefs therefore show the process of creation. Some of the details are finely carved; others seem to be merely roughed in, while certain details are only sketched on the stone with reddish paint.

West Wing, Fifth Floor

Contemporary Painting and Sculpture
Installations in the galleries are changed occasionally; the alphabetical list that follows reflects major holdings in the collection. Dottie Attie,

Barred from the Studio (1987). Francis Bacon, *Personnage* (1955–56). Romare Bearden, *At Connie's Inn* (1974). Robert Colescott, *Havana Corona* (1970). Joseph Cornell, *Starfish* (1954). Petah Coyne, *The Twins* (1987). Richard Diebenkorn, *Ocean Park No. 27* (1970). Helen Frankenthaler, *Lorelei* (1951).

Leon Golub, *Riot IV* (1983). Adolph Gottlieb, *Premonition of Evil* (1946); though best known as an Abstract Expressionist, Gottlieb was a member of The Ten (along with William Merritt Chase and Childe Hassam). Nancy Graves, *Mummy* (1969–70). Philip Guston, *Red Cloth* (1976). Hans Hofmann, *Towering Spaciousness* (1956). Alex Katz, *Ann* (1956). Yves Klein, *Accord Bleu (Relief)* (1958). Win Knowlton, *Untitled (Arms and Legs)* (1986). Barbara Kruger, *We Are Notifying You of a Change of Address* (1986). Sylvia Plimack Mangold, *The Inversion* (1984). Louise Nevelson, *First Personage* (1956). Tom Otterness, *Head* (1984).

Ad Reinhardt, *Untitled (Composition #104)* (1954–60). Larry Rivers, *July* (1956). Ursula von Rydingsvard, *Umarles (You Went and Died)* (1987–88). George Segal, *Girl on a Chair* (1970). David Smith, *Hero* (1952). Pat Steir, *Everlasting Waterfall* (1989).

EXHIBITION PROGRAM

The Museum has a varied and resourceful program of exhibitions and in recent years has offered some of the city's more engaging shows, some originating with the Museum, others traveling from elsewhere. The GRAND LOBBY, originally the main foyer of the Museum, offers site-specific installations by significant contemporary artists and has become an important venue for large-scale work of this kind. Among the installations have been Jenny Holzer's electronic signs and inscribed granite benches and Chris Burden's 5-ton sphere of rock and concrete suspended from the ceiling by a thick chain. Other artists who have created installations in the lobby include Ida Applebroog, Dale Chihuly, Alain Kirili, and Alison Saar.

In the LOBBY GALLERY, behind the Grand Lobby, Red Grooms mounted a long-term exhibition (1992–95), "Dame of the Narrows." This fanciful large-scale installation turned the gallery into a cheerful version of New York Harbor.

Other exhibitions are related to specific departments within the Museum. "Objects of Myth and Memory" brought from the storerooms some 250 American-Indian artifacts accumulated by R. Stewart Culin, an indefatigable collector, to whom the Museum owes many of its ethnological collections. "Biomorphism and Organic Abstraction in 20C Decorative Arts" drew on the permanent collection to explore designs of tableware, furniture, and other objects whose forms alluded to the sinuous curves found in nature. Included were examples of the work of Louis Comfort Tiffany, Alvar Aalto, and Frederick Kiesler. "Sigmar Polke," the first North American retrospective of this important contemporary German painter, filled a large area of the fifth floor with the work of a prolific yet enigmatic artist.

HISTORY

The Museum had its beginnings as a humble institution, the Brooklyn Apprentices' Library, founded (1824) when Brooklyn was a village at the western tip of Long

Island. The library had as its goal the collection of "books, maps, drawing apparatus, models of machinery, tools, and implements" that the youth of Brooklyn could
use "in learning the mechanic arts and . . . becoming useful and respectable members of society." By 1831 the library had decided to broaden its collections and commissioned its first painting, a portrait of one of the founders. In 1843 the
Apprentices' Library was consolidated with the Brooklyn Lyceum and renamed the
Brooklyn Institute, whose interests embraced natural history as well as fine arts.
The collection included birds, reptiles in jars in alcohol, a few mammals, various
fishes beautifully mounted, a large number of shells, and some minerals. Its exhibitions (which drew on loans from the citizens of Brooklyn) included "models of
machinery, curious specimens of nature and art . . . pieces of sculpture, and many
superior works in painting."

As the century progressed, the Institute suffered a dry period as enthusiasm for
its intellectual goals ebbed. When Francis Guy's famous *View of Brooklyn* was presented to the Institute by some of the painter's friends in 1878, the collection consisted of only 15 works, 7 of them portraits of Museum officers.

But when the Brooklyn Bridge linked the city to Manhattan, Brooklyn saw for
itself a great future as the residential outpost of New York. In keeping with Brooklyn's future as the "Home City of America," a city with its own cultural resources,
the Institute was reorganized as the Brooklyn Institute of Arts and Sciences, whose
departments ranged from anthropology to zoology.

In 1893 the Institute organized an architectural competition to provide a design
for the Museum building, to be constructed on land earlier set aside for a public
park. The City of Brooklyn appropriated funds for construction, an obligation
assumed by the City of New York when Brooklyn became a borough (1898). The
prestigious firm of McKim, Mead & White was selected. In 1897 the West Wing was
completed, the collections which had been in storage in nearby institutions were
installed, and the building was opened to the public.

Thereafter the Museum began an active program of excavations in Egypt; it also
continued collecting specimens for the natural history collection (including a model
of a humpback whale), and art, particularly Asian art. The opening of a subway stop
at the Museum (1920) boosted attendance. In 1934 the Museum decided to discon-
tinue the natural history collections, and to emphasize the fine arts, cultural history, and the social and industrial aspects of art.

In 1986 the Museum announced a competition to devise a new master plan to
provide for the Museum's growth into the 21C. The firm of Arata Isozaki & Assocs
with James Stewart Polshek & Partners was chosen for a design that has been much
admired by the architectural community at large. The first phase, the redesign of
the galleries in the West Wing and the reinstallation of the Egyptian collection, was
completed in 1993.

The Coney Island Museum (7)

1205–11 Riegelmann Boardwalk (at W. 12th St), Brooklyn, N.Y. 11224. Tel:
(718) 372-5159.

ADMISSION: Open Labor Day–Memorial Day: Sat and Sun 12–5, weather
permitting; Memorial Day–Labor Day: Wed–Sun 12–7. Closed Mon–Tues in
summer; weekdays in winter; winter weekend holidays. Admission charge.

Permanent exhibition. Arts Center with 150-seat theater has live shows,
often with Coney Island themes: circus sideshow, tattoo conventions,
annual Mermaid Parade, music series.

✘ Snack bar.

▥ Gift shop, with Coney Island T-shirts, antique postcards, souvenirs.

&. Museum accessible to wheelchairs. Restrooms not accessible.

⊘ No photography.

🚇 IND 6th Ave express or local (D or F train) to W. 8th St in Brooklyn; a pedestrian bridge from the subway station crosses Surf Ave and leads to Boardwalk. Turn right and walk west to W. 12th St.

🚗 Belt Pkwy, exit 7S (Ocean Pkwy South). Follow blue Beluga Whale signs to the Aquarium. Parking lot for Aquarium (fee) or on street.

The small Coney Island Museum (1991) offers a permanent exhibit that recalls the glory that was Coney Island, once America's premier amusement park. On view in about a dozen display cases are photos, postcards, souvenirs, and pieces of equipment that document the exhibits and amusements of Coney Island's former attractions, some of them of questionable taste by today's politically cautious standards.

PERMANENT EXHIBITION AND COLLECTION

The collection contains some 1,000 objects, not all on display. Among the big-ticket items are an original wicker Rolling Chair, in which leg-weary tourists could be pushed along the boardwalk; a Fun House mirror; and a Bumping Car from the 1950s, which allowed early off-road drivers to crash maniacally into one another. Perhaps the crowning item in the exhibit is a wooden racing horse from George C. Tilyou's Steeplechase Park, a 15-acre collection of rides and amusements fenced around by the gravity-driven steeplechase race. The Steeplechase itself was a scaled-down roller-coaster ride, though the horses are reputed to have achieved speeds of 60 mph.

Smaller exhibits include photos of Coney Island oddities, freak shows, and pleasure seekers. Also on view are videos, including a 4-min clip from 1904 engineered by Thomas Edison himself, and newsreels and documentaries from the '40s and '50s.

HISTORY

The Museum is an offshoot of Coney Island U.S.A., a nonprofit theater group that has been operating sideshows and other entertainments on the boardwalk since 1980. In 1985, the group moved into the present building and began offering exhibits of Coney Island memorabilia along with its shows; major renovations in 1991 allowed the group to open a separate gallery with a permanent exhibition.

Museum founder Dick D. Zigun began gathering Coney Island memorabilia during the late '70s. The collection now includes objects purchased from dealers, objects given by donors, and objects acquired by Coney Island fans who simply picked them up from derelict buildings and exhibits.

The Harbor Defense Museum of New York City (8)

Fort Hamilton (101st St and Fort Hamilton Pkwy), Brooklyn, N.Y. 11252. Tel: (718) 630-4349.

ADMISSION: Open Mon–Fri 1–4. Closed weekends, holidays except Memorial Day, July 4, and Veterans Day; closed for ten days over the Christmas holiday. Free.

Brochure for self-guided tour of post. Group tours by appointment. Changing exhibitions.

✗ Cafeteria on post nearby open to the public; closes at 3 P.M. on Sun.

†↑↘ Restroom on post nearby.

🖻 Sales desk with prints, booklets, pins, military insignia, T-shirts. Tours by appointment.

&. Accessible to wheelchairs.

◎ BMT Broadway local (R train) to 95th St / Fort Hamilton (4th Ave) in Brooklyn.

🚙 **From Manhattan:** Take Brooklyn Bridge to Brooklyn-Queens Expwy; east to Belt Pkwy, exit at Fort Hamilton / 4th Ave. Take 4th Ave; right onto Marine Ave, right again onto Fort Hamilton Pkwy; follow to end. Once within the fort, follow signs to the Museum near the Fort Hamilton Community Club. Parking available.

The only military museum (1980) in the city is located on Fort Hamilton (1825), an active army post, and housed in a renovated battery within the walls of the original fort. Changing exhibitions focus on the history of the fort and on local and state military units.

CHANGING EXHIBITIONS

There are about three exhibitions a year, which focus on military themes with an emphasis on local people and local military units. An exhibition on the 50th anniversary of Pearl Harbor, for example, focused on the experiences of a Brooklyn sailor stationed there during the attack.

PERMANENT COLLECTION

The Museum maintains a small permanent collection of arms and armor, guns, uniforms, banners, and other military equipment and memorabilia. It includes a helmet and body armor from the 16C, a polished brass-sheathed Gatling gun and other early machine guns, a Civil War torpedo (mine), and an 1841 flank howitzer, which was part of the original armament of Fort Hamilton.

Outside the fort on Fort Hamilton Pkwy is an experimental Rodman gun, the largest artillery piece of the Civil War. The bottle-shaped muzzle-loader with a 20-in bore bears the name of its designer, Thomas J. Rodman. The iron projectiles stacked by it weigh over 1,000 lbs apiece. At the Seventh Ave gate on the other side of the fort are two 16-in shells used by later breech-loading seacoast guns and by battleships.

THE BUILDING

The exhibits are housed in a building once known as the caponier (literally, "chicken coop"), a term that describes both its low structure and its function as a flank battery to protect the fort against attack from land.

HISTORY

The defense of New York's harbor began with the arrival of the Dutch, who built Fort Amsterdam where the Alexander Hamilton Custom House now stands at the foot of Broadway in Manhattan, and shortly afterwards added small blockhouses at strategic points some distance from their settlement. From then on, New York's defense has consisted of developing fortifications ever more distant from the center of the city, a process made possible by increasingly sophisticated technology.

The site where the present Fort Hamilton stands was used during the Revolutionary War, when a small battery fired (July 4, 1776) on the British warship *Asia,* inflicting modest damage before being silenced. During the rest of the Revolution, the site was held by the British.

Fort Hamilton itself (1825–31) dates from a period after the War of 1812, when the federal government undertook to defend the coastline by placing paired fortifications across strategic waterways. Constructed of granite, the fort faces the former Fort Wadsworth on Staten Island across the Narrows, a distance so short that even early muzzle-loaders could fire effectively on ships approaching the city.

Robert E. Lee served here in the 1840s, supervising waterproofing and the construction of new gun emplacements. Thomas "Stonewall" Jackson also served a tour of duty at Fort Hamilton, as did Abner Doubleday, who probably did not invent baseball but certainly was a hero at Gettysburg.

During the early years of this century, Forts Hamilton and Wadsworth were considered among the most powerful coastal defense complexes in the world, poised to rake any hostile ship passing through the Narrows with an estimated 100 hits per minute.

Memorial Arch, Grand Army Plaza (9)

Grand Army Plaza (intersection of Flatbush Ave and Eastern Pkwy at Prospect Park), Brooklyn, N.Y. 11225. Tel: (718) 965-8999 for recorded information about park events. To reach a live person, call (718) 965-8951.

ADMISSION: Open only during exhibitions: spring–fall weekends, holidays 11–5. Arch has no heating system, no running water; closed late autumn–late spring. Call ahead for information. Free.

Changing exhibitions of sculpture, community art.

✗ No restaurant.

🛗 Not accessible to wheelchairs.

🚊 IRT 7th Ave express (train 2 or 3) to Eastern Pkwy / Brooklyn Museum at Grand Army Plaza.

🚌 **From Manhattan:** Take Brooklyn Bridge left onto Tillary St, right onto Flatbush Ave to Grand Army Plaza. **Parking** on the street or in large lot (fee) behind Brooklyn Museum, a few blocks away; lot accessible from Washington Ave.

The triumphal arch in Grand Army Plaza, built to honor the Union dead in the Civil War, has served since 1981 as an unusual art gallery. Originally the arch was intended to display Civil War memorabilia, but the dank, windowless interior remained unused until the New York City Department of Parks and Recreation determined to use the space for sculpture exhibitions.

Two six-story circular staircases with newel posts shaped like battle-axes lead to the exhibition rooms. In nice weather an outdoor observation deck atop the arch offers a splendid view of Brooklyn and the Manhattan skyline.

THE ARCH

John H. Duncan (architect of Grant's Tomb in Manhattan) designed the 80-ft arch, erected in 1892. Six years later a sculptural group by Frederick W. MacMonnies was added atop the structure. The winged female figure driving a four-horse chariot *(quadriga)* and flanked by winged trumpet-

The Memorial Arch at Grand Army Plaza in Brooklyn was erected to
celebrate the Union Victory, and its interior rooms were intended to
display Civil War memorabilia. Its architect, John H. Duncan,
designed Grant's Tomb. Today, it holds changing exhibitions of art.
(Photo: Tom McGovern)

ers is commonly believed to represent Victory, but according to park
archives she is Columbia, the Union.

On pedestals on the arch's legs two monumental groups (1901) also by
MacMonnies represent the Army (west leg) and the Navy (east leg). Above
the inner doorway to the arch are bas-reliefs of Abraham Lincoln and
Ulysses S. Grant (both 1894; Thomas Eakins and William R. O'Donovan).

EXHIBITION PROGRAM

In recent years, there have been exhibitions of contemporary sculpture. A belated centennial celebration in 1994 explored the arch's historic sculpture. Other shows focus on community art, e.g., "Who Lives Here," a doll exhibit with mural backdrops created by children working on projects at the Lefferts Homestead Children's Museum.

The New York Transit Museum (10)

In former subway station at corner of Boerum Place and Schermerhorn St, Brooklyn, N.Y. 11201. Tel: (718) 330-3060.

ADMISSION: Open Tues–Fri 10–4; Sat–Sun 12–5. Closed Mon, major holidays. Admission charge.

Guided tours for groups, occasional lectures and workshops, changing exhibitions.

✗ No restaurant.

🛍 Gift shop with transit souvenirs, toys, T-shirts, postcards. Also transit memorabilia (old tokens, even old bus-fare boxes).

♿ Not accessible to wheelchairs.

🚇 IRT Broadway-7th Ave local or express (train 2 or 3) or IRT Lexington Ave express (train 4 or 5) to Borough Hall. IND 8th Ave express or local (A or C train) or 6th Ave (F train) to Jay St / Borough Hall. BMT Nassau line (M train) or Broadway line (N or R train) to Court St.

This two-level subterranean Museum (opened 1976) offers subway buffs the chance to explore the history of the world's second-largest mass transit system (704 miles of track serving 458 stations in four boroughs).

PERMANENT COLLECTION

Berthed at the platforms of what was once the Hoyt-Schermerhorn Station are 18 classic *subway and trolley cars,* dating back to 1903, a year before the first subway began running. The cars have been completely restored and refurbished. Other exhibits include examples of turnstiles (some anticipating a long-vanished 5-cent fare) and collection boxes. Displays of the mosaics from IRT and BMT stations include graphic representations of stations (e.g., the beaver for Astor Place), which were intended partly as decoration and partly as visual aids for immigrants who could not read English. A display of antique maps from the late 1800s, printed privately by hotels and banks, not only shows the development of the system but suggests the importance of public transit to the city's commerce.

Other displays include historical photographs, architectural drawings of the under-river tunnels and over-valley viaducts that were designed in the early 20C for the first section of the IRT line, and an informal narrative history of unusual subway events.

EXHIBITION PROGRAM

On occasion the Museum mounts a special program, e.g., the Bus Festival, for which the Transit Authority scrubbed and waxed eight vintage buses

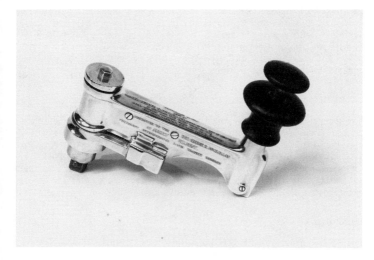

The New York Transit Museum. Controller's handle, made of silver and designed by Tiffany and Co., 1904, used to start the first New York subway train from City Hall station.
(Permanent Collection of the New-York Historical Society)

and parked them outside the Museum. Visitors could climb aboard a 1917 wooden double-decker model or inspect a Transit Police "bust" bus, a mobile police station. One highlight was a model of the 1949 bus that Jackie Gleason drove in the television show *The Honeymooners*.

Other exhibitions have focused on subjects less strictly related to the transit system, e.g., photographs of the city's boroughs by Harvey Wang, who documented the outlying regions of the city from Breezy Point to the Brooklyn Bridge.

Prospect Park: The Boathouse Visitor Center (11)

Prospect Park, on the Lullwater (near Lincoln Rd entrance), Brooklyn, N.Y. 11225. Tel: (718) 287-3474.

ADMISSION: Open only mid-May–mid-Oct: holidays and Sat 11–6; Sun 9–6. Closed in winter.

Changing exhibitions; Prospect Park has an extensive program of events for children and adults.

✗ Cafe with snacks, sodas, coffee.

🛍 Shop with T-shirts, postcards, maps, books about Prospect Park.

♿ Accessible to wheelchairs.

🚊 IND 6th Ave express (D train) or Franklin Ave shuttle to Prospect Park stop. Walk south through park.

Prospect Park, 526 acres of meadows, woods, and lakes laid out by Frederick Law Olmsted and Calvert Vaux in 1866–67 after they had already designed Central Park, is thought by many to be their masterpiece. The Boathouse Visitor Center (built 1905; opened as Visitor Center 1984) offers information about the park, its history, and its programs, and occasional changing exhibitions.

EXHIBITION PROGRAM

For several years an outdoor Sculpture Walk near the Boathouse offered contemporary sculpture based on park-related themes. Current exhibits are geared to the community and park preservation. In "Letters to a Forest," mounted in conjunction with a woodlands restoration project, letters from local children and prominent writers were pinned to a fence enclosing a 40-ft area where native species were replanted. As one area is reforested, the fence will be moved to a new location in the park.

THE BUILDING

Built by architects Frank J. Helmle and Ulrich J. Huberty, who designed other architecture in Prospect Park, the center originally served as a boat-renting office, with a soda fountain and enclosed kitchen on the ground floor and a dining hall upstairs, served by dumbwaiters at the east corners of the building. French doors opened onto the terrace upstairs; downstairs the building was open, except for the kitchen. As patterns of park usage changed, the Boathouse fell into disuse and deteriorated until it was refurbished for its present use.

Prospect Park: Lefferts Homestead Children's Museum (12)

In Prospect Park (on Flatbush Ave near the intersection with Empire Blvd, next to Prospect Park Carousel), Brooklyn, N.Y. 11215. Tel: (718) 965-6505.

ADMISSION: Open Sat and Sun 12–4; hours may vary seasonally. Arrange for tours at other times by calling (718) 965-6505. Free.

Craft workshops and demonstrations, children's programs, lectures, seasonal festivals.

✗ No restaurant. Food available at Boathouse Visitor Center and Carousel.

▥ Gift items include notecards, reproductions, items related to current exhibitions.

♿ Not currently accessible to wheelchairs; call for most recent information.

🚇 IND 6th Ave express (D train) to Prospect Park station.

The Lefferts Homestead (opened as a museum 1918), a clapboarded farmhouse built in 1777–83, offers a glimpse into Brooklyn's past, with period rooms, workshops and demonstrations (many of which explore crafts of the early 19C), and changing exhibitions. Built during the American Revolution, the homestead is a fine example of Dutch-American architecture.

THE BUILDING

The homestead exemplifies the last stage of Dutch vernacular architecture on Long Island. The smaller wing, now used as a caretaker's apartment, may have been built first, as the steeply sloping roof, large cooking fireplace (now bricked up), and overhanging eaves suggest. During a recent renovation of the roof, it was discovered that the two wings were originally separate buildings.

The larger wing has a gambrel (double-pitched) roof, a feature of Dutch Colonial architecture that dates back to the beginning of the 18C. The leaded transom and sidelights decorating the front door and the arched dormer windows are features of the American Federal style. Although its origin is not known, the split front door, commonly called a "Dutch door," is probably not original.

PERIOD ROOMS

The floor plan is typically Dutch, with a central hall and four rooms. The FRONT PARLOR to the left of the entrance hall is the most formal room in the house. Included among the furnishings is a tall clock that belonged to the Lefferts family. Behind this PARLOR is a BEDROOM with a corner fireplace, used for heating. On the other side of the central hallway is the DOUBLE PARLOR, where the Lefferts family dined. The room is fitted out as a playroom and is used for changing exhibitions and public programs.

EXHIBITION PROGRAM

The Museum offers a program of changing exhibitions that focus on family life in the Lefferts Homestead during the early decades of the 19C. An exhibition on the paper cutouts or silhouettes by Abigail Lefferts (1759–1847) recalled a popular 19C craft. Other exhibitions have examined the lives of women and children in the early 19C. A selection of household implements and decorative arts from the permanent collection is always on display, the choice influenced by the seasons. "The Unsolved Mystery of History" uses paintings, documents, and objects to explore the writing of history and the story of people who lived in the homestead.

HISTORY

By the time of the Revolutionary War, the Lefferts family, originally of Dutch descent, had become prominent in King's County (modern Brooklyn). Peter Lefferts, a wealthy farmer and county judge, lived in a farmhouse that had been built by his great grandfather on what is now Flatbush Ave. On Aug 23, 1776, three days before the Battle of Long Island, American soldiers burned the Lefferts House to prevent its being used by the British.

In 1777, Peter Lefferts began rebuilding the homestead on the old foundations, a reconstruction completed in 1783. After the war, Lefferts, a lieutenant in the Continental Army, became one of the county's most prosperous farmers, working some 250 acres with the help of perhaps a dozen slaves. His principal cash crops were flax, wheat, and rye, at least until the mid-1820s, when the Erie Canal diminished the importance of the Atlantic seaboard as an agricultural producer. Thereafter the kitchen garden with its fruits and vegetables became a principal source of income from the property.

Lefferts, who served as a county judge, a pillar of the Dutch Reformed Church in Flatbush, and a delegate to the state convention in Poughkeepsie (1788) where New

York ratified the U.S. Constitution, died in 1791, and the property passed to his second wife, Femmetje Suydam Lefferts, and their son John, then six years old.

John, who grew up to become an attorney and a state senator, married Maria Lott and had two children, Gertrude (b. 1824) and John (b. 1826). It is this phase in the history of the house that the Museum interprets through its period rooms, craft programs, and other exhibitions. As a married woman, Gertrude Lefferts Vanderbilt wrote *A Social History of Flatbush* (1881), which the Museum uses extensively in researching its programs.

The Lefferts family continued to occupy the homestead, making occasional improvements, until 1918, when they donated it to the city. The city moved the building from its location at 563 Flatbush Ave (between Maple and Midwood Sts) to its present site in the park.

Prospect Park Wildlife Center (formerly Prospect Park Zoo) (13)

450 Flatbush Ave, Brooklyn, N.Y. 11215. Entrances on Flatbush Ave near Empire Blvd and Ocean Ave and in the park near Lefferts Homestead. Tel: (718) 399-7333.

ADMISSION: The Wildlife Center opens every day of the year at 10 A.M. Closing times: April–Oct: weekdays at 5; weekends and holidays at 5:30. Nov–March: every day at 4:30. Admission charge. Children under 3 free.

Educational programs. Weekend family activities.

✖ Cafeteria.

🏛 Gift shop, with souvenirs, hats, gifts with zoological themes.

♿ Accessible to wheelchairs.

⊘ No bicycles, radios, skateboards, or pets. Children under 16 must be accompanied by an older chaperone.

🚇 IND 6th Ave express (D train) to Prospect Park station.

🚗 **From Manhattan:** Take the Manhattan Bridge to Flatbush Ave. Follow Flatbush Ave south through the park to the Wildlife Center. **Parking** available on Flatbush Ave or in the parking lot (fee) behind the Brooklyn Museum, accessible from Washington Ave.

After a four-year renovation the Prospect Park Zoo (1895) reopened in 1993 as the Prospect Park Wildlife Center, a 14-acre state-of-the-art zoo, whose engaging and educational exhibits are directed especially at children.

EXHIBITIONS

In the center of the exhibit space is the *Sea Lion Pool,* twice as large as its predecessor, furnished with new rockwork suggesting a California coastal environment. The *World of Animals,* an outdoor exhibit, encourages young visitors to explore the relationship between animals and their habitat. Visitors can climb into child-sized birds' nests or enjoy the sociability of a prairie dog town. *Animal Lifestyles,* an indoor exhibit, presents reptiles, fish, birds, and mammals in settings that suggest how an animal's habitat determines its lifestyle. A highlight of the area is the exhibition of Hamadryas baboons; visitors can watch these intelligent and sociable primates in a naturalistic setting. Other animals displayed are blind cave fish, snapping turtles, tortoises, lizards, and red-headed parrot finches. *Animals in Our Lives* includes an outdoor barnyard exhibit with goats, sheep, and cows, and a pet exhibit, where volunteers from the Education Department discuss the history of domestication and give tips on pet care.

Near the south entrance to the zoo are colored aluminum sculptures by Mags Harries, including an Octopus Gateway, a chameleon, a snake eating a frog, and some garden eels. Boxwood has been planted near the sculptures: it will grow into the work, creating large topiary animals.

HISTORY

By the end of the 19C a small urban menagerie was growing in Prospect Park. The park had been laid out (1866–67) by Frederick Law Olmsted and Calvert Vaux, also the designers of Central Park. An 1895 report mentions a collection of geese, ducks, swans, eagles, elk, white deer, one Brahma cow, and one "buffalo bull," as well as rabbits and dogs. Donations of animals to the menagerie continued, and by 1902 included an alligator, a ring tailed monkey, flamingos, a silver fox, and porcupines.

By 1915 the zoo also contained bears, but no lions or members of the cat family, and so $3,000 was raised to purchase about 90 animals from a European collection. A public subscription brought in more than $16,000 needed to build an appropriate shelter for the animals.

During the Depression under the aegis of powerful Parks Commissioner Robert Moses, the zoo was completely rebuilt. Rocky dens of huge boulders were constructed for the bears and barrier moats 18 ft deep replaced barred cages. A grouping of neat brick buildings was created around a large rotunda for elephants and hippos. WPA artists decorated the buildings with murals and bas-reliefs illustrating scenes from Kipling's *Jungle Books*. The new zoo was dedicated with fanfare and celebration on July 3, 1935. Among its favorite attractions were the sea lion pool and huge decorative cages with hawks and eagles.

By the 1980s the Zoo had become obsolete and its animal enclosures were no longer considered adequate or humane. The Zoo closed (1989) for a major renovation, jointly undertaken by the New York City Parks and Recreation Department and the New York Zoological Society. Important structures from the 1935 restoration were refurbished, old statuary was reinstalled. The Center is now managed by the Wildlife Conservation Society.

The Rotunda Gallery (14)

1 Pierrepont Place, entrance at 33 Clinton St, Brooklyn, N.Y. 11201. Tel: (718) 875-4047.

ADMISSION: Open Tues–Fri noon–5; Sat 11–4. Closed Sun, Mon, summer months, and holidays. Free.

Changing exhibitions. Occasional lectures, gallery talks, and performances to supplement particular exhibitions.

✗ No restaurant.

🏛 No gift shop.

♿ Accessible to wheelchairs.

🚇 IRT 7th Ave express (train 2 or 3) to Borough Hall. IRT Lexington Ave express (train 4 or 5) to Borough Hall. BMT Broadway Nassau St local (M train) or BMT Broadway local (R train) to Court St. IND 8th Ave express (A train) or 6th Ave local (F train) to Jay St / Borough Hall.

Founded in 1981, the Rotunda Gallery offers four exhibitions each year of work by artists who are connected to Brooklyn by birth, residence, training, subject matter, or even by studio space. The artists range from the well known, e.g., Judy Pfaff, who maintains a studio in the Greenpoint section of the borough, to emerging artists, to Brooklyn children.

In 1993, the gallery moved from its former home in the Brooklyn War Memorial to its present location.

The Pieter Claesen Wyckoff House Museum (15)

5902 Clarendon Rd (Ralph Ave), Brooklyn, N.Y. 11203; mailing address P.O. Box 100-376, Brooklyn, N.Y. 11210. Tel: (718) 629-5400.

ADMISSION: Open Thurs and Fri 12–5. Groups by appointment. Admission charge.

Educational programs; craft demonstrations; lectures; community events. Group tours by appointment.

✗ No restaurant.

🏛 No gift shop. Mail order catalogue.

⚜ Not accessible to wheelchairs.

🚇 IND 6th Ave express (D train) to Newkirk Ave. Take B8 bus to E. 59th St / Beverly Rd. Follow 59th St one block south to museum.

🚗 **From Manhattan:** Take Brooklyn-Battery Tunnel to Gowanus Expwy; continue south to Shore Pkwy; go east on Shore (Belt) Pkwy. Belt Pkwy to Flatbush Ave exit. Continue north on Flatbush Ave to Clarendon Rd; turn right onto Clarendon Rd and follow it to house, located between E. 59th St and Ralph Ave. Street parking only.

The Pieter Claesen Wyckoff House in the Flatlands section of Brooklyn is the oldest building in New York City and one of the oldest wooden structures in the nation. Rescued from demolition, restored, and opened as a museum (1982), the house offers a collection of furniture and artifacts that reflect life in the town of New Amersfoort (later Flatlands) during the 17–18C.

THE BUILDING

The oldest part of the house, the kitchen wing, dates from about 1652, with additions made c. 1740 and 1819. The exterior exemplifies Dutch Colonial vernacular architecture, with wide overhanging eaves, a double-hung ("Dutch") door, and "fish scale" shingles, some original. Although only one story high, the house has a full attic (not open to the public), reached by a boxed-in stairway. The walls of the original house are insulated with mud and wattles (reeds, corn cobs, even acorns) and the floors are laid with wide pine flooring.

PERIOD ROOMS

On display are the FORMAL PARLOR, seldom used by the family, and the MIDDLE PARLOR, a kind of family room. In the parlors are examples of

Dutch and Federal period furniture, which suggest domestic life in the house during different eras of its long history. No room is furnished strictly according to a particular period; each contains objects similar to those used by the family during its long residence. The *cradle* (1700s) in the Middle Parlor was made by one of several Pieter Wyckoffs in the family. The KITCHEN has an unusual open or jambless fireplace. Some of the implements belonged to the Wyckoffs; of particular interest are patterned *waffle* and *wafer irons* (1700s), initialed "PW" and "GW," probably the initials of the bride and groom who received this traditional wedding gift.

HISTORY

In 1636, Wouter van Twiller, governor general of New Amsterdam (as New York was called during the period of Dutch domination), purchased from the Canarsie Indians some 15,000 acres, including the land on which the house presently stands. A year later Pieter Claesen came to America as an illiterate indentured servant. Claesen rose to prosperity as a farmer, eventually becoming superintendant of the estates of Peter Stuyvesant, who succeeded van Twiller as governor. Some time after 1664, when the English took the colony from the Dutch, Claesen took the name Wyckoff. The English required that all Dutch property holders use a "proper" surname, as opposed to a patronymic, and since "Claesen" simply meant that Pieter was Nicholas's son (his own first four children had been baptized Pieterse after their father), Claesen chose "Wyckoff" from the place in East Friesland (now Germany) whence he had emigrated.

The house remained in the Wyckoff family until 1902. In the 1960s, the Wyckoff House and Assoc. purchased it and subsequently donated it to the City of New York, which restored the building (1982), analyzing original construction techniques and preserving as many of the original materials as possible. New beams were crafted by hand, nails were forged on site, old glass was used to replace broken windowpanes, and the original fireplace tiles and paint colors were replicated.

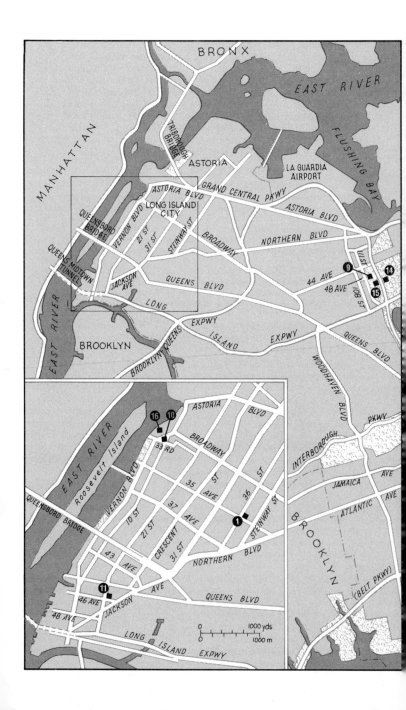

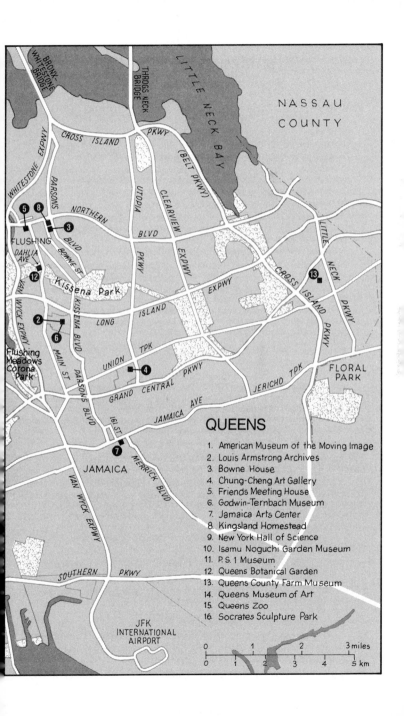

QUEENS

1. American Museum of the Moving Image
2. Louis Armstrong Archives
3. Bowne House
4. Chung-Cheng Art Gallery
5. Friends Meeting House
6. Godwin-Ternbach Museum
7. Jamaica Arts Center
8. Kingsland Homestead
9. New York Hall of Science
10. Isamu Noguchi Garden Museum
11. P.S. 1 Museum
12. Queens Botanical Garden
13. Queens County Farm Museum
14. Queens Museum of Art
15. Queens Zoo
16. Socrates Sculpture Park

NASSAU COUNTY

LITTLE NECK BAY

BRONX WHITESTONE BRIDGE

THROGS NECK BRIDGE

CROSS ISLAND PKWY

(BELT PKWY)

WHITESTONE EXPWY

PARSONS BLVD

NORTHERN BLVD

FLUSHING

DAHLIA AVE

VAN WYCK EXPWY

BOWNE ST

Kissena Park

KISSENA BLVD

LONG ISLAND EXPWY

UTOPIA PKWY

CLEARVIEW EXPWY

CROSS ISLAND PKWY

LITTLE NECK PKWY

Flushing Meadows Corona Park

MAIN ST

PARSONS BLVD

UNION TPK

GRAND CENTRAL PKWY

JERICHO TPK

FLORAL PARK

JAMAICA AVE

161 ST

MERRICK BLVD

JAMAICA

VAN WYCK EXPWY

SOUTHERN PKWY

JFK INTERNATIONAL AIRPORT

| 0 | 1 | 2 | 3 miles |
| 0 | 1 | 2 | 3 | 4 | 5 km |

MUSEUMS IN QUEENS

The American Museum of the Moving Image (1)

35th Ave at 36th St, Astoria, N.Y. 11106. Tel: (718) 784-0077.

ADMISSION: Open Tues–Fri 12–5; Sat and Sun 11–6. Closed Mon, New Year's Day, July 4, Thanksgiving, and Christmas Day. Admission charge.

Changing exhibitions; video and film screenings; lectures, symposia, demonstrations, conferences. Tours of Museum highlights available for adults Wed–Sat afternoons by appointment only.

✗ No restaurant.

🏛 Gift shop well stocked with historical and critical books on movies and TV, biographies, children's books, gift books. Posters, notecards, toys, games, and jewelry.

♿ Accessible to wheelchairs.

🚫 No strollers permitted. Children under 12 must be accompanied by an adult.

🚇 BMT Broadway local (R train) or Brooklyn-Queens crosstown (G train) to Steinway St in Astoria (exit at 34th Ave end of station). Walk along Steinway St to 35th Ave. Turn right on 35th Ave. Proceed to 36th St. IND 8th Ave local (E train) or 6th Ave local (F train) to Queens Plaza (from Manhattan) or Roosevelt Ave (from points east). Cross platform to R or G train. Exit at Steinway St. Proceed as above. BMT Broadway express (N train) to Broadway in Astoria. Walk along Broadway to 36th St. Turn right on 36th St. Proceed to 35th Ave.

🚗 From Manhattan via Queensborough Bridge: Lower roadway; exit onto Northern Blvd; follow it to Steinway St. Turn left onto Steinway St, then left onto 35th Ave. Proceed to 36th St. Upper roadway; follow signs to 21st St to 35th Ave; then right onto 35th Ave. Proceed to 36th St. From Upper Manhattan via Triborough Bridge: Exit at 31st St (first exit). Turn right onto 31st St. Follow it to 35th Ave. Turn left onto 35th Ave. Proceed to 36th St. Street parking only.

The American Museum of the Moving Image (1988), located in the former East Coast facility of Paramount Pictures, is currently the only museum in the country specifically dedicated to film, television, and video. Its programs include screenings of film and video programs, installations, tours, and changing exhibitions from a collection of more than 80,000 artifacts of movie and TV memorabilia.

PERMANENT COLLECTION

The permanent collection is a vast gathering of memorabilia relating to films, TV, and video, much of it donated. Paul Newman gave parts of the set for the TV remake of *The Glass Menagerie* which he directed in 1987; Maurice Seiderman, whom Orson Welles hailed as the greatest makeup man in the world, left an extensive collection.

Treasures from the collection are displayed in the permanent exhibition, entitled "Behind the Screen: Producing, Promoting, and Exhibiting Motion Pictures and Television." The exhibition highlights the contributions of writers, directors, makeup artists, and others, who collaborate in the gigantic effort of filmmaking. It also explores the impact of movies and TV on popular culture. On view are such collectibles as Shirley Temple dolls, *Star Wars* teacups, and lunch boxes sporting images of Gomer Pyle and Darth Vader. Computerized interactive displays offer starstruck visitors the opportunity to see how they would look if they were as well endowed as Marilyn Monroe *(Seven Year Itch)* or as muscular as Sylvester Stallone *(Rocky)*. There are costumes (Don Johnson's Armani suits from *Miami Vice*), vintage fan magazines, the actual Yellow Brick Road (though not the ruby slippers) from *The Wizard of Oz*, and the production drawings from *The Age of Innocence*.

Among the three installations especially commissioned for the Museum are Nam June Paik's 80-monitor *Get-away Car*, Jim Isermann's *TV Lounge*, a recreation of a 1960s-style viewing room complete with conversation pit, yellow linoleum floor, and built-in seating covered in cowhide and protected with plastic. The *pièce de résistance*, however, is *Tut's Fever*, a tongue-in-cheek rendering by Red Grooms and Lysiane Luong of a 1920s movie palace. Egyptoid figures of movie greats (Mae West behind the candy counter selling Tut's Nuts, James Dean laid out in a mummy case, rows of seats slipcovered with fabric that depicts Rita Hayworth as Cleopatra), and a painted audience wearing 3-D glasses fill the theater.

CHANGING EXHIBITIONS

Special exhibitions concentrate on a specific profession within the industry, a cultural or social theme, or a particular film or TV genre. "Masterpieces of Moving Image Technology" offered 58 technological achievements ranged from the simple Zoetrope (with images inside a spinning drum with viewing slits) to sophisticated modern equipment. "Changing Faces" focused on the work of makeup artists and hairstylists who have influenced notions of beauty or created monsters from earth and elsewhere. On view were plaster casts of Orson Welles's nose—during *Citizen Kane*, he was transformed from a man in his 20s to an octogenarian—a full-size mechanical figure of the possessed Linda Blair for *The Exorcist*, the wigs Elizabeth Taylor wore in *Cleopatra*, and glamour photographs, including a before-and-after sequence of Joan Crawford which suggests that beauty was, at least in part, in the hand of the makeup artist.

SCREENINGS

The Museum offers programs of film and video screenings in two state-of-the-art facilities. In addition to the short subjects and serials shown in Tut's Theater, there are weekend programs that may deal with specific themes or showcase the work of a particular director, actor, or cinematographer. "The Black New Wave" was the first major museum retrospective to explore the contemporary resurgence of black filmmaking by such directors as John Singleton, Spike Lee, and Matty Rich.

HISTORY

In the days before Hollywood became the mecca of the film industry, the Astoria Studios were an important center for film production. The Famous Players-Lasky Company, which released films through Paramount and later adopted that name, opened here in 1920. The location, convenient to Manhattan, brought technical crews and extras, stars, writers, and executives to the area. Between the two world wars, Billie Burk, Lillian and Dorothy Gish, W. C. Fields, Clara Bow, Fay Wray, Adolphe Menjou, Claudette Colbert, Jimmy Durante, Gloria Swanson, Maurice Chevalier, Paul Robeson, Rudy Vallee, and Rudolf Valentino, among others, deployed their talents before the cameras of Astoria.

When the movie industry gravitated westward, the fortunes of the studios declined. As the Eastern Service Studios, its facilities were devoted to educational films and comic shorts, and during World War II the Signal Corps of the U.S. Army took over, cranking out training films and propaganda. Such hopefuls as Jack Lemmon and Charlton Heston found work in front of the army's cameras, while waiting for fame and fortune to find them.

But when the government abandoned the property (1971), the buildings fell into disrepair and were virtually forgotten until 1976, when a salvage team, headed by a city planner and leaders of New York movie unions, decided to restore the facility to its original purpose and bring the movies back to Queens. The following year the Astoria Motion Picture and Television Foundation was formed, the buildings secured landmark designation and were placed on the National Register of Historic Places, and arrangements were worked out for commercial development. The Kaufman / Astoria Studios, outfitted with new sound stages and recording studios, saw the production of *The Wiz, All That Jazz, Hair,* and *Hannah and Her Sisters.* It also became the home of the weekly tapings of *The Cosby Show.*

Inclusion on the National Register demanded that part of the site be reserved for educational purposes; in 1981, the foundation resolved to establish a museum of the moving image. Building 13, once a film-processing center, was chosen to house the Museum.

Louis Armstrong Archives and Louis Armstrong House: Queens College (2)

Archives in Rosenthal Library on the campus of Queens College, Kissena Blvd, Flushing, N.Y. 11367. Tel: (718) 997-3670. Louis Armstrong House, 34–56 107th St (bet. 34th / 37th Aves), Corona, N.Y. 11368. Tel: (718) 478-8274.

ADMISSION: Archives open Mon–Fri 10–5. Hours may vary with college schedule; appointments recommended. Closed weekends, some college holidays, New Year's Day, Thanksgiving, and Christmas Day. Free. Louis Armstrong House not currently open to the public except for special programs.

Changing exhibitions, reading room.

✗ No restaurant; cafeteria on campus.

⛫ No gift shop.

♿ Accessible to wheelchairs.

🚇 IRT Flushing line (train 7) to Flushing; then bus Q17 or Q25 to Queens College. IND 8th Ave express (E train) or 6th Ave express (F train) to 71st St / Continental Ave; then Q65A, Jewel Ave bus, to Kissena Blvd, where there is a gate to the college.

🚗 **From Manhattan via Queens-Midtown Tunnel:** Long Island Expwy to exit 24, Kissena Blvd. Parking on campus only during special events; otherwise street parking.

The Louis Armstrong Archives (1991) contain the personal collections—papers, photographs, recordings, musical instruments, and other memorabilia—of this important figure in the history of jazz and American popular culture. Queens College is presently renovating the house, in the nearby Corona section of the borough, where Armstrong and his wife lived for 28 years. When renovations are completed (target date 1997), the house, designated a national historic landmark in 1977, will become the primary exhibition site.

HISTORY

Louis ("Satchmo") Armstrong (1901–1971), jazz trumpeter and vocalist, worked as a musician for more than 60 years. During the '20s he shaped the direction of jazz, bringing to it stylistic elements from his native New Orleans. As a trumpet player, he became a model for a generation of soloists; as a vocalist, he introduced "scatting" (improvising a jazz vocal line, with meaningless syllables instead of words) and influenced singers as different as Billie Holiday and Frank Sinatra. Armstrong performed all over the world, earning the affection of a global audience and the nickname "Ambassador of Jazz."

In 1943, he and his wife Lucille moved to 107th St in Corona, where they lived the rest of their lives. A prolific writer and inveterate collector, Louis Armstrong seems to have kept almost everything that pertained to his career. When Lucille Armstrong died in 1983, the archive went to the City of New York and the Louis Armstrong Educational Foundation. In 1987, Queens College took over administration of the house and archive.

PERMANENT COLLECTION

Highlights include a 200-page autobiography in Armstrong's own hand, 5,000 photographs of him and his contemporaries, 82 scrapbooks of clippings and memorabilia, 650 reel-to-reel tapes, 1,000 recordings, 270 sets of manuscript band parts, 5 trumpets, 14 trumpet mouthpieces, and 105 awards and plaques. Also in the collection are tape recordings of the ebullient Armstrong telling his favorite jokes and stories, as well as material donated by private collectors.

EXHIBITION PROGRAM

The Archive mounts about four shows yearly, which examine Armstrong's work and his impact on American culture. "Armstrong Akwaba" (which means "Welcome, Armstrong" in the language of the Ga people of Ghana) explored his relationship with Africa, which he visited repeatedly on tours sponsored both by the government and by private institutions. "Breaking the Barriers" used photos and other memorabilia to follow Armstrong's career as he became a mainstream figure in popular music and film, creating opportunities for African-American artists who followed him. Although African-American actors had appeared in films before, it was Armstrong who expanded their participation beyond bit parts and stereotypical roles.

Bowne House (3)

37-01 Bowne St (37th Ave), Flushing, N.Y. 11354. Tel: (718) 359-0528.

ADMISSION: Open Sat and Sun 2:30–4:30. Groups by appointment. Closed weekdays, national holidays, and mid-Dec–mid-Jan. Admission charge.

Changing exhibitions, lectures, craft demonstrations, historic walking tour, group tours by appointment.

✗ No restaurant.

♦♦⤸ No restrooms.

▥ Gift shop with mugs, postcards, reproductions of items in collection.

&. Accessible to wheelchairs.

⊘ No photography inside house.

🚊 IRT Flushing line (train 7) to Main St in Flushing. Walk 2 blocks east (uphill) on Roosevelt Ave to Bowne St; go left on Bowne St to house.

🚌 **From Manhattan via Triborough Bridge:** Take Grand Central Pkwy to Northern Blvd; go east on Northern Blvd; turn right on Bowne St; continue a half block to Bowne House. Street parking only.

Bowne House, built in 1661 (with later additions), is the oldest house in Queens, constructed by John Bowne and maintained in the Bowne family until 1945, when it opened as a museum. The house has further importance as a historic site in the establishment of freedom of religion in this country.

THE BUILDING

Nine generations of Bownes lived in the house and used the furnishings and utensils on display today. Among the fine 17–18C furnishings are a Chippendale secretary and a William and Mary highboy, a wedding gift in 1695 to Hannah Bowne from Leticia Penn, daughter of William Penn. The 1680 PARLOR has its original oak pegged floors and hand-hewn beams. In 1695 the house passed to John Bowne's son, Samuel, who added the present entry and the FRONT PARLOR (1696). The 18C painted wood paneling, later added to this room, is decorated with a cross and Bible motif and has a built-in china cabinet. On the walls are Bowne family portraits.

The oldest part of the house is the KITCHEN, which retains its original large fireplace and beehive oven fitted out with cranes, kettles, and pewter and ceramic utensils, some of which were brought from Holland in the 17C.

There is an exhibition of photos showing the house at various times in its history; in the garden is a plaque inscribed with the *Flushing Remonstrance* (see **History** below).

CHANGING EXHIBITIONS

Exhibitions, which change twice yearly, focus on items in the collection, the history of Flushing, and religious tolerance. On display have been the tea service of Walter Bowne, mayor of New York 1829–33, a photographic display documenting the restoration of the parlor, and a show relating the principle of religious tolerance as set forth in the Flushing Remonstrance to its inclusion in the Bill of Rights.

HISTORY

Flushing, named for the Dutch town of Vlissingen, was chartered (1645) by the Dutch West India Company under terms that specifically ensured freedom of worship for its inhabitants; they were to "have and enjoy liberty of conscience, according to the custom and manner of Holland, without molestation or disturbance." Two years later Peter Stuyvesant, noted for his hot temper and his lack of religious tolerance, became governor, with jurisdiction over the small village of Flushing.

Stuyvesant was unhappy when the first Jews arrived in the colony in 1654 and even angrier when a group of Quakers came three years later. What he saw as their fanaticism and frenzied habits of worship, along with their heretical beliefs, made their religion particularly repugnant to him. Though Stuyvesant refused to let the Quakers land in New Amsterdam, he could not prevent members of the sect from settling in Long Island or from meeting secretly to practice their religion, though he tried to stifle the spread of Quakerism by arresting anyone who allowed them to meet in their homes.

In 1657 the citizens of Flushing remonstrated with their governor, stating that in the light of the earlier charter, if people of any faith "come in love unto us, we cannot in conscience lay violent hands upon them, but give them free egress into our town and houses as God shall persuade our Conscience." This document, known as the *Flushing Remonstrance,* is considered an early milestone in the history of American religious toleration.

John Bowne himself, who arrived in this country in 1655, built the house in 1661 and allowed Quakers to meet there. For this violation of Governor Stuyvesant's edicts, Bowne was expelled from the colony. He appealed his deportation to the Dutch West India Company in Amsterdam, and in 1663 the company, which was after all running the colony for profit, admonished Stuyvesant that religious intolerance was bad business for an underpopulated colony.

Chung-Cheng Art Gallery: St. John's University (4)

In Sun Yat Sen Hall, on the campus of St. John's University, Utopia and Grand Central Pkwys, Jamaica, N.Y. 11439. Tel: (718) 990-1526.

ADMISSION: Open Mon–Fri 10–8; Sat and Sun 10–4. Closed major holidays, Thanksgiving, and Christmas Day.

Lectures, films, demonstrations, performing arts events.

✘ No restaurant. Food available on campus.

⌂ No gift shop.

&. Accessible to wheelchairs.

🚇 IND 8th Ave local (E train) or 6th Ave local (F train) to Union Turnpike / Kew Gardens station in Queens. Then transfer to the Q46 bus to St. John's University. Or IND 6th Ave local (F train) to 169th St; transfer to Q30 or Q31 bus to St. John's University.

🚗 **From Manhattan via Queens-Midtown Tunnel:** Take Long Island Expwy to Utopia Pkwy exit. Follow Utopia Pkwy south to St. John's University. Parking available.

> **NOTE:** Sun Yat Sen Hall is between St. Augustine Hall (the main library facing the campus quadrangle) and the stadium.

The Chung-Cheng Gallery (founded 1977) is the centerpiece of the arts program for the Institute of Asian Studies at St. John's University. It is located in Sun Yat Sen Hall (1973), modeled after the Great Peace Palace of the Forbidden City of Beijing and named for Chiang Kai-shek, whose official name was Chiang Chung-cheng.

PERMANENT COLLECTION

About half the collection, now numbering over 1,000 objects, was donated by Henry C. Goebel, a New York lawyer and collector whose interests included jade, ivory carvings, netsuke, lacquer ware, and paintings. To this nucleus have been added contemporary Chinese porcelains, painting, photography, calligraphy, stamps, currency, and sculpture. About 200 objects from the collection (approx. half Japanese and half Chinese) are on display at a given time. Highlights include an exquisite jade elephant (from the Goebel Collection), Ming Dynasty landscape paintings, and lavish 19C robes that belonged to members of the imperial family.

EXHIBITION PROGRAM

The Gallery also has a program of changing exhibitions, which feature the work of Asian artists from here and abroad, as well as occasional community shows.

The Friends Meeting House (5)

137–16 Northern Blvd (Main St), Flushing, N.Y. 11354. Tel: (718) 358-9636.

ADMISSION: Open first Sun of every month 12–1 or by appointment. There is a worship service Sun at 11. Free.

Guided tour; library on Quaker thought.

✗ No restaurant.

🍴 No restrooms.

🏛 No gift shop.

♿ Not accessible to wheelchairs.

🚇 IRT Flushing line (train 7) to Main St.

🚌 **From Manhattan via Triborough Bridge:** Take Grand Central Pkwy to Northern Blvd exit. Follow Northern Blvd east to Meeting House. Street parking only.

The Friends Meeting House (1694; enlarged 1716–19), like Bowne House a few blocks away (see p. 395), harks back to the Colonial period, when Long Island saw the arrival of groups of Quakers seeking freedom from religious persecution. The land was purchased in the names of John Bowne and John Rodman, since the Society of Friends, as the Quakers are more correctly called, were forbidden to own land in the colony. The Meeting House became the Quaker house of worship when the congregation outgrew John Bowne's kitchen.

The house is a simple wooden building with a steep hipped roof and very small windows. Its rear faces Northern Blvd, while the front opens onto a small graveyard, whose stones were unmarked until 1848 in accordance with the Quaker belief that death levels all personal distinctions. Except for the period of British occupation during the Revolutionary War (1776–83), when it was used as a prison, hay barn, and hospital, the Meeting House has been used continuously for religious services since its construction, the oldest such house of worship in the city. The simplicity of the building, its furnishings, and its construction all reflect the austerity of the religion.

The Godwin-Ternbach Museum at Queens College (6)

In Paul Klapper Hall on the campus of Queens College, Kissena Blvd, Flushing, N.Y. 11367. Tel: (718) 997-4747.

ADMISSION: Open during exhibitions Mon–Thurs 11–7; Fri 11–5. Call for exhibition schedule. Free.

Changing exhibitions, occasional lectures.

✗ No restaurant; cafeteria on campus.

⛫ No gift shop; sales desk with catalogues.

♿ Accessible to wheelchairs.

🚊 IRT Flushing line (train 7) to Flushing; then bus Q17 or Q25 to Queens College. IND 8th Ave express (E train) or 6th Ave express (F train) to 71st St and Continental Ave; then Q65A, Jewel Ave bus, to Kissena Blvd, where there is a gate to the college.

🚗 **From Manhattan via Queens-Midtown Tunnel:** Take Long Island Expwy to exit 24, Kissena Blvd. Parking on campus only during special events; otherwise street parking.

The Godwin-Ternbach Museum (1981), the exhibition center for Queens College of the City University of New York, reopened in 1993 after a four-year hiatus for reconstruction of the building in which it is located. The Museum offers a small permanent collection, as well as changing exhibitions of historical and contemporary art. The facility takes its name from its founders, Frances Godwin, a professor at the college, and Joseph Ternbach, an art restorer and collector.

PERMANENT COLLECTION

Highlights of the permanent collection include some 200 pieces of ancient and antique glass, prints by American artists commissioned by the WPA, and examples of Asian and Egyptian art. The approximately 2,500 objects in all media range chronologically from ancient Mesopotamia to the present.

EXHIBITION PROGRAM

The exhibition program offers some three to five shows yearly, curated by the staff, as well as loan shows. Shows may be thematic or historical in nature, or on occasion may focus on individual contemporary artists. The Museum draws on its own collections and the holdings of other museums and private collectors.

The inaugural show in the new space was the first New York exhibition since 1979 of the work of John Ferren, a pioneering American abstractionist who bridged the gap between European modernism and the Abstract Expressionism of the New York School; in his later years Ferren taught at Queens College.

Other shows have included "From Under Wraps," exhibiting works acquired in 1988–93 when the Museum was closed, and exhibitions of contemporary posters. Some shows highlight the borough's ethnic communities. There have been exhibits of Latin-American and African art, Japanese woodcuts, and historical photos taken by Arnold Genthe showing San Francisco's Chinatown before the Great Fire.

The Jamaica Arts Center (7)

161–04 Jamaica Avenue (161st St), Jamaica, N.Y. 11432. Tel: (718) 658-7400.

ADMISSION: Open Tues–Sat 10–5. Closed Sun, Mon, major holidays. Donation requested.

Changing exhibitions, outreach programs, workshops and classes; lectures, demonstrations, children's programs.

✘ No restaurant.

🏛 No gift shop.

🚇 IND 8th Ave local (E train) or BMT Nassau St express (J train) to Jamaica Center (Parsons Blvd / Archer Ave).

🚗 **From Manhattan via Queens-Midtown Tunnel:** Take Long Island Expwy to Van Wyck Expwy south. Exit at Jamaica Ave. Follow Jamaica Ave east to Arts Center.

Founded in 1974, the Jamaica Arts Center (JAC) is a community arts and cultural center with an active schedule of exhibitions and educational programs. Gallery exhibitions include thematic shows (many focused on topics of interest to the African-American, Latino, Native American, and Asian communities), community gallery shows featuring the work of local artists or local groups, and a show of work by artists in the co-op gallery. Artists whom the Center has showcased before they were absorbed into the mainstream have included such now established contemporary figures as David Hammons and Glenn Ligon.

On occasion the Center mounts exhibitions curated in cooperation with other institutions in the city, e.g., "Re-Discoveries: The Mythmakers," for the Columbus quincentennial, which drew on the resources of INTAR Latin American Gallery and the American-Indian Community House.

THE BUILDING

The Center occupies a landmark building that once housed the *Jamaica Register,* a local newspaper.

Kingsland Homestead: The Queens Historical Society (8)

143–35 37th Ave, Flushing, N.Y. 11354. Tel: (718) 939-0647.

ADMISSION: Open for tours Tues, Sat, and Sun 2:30–4:30. No tours Mon, Wed–Fri; Easter; all federal holidays. Historical Society offices in building open Mon–Sat 9–5, except federal holidays. Admission charge.

Changing exhibitions, lectures, workshops, walking tours. Library and research services open to public.

✘ No restaurant. Neighborhood restaurants on Main St in Flushing.

📖 Bookstore with historical publications, focusing on Queens.

♿ The ground floor is accessible to wheelchairs, but the Victorian Parlor and restrooms are not.

🚇 IRT Flushing line (train 7) to Main St.

🚗 **From Manhattan via Queens-Midtown Tunnel:** Take Long Island Expwy to Main St. Follow Main St north to Northern Blvd. Turn right to Parsons Blvd; go right one block to 37th Ave, turn right. The house actually is on 37th Ave west of Parsons Blvd. Street parking only.

Kingsland Homestead (c. 1785), home of the Queens Historical Society (1968), offers an intriguing history, a program of changing exhibitions, and, in a small backyard park, a landmark Weeping Beech tree (c. 1847) of imposing proportions.

EXHIBITION PROGRAM

In the permanent collection are memorabilia from early owners Joseph King and the Murray family, photographs and maps of Queens, and examples of decorative arts; there is a video library which documents Queens history and landmarks. On the second floor is a VICTORIAN PARLOR furnished with period pieces, some of which came from the Murray estate. The ground-floor parlors of the Museum are used for changing exhibitions of local history and decorative arts. Two past themes were "Queens Movie Palaces" and "350 Years of Queens Landmarks," which included the Weeping Beech, the borough's only living landmark.

THE BUILDING

Like the settlers of Long Island, the house is a mixture of English and Dutch elements. The split door, the long porch supported by columns, and the general proportions of the building suggest Dutch influence, while the central chimney and the proportions of the windows are English Colonial in style.

HISTORY

The house was built (c. 1785) by Charles Doughty, a Quaker farmer reputed to have been the first person in the area to free a slave. Doughty's son-in-law Joseph King inherited the house and settled down to a comfortable life in Queens after a career as a sea captain, whose most harrowing moments came during the French Revolution when he was captured by privateers. Imprisoned in Paris, he was eventually smuggled out to freedom by an unidentified American. His daughter Mary King married Lindley Murray, whose family gave Murray Hill in Manhattan its name. Descendants of the couple owned the house until it was sold to a developer and slated for demolition in favor of a shopping center. Preservationists had the house moved from its original location (Northern Blvd and 155th St) to Weeping Beech Park, where it opened as a museum in 1968.

The massive *Weeping Beech* (c. 1847), whose boughs droop in mournful splendor, dates back to the time when Samuel B. Parsons ran a tree nursery in Queens, supplying shrubs and trees for Central and Prospect Parks. According to legend, the tree was first planted along an avenue of beeches belonging to the Belgian baron de Man. When the baron noticed one seedling drooping, he ordered his gardener to destroy it, but instead the gardener put it in a secluded spot, where it flourished; its unusual form is the result of a spontaneous mutation. Parsons brought back a cutting in a flower pot. From that small beginning grew the present tree, now more than 60 ft tall, with a spread of some 85 ft and a trunk circumference of 14 ft.

The New York Hall of Science (9)

47–01 111th St in Flushing Meadows Corona Park, N.Y. 11368. Tel: (718) 699-0005.

ADMISSION: Open Wed–Sun 10–5. Group visit hours Mon–Tues 9:30–2 and Wed–Sun 9:30–5. Closed New Year's Day, Labor Day, Thanksgiving, and Dec 24–25. Admission charge, except Wed and Thurs 2–5, when Museum is free.

Changing exhibitions, live demonstrations, make-it-and-take-it activities, videos and films, special events, workshops, family workshops, newsletter. Science Access Center: a multimedia library featuring books, videos, periodicals, and tabletop activities for all ages. Rental programs for teachers, teacher training, membership with benefits.

✖ Snack automat.

⌸ Gift shop with toys, science apparatus, posters, books, gifts.

♿ Accessible to wheelchairs. Visitors with special needs call (718) 669-0005, Mon–Fri 9–5.

🚇 IRT Flushing line (train 7) to 111th St station. Walk south five blocks to the Hall of Science at 48th Ave and 111th St.

🚗 **From Manhattan via Queens-Midtown Tunnel:** Take Long Island Expwy to 108th St exit. Left onto 108th St. Right at 48th Ave to 111th St. Follow signs into Hall of Science parking lot (fee). **From Manhattan via Triborough Bridge:** Take Grand Central Pkwy to the Long Island Expwy / Midtown Tunnel exit. Immediately bear right off the exit ramp and proceed one block to the light. Right onto 111th St. Turn right into Hall of Science parking lot (fee) across from 48th Ave.

The New York Hall of Science (founded 1964; opened in its present form 1986) offers hands-on exhibits to dazzle the eye, entice the hand, and intrigue the brain. The originality and creativity of the Museum have attracted international attention and it has been described as one of the best of its kind in the world.

EXHIBITION PROGRAM

Participatory exhibits allow visitors to explore major phenomena of physics and biology. One group of experiments demonstrates the mechanism of feedback by which machines and living creatures sense changes in their environment and adapt to them; visitors can experiment with the concept by pedaling a bicycle which turns a full-size airplane propeller from a 1930s De Havilland "Otter" while a flyball governor (a system of spinning weights) regulates the speed of the propeller by changing the angle of the blades. "Seeing the Light" offers experiments with light, color, and perception, e.g., a "Distorted Room," where perspective fools the eye into perceiving the room as normal while the people in it grow and shrink as they move around.

The New York Hall of Science in Flushing Meadows, Corona Park, orig-
inally a pavillion at the World's Fair of 1964, is filled with exhibits to
trick the eye and vex the mind.
(New York Hall of Science)

"Hidden Kingdoms—The World of Microbes" offers a 14-ft sewing needle with models of microbes on its surface to suggest the scale of the
microscopic world. The Microbial Zoo displays live shows of ten species
of protozoa under specially designed microscopes.

Four artistic works, created using different technologies, remain on
permanent display. One of the most popular, *Temple of the Whirlwind*
(1989) by Ned Kahn, utilizes air blowers, humidifiers, and a fan to create
a 17-ft tornado of water vapor that twists and turns inside what looks
like a modern Greek temple.

In addition to these ongoing exhibits the Museum mounts an entertaining (though, of course, informative) series of events and programs. In
1989, visitors could send messages into space recorded onto an optical
disk and sent aboard the Space Shuttle Atlantis.

The newest exhibition, "SoundSensations—The Inside Story of Audio,"
explains the workings of tape cassettes and CDs. Visitors can enter a
special phone booth, press a button, and transform their voices to resemble, e.g., a sad Mickey Mouse. They can enter a room-sized installation
designed by composer Ron Kuivila, where the movements of their shadows fall on translucent panels that activate computer-controlled synthesized music.

In June 1994, the Hall of Science opened a sidewalk exhibition on 34th
St in Manhattan, with exhibits that allowed people to discover the secrets
of the city's technology. Viewers could peer down through the sidewalk

with periscopes to view simulations of the city's utility service just below the surface, the subways 50 ft down, and the water tunnel under construction in bedrock 100 ft below. Accompanying the outdoor exhibit at Herald Sq. was a more traditional exhibit in the Museum, also focusing on the technology that makes the city work.

THE BUILDING

The New York Hall of Science was built for the 1964–65 World's Fair and held exhibits on the space program and other marvels of the future.

The Isamu Noguchi Garden Museum (10)

32–37 Vernon Blvd (bet. 33rd Rd / 10th St), Long Island City, N.Y. 11106. Tel: (718) 204-7088.

ADMISSION: Open April–Nov: Wed, Sat, Sun 11–6. Suggested contribution.

Gallery talks. Educational programs, programs for visually impaired and handicapped visitors. Group tours by appointment.

✘ No restaurant. There are restaurants in the Astoria section of Queens on Broadway, easily reached by car and accessible on foot (about a 15-min walk).

🏛 Gift shop with notecards, catalogues, books, postcards, and Akari light sculptures.

♿ Ground floor and garden (two-thirds of the collection) accessible to wheelchairs. Upstairs galleries accessible only by stairway.

⊘ Photography by permission.

🚇 BMT Broadway line (N train) to Broadway station in Queens. Walk west toward the Manhattan skyline for nine blocks until Broadway ends at Vernon Blvd. The Museum is two blocks south of this intersection.

🚐 Shuttle bus service from Manhattan, Sat only, leaves from Asia Society (Park Ave at 70th St); call (718) 204-7088 for information and schedule.

🚗 **From Manhattan via Queensborough Bridge (lower roadway):** Take first right exit off the bridge, Crescent St. Go straight to 43rd Ave; turn right and follow 43rd Ave to Vernon Blvd. Turn right on Vernon Blvd and continue to Museum at 33rd Rd. Street parking only.

Located in a quiet, low-rise industrial neighborhood near the East River, the Museum (1985) houses more than 250 works by Japanese-American sculptor Isamu Noguchi (1904–1988). On view in the galleries and in the walled garden are sculptures in wood, clay, marble, and metal, as well as Noguchi's famous *Akari light sculptures*. A collection of models, drawings, and photographs demonstrates the artist's designs for gardens, plazas, and public sculptures, some of which have been realized, others that exist only as designs.

The galleries are organized roughly in reverse chronological order, with more recent pieces on the ground floor and earlier ones upstairs. Noguchi's interest in the environment of his art was as powerful as his interest in sculpture itself, and the building with its various galleries of different sizes and materials reflects a setting the artist deliberately created for his work.

PERMANENT COLLECTION

The collection includes work from all phases of Noguchi's career, from early brass sculpture in the '20s that shows the influence of Brancusi, for whom he acted as a studio assistant, to his most mature and austere pieces of basalt and granite.

First Floor

The INDOOR / OUTDOOR GALLERY (AREA 1), with windows permanently open to the elements, an unroofed corner that allows rain and snow to fall within the Museum, and some slender birch trees growing inside, blurs the distinction between a traditional indoor art gallery and a sculpture garden. Installed here are a number of large pieces in granite and basalt.

The GARDEN (AREA 2), like a traditional Japanese garden, contains objects of both visual and aural pleasure, though the rocks here have been chiseled and worked with tools, in contrast to those in a classical Japanese garden, which remain in their natural forms. The *Well* (1982) is a variant on the Japanese *tsukubai,* a hollowed stone into which water trickles, though in Noguchi's rendering the water rises to the surface of the stone and slides down the outside.

AREA 4, whose ceiling retains the metal plates of the original chemical plant, contains *Life of a Cube #5* (1968), part of a series of studies of distortions of the cube that occupied the sculptor's attention while he was working on *Red Cube,* a site-specific work installed in front of 140 Broadway in Manhattan.

Second Floor

AREA 8. When Noguchi agreed to represent the United States at the Venice Biennale in 1986, he decided to show a spiral slide he had devised in 1966 to illustrate the idea of play as it relates to sculpture. The gallery documents several unsuccessful attempts at the spiral slide, and a final working model.

AREA 11. This large gallery contains models, photographs, and drawings of Noguchi's projects for stage sets, public sculpture, parks, gardens, and playgrounds. Included are a stage set for *Frontier,* designed for Martha Graham in 1935, and photos documenting the once scandalous Peter Hall / Royal Shakespeare Company production of *King Lear.*

AREA 13 contains Noguchi's famous *Akari lights,* which originated when he traveled to Hiroshima to design the bridges for the Peace Park. Noguchi stopped by the town of Gifu, whose mayor asked him to help modernize their traditional paper lanterns. The shapes of the *Akari* (the Japanese word for light) lamps echo other forms (e.g., the twisted column) found in Noguchi's work in different media.

HISTORY

In the early 1960s, sculptor Isamu Noguchi moved his studio from Manhattan to a building in this Queens neighborhood to be close to the marble suppliers on Vernon Blvd. In 1975 he bought a small building, formerly a photo-engraving plant, which he used for studio space and storage. Over the years Noguchi nurtured the idea of creating a museum to display examples of his work that he had kept for himself; with his friend, architect Shoji Sadao, he eventually converted the studio into the present Museum and Garden.

P.S. 1 Museum: The Institute for Contemporary Art (11)

46-01 21st St (46th Ave), Long Island City, N.Y. 11101. Tel: (718) 784-2084 or (212) 233-1440.

Information Desk. Gallery talks. Performances, special events, lectures, educational programs.

✘ No restaurant.

🛍 Bookshop.

♿ Accessible to wheelchairs.

⊘ IRT Flushing line (train 7) to 45th Rd / Courthouse Sq. IND 8th Ave local (E train) or 6th Ave local (F train) to 23rd St / Ely Ave. Brooklyn-Queens crosstown (G train) to 21st St / Van Alst.

🚗 **From Manhattan via Queens-Midtown Tunnel:** Exit at 21st St, follow 21st St across Jackson Ave to Museum. Street parking only.

> NOTE: P.S. 1 is closed for renovations. The projected reopening date is early 1997.

P.S. 1 (1976) is an alternative art space that offers studio facilities to artists and changing exhibitions of contemporary art to the public. Originally called Project Studios 1, P.S. 1 (opened 1976) occupies a former school building (Queens P.S. 1, formerly the Ward 1 School), whose three floors of large, high-ceilinged white galleries give the Museum ample exhibition space for installations and shows of practically any scale.

EXHIBITION PROGRAM

Major exhibitions have included surveys of influential mid-career artists, presentations of artists not well known in New York, and shows that suggest important movements in international art. The Studio Program, which offers studio space, and the Special Projects series support the work of emerging artists. Both geographically and imaginatively, P.S. 1 is off the beaten path, and worth the extra steps it takes to get there.

The Museum mounted a highly regarded retrospective of African-American artist David Hammons, whose sculpture incorporates humble objects—shovels, human hair, bottle caps, Venetian blinds, chicken wings—to comment with both wit and penetration on issues—the drug culture, racism, poverty—that affect African Americans. Lewis Baltz, a photographer who specializes in mapping the decay of the industrial landscape, offered an exhibition that focused on tract housing and new industrial parks. The Museum has shown the dissident work of Czech artists whose exhibitions in Prague were closed or demolished by the police, as well as the politically acceptable work of "Stalin's Choice: Soviet Socialist Realism, 1932–1956."

On occasion the Museum makes use of nongallery space—the boiler room, the stairwells, the Boys' Entrance to the former school, and its unused bathrooms—for site-specific installations. "Slow Art: Painting in New York Now" took a sweeping look at 103 New York painters represented by one canvas apiece; names ranged from the famously familiar (Jasper Johns, James Rosenquist, Roy Lichtenstein) to relatively unknown artists at the beginning of their careers.

PERMANENT EXHIBITIONS

In addition to its program of changing exhibitions, the Museum maintains several permanent installations. Two are by Alan Saret: *Fifth Solar Chto-honic Wall Temple* (1976) and *Ascending Number Spirit Fountain* (1980–81). Also permanently on view is James Turrell's *Meeting* (1980–86), one of two permanent sky pieces by that artist in the United States. The installation is in an upper room with shapes cut out of the ceiling to open it to the sky; as the sun sets, the light within the room changes quickly and sometimes dramatically (installation open at sunset, during good weather).

HISTORY

In 1971, at a time of artistic and political ferment, Alanna Heiss founded the Institute for Contemporary Art and Urban Resources, the parent organization of P.S. 1, to reclaim abandoned or underused city buildings for use as studio, exhibition, and performance space by contemporary artists. Today, the Institute—renamed the Institute for Contemporary Art, is one of the oldest surviving alternative art organizations in the city. It oversees two galleries, the P.S. 1 Museum in Queens and the Clocktower Gallery in Manhattan.

The Queens Botanical Garden (12)

43–50 Main St (Dahlia Ave), Flushing, N.Y. 11355. Tel: (718) 886-3800.

ADMISSION: Open Tues–Sun 10–7. Closed Mon except legal holidays. Free.

Lectures, exhibits, workshops, gardening classes, educational programs, concerts and films. Victorian-style garden for weddings and other ceremonies.

✘ No restaurant.

🏛 Plant and gift shop.

& Accessible to wheelchairs.

⊘ No bicycles. No ball games.

🚇 IRT Flushing line (train 7) to Main St, Flushing. Transfer to bus Q44 to Elder Ave.

🚗 **From Manhattan via Queens-Midtown Tunnel:** Take Long Island Expwy to Main Street North, Flushing; turn left onto Dahlia Ave and continue to parking lot. Free parking.

The Queens Botanical Garden (founded 1963) encompasses 39 acres of plantings, including a 19-acre Arboretum with dogwoods, maples, magnolias, and other naturalized woodland plants. Seasonal displays include blossoming crabapple and cherry trees in spring, a 4-acre Rose Garden (some 5,000 plants) in summer, and displays of chrysanthemums and ornamental cabbages in the autumn.

Along Elder Ave a BEE GARDEN contains flowers and plantings that attract honey-producing bees. Along Crommelin St varieties of shrubs and trees have been selected to attract birds. The WEDDING GARDEN, with its white gazebo and small stream, has been designed from documented Victorian sources and serves as a background for ceremonies and parties in addition to pleasurable strolling. The formally designed HERB GARDEN offers medicinal and culinary herbs as well as plants traditionally used for dyes.

HISTORY

The Queens Botanical Garden got its start as an exhibit entitled "Gardens on Parade" in the 1939 World's Fair, whose grounds occupied what is now Flushing Meadows Corona Park. The 5-acre exhibit remained after the Fair closed, and in 1946 the Queens Botanical Garden Society took over its upkeep. When the old Fair site was pressed into service for the 1964 World's Fair, the Garden was moved outside the park but given more spacious grounds. Two Mt Atlas cedars from the 1939 Fair flanking the present entrance and a walkway connecting the present site to the park link the Garden to its past.

The Queens County Farm Museum (13)

73–50 Little Neck Pkwy, Floral Park, N.Y. 11004. Tel: (718) 347-3276.

ADMISSION: Grounds open Mon–Fri 9–5 all year round. House open Sat–Sun 12–5; closed sometimes in late winter; call ahead. Donation requested.

House tours weekends 12–5. Seasonal programs, educational programs for children, workshops, craft classes; antique car show (late April), motorcycle show, Indian Pow Wow (end of July); summer drop-in arts and crafts programs for children; Queens County Fair; Children's Fall Festival; holiday week at Christmas, drop-in wreath-making classes; group tours.

✗ No restaurant.

🏛 Gift shop with souvenirs, T-shirts, gift items. Seasonal fresh produce and eggs for sale. Plant sales in spring.

♿ Limited wheelchair accessibility.

⊘ No bicycles or dogs.

🚇 IND 8th Ave local (E train) or 6th Ave (F train) to Kew Gardens / Union Turnpike station. Transfer to Q46 bus to Little Neck Pkwy. Walk north three blocks to Museum entrance.

🚗 **From Manhattan via Triborough Bridge:** Take Grand Central Pkwy to Little Neck Pkwy (exit 24). South on Little Neck Pkwy three blocks to Museum entrance. **From Manhattan via Queens-Midtown Tunnel:** Take Long Island Expwy to Little Neck Pkwy (exit 32); south on Little Neck Pkwy 1 mile to Museum entrance. Parking available.

This 47-acre working farm, the site of continuous farming for more than 200 years and the only working farm within New York City, was opened as a museum (1975) dedicated to the agricultural history of New York City. The landmark farmhouse (earliest part c. 1772) has been restored and furnished with period artifacts and some period furniture. In addition to the house there is a 3,000-sq-ft barn, gardens producing fruit and vegetables, an accumulation of farm animals, and a 3-acre orchard.

Guided house tours focus on the historic details of the restored building, which features a Colonial fireplace. Visitors may take self-guided tours of the farmyard. Programs at the Museum, designed to teach visitors about the agrarian past of Long Island, include experiments in cider pressing, carding and spinning, candlemaking, and quilting.

HISTORY

The earliest part of the house, known as the Adriance Farmhouse, dates to c. 1772, when this part of Long Island was settled primarily by the Dutch, who farmed the land. The house, believed to have been built by Jacob Adriance, conforms to the Dutch Colonial style, with a long front and, on the north side, an overhanging roof. It departs from the usual type in that it faces north instead of south and its fireplace is located toward the middle of the floor instead of against an end wall. Over the years the original simple house acquired various wings and porches, a new roof line, and other adornments. In 1926 the Creedmoor branch of the Brooklyn State Hospital, a psychiatric facility, acquired the property and used it to cultivate vegetables for the patients, some of whom worked in the gardens as therapy. New York City took over the property in 1982. It is now operated by the nonprofit Colonial Farmhouse Restoration Society of Bellerose, Inc.

The Queens Museum of Art (14)

New York City Building, Flushing Meadows Corona Park, Flushing, N.Y. 11368. Tel: (718) 592-5555 for recorded information; to reach a live person, call (718) 592-9700.

ADMISSION: Open Wed–Fri 10–5; Sat and Sun 12–5. Tues open only to groups by appointment. Closed Mon, New Year's Day, Thanksgiving, and Christmas Day. Suggested admission charge. Children under five free.

Gallery talks, lectures, performances, children's activities, family events, musical events.

✘ No restaurant.

❧ Gift shop with posters, catalogues, postcards, books, craft items (replica African instruments, baskets), T-shirts, mugs, New York items, jewelry.

♿ Accessible to wheelchairs. Programs for the handicapped and the visually impaired; call (718) 592-9700 and ask for the Education Department. For TT / TDD service, call (718) 592-2847.

⊘ No photography; number of strollers limited when Museum is crowded.

🚇 IRT Flushing line (train 7) to Willets Point-Shea Stadium. Ten-min walk to Unisphere; Museum is directly adjacent.

🚗 **From Manhattan via Triborough Bridge:** Take Grand Central Pkwy to Northern Blvd / Shea Stadium exit. Follow signs through the park to Museum. Free parking lot at Museum.

The Queens Museum of Art (1972) is the borough's only art museum, the offspring of the two World's Fairs that filled Flushing Meadows-Corona

Park in 1939 and 1964. The Museum offers changing exhibitions of contemporary art and works from the permanent collection, including the famous *Panorama of New York City*, the world's largest architectural replica.

HISTORY

Before 1939, when the most famous of all World's Fairs opened in Flushing Meadows, the park was the huge Corona Dump, occupying the saltmarsh surrounding the Flushing River. By the 1920s, trainloads of trash and garbage which arrived daily from Brooklyn were burned there at night, inspiring F. Scott Fitzgerald to call it the Valley of Ashes.

Park Commissioner Robert Moses determined that the dump would become a great park. With Herculean effort, the site was converted for the 1939–40 World's Fair, a project that involved channeling the river through a conduit as large as the tube of the Holland Tunnel and carting off hundreds of thousands of tons of debris and garbage. New York City's exhibition space at the Fair, a $4 million permanent building, with room for an ice- and roller-skating rink, was built by parks' architect Aymar Embury.

In 1946, the United Nations used the New York City Building while awaiting completion of its headquarters in Manhattan. Again during the World's Fair of 1964–65 the building housed the New York City exhibit, whose outstanding feature was the *Panorama of New York City*, constructed on the 300th anniversary of the arrival of the Dutch in 1664.

By 1971, several borough planning boards felt that Queens needed a museum of its own. The City Department of Parks, Recreation, and Cultural Affairs paid to renovate the building as a museum. In 1994 the Museum reopened after a second renovation that doubled exhibition space and added three new permanent galleries.

EXHIBITION PROGRAM

The exhibition program focuses on contemporary art, and includes shows curated by the Museum staff as well as loan shows from other institutions. Some shows are issue-oriented, e.g., "Fragile Ecologies: Artists' Interpretations and Solutions," which included artists' projects that actually assisted in protecting the environment.

Other shows reflect the ethnic diversity of the borough and the vitality of the city; the Museum has sponsored exhibitions of contemporary Irish, Korean, Japanese, and Colombian art. One show entitled "Keith Haring: Future Primeval" brought together the work of this artist who began his career painting in the New York subways, and who went on "to compete with television" (he said) as an artist who bridged the gap between "high" and popular art. The Museum inaugurated the revitalized exhibition space with "Louis Armstrong: A Cultural Legacy," which documented the career of the famous jazz trumpeter, who lived for many years in Queens. The show combined memorabilia, photographs, pages from the handwritten manuscript of his autobiography, and audiotapes of broadcasts, rehearsals, and private music lessons.

PERMANENT EXHIBITION

The Museum has a permanent collection of some 5,000 works, focusing on contemporary art, especially by New York City artists, and art related to the city, its history, and popular culture. *The Panorama of New York City* is the centerpiece of the Museum. Constructed by the firm of Raymond Lester & Assocs for the 1964–65 Fair, the *Panorama* is the world's largest architectural scale model (9,335 sq ft, at a scale of 1 in to 100 ft). Updated to 1992, it contains more than 865,000 buildings, bridges, roads, parks, and airports in all five boroughs.

Adjacent to the *Panorama* is a historical gallery entitled "A Panoramic View: The History of the New York City Building and Flushing Meadows-Corona Park," with memorabilia of the World's Fairs of 1939 and 1964, as well as objects commemorating the history of the building and the park. The Plaster Cast Gallery overlooking the park contains replicas of important classical and Renaissance statues, examples from a group of some 283 casts of Greek, Roman, and Renaissance originals (including Michelangelo's *Pietà,* currently in storage) on long-term loan from the Metropolitan Museum of Art. These casts were originally intended for the use of art students.

SATELLITE GALLERY

The Museum also maintains two exhibition spaces at Bulova Corporate Center.

> The Queens Museum at Bulova Corporate Center, 75–20 Astoria Blvd, Jackson Heights, N.Y. 11370. Tel: (718) 899-0700. Open Mon–Fri 7 A.M.–7 P.M.; Sat 10–4. Closed Sun and major holidays. Free.
>
> 🚇 BMT Broadway express to Astoria Blvd / Hoyt Ave. Change to bus M60 eastbound on Astoria Blvd.
>
> 🚌 **From Manhattan:** M60, from 116th St-Broadway, crosstown on 125th St, via Triborough Bridge to Astoria Blvd.
>
> 🚗 **From Manhattan via Triborough Bridge:** Take Grand Central Pkwy; exit at 94th St. Follow 94th St south to Astoria Blvd. Turn right and follow Astoria Blvd west to the Bulova Corporate Center, near 77th St. Free parking lot.

In the Atrium are examples of the plaster casts on loan from the Metropolitan Museum of Art. In the West Concourse Gallery, the Museum mounts about three shows yearly by emerging artists.

The Queens Wildlife Center (formerly Queens Zoo) (15)

> 53–51 111th St in Flushing Meadows Corona Park, N.Y. 11368. Tel: (718) 271-7761.
>
> ADMISSION: Open every day of the year. April–Oct: weekdays 10–5; weekends and holidays 10–5:30. Nov–March: 10–4:30 daily. Admission charge. Lower rates for senior citizens and children 3–12; children under 3 are free.
>
> Self-guided tour. Domestic animal area with educational programs.
>
> ✗ Cafe with light refreshments.
>
> 🏛 No gift shop.
>
> ♿ Accessible to wheelchairs.
>
> 🚫 No pets, radios, or skateboards.
>
> 🚇 IRT Flushing line (train 7) to 111th St. Walk south to zoo.
>
> 🚗 **From Manhattan via Queens-Midtown Tunnel:** Take Long Island Expwy to 108th St exit. Left onto 108th St. Right at 48th Ave to 111th St. Follow signs into Hall of Science parking lot (fee). **From Manhattan via**

Triborough Bridge: Take Grand Central Pkwy eastbound to the Long
Island Expwy / Midtown Tunnel exit. Immediately bear right off the exit
ramp and proceed one block to the light. Right onto 111th St. Turn right
into Hall of Science parking lot (fee) across from 48th Ave.

The Queens Zoo (1968) is a small (11-acre) zoo with displays of North
American wildlife. In its handsomely designed habitat areas are approximately 250 animals of some 40 species, including sandhill cranes, bob-
cats, bison, mountain lions, Roosevelt elk, and coyotes.

EXHIBITS

In the forested *Aviary,* a geodesic dome designed by Buckminster Fuller
for the 1964–65 World's Fair, are such familiar species as the northern
cardinal and such unfamiliar ones as the cattle egret. Mountain lions
enjoy artificially warmed basking rocks, which attract them closer to the
public. There is a sea lion pool, with a waterfall and rock background.
The marsh habitat includes ducks, geese, herons, and a few turtles, as
well as native wildlife.

The "signature" animal of the zoo is the American bison, an animal
helped back from the brink of extinction a century ago by the New York
Zoological Society, whose successor, the Wildlife Conservation Society,
today operates the Queens Zoo. Near the bison exhibit is a prairie dog
town, with cutaways so that visitors can observe the underground habitat of these social animals. Other exhibits include black bears and wild
turkeys. There is a *Domestic Animal Area,* where children can pet goats,
sheep, and rabbits.

HISTORY

The Queens Zoo originally opened in 1968 on the grounds of the 1964–65 World's
Fair. Newer than the other two city-owned zoos in Prospect and Central Parks, the
Queens Zoo nonetheless quickly became outdated as advances were made in zoo
design and animal management. In 1988 Wildlife Conservation Society, which now
operates the Bronx, Prospect Park, and Central Park zoos, took over the Queens Zoo
and began a major renovation. The new zoo reopened in 1992.

Socrates Sculpture Park (16)

Vernon Blvd (Broadway), Long Island City, N.Y. 11106. Mailing address:
P.O. Box 6259, Long Island City, N.Y. 11106. Tel: (718) 956-1819.

ADMISSION: Open all year 10–dusk. Free.

Changing exhibitions of sculpture, two opening celebrations a year (one
spring, one fall), with performance events, music.

✗ No restaurant.

🍴 No restrooms.

🏛 No gift shop. Catalogues and T-shirts available at openings.

⊘ Accessible to wheelchairs. Park terrain is flat; some areas have gravel
and wood chips.

🚇 BMT Broadway line (N train) to Broadway station in Queens. Walk west toward the Manhattan skyline for eight blocks until Broadway ends at Vernon Blvd. The park is visible across Vernon Blvd.

▄▄▄ Take the Queens Surface Q101 (not the bus labeled Rikers Island) from 59th St / 2nd Ave on the south side of the Queensboro Bridge; ask for a transfer. At Broadway / Steinway St in Queens, transfer to the Q104. Exit at Broadway / Vernon Blvd. For more information, call Queens Surface: (718) 445-3100.

The park is only two blocks away from the Noguchi Museum, for which there is shuttle bus service from Manhattan, Sat only, leaving from the Asia Society (Park Ave at 70th St); call (718) 204-7088 for information and schedule.

🚗 **From Manhattan via Queensborough Bridge (lower roadway):** Take first right exit off the bridge, Crescent St. Go straight to 43rd Ave; turn right and follow 43rd Ave to Vernon Blvd. Turn right on Vernon Blvd and continue to park at 33rd Rd. Street parking only.

Socrates Sculpture Park, founded in 1985 and named for the philosopher who dedicated himself to a search for truth, is one of the few places in the city to see exhibitions of large-scale, even monumental, sculpture by established and emerging artists. The park is laid out in a 4-acre windswept field that faces the East River and commands a view of the Manhattan skyline on one side and the low-rise industrial landscape of Long Island City on the other.

The site itself is striking—remote, a little wild, exposed. Formerly a marine terminal, then an abandoned lot filled with garbage and rubble, the land was leased (1985) for five years from the city (with later extensions) and developed as a park largely through the efforts of sculptor Mark di Suvero, whose studio is nearby. Though this area of Long Island City has historically been an industrial zone, in recent years it has become an enclave of art, with the Isamu Noguchi Museum, artists' studios, and P.S. 1, the alternative art space, in the vicinity.

EXHIBITION PROGRAM

Each year two major exhibitions, whose openings attract between 2,000 and 5,000 people, bring an influx of new works to the park, but some pieces from previous seasons also remain in place. Some exhibitions have a specific focus, e.g., " '93 New York 50," which surveyed contemporary work in and around New York. Other shows are more wide-ranging and eclectic, giving new opportunities in scale and venue to sculptors from the wider American and international scenes, many of whom are normally seen only in gallery settings. Artists participating in the on-site studio program are invited to come to the park to create pieces on the spot, which gives visitors the opportunity to watch work in process.

Sculptors who have exhibited in the park have distinguished themselves for their choice of materials, making use of strips of shredded tires, bales of hay, giant wooden wheels, and mounds of earth planted with grass. Other works have responded to the site, with its view of the city and the river, by referring to such themes as ancient architecture, the bones of whales, and agriculture. Among those whose works have been displayed here are Vito Acconci, Mark di Suvero, Mel Edwards, Grace Knowlton, Helen Lessick, Alison Saar, Alan Sonfist, and Richard Stankiewicz.

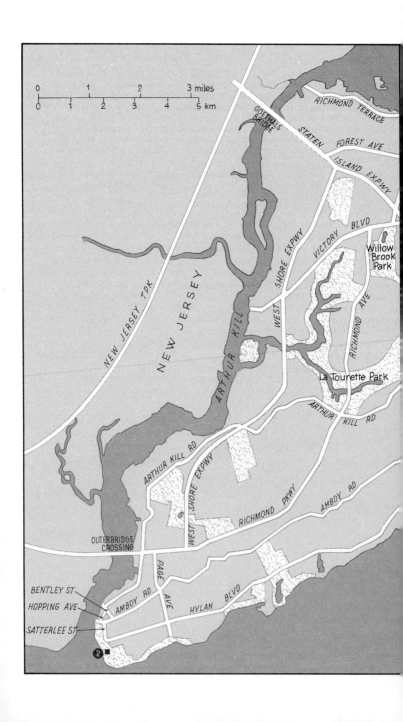

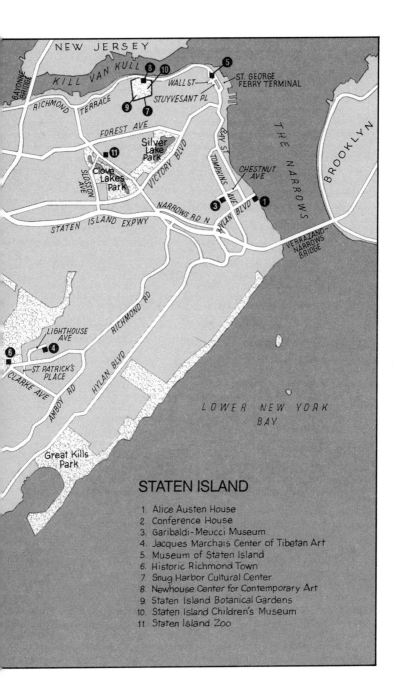

STATEN ISLAND

1. Alice Austen House
2. Conference House
3. Garibaldi-Meucci Museum
4. Jacques Marchais Center of Tibetan Art
5. Museum of Staten Island
6. Historic Richmond Town
7. Snug Harbor Cultural Center
8. Newhouse Center for Contemporary Art
9. Staten Island Botanical Gardens
10. Staten Island Children's Museum
11. Staten Island Zoo

MUSEUMS IN STATEN ISLAND

To get to Staten Island from Manhattan, you must either drive or take the ferry. The Manhattan terminus of the Staten Island Ferry is near Battery Park at the foot of State St (extension of Broadway). Bus directions on Staten Island, where appropriate, are given from the St. George Ferry Terminal. For further information about public transportation, call the Staten Island Travel Information Center (open 6 A.M.–9 P.M. daily) at (718) 979-0600.

🚇 **To ferry terminal in Manhattan:** IRT Broadway–7th Ave local (train 1 or 9) to South Ferry. IRT Lexington Ave local (train 4 or 5) to Bowling Green. BMT Broadway express or local (N or R train) to Whitehall St.

🚌 **To ferry terminal in Manhattan:** M1 (make sure you get a bus marked South Ferry), M6 via Broadway, M15 via 2nd Ave to South Ferry.

⛴ **The Staten Island Ferry** leaves at frequent intervals from both the Staten Island (St. George) and the Manhattan terminals during normal working hours, and at less frequent intervals during the evenings, on weekends, and on holidays. The trip takes about 25 min oneway; round trip fare is 50¢, paid at the Staten Island terminal.

It is difficult to reach some of Staten Island's museums without a car. Directions to museums by car are given from the Verrazano-Narrows Bridge. To reach the Brooklyn end of the bridge from Manhattan, take the Brooklyn-Battery Tunnel, the Brooklyn Bridge, or the Manhattan Bridge to the Brooklyn-Queens Expwy. Follow the expressway to the Verrazano-Narrows Bridge entrance. It is also possible but less convenient to reach Staten Island by car via the ferry; for schedule of ferries taking cars, call (212) 806-6940.

Alice Austen House (1)

2 Hylan Blvd, Staten Island, N.Y. 10305. Tel: (718) 816-4506.

ADMISSION: House open year round Thurs–Sun, 12–5. Closed major holidays. Suggested donation. Grounds open daily until dusk.

House tour, workshops, lectures, special events, exhibitions, semiannual antiques fair, musical events.

✗ No food service at house. Hot dog vendor near entrance in warm weather. Informal restaurants on Bay St.

🏛 Gift shop, Alice's World, offers postcards, catalogues, Victorian-style items, ornaments, toys, picture frames, jewelry.

♿ Accessible to wheelchairs, entrance at rear of house; call ahead to arrange visit.

⊘ No unaccompanied children. No picnicking or pets in park.

🚌 **From St. George Ferry Terminal in Staten Island:** S51 bus (15 min) via Bay St to Hylan Blvd. Walk one block east toward the water and Alice Austen House.

From Verrazano-Narrows Bridge: Stay in right lane on bridge and take Bay St exit, the first exit after the tollbooths. Continue to end of road, School Rd, and turn left onto Bay St. Follow Bay St to Hylan Blvd. Turn right on Hylan Blvd and continue one block to the water and Alice Austen House. Street parking only.

Clear Comfort, Alice Austen's cottage overlooking New York Harbor, photographed c. 1888 by Austen herself.
(Alice Austen Collection, Staten Island Historical Society)

Exhibits in the Alice Austen House Museum (opened 1985) document the life and work of Alice Austen (1866–1952), a lifelong Staten Island resident and pioneering woman photographer. The restored Austen cottage, situated on the shore just north of the Verrazano-Narrows Bridge, offers a glorious view of New York Harbor and the ships passing through the Narrows.

HISTORY

It is only by good luck that Alice Austen and her work are known today. Born to a well-to-do Victorian family in what is today the Rosebank section of Staten Island, she seems to have been remarkable for a certain high-spiritedness and a passion for photography. Given a camera at ten, she grew up to become one of the first female photographers in the country to work outside the studio documenting the world around her, her interest in the human condition taking her beyond the boundaries of Staten Island and the restrictions of her upbringing. She took some 9,000 photos in her lifetime, many recording (and occasionally poking gentle fun at) the social mores of her generation, others documenting the influx of immigrants to New York City, still others focusing on the workings of the former Quarantine Stations on Staten, Hoffman, and Swinburn Islands (in the Narrows).

Though Alice Austen's early life was very comfortable, her finances became increasingly straitened as she grew older. The value of her inheritance dwindled and the 1929 stock market crash dealt her a blow from which she never recovered. Increasingly afflicted by arthritis, she was forced to mortgage and re-mortgage her house until, in 1945, she eventually lost it. Later she moved to the Staten Island Farm Colony, the poorhouse. Here she would have remained until the end of her life, had not her photography been discovered by Constance Foulk Robert, a writer doing research for *Life* magazine. In 1951, *Life* published an illustrated story on Austen's extraordinary work, and with the proceeds from this sale Austen was able to spend the last six months of her life in a private nursing home.

When Alice Austen was evicted from her house (1945), she appealed to the Staten Island Historical Society to take for safekeeping some 4,800 negatives, including 2,105 vintage glass dryplates exposed between 1884 and c. 1915; in 1950, formal title was transferred to the Historical Society. The Society also owns about 2,700 film sheets dating from c. 1900–36, as well as many of Miss Austen's hand-annotated negative envelopes, prints, and photo albums.

THE HOUSE

The house of the Austen family, "Clear Comfort," is a Victorian Gothic cottage, whose oldest portion dates back to c. 1690–1710, but which was bought by Alice's grandfather and substantially "modernized" around 1850. Designated a New York City landmark in 1971, the house is gradually being restored by the Friends of Alice Austen House, Inc., who operate the Museum. Though Austen's possessions were dispersed through the years, her careful photographic documentation of the house and its contents today serves as a guideline for refurnishing the rooms.

Within the house, selections of Alice Austen's photographs are shown in a series of changing exhibitions, accompanied by a videotaped documentary of her life and work.

The Conference House (2)

7455 Hylan Blvd (Satterlee St), Staten Island, N.Y. 10307. Tel: (718) 984-2086.

ADMISSION: Open March 15–Dec 15: Thurs–Sun 1–4. Closed Mon and Tues. Open Labor Day and some Mon holidays, but call to check hours. Closed Dec 16–March 14. Entrance fee.

Guided tours of house. Special events including park tours, craft demonstrations and workshops, concerts, lectures. Programs for elementary school children.

✘ No food service. Conference House Park is a pleasant picnic site. Nearest restaurants in Tottenville, about a 15-min walk away.

⚦ No restroom. Toilet facilities in park.

🏛 Postcards, a few gift items for children.

♿ Not accessible to wheelchairs.

⊘ Visitors must join guided groups to tour house. No photography permitted.

� **From St. George Ferry Terminal:** Take Staten Island Rapid Transit to the last stop, Tottenville. Follow walking directions below.

🚌 **From St. George Ferry Terminal:** It is possible, but not very convenient, to reach the Conference House by bus. Take bus S78 the entire length of Staten Island to the end of Hylan Blvd. The bus leaves Ramp D at approximately 30-min intervals on weekdays and Sat; at 40-min intervals on Sun.

⋏ From Staten Island Rapid Transit, Tottenville Station: Exit onto Bentley St. Walk up Bentley St and turn right onto Hopping Ave. Make the first left onto Amboy Rd. Turn right onto Satterlee St. The Conference House is at the corner of Satterlee St and Hylan Blvd.

🚗 From Verrazano-Narrows Bridge: Follow the Staten Island Expwy (I-278) for about 6 miles. Take the West Shore Expwy exit and follow the signs for the Outerbridge Crossing. Stay to the right as exit 2 goes off to the left; take exit 1 for Arthur Kill Rd. At the end of the exit ramp, turn right. At the next intersection, turn right again. At the next stop sign, turn right onto Page Ave. Follow Page Ave to Hylan Blvd. Turn right and follow Hylan Blvd to Satterlee St. Turn right onto Satterlee St and park. The house is across the street in Conference House Park.

In a 242-acre park at the southern tip of Staten Island stands one of the city's oldest houses (c. 1680) and one of its most historic, the site of an abortive peace conference between His Majesty's Government and the American colonies. The park, which overlooks the Arthur Kill, must have enjoyed a magnificent view before northern New Jersey was industrialized, but even now its sloping lawns and stately trees give it an aura of serenity.

The house, formerly known as the Billop House for its pre-Revolutionary owner, is the most impressive 17C manor house surviving on Staten Island. Two and a half stories high, with a central hallway, a large attic, and an impressive basement kitchen, it is built of local rubblestone with ground seashells mixed into the mortar. Inside are period furnishings, including a portrait of a Billop family descendant, and a handsome, working 17C kitchen.

HISTORY

Capt. Christopher Billop, a distinguished officer of the Royal Navy, immigrated to Staten Island in 1674, where he was awarded a patent for 932 acres. Three years later he commanded a local garrison in New Castle on the Delaware River, returning thereafter to Staten Island where he was further rewarded by a grant increasing his holdings to 1,600 acres. His descendants lived in the house until the time of the Revolution. After the war the property was confiscated by the State of New York.

The Staten Island Peace Conference, which took place on Sept 11, 1776, was destined to fail before it began. In May of that year Gen. William Howe and his brother Adm. Richard Howe were appointed peace commissioners by the king. In August, when Gen. Howe routed Washington's forces and took control of the western part of Long Island, it seemed that Britain had an excellent chance of winning the war. In early September the British sent their prisoner, Gen. John Sullivan, to the Congress proposing an informal peace conference. On Sept 6, the Continental Congress, hearing that Britain might offer generous terms, sent Benjamin Franklin, John Adams, and Edmund Rutledge to Staten Island to find just what negotiating powers the Howe brothers had. As it turned out, the Howes could pardon American rebels who wanted to return to the fold, but they could not negotiate a treaty with any colony. Adm. Howe's demand that the Declaration of Independence be revoked before any further peace talks take place left no room for further diplomatic approaches.

The Garibaldi-Meucci Museum (3)

420 Tompkins Ave (Chestnut Ave), Staten Island, N.Y. 10305. Tel: (718) 442-1608.

ADMISSION: Open Tues–Sun 1–5. Closed Mon and national holidays. Free admission; donations accepted.

Group tours of house, special events, Italian language and culture classes for adults and children, lecture series, films, video programs, library, community programs.

✗ No restaurant.

🛍 Postcards, stationery, souvenirs.

♿ 1st floor accessible to wheelchairs; restrooms and 2nd floor not accessible.

🚍 **From St. George Ferry Terminal:** Bus S52 or S78.

🚗 **From Verrazano-Narrows Bridge:** Take the Hylan Blvd exit. Continue straight ahead on Narrows Rd (the service road) to Hylan Blvd. Bear right onto Hylan Blvd. Follow it to Tompkins Ave and turn left. Continue on Tompkins Ave, past the Church of St. Joseph, to Chestnut Ave. The Museum is on the left.

This modest clapboard farmhouse (c. 1845; opened as a museum 1956) once sheltered two remarkable men, Antonio Meucci, perhaps the unacknowledged inventor of the telephone, and for a period of 18 months, Giuseppe Garibaldi, the Italian patriot and hero. Meucci still remains an obscure figure in the annals of technological history, but his achievements would be utterly unknown had he not extended his hospitality to Garibaldi. The house has been restored with period furniture and artifacts relating to the two men.

PERMANENT EXHIBITION

The first room of the Museum is devoted to the story of Antonio Meucci's unhappy life. On display are a prototype of the telephone, Meucci's death mask, a chair crafted from twisted roots by Meucci possibly with Garibaldi's assistance (the two men were too poor to afford lumber), and other pictures and documents relating to the inventor's life.

The two other downstairs galleries focus on the career of Giuseppe Garibaldi (1807–1882). There are photographs, prints, paintings, and personal memorabilia, including the chair on which he was carried from the ship on his arrival (1850) in the United States. One display contains a lock of his hair (reddish); another outlines the relationship between Garibaldi and Abraham Lincoln, who asked the Italian fighter to join forces with the Union Army during the Civil War. In the RED GALLERY, a series of lithographs recounts the hero's major military victories; a ceremonially embroidered red shirt recalls his guerrilla organization, the Red Shirts.

Upstairs, a humble BEDROOM under the eaves has been furnished with period antiques to suggest its appearance when Garibaldi slept there.

HISTORY

Born 1808 near Florence, Antonio Meucci came to Staten Island in 1850 after a stint as a scenic designer and stage technician for a theater in Havana, Cuba. While in Cuba, Meucci, an inveterate tinkerer and an avid reader of scientific literature, became curious about the therapeutic uses of electric shock. One day, while experimenting on a friend by this somewhat dubious procedure, he heard the friend's exclamation transmitted over a copper wire from the next room. Realizing this was significant, he spent the next ten years trying to implement his discovery.

Meucci's lack of entrepreneurial skill, his inability to speak English, and his increasing poverty all worked against him. Although he filed a notice of intent to take out a patent on his invention in 1871, six years before Alexander Graham Bell filed for his patent, Meucci could not come up with the $250 necessary to register his invention officially. Through a series of Kafkaesque bureaucratic blunders (including the loss of Meucci's prototypes and repeated delays), Bell received credit for the invention of the telephone and the rights to the financial rewards that went with it. Meucci sued to regain his commercial rights, but not unexpectedly, the court found in Bell's favor. Investigations eventually uncovered collusion between employees of the Patent Office and officials of Bell's company; the government in 1886 upheld Meucci's claim and initiated prosecution for fraud against Bell's patent. But Meucci died in 1889 and the case was eventually dropped.

Although Meucci's story is a sad one, his generosity of spirit in the face of adversity is apparent in the hospitality he extended to Giuseppe Garibaldi. After the defeat of the republican forces in the Italian uprisings of 1848–49, Garibaldi, fled to the United States (summer 1850), where Meucci, who knew the Italian rebel by reputation, took him in. The two eked out a living hunting and making candles (the vat for melting the tallow can still be seen in the backyard), until Garibaldi was well enough to resume his career as a merchant sea captain the following summer. Garibaldi returned to Italy in 1854 to achieve his greatest victories.

Defrauded by a business partner, Meucci eventually lost the ownership of his house, which was bought by a friend, brewer Frederick Bachman. At Garibaldi's death (1882) a committee was formed to commemorate the hero's stay on Staten Island, and two years later (1884) the marble plaque over the door was installed. Bachman donated the house to the Italian community as a memorial to Garibaldi, insisting that Meucci be allowed to live there rent-free until his death.

In 1907, the Giuseppe Garibaldi Society of Staten Island moved the house to its present location. The Order Sons of Italy in America, a fraternal organization of men and women dedicated to the preservation of Italian-American culture, took over the building in 1919.

The Jacques Marchais Center of Tibetan Art (4)

338 Lighthouse Ave, Staten Island, N.Y. 10306. Tel: (718) 987-3478 for recorded information; to reach a live person, call (718) 987-3500.

ADMISSION: Open Wed–Sun 1–5. Closed Easter, Memorial Day, Independence Day, Labor Day, Thanksgiving Day and the day following. The Center closes for the winter from the last Sun in Nov until April 1, but individuals and groups may visit by appointment. Admission charge.

Lectures, art demonstrations, performances of music and dance, special events (programs have included a Harvest Festival, Buddhist chanting, exhibitions of yoga and tai ch'i, and other aspects of Oriental culture), video programs. Children's programs, including storytelling, crafts, and calligraphy. Museum tours, programs for the elderly, the visually and hearing-impaired, and children's groups.

✗ No restaurant. Neighborhood is residential, with no restaurants convenient within walking distance.

⌂ Gift shop with books on Oriental art and culture, cassettes of Tibetan music, postcards, stationery, toys, jewelry, T-shirts, tote bags, and craft items from Tibet, Nepal, Indonesia, China, India, and other Asian countries.

&. Not accessible to wheelchairs.

🚌 **From St. George Ferry Terminal:** Bus S74 to Lighthouse Ave (ask the driver to let you off). Turn right; walk up the hill to the Center, which is on the right-hand side of the street. From Manhattan the trip takes 1½–2 hrs, including the ferry ride.

🚗 **From Verrazano-Narrows Bridge:** Take the Staten Island Expressway (I-278) west to the Richmond Rd / Clove Rd exit. From the exit ramp, turn right at the second traffic light onto Richmond Rd and follow the signs marked Richmondtown to Lighthouse Ave (about 5 miles). Turn right up the hill to No. 338 on the right. Limited street parking. Visitors are requested not to block neighboring driveways.

High on the rocky spine of Staten Island sits the Jacques Marchais Center of Tibetan Art (founded 1947), the creation of a midwestern woman enamored of Eastern art. Cloaked in an air of serenity and remoteness, the Center seems an unlikely denizen of suburban Staten Island, but its founder was a woman with an unusual vision. The Center has two small buildings: one contains administrative offices; the other houses the collection.

HISTORY

Jacques Marchais, née Edna Coblentz, was born (1890) in Illinois. As a child she was captivated by a collection of 13 bronze Tibetan figures she found stashed away in a trunk in the attic, apparently souvenirs her great-grandfather brought back from Asia. Edna Coblentz grew up to become a successful dealer in Asian art. Using the professional name Jacques Marchais (her married name was Jacqueline Klauber), she ran a gallery on Madison Ave and gradually built up her personal collection, later concentrating on Tibetan work and selling off pieces from other parts of the Far East. Though she was absorbed by Asian culture and religion, Marchais never visited the Far East, but bought pieces from other collections in private sales or auctions, or by working closely with dealers. Her timing was fortunate since during the early 20C the many Lamaist temples in Beijing were being closed, falling into ruin, and being looted, and their contents came onto the Western market.

PERMANENT COLLECTION

On tiered stone shelves in the museum building stand rows of sacred objects—prayer wheels, offering bowls, gilded images of deities, and incense burners. Around the walls, exhibit cases contain the major part of the collection. Among the pieces of sculpture are the 13 bronze figurines that originally awoke Jacques Marchais's interest. There are ceremonial pieces that range from elaborate jewel-encrusted images to humble devotional objects made of human and animal bone. One case contains an ethnographic exhibit on modern Tibet.

Among the masterpieces of the collection is a Tibetan *thanka,* or scroll painting, depicting the goddess of universal compassion. Beginning in 1988, the *thanka* was restored by Tibetan artist Pema Wangyal, using only traditional techniques and materials. The process took about a year, and in 1989 the Dalai Lama blessed the restored work. Outside the buildings is a small garden with stone and metal statuary.

THE BUILDINGS

One of the great pleasures of the Center is its architecture, which recalls the style of Tibetan mountain monasteries: sturdy buildings whose thick stone walls are pierced with small windows and overhung by cedar roofs. The Klaubers' home was next door, but it is not part of the museum. The first museum building contains the administrative offices and the gift shop. The second is constructed like a small Tibetan temple, with a large altar on the north wall.

The Museum of Staten Island (5)

75 Stuyvesant Place, Staten Island, N.Y. 10301. Tel: (718) 727-1135.

ADMISSION: Open Mon–Sat 9–5; Sun 1–5. Closed New Year's Day, Memorial Day, Independence Day, Labor Day, Thanksgiving, and Christmas Day. Admission charge, suggested amount; children under 5 free.

Lectures, walking tours of Staten Island, educational and school programs, group programs, tours of other museums, children's events, special events, films.

✘ No restaurant in Museum; several informal restaurants in neighborhood.

⌂ A small gift shop carries books, jewelry, toys, crafts, postcards, souvenirs.

♿ Limited wheelchair access; one step up from street. 2nd floor not accessible.

⊘ Photography by permission only.

🚶 **From St. George Ferry Terminal:** Walk up the pedestrian ramp to Richmond Terrace. Turn right, walk two blocks to Wall St; turn left and walk one block to Stuyvesant Place. Turn right at the corner of Stuyvesant Place and Wall St; the Museum is on the corner, about a 5-min walk from the ferry.

🚗 **From Verrazano-Narrows Bridge:** Take the first exit (Bay St). Follow Bay St until it becomes Richmond Terrace. Four blocks past ferry terminal, turn sharply left onto Stuyvesant Place. Limited street parking available.

The oldest cultural institution on Staten Island (founded 1881), the Museum of Staten Island is operated by the Staten Island Institute of Arts and Sciences. Its changing exhibitions, which emphasize the heritage of the island and its people, often focus on the interrelationship between art, science, and history.

EXHIBITION PROGRAM

Exhibitions have included "Beyond the Bridge: A Celebration of Recent Staten Island History," which used photos, original artwork, and contemporary artifacts to trace recent Staten Island history, casting a critical eye at the changes brought by the opening of the Verrazano-Narrows Bridge in 1964. Another exhibition offered scale models of ferry boats, historic photographs, postcards, and assorted memorabilia to illustrate the history of the Staten Island Ferry. "Black Photographers: 1840–1940," organized by the Schomburg Center for Research in Black Culture, brought a chronological exhibition of images from African-American photographers to the Museum, while "Brass Candlesticks from the Collection of George Way" featured exquisite Dutch, English, and Spanish candlesticks gathered by a passionate local collector. "From Cicadas to Chagall: A Century of Collecting" reviewed the history of the collection, and included such disparate items as Roman glass, beetles, maps, atlases, local and European art, 19C silver, and, of course, cicadas.

The Manteo Family Sicilian Marionette Theater, which operates under the auspices of the Museum, is virtually unique in the United States. Its programs employ traditional Sicilian marionettes and techniques to enact the stories of Italy's great chivalric romances, e.g., the *Orlando Furioso*.

PERMANENT COLLECTION

The Museum has a permanent collection of more than 2 million items (including ½ million insects). In addition to its plant and animal specimens, the collection houses a historical archive and library, which is the most comprehensive repository of Staten Island history anywhere. Today there are 55,000 photographs, oral history tapes, transcripts, and historical artifacts. The art collection got under way in the early 20C with the acquisition of Greek and Roman art; it has since broadened to include 19C painting, sculpture, and decorative arts.

Historic Richmond Town: Staten Island Historical Society (6)

441 Clarke Ave (bet. Richmond / Arthur Kill Rds), Staten Island, N.Y. 10306. Tel: (718) 351-1611.

ADMISSION: Open Jan–March: Sat–Sun 1–5; April–June: Wed–Sun 1–5; July–Aug: Wed–Fri 10–5, Sat–Sun 1–5; Sept–Dec: Wed–Sun 1–5. Closed New Year's Day, Thanksgiving, and Christmas Day. Admission charge; children under 6 free.

Visitors Center in Third County Courthouse near parking lot. Festivals, county fair, children's programs, craft demonstrations, workshops, musical programs. For information about special events, inquire at Visitors Center or call (718) 351-1617. Dinners with traditional American menus by reservation; call (718) 351-9414.

✖ Snack bar open for sandwiches and light meals. Picnic area near visitor parking lot. No fires allowed in the picnic area.

♯↰ Restrooms in lower level of the Historical Museum.

🏛 Museum store in the Transportation Museum has books, postcards, jewelry, traditional toys, period reproductions by Richmondtown craftspeople, prints and photographs of historic Staten Island, seasonal items.

♿ Historical Museum building accessible to wheelchairs; portable ramp available for other locations.

⊘ No flash photography within buildings. Pets must be on leashes and are not permitted in exhibit buildings. No strollers in historic buildings. No bicycle riding in the Restoration area. No radios to be played on grounds. No smoking, eating, or drinking in historic buildings.

From St. George Ferry Terminal: Bus S74 to Richmond Rd and Court Place in the middle of the Restoration area.

From Verrazano-Narrows Bridge: Follow the New Jersey West route; take Richmond Rd / Clove Rd exit. Continue to second traffic light and turn left onto Richmond Rd. Continue about 5 miles; turn left onto St. Patrick's Place. Follow signs to parking lots.

Historic Richmond Town, formerly the Richmondtown Restoration (1936), is a 100-acre outdoor museum whose buildings recall the evolution of village life on Staten Island from the 17C through the 19C. Some of the buildings were moved to the restoration from other parts of the island.

HISTORY

The village, first known as "Cocclestown," dates back to c. 1690. Though the name probably referred to the island's abundant oysters and clams, it degenerated in popular slang to "Cuckoldstown," and the residents prudently renamed their town Richmondtown by the end of the Revolution. Located at a crossroads in the middle of the island, Richmondtown grew and prospered until 1730, when it became the seat of Richmond County (i.e., Staten Island).

In the 1830s, as New York City across the bay began to grow and feel the pressures of its own boundaries, Staten Island became a suburban resort for well-to-do New Yorkers. During this period Richmondtown raised a series of new municipal buildings, including the Third County Courthouse (1837) and the County Clerk's and Surrogate's Office (1848), built a bigger jail (1860; demolished 1953), and subdivided some farmland to make way for a planned residential development.

In the later 19C the population of the island shifted to the coastal areas, leaving Richmondtown as a rural backwater. By 1898, when Staten Island had joined Greater New York as the borough of Richmond, St. George, just across the bay from Manhattan, had superseded Richmondtown as the seat of government, curtailing its development but making it an attractive prospect for restoration a few decades down the line.

PERMANENT EXHIBITION

Just beyond the parking lot is the Visitors Center in the **Third County Court House** (1837), a fine Greek Revival building dating from Richmondtown's heyday as a seat of political power. The central section is built of local trap rock. To its left near Tysen Court is the **Reseau-Van Pelt Cemetery,** a small graveyard originally set aside on a remote part of a farm and used for burials of two of Richmondtown's early families.

Across Center St from the Third Court House is the **Second County Clerk's and Surrogate's Office** (1848), now the **Staten Island Historical Museum,** the main exhibition space of the Staten Island Historical Society. The museum has a permanent exhibit recording the history of Staten Island, as well as changing exhibitions drawn from the Historical Society's collections.

Across Court Place is the Greek Revival **Stephens-Black House** (c. 1838–40) and **General Store** (c. 1840–60). Inside are antique furnishings and demonstrations of mid-19C textile arts. Behind it is probably New York's only historic **Outhouse** (date unknown), moved from its original site on Amboy Rd. The General Store is outfitted with its original coffee grinder, iron stove, and cracker barrel.

Next to the General Store is the small **Colon Store** (c. 1840–50), now used as a tinsmith shop. Just beyond it is the **Transportation Museum,** whose collection includes carriages, firefighting equipment, and old-time commercial vehicles.

Walk up Court Place past the Stephens-Black House and Store to the **Eltingville Store** (c. 1860), originally a one-room frame country store on Amboy Rd, now fitted out as a print shop with an early 19C press. Equally small is the adjacent **Carpenter Shop** (c. 1835), once part of a farmhouse in New Springville, now featuring exhibits of traditional carpentry techniques. On the same side of the street at the corner of Richmond Rd is the **Bennett House** (1839, with c. 1854 addition), on its original site. The large brick oven in the basement suggests that the house had an early bakeshop. Upstairs are exhibits of dolls, toys, and other remnants of 19C childhood.

Facing the Bennett House on the other side of Richmond Rd is the **Guyon-Lake-Tysen House** (c. 1740, with kitchen addition c. 1820 and dormers c. 1840), an outstanding example of Dutch Colonial architecture, complete with gambrel roof and springing eaves.

Next door is the **Britton Cottage** (c. 1670, with additions in c. 1755, c. 1765, and c. 1800), whose oldest section is believed to have been the Town House where public meetings were held. Facing the Britton Cottage across Richmond Rd are the **Edwards-Barton House** (c. 1870), a Gothic Revival house on its original site decorated with Victorian furnishings, and the **Guyon Store** (c. 1815–20, with additions c. 1835–50), also on its original site, used as a barter market until 1835, when it was converted into a house.

Across Richmond Rd from the Guyon Store, between the Britton Cottage and the pond is the **Basketmaker's House** (c. 1810–20), a Dutch-influenced house moved here from New Springville. It is furnished to suggest a Methodist household of c. 1815–25, for whom basketmaking was a source of supplemental income. Next door is the **Kruser-Finley House** (c. 1790, with addition c. 1820) and **Shop** (c. 1850–60). Oral tradition says the house, which was moved here from Egbertville (near the intersection of Richmond Rd and Rockland Ave), belonged to a cooper.

Walk toward Richmond Hill Rd past **Dunn's Mill,** a partial reconstruction of an early 19C sawmill. The **Treasure House** (c. 1700, with additions c. 1740, c. 1790, and c. 1860) originally belonged to Samuel Grasset, a tanner and leather worker. According to tradition, around 1850 a cache of British coins was discovered within the walls, hidden during the Revolution.

Set back from the road is the **Christopher House** (c. 1720 with c. 1730 addition), a fieldstone farmhouse. The **Boehm House** (c. 1750, with addition c. 1840) belonged to Henry M. Boehm, a teacher, and was moved here from Greenridge (west of Richmondtown on the Arthur Kill Rd). The oldest part is faced with wide hand-hewn boards, the newer with narrow, sawn clapboards.

Facing Arthur Kill Rd is one of the most important structures in Richmondtown, the little frame **Voorlezer's House** (c. 1695), built by the Dutch Reformed congregation for its *voorlezer* or lay reader, who lived and also taught school there. It is the oldest elementary school building still standing in the nation. **The Parsonage** (1855) on Arthur Kill Rd at Clarke Ave, a gabled, two-story Gothic Revival house on its original site, was built for the minister of the Dutch Reformed Church but became a private residence in 1875 when the church could no longer support a resident pastor.

At the other end of the restoration is **St. Patrick's Church** (1860–62), at 53 St. Patrick's Place between Center St and Clarke Ave, a white brick Romanesque Revival church with unusually narrow round-headed windows. It was built just before the Civil War, when the Roman Catholic population of Staten Island was increasing rapidly. In the churchyard are the graves of prominent Staten Islanders, including Dr. Richard Bayley, father of St. Elizabeth Ann Seton.

Snug Harbor Cultural Center (7)

1000 Richmond Terrace, Staten Island, N.Y. 10301. Tel: (718) 448-2500.

ADMISSION: The grounds are open daily, free, 8 A.M. until dusk. See also listings under individual museums.

Information Desk at the Visitors Center. For other sources of information, see individual listings. In the summer there is an outdoor kiosk. Tours (free) of buildings and site, Sat and Sun at 2. Lectures, concerts, film festivals, art exhibitions, educational programs for adults and children, workshops, special events. Outdoor and indoor concerts. For concert information, call HarborCharge at (718) 448-2500.

✘ Cafe in Visitors Center offers light meals; open Tues–Fri 11–2; Sat–Sun 11–5. Vending machines in the Visitors Center. Picnicking permitted in grounds; no barbecues or cooking fires. Food and beverages for purchase at outdoor events and performances.

♦♦�‸ Restrooms in the Visitors Center, Veterans Memorial Hall, the Staten Island Children's Museum, and the Great Hall.

🏛 Gift shop in Visitors Center open Wed–Sun 1–4:30. The shop offers jewelry, original art, cards, books, souvenirs, catalogues, gift items. Also at the Center are the Staten Island Children's Museum Gift Shop and the Staten Island Botanical Garden Gift Shop.

♿ Main Hall, the Visitors Center, Veterans Memorial Hall, and the Staten Island Children's Museum are accessible to handicapped visitors. Ground floor of Great Hall accessible.

⊘ No flash photography during concerts, no recording of concerts. No food in upper level of Veterans Memorial Hall or in the Newhouse Center.

🚌 **From St. George Ferry Terminal:** Bus S40.

🚗 **From Verrazano-Narrows Bridge:** Take the lower level of the bridge to first exit (Bay St). Follow Bay St, with the harbor on your right, until it becomes Richmond Terrace (at the ferry terminal). Continue 2 miles to Snug Harbor. Ample parking available.

Snug Harbor Cultural Center, built on the grounds of the former Sailors' Snug Harbor, a retreat for retired seamen, has since 1976 offered an expanding program of art, theater, and music in magnificent surroundings. The Center attracts, first, because of its setting—83 acres of park and lawn overlooking the Kill Van Kull (unfortunately recently synonymous with oilspills and industrial pollution)—and for its architecture, the 19C Greek Revival, Gothic Revival, Italianate, and Beaux-Arts buildings constructed to house and care for the retired sailors and now included within a National Historic District. Finally, Snug Harbor draws visitors with its year-round schedule of art exhibitions in the Newhouse Center for Contemporary Art, and concerts (jazz, folk, classical, and chamber music) presented either in the restored Veterans Memorial Hall, an intimate performance space, or on the lawn. The Staten Island Botanical Garden maintains the lawns and gardens. The Staten Island Children's Museum offers the young a wealth of hands-on exhibitions and activities.

The Newhouse Center for Contemporary Art (8)

1000 Richmond Terrace, Staten Island, N.Y. 10301. Tel: (718) 448-2500.

ADMISSION: Galleries open Wed–Sun 12–5. Closed Mon and Tues, New Year's Day, Thanksgiving, and Christmas Day.

Information Desk at the Visitors Center. Lecture and video programs, gallery talks, poetry readings, concerts of avant-garde music.

🛍 Gift shop in Visitors Center open Wed–Sun 1–4:30. The shop offers jewelry, original art, cards, books, souvenirs, gift items, and catalogues and postcards relating to exhibitions.

&. Accessible to handicapped visitors.

⊘ No photography of works of art.

The Newhouse Center for Contemporary Art, founded (1977) as a community gallery, is the focus of the visual arts programs in the Snug Harbor Cultural Center. The buildings that house the galleries are old, but the art shown within is resolutely contemporary.

The galleries occupy two buildings of the former Sailors' Snug Harbor. *Main Hall* (1833), the oldest of the buildings on the Snug Harbor campus, was designed by Minard Lafever, a renowned architect of the Greek Revival period; the building behind it originally served the old salts as a *Dining Hall* (1879), and the sailors gathered to wait for their meals in the long-windowed corridor, *Shinbone Alley*, that joins the two structures.

EXHIBITION PROGRAM

The location of the Center in these historic buildings and its nonprofit status gives the program a unique character. Some of the six exhibitions mounted yearly focus on themes related to the architecture of Snug Harbor and its history as a charitable institution. "Contemporary Fresco Painting" coincided with the unveiling of the newly restored 19C painted ceilings. Other exhibitions have examined issues of regional and national as well as local interest: pollution, the environment, changing family patterns. "In the Ring," for example, looked at boxing as a metaphor for violence and confrontation in our society, using photos, paintings, and multimedia installations by contemporary artists.

The Center highlights emerging and mid-career artists who have not achieved wide commercial recognition. An annual *Sculpture Exhibition* is installed on the lawns during the summer. Although it includes occasional pieces loaned from other institutions, the exhibition emphasizes new work by emerging artists, usually site-specific, and emphatically experimental pieces. In October a juried craft exhibition and sale of jewelry, wearables, and small decorative objects showcases the work of 50 of the country's leading contemporary craft artists.

The Staten Island Botanical Garden (9)

1000 Richmond Terrace, Staten Island, N.Y. 10301. Tel: (718) 273-8200.

ADMISSION: The grounds are open daily 8 A.M. until dusk. Greenhouse open 9–5 weekdays; weekends 12–4. Free.

Information at Botanical Garden offices in Visitors Center. Lectures, exhibits, gardening workshops and courses, special events, trips. School programs. Tree tours, plant sales (fall, spring, Christmas, and Easter).

🏛 Gift shop in Cottage beyond Gazebo, open Wed–Sun 12–4. Wreaths, some made by staff members and volunteers, floral stationery and china, gardening tools, jewelry, books, and items for children.

♿ Gardens accessible to handicapped visitors.

Some of the greatest pleasures at the Snug Harbor Cultural Center are horticultural. The grounds offer natural woodlands, ponds, and wetlands, as well as landscaped areas overseen by the Staten Island Botanical Garden (founded 1973). On the front lawn formal plantings of annuals surround the statue of Sailors' Snug Harbor founder Robert Richard Randall and the fountain of Neptune. These beds, with their ribbons of coleus, and stands of pampas grass, canna, and castor beans, recall the botanical preferences of the Victorians. The Lynne Steinman Rhododendron Collection blooms seasonally at the main entrance.

There are also specialized gardens. The *Perennial Garden* contains 3,000 plants; mid-season flowering garden, high summer season at its peak. The *White Garden,* modeled after the one designed by Vita Sackville-West at Sissinghurst in Kent, England, contains only plants with white blossoms or pale gray-green foliage. Plants in the *Butterfly Garden* have been selected to provide nutrition for butterflies in the various stages of their life cycle. The *Lions Sensory Garden for the Disabled* is filled with unusually fragrant plants and shrubs, plants with interesting tactile qualities, or those that rustle pleasingly when moved by the breeze. The restored *Greenhouse* was built (c. 1935) when retired sailors still strolled the grounds of Snug Harbor. Inside is the *Neil Vanderbilt Orchid Collection,* containing orchids and bromeliads gathered during Vanderbilt's travels in the Amazon and the Caribbean. Behind the Greenhouse is the *Lower Pond,* a quiet and secluded area kept as a wildlife refuge and furnished with plants attractive to birds.

Like other facilities at Snug Harbor, the Staten Island Botanical Garden is still expanding. Among its newly designed gardens is the *Pond Garden,* based on a 19C prototype, with shrubs and perennials popular in the late 19C, and a large variety of aquatic and marsh plantings surrounding a 100-year-old pond dug for the now-departed sailors. The *Heritage Rose Garden* (1993) contains rare and unusual varieties, demonstrating the history of the rose from ancient times to the end of the 19C. The climbing roses are supported by latticework and the whole garden is surrounded by flowering apple trees, suggesting popular 19C plantings of fruit trees at Sailors' Snug Harbor. The *Chinese Scholar's Garden* (scheduled to open in 1997) will be unique in this country, a walled courtyard with small pavilions, pools, and plant materials from China.

In addition to its horticultural exhibits, the Staten Island Botanical Garden offers a program of fine arts whose monthly shows (mounted in the entrance corridor to the Visitors Center) focus on Staten Island and its landscape, on horticultural subjects, or on the environment.

The Staten Island Children's Museum (10)

1000 Richmond Terrace, Staten Island, N.Y. 10301. Tel: (718) 273-2060.

ADMISSION: *During the school year:* Open Tues–Sun 12–5. Closed Mon, New Year's Day, Thanksgiving, and Christmas Day. *Summer:* Open Tues–Sun 11–5; Thurs until 7. Closed Mon, July 4, Labor Day. Admission charge; children under 2 free.

Changing exhibits, indoor and outdoor workshops, special events (e.g., Young Magicians' Convention, Kidstock, Meadow Fair), story hours, art programs, family workshops. Call Museum for information about reservation policy for workshops and performances.

✗ Vending machines.

🏛 Excellent gift shop with books, educational toys, crafts, souvenirs.

♿ Accessible to wheelchairs.

🚫 No strollers in the Museum. Strollers can be stored in lobby.

If children learn by doing, the Staten Island Children's Museum (1974), with its interactive exhibits, workshops, and special events, is one of the outstanding educational facilities in the city. Its programs, geared for children ages 2–12, focus on the arts, science, and the humanities.

The Museum moved to its permanent home at Snug Harbor in 1986. Its three-story brick building, officially known only as Building M, was once a maintenance facility. Now it is a lively, compact exhibition space packed with activity rooms and galleries joined by bridges and flights of stairs that make the building physically an exciting place to explore.

EXHIBITION PROGRAM

The Museum generally mounts four major exhibits simultaneously. "Bugs and Other Insects" allowed children a bug's-eye view into the insect world. One appealing model was a child-sized, crawl-through ant colony, filled with ant eggs enlarged to the size of chicken eggs and zippered cocoons holding ft-long pupae. Another part of the exhibit compared insects with their external skeletons to their closest human counterparts, knights in (green) armor.

"Wonder Water" allowed children to discover how much water their own bodies contain and to go paddling in a gurgling brook. "Adventures in Three Dimensions," the newest exhibit, offers opportunities for exploring texture, scale, geometry, and simple technology. A large sculptural environment presents shape as three-dimensional volume, as negative space, and as silhouette. Another walk-through exhibit progresses through geometric forms that gradually change from one shape to another. Modular plantlike forms that children can take apart and put together in different patterns illustrate the underlying geometry of nature.

With its full program of exhibitions, workshops, and performances— puppet shows, storytelling, dance, drama, and concerts—the Museum attracts some 100,000 visitors yearly.

Staten Island Zoological Park (11)

614 Broadway (bet. Forest Ave and Clove Rd), Staten Island, N.Y. 10310. Tel: (718) 442-3100.

ADMISSION: Open daily 10–4:45. Closed New Year's Day, Thanksgiving, and Christmas Day. Admission charge, except Wed after 2 when admission is by donation. Children under three free.

Educational programs, lectures, children's activities, family activities, after school programs, adult programs, feeding times for animals.

✗ Food concession with hot and cold food, snacks, soda.

🏛 Gift shop with souvenirs.

♿ Accessible to wheelchairs.

🚫 No radios.

🚌 From **St. George Ferry Terminal:** Bus S48 along Forest Ave to Broadway; walk three blocks southeast on Broadway to zoo entrance.

🚗 From **Verrazano-Narrows Bridge:** Follow I-276 west to Slosson Ave exit. Turn right onto Slosson Ave and continue to Clove Rd. The entrance is ahead; parking lot on right.

The 8-acre Staten Island Zoo (1936), with its famous reptile collection and fine exhibits of smaller animals, draws some 300,000 visitors annually. Its extensive educational programs have made it an important cultural and recreational resource. In recent years the zoo (administered by the Staten Island Zoological Society) has embarked on a program of modernization and now boasts handsome new habitat exhibits.

PERMANENT EXHIBITION

Indoor exhibitions include the **Aquarium,** a modern wrap-around exhibit with marine life from all over the world ranging from shrimp to sharks. Aquarium exhibits change from time to time, but usually include a coral reef exhibit with colorful fish and invertebrates. The **Tropical Forest** allows visitors to walk through a simulated forest planted with exotic fauna including bromeliads and flowering orchids. Fauna include piranhas and caimans in the river-bend area and blind cave fish and fruit bats in a simulated cave environment. The walkway is designed so that it appears to ascend to the forest canopy, populated with birds (including toucans) as well as other tree-dwelling creatures like sloths, ocelots, and spider monkeys.

Scheduled for completion in the spring of 1997 is the **African Savannah** exhibit, which will simulate this dramatic environment at twilight and focus on such African animals as panthers and monkeys.

Also indoors is the **Serpentarium,** known for its extensive collections of North American rattlesnakes. A memorial exhibition contains turtle and tortoise miniatures dedicated to "Jalopy," a Galapagos turtle who lived in the zoo for 48 years, 1936–84.

Outdoor exhibits include porcupines, raccoons, otters, and prairie dogs, animals known for their interesting social behavior. There is a pony barn and track, and in the **Children's Center,** a New England farm with a duck pond and domestic animals, which visitors may experience close up. Animals being cared for in the hospital are visible through a viewing window.

COMMERCIAL ART GALLERIES

If you are interested in contemporary art you should explore New York's commercial art galleries, where you can search out emerging talent or view the work of established major artists. You can see historical or thematic exhibitions, some of museum quality, that explore in depth a particular artist or a particular aspect of art. And, of course, you can buy art.

Geographically, there are two major concentrations of galleries within the city, around 57th St and in SoHo. Until the burgeoning of SoHo in the '70s, New York's prime art territory ranged along Madison Ave above 57th St and around Fifth Ave on East and West 57th St. For a while in the early '80s the East Village became a hotbed of artistic activity, but today SoHo is the center, and building for building has an astonishing concentration of art galleries. Recently, however, less expensive neighborhoods have begun luring both artists and galleries. TriBeCa, lower Manhattan, and Long Island City, Queens, all have art enclaves. The most recent candidate for the "Next SoHo" is West Chelsea, around 22nd St between 11th and 12th Aves, where low rents and the presence of the Dia Center for the Arts are drawing new galleries.

Although it is hard to generalize about what kinds of galleries are in what neighborhoods, many of the galleries that made their reputations with the Abstract Expressionists and the various styles of the '60s are located uptown, while younger galleries tend to be located in SoHo. In the '60s artists began moving to the then-rundown neighborhood, finding its abandoned or underused 19C industrial buildings, with their open floor spaces and large windows, ideal for studio space. By the late '60s a few dealers had ventured downtown, some of whom (e.g., Paula Cooper and Ivan Karp of the O. K. Harris Gallery) have become almost legendary.

TYPES OF GALLERIES

There are more than 500 art galleries in New York; the art they sell ranges from artist-designed jewelry and clothing, to inexpensive posters, to museum-quality works with prices soaring into six and seven figures. Some galleries are involved in the resale or secondary market, handling what might be called pre-owned art. Their inventories come from individual or corporate collectors who either wish to reshape their holdings or raise money; occasionally museums "deaccession" or sell off works, for the same reasons. Works that appear in these galleries range from Old Masters to contemporary work.

Other galleries are more directly involved with artists, selling their works for a commission, or in some cases offering stipends to support artists while they work on new projects. Some galleries do both, using the profits from resales to support working artists. Though dealers must be interested in the bottom line to survive, those who are directly involved with artists are ultimately the people who keep alive the tradition of the visual arts within the city.

Some galleries are known for their connection with particular media or particular movements in the history of art. For example, Galerie St. Etienne specializes in Austrian and German Expressionism as well as 19–

20C naïve art; the Laurence Miller Gallery shows photography; the Max Protetch Gallery is known for its involvement with artists who have some connection with architecture or design, though it certainly shows other art. Other galleries have particular images, though these images may blur around the edges sometimes. Mary Boone is known for big-ticket, "hot," usually young, contemporary artists; O. K. Harris is genial and user-friendly.

The list below is merely a place to begin. It offers a selection of Manhattan galleries, which reflect the scope of what is available. Some are well known, in this country and even abroad. Others, perhaps because of art world politics, are less recognized than they ought to be. There are many fine galleries not on the list, simply because of the demands of space. Since artists move quite frequently from gallery to gallery, the lists published here reflect affiliations at the time of publication.

GALLERY INFORMATION

The best place to discover what is going on is to pick up a copy of *Art Now: New York Gallery Guide,* published monthly. You can usually ask for a copy in the galleries or order it by subscription. The Sunday edition of the *New York Times* lists important exhibitions, as does *New York* magazine and *The New Yorker.*

During the fall, winter, and spring, most galleries are open Tues through Sat, from 10 or 11 A.M. until 5 or 6 in the evening. Saturday is traditionally "the" day for gallery-hopping, and on sunny Saturdays SoHo assumes a carnival atmosphere as imaginatively dressed art aficionados throng the streets, stopping here and there at their favorite haunts. In the summer, galleries are generally open Mon through Fri, from 10 or 11 until 5 or 6.

Galleries Uptown

George Adams Gallery

50 W. 57th Street (bet. 5th / 6th Aves), New York 10019. Tel: (212) 757-6655.

Artists: Frederic Amat, Robert Arneson, Luis Cruz Azaceta, Jim Barsness, Jack Beal, Jose Bedia, Joan Brown, Roy De Forest, Leslie Dill, David Krueger, James McGarrell, Arnaldo Roche Rabell, Peter Saul, Richard Shaw, James Valerio, H. C. Westermann, Sandy Winters, and Philip Wofford.

The George Adams Gallery, formerly the Frumkin / Adams Gallery, which originally opened in Chicago (1953) as the Allan Frumkin Gallery, has been through several transformations. Frumkin's first years in Chicago were taken up mainly with showing European and New York artists: from Europe, the gallery brought a group of Surrealists and German Expressionists, neither group well known in that city at the time; and from New York, the work of Joseph Cornell and Esteban Vincente. Then, in 1960, Frumkin moved to New York to pursue the market and the artists there. George Adams joined the gallery in 1980 and in 1995 became its director.

The Frumkin / Adams never had a particular slant or set of aesthetic criteria to guide its stable of artists, though as the gallery matured, its style evolved, embracing many types of American and European art. Now the stable is composed primarily of artists, including painters, sculptors, and a few photographers, whose work has some figurative reference. Geographically, Latin American and the San Francisco Bay Area are well represented. To encourage younger artists and seek out new talent, Adams sets aside a morning each week to look at slides of new work by anyone who wants to bring them in, a policy unusual among dealers in the city.

Marisa Del Re Gallery

41 East 57th St (bet. Madison / Park Aves), New York 10022. Tel: (212) 688-1843.

Artists: Valerio Adami, Arman, Nobu Fukui, Judith Godwin, Robert Indiana, Les Lalannes, Paul Manes, Conrad Marca-Relli, Kenzo Okada, Sacha Sosho, George Tooker, and Bettina Werner.

The Marisa Del Re Gallery (founded 1968) shows an impressive array of modern and contemporary artists working in a broad range of styles. European and American artists, painters and sculptors are all represented, and Abstract Expressionism, Pop Art, and Photo Realism all fall within the gallery's aesthetic. The emphasis here is on high quality and a refined, sophisticated sensibility, not on a particular movement or period. Historical shows of museum caliber appear with some frequency.

Because the gallery deals both in its own artists and in the secondary market, shows exhibit well-known artists like Robert Motherwell or Arman as well as lesser-known young New York painters. Nor is the gallery timid about exhibiting artists who may not be currently in vogue.

Andre Emmerich Gallery

41 East 57th St (bet. Park / Madison Aves), 5th and 6th floors, New York 10022. Tel: (212) 752-0124.

Artists: Josef Albers, Pierre Alechinsky, Karel Appel, William Bailey, Willard Boepple, Stanley Boxer, Roberto Caracciolo, Anthony Caro, Friedel Dzubas, Stephen Ellis, Sam Francis, Al Held, David Hockney, Hans Hofmann, Alexander Liberman, Morris Louis, Andrew Masullo, John McLaughlin, Beverly Pepper, Joel Perlman, Judy Pfaff, Dorothea Rockburne, David Row, Anne Truitt, Jack Tworkov, Bernard Venet, and Stephen Westfall.

Though his parents were collectors and his grandfather was an art dealer in Europe before World War I, Andre Emmerich only decided to go into the art business (1954) after first establishing a career as a writer. Emmerich became known for his interests in Color Field painters like Helen Frankenthaler, Morris Louis, and Kenneth Noland, and for his expertise in pre-Columbian art, which he had been collecting for a long time. He is the author of two books on the subject, *Art Before Columbus* (1963) and *Sweat of the Sun and Tears of the Moon* (1965).

Today the gallery shows many styles of painting as well as abstract sculpture, and is especially renowned for the catalogues it publishes to accompany exhibitions.

Forum Gallery

745 Fifth Ave (bet. 57th / 58th Sts), New York 10151. Tel: (212) 355-4545.

Artists: Robert Bauer, William Beckman, Chris Darton, Philip Evergood, Alan Feltus, Gregory Gillespie, Jeffrey Gold, Chaim Gross, George Grosz, Raymond Han, Bernard Karfiol, David Levine, Bruno Lucchesi, Jane Lund, Odd Nerdum, Elliot Offner, Carole Robb, Hugo Robus, Wade Schuman, Honoré Sharrer, Sarai Sherman, Raphael Soyer, Volker Stelzmann, Marina Stern, Christian Vincent, Albert Walkowitz, Max Weber, and Laura Ziegler.

The Forum Gallery (founded 1961) is one of the most consistent galleries in New York. It has managed to maintain a single focus on several generations of American figurative artists and over the years has built a coherent stable of artists who, while working in traditional modes and media, also remain contemporary and relevant. There is nothing controversial about the art here; it is not at the "cutting edge." However, the common focus of the work and its high quality makes for some of the best group shows in New York. A collection of self-portraits or nudes or landscapes often has the feel of a small museum show.

A move from Madison Ave to a large and beautifully appointed space at Fifth Ave and 57th St has helped to emphasize the continuing vitality of this older, traditional gallery, as it continues to show the works of painters prominent in the '30s and '40s, like Raphael Soyer and Max Weber, alongside contemporary artists.

Gagosian Gallery

980 Madison Ave (76th St), New York 10021. Tel: (212) 744-2313. Also at 136 Wooster St (bet. Houston / Prince Sts), New York 10012. Tel: (212) 228-2828.

Artists: Chris Burden, Francesco Clemente, Walter de Maria, Mark di Suvero, Howard Hodgkin, Yves Klein, Andrew Lord, David Salle, Richard Serra, Philip Taaffe, Andy Warhol, and Elyn Zimmerman.

Today Larry Gagosian is one of the city's high-profile dealers, known for exhibitions of astonishingly high quality and for the sale and resale of blue-chip paintings. Surprisingly enough, the Gagosian Gallery has been in the city only since 1985, when its owner arrived from Los Angeles where he ran a small gallery that sold prints, photographs, and drawings. In New York he opened his first establishment on West 23rd St in Chelsea, far from the established art precincts, where he quickly gained a reputation as a mover in the secondary market (reselling paintings that already belonged to collectors) and mounted important historical shows.

By February 1989 when he moved to the skylit penthouse of 980 Madison Ave (former home of the Parke Bernet auction house), Gagosian was well up the ladder of the power structure of New York's commercial galleries. His first show in that space was of Jasper Johns maps, which brought together paintings from private collections all over the country. The exhibition was a particularly fine example of Gagosian's trademark show, which develops historical aspects of postwar American painters.

Gagosian also represents firmly established living artists, some of whom are stars of an earlier generation like Lichtenstein and Frank Stella, others who are younger like Brice Marden, Philip Taaffe, and David Salle.

In addition to his Madison Ave and SoHo spaces, Gagosian owns with Leo Castelli a gallery at 65 Thompson St, whose size permits installations and other large-scale works.

Galerie St. Etienne

24 West 57th St, 8th floor (bet. 5th / 6th Aves), New York 10019. Tel: (212) 245-6734.

Artists: Sue Coe, Lovis Corinth, Earl Cunningham, Oskar Kokoschka, Gustav Klimt, Kathe Kollwitz, Alfred Kubin, Paula Modersohn-Becker, Grandma Moses, Egon Schiele, and Art Spiegelman.

Tucked away on the eighth floor of the New York Gallery Building is the Galerie St. Etienne. It was founded (1939) by Otto Kallir, who after enjoying 15 years of success as the owner of Vienna's modernist Neue Gallerie was forced to flee the Nazis. He left behind not only the Neue Gallerie but also the original Galerie St. Etienne, a space he had opened in Paris to show Austrian art. The New York gallery was originally intended to be a branch of the Paris concern, but the European end of the business was never resumed.

It became Kallir's mission in America to promote the Austrian Expressionist art he had represented in Vienna, which was often overlooked in this country in favor of German Expressionism. Kallir did a spectacular job, mounting the first American exhibitions of work by Oskar Kokoschka (1940), Egon Schiele (1941), Gustav Klimt (1959), and the Weiner Werkstätte (1966). Not content to narrow his focus, Kallir branched out and began investigating American folk art. In 1940 he gave Grandma Moses her first gallery show, and added her and other so-called primitive or naïve artists to the gallery's roster.

St. Etienne is now run by Hildegard Bachert and Jane Kallir, Otto Kallir's daughter, a respected art historian and the author of several books on gallery artists. These two women continue to put together museum-quality exhibitions of European and American work. A survey of the work of Art Spiegelman, including an exploration of the development of his Pulitzer Prize-winning *Maus;* and a show entitled "Dance of Death: Images of Mortality in German Art," with works by Beckmann, Dürer, Grosz, Holbein, and Kollwitz, suggests the range of this gallery.

Marian Goodman Gallery

24 West 57th St (5th Ave), New York 10019. Tel: (212) 977-7160.

Artists: Giovanni Anselmo, Art & Language, Lothar Baumgarten, Christian Boltanski, Marcel Broodthaers, James Coleman, Tony Cragg, Richard Deacon, Dan Graham, Rebecca Horn, Anselm Kiefer, Jannis Kounellis, Juan Muñoz, Maria Nordman, Gabriel Orozco, Giulio Paolini, Giuseppe Penone, Gerhard Richter, Thomas Schütte, Thomas Struth, Niele Toroni, Jeff Wall, and Lawrence Weiner.

Marian Goodman came into the gallery world of painting and sculpture by way of prints. While still a graduate student, Goodman published her first portfolio of prints. In 1965, she established Multiples, Inc., to publish the work of important American artists. The first catalogue, with a cover by Josef Albers, presented editions of prints by Barnett Newman, Larry Rivers, Claes Oldenburg, and Philip Guston. In addition to publishing limited-edition prints by such now world-famous artists, Goodman expanded into other kinds of multiple editions, including sculpture, books, anthologies, and objects.

In 1968, Goodman attended the Documenta Exhibition, the influential German show of contemporary art where she first saw the work of Joseph Beuys and other European artists who were doing important and interesting work but who were not exhibiting in New York. To change this situation, Goodman finally opened her own gallery in 1977, with an exhibition of Marcel Broodthaers, soon followed by Anselm Kiefer, and thereafter by Sigmar Polke, Gerhard Richter, Rebecca Horn, and many of the most important European artists. She also began to work with seminal and influential American artists, such as Dan Graham and Lawrence Weiner.

Her gallery continues to emphasize both European and American painters and sculptors. Important exhibitions in recent years have included major exhibitions of paintings by Kiefer and Richter and sculpture by Jannis Kounellis.

Hirschl & Adler Gallery + Hirschl & Adler Modern

21 East 70th St (bet. 5th / Madison Aves), New York 10021. Tel: (212) 535-8810.

Artists: Works available by 18–20C American artists, e.g., Mary Cassatt, Frederic Edwin Church, John Singleton Copley, Marsden Hartley, Childe Hassam, Winslow Homer, Edward Hopper, Martin Johnson Heade, Georgia O'Keeffe. Also Pablo Picasso; Jean-Baptiste-Camille Corot and Pierre-Auguste Renoir.

Contemporary Artists: Gregory Amenoff, Polly Apfelbaum, Forest Bess, Joseph Beuys, Rackstraw Downes, Charles Garabedian, Gilbert & George, Ellsworth Kelly, John Lees, Chris Macdonald, Piero Manzoni, John Moore, Fairfield Porter, David Robilliard, Joan Snyder, David Storey, Bill Traylor, Cy Twombly, Christopher Wilmarth, and Joe Zucker.

The Hirschl & Adler Gallery, founded (1955) by Norman Hirschl and Abraham Adler, is one of the city's most respected dealers in American art and an important player in the secondary market, reselling works of art that have already belonged to at least one owner. The gallery acquires its impressive inventory from individual collectors, corporate collections, and museums that are deaccessioning works. At any given time Hirschl & Adler may hold literally thousands of paintings, watercolors, prints, drawings, and examples of sculpture by artists from the 18C to the 20C. The gallery also has a department of decorative arts and museum-quality examples of American folk art. In addition to American artists, Hirschl & Adler shows Impressionists, Post-Impressionists, and modern European masters.

The exhibition program of some five to six yearly shows includes monographic shows on American artists, e.g., a collection of works by Ralston Crawford that included Tour of *Inspection, Bikini,* created after the artist had witnessed the nuclear bomb tests on that atoll in 1946. Survey exhibitions, which draw on the inventory but sometimes also include works from outside sources, focus on broader themes, e.g., American painters in Paris between the turn of the century and the outbreak of World War II, or paintings and sculpture by or about women. Shows are often accompanied by detailed catalogues, some of which have won awards for their scholarship.

After a long period of residence on 57th St, Hirschl & Adler moved further uptown (1983) to its present landmark town house on East 70th St, between Madison Ave and the Frick Collection. The building it occupies is part of a row built on land held for a long time by the estate of James Lenox, a wealthy collector of rare books. In 1907, the Lenox estate started selling off the real estate to wealthy New Yorkers who built elaborate homes for themselves. Designed by architect William J. Rogers, this house was completed in 1919.

The galley currently incorporates Hirschl & Adler Modern (founded 1981), which shows work by important 20C masters and contemporary painters.

Sidney Janis Gallery

110 West 57th St (bet. 6th/7th Aves), New York 10019. Tel: (212) 586-0110.

Artists: Josef Albers, Jean Arp, Constantin Brancusi, Georges Braque, Eduardo Chillida, Willem de Koning, Jean Dubuffet, Oyvind Fahlstrom, Alberto Giacometti, Arshile Gorky, Auguste Herbin, Edward Hicks, Morris Hirschfield, Valerie Jaudon, Franz Klein, Fernand Léger, Maya Lin, Marisol, Duane Michals, Piet Mondrian, Pablo Picasso, Jackson Pollock, Kurt Schwitters, George Segal, Tom Wesselmann, and Christopher Wilmarth.

The Sidney Janis Gallery was begun (1948) by Janis and his wife Harriet, as a space to show 20C American and European art. At the time Janis was 52 years old, a retired shirt manufacturer and a collector with interests in modern European masters and American folk art. Since the late '20s he and his wife had visited Europe, where they had met leading painters including Mondrian and Léger. Janis began collecting folk painting in the

'30s and abstract art a decade later. During the '40s he came to know many of the European artists who had fled the war, including Mondrian and Matta. He organized a show of Surrealism in 1942 and in 1944 published *Abstract and Surrealist Art in America,* which included many artists who had not yet achieved the style for which they would become known. Among them was Jackson Pollock, whose drip paintings lay in the future.

The first exhibition in the Janis Gallery focused on Fernand Léger and contained paintings that Janis had on loan from European collections. Later shows focused on Mondrian, Schwitters, Albers, and Kandinsky; Janis also became known for mounting historical exhibitions on important movements in 20C art, such as Dada, Futurism, and Cubism. Although sales were slow in the early days, Janis did sell three great paintings by Mondrian and one by Léger to Baroness Hilla Rebay and Solomon Guggenheim, a sale that encouraged Janis to continue as a dealer at a time when he was contemplating leaving the business.

Later Janis became interested in American painters, and starting in the early '50s he began to include one-person shows of painters of the New York School. Eventually the Janis Gallery represented Pollock, Kline, de Kooning, and Mark Rothko.

Janis's interests continued to develop and he put together one of the first major Pop Art shows (1961). The show, entitled "The New Realism," brought into the gallery a number of younger artists, including Jim Dine, Tom Wesselmann, Claes Oldenburg, and George Segal.

Janis died in 1989. His son, Carroll Janis, is now the director, and Carroll's son, David, is assistant director. Under the guidance of the second and third generations, the gallery still emphasizes modern masters as well as a strong group of established living artists.

In 1967, Sidney Janis gave his private collection to the Museum of Modern Art; among the paintings were important works by Umberto Boccioni, Picasso, Piet Mondrian, and Paul Klee.

Knoedler & Company

19 East 70th St (5th Ave), New York 10021. Tel: (212) 794-0550.

Artists: Michael David, Richard Diebenkorn, Herbert Ferber, Helen Frankenthaler, Glenn Goldberg, Adolph Gottlieb, Nancy Graves, Robert Motherwell, Richard Pousette-Dart, David Smith, Frank Stella, Donald Sultan, and John Walker.

Knoedler & Company (founded 1846) is the oldest exhibition space in the city, almost a quarter century older than the Metropolitan Museum of Art. The gallery has a long and illustrious history of exhibiting outstanding American artists, and today it continues to represent a small group of world-famous painters and sculptors.

In the 19C, most European dealers ignored the possibility of a market for European art in the United States. An exception was the French print firm of Goupil, Vibert et Cie, which sent Michael Knoedler to New York as its representative. Realizing that the American public had an interest in

French landscape painters of the Barbizon School, Knoedler quickly began importing works by these artists while continuing to sell prints. In the 1850s Knoedler bought out the Goupil interest, and in 1877 he formed his own company. The timing was fortunate, for in the decades after the Civil War New York was rising to power as a center of banking, finance, and industry, and a class of newly wealthy industrialists was turning to art collecting as a means for displaying money and culture. Although Knoedler died in 1878, his sons and grandsons continued in the firm, which became known for handling fine paintings and Old Master prints. Among its prestigious clients were Henry Clay Frick, Andrew Mellon, John J. Astor, Jay Gould, and Samuel Kress.

Knoedler & Company later became known for its support of American artists, exhibiting works by Winslow Homer, James McNeill Whistler, Charles Prendergast, Frederic Remington, and Andrew Wyeth. In 1930 the gallery carried out major negotiations with the Soviet Union which resulted in Andrew Mellon's purchase of 21 paintings from the Hermitage, later to form the nucleus of the National Gallery of Art in Washington, D.C.

In the 1960s Knoedler represented Willem de Kooning, Barnett Newman, Salvador Dali, Henry Moore, and Arshile Gorky. The firm moved (1970) from 57th St to its present location in a landmarked building on 70th St, between Madison Ave and the Frick Collection. That same year Armand Hammer, the industrialist and collector, bought the firm from the Knoedler family, and subsequently (in 1973, 1975, and 1979) was responsible for bringing three important exhibitions of work from the Hermitage in the former Soviet Union. In 1977, Hammer brought in Lawrence Rubin, under whose leadership Knoedler changed its focus to contemporary art.

Today, Knoedler is one the city's most respected galleries. Though it has a relatively small stable of artists, it nonetheless has an international reputation, representing primarily artists who are well established and highly regarded. Gallery artists have solo shows about every other year. Many have remained with Knoedler for a long time and it is possible to follow the development of their careers and styles through their gallery exhibitions.

Occasionally the gallery will mount a thematic show. "Modernism in Russia, Italy and Czechoslovakia, 1915–1935," for example, included drawings, architectural and graphic design, collages, ceramics, glassware, and books by such well-known figures as Balla, Kupka, Lissitzky, Malevich, and Rodchenko.

Matthew Marks Gallery

1018 Madison Ave (bet. 78th / 79th Sts), New York 10021. Tel: (212) 861-9455.

Artists: David Armstrong, Nayland Blake, Richmond Burton, Peter Cain, Willem de Kooning, Lucian Freud, Katharina Fritz, Nan Goldin, Jonathan Hammer, Roni Horn, Gary Hume, Ellsworth Kelly, Brice Marden, Richard Serra, David Smith, Tony Smith, and Cy Twombly.

The Matthew Marks Gallery (opened 1990) is a young gallery and Matthew Marks himself is undoubtedly the youngest major art dealer in New York City. His very early involvement in the art world, as a collector of American prints while he was still in his teens and as a curator of prints at the Pace Gallery in his early 20s, gave Marks enough experience and expertise to open his own gallery at the ripe age of 27.

Marks's gallery reflects his early interest in works on paper. He continues to assemble shows of graphic work, whether drawings, prints, or sketchbooks, by American and European artists of stature. Exhibitions have featured Roni Horn's watercolors based on Kafka's notebooks and Emily Dickinson's poems and works on paper by Julian Schnabel.

Marks has also put together a small stable of younger artists working in paint and mixed media. For people interested in buying art, the gallery offers a combination of blue-chip art, e.g., works by Brice Marden, along with less expensive pieces that beginning collectors can afford.

The Marks has expanded from one to two floors (the second and fifth) of the Wittenborn Building. It is a comfortable place to visit, with shows that are often surprising and entertaining. In 1995, the gallery opened a second space in West Chelsea.

Marlborough Gallery

40 West 57th St (bet. 5th / 6th Aves), New York 10019. Tel: (212) 541-4900.

Artists: Magdalena Abakanowicz, John Alexander, Avigdor Arikha, Frank Auerbach, Francis Bacon, Fernando Botero, Christopher Bramham, Claudio Bravo, Grisha Bruskin, Steven Campbell, Lynn Chadwick, Stephen Conroy, Christopher Couch, John Davies, Vincent Desiderio, Richard Estes, Juan Genoves, Luis Gordillo, Red Grooms, Dieter Hacker, Barbara Hepworth, Israel Hershberg, Bill Jacklin, Alex Katz, Ken Kiff, R. B. Kitaj, Oskar Kokoschka, Christopher LeBrun, Francisco Leiro, Jacques Lipchitz, Antonio Lopez Garcia, Marisol, Raymond Mason, Lucio Munoz, Therese Oulton, Victor Pasmore, Celia Paul, John Piper, Arnaldo Pomodoro, Daniel Quintero, Joaquin Ramo, Paula Rego, Larry Rivers, Kurt Schwitters, Altoon Sultan, James Surls, Manolo Valdes, and Neil Welliver.

The Marlborough Gallery, originally established in London (1946), is one of the city's largest galleries. With divisions in London, Madrid, and Tokyo, Marlborough is also one of the world's most international galleries, whose contemporary artists enjoy worldwide reputations. The New York branch (opened 1963) has been twice renovated and expanded, and now covers 19,000 sq ft.

Most of the artists shown at Marlborough are representational, though within that mode they cover a wide range of styles. Many of the living artists, such as Fernando Botero and R. B. Kitaj, are household names among the artistically literate; others are less famous; but all are well established. In addition to its contemporary artists, the gallery also shows major 19C and 20C work by Impressionists, 20C European masters, German Expressionists, post-World War II American artists, and 19C and 20C photographers. Periodic exhibitions feature the work of such well-known photographers as Berenice Abbott, Brassai, and Irving Penn. The graphics division offers works by Red Grooms, Alex Katz, Rufino

Tamayo, and others. The gallery is well lit, comfortable, and upbeat in feeling.

Midtown-Payson Galleries

745 Fifth Ave (bet. 57th / 58th Sts), New York 10151. Tel: (212) 758-1900.

Artists: Leonard Baskin, Michael Bergt, Debra Bermingham, Isabel Bishop, Bernada Bryson-Shahn, Paul Cadmus, David Driskell, Mary Frank, Jared French, Beverly Hallam, Cynthia Knott, Joyce Kozloff, Walter Kuhn, Robert Kushner, Jacob Lawrence, Jack Levine, Whitfield Lovell, Reginald Marsh, Hans Moller, Gregorio Prestopino, Pavel Tchelitchew, William Thon, and Jimmy Wright.

Midtown-Payson Galleries was among the first galleries in New York to show American art exclusively. It opened (1932) as the Midtown Gallery, owned and directed by Alan Gruskin, who realized that American art at the time was underrepresented and generally neglected in American galleries. Gruskin cultivated a stable of figurative, Social Realist artists in the '30s and '40s, among them Isabel Bishop and Paul Cadmus, both of whom are still represented by the gallery. He encouraged collectors to reevaluate their negative attitudes toward American art, first through the strong shows he put together, and then in his notable book *Painting in the U.S.A.* (1946). After Gruskin's death (1970), his wife Mary Gruskin took over as director, but in 1985, concerned about Midtown's future, she sold it to John Payson.

Though Midtown remains solid and conservative in the best sense of that word, Payson has spiced up the gallery considerably, adding many younger figurative artists to the existing stable. In 1990, he moved the newly christened Midtown-Payson Galleries to larger quarters. Its more than 5,000 sq ft of space make it large enough to mount simultaneous shows of early-20C art and brand-new work. The roster now includes such artists as Jack Levine and Mary Frank, but Midtown-Payson remains true to its roots while embracing younger artists.

At press time, the gallery had relocated to Florida.

Robert Miller Gallery

41 East 57th St (bet. Park / Madison Aves), New York 10022. Tel: (212) 980-5454.

Artists: Diane Arbus, Jean-Michel Basquiat, Louise Bourgeois, Saint Clair Cermin, Martha Diamond, William Eggleston, Louise Fishman, Lee Friedlander, Adam Fuss, Jedd Garet, Gilbert & George, Robert Graham, Robert Greene, Jan Groover, Al Held, Eva Hesse, Roberto Juarez, Alex Katz, Lee Krasner, Robert Mapplethorpe, Clarence John Laughlin, Herbert List, Joan Mitchell, Alice Neel, Joan Nelson, Philip Pearlstein, Milton Resnick, David Seidner, Pat Steir, and Bruce Weber.

The Robert Miller Gallery (founded 1977) shows one of the most interesting collections of contemporary art in New York. Taken individually, each artist is fairly straightforward, salable, and popular, but the beauty here is in the creative mix of generations and mediums, often seen side by side at the same time. The bizarre photographs of Diane Arbus might rub shoulders with the delicate paintings of Joan Nelson. Louise Bourgeois and Alex Katz are both represented, along with the estate of the controversial Robert Mapplethorpe. This is one of the few galleries in the city to divide its attention almost equally between photography and other mediums. Nearly 50% of the artists represented are photographers and there is almost always a room or two of photography on display.

For the most part the art shown is as aesthetically pleasing and polished as the gallery itself. The space, broken up into four small rooms, is one of the most beautiful in New York. The entrance room is a comfortable place to sit and peruse the handsome books and catalogues put together by the gallery and displayed in bookcases on either side of the front door.

Miller himself, formerly a partner of Andre Emmerich, brought to the gallery a strong sense of his tastes and beliefs. Today, the gallery's image is largely the work of John Cheim, its director. Attention to details, and especially to its publications, has given the gallery considerable power in the art world; vigorous promotion of gallery artists like Alice Neel and Ed Ruscha has helped push these artists to the forefront. The gallery is known for its emphasis on painterliness, for its multigenerational stable, and for its rediscovery of older artists.

Pace Wildenstein Gallery

32 East 57th St (bet. Park / Madison Aves), New York 10021. Pace Gallery, tel: (212) 421-3292. Pace Prints, tel: (212) 421-3237. Pace MacGill, tel: (212) 759-7999. Pace Master Prints, tel: (212) 421-3688. Pace Primitive, tel: (212) 421-3688. The Wildenstein Gallery, 19 East 64th St (Madison Ave), New York 10021.

Artists: *Pace Gallery:* Georg Baselitz, Alexander Calder, John Chamberlain, Chuck Close, George Condo, Joseph Cornell, Jim Dine, Jean Dubuffet, Barry Flanagan, Dan Flavin, Robert Irwin, Alfred Jensen, Donald Judd, Robert Mangold, Agnes Martin, Louise Nevelson, Isamu Noguchi, Claes Oldenburg, Pablo Picasso, Ad Reinhardt, Mark Rothko, Robert Ryman, Lucas Samaras, Julian Schnabel, Richard Serra, Joel Shapiro, Saul Steinberg, and Antoni Tàpies. *Wildenstein Gallery:* A large inventory of paintings, drawings, and sculpture of artists of the 16–19C; artists in the inventory have included Rubens, Rembrandt, Leonardo, Monet, van Gogh, and Caravaggio.

If you have time to visit only one gallery, the Pace is probably the best choice. Under one roof are five different divisions: the main gallery on the second floor, Pace Prints, Pace MacGill, which shows photography, Pace Master Prints, and Pace Primitive. Like a small museum, the many parts of Pace show highest-quality work in a full range of mediums and styles. In its stable, the Pace Gallery has famous and highly respected contemporary artists and modern masters.

Founded in Boston (1960) by Arne Glimcher, Pace made its reputation with its first show, a collection of work by the then little-known Louise

Nevelson that sold out in record time. In 1963, Pace opened in New York and has been growing in both size and stature ever since, adding artists and new divisions.

The work shown in the main gallery is often by modern masters, e.g., Alexander Calder, Jean Dubuffet, or Louise Nevelson, or by more contemporary, less famous artists, but no one in the Pace stable is up and coming; all have most definitely "arrived." The gallery shows a wide range of artistic styles, from the cheerfully Technicolor representationalism of Malcolm Morley to the cool Minimalist constructions of Donald Judd. The only common factors here are quality and salability.

A spiral staircase in the center of the main gallery leads to Pace Prints, the gallery's graphics division, remarkable for the number of artists it represents. Over 100 sell their work and many actually create their work under the aegis of Pace, which runs an enormous print shop downtown on Spring Street, Pace Editions.

The two exhibition rooms hold well-organized, often inspired shows, which may combine contemporary pieces with works from Pace Master Prints upstairs, and it is not unlikely to see prints by Rembrandt and David Hockney hanging side by side. Close to the exhibition space is the rack room, where framed prints are arranged alphabetically by artist for visitors to peruse.

Pace MacGill, the photography gallery, named for its director Peter MacGill, is run in much the same way, on a slightly smaller scale. There is a lot of work on view and available for viewing, including drawers full of prints, each labeled with a photographer's name. The exhibition space, a collection of small rooms, makes it easy for the gallery to show more than one artist at a time. Photographers represented run the gamut from the earliest practitioners of the art to those working today.

On the tenth floor are the two smallest divisions of Pace, Pace Master Prints and Pace Primitive. Each has an exhibition room of its own. Pace Master Prints exhibits prints and drawings from the 15c through the 18c with work by artists like Dürer, Tiepolo, and Goya; the gallery also shows prints by 19C and 20C greats like Miró, Chagall, Picasso, and Gauguin. Pace Primitive exhibits exceptional pieces of turn-of-the-century African, Himalayan, and Oceanic art. Pieces are most often small sculptures, masks, or textiles.

In 1993, Pace merged with Wildenstein & Company, an international house (founded 1875) that offers a stellar inventory of Impressionist paintings and top-flight Old Master paintings and drawings. Wildenstein has galleries in London, Tokyo, and Buenos Aires, and plans to open more in Los Angeles and the Far East.

Schmidt-Bingham Gallery

41 East 57th St (bet. 5th / Madison Aves), New York 10022. Tel: (212) 888-1122.

Artists: Adele Alsop, Dozier Bell, Gordon Cook, Morris Graves, Holly Lane, Norman Lundin, James B. Moore, Peter Poskas, Joyce Treiman, Tom Uttech, Idelle Weber, and John Wilde.

The Schmidt-Bingham Gallery is unusual within the city's galleries: a relatively new space (opened 1985), with a total commitment to idiosyncratic, representational art. The published statement of the gallery's outlook describes this as "art that conveys poetical insight and a personal truth." This is not the place to come to see anything risqué or shocking, nor to see household names of the contemporary art world. It is, however, the place to come to see high-quality representational work, including landscapes and still lifes, by many artists who don't quite get the recognition they deserve. Traditional materials and techniques dominate the collection here. Much of the work conveys a sense of the craft of creating art.

Alice Bingham, co-owner of the gallery with Penelope Schmidt, is also the owner of the Bingham Gallery in Memphis, Tenn. The two galleries share some artists, and the influence of a non-New York sensibility may help explain Schmidt-Bingham's uniquely varied stable of artists.

After seven years in a smaller space, 41 West 57th St, the gallery moved a block east to larger quarters in the Fuller Building, one of the most prominent gallery buildings in the city. An exhibition of paintings by Tom Uttech, who lives on a farm near Saukeville, Wis., inaugurated the new space and suggested the focus of the gallery and its particular handle on representational art. Uttech's large-scale paintings of the northern woods, peopled with forest creatures and atmospheric pyrotechnics (like the Northern lights), both celebrated nature and made pointed political comment about its uses.

The staff at Schmidt-Bingham is uncommonly pleasant, happy to talk about the artists and their work.

Galleries Downtown

A.I.R. (Artists in Residence)

40 Wooster St (bet. Broome / Grand Sts), New York 10012. Tel: (212) 966-0799.

Artists: Nancy Azara, Stephanie Bernheim, Sharon Brant, Daria Dorosh, Jessie Nebraska Gifford, Lenore Goldberg, Regina Granne, Barbara Grinell, Michi Itami, Louise Kramer, Carolyn Martin, Louise McCagg, Sylvia Netzer, Ann Pachner, Carol Ross, Barbara Roux, Elke Solomon, Nancy Storrow, Tenesh Webber, Madeline Weinrib, and Janise Yntema.

A.I.R. (founded 1972) was the first women's cooperative gallery in the United States, arriving on the scene simultaneously with a wave of concern by women about women's issues. The gallery was begun by two artists, Barbara Zucker and Susan Williams, who were frustrated dealing with the commercial gallery system and who recognized that female artists had certain shared needs.

Its functional, no-frills gallery space in SoHo has served since the co-op's beginnings as the professional home of its New York members and as the spiritual home of a very different kind of art promotion. As a non-profit organization supported by grants and membership dues, the gallery need not concern itself with salability or prevailing trends in art. The shows that result from this independence are often quite interesting, and focus on nontraditional, even eccentric art. Ten group shows by emerging women artists are curated each year and an annual invitational features small works by up-and-coming male and female artists. Thematic shows often feature art that highlights political issues, particularly those of interest to women.

The 20 co-op members, whose names are posted on the wall of the gallery, are each given solo shows as at a commercial gallery. Visitors stopping at the front desk will find information about gallery artists: a bookshelf holds three-ring binders containing résumés and exhibition histories; there is also a standing slide file of artists' work.

The gallery has links to an extended family of "National Affiliates," 15 members from around the country, who are also exhibited here. Women from around the world are organized into group shows, which highlight art from specific nations. All of these activities are part of the gallery's original mission: "to advance the status of women artists by exhibiting diverse works of the highest quality and by providing leadership and a sense of community to women artists."

Brooke Alexander Gallery

59 Wooster St (bet. Broome / Spring Sts), New York 10012. Tel: (212) 925-4338. Brooke Alexander Editions at 476 Broome St (bet. Wooster / Greene Sts), New York 10013. Tel: (212) 925-2070.

Artists: Richard Artschwager, John Baldessari, Raoul De Keyser, Helmut Dorner, Michael Joaquin Grey, Jasper Johns, Donald Judd, Annette Lemieux, Sol LeWitt, Richard Long, Robert Longo, Robert Mangold, Bruce Nauman, Claes Oldenburg, Tom Otterness, Markus Raetz, Andrei Roiter, Lorna Simpson, Richard Tuttle, and Rémy Zaugg.

The Brooke Alexander Gallery (1968) is one of the city's premier spaces, whose stable of artists reflects the owner's eye and tastes rather than what is currently in fashion or what is immediately salable. Alexander's interests include prints and contemporary painting, drawing, and sculpture. After working with prints and graphics at the Marlborough Gallery and serving as director of the American branch of a British publisher, Alexander decided to strike out on his own as a publisher and dealer of prints, and with his wife Carolyn put together and published their first venture, a portfolio based on a Milwaukee exhibition of painting called "Aspects of New Realism." While dealers of Old Master prints had long published catalogues of the work they handled, Alexander was one of the first to do the same for contemporary American prints, an effort that acknowledged the medium as serious art and also recorded the occasion of publication. Among the artists published by Brooke Alexander, Inc., have been Joseph Albers, Jack Beal, Sam Francis, Red Grooms, Jasper Johns, Robert Motherwell, Fairfield Porter, Richard Tuttle, and Neil Welliver.

In 1975, Alexander opened a gallery on 57th St and began to show painting and sculpture, focusing on the work of emerging artists, while continuing to publish and exhibit prints. In 1985, the gallery moved to larger quarters at 59 Wooster St in SoHo, and four years later opened a second space, at 476 Broome St, to exhibit and handle prints. In 1995, the two galleries were consolidated.

In addition to prints and other works on paper, the gallery shows contemporary painting and sculpture, both American and European. Some artists in the stable are of world-class rank, engaged in major commissions, their work collected and exhibited by museums. One show of large-scale sculpture by Tom Otterness, for example, was part of a commission for the public library in Münster, Germany; the exhibition also coincided with the opening of a permanent outdoor installation of Otterness's animal sculptures at Battery Park City.

Mary Boone Gallery

417 West Broadway (bet. Spring / Prince Sts), New York 10012. Tel: (212) 752-2929.

Artists: Richard Artschwager, Ross Bleckner, Eric Fischl, Roni Horn, Bill Jensen, Barbara Kruger, Brice Marden, Malcolm Morley, Tim Rollins & K.O.S., David Salle, Sean Scully, and Richard Tuttle.

After opening her gallery in 1977, Mary Boone became the *wunderkind* of the New York art scene. Originally a painter herself, Boone began selling art while in her mid-20s and quickly became known for her ability to discover exceptional young talents, including Julian Schnabel, Jean Michel Basquiat, and David Salle. As she built her career, Boone was helped and encouraged by Leo Castelli, probably New York's most influential dealer, whose building she originally shared and with whom she collaborated on several shows. Now that her early "discoveries" have matured into some of the priciest, most-sought-after contemporary artists in the United States, she has become one of the most powerful dealers in New York and an art world celebrity whose words and actions attract media attention. The work she shows is always central to current trends and developments in contemporary art.

The gallery is a cavernous space in its own one-story building on West Broadway, just across from the Castelli Gallery, and on a given Saturday, hordes of gallerygoers cross the street from one place to the other. Not surprisingly the gallery is a popular place for people-watching, and on occasion the fashionable New Yorkers who throng to Boone pay more attention to each other than they do to the art on the wall.

At press time, Mary Boone Gallery moved to 745 Fifth Avenue (bet. 57th / 58th Sts).

Leo Castelli Gallery, Castelli Graphics

Leo Castelli Gallery, 2nd floor, 420 West Broadway (bet. Spring / Prince Sts), New York 10012. Tel: (212) 431-5160. Leo Castelli Graphics, 3rd floor, 578 Broadway (bet. Houston / Prince Sts), New York 10012. Tel: (212) 431-6279. Castelli Graphics, tel: 941-9855.

Artists: *Leo Castelli Gallery:* Sophie Calle, Hannah Collins, Nassos Daphnis, Hanne Darboven, Jasper Johns, Ellsworth Kelly, Joseph Kosuth, Roy Lichtenstein, Robert Morris, Bruce Nauman, James Rosenquist, Ed Ruscha, Richard Serra, Keith Sonnier, Mike and Doug Starn, Frank Stella, Robert Therrien, Meyer Vaisman, and Lawrence Weiner. *Castelli Graphics·* Artists exhibited include Richard Artschwager, James Brown, Jasper Johns, Ellsworth Kelly, Bruce Nauman, Claes Oldenburg, Robert Rauschenberg, James Rosenquist, Edward Ruscha, David Salle, Richard Serrsa, Frank Stella, and Andy Warhol.

Leo Castelli is probably the most famous and influential dealer in New York, known for his uncanny ability to sense changes in aesthetic points of view just as they are about to happen and to find the foremost practitioners of the "next" style before anyone else became aware of a shift at all.

Castelli, who opened his first gallery in Paris before World War II, came to the United States in 1939. In the '50s he became involved with the Abstract Expressionists and opened his first New York gallery at 4 East 77th St in 1957. In 1958, Castelli had his first Jasper Johns show—a watershed event both in Castelli's career and in the course of American art. Thereafter he began to show such important artists as Robert Rauschenberg, Roy Lichtenstein, and Andy Warhol, and through his support of these artists he is generally considered the dean of the Pop Art movement.

During the mid-'60s at the same time that Castelli was exhibiting the stars of Pop Art, he again foresaw a major change in artistic sensibility, the reaction against many of the tenets of Pop Art now known as Minimalism. Castelli began showing Minimalist art by Dan Flavin, Donald Judd, Robert Morris, and others. In 1971, Castelli moved his gallery downtown to SoHo, and began exhibiting some of the first Conceptual art, including work by Joseph Kosuth, Robert Barry, and Lawrence Weiner. Despite all his success, Castelli has, remarkably, never been content to rest on his laurels; whereas many galleries capitalize on early discoveries and then stagnate, Castelli has continued to seek out and show new work. Thus the stable still includes superstars of the '60s like Johns, Rauschenberg, and Lichtenstein, but it also features younger artists who emerged in the late '80s. Part of Castelli's genius seems to be his ability to evaluate artists who will work well with him and who will continue to develop through long careers.

The graphics department of the Leo Castelli Gallery is a few blocks away, at 578 Broadway. A large space, it shows drawings and prints by gallery artists, as well as photography. Leo Castelli's own collection is kept in an adjoining space and on occasion pieces may be seen in gallery shows. In the spring of 1989 Castelli joined with Larry Gagosian to open 65 Thompson St, a gallery that draws on artists represented by both dealers as well as outside sources to present shows of historical and thematic interest.

Paula Cooper Gallery

155 Wooster St (bet. Prince / Houston Sts), New York 10012. Tel: (212) 674-0766.

Artists: Carl Andre, Burt Barr, Jennifer Bartlett, Lynda Benglis, Jonathan Borofsky, Peter Campus, Robert Gober, Robert Grosvenor, Michael Hurson, Zoë Leonard, Julian Lethbridge, Elizabeth Murray, Cady Noland, Andres Serrano, Tony Smith, Rudolf Stingel, Dan Walsh, Robert Wilson, and Jackie Winsor.

Paula Cooper is virtually a legend in the New York art world. One of the few ground-breaking dealers who emerged in the 1960s and 1970s, she was the first to open a gallery in SoHo (1968), a move that presaged the emergence of SoHo as the city's artistic center.

Cooper began her career uptown working for the now-defunct World House Gallery. She set out on her own as a dealer in 1964, working from her apartment on East 64th St, where she showed work by Robert Smithson, Sol LeWitt, and Walter De Maria.

In 1965 Cooper moved downtown, working as director of the Park Place Gallery, a cooperative gallery owned and run by artists, and located in lower Manhattan before it moved to SoHo. The Park Place Gallery became a community center of sorts, the site of performances and political and community meetings, and its activities suggested to Cooper the many roles a gallery could play besides merely selling art.

When Cooper opened her first downtown space on Prince St (1968), much of the spirit of Park Place continued there. The Paula Cooper Gallery became known for readings, concerts, and performance pieces, as well as a showplace for top-notch contemporary art in all media. There were experimental films by Stan Brakhage, Hollis Frampton, and others, performances by Vito Acconci, Mabou Mines, and a traditional all-night reading of Gertrude Stein's *The Making of Americans.*

Cooper's gallery currently shows work by both established and younger artists, including some of the artists with whom she began her career. She is known for her good eye and her adventurous spirit.

The two Paula Cooper spaces on Wooster St are relatively small, both on the ground floor with storefront windows, a few doorways away from each other. The smaller space, at No. 149, is a square room which usually holds small works and one-man shows. No. 155 is a series of rooms, with a garage-style door at the front allowing for the installation of larger pieces, especially sculpture.

Ronald Feldman Fine Arts Inc.

31 Mercer St (bet. Canal / Grand Sts), New York 10013. Tel: (212) 226-3232.

Artists: Vincenzo Agnetti, Eleanor Antin, Ida Applebroog, Arakawa, Conrad Atkinson, Joseph Beuys, Brodsky and Utkin, Nancy Chunn, Keith Cottingham, Douglas Davis, Jud Fine, Terry Fox, Leon Golub, Helen and Newton Harrison, Margaret Harrison, Ilya Kabakov, Peggy Jarrell Kaplan, Komar and Melamid, Piotr Kowalski, The Martinchiks, Roxy Paine, Panamarenko, The Peppers, Tomas Ruller, Edwin Schlossberg, Todd Siler, Mierle Laderman Ukeles, Andy Warhol, Clemens Weiss, Allan Wexler, and Hannah Wilke.

Ronald Feldman Fine Arts was founded (1971) on East 74th St by Feldman and his wife Frayda. Although Feldman had recently become partner in a law firm, he was dissatisfied with the practice of law and had decided to change professions. He headed for Europe and brought back a group of lithographs and etchings by Picasso, Chagall, Giacometti, and others, from which his business grew.

Feldman seems drawn to artists who explore different disciplines and who take an interest in the outside world, and exhibitions at the gallery reflect these varied interests rather than just a selection of salable, collectible art. The gallery can be considered a barometer of current sensibility and its shows, some of which have political overtones, can be provocative. One landmark show of the work of Joseph Beuys consisted of the gallery space with no art objects in it, only spectators. Beuys, who is known for shifting his emphasis from the artist's production to his persona and opinions, called the exhibition his first social sculpture. In 1982 the gallery produced a record album entitled *Revolutions Per Minute (The Art Record)*, put together by all the artists in the gallery using the medium of sound to create a composition. Among the exhibitions have been several large thematic group shows in collaboration with *The Village Voice*.

In addition to these special projects, the gallery shows all kinds of contemporary art from paintings to major installations. The roster includes contemporary, mostly Conceptual artists; publications and videos by and about them are available through the gallery. The gallery publishes graphic works, editions of prints by Andy Warhol and others, as well as books on gallery artists, several of which have been edited by Frayda Feldman.

Barbara Gladstone Gallery

99 Greene St, New York 10012. Tel: (212) 431-3334.

Artists: Vito Acconci, Matthew Barney, Luciano Fabro, Patrick Faigenbaum, Michael Joaquín Grey, Gary Hill, Jenny Holzer, Craigie Horsfield, Anish Kapoor, Sarah Lucas, Mario Merz, Marisa Merz, Matt Mullican, Richard Prince, Georgina Starr, and Rosemarie Trockel.

The Barbara Gladstone Gallery (first opened 1979) is known for its unity of focus. Its stable consists of a group of well-known American and European painters and sculptors, most of them Conceptualists, as well as several photographers. Since Conceptualism is often a deliberately provocative style, posing questions about the nature and limits of art and employing unusual materials to frame those questions. it is not surprising that shows at Gladstone sometimes arouse controversy and attract considerable attention.

Most of the artists in the stable are firmly established, their work splashed across the covers of art magazines or displayed in prestigious national and international exhibitions, but many have been with her for years. In 1986, before Jenny Holzer achieved the fame she presently enjoys, Gladstone mounted an installation of Holzer's electronic light boards across which ran her gnomic sayings in a variety of colors and configurations.

In 1991, Gladstone mounted the first New York exhibition of Matthew Barney's multimedia work in an installation that included videos showing the controversial young artist in a 3-hr climb—facilitated by pitons screwed into the architecture—over the ceiling, down a wall, and into a stairwell. Also in the installation was a weightlifter's bench coated with thick layers of petroleum jelly. Equally flamboyant was an exhibition of Vito Acconci's *Adjustable Wall Bras,* a sculptural installation whose metal, plaster, and canvas structures resembled huge bras with canvas seats in their cups. Nearby stereo speakers played the recording of a woman breathing. The works, both humorous and provocative, invited viewer participation while referring to images of the past, perhaps the 1950s. The gallery also shows photography, e.g., Patrick Faigenbaum's depictions of Italian aristocrats or shots of marble busts of Roman emperors, taken as close-up portraits.

Stephen Haller Gallery

560 Broadway (corner of Prince St), New York 10012. Tel: (212) 219-2500.

Artists: Elaine Anthony, Eric Blum, Power Boothe, James Brown, Caroline Chandler, Richard Diebenkorn, Ron Ehrlich, Lothar Fischer, Johannes Giradoni, Laurie Kaplowitz, Giorgio Morandi, Melinda Stickney-Gibson, Linda Stojak, Judith Streeter, Osami Tanaka, Stephanie Weber, and Hiro Yokose.

The Stephen Haller Gallery (founded 1972) reflects the particular vision of its owner rather than following what is trendy or fashionable. The stable of artists, which includes painters and sculptors, is weighted toward abstractionists, artists who are concerned with the implications of the materials with which they work and with the mysterious aspects of the images and objects they render. The work exhibited here is often subtle and introspective.

Artists, both established and emerging, American and European, are selected for a sensibility that coincides with the gallery vision. Many have been recommended by other gallery artists. All are people on whose abilities Haller is willing to take a risk. This openness places Haller among those dealers whose work contributes overall to the visual arts culture of the city.

Haller relocated his uptown gallery about ten years ago to SoHo, where he felt the energy had moved. Today the gallery occupies three rooms on one of SoHo's more important gallery buildings on Broadway. The space, flooded with natural light, is especially well designed and, like the work on its walls, does not reveal everything on exhibition at once, but allows the visitor to view the art from different perspectives. Exhibitions generally focus on artists represented by the gallery; occasionally they include guest artists whose work expresses the gallery aesthetic.

Pat Hearn Gallery

530 West 22nd St (bet. 10th / 11th Aves), New York 10011. Tel: (212) 727-7366. Open Wed–Sun 12–6.

Artists: Jimmy De Sana, Gretchen Faust, Renee Green, Mary Heilmann, Lisa Hein, Susal Hiller, Tishan Hsu, Patty Martori, Thom Merrick, J. St. Bernard, and Julia Scher.

The Pat Hearn Gallery opened (1983) in the East Village, one of many galleries that sprang up in that neighborhood during a time when the art market was enjoying a period of phenomenal growth. Unlike many of its cohorts, however, Hearn's gallery survived the dissolution of the East Village scene and moved down to SoHo. Nevertheless it retained something of the experimental feel it had in the East Village. Its address was at the edge of the neighborhood and its cement-floored exhibition space seemed more like a warehouse than the usual elegantly finished SoHo gallery. In 1995 Hearn moved again, to a larger but equally spare space in West Chelsea, an industrial neighborhood targeted by some as the "next SoHo."

Before becoming a dealer, Pat Hearn was an artist herself, and while in the East Village her gallery showed primarily painters. In SoHo the gallery leaned toward nontraditional art forms, exhibiting young American and European artists, an emphasis that continues in its West Chelsea location. The new gallery opened with a show of Jutta Koether, a painter from Cologne; the second show recapitulated the gallery's history.

Phyllis Kind Gallery

136 Greene St (bet. Prince / Houston Sts), New York 10012. Tel: (212) 925-1200.

Artists: William A. Blaney, Roger Brown, Eric Bulatov, Carlo, Robert Colescott, Thornton Dial, Mark Greenwold, Richard Hull, J. B. Murry, Gladys Nilsson, Jim Nutt, Ed Paschke, Martin Ramirez, Alison Saar, Oleg Vassilyev, Adolf Wolfli, and Joseph Yoakum.

Phyllis Kind opened her first gallery in Chicago (1967), selling Old Master prints and drawings. Within a short time, she became involved in the local art scene and began showing the work of several Chicago artists who were making personal narrative art in defiance of the prevailing New York movements of Minimalism and Pop Art.

By the time she opened her New York gallery (1975), Kind had a full complement of living artists from Chicago and elsewhere around the United States, all well outside the New York mainstream aesthetic. Kind has always shown quirky, expressive art, sometimes humorous, sometimes irreverent.

A product of Kind's openness to different types of work was her early involvement with "outsider" artists, people without formal training, and she has shown naïve art by artists from places like New Orleans, Wichita, and Albany. She continues to show this kind of work by a range of people, including the Rev. Howard Finster, the Georgia religious folk artist who has received wide attention in recent years.

A trip to the USSR in 1986 spurred Kind to mount a large show of contemporary Soviet art in 1987. In 1990, as the former Soviet Union was disintegrating politically, Kind mounted a show of art in the age of *peres-*

troika. Now she represents several of artists from the former Soviet Union and continues to assemble solo and group shows of their work.

Matthew Marks Gallery

522 West 22nd St (bet. 10th / 11th Aves), New York 10011. Tel: (212) 243-1650.

This downtown satellite (opened 1995) of a well-regarded uptown gallery (see p. 441) is a pioneer in West Chelsea, an up and coming art neighborhood. Exhibition policies are much the same as those uptown, though the space is larger and permits greater freedom in installation. The inaugural show featured minimal paintings of Ellsworth Kelly; it was followed by a show of the photographs of Nan Goldin, made during trips to Berlin, Tokyo, and Salzburg. The gallery is open Thurs–Sun 12–6, reflecting the hours of the Dia Art Center nearby.

Laurence Miller Gallery

138 Spring St (Wooster St), New York 10012. Tel: (212) 226-1220.

Artists: Lois Conner, William Eggleston, Robert Frank, Helen Levitt, Ray Metzker, Eadweard Muybridge, Toshio Shibara, Michael Spano, Alfred Stieglitz, and. Ruth Thorne-Thomsen

The Laurence Miller Gallery is one of the foremost photography galleries in showing works from the turn of the century to the present. The gallery originally opened (1984) on 57th St in a space that showed painting and other mediums as well as photography. But the photographs soon took precedence, and by the time the gallery had moved downtown (1986) to its present location, Miller had fully committed himself to advancing the cause of fine photographers and encouraging novice collectors of the medium.

As a result of this desire to encourage collecting, the gallery shows an interesting mix of fairly traditional, accessible photography: established artists, such as William Eggleston and Lee Friedlander, make up the bulk of the gallery's stable. Works are available from some of the "masters" like Henri Cartier-Bresson, Walker Evans, Robert Frank, and Minor White.

Laurence Miller, once a photographer himself, also publishes a 4-page quarterly newsletter titled *Flash, Chroma, and the Inner Sanctum,* which discusses upcoming shows at the gallery, developments in the photo world, and recent releases of photographic editions and books. A small part of each issue is devoted to important aspects of collecting photography and serves as a "how-to" guide, explaining editions, values, historical importance, and other details of buying, selling, and looking at photographs.

The two rooms of the gallery allow it to mount either two small shows or a single larger one. A large bookcase in the inner room displays de luxe editions of books and prints on or by gallery artists. Current issues of the newsletter are around for the taking, and back issues are available from the front desk.

O. K. Harris Gallery

383 West Broadway, New York 10012. Tel: (212) 431-3600.

Artists: Thomas Bacher, John Baeder, Robert Bechtle, Douglas Bond, Muriel Castanis, Don Celender, Daniel Chard, Y. J. Cho, Davis Cone, Greg Constantine, Jamie Dalglish, James Del Grosso, Mariano Del Rosario, Daniel Douke, Randy Dudley, Leonard Dufresne, Stephen Fox, Kevin Franke, Marilynn Gelfman, David Giese, Robert Ginder, Ralph Goings, Masao Gozu, D. J. Hall, Allen Harrison, Sookjin Jo, John Kacere, Jay Kelly, Aris Koutroulis, Oscar Lakeman, Josef Levi, Marilyn Levine, Robert Lowe, Clyde Lynds, John Mackiewicz, Nicholas Maravell, Richard McLean, Jack Mendenhall, William Nichols, R. E. Penner, Joseph Richards, Lance Richbourg, Robert Rohm, Arsen Roje, John Salt, Masaaki Sato, Keung Szeto, Boaz Vaadia, Robert Van Vranken, Tom Wesselman, John T. Young, and Tino Zago.

Established in 1969, the O. K. Harris Gallery with its maverick spirit still reflects some of the atmosphere and energy of those pioneering days in SoHo. A plaque on the door announces that the gallery has been there since 1493; another, in Latin, warns visitors to beware of the dog. Karp himself has been called the unofficial mayor of SoHo, known for his knowledge of the neighborhood and its residents, including artists and dealers. His gallery, which occupies 11,000 sq ft, is one of the larger in New York and allows him to show four or five artists at once. A portrait of the eponymous Oscar Klondike Harris, a fictional character dreamed up by Karp, hangs in the office where it serves as a suitable gallery symbol.

Karp began his career in the art world writing reviews for *The Village Voice* in the 1950s. Before opening his own gallery, Karp had short stints at the small but historically significant Hansa Gallery and a mainline Madison Ave gallery; he also had an 11-year working relationship with Leo Castelli, along with whom he pioneered the discovery of Pop artists Roy Lichtenstein, Jasper Johns, and James Rosenquist.

Today O. K. Harris maintains its nonconformist position. Karp does not advertise and receives minimal press attention, and unlike many art dealers, he still looks at slides by unknown artists, of whom some 50–60 arrive weekly, unannounced, to show him their work. The gallery embraces the public with unusual energy and hospitality. In addition to viewing the art, you can buy postcards and O. K. Harris T-shirts. A sign on the wall announces that it is "O.K." to smoke. In fact, Karp maintains a collection of some 350 objects bearing the "O.K." signature. Saturday mornings the place is crowded with everyone from tourists to artists to collectors.

Although O. K. Harris has a reputation for figurative art, and especially hyperrealism, the art shown in the several rooms at the gallery is eclectic, including installations, figurative and abstract sculpture, as well as painting and photography. Karp's gallery remains a prime SoHo destination and a place that expresses the particular vision of its founder.

Pace Wildenstein Gallery

142 Greene St (near Houston St), New York 10012. Tel: (212) 431-9224.

This is the downtown branch of the renowned Pace Wildenstein Gallery on East 57th St (see p. 444). Located in a beautifully refurbished SoHo cast-iron building, the gallery shows the same stable of world-famous artists as the uptown space.

P.P.O.W.

532 Broadway (bet. Prince / Spring Sts), New York 10012. Tel: (212) 941-8642.

Artists: Dotty Attie, Bo Bartlett, Carole Caroompas, Lynne Cohen, Dorothy Cross, Michael DeJong, Michael Flanagan, Judy Fox, Lynn Geesaman, Teun Hocks, Joe Houston, Katharine Kuharic, Walter Martin / Paloma Munoz, Nic Nicosia, Erika Rothenberg, Gary Schneider, Sandy Skoglund, David Smith, Carrie Mae Weems, Pat Ward Williams, David Wojnarowicz, Martin Wong, and Thomas Woodruff.

In the 1980s many small storefront galleries opened in New York's East Village. While they prospered for several years, generating a new, youthful art scene, few survived into the next decade. Those that did move to SoHo to take advantage of the traffic generated by the galleries already established there. Foremost among the survivors is P.P.O.W.

The name comes from the initials of the gallery's co-directors, Penny Pilkington and Wendy Olsoff. Originally founded (1983) on East 10th St, P.P.O.W. has been at its present location since 1988; although P.P.O.W. may have moved physically into the mainstream, its stable of artists remains varied and outside the SoHo norm. Many who show here are confrontational and political, making art that deals with issues like racism, sexism, or the environment.

P.P.O.W. shows works in many mediums: paintings of all kinds vie for one's attention with sculpture, photography, and mixed media. Many of the gallery's artists have received wide acclaim, some participating in the Whitney Biennial, others garnering cover stories in art magazines, but the gallery remains committed to its low-key East Village roots.

Max Protetch Gallery

560 Broadway (Prince St), New York 10012. Tel: (212) 966-5454.

Artists: Siah Armajani, Scott Burton, Richard DeVore, Oliver Herring, Byron Kim, Glenn Ligon, Marilyn Minter, Thomas Nozkowski, David Reed, Judith Shea, Andrew Spence, William T. Wiley, and Betty Woodman.

Max Protetch opened his first gallery in Washington, D.C., where he showed the work of Minimalists and Pop artists, but when he came to New York and opened a gallery (1979) on 57th St, he quickly became known for his interest in architecture. Museums and alternative exhibition spaces had already shown architectural drawings and models as art, but Max Protetch was the first to do so commercially. Consequently the gallery attracted a following among architects and people interested in the profession.

The gallery moved downtown to SoHo in 1987, taking its reputation and its following with it. On its walls you can still see the work of early 20C masters like Ludwig Mies van der Rohe and Frank Lloyd Wright, as well as drawings or models by such contemporary architects as Michael Graves, Arata Isozaki, and Rem Koolhaus.

Today the gallery has a broader focus. Some of its artists create work that lies between traditional "fine art" and functional design, e.g., the late Scott Burton, whose furniture was often designed to fit specific architectural sites. Others focus on traditional nonutilitarian kinds of art. Thus exhibitions may include anything from architects' drawings to commissions for architectural sites, to traditional painting and sculpture, to ceramics. Some shows are academic or scholarly in nature, while others offer the latest work of gallery artists.

The gallery space is divided into several rooms, which allows several small individual shows to take place simultaneously.

Holly Solomon Gallery

172 Mercer St (Houston St), New York 10012. Tel: 941-5777.

Artists: Nicholas Africano, Laurie Anderson, Robert Barry, Brad Davis, Douglas Huebler, Peter Hutchinson, Neil Jenney, Robert Kushner, Thomas Lanigan-Schmidt, Kim MacConnel, Frank Majore, Gordon Matta-Clark, Melissa Meyer, Nam June Paik, Izhar Patkin, Elsa Rady, Thomas Lanigan-Schmidt, and William Wegman.

Holly Solomon is one of the New York art world's more famous figures. By the mid-'60s she and her husband Horace, a successful plastics manufacturer, had gained attention in art circles as collectors of Pop Art. (In 1963 she asked her husband for a portrait by Andy Warhol as a wedding anniversary present.) Later the Solomons turned their collecting attention to Conceptual and Earth Art.

In 1969, when SoHo was a wide-open artistic community, the Solomons introduced a new kind of art patronage with the opening of a loft space which for four years served as an exhibition and performance space for emerging artists, writers, and performers. The Solomons felt this was a more productive way of investing in the art world than straightforward collecting, and the venture reflected Holly Solomon's own interests in performance and the theater.

When the Holly Solomon Gallery opened (1975), many of the artists who had participated at the performance space went onto the roster. The gallery continued to reflect Solomon's theatrical interests, emphasizing installation, performance art, and narrative art.

In 1977, when the reigning styles were Conceptualism and Minimalism, Solomon presented a group of gallery artists at the Basel Art Fair in an exhibition entitled "Pattern and Decoration." Because decorative art stood low on the hierarchy, the show became immediately controversial, but Solomon persevered in the belief that decoration was an instrumental force in turning artists away from the narrow intellectual goals of Conceptualism and Minimalism.

After a stint uptown on Fifth Ave, the gallery has returned to SoHo where Solomon continues to show artists from the original stable as well as younger talents. The art at Solomon ranges from Conceptual to Decorative to Neo-Realist, yet there is still a real sense that the vision behind the work is the aesthetic sense of Holly Solomon herself.

Sonnabend Gallery

420 West Broadway (bet. Prince / Spring Sts), New York 10012. Tel: (212) 966-6160.

Artists: John Baldessari, Bernd and Willa Becher, Ashley Bickerton, Mel Bochner, Wim Delvoye, Carroll Dunham, Peter Fischli / David Weiss, Gilbert & George, Jannis Kounellis, Barry Le Va, Robert Morris, Anne and Patrick Poirier, Robert Rauschenberg, Haim Steinbach, Hiroshi Sugimoto, Meyer Vaisman, Boyd Webb, Matthew Weinstein, Terry Winters, Robert Yarber, and Gilbert Zorio.

Ileana Sonnabend is a legendary figure in the SoHo art world. She was born to a wealthy and cultured family in Romania, becoming familiar with art even as a child. With her first husband Leo Castelli she opened a gallery in Paris in 1939, showing Art Deco decorative arts and works by the Surrealists. With the coming of World War II, Sonnabend and Castelli emigrated to the United States. They continued to work together until 1960.

In 1962 she started her own venture in Paris, opening a gallery on the rue Mazarine, which showed American art, neglected at the time in Europe. The first exhibition of Jasper Johns flags, a bold choice because the flags were considered by the French a symbol of American imperialism, was followed by shows of such American superstars as Andy Warhol, Robert Rauschenberg, Roy Lichtenstein, and Claes Oldenburg.

The SoHo gallery was founded in 1970 and immediately attracted attention with its opening exhibition, a performance piece by English artists Gilbert & George. The two men, painted completely gold, stood on a table in the center of the room making stylized gestures and singing "Underneath the Arches" over and over again for hours. As Sonnabend had shown American artists in her Paris gallery, she now shows European artists in New York; she has introduced to this country such figures as Jannis Kounellis, a Greek artist who for many years lived and worked in Rome, and the German painter A. R. Penck.

Sonnabend also was one of the first to show adventurous contemporary photography, including the serial photos of industrial architecture by Hilla and Bernd Becher.

Sperone Westwater Gallery

121 and 142 Greene St, New York 10012. Tel: (212) 431-3685.

Artists: Alighiero e Boetti, Donald Baechler, Domenico Bianchi, David Bowes, Sandro Chia, Francesco Clemente, Greg Colson, Gianni Dessi, Giuseppe Gallo, Don Gummer, On Kawara, Guillermo Kuitca, Wolfgang Laib, Jonathan Lasker, Richard Long, McDermott & McGough, Mario Merz, Aldo Mondino, Bruce Nauman, Luigi Ontani, Mimmo Paladino, Gerhard Richter, Susan Rothenberg, Peter Schuyff, Michael Singer, Ray Smith, Cy Twombly, and William Wegman.

The art on the walls of this important SoHo gallery reflects the backgrounds as well as the taste of its owners, Gianenzo Sperone of Turin and Rome, and Angela Westwater, an American. Before opening his own gallery in SoHo (1975), Sperone exhibited American art in his galleries abroad and is closely associated with the career of Cy Twombly, long based in Rome. His partner Angela Westwater came to the gallery after a stint as managing editor of *ArtForum* magazine.

The first gallery opened upstairs at 142 Greene St; later the gallery expanded to its second space up the block. Sperone Westwater has a very cosmopolitan feeling and an international sensibility, showing both established American artists and some European artists who are less frequently seen in America. Shows include one-person exhibitions of artists in the stable and more ambitious group shows, e.g., one entitled "The Spirit of Drawing," which included work from a wide range of artists, from Giorgio di Chirico and Pablo Picasso to Roy Lichtenstein and Francesco Clementi.

John Weber Gallery

142 Greene St (near Houston St), New York 10012. Tel: (212) 966-6115.

Artists: Terry Allen, Massimo Antonaci, Alice Aycock, James Biederman, Alighiero e Boetti, Daniel Buren, Victor Burgin, Hamish Fulton, Charles Gaines, Marco Gastini, Jack Goldstein, Hans Haacke, Nancy Holt, Pello Irazu, Magdalena Jetelova, Barbara Kasten, Mel Kendrick, Susan Leopold, Sol LeWitt, Allan McCollum, John Murphy, Roman Opalka, Adrian Piper, Carole Seborovski, Robert Smithson, Sara Sosnowy, Franz Erhard Walther, and Kes Zapkus.

The John Weber Gallery, founded (1971) by a SoHo pioneer, is known for the astuteness and vision of its owner and for its long association with Minimal and Conceptual art. Weber, born in California, received a business degree in college and came to New York after a stint as associate curator at the Dayton Art Institute. He worked first for the Martha Jackson Gallery, a respected uptown establishment whose owner's tastes ran to European painters. Weber attempted to change the focus of the gallery, mounting solo shows for young American Pop artists like Robert Indiana and Jim Dine. In the mid-'60s Weber went to work for Virginia Dwan, who had galleries in Los Angeles and eventually in New York, and who boldly supported artists at the cutting edge, including Robert Smithson, known for his earthworks art, and the Minimalists.

When the Dwan Gallery in New York closed in 1971, Weber opened his own place in SoHo, where he continued in the directions established by Dwan and brought in Europeans, including the Arte Povera group and Conceptual artists from Poland, Germany, and elsewhere. Many of Weber's first customers were Europeans; the renowned Count Giuseppe Panza's collection of Minimal art was acquired by the Guggenheim.

Today the gallery handles many of the artists with whom Weber has been associated since the beginning, artists whose work has matured over the years. But the stable also includes artists whose reputations are still young, maintaining a good balance of the well-known, the fairly-well-known, and the unknown. This balance makes the gallery a place to see controversial and energetic work, much of which uses unconventional materials in unusual ways.

The gallery is divided into a larger main space and a smaller Project room. The Project room serves a variety of purposes: highlighting work of gallery artists for which its smaller scale is especially appropriate, or showing work by artists not represented by the gallery but whose work reflects its sensibility.

AUCTION HOUSES

The city's auction houses provide another venue for seeing fine art in a commercial setting. Works on view in the major houses can range from major Impressionist paintings that command prices in the millions of dollars, to tribal art, to French decorative art and tapestries, to jewelry, armor, printed books, and silver. Occasionally the collections of renowned collectors or celebrities come on the market and generate interest not entirely based on the objects on sale. Auction houses hold regular viewing hours in the week or few days before each sale, so that you can look at what is for sale at close hand, even if you do not want to attend the auction.

The auction season runs from September through June, with the most important sales taking place in October, November, and December, April, May, and June. A major house, like Sotheby's or Christie's, may hold as many as ten auctions a week during the peak season, each auction including 200–300 "lots" (items or groups of items sold together). Auction sessions usually last 2 or 3 hrs, and visitors are free to come and go during the sale.

Christie's, Sotheby's, and William Doyle's all have special galleries for objects of lesser quality and more modest price than those sold in the main gallery. Auction houses publish schedules of sales, but if you decide to go on a whim, check *The New Yorker, New York* magazine, or the Sunday edition of the *New York Times* for a current schedule. Auction houses also put out catalogues describing the objects for sale and suggesting the prices they may bring.

Even if you do not plan to bid, it is undeniably entertaining to see large sums of money at stake, especially when several bidders are vying for a single object. High-profile sales, such as the auction of the Andy Warhol Collection or the duchess of Windsor's jewelry at Sotheby's, are covered by the media, as are sales of major paintings. In 1990, the sale of Vincent van Gogh's *Portrait of Dr. Gachet,* which brought a record $82.5 million at Christie's, was a media event.

Sotheby's

1334 York Ave (72nd St), New York 10021. Tel: (212) 606-7000.

Sotheby's was founded (1744) by a London book dealer, Samuel Baker, who established an auction room in order to find buyers for the private libraries he was selling. His business thrived, handling the collections of such important figures as Talleyrand and Napoleon. When Baker died in 1778, his nephew, John Sotheby, took over.

In 1964, Sotheby's merged with an American company, Parke-Bernet, founded (1883) as the American Art Association (AAA). By the turn of the century the AAA was serving the well-funded collecting interests of the nation's industrial barons, the Rockefellers, Morgans, Vanderbilts, and Whitneys. In 1937, Otto Bernet, who had begun as a lowly employee and enhanced his prospects by studying art history at night, and Hiram Haney Parke, one of the nation's greatest auctioneers, founded their own business.

In recent years Sotheby's has had spectacular sales. Among them have been van Gogh's, *Irises* knocked down for $53.9 million in 1987; the Andy Warhol Collection, which brought $25.3 million in 1988; and Greta Garbo's collection of Impressionist and modern paintings, French furniture, and porcelain, which went for $20.7 million in 1990.

Christie's

502 Park Ave (59th St), New York 10022. Tel: (212) 546-1000. Christie's East, 219 East 67th St (3rd Ave), New York 10021. Tel: (212) 606-0400.

James Christie opened an auction house in London in 1766, and his auction rooms in Pall Mall swiftly became a center of fashionable society and a gathering place for collectors and artists of Georgian England. Christie enjoyed the friendship of Thomas Gainsborough, Sir Joshua Reynolds, and Thomas Chippendale, friendships which can only have augmented his business. When Christie died (1803), he left the firm to his son, also named James, who moved it to its present London location at 8 King St.

In the late 18C, Christie's dealt with a number of fabled collections, including the paintings gathered by Sir Robert Walpole that were sold to Catherine the Great. After the French Revolution, Mme du Barry, formerly the mistress of Louis XV, confided her jewels to Christie's for auction, but unfortunately was guillotined before she could realize the profits from the sale. The contents of Sir Joshua Reynolds's studio were auctioned after the painter's death in a sale that lasted five days, short in comparison with the auction of the extravagant and spendthrift duke of Buckingham's famous collection of paintings, which took 40 days to sell off in 1848.

Christie's opened New York salesrooms in 1977 at its present Park Ave location. Christie's East followed two years later, offering more modestly priced objects. Major sales in America include the Impressionist and modern painting collections of Hal B. Wallis, Billy Wilder, Henry Ford II, and Paul Mellon. The Tremaine Collection of Contemporary Art sold in 1988 for $25.8 million, a record price for a contemporary collection. The following year, Christie's New York sold a desk and bookcase by Nicholas Brown for $12.1 million, a record for American furniture, and Pontormo's *Portrait of Duke Cosimo I de' Medici* for $35 million, a record for an Old Master painting. In 1995, the sale of Rudolf Nureyev's effects brought $7.9 million, including $9,200 for a single pair of his pink ballet slippers.

Today Christie's has offices in 30 countries and salesrooms in 10 of them. Its annual sales top $2 billion. In addition to selling art, the firm offers lectures, publications, and appraisal services.

William Doyle Galleries

175 East 87th St (3rd Ave), New York, 10028. Tel: (212) 427-2730.

William Doyle Galleries opened in the Yorkville section of Manhattan in 1973. Smaller and perhaps less formal than Christie's or Sotheby's, the house deals for the most part in estate sales. It is particularly known for its sales of porcelain and silver, and its auctions of the estates of celebrities, such as Gloria Swanson, Bette Davis, and Rock Hudson, cookbook author James Beard, and former New York Mets owner Joan Whitney Payson. Doyle's will appraise and sell an entire estate and so offers a great variety of furniture, jewelry, watches, stamps, coins, and silver.

Swann Galleries

104 East 25th St (Lexington Ave), New York 10010. Tel: (212) 254-4710.

Swann Galleries was founded (1941) as an auction house specializing in rare books. The business has since expanded into related fields, including photographs, autographs and manuscripts, Hebraica and Judaica, but Swann's is still the largest rare-book auction house in the United States. Swann book auctions also focus on areas of collecting other than rare books, e.g., modern literature, travel and exploration, art and architecture, medicine, Americana, maps and atlases, and the performing arts. There are major auctions each spring and fall, with annual sales topping $6 million.

Among the historic items sold through Swann's have been letters from Anne Frank and her sister to their American pen pals in Iowa, written just before the Nazi invasion of the Netherlands, the first Anne Frank material ever auctioned. *Moses and the "Burning" Bush,* a folio of 24 color lithographs by Marc Chagall, sold (1987) for $17,000, while a historic daguerreotype showing photographer Mathew Brady and his wife was bought by the National Portrait Gallery (1985) for $59,400, at the time a record price for a daguerreotype. The gallery also publishes an occasional newsletter, *The Trumpet,* describing recent and upcoming sales.

WHERE TO FIND . . .

African Art

Brooklyn Museum
Metropolitan Museum of Art
Museum for African Art
Studio Museum in Harlem

African-American Art and Culture

Bronx Museum of the Arts
Brooklyn Historical Society
Henry Street Settlement Gallery
INTAR Latin American Gallery
Jamaica Arts Center (Queens)
Louis Armstrong Archives and
    House: Queens College
Museum for African Art
Schomburg Center for Research
    in Black Culture
Studio Museum in Harlem

American Art

American Academy and Institute
    of Arts and Letters
American Craft Museum
Baruch College: Sidney Mishkin
    Gallery
Brooklyn Museum
City Hall: The Governor's Room
Cooper-Hewitt, National Design
    Museum
Forbes Magazine Galleries
Chaim Gross Studio Museum
Godwin-Ternbach Museum at
    Queens College
Solomon R. Guggenheim
    Museum
Guggenheim Museum SoHo
Jewish Museum
Metropolitan Museum of Art
Museum of American Folk Art
Museum of Modern Art
Museum of Staten Island
Museum of the City of New York
National Academy of Design
New-York Historical Society
New York Public Library, 42nd
    St
Isamu Noguchi Garden Museum
    (Queens)
Nicholas Roerich Museum
Schomburg Center for Research
    in Black Culture

	Society of Illustrators: Museum of American Illustration
	Whitney Museum of American Art
	Whitney Museum at Philip Morris
American History	American Numismatic Society
	Castle Clinton National Monument
	Conference House (Staten Island)
	Dyckman Farmhouse Museum
	Ellis Island Immigration Museum
	Federal Hall National Memorial
	Friends Meeting House (Queens)
	Fraunces Tavern Museum
	General Grant National Memorial
	Hall of Fame for Great Americans (Bronx)
	Hamilton Grange National Monument
	Intrepid Sea Air Space Museum
	National Museum of the American Indian
	New-York Historical Society
	Theodore Roosevelt Birthplace
	South Street Seaport Museum
	Statue of Liberty National Monument
	Van Cortlandt House Museum (Bronx)
Ancient Near Eastern Art	Brooklyn Museum
	Metropolitan Museum of Art
	Pierpont Morgan Library
Anthropology	American Museum of National History
	National Museum of the American Indian
Arms and Armor	Metropolitan Museum of Art
	Wave Hill (Bronx)
Asian Art	American Museum of Natural History
	Asia Society
	Brooklyn Museum
	China House Gallery
	Chung-Cheng Art Gallery, St. John's University (Queens)

Frick Collection (ceramics)
Japan Society Gallery
Jacques Marchais Center of
Tibetan Art (Staten Island)
Metropolitan Museum of Art

Asian-American Art and Culture

Asian American Arts Centre
Brooklyn Historical Society
Chinatown History Museum

Books and Manuscripts

American Academy-Institute of
Arts and Letters
American Bible Society: Museum
Gallery
Franklin Furnace
Grolier Club
Pierpont Morgan Library
New-York Historical Society
New York Public Library, 42nd
St
New York Public Library for the
Performing Arts (Lincoln
Center)
Theodore Roosevelt Birthplace
Schomburg Center for Research
in Black Culture

Ceramics

American Craft Museum
Asia Society
Brooklyn Museum
Cooper-Hewitt, National Design
Museum
The Frick Collection
Hispanic Society of America
Japan Society
Metropolitan Museum of Art
Pierpont Morgan Library
Yeshiva University Museum

Children [of interest to]

American Museum of Natural
History
Aquarium for Wildlife Conserva-
tion (Brooklyn)
Bronx Zoo (Wildlife Conservation
Park)
Brooklyn Children's Museum
Brooklyn Museum
Central Park Zoo (Wildlife
Center)
Children's Museum of Man-
hattan
Children's Museum of the Arts
Con Edison Energy Museum

Cooper-Hewitt, National Design
 Museum
Ellis Island Immigration
 Museum
Forbes Magazine Galleries
Guinness World of Records Exhi-
 bition
Harbor Defense Museum of New
 York City
Hayden Planetarium
Intrepid Sea Air Space Museum
Lower East Side Tenement
 Museum
Metropolitan Museum of Art
Museum of American Folk Art
Museum of Television and
 Radio
Museum of the City of New York
National Museum of the Ameri-
 can Indian
New York City Fire Museum
New York City Police Museum
New York Hall of Science
 (Queens)
New-York Historical Society
New York Transit Museum
 (Brooklyn)
New York Unearthed
Prospect Park Zoo (Wildlife Cen-
 ter) (Brooklyn)
Queens County Farm Museum
Historic Richmond Town (Staten
 Island)
Sony Wonder Technology Lab
Staten Island Children's
 Museum
Staten Island Zoological Park
Statue of Liberty National Monu-
 ment
Van Cortlandt House Museum
 (Bronx)
Pieter Claesen Wyckoff House
 Museum (Brooklyn)

Coins and Medals

American Numismatic Society
Jewish Museum
Metropolitan Museum of Art
Ukrainian Museum

Community Gallery, Work by
 Local Artists

Bronx Museum of the Arts
Henry Street Settlement Gallery
Jamaica Arts Center (Queens)
El Museo del Barrio

Contemporary Art

Alternative Museum
Americas Society Art Gallery
Arsenal Gallery
Art in the Anchorage (Brooklyn)
Artists Space
Asian American Arts Centre
Bronx Museum of the Arts
Brooklyn Museum
Clocktower Gallery: Institute for
    Contemporary Art
Columbia University: Wallach
    Art Gallery
Dia Center for the Arts
Drawing Center
80 Washington Square East Gal-
    leries
Franklin Furnace
Godwin-Ternbach Museum at
    Queens College
Goethe House New York
Grey Art Gallery and Study
    Center
Chaim Gross Studio Museum
Solomon R. Guggenheim
    Museum
Guggenheim Museum SoHo
INTAR Latin American Gallery
Jamaica Arts Center (Queens)
Memorial Arch, Grand Army
    Plaza (Brooklyn)
Metropolitan Museum of Art
El Museo del Barrio
New Museum of Contemporary
    Art
Newhouse Center for Contempo-
    rary Art (Snug Harbor, Staten
    Island)
New York Academy of Sciences
PaineWebber Gallery
Pratt Manhattan Gallery
P.S. 1: Institute for Contempo-
    rary Art (Queens)
Queens Museum of Art
Rotunda Gallery (Brooklyn)
Snug Harbor Cultural Center
    (Staten Island)
Socrates Sculpture Park (Queens)
Spanish Institute
Studio Museum in Harlem
Tweed Gallery
White Columns
Whitney Museum at Philip
    Morris

Whitney Museum of American
Art
World Financial Center: Arts and
Events Program

Costume and Textiles

American Museum of Natural
History
Brooklyn Museum
Cooper-Hewitt, National Design
Museum
Metropolitan Museum of Art
Museum at the Fashion Institute
of Technology

Craft

American Craft Museum
American Museum of Natural
History
Museum of American Folk Art
National Museum of the Ameri-
can Indian
Historic Richmond Town (Staten
Island)

Decorative Arts

American Craft Museum
Bartow-Pell Mansion Museum
(Bronx)
Bowne House (Queens)
Brooklyn Museum
The Cloisters (Metropolitan
Museum of Art)
Cooper-Hewitt, National Design
Museum
Fraunces Tavern Museum
Frick Collection
Hispanic Society of America
Japan Society Gallery
Jewish Museum
Judaica Museum (Bronx)
Merchant's House Museum
Metropolitan Museum of Art
Pierpont Morgan Library
Morris-Jumel Mansion
Museum of American Folk Art
Museum of the City of New York
Museum of Modern Art
New-York Historical Society
Historic Richmond Town (Staten
Island)
Abigail Adams Smith Museum
Ukrainian Museum

Dinosaurs

American Museum of Natural
History

Eastern European Art and Culture

Ellis Island Immigration Museum
Ukrainian Institute of America
Ukrainian Museum
YIVO Institute for Jewish Research

Egyptian Art

Brooklyn Museum
Godwin-Ternbach Museum at Queens College
Metropolitan Museum of Art

European Painting

Brooklyn Museum
The Cloisters (Metropolitan Museum of Art)
Dahesh Museum
Frick Collection
Hispanic Society of America
Metropolitan Museum of Art
Pierpont Morgan Library
Museum of Modern Art

Firefighting

Museum of the City of New York
New York City Fire Museum

Folk Art

American Museum of Natural History
El Museo del Barrio
Metropolitan Museum of Art
Museum for African Art
Museum of American Folk Art
Ukrainian Museum

Furniture

Bartow-Pell Mansion Museum (Bronx)
Brooklyn Museum
City Hall: The Governor's Room
The Cloisters (Metropolitan Museum of Art)
Cooper-Hewitt, National Design Museum
The Frick Collection
Gracie Mansion
Lefferts Homestead (Brooklyn)
Metropolitan Museum of Art
Morris-Jumel Mansion
Museum of American Folk Art
Museum of Modern Art
Museum of the City of New York
New-York Historical Society
Theodore Roosevelt Birthplace
Abigail Adams Smith Museum

<table>
<tr><td></td><td>Van Cortlandt House Museum (Bronx)</td></tr>
<tr><td>Gardens</td><td>Alice Austen House (Staten Island)
Bartow-Pell Mansion Museum (Bronx)
Brooklyn Botanic Garden
The Cloisters (Metropolitan Museum of Art)
New York Botanical Garden (Bronx)
Isamu Noguchi Garden Museum (Queens)
Queens Botanical Garden
Snug Harbor Cultural Center (Staten Island)
Staten Island Botanical Garden
Wave Hill (Bronx)</td></tr>
<tr><td>Gems and Jewelry</td><td>American Museum of Natural History
The Cloisters (Metropolitan Museum of Art)
Cooper-Hewitt, National Design Museum
Forbes Magazine Galleries
Metropolitan Museum of Art</td></tr>
<tr><td>Glass</td><td>American Craft Museum
Brooklyn Museum
The Cloisters (Metropolitan Museum of Art)
Cooper-Hewitt, National Design Museum
Godwin-Ternbach Museum at Queens College
Hispanic Society of America (Audubon Terrace)
New-York Historical Society</td></tr>
<tr><td>Greek and Roman Art</td><td>Brooklyn Museum
Godwin-Ternbach Museum at Queens College
Metropolitan Museum of Art</td></tr>
<tr><td>Hispanic Art</td><td>Americas Society Art Gallery
Brooklyn Museum
Hispanic Society of America (Audubon Terrace)
Metropolitan Museum of Art
El Museo del Barrio</td></tr>
</table>

Historic Buildings and Houses;
    Local History

Alice Austen House (Staten
    Island)
Arsenal Gallery (Central Park
    Arsenal)
Art in the Anchorage (Brooklyn
    Bridge Anchorage)
Bartow-Pell Mansion Museum
    (Bronx)
Boathouse Visitor Center (Pros-
    pect Park Boathouse,
    Brooklyn)
Bowne House (Queens)
Brooklyn Historical Society
Brooklyn Museum
Castle Clinton National Monu-
    ment
City Hall: The Governor's Room
Conference House (Staten Island)
Cooper-Hewitt, National Design
    Museum (Andrew Carnegie
    Mansion)
The Dairy (Central Park)
Dyckman Farmhouse Museum
Ellis Island Immigration
    Museum
Federal Hall National Memorial
Fraunces Tavern Museum
Friends Meeting House (Queens)
The Frick Collection
Garibaldi-Meucci Museum
    (Staten Island)
Gracie Mansion
General Grant National Memo-
    rial
Solomon R. Guggenheim
    Museum
Hall of Fame for Great Ameri-
    cans
Hamilton Grange National Monu-
    ment
Harbor Defense Museum of New
    York City (Fort Hamilton,
    Brooklyn)
Hispanic Society of America
    (Audubon Terrace)
Jewish Museum (Felix Warburg
    Mansion)
Kingsland Homestead: Queens
    Historical Museum
Lefferts Homestead (Brooklyn)
Lower East Side Tenement
    Museum

Memorial Arch (Grand Army
  Plaza, Brooklyn)
Merchant's House Museum
Metropolitan Museum of Art
Pierpont Morgan Library
Morris-Jumel Mansion
Museum of Bronx History (Valen-
  tine-Varian House)
Museum of Staten Island
National Museum of the Ameri-
  can Indian (Alexander Hamil-
  ton Custom House)
New York Botanical Garden (Con-
  servatory) (Bronx)
New York Public Library, 42nd St
Edgar Allan Poe Cottage (Bronx)
Pratt Manhattan Gallery (Puck
  Building)
Historic Richmond Town (Staten
  Island)
Theodore Roosevelt Birthplace
Abigail Adams Smith Museum
Snug Harbor Cultural Center
  (Staten Island)
South Street Seaport Museum
Statue of Liberty National Monu-
  ment
Trinity Church Museum
Tweed Gallery
Van Cortlandt House Museum
  (Bronx)
Wave Hill (Bronx)
Pieter Claesen Wyckoff House
  Museum (Brooklyn)

Immigration	Castle Clinton National Monu-
	  ment
	Chinatown History Museum
	Ellis Island Immigration
	  Museum
	Lower East Side Tenement
	  Museum
	Statue of Liberty National Monu-
	  ment and Museum

Islamic Art	Brooklyn Museum Metropolitan Museum of Art

Judaica and Jewish History	Ellis Island Immigration
	  Museum
	Hebrew Union College-Jewish
	  Institute of Religion

	Jewish Museum
	Judaica Museum (Bronx)
	Lower East Side Tenement Museum
	Yeshiva University Museum
	YIVO Institute for Jewish Research
Latino Art and Culture	Bronx Museum of the Arts
	Brooklyn Historical Society
	Henry Street Settlement: Arts for Living Center
	INTAR Latin American Gallery
	El Museo del Barrio
	Museum of American Folk Art
Literary Interest	Grolier Club
	Pierpont Morgan Library
	New York Public Library, 42nd St
	Edgar Allan Poe Cottage (Bronx)
Locks	Cooper-Hewitt, National Design Museum
	J. M. Mossman Collection of Locks
Maritime History	Harbor Defense Museum of New York City (Brooklyn)
	Intrepid Sea Air Space Museum
	Museum of the City of New York
	South Street Seaport Museum
Medieval Art	The Cloisters (Metropolitan Museum of Art)
	Hispanic Society of America (Audubon Terrace)
	Metropolitan Museum of Art
	Pierpont Morgan Library
Metalwork	American Craft Museum
	Brooklyn Museum
	The Cloisters (Metropolitan Museum of Art)
	Cooper-Hewitt, National Design Museum
	The Frick Collection
	Metropolitan Museum of Art
	Pierpont Morgan Library
Military History	Castle Clinton National Monument
	General Grant National Memorial

Harbor Defense Museum of New
York City (Brooklyn)
Intrepid Sea Air Space Museum

Modern Art

Baruch College: Sidney Mishkin
Gallery
Brooklyn Museum
Drawing Center
Equitable Gallery
Chaim Gross Studio Museum
Solomon R. Guggenheim
Museum
Guggenheim Museum SoHo
Jewish Museum
Metropolitan Museum of Art
Museum of Modern Art
National Academy of Design
PaineWebber Gallery
Queens Museum of Art
Spanish Institute
Whitney Museum of American
Art
Whitney Museum at Philip
Morris

Music and Theater

Pierpont Morgan Library
Metropolitan Museum of Art
Museum of the American Piano
Museum of the City of New York
New York Public Library for the
Performing Arts (Lincoln
Center)

Musical Instruments

American Museum of Natural
History
Museum of the American Piano
Metropolitan Museum of Art

Native American Art and Culture

American Museum of Natural
History
Brooklyn Museum
Museum of American Folk Art
National Museum of the Ameri-
can Indian (Alexander Hamil-
ton Custom House)

Natural History

American Museum of Natural
History
Aquarium for Wildlife Conserva-
tion (formerly New York
Aquarium) (Brooklyn)
Bronx Zoo (Wildlife Conservation
Park)

Brooklyn Botanic Garden
Central Park Zoo (Central Park
   Wildlife Center)
Hayden Planetarium: American
   Museum of Natural History
New York Botanical Garden
New York Hall of Science
Prospect Park Zoo (Prospect Park
   Wildlife Center)
Queens Zoo (Queens Wildlife
   Center)
Staten Island Botanical Garden
Staten Island Zoological Park

Parks and Urban Planning

Arsenal Gallery
The Dairy (Central Park)
Tweed Gallery
Urban Center Galleries

Period Rooms

Alice Austen House (Staten
   Island)
Bartow-Pell Mansion Museum
   (Bronx)
Bowne House (Queens)
Brooklyn Museum
Castle Clinton National Monu-
   ment
City Hall: The Governor's Room
The Cloisters (Metropolitan
   Museum of Art)
Conference House (Staten Island)
Dyckman Farmhouse Museum
Fraunces Tavern Museum
The Frick Collection
Friends Meeting House (Queens)
Garibaldi-Meucci Museum
   (Staten Island)
Gracie Mansion
Harbor Defense Museum of New
   York City (Brooklyn)
Kingsland Homestead: Queens
   Historical Society
Lefferts Homestead (Brooklyn)
Lower East Side Tenement
   Museum
Merchant's House Museum
Metropolitan Museum of Art
Pierpont Morgan Library
Morris-Jumel Mansion
Museum of Bronx History, Valen-
   tine-Varian House
Museum of the City of New York
Edgar Allan Poe Cottage (Bronx)

Queens County Farm Museum
Historic Richmond Town: Staten
   Island Historical Society
Theodore Roosevelt Birthplace
Abigail Adams Smith Museum
Van Cortlandt Mansion House
   Museum (Bronx)
Pieter Claesen Wyckoff House
   Museum (Brooklyn)

Photography

Alice Austen House (Staten
   Island)
Brooklyn Historical Society
Brooklyn Museum
International Center of Photog-
   raphy
International Center of Photogra-
   phy, Midtown
Metropolitan Museum of Art
Museum of Modern Art
New-York Historical Society
Schomburg Center for Research
   in Black Culture

Planetarium

Hayden Planetarium: American
   Museum of Natural History

Police History

New York City Police Museum

Prints and Drawings

Asia Society
Brooklyn Historical Society
Brooklyn Museum
Cooper-Hewitt, National Design
   Museum
Drawing Center
The Frick Collection
Metropolitan Museum of Art
Museum of Modern Art
New-York Historical Society
New York Public Library, 42nd
   St
Pierpont Morgan Library
Society of Illustrators: Museum
   of American Illustration

Radio, Television, and Movies

American Museum of the Moving
   Image (Queens)
Museum of Television and Radio
New York Public Library for the
   Performing Arts (Lincoln
   Center)

Religion

American Bible Society: Museum
   Gallery

The Cloisters (Metropolitan
Museum of Art)
Friends Meeting House (Queens)
Hebrew Union College-Jewish
Institute of Religion
Jewish Museum .
Judaica Museum (Bronx)
Metropolitan Museum of Art
Pierpont Morgan Library
Trinity Church Museum
Yeshiva University Museum

Science and Technology

American Museum of Natural
History
Brooklyn Children's Museum
Children's Museum of Man-
hattan
Con Edison Energy Museum
Hayden Planetarium: American
Museum of Natural History
Intrepid Sea Air Space Museum
Museum of Staten Island
New York Academy of Sciences
New York Hall of Science
(Queens)
Sony Wonder Technology Lab
Staten Island Children's
Museum

Sculpture

American Academy / Institute of
Arts and Letters (Audubon Ter-
race)
American Craft Museum
Asia Society
Brooklyn Museum
The Cloisters (Metropolitan
Museum of Art)
The Frick Collection
Chaim Gross Studio Museum
Solomon R. Guggenheim Museum
Guggenheim Museum SoHo
Hall of Fame for Great Ameri-
cans (Bronx)
Hispanic Society of America
(Audubon Terrace)
Jewish Museum
Memorial Arch, Grand Army
Plaza (Brooklyn)
Museum of American Folk Art
Museum of Modern Art
Newhouse Center for Contempo-
rary Art (Snug Harbor Cultural
Center, Staten Island)

Isamu Noguchi Garden Museum
(Queens)
Queens Museum of Art
Sculpture Center
Socrates Sculpture Park (Queens)
Whitney Museum of American
Art
Whitney Museum at Philip
Morris

Silver

Brooklyn Museum
The Cloisters (Metropolitan
Museum of Art)
Metropolitan Museum of Art
Museum of the City of New York
New-York Historical Society

Toys and Dolls

Cooper-Hewitt, National Design
Museum
Museum of the City of New York
New-York Historical Society

Urban Archeology

New York Unearthed

Zoos

Aquarium for Wildlife Conserva-
tion (Brooklyn)
Bronx Zoo (Wildlife Conservation
Park)
Central Park Zoo (Wildlife
Center)
Prospect Park Wildlife Center
(Brooklyn)
Queens Wildlife Center
Staten Island Zoological Park

INDEX OF ARTISTS IN PERMANENT COLLECTIONS

INDEX OF MUSEUMS

(alphabetical)

COMMERICAL ART GALLERIES

INDEX OF MUSEUMS

(by location)

Manhattan: Battery Park to 13th St

Manhattan: Midtown: 14th St to 58th St

Manhattan: Upper East Side: 59th St to 110th St

Manhattan: Upper West Side: 59th St to 110th St

Upper Manhattan: North of 110th St

The Bronx

Brooklyn

Queens

Staten Island